POSTURE OF EUROPE, 1815–1940

Readings in European Intellectual History

THE DORSEY SERIES IN EUROPEAN HISTORY

EDITOR THEODORE S. HAMEROW *University of Wisconsin*

STROMBERG *A History of Western Civilization*

BLACK *Posture of Europe, 1815–1940: Readings in European Intellectual History*

POSTURE OF EUROPE
1815–1940

Readings in
European Intellectual History

Edited by

EUGENE C. BLACK
Brandeis University

1964 • HOMEWOOD, ILLINOIS

THE DORSEY PRESS

First Printing, September, 1964

Library of Congress Catalog Card No. 64–24704

PRINTED IN THE UNITED STATES OF AMERICA

IN MEMORY OF J. B.

PREFACE AND ACKNOWLEDGMENTS

Two principles have governed the selection of these readings. They should be significant, and they should stand, insofar as possible, on their own. The readings presume sufficient familiarity with the historical context to preclude ponderous annotation. Selection by definition means omission, and many will doubtless search in vain for a favorite author or a preferred title. Some items not included are readily available in other volumes; others can be found in inexpensive paperback editions. My preference for longer, self-defining selections has also created limitations of space.

Many friends and colleagues made my task easier. In particular, Professors David Owen of Harvard, Raymond Grew of Michigan, and Heinz Lubasz of Brandeis offered valuable suggestions and criticism. Much of the credit for what is good in this volume belongs to them, and they carry no blame for its flaws. Mr. George Kelly of Harvard executed the splendid translation of Péguy. Mrs. Angeliki Laïou-Torode aided in the selection and preparation of several items. Miss Sally Phillips has helped with much of the drudgery that must accompany the preparation of any volume.

Acknowledgment for the use of specific material is due to the following:

Léon Blum, *For All Mankind* (New York: The Viking Press), translated by W. Pickles, 1946, chapter viii, pp. 163–86. © The Viking Press. Reprinted by permission.

Albert Einstein, *The World As I See It* (New York: Convici, Friede, 1934) translated by Alan Harris, pp. 18–30, 73–82. © Crown Publishers, New York. Reprinted by permission.

Adolph Hitler, *Mein Kampf* (Boston: Houghton Mifflin Co.), edited and translated by John Chamberlain, Sidney B. Fay, *et al.*, unabridged edition, 1939, pp. 630–51. © Houghton Mifflin Co. Reprinted by permission.

Sigmund Freud, "Thoughts for the Times on War and Death," *Collected Papers* (New York: Basic Books, Inc., 1959), authorized translation under the supervision of Joan Riviere, New York, Volume IV, *Papers on Metapsychology. Papers on Applied Psycho-Analysis*, pp. 288–317. © For the United States, Basic Books, Inc.; For the world market in English, The Hogarth Press Ltd., London, England. Reprinted by permission.

Georg Wilhelm Friedrich Hegel, "Concerning the English Reform Bill," *The Philosophy of Hegel* (New York: Modern Library), edited by Carl J. Friedrich, 1954, pp. 540–45. © Random House, Inc., 1953. Reprinted by permission.

Oswald Spengler, "The State. (C) Philosophy of Politics," *Perspectives of World History* (New York: Alfred A. Knopf, Inc.), translated by Charles Francis Atkinson, 1938, Volume II, *The Decline of the West*, chapter xii, pp. 439–65. © Alfred A. Knopf, Inc. Reprinted by permission.

"The Spartacist Manifesto" (New York: *The New York Times*, December 26, 1918), published and translated January 24, 1919, page 3. © *The New York Times*. Reprinted by permission.

Leo XIII, "*Rerum Novarum:* Encyclical Letter (May 15, 1891) on the Condition of the Working Classes" in *The Pope and the People* (London, England: The Catholic Truth Society, 1931), pp. 133–68. © The Catholic Truth Society. Reprinted by permission.

Heinrich von Treitschke, "Races, Tribes, and Nations," *Politics*, (London, England: Constable & Co., Ltd.), translated by Blanche Dugdale and Torben de Billie, 1916, Volume I, pp. 270–302. © Constable & Co., Ltd. Reprinted by permission.

BRANDEIS UNIVERSITY   EUGENE C. BLACK
September, 1964

TABLE OF CONTENTS

xi

INTRODUCTION

I

REVOLUTIONARY CHANGE is a contemporary commonplace. Some lead it; some follow; others resist. Change has colored every aspect of man's life and thought. Historic political institutions have vanished. Economic developments have altered conditions and ways of life. Science has challenged man; in the minds of some, even God. Man ventures into space, watched by a generation born before the airplane. Contemporary doubts revolve less around change—an accepted fact—than around direction. This was not the case for the statesmen and thinkers who contemplated the French revolutionary and Napoleonic era or heard the hum of English textile mills.

The French revolution sundered the traditional fabric of politics, society, even economics. New answers were posed for old questions. Reason displaced historic hierarchical order. There was a new concept of the nation as sovereignty of the people rather than the dynastic domain of princes. Social categories and restrictions were swept away. The traditional vocabulary proved insufficient to cope with the force of change. An Irish judge at the end of the eighteenth century unconsciously reflected the inadequacy of the past. Since the subject, he charged the jury, had ceased to be a breeches-maker without becoming a gentleman, he must be a yeoman. As the smoke drifted from the scene at Waterloo in 1815, the confusion in men's minds equaled only the chaos of that battlefield. Most of European thought through subsequent years was a commentary on this world of revolutions. The concept of change was itself challenged, and men wondered by what lights to set their course. Men who made revolutions and men who contemplated them assumed intellectual positions to storm or defend the citadel of the past.

Western ideology was translated into other cultures during the course of the nineteenth century. Western technology seized the untapped resources of the world. The nineteenth century was Europe's century, and one of the cardinal features of the twentieth century has been the emergence of semi-European powers, particularly the United States and Russia. Even Japan, when it emerged to major power status, did so by adopting western technology and, to a greater degree than the Japanese might care to admit, western ideology. Repeatedly in the past half century we have seen western technology and western ideology employed to repulse western physical domination.

Technological change reinforced, even promoted ideological development. The railroad destroyed provincial particularism in a way that centuries of dynastic ambition could not. Commerce, towns, and money economy slowly eroded the bases of feudalism, but rolling mills and machine

1

shops, agricultural machinery and artificial fertilizer swept away institutions centuries old within a few decades. City burgeoned into megalopolis swallowing the countryside. Mass man replaced ordered man. This is not to argue that the past was "better," although many did and still do so argue. The eighteenth century was not superior to the twentieth unless one regards the potential reality of universal destruction as impossible in that ordered and elegant age.

At the same time there is a fundamental difference between the requirements of ideology and technology—a difference that bespeaks a problem. Ideologues live at least part of their lives in a world of dreams. Only thus can they transcend the mundane. Technological society requires for its maintenance men living very much in the present and foreseeable future—a short-term view at best, although the gap between the two can narrow as $E = mc^2$ will testify. In foreign affairs Bismarck may have maintained a generation of peace, but his less talented successors, attempting to apply half-learned lessons, bumbled down the road to war. The authors of the covenant of the League of Nations, be it observed, did no better. Their handiwork collapsed in less time than that of Bismarck or even Metternich.

Nineteenth-century ideas developed against a background of overwhelming technological change. Europe had long known the chaos and dislocation of war. She had witnessed revolution before—in politics, in society, and in values. For the nineteenth century, "steam and credit" was as compelling a concept as the "rights of man." The process of economic revolution dictated change, but of what sort and to what end? These were questions for which men sought answers for themselves, their world, and their cosmos. The political tidal wave of the French revolution demanded accommodation or resistance. Traditional social relationships and economic functions ceased to be meaningful. In despair some radicals and conservatives hoisted the banner "Back to Stonehenge!" But only in *Erewhon* was the industrial revolution suppressed. Samuel Butler's novel attracted anti-utopian imitators, but the process of invention ground on.

The greatest thinkers transcend their times, although they are often simultaneously very much a part of them. Friedrich Hegel was a good Prussian, a servant of the monarchy, socially conservative, and economically naïve. While this affected his political views it had little bearing upon his philosophy. It is timeless, whatever its immediate influence. This suggests a corollary problem. What men say or think may be less important in historical terms than what they were presumed to have meant or than the doctrine as refined by popularizers. The notions of classical economy held by most Englishmen who had any such ideas derived from Jane Marcet or the Society for the Diffusion of Useful Knowledge rather than Smith, Sismondi, Malthus, and Ricardo. The penalty of original thought is often to be misunderstood or abused. Friedrich Nietzsche was no racist, an anti-German nationalist, but his slashing paragraphs could be ripped from context (as they were) to become the rhetoric of demonic creeds. Few Englishmen understood the German metaphysicians (fewer read them), but many Englishmen understood or thought they understood the confused popularization of Thomas Carlyle. Generations of socialists expound and explicate the work of Karl Marx and Friedrich Engels just as countless Christians explain scripture. Are Lenin and Bernstein talking about the same body of ideas? Of course they are. So, for that matter, are Trotsky and Stalin, Khrushchev and Mao Tse-tung. The *Syllabus of Errors* and *Rerum Novarum* derive from the same corpus of Christian doctrine, although they point in different directions and have contradictory implications.

Rare is the age that produces original ideas, for most ideas are rationalizations of social, economic, and political developments to a much greater degree than most intellectuals are willing to admit. They are, if you will, an attempt to order the past and present for the future. Classical economy was refined in a developing age of machinery—an era in which we still live—but it was not an economist who first comprehended the meaning of industrial revolution. Credit should go to social visionaries, particularly to Robert Owen and Henri, Comte de Saint-Simon. The term "profound" cannot apply to Thomas Babington Macaulay or Samuel Smiles, but they articulated the notions and prejudices of the liberal English middle class.

There is an important place for banal or ill-conceived ideas in intellectual history. Conservative views, the justification of the status quo, are rarely inspiring but are often more important than the penetrating critique of social dissent. One feature of the child's mind is the capacity to hold contradictory ideas as simultaneous truths. The public mind, inchoate as it is, works much the same way. There is such a thing as "climate of opinion" or "notions in the air," albeit they are rarely well formulated or entirely consistent. Charles Péguy offers an extremely sophisticated version of what many Frenchmen instinctively felt at the opening of the twentieth century. Robert Owen reflects fundamental enlightenment beliefs, although it is not demonstrable that he read or understood any major enlightenment thinkers. John Atkinson Hobson's devastating attack on imperialism and John Maynard Keynes's indictment of the Treaty of Versailles touched a widespread feeling of guilt after the orgy of superpatriotism and war.

II

During the first half of the nineteenth century Europe evolved a new vocabulary that includes most of our "isms." Words to describe changes in fact and thought were needed to cope with the impact of political, social, and economic revolution. The words remain, although the meanings and context are demonstrably different. Most are in current use. Some like "monarchism" persist only as antiques. What is conservatism? It varies according to historical context, even according to the individual employing the term. The words outlived the ideas that gave them birth but remained through linguistic and rhetorical usage. Their meaning is never absolute, only historically relative.

From the Napoleonic era through the revolutions of 1848, European thinkers and statesmen attempted to come to terms with the changing facts and forces about them: the liquidation of feudalism, the advent of industrialism, the population explosion, demands of propertied and nonpropertied elements for political and social status, national claims and assertions, the demands of a Europe remade. Talleyrand laid down a set of principles (although he was prepared to jettison them) for the reshaping of Europe at the Congress of Vienna. Metternich defined his version of conservative principles for Europe after the failure of the congress system. Macaulay preached Whig-Liberalism, reforms intended to maintain the rule of property. Hegel had reservations and wondered if reformers were asking the right questions. The exiled Adam Mickiewicz placed overtones of anguish and vindictive racism in the national mission of the Christ among nations, his native Poland. Mazzini, the most humane of nineteenth-century nationalists, saw the joint victory of liberalism and nationalism in Italy leading to a world at peace.

Many saw more profound problems underlying political forms and forces. Jane Marcet sought to teach the common man to accept the fixed and immutable principles of political economy in the coming industrial age. William Cobbett, on the other hand, rejected this world and everything for which it stood. There was something noble and humane in the rural past worth the cost of resurrection. Saint-Simon and Owen believed that the new world of the nineteenth century demanded total social reorganization and regeneration. Society must be rebuilt from the ground up. List argued for national economic systems drawing on his American experience and European observations. Laissez-faire could only mean British world domination. The Reverend Daniel Corrie translated the Protestant evangelical ethic into missionary imperialism. Some did good; many sought to do well. Schlegel added his voice to the outcry against past cultural values with a classic, metaphysical statement for romanticism.

Everything seemed possible to the idealist of 1848. In that year of expectations when heaven seemed very close to earth, revolutions came and went. Few dreams were realized. Ideas lost, there was always reality. The ensuing decades saw the making of modern states, the expansion of finance capitalism and industrialization, Europe's "liberal era," European world domination, and an accelerating scientific revolution. Thought tended to move in one of two ways—either to become pragmatic, immediately involved with current conditions and problems, or to reject the materialistic world in its entirety. Positivistic commitment or quietistic withdrawal came more and more to characterize late nineteenth-century thought and culture.

John Stuart Mill, the Victorian paragon, defined classical liberalism in its most eloquent terms. Treitschke, a veteran of defeated German liberal struggles, found freedom in authority. Joseph Chamberlain, on the other hand, believed that nineteenth-century liberalism could survive if it were to adopt social and economic collectivism. Since one lesson of 1848 appeared to be the incompatibility of traditional liberalism and linguistic or racial nationalism, late nineteenth-century nationalism and its concomitant imperialism assumed a foggy, dangerous aura. Dostoevsky contributed to the mystique of Pan-Slavism. Treitschke discovered a new form of liberty in the freedom to tyrannize over lesser peoples. Cecil Rhodes built empires; Hobson denounced them.

For those who accepted the Victorian compromise in social values—and to a considerable extent we still do—Samuel Smiles proposed a practical ethical imperative. Marx and Engels built on earlier foundations to formulate a new critique and alternative way of life. Kropotkin rehabilitated the communitarian tradition, rejecting both liberalism and socialism. E. E. Williams mixed economic and political bellicosity in threatening proportions. Sorel capped anarchism with syndicalism, pointing to if not understanding the coming age of violence. Péguy sought verity and virtue behind the debased and corrupt in national political life.

The Roman Catholic Church achieved unprecedented centralization during the nineteenth century, but it won control of its component parts at some cost. The Catholic Church set itself against the most dynamic currents of the century. The *Syllabus of Errors,* reinforced by the doctrine of papal infallibility, seemed to some a threat to repeal the nineteenth century. Not until 1891 with *Rerum Novarum* did the papacy forcefully come to grips with a positive program for the age. These were unfortunate years to have the moral force of the Church—a factor of great weight throughout European history—out of tune with so much of life. Scientific advance, positivist analysis, historical scholarship, and simple ethics seemed to clash with traditional religious beliefs. Renan was but one of many who question Christian cosmogony in his scholarly quest for truth. Newman wondered if a revolution in the sum of human knowledge really meant human improvement. Huxley, a major participant in the unbecoming debate on science and faith, was certain that it would. Nietzsche attempted to emancipate himself and the human mind from the encumbrances and limitations of the present.

Every element in the collapse of nineteenth-century Europe can be traced to before the first world war, although that event proved crucial. The so-called great depression of 1873–95 (a far cry from later economic collapse) and the rise of economic nationalism ended unquestioning acceptance of free-wheeling finance capitalism, although form and rhetoric persisted well into the twentieth century. Material prosperity meant increasing aspiration; every improvement excited still greater expectations. Productivity could be a blessing and a curse. The maldistribution of social resources remained a problem. Human irrationality seemed more important than reason and virtue as civilization burned away in the furnace of war.

The succession states—heirs of the central and east European empires—appeared to be the fulfillment of the national principle so prized in nineteenth-century thought, but far from resolving problems, they created new ones. The war reinforced the demand for social change while it eroded the bases of material prosperity and undermined the structure of international capitalism. Political forms appeared inadequate; totalitarian alternatives, attractive.

Irresolution was a feature of this generation afraid—fearful of the present, longing for a past apparently stable but unattainable, despairing for the future. Scientific and technological advance accelerated, making more apparent the gap between man's achievements in the material and humane spheres. Many feared the products of human capacities.

The postwar era offered a spectrum of alternatives. For the traditional and new left, two party manifestos—the Spartacists in Germany, the Labour party in Britain—show the range of views and attitudes. Lenin, about to confront the realities of state-making, denounced all non-Communist alternatives. Keynes warned that the Treaty of Versailles carried the seeds of future disaster. Stalin translated ideas into power. Hitler contributed to the new Armageddon by appealing to the most dangerous perversions of nineteenth-century doctrine. The papacy viewed the rise of new mass doctrines with distaste, although with unfortunately mixed feelings. Léon Blum, from a secular approach, hoped to preserve the humane tradition in the conduct of affairs.

Politics, however, were but the external manifestations of deep social, economic, and cultural problems. Freud insisted that we look inside of man to understand and meet his deepest wants and needs. Spengler despaired for the survival of western civilization but drew consolation from the possibilities of purification by violence. Keynes recognized the need for a new approach to society and economics fitted to the twentieth century if liberal and humane forms were to survive. The papacy reiterated and expanded its social views in *Quadragesimo Anno* to meet the spiritual and mundane requirements of the age. Orwell left an unforgettable description of what a depression means to many. Scientists like Einstein made contributions of supreme originality that offered hopes and fears for mankind.

These documents speak for themselves, but they can be understood only in historical context. Many questions and issues raised overleap the boundaries of simple categories—chronological, political, social and economic, cultural—and are sometimes brilliantly perceptive, sometimes naïve. But they are, in all cases, ways in which the European mind has thought about itself. They are mirrors and landmarks of an age.

PART I

BETWEEN TWO WORLDS
1815–50

A. *Old and New Visions of Politics*

Dynastic Conservatism:
The Congress of Vienna

> Charles Maurice de Talleyrand-Périgord, Prince de Bénévent, "In-
> structions for the King [of France]'s Ambassadors at the Congress
> (August, 1814)," Memoirs of the Prince de Talleyrand, ed. duc de
> Broglie, trans. M. de Deaufort (New York: G. P. Putnam's Sons, 1891),
> Vol. II, pp. 157–84. The text has been checked and corrected against
> the original French as given in Talleyrand, Mémoires, II, 1807–1815,
> ed. P.-L. and J.-P. Couchoud (Paris: Librarie Plon, 1957), pp. 351–71.
> Occasional cuts of detail have been made.

Diplomatic instructions scarcely seem a medium of intellectual history. The
Congress of Vienna (1814–15), however, was the occasion for remaking a
world. Some statesmen conceived it to be the opportunity to turn back the
clock, to rid themselves of that enigma, the French Revolution. They could
not do so, as the wiser among them knew. One of the ablest statesmen at
the Congress was Charles Maurice de Talleyrand-Périgord, Prince de Béné-
vent (1754–1838). This representative of the most enlightened eighteenth-
century aristocratic tradition had been a nonbelieving bishop under the old
regime, a revolutionary statesman, a real-estate promoter in American exile,
Napoleon's foreign minister, and one of those most instrumental in restoring
the Bourbons to the throne of France. Corrupt, clever, cynical—historians
have often asked whether Talleyrand really believed in anything. He believed in himself. He believed in France. He believed in European order. He
also realized that the new world of the nineteenth century could never be
quite the same, no matter what men might wish, as the world that had died.

Talleyrand and his king, Louis XVIII, had some very specific ends in view.
By the first Peace of Paris (1814), France had conceded to the Grand Alliance
(Great Britain, Russia, Austria, and Prussia) the right to reorder Europe without regard to French wishes. Through skillful diplomacy, Talleyrand was to
work France back into the circle of great powers, giving his nation a significant voice in the final settlement by rather unscrupulously playing on the
rights of the lesser states. At Vienna, France had nothing to lose but much
to gain—principally her position as a great power. Talleyrand, in his instructions, spoke of more than French interests (such as the restoration of Bourbon princes). He touched on the general principles that must guide the remaking of Europe.

INSTRUCTIONS

For the King's Ambassadors at the Congress

No ASSEMBLY invested with powers can do anything legitimate unless it
be legitimately constituted, and consequently, unless none of those who

have a right to be there be excluded therefrom, and none of those who have not such right be admitted; let it confine itself scrupulously to its province, and proceed according to prescribed rules, or failing such rules, according to those which may be drawn from the purpose for which it was constituted, and from the nature of things. It is the nature of things to fix the order in which it is indispensable to regulate them, by the various degrees of connection of dependence that it places between different objects, seeing that a subordinate question cannot be treated and decided before that upon which it depends. Finally the most legitimate and wisest acts would be useless and fail in their object if, for want of means of execution, they were not enforced.

It is then most necessary that the congress should determine first of all,

1. Which are the states which may send plenipotentiaries.

2. What subjects should or might be settled there.

3. By what means they can be settled; if by decision or arbitration, or by means of negotiations, or again partly by both these means, and the cases in which each of those means should be employed.

4. In cases in which the means of decision shall be employed, in what manner the votes are to be taken.

5. The order in which the subjects are to be treated.

6. The form to be given to the decision.

7. The mode and means of execution in case obstacles of any description should be met with.

According to Article XXXII of the treaty of May 30th, the congress should be 'general,' and 'all the powers engaged in the war' that that treaty terminated should send their plenipotentiaries there. Although the term *powers* carries with itself an indeterminate idea of greatness and of strength, which seems to render it inapplicable to many states deprived of the one and the other, employed as it is in Article XXXII in an abstract and general sense, restrained only by the expression of a connection entirely independent of the comparative strength of States and common to the smallest and the largest, it comprises incontestably all those between which that connection exists, that is to say, that have been in one way or another engaged in the war that the treaty of May 30th terminated.

If one excepts Turkey and Switzerland, for the republic of San-Marino cannot be reckoned, all the States of Europe, great and small, have been engaged in that war. The right of the smallest to send a plenipotentiary to the congress results then from the provision of the treaty of May 30th. France has not thought of excluding them, and the other contracting powers have not been able to do so, since stipulating for them and in their name they were not able to stipulate against them. The smallest states, being those which would most readily be excluded because of their weakness, are all, or nearly all, in Germany. Germany intends to form a confederation of which they are members; the organization of this consequently interests them in the highest degree. It could not be done without them without violating their natural independence and Article VI of the treaty of May 30, which by implication lays great stress upon it, by saying that the states of Germany should be independent and united by a federal link. That organization will be made at the congress; it would then be unjust to exclude them from it.

To these motives of justice a more practical motive of utility to France must be added. That which is of interest to the small state is of interest to her also. All wish to preserve their existence, and she should wish that they preserve it. Some of them might desire to be enlarged, and that would suit her, inasmuch as it would diminish the growth of the large states. Her policy would be to protect and favour them, but without any one being able to take umbrage on that account, which would be less easy if they did not attend the congress, and, instead of having to support their requests, she should even be obliged to make their requests for them. From another point of view, the need they would have of her assistance would give her an influence over them. Thus the question of their votes being or not being counted, is not indifferent to her.

In pursuance of which, if it should occur that, under the pretext of the smallness of any State engaged in the last war, the plenipotentiaries of the sovereign of that State be excluded from the congress, the king's ambassadors shall oppose, and shall insist on their being admitted.

The nations of Europe do not yet acknowledge in their mutual intercourse the moral law alone, nor yet that of nature alone, but are still under a law that they have made for themselves, and which gives to the first a sanction which it otherwise lacks; it is a law established by written conventions, or by usage constantly, universally, and reciprocally followed, which is always founded on mutual consent, whether tacit or expressed, and which is obligatory for all. This law is the law of public right.

Now there are in this right two fundamental principles: the one that the sovereignty cannot be acquired by the simple fact of conquest, nor pass to the conqueror if the sovereign does not cede it; the other, that any title of sovereignty, and consequently the right that it supposes, are binding for the other states only in so far as they may recognize it.

Whenever a conquered country has a sovereign, cession is possible, and it follows from the first of the principles cited, that it cannot be replaced, or supplied by anything.

But a conquered country can be without a sovereign, either because he who was sovereign has for himself and his heirs renounced his right simply, without ceding it to another; or because the reigning family has just died out without any one being legally called to reign after it. The moment a republic is conquered, the sovereign ceases to exist,[1] because his nature is such that liberty is a necessary condition of his existence, and because it is

---

[1] This refers to the former republics like Genoa, Lucca, or the Hanseatic towns, not to popular rights or sovereignty of the people.

an absolute impossibility for him to have one moment of liberty so long as the conquest lasts.

The cession by the sovereign is then impossible.

Does it therefore follow that in this case the right of conquest can prolong itself indefinitely, or convert itself into the right of sovereignty? By no means.

Sovereignty is, in the general society of Europe, what private property is in civil society. A country or state under conquest and without a sovereign, and a property without a master, are unclaimed goods; but forming both the one and the other a portion of a territory which is not unclaimed, and consequently subject to the law of that territory, and can be acquired only in conformity with that law; for example, private property, in conformity with the public law of the special state in which it is situated, and the country or state only in conformity with the European public law, which is the general law of the territory forming the common domain of Europe. Now it is one of the principles of this law that the sovereignty cannot be transferred by the mere act of conquest. Therefore, when the cession by the sovereign is impossible, it is of the fullest necessity that it be supplied. And this can only be done by the sanction of Europe.

A sovereign whose states are under conquest (if he be an hereditary sovereign) does not cease to be sovereign, unless he has ceded his right or has renounced it, nor does he lose by the conquest anything beyond actual possession, and consequently preserves the right to do all that does not presuppose this possession. The sending of plenipotentiaries to the congress presupposes it so little, that it could even have for object to demand it.

Thus the King of Saxony and the prince-primate, as legitimate sovereign of Aschaffenburg [a Napoleonic creation] (at least if he has not abdicated in the meantime), could send theirs there, and not only could they do so, but it is even necessary that they should, for in case, which is more than probable, one wished to dispose entirely, or in part of their possessions, since it would be impossible to legitimately dispose of them, without a cession or renunciation on their part, it is necessary that some one, invested with their power, cede or renounce them in their name; and as it is a third principle of the public law of Europe, that a cession or renunciation is null, if it has not been freely made, that is, by a sovereign at liberty, the king's ambassadors shall take the necessary steps that some envoy claim, in conformity with this principle, for the King of Saxony, the authorization to repair immediately wherever he may deem fit, and they shall personally second that request, and if needed, shall themselves make it.

The Duke of Oldenburg and the Duke of Arenberg, the Princes of Salm, possessed in sovereignty countries that were seized in open peace by him who named himself and who should have been their protector, and they were annexed to France, but their sovereigns did not yield. The allies do not appear to have, up to the present, recognized the rights of the houses of

Arenberg and Salm; but those rights exist, as well as those of the Prince of Isenburg, who, absent from home and in the service of France, was treated like an enemy, and whose estates are under conquest.

The princes and counts of the old German empire who have become subjects of the members of the Rhine Confederation in virtue of the act which constituted it, cannot be considered as dispossessed sovereigns, seeing that they were not sovereigns, but simply vassals and subjects of the emperor and of the Empire, whose sovereignty over them has been transferred to their new masters. The attempts that they might make to have themselves recognized as dispossessed sovereigns, and that certain powers might be willing to support, ought to be rejected as illegitimate and even dangerous. Mere hesitation on that point would suffice to agitate, and perhaps, to set on fire the whole of Southern Germany.

The order of St. John of Jerusalem might desire to send representatives to the congress, but considering that the island of Malta and its dependencies were the only territory that it possessed; that it yielded them, and that there can be no sovereign without territory, as there can be no property without an owner, it has ceased to be sovereign and can only become one by acquiring a territory.

The deliverance of a conquered country, in whatever manner it be done, returns immediate possession to the sovereign who has only lost that, and to the republic its existence. They can only retake possession, the one and the other, of that which belonged to them, and not to any one else.

The Electors of Hanover and of Hesse, the prince of Nassau-Orange as prince of Germany, the Dukes of Brunswick and of Oldenburg, who all, in consequence of the dissolution of the German Empire were independent when their countries were invaded, or disposed of, possess them to-day as legitimately as formerly.

The cities of Lübeck, Bremen, and Hamburg, had become independent by reason of the dissolution of the German Empire: that of Danzig, by the peace of Tilsit. The republics of Valais, of Genoa, Lucca, and Ragusa, were independent for centuries. All have fallen under the conquest, unless the documents by which Genoa and Lucca seemed to give up their own sovereignty be regarded as valid.

Those that are not now occupied by any foreign force, nor governed by any foreign authority, have again become what they were, and can have ministers at the congress. The others cannot.

Geneva has recovered her former independence; but she has not been engaged, as a state, in the war that the treaty of May 30 has terminated; and she is to be included in the Helvetic confederation, which also was not engaged therein.

The island of Elba forms an independent state only since the war has ceased.

Conquest being unable by itself to give sovereignty cannot return it. The sovereign who enters by conquest into a country which he has ceded cannot again become sovereign of that country, any more than a private owner can seize upon property he has already disposed of.

That which conquest cannot give to one it cannot give to several. If then several fellow-conquerors attribute to themselves or give to themselves reciprocally a sovereignty over the country which they have conquered, they commit an act which public law disapproves and annuls.

The Prince of Orange ceded all his rights to Holland, but the treaty of May 30, signed by eight of the principal powers of Europe and agreed to in the names of all, returns him that country (Open Treaty, Art. 6).

That treaty on laying down the bases of several dispositions to made by the congress, says that the former states of the King of Sardinia a portion only of which he had ceded, shall be returned him (Art. 2, Secret), and that Austria shall have as limits, beyond the Alps, the Po, Logo Maggiore, and the Tessin, which will be returning her countries that belonged to her and that she had yielded on the Adriatic Gulf and in Italy (Art. 6, Open, and 2, Secret).

The Prince of Orange possesses therefore a legitimate and actual right, and the King of Sardinia and Austria an almost actual right of sovereignty over the countries which had ceased to belong to them because they had ceded them.

But the treaty has not returned to Prussia any of the countries that she ceded at various times on this side of the Elbe. She has then no real right of sovereignty over those countries, if we except the principality of Neufchâtel, for which the last and legitimate possessor has made an arrangement with her that may be considered as a cession. The treaty has not given Tuscany and Modena back to the Archdukes Ferdinand and Francis, who consequently have not, nor can have any legitimate right as sovereign over them.

A prince who attributes to himself the sovereignty of a conquered country that has not been ceded to him usurps it. If the country previously belonged to him, and if it be vacant the usurpation is less odious; but it is still usurpation, which cannot confer legal right.

The country about Modena having been yielded, and having become an integrant portion of another state, before the war which the treaty of May 30th terminated, was not engaged in that war as a state. Thus if it possessed now a legitimate sovereign, that sovereign could not have a minister at the congress.

The country about Parma, which was likewise ceded, had likewise ceased before the war to form a separate state, and became one only after the war was over.

Tuscany is not a vacant country, though France to whom she has been ceded and united, has renounced her, because it was ceded under a condition which has not been fulfilled, on condition to furnish a determinate equivalent, which has not been furnished, and which caused the Queen of Etruria to recover her right of sovereignty over that country.

The most legitimate right can be contested, it then becomes and remains doubtful, as long as the dispute is not terminated; and the effect of that right is suspended for all cases, and everywhere when it is necessary for it to be made evident. A sovereign who is such only for the states which acknowledge him, cannot send an envoy where the representatives of all meet a portion of which do not recognize his rights.

Ferdinand IV can therefore have representatives at the congress only as King of Sicily. It is not necessary to add that he who reigns at Naples cannot have any.

From all that precedes, the following general rule can be drawn:

That every prince possessing over states engaged in the last war, a right of sovereignty which has been universally recognized, that he has not ceded, and which is not recognized in any way (be those states under conquest or not), can, as well as all states that the war found free, which have been engaged in it, and are actually free, have a plenipotentiary at the congress, and that all other princes or states cannot.

The king's ambassador shall abide by this rule, and arrange that it be adopted and followed.

The treaty of May 30th mentions as the points to be regulated at congress only the following:

1. The disposal of the territories which France had renounced (Art. 1, Secret).

2. The establishment of relations from which should result a real and durable system of equilibrium in Europe (Same Article).

3. The organization of the confederation of the German States (Art. VI, Open).

4. The guarantee of the organization that Switzerland has or shall have given herself since the treaty (Art. II, Secret).

5. The duties to be levied on the navigation of the Rhine by the bordering states (Article V, Open).

6. The application, (if it be judged practicable,) to the rivers that separate or cross different states, of the clause which provides for the free navigation of the Rhine (Same Article).

7. The universal abolition of the slave trade (Treaty with England, 1st additional Article).

But the territories which France has renounced are not the only ones to be disposed of. There are yet those to dispose of which belonged to Napoleon, in another capacity than that of ruler of France, where or to the members of his family, and over which as well for the latter as for himself, he has renounced all claim.

Outside of these territories there are many others which are under conquest. If the congress should not regulate their fate, how can it establish that equilibrium, which ought to be the main and final object of its operations? Is not a determined ratio between the forces, and consequently between the possessions of all the states, a necessary condition of it? Can certain proportions exist between the possessions of all, if the right of possession be uncertain for some? It is not a momentary equilibrium that should be established, but a durable one. It can endure only as long as the proportions upon which it is founded; and these proportions can themselves endure only as long as the right of possession shall be transmitted in such a way that they shall not be changed. The order of succession in each state ought to be entered as a necessary element in the calculation of the equilibrium, not so as to be changed, if it is certain, but in such a manner as to be rendered certain, if it is not that. There is all the more reason for fixing it, if the state where it is doubtful is a state that is about to be aggrandized; for, by giving to its present possessor, one gives to the heir of the latter, and it is necessary to know to whom one gives. The ordinary and almost inevitable effect of a right of uncertain succession is to produce civil and foreign wars, and often the one and the other at the same time, which is not only a just motive for, but again makes a necessity to remove all uncertainty on that point.

The King of Sardinia took among his titles that of prince and perpetual vicar of the Holy Roman Empire. Savoy and Montferrat, some districts of Piedmont were the fiefs of it. The right to succeed to them was regulated by the law of the Empire, and that law excluded women for ever.

The King of Sardinia possessed his other states as independent prince. The right to succeed to them could be regulated only by the laws of the Empire to which they were not subjected. Was the order of succession there established by an express law which might be applied to a circumstances for which the tacit law of usage could not replace it, because that circumstance never offered before? namely that in which the house of Savoy being divided into two lines, there would only remain women in the reigning line, a circumstance which, to say the truth, still belongs to the future, but to a future so certain and so near that, in the eyes of Europe, and respecting the points which the congress should settle, it ought to be considered as present.

. . . .

The same principle of public right which renders all claim to sovereignty null for the states which have not recognized it, applies, as a necessary consequence, to every means of acquiring sovereignty, and, therefore, to the laws of inheritance than transmit it. It is known what happened when the last prince of each of the two branches of the first house of Austria substituted (Charles II by his testament, and Charles VI by his pragmatic) a new order of succession to that which should have ended with his person. Recognized by some, rejected by the others, the new law of inheritance became the cause of a bloody contest, that did not and could not terminate except when all the states were of one accord on the right that the disposition made by each prince tended to establish.

To terminate a contest being only to acknowledge a right, those without whose recognition a right should be reputed not to exist, can proclaim it, and are indeed the only ones who can do so. And by the same means (and because it is not of Europe as of a particular state, where disputes relative to the right of property cannot have very serious results, which may not easily and quickly be terminated, and where those who can terminate them are always present) to the power of terminating the present disputes relative to the right of sovereignty, is added for the congress, not only the right but even the power of preventing them, as much as the nature of things will permit, by removing that of all causes that could most infallibly produce them, namely: uncertainty regarding the right of succession.

Switzerland enjoyed, during several centuries, amidst the wars of Europe, and though situated between two great rival powers, a neutrality constantly respected, and not less profitable to others than to herself. Not only by that neutrality the arena of war was restrained, but again many causes of war were prevented, and France found herself dispensed with devoting a portion of her means and forces to defend that portion of her frontiers, the most vulnerable, which Switzerland, always neutral, protected. If, in the future, Switzerland was no longer to be free to remain neutral, or, what amounts to the same thing, if her neutrality should not be respected, such a state of things, by the influence that it would necessarily have on the relative power of the neighbouring states, would disturb and perhaps even destroy that equilibrium which it is to establish. The treaty of May 30 only speaks of guaranteeing the organization of Switzerland; but it is necessary that her future neutrality be also guaranteed.

The Ottoman Porte was not engaged in the last war, but it is a European power, whose preservation is important for the European equilibrium. It is then useful that its existence should also be assured.

Thus the Congress should decide:—

1. The fate of the states under conquest and not vacant, of which there are two classes, including: the first, the states in litigation, that is to say, the states over which the same right of sovereignty is recognized to several persons, by different powers.

To this class belong the realms of Naples and Tuscany.

The second, the states or countries the possession of which the sovereign has lost, without having ceded them and without another person claiming sovereignty over them.

The kingdom of Saxony, the duchy of Warsaw, the provinces of Holy-See situated on the Adriatic, the principalities of Orenberg, Isenberg, and Salm, to which must be added that of Aschaffenburg (if the prince primate has not abdicated) compose the second class.

2. Doubtful rights of succession.

3. The disposal to be made of those states or vacant countries, that is to say, the states which the legitimate sovereign has renounced, without ceding them, or those over which no actual right of sovereignty has been conferred upon any one with the consent of Europe.

They form also two classes; in the first of which are included those which have not been actually assigned, but destined by the treaty of May 30, namely:—

To the King of Sardinia, the portion of his old states ceded to France, that is to say, Savoy and the country of Nice, (his other possessions not having been ceded, he remained lawful sovereign of them), and an indeterminate portion of the state of Genoa.

To Austria, the Illyrian provinces and the portion of the realm of Italy to the left of the Po, and to the east of Lago Maggiore and of Tessin.

To Holland, Belgium, with a frontier to fix to the left side of the Meuse.

Finally, to Prussia and other German states that have not been mentioned, to serve them as compensation and to be divided among them in a proportion that has not been indicated, the countries situated between the Meuse, the frontiers of France and the Rhine.

To the other class belongs the rest of the vacant countries, namely:—

The undetermined part of the state of Genoa which has not been destined to the King of Sardinia; the part of the former realm of Italy not destined to Austria; Lucca; Piombino; the Ionian Isles; the Grand Duchy of Berg, such as it existed before January 1, 1811; Ost-Frise; all of the provinces formerly Prussian, which formed a portion of the kingdom of Westphalia; the principality of Erfurt and the town of Danzig.

4. The future destiny of the Island of Elba, which, given to him who possesses it for life only, shall, at his death, become a vacant country.

5. The organization of the German Confederation:—

All those points should be so settled as to bring about a real equilibrium, into the composition of which shall enter as necessary elements the organization of Switzerland, its future neutrality, and the integrity of the recognized and guaranteed Ottoman possessions in Europe.

6. The toll dues on the Rhine the Scheldt, and the other rivers the navigation of which is to be made free.

7. The universal abolition of the slave-trade.

Neither an obligation can be created, nor a certain right of a state removed, without its consent.

In every case where it is necessary to do the one or the other, all the powers together have no more power than one alone. The consent of the party iinterested being necessary, it must be obtained or to that which, without it, would not be just must be renounced. Means of negotiations is then the only one permitted.

The means of decision is, on the contrary, the only one that can be taken when the competence, having been established (and that of the congress is an obvious consequence of the principles set forth above), the question at issue is either to proclaim a disputed right of sovereignty or to dispose of territories which belong to no one, or to regulate the exercise of a right common to several states, which, by explicit consent made it subordinate to the interest of all. For if it were necessary to secure, in the first case, the consent of him whose right is declared null, in the second, the consent of all those who pretend to a vacant territory, and, in the third, that of all concerned, never could a different be terminated, a vacant territory could never cease to be so, never could a right the exercise of which should have to be regulated according to the interest of all, be discharged.

The fate of states in litigation,

the doubtful rights of succession,

the disposal of vacant states,

and the toll dues to establish on the Rhine,

should be settled by means of *decision*, with this difference, which arises from the disparity of objects, namely that, in the first case, the litigation cannot be terminated only in so far as the right of one of those between which it exists, is *unanimously* recognized; that in the second case, the decision ought to be likewise *unanimous*; and that it should be so again, in the third, with the exception of the votes of the co-claimants, which ought not to be counted; finally that, in the fourth case, the *majority* should suffice.

The other points can only be settled by means of *negotiation:*

the fate of the countries that are neither vacant, nor in litigation, because for disposing of them otherwise than by returning them to their respective sovereigns, the consent of the latter is necessary;

the organization of the German Confederation, because that organization shall become, for the German states, a law which cannot be imposed upon them without their consent;

the abolition of the slave-trade, because it has been hitherto a matter foreign to the public law of Europe, under which the English wish to bring it now.

Out of about one hundred and seventy millions of inhabitants that Christian Europe contains, more than two-thirds of them belong to France and to the seven states that signed with her the treaty of May 30, and the half of the other third to countries under conquest, which not having been engaged in the war, have no ministers at the congress; the surplus forms the population of more than forty states, of which some would be scarcely the hundredth part of the smallest of those which signed the treaty of May 30, and which all united would not constitute a power equal to one of the great powers of Europe. What part shall they play in the deliberations? What share in the right of voting?

Shall each one have a share equal to that of the largest states? This indeed would be unwarrantable. Shall they have but one vote in common? They would never succeed in coming to an agreement. Shall they have none? It would be better, then, not to admit them. But which shall be excluded? The ministers of the pope, of Sicily, of Sardinia? or that of Holland, or that of Saxony, or only those who are not ministers of crowned heads? But who would cede on behalf of those princes if they should have to cede? Who would, on their behalf, give to the obligation, that was about to be imposed upon them, the consent that they should give? Shall their states be disposed of without their ceding them? Shall their consent be passed over when public law renders it necessary? Shall Europe thus have met to violate the principles of the law which governs her? It is on the contrary most important to enforce them more strictly now that they have been so long ignored and so ruthlessly violated. A simple means of conciliating at the same time, law and propriety would be to value the share that the states of the third or fourth order should take in the arrangements about to be made, not by the scale of power, but by that of their interest.

The general equilibrium of Europe cannot be composed of simple elements. It can only be a system of partial equilibrium. The small or medium states should be allowed a vote only in the questions concerning the particular system to which they belong—the states of Italy in the arrangements relative to Italy, and the German states in the arrangements relative to Germany. The great powers alone, being interested in the whole, should co-ordinate each part with regard to the whole.

The order which appears the most natural and suitable for treating those points, is that in which they have been presented above. That which each one has and that which he ought to keep must first be determined to know if it is necessary and what is necessary to add to it; not to dispose of vacant countries except when having good grounds for doing so to divide afterwards that which is to be divided, and thus to fix the general state of possession which is the first principle of all equilibrium. The organization of Germany can only come afterwards, for it is necessary that it be relative to the reciprocal power of the German States, and consequently that that power be previously fixed. Finally, the guarantees should follow and not precede the arrangements on which they bear.

A protocol should be kept of the deliberations, acts and decisions of the congress.

These decisions ought not to be expressed in other languages than that of ordinary treaties. To return the realm of Naples to Ferdinand IV, it will suffice that the treaty recognize that prince as King of Naples, or simply name him with that title in the following style, "His Majesty Ferdinand IV, King of Naples and Sicily."

In like manner, to proclaim the right of the house of Carignano, the treaty has only to say, "Such part of the state of Genoa is for ever united to the states of his Majesty the King of Sardinia, to be, like them, possessed in full ownership and sovereignty, and to be inherited from male to male, by order of primogeniture, in both branches of his house."

For that which concerns the manners and means of execution a guarantee common to all the recognized rights, will be sufficient, since it forces the guarantees to uphold those rights, and that it deprives from all external support the pretensions opposed to them.

After having indicated what points the congress can and should decide, and pointed out that its competence results from the very principles of law that are to serve to decide those points, it remains to consider them in the light of the interest of France, and to show that fortunately for France she sees no reason why justice and utility should be antagonistic, and does not seek her own utility save in that justice which is the utility of all.

An absolute equality of power between all the states, not only can never exist, but is not necessary to the political equilibrium, and would perhaps, in some respects, be hurtful to it. That equilibrium consists in a relation between the power of resistance and forces of aggression reciprocal of the various political bodies.

If Europe were composed of states being so related to one another that the minimum of the resisting power of the smallest was equal to the maximum of the aggressive force of the largest, there would then be a real equilibrium, that is to say resulting from the very nature of things. But the situation of Europe is not and will never become such. Contiguous to large territories belonging to one single power there are territories of a greater or less size divided in a greater or less number of states, often of diverse natures. To unite these states by a federal link is often impossible, and it is always impossible to give those which are thus united the same unity of will and the same power of action as though they were a simple body. Therefore, they only contribute to the formation of the general equilibrium as imperfect elements; in their capacity of composite bodies, they have their own equilibrium, subject to a thousand modifications, which necessarily affect that of which they form a part.

Such a situation admits solely of an equilibrium quite artificial and precarious, that can endure only so long as certain large states are animated with a spirit of moderation and justice which will preserve that equilibrium.

The policy of preservation was that of France, during the whole of the past century, until the outbreak of the events which produced the last war; and it is that policy which the king wishes constantly to follow. But before preserving, one must establish.

If Austria were to ask for the possession of all Italy, there would be no one perhaps who would not denounce such a demand, think it monstrous, and regard the union of Italy to Austria as fatal to the independence and safety of Europe. Nevertheless, by giving all Italy to Austria, the independence of the former would simply be assured. Once united in one body, Italy, by whatever right she belonged to Austria, would escape her, not sooner or later, but in a very few years, perhaps in a few months, and Austria would have acquired her only to lose her.

On the other hand, let Italy be divided into seven territories, of which the two principal shall be at the extremities and the four smallest contiguous to the largest; give the latter to Austria, and three of the smallest to the princes of her house, this would offer her a pretext by the aid of which she cause the fourth one to fall to the share of one of the princes. Let the territory at the other extremity be occupied by a man, who because of his personal position towards a number of the sovereigns of Europe, can have no hope except in Austria nor any support but hers; let the seventh territory belong to a prince whose sole strength rests in the respect due to his character, is it not manifest that in appearing to give but a portion of Italy to Austria she will really have been given the whole? and that her apparent division into different states would be, in reality, but a means given to Austria to possess that country in the only manner in which she can possess it, without losing it. Such, indeed, would be the state of Italy, where Austria is to have the Po, Lago Maggiore, and Tessin as limits, if Modena, Parma and Piacenza, if the grand-duchy of Tuscany had princes of her house for sovereigns, if the right of succession in the house of Sardinia remained doubtful, if he who reigns at Naples continued to reign there.

Italy divided into non-confederate states is not susceptible for a real but only for a relative independence, which consists in being submitted not to one influence only, but to several. The relation which causes those influences to balance each other is that which constitutes her equilibrium.

That the existence of this equilibrium is of importance to Europe is a thing so obvious that it is unnecessary to question it; and it is no less obvious that, were Italy situated as has just been surmised, all kind of equilibrium would cease for her.

What is necessary, and what can be done to establish it? Nothing except what justice requires or authorizes.

Naples must be restored to her legitimate sovereign;

Tuscany to the Queen of Etruria;

not only the provinces on the Adriatic that have not yet been ceded, but also the legations of Ravenna and of Bologna, now vacant must be returned to the Holy See;

Piombino must go back to the prince of that name to whom it belonged, as well as the mines of the Island of Elba, under the suzerainty of the crown of Naples, and who having been deprived of both properties without indemnity, has been reduced to a state bordering upon indigence.

To remove all doubts concerning the rights of the house of Carignano, and to aggrandize Sardinia.

If it were proposed to assembled Europe to declare:

"that the sovereignty is acquired by the sole fact of conquest; and that the patrimony of a prince who only lost it through his unswerving fidelity to the cause of Europe, should with the consent of Europe, belong to him into whose hands the misfortunes of Europe have alone caused it to fall,"

it is impossible to suppose that such a proposition would not be at once received with an unanimous cry of reprobation. All would feel that it tended to nothing less than an overthrow of the only barrier that the natural independence of the people has permitted reason to raise between the right of sovereignty, and force, in order to restrain the one and preserve the other, and to the undermining of the very foundations of morality itself.

[There follows a section dealing specifically with the Italian, Saxon-German, and Polish problems. Part of the last only is included here, although the questions were related.]

The re-establishment of the realm of Poland, would be a good and very great improvement, but only under the three following conditions:

1. That it be independent;
2. That it have a strong constitution;
3. That it be not necessary to compensate Prussia and Austria for the part that had respectively fallen to them.

Those conditions are all impossible, and the second more so than the two others.

In the first place, Russia does not wish for the re-establishment of Poland, in order to lose what she has acquired of it. She wishes it so as to acquire what she does not possess of it. Thus, to re-establish Poland in order to give it entirely to Russia, and carry the population of the latter, in Europe, to forty-four millions of subjects, and extend her frontiers to the Oder, that would mean creating so great and imminent a danger for Europe, that although we must do everything to preserve peace, if the execution of such a plan could only be stopped by force of arms, not a single moment should be lost in taking them up. It would be vainly hoped that Poland, thus united to Russia, would detach herself from her of her own accord. It is not certain that she would wish to do so, it is less certain still that she could, and it is certain that, if she could, and would do so at a given time, she would escape one yoke, only to carry a new one; for Poland restored to independence would be invincibly delivered to anarchy. The size of the country excludes the existence of an aristocracy properly speaking, and there can exist no monarchy where the people are without civil liberty, and where the nobles possess political liberty or be independent, and where anarchy do not reign. Reason alone tells it and the history of all Europe proves it. Thus, how on re-establishing Poland can political liberty be taken from the nobles, or civil liberty be given to the people? The latter could not be given by a declaration or by a law, it is but a vain word, if the people, to whom it is given, have no independent means of existence, no property, no industry, and no arts, all of which no declaration nor law can give, and which can only be the work of time. Anarchy was a condition from which Poland could emerge only by the aid of an absolute power; and as there did not exist in her the elements of that power, it was necessary that it came to her from outside, that is to say, that she fell under conquest. And she fell under it as soon as her neighbours wished, and the progress that has been made by those portions of her, that have been allotted to nations more advanced in civilization, proves that it was fortunate for them to have fallen in their power. Let her be restored to independence and be given a king no longer elective but hereditary; let their be added all imaginable institutions; the less free the latter shall be, and the more they shall be opposed to the genius, customs, and recollections of the nobles who shall have to be submitted to them by force—and where is that force to come from? And on the other hand, the more liberty is given to those institutions the more inevitably Poland will be plunged anew in anarchy, to end anew by being conquered. All this is because there is in that country like two peoples from whom there must be two institutions that exclude each other. Not being able to arrange that these two peoples be as one, nor to create the one power that could conciliate all; being on the other hand, without evident peril to Europe, unable to give all Poland to Russia (and the mere addition of the duchy of Warsaw to that which she already possesses would mean giving her all Poland), what better can be done than to replace things in the same state in which they were before the last division? That would be all the more advisable that it would put an end to the pretensions of Prussia on the realm of Saxony; for it is only as compensation, for what she should not recover, in the event of the re-establishment of Poland, that she dares to ask for Saxony.

Austria would also surely demand compensation for the five millions of subjects that the two Gallicias contain, or if she did not ask for it, she would become all the more exacting in all questions relative to Italy.

If nevertheless, contrary to all probability, the Czar of Russia consented to renounce that which he possesses of Poland (and it is clear that he could not do so without exposing himself to personal dangers on the part of the Russians), and if it were wished to make an experiment, the king, without expecting any favourable result from it, would not oppose it. In that case, it would be desirable that the King of Saxony, already sovereign of the duchy of Warsaw, whose father and ancestors have occupied the throne of Poland, and whose daughter was to bring the Polish crown as portion to her husband, should be made King of Poland.

But, with the exception of the case where Poland could be re-established in a complete independence of each of the three co-possessing courts, the only admissible proposition, and the only one to which the king could consent, is (save several rectifications of frontiers) to restore everything in Poland on the footing of the last division.

By remaining divided Poland will not be annihilated for ever: the Poles no longer forming a political society shall continue to form a family. They will no longer have the same country, but they will have the same language, they will thus remain united by the strongest and most durable of all links. They will arrive under foreign dominations, at the virile age which they have not been able to reach during nine centuries of independence, and the moment when they attain will not be far from that of their emancipation, when they will all converge to the same centre.

Danzig must follow the destiny of Poland of which she was only a warehouse; she will have to be free, if Poland recover her independence, or to submit again to the domination of Prussia, if the old division be maintained.

A disposition which could be made of the Ionian Islands, has already been indicated; it is important that those islands, and especially that of Corfu, should belong neither to England nor to Russia, who both covet them, nor to Austria. Corfu is the key of the Adriatic Gulf. If to the possession of Gibraltar and Malta, England added that of Corfu, she would be absolute mistress of the Mediterranean. Those islands would furnish Russia with a point of aggression against the Ottoman Empire, and with a point of support for fomenting an uprising among the Greeks. In the hands of Austria, Corfu would serve to establish and consolidate her dominion over Italy.

The order of Saint John of Jerusalem is without a capital, and it might be said, without asylum, since it lost Malta. The Catholic powers have an interest that it be restored and resuscitated from its ruins. It is true that it ceded Malta, but it is equally true that it did so only as the result of an invasion that no motive of right or even of utility could justify nor excuse. It would be to the honour of England, who, by the way, profits by that injustice, to contribute towards a separation by uniting with the Catholic powers to obtain a compensation for the order. Corfu could be given her without compromising the interests of any Christian state. It will ask the possession of it, and the king's ambassadors shall support this claim.

The island of Elba, being a possession which, at the death of him who occupies it, shall become vacant, and only at the time when it shall become so, could be restored to its former masters, Tuscany and Naples, or given alone to Tuscany.

The future of all countries under conquest, of those which are not vacant, of those which are, and of those which will become so, shall thus be completely settled.

In some of those countries, certain Frenchmen possessed, by right of endowment, estates which the treaty of May 30th caused them to lose. That harsh measure, which might be considered as unjust, relative to the endowments, situated in those countries that had been ceded, has been aggravated by the retro-active effect that was given it, in applying it to rents and revenues fallen due. The king's ambassador shall protest against such injustice, and shall do all in their power that it be repaired. The sovereign allies having given occasion to hope that they shall make, and several having already made exceptions to the clause which deprived the donors of their endowments, the king's ambassadors shall again do all in their power in order that that favour be extended and accorded to as many donors as possible.

As to the right of navigation on the Rhine and on the Scheldt, as they are to be the same for all, France has nothing to desire, as long as they be very moderate. Owing to the free navigation of the Rhine and of the Scheldt, France will have the advantages that the possession of the countries crossed by those rivers would have given her, and which she has renounced, and will not have the charges of their possession. She cannot thus reasonably regret it.

The question of the abolition of the slave-trade is decided relative to France, who, on that point, has no more concessions to make, for, if it were asked simply to remove or merely abridge the agreed delay, she could not consent. But the king has promised to unite all his efforts to those of England so as to obtain that the universal abolition of slavery be pronounced. That promise must be discharged because it has been made, and because it is of importance to France to have England on her side in the questions that interest her the most.

England, who has given herself up to conquest outside of Europe, carries a conservative spirit in the affairs of Europe. That proceeds, perhaps, simply from her insular position that does not permit of any territory be added to her own, and from her relative weakness that would not enable her to retain on the Continent the conquests she might already have made there. But, be it with her necessity or virtue, she has shown herself to be animated with a conservative spirit, even towards France, her rival, under the reign of Henry VIII, of Elizabeth, of Queen Anne, and perhaps a much more recent period.

France bringing before the congress only thorough conservative views, has then occasion to hope that England will second her, provided that she herself satisfy England on the points she has most at heart, and England has nothing more at heart than the abolition of slavery. That which was, in the origin, but a matter of interest and speculation, has become for the English people a passion carried to fanaticism, and one which the ministry is no longer at liberty to check; that is why the king's ambassadors shall give every satisfaction to England on that point, in pronouncing themselves frankly and energetically for the abolition of slavery. But if Spain and Portugal, which are the only powers that have not yet bound themselves in that direction, consented only to cease the slave-trade after the expiration of a delay of more than five years, and if that delay were granted, the king's ambassadors should arrange that France be admitted to take advantage of it.

The present instructions are not given to the king's ambassadors as an absolute rule from which they must not deviate in any degree. They can relinquish that which is of a less interest to obtain that which is of a greater one. The points the most important to France are classified according to their relative importance as follows:

1. That no opportunity be left to Austria to obtain possession for the princes of her house, or rather for herself, of the estates of the King of Sardinia;

2. That Naples be restored to Ferdinand IV;

3. That the whole of Poland do not or cannot pass under the sovereignty of Russia;

4. That Prussia neither acquire the realm of Saxony, at least in totality, nor Mayence.

In making concessions on the other points, the king's ambassadors will make them bear only on simple utility and not on obligation; in the first place, because, for nearly the totality of the points to be decided by the congress, right results from one and the same principle, and that to forego that principle with regard to one point, would be to forego it with regard to all; in the second place, because recent times have left impressions that it is of importance to efface. France is such a powerful state, that other nations can be tranquillized only by the idea of her moderation—an idea which they will form all the more easily, that she shall have given them a greater one of her justice.

The king having decided on having at the congress several representatives of his will, which must be one; his intention is, that no overture, proposal, or concession be made except with the consent of his Minister of Foreign Affairs, who himself is to go to Vienna, and only inasmuch as he shall have decided what overtures, proposals, and concessions shall be made.

Approved: signed, Louis
And below: signed: Prince de Talleyrand

Paris, August, 1814

SUPPLEMENTARY INSTRUCTIONS

From the King to his Ambassadors and Plenipotentiary Ministers

at the Congress of Vienna

The king, conforming to the instructions given to his plenipotentiary ministers before their departure for the Vienna Congress, and informed by their correspondence of an agreement formed between Russia and Prussia to establish the semblance of Poland under Russian dependence, and to increase Prussia by Saxony, has judged it advisable to address to his plenipotentiaries the following supplementary instructions:—

It appearing that the same reasons that induced his Majesty to think that the aggrandizement of Russia by Poland submitted to her dependence, and the union of Saxony to the Prussian monarchy, would be equally contrary to the principles of justice and of public law, and to the establishment of a system of solid and durable equilibrium in Europe, have been taken into consideration by other powers, and that it will be possible perhaps to cause, without disturbing the peace, Russia and Prussia to adopt views more moderate and more consonant with the general interest of Europe, by an agreement formed in opposition to that which now exists between them; his Majesty authorizes his plenipotentiaries to declare to the Austrian and Bavarian plenipotentiaries that their courts can count on the most active military co-operation, on his part, to oppose the views of Russia and Prussia, as well on Poland as on Saxony. The king's plenipotentiary ministers can confide the contents of the present instructions to the English plenipotentiaries, if they be of opinion that that might determine the cabinet of St. James to act in concert with France, Austria, and Bavaria, or at least, to remain neutral. It would be especially well to make this confidence to Count von Münster, the Hanoverian plenipotentiary.

Signed, Louis

And underneath:—

The State-minister, charged *ad interim* with the portfolio of Foreign Affairs.

Signed, Comte François de Jaucourt

Paris, October 25, 1814

The Statesmanship of the Old Order: Metternich's Conservatism

Clemens von Metternich to Tsar Alexander I, December 15, 1820,
Memoirs of Prince Metternich 1815–1829, ed. Richard Metternich,
trans. Mrs. Alexander Napier (London: Richard Bentley & Son, 1881),
Vol. III, pp. 453–76.

With the growing rift between Great Britain and the continental powers that would shortly end the system of international government by great power congress, Clemens von Metternich (1773–1859) sought to define the values for which Austria, Russia, and Prussia must stand to prevent Jacobin anarchy and war. Castlereagh, Britain's foreign minister, warned, "The principle of one State interfering in the internal affairs of another in order to enforce obedience to the governing authority is always a question of the greatest moral, as well as political delicacy. . . . To generalize such a principle, to think of reducing it to a system, or to impose it as an obligation, is a scheme utterly impracticable and objectionable." Metternich persisted, and the Troppau Protocol of November 1820 consecrated the principle of intervention by the great powers to prevent revolution. British interests in the revolutions in Greece and Latin America precluded reconciliation.

Metternich was left with no choice but to redefine the relationship between the three east European autocratic powers. Conservative thought rarely makes exciting reading, for it endorses the state of things as they are. The critique of radical or liberal weaknesses may be vigorous, but positive conservative statements seem shallow—particularly when the tide of history has already eroded the position. Metternich's notions were more important, for his time, than revolutionary doctrine. He spoke with authority on a cause he defended for a generation. More recently his position has come back into favor. Substitute *Communist* for *Jacobin*, and Metternich's views seem less out of date.

"Presumptuous man," the target of Metternich's sharpest thrusts, finally drove the statesmen of the old order from power. Metternich's position was impossible. The Habsburg monarchy could not survive the coming of liberalism and nationalism, and no man knew it better than he. The partner autocracies could and did seize nationalism as a weapon. Austria could not. Metternich argued that repression was not his stock in trade. His policy was one of "prevention" as opposed to concession. Even the British, he observed, who granted constitutional concessions were forced at times to fall back to domestic repression. Far better to do so from an uncompromised position.

Principles of government are like religious dogmas. Any discussion about them is often dangerous and always useless. The wisdom of a Government should consist in living in peace and harmony; and the surest way to attain this object is carefully to avoid all those subjects of discussion on which agreement is hopeless, and as carefully to seek out those objects in which all have a common interest. [Metternich to Neumann, October 31, 1832, *Memoirs*, Vol. V, p. 269.]

Metternich's principles dominated continental Europe for more than a decade. They were carried by momentum from the revolutions of 1830 to the revolutions of 1848. By that time everyone knew, including Metternich, that upheaval meant the end of the old order. It no longer had meaning within the realities of the economic, social, and political situation. The residual hold of Metternichian conservatism was gone.

METTERNICH TO THE EMPEROR ALEXANDER, TROPPAU, DECEMBER 15, 1820

SIRE, I have the honour to send to your Imperial Majesty the enclosed statement. I received your Majesty's commands, and have fulfilled them with an ardour which gives full liberty to my thoughts. Your Imperial Majesty will find it complete on all the questions most worthy of the meditations of every public man, of every man entrusted with grave interests—in short, of every man sufficiently enlightened to feel that to a world of folly he should oppose another full of wisdom, reason, justice, and reformation. I should have despised myself, Sire, long ago, if I did not say what I think. What in a private individual might appear a merit is simply a duty to a man in my position.

What is contained in this statement would excite a disdainful smile from the superficial persons who, full of complacency at their own imperfect knowledge, are impudent criticisers of the first interests of Society—that crowd of bawlers with crude ideas, who are the victims of their own errors, and false prophets, whenever they allow themselves to predict anything but groundless errors. This same smile would appear on the lips of a better class of men—those men who think that the most useless of all enterprises is to say what is self-evident. My conviction, Sire, is that it is always the duty of men who wish to do good to speak, for at all times, and above all at times disturbed by passion, those men who wish to do evil, the vain and the foolish, will speak. It is therefore necessary not to abandon the moral atmosphere to them altogether.

Deign, Sire, while receiving this paper, dictated by my conscience, to accept the homage of my profound respect.

CONFESSION OF FAITH

METTERNICH'S SECRET MEMORANDUM TO THE EMPEROR ALEXANDER

'L'EUROPE,' a celebrated writer has recently said, '*fait aujourd'hui pitié à l'homme d'esprit et horreur à l'homme vertueux.*'

It would be difficult to comprise in a few words a more exact picture of the situation at the time we are writing these lines!

Kings have to calculate the chances of their very existence in the immediate future; passions are let loose, and league together to overthrow everything which society respects as the basis of its existence; religion, public morality, laws, customs, rights, and duties, all are attacked, confounded, overthrown, or called in question. The great mass of the people are tranquil spectators of these attacks and revolutions, and of the absolute want of all means of defence. A few are carried off by the torrent, but the wishes of the immense majority are to maintain a repose which exists no longer, and of which even the first elements seem to be lost.

What is the cause of all these evils? By what methods has this evil established itself, and how is it that it penetrates into every vein of the social body?

Do remedies still exist to arrest the progress of this evil, and what are they?

These are doubtless questions worthy of the solicitude of every good man who is a true friend to order and public peace—two elements inseparable in principle, and which are at once the first needs and the first blessings of humanity.

Has there never been offered to the world an institution really worthy of the name? Has truth been always confounded with error ever since society has believed itself able to distinguish one from the other? Have the experiences bought at the price of so many sacrifices, and repeated at intervals, and in so many different places, been all in error? Will a flood of light be shed upon society at one stroke? Will knowledge come by inspiration? If one could believe in such phenomena it would not be the less necessary, first of all, to assure oneself of their reality. Of all things, nothing is so fatal as error; and it is neither our wish nor our intention ever to give ourselves up to it. Let us examine the matter!

THE SOURCE OF THE EVIL

Man's nature is immutable. The first needs of society are and remain the same, and the differences which they seem to offer find their explanation in the diversity of influences, acting on the different races by natural causes, such as the diversity of climate, barrenness or richness of soil, insular or continental position, &c. &c. These local differences no doubt produce effects which extend far beyond purely physical necessities; they create and determine particular needs in a more elevated sphere; finally, they determine the laws, and exercise an influence even on religions.

It is, on the other hand, with institutions as with everything else. Vague in their origin, they pass through periods of development and perfection, to arrive in time at their decadence; and, conforming to the laws of man's nature, they have, like him, their infancy, their youth, their age of strength and reason, and their age of decay.

Two elements alone remain in all their strength, and never cease to exercise their indestructible influence with equal power. These are the precepts of morality, religious as well as social, and the necessities created by locality. From the time that men attempt to swerve from these bases, to become rebels against these sovereign arbiters of their destinies, society suffers from a *malaise* which sooner or later will lead to a state of convulsion. The history of every country, in relating the consequences of such errors, contains many pages stained with blood; but we dare to say, without fear of contradiction, one seeks in vain for an epoch when an evil of this nature has extended its ravages over such a vast area as it has done at the present time. The causes are natural.

History embraces but a very limited space of time. It did not begin to deserve the name of history until long after the fall of great empires. There, where it seems to conduct us to the cradle of civilisation, it really conducts us to ruins. We see republics arise and prosper, struggle, and then submit to the rule of one fortunate soldier. We see one of these republics pass through all the phases common to society, and end in an almost universal monarchy—that is to say, subjugating the scattered portions of the then civilised world. We see this monarchy suffer the fate of all political bodies: we see its first springs become enfeebled, and finally decay.

Centuries of darkness followed the irruption of the barbarians. The world, however, could not return to barbarism. The Christian religion had appeared; imperishable in its essence, its very existence was sufficient to disperse the darkness and establish civilisation on new foundations, applicable to all times and all places, satisfying all needs, and establishing the most important of all on the basis of a pure and eternal law! To the formation of new Christian States succeeded the Crusades, a curious mixture of good and evil.

A decisive influence was shortly exercised on the progress of civilisation by three discoveries—the invention of printing, that of gunpowder, and the discovery of the New World. Still later came the Reformation—another event which had incalculable effects, on account of its influence on the moral world. From that time the face of the world was changed.

The facilitation of the communication of thoughts by printing; the total change in the means of attack and defence brought about by the invention of gunpowder; the difference suddenly produced in the value of property by the quantity of metals which the discovery of America put in circulation; the spirit of adventure provoked by the chances of fortune opened in a new hemisphere; the modifications in the relations of society caused by so many and such important changes, all became more developed, and were in some sort crowned by the revolution which the Reformation worked in the moral world.

The progress of the human mind has been extremely rapid in the course of the last three centuries. This progress having been accelerated more rapidly than the growth of wisdom (the only counterpoise to passions and to error); a revolution prepared by the false systems, the fatal errors into which many of the most illustrious sovereigns of the last half of the eighteenth century fell, has at last broken out in a century advanced in knowledge, and enervated by pleasure, in a country inhabited by a people whom one can only regard as frivolous, from the facility with which they comprehend and the difficulty they experience in judging calmly.

Having now thrown a rapid glance over the first causes of the present state of society, it is necessary to point out in a more particular manner the evil which threatens to deprive it, at one blow, of the real blessings, the fruits of genuine civilisation, and to disturb it in the midst of its enjoyments. This evil may be described in one word—presumption; the natural effect of the rapid progression of the human mind towards the perfecting of so many things. This it is which at the present day leads so many individuals astray, for it has become an almost universal sentiment.

Religion, morality, legislation, economy, politics, administration, all have become common and accessible to everyone. Knowledge seems to come by inspiration; experience has no value for the presumptuous man; faith is nothing to him; he substitutes for it a pretended individual conviction, and to arrive at this conviction dispenses with all inquiry and with all study; for these means appear too trivial to a mind which believes itself strong enough to embrace at one glance all questions and facts. Laws have no value for him, because he has not contributed to make them, and it would be beneath a man of his parts to recognise the limits traced by rude and ignorant generations. Power resides in himself; why should he submit himself to that which was only useful for the man deprived of light and knowledge? That which, according to him, was required in an age of weakness cannot be suitable in an age of reason and vigour, amounting to universal perfection, which the German innovators designate by the idea, absurd in itself, of the Emancipation of the People! Morality itself he does not attack openly, for without it he could not be sure for a single instant of his own existence; but he interprets its essence after his own fashion, and allows every other person to do so likewise, provided that other person neither kills nor robs him.

In thus tracing the character of the presumptuous man, we believe we have traced that of the society of the day, composed of like elements, if the denomination of society is applicable to an order of things which only tends in principle towards individualising all the elements of which society is composed. Presumption makes every man the guide of his own belief, the arbiter of laws according to which he is pleased to govern himself, or to allow some one else to govern him and his neighbours; it makes him, in short, the sole judge of his own faith, his own actions, and the principles according to which he guides them.

Is it necessary to give a proof of this last fact? We think we have furnished it in remarking that one of the sentiments most natural to man, that of nationality, is erased from the Liberal catechism, and that where the word is still employed, it is used by the heads of the party as a pretext to enchain Governments, or as a lever to bring about destruction. The real aim of the idealists of the party is religious and political fusion, and this being analysed is nothing else but creating in favour of each individual an existence entirely independent of all authority, or of any other will than his own, an idea absurd and contrary to the nature of man, and incompatible with the needs of human society.

THE COURSE WHICH THE EVIL HAS FOLLOWED AND STILL FOLLOWS

The causes of the deplorable intensity with which the evil weighs on society appear to us to be of two kinds. The first are so connected with the nature of things that no human foresight could have prevented them. The second should be subdivided into two classes, however similar they may appear in their effects.

Of these causes, the first are negative, the others positive. We will place among the first the feebleness and the inertia of Governments.

It is sufficient to cast a glance on the course which the Governments followed during the eighteenth century, to be convinced that not one among them was ignorant of the evil or of the crisis towards which the social body was tending. There were, however, some men, unhappily endowed with great talents, who felt their own strength, and were not slow to appraise the progressive course of their influence, taking into account the weakness or the inertia of their adversaries; and who had the art to prepare and conduct men's minds to the triumph of their detestable enterprise—an enterprise all the more odious as it was pursued without regard to results, simply abandoning themselves to the one feeling of hatred of God and of His immutable moral laws.

France had the misfortune to produce the greatest number of these men. It is in her midst that religion and all that she holds sacred, that morality and authority, and all connected with them, have been attacked with a steady and systematic animosity, and it is there that the weapon of ridicule has been used with the most ease and success.

Drag through the mud the name of God and the powers instituted by His divine decrees, and the revolution will be prepared! Speak of a social contract, and the revolution is accomplished! The revolution was already completed in the palaces of Kings, in the drawing-rooms and boudoirs of certain cities, while among the great mass of the people it was still only in a state of preparation.

It would be difficult not to pause here to consider the influence which the example of England had for a long time exercised on France. England is herself placed in such a peculiar situation that we believe we may safely say that not one of the forms possible to that State, not one of its customs or institutions, would suit any Continental State, and that where we might wish to take them for models, we should only obtain inconvenience and danger, without securing a single one of the advantages which accompany them.

According to the bent of minds in France, at the time of the convocation of the *notables,* and in consequence of the direction which public opinion had received for more than fifty years—a direction which, latterly, had been strengthened and in some sort adapted to France by the imprudent help which her Government had given to the American revolution— all reform in France touching the very foundations of the monarchy was soon transformed into a revolution. What might have been foreseen, and what had been foretold by everybody, the Government alone excepted, was realised but too soon. The French Revolution broke out, and has gone through a complete revolutionary cycle in a very short period, which could only have appeared long to its victims and to its contemporaries.

The scenes of horror which accompanied the first phases of the French Revolution prevented the rapid propagation of its subversive principles beyond the frontiers of France, and the wars of conquest which succeeded them gave to the public mind a direction little favourable to revolutionary principles. Thus the Jacobin propaganda failed entirely to realise criminal hopes.

Nevertheless the revolutionary seed had penetrated into every country had spread more or less. It was greatly developed under the *régime* of the military despotism of Bonaparte. His conquests displaced a number of laws, institutions, and customs; broke through bonds sacred among all nations, strong enough to resist time itself; which is more than can be said of certain benefits conferred by these innovators. From these perturbations it followed that the revolutionary spirit could in Germany, Italy, and later on in Spain, easily hide itself under the veil of patriotism.

Prussia committed a grave fault in calling to her aid such dangerous weapons as secret associations always will be: a fault which could not be justified even by the deplorable situation in which that Power then found itself. This it was that first gave a strong impulse to the revolutionary spirit in her States, and this spirit made rapid progress, supported as it was in the rest of Germany by the system of foreign despotism which since 1806 has been there developed. Many Princes of the Rhenish Confederation were secretly auxiliaries and accomplices of this system, to which they sacrificed the institutions which in their country from time immemorial had served as a protection against despotism and democracy.

The war of the Allies, by putting bounds to the predominance of France, was vigorously supported in Germany by the same men whose hatred of France was in reality nothing but hatred of the military despotism of Bonaparte, and also of the legitimate power of their own masters. With wisdom in the Governments and firmness in principles, the end of the war in 1814 might nevertheless have insured to the world the most peaceful and happy future. Great experiences had been gained and great lessons, which might have been usefully applied. But fate had decided otherwise.

The return of the usurper to France, and the completely false steps taken by the French Government from 1815 to 1820, accumulated a mass of new dangers and great calamities for the whole civilised world. It is to the first of these misfortunes that is partly due the critical state in which France and the whole social body is placed. Bonaparte destroyed in a hundred days the work of the fourteen years during which he had exercised his authority. He set free the revolution which he came to France to subdue; he brought back men's minds, not to the epoch of the 18th Brumaire, but to the principles which the National Assembly had adopted in its deplorable blindness.

What Bonaparte had thus done to the detriment of France and Europe, the grave errors which the French Government have since committed, and to which other Governments have yielded—all these unhappy influences weigh heavily on the world of to-day; they threaten with total ruin the work of restoration, the fruit of so many glorious efforts, and of a harmony between the greatest monarchs unparalleled in the records of history, and they give rise to fears of indescribable calamities to society.

In this memoir we have not yet touched on one of the most active and at the same time most dangerous instruments used by the revolutionists of all countries, with a success which is no longer doubtful. I refer to the secret societies, a real power, all the more dangerous as it works in the dark, undermining all parts of the social body, and depositing everywhere the seeds of a moral gangrene which is not slow to develop and increase. This plague is one of the worst which those Governments who are lovers of peace and of their people have to watch and fight against.

Do Remedies for this Evil exist, and What are They?

We look upon it as a fundamental truth, that for every disease there is a remedy, and that the knowledge of the real nature of the one should lead to the discovery of the other. Few men, however, stop thoroughly to examine a disease which they intend to combat. There are hardly any who are not subject to the influence of passion, or held under the yoke of prejudice; there are a great many who err in a way more perilous still, on account of its flattering and often brilliant appearance: we speak of *l'esprit de système*; that spirit always false, but indefatigable, audacious and irrepressible, is satisfactory to men imbued with it (for they live in and govern a world created by themselves), but it is so much the more dangerous for the inhabitants of the real world, so different from that created by *l'esprit de système*.

There is another class of men who, judging of a disease by its outward appearance, confound the accessory manifestations with the root of the disease, and, instead of directing their efforts to the source of the evil, content themselves with subduing some passing symptoms.

It is our duty to try and avoid both of these dangers.

The evil exists and it is enormous. We do not think we can better define it and its cause at all times and in all places than we have already done by the word 'presumption,' that inseparable companion of the half-educated, that spring of an unmeasured ambition, and yet easy to satisfy in times of trouble and confusion.

It is principally the middle classes of society which this moral gangrene has affected, and it is only among them that the real heads of the party are found.

For the great mass of the people it has no attraction and can have none.

The labours to which this class—the real people—are obliged to devote themselves, are too continuous and too positive to allow them to throw themselves into vague abstractions and ambitions. The people know what is the happiest thing for them: namely, to be able to count on the morrow, for it is the morrow which will repay them for the cares and sorrow of to-day. The laws which afford a just protection to individuals, to families, and to property, are quite simple in their essense. The people dread any movement which injures industry and brings new burdens in its train.

Men in the higher classes of society who join the revolution are either falsely ambitious men or, in the widest acceptance of the word, lost spirits. Their career, moreover, is generally short! They are the first victims of political reforms, and the part played by the small number among them who survive is mostly that of courtiers despised by upstarts, their inferiors, promoted to the first dignities of the State; and of this France, Germany, Italy, and Spain furnish a number of living examples.

We do not believe that fresh disorders with a directly revolutionary end —not even revolutions in the palace and the highest places in the Government—are to be feared at present in France, because of the decided aversion of the people to anything which might disturb the peace they are now enjoying after so many troubles and disasters.

In Germany, as in Spain and Italy, the people ask only for peace and quiet.

In all four countries the agitated classes are principally composed of wealthy men—real cosmopolitans, securing their personal advantage at the expense of any order of things whatever—paid State officials, men of letters, lawyers, and the individuals charged with the public education.

To these classes may be added that of the falsely ambitious, whose number is never considerable among the lower orders, but is larger in the higher ranks of society.

There is besides scarcely any epoch which does not offer a rallying cry to some particular faction. This cry, since 1815, has been *Constitution*. But do not let us deceive ourselves: this word, susceptible of great latitude of interpretation, would be but imperfectly understood if we supposed that the factions attached quite the same meaning to it under the different *régimes*. Such is certainly not the case. In pure monarchies it is qualified by the name of 'national representation.' In countries which have lately been brought under the representative *régime* it is called 'development,' and promises charters and fundamental laws. In the only State which possesses an ancient national representation it takes 'reform' as its object. Everywhere it means change and trouble.

In pure monarchies it may be paraphrased thus:—'The level of equality shall pass over your heads; your fortunes shall pass into other hands; your ambitions, which have been satisfied for centuries, shall now give place to our ambitions, which have been hitherto repressed.'

In the States under a new *régime* they say:—'The ambitions satisfied yesterday must give place to those of the morrow, and this is the morrow for us.'

Lastly, in England, the only place in the third class, the rallying cry—that of Reform—combines the two meanings.

Europe thus presents itself to the impartial observer under an aspect at the same time deplorable and peculiar. We find everywhere the people praying for the maintenance of peace and tranquillity, faithful to God and their Princes, remaining proof against the efforts and seductions of the factious who call themselves friends of the people and wish to lead them to an agitation which the people themselves do not desire!

The Governments, having lost their balance, are frightened, intimidated, and thrown into confusion by the cries of the intermediary class of society, which, placed between the Kings and their subjects, breaks the sceptre of the monarch, and usurps the cry of the people—that class so often disowned by the people, and nevertheless too much listened to, caressed and feared by those who could with one word reduce it again to nothingness.

We see this intermediary class abandon itself with a blind fury and animosity which proves much more its own fears than any confidence in the success of its enterprises, to all the means which seem proper to assuage its thirst for power, applying itself to the task of persuading Kings that their rights are confined to sitting upon a throne, while those of the people are to govern, and to attack all that centuries have bequeathed as holy and worthy of man's respect—denying, in fact, the value of the past, and declaring themselves the masters of the future. We see this class take all sorts of disguises, uniting and subdividing as occasion offers, helping each other in the hour of danger, and the next day depriving each other of all their conquests. It takes possession of the press, and employs it to promote impiety, disobedience to the laws of religion and the State, and goes so far as to preach murder as a duty for those who desire what is good.

One of its leaders in Germany defined public opinion as 'the will of the strong man in the spirit of the party'—a maxim too often put in practice, and too seldom understood by those whose right and duty it is to save society from its own errors, its own weaknesses, and the crimes which the factious commit while pretending to act in its interests.

The evil is plain; the means used by the faction which causes these disorders are so blameable in principle, so criminal in their application, and expose the faction itself to so many dangers, that what men of narrow views (whose head and heart are broken by circumstances stronger than their calculations or their courage) regard as the end of society may become the first step towards a better order of things. These weak men would be right unless men stronger than they are come forward to close their ranks and determine the victory.

We are convinced that society can no longer be saved without strong and vigorous resolutions on the part of the Governments still free in their opinions and actions.

We are also convinced that this may be, if the Governments face the truth, if they free themselves from all illusion, if they join their ranks and take their stand on a line of correct, unambiguous, and frankly announced principles.

By this course the monarchs will fulfil the duties imposed upon them by Him who, by entrusting them with power, has charged them to watch over the maintenance of justice, and the rights of all, to avoid the paths of error, and tread firmly in the way of truth. Placed beyond the passions which agitate society, it is in days of trial chiefly that they are called upon to despoil realities of their false appearances, and to show themselves as they are, fathers invested with the authority belonging by right to the heads of families, to prove that, in days of mourning, they know how to be just, wise, and therefore strong, and that they will not abandon the people whom they ought to govern to be the sport of factions, to error and its consequences, which must involve the loss of society. The moment in which we are putting our thoughts on paper is one of these critical moments. The crisis is great; it will be decisive according to the part we take or do not take.

There is a rule of conduct common to individuals and to States, established by the experience of centuries as by that of everyday life. This rule declares 'that one must not dream of reformation while agitated by passion; wisdom directs that at such moments we should limit ourselves to maintaining.'

Let the monarchs vigorously adopt this principle; let all their resolutions bear the impression of it. Let their actions, their measures, and even their words announce and prove to the world this determination—they will find allies everywhere. The Governments, in establishing the principle of *stability*, will in no wise exclude the development of what is good, for stability is not immobility. But it is for those who are burdened with the heavy task of government to augment the well-being of their people! It is for Governments to regulate it according to necessity and to suit the times. It is not by concessions, which the factious strive to force from legitimate power, and which they have neither the right to claim nor the faculty of keeping within just bounds, that wise reforms can be carried out. That all the good possible should be done is our most ardent wish; but that which is not good must never be confounded with that which is, and even real good should be done only by these who unite to the right of authority the means of enforcing it. Such should be also the sincere wish of the people, who know by sad experience the value of certain phrases and the nature of certain caresses.

Respect for all that is; liberty for every Government to watch over the well-being of its own people; a league between all Governments against factions in all States; contempt for the meaningless words which have become the rallying cry of the factious; respect for the progressive development of institutions in lawful ways; refusal on the part of every monarch to aid or succour partisans under any mask whatever—such are happily the ideas of the great monarchs: the world will be saved if they bring them into action—it is lost if they do not.

Union between the monarchs is the basis of the policy which must now be followed to save society from total ruin.

What is the particular object towards which this policy should be directed? The more important this question is, the more necessary it is to solve it. A principle is something, but it acquires real value only in its application.

The first sources of the evil which is crushing the world have been indicated by us in a paper which has no pretension to be anything more than a mere sketch. Its further causes have also there been pointed out: if, with respect to individuals, it may be defined by the word *presumption*, in applying it to society, taken as a whole, we believe we can best describe the existing evil as the *confusion of ideas*, to which too much generalisation constantly leads. This is what now troubles society. Everything which up to this time has been considered as fixed in principle is attacked and overthrown.

In religious matters criticism and inquiry are to take the place of faith, Christian morality is to replace the Law of Christ as it is interpreted by Christian authorities.

In the Catholic Church, the Jansenists and a number of isolated sectarians, who wish for a religion without a Church, have devoted themselves to this enterprise with ardent zeal: among the Protestant sects, the Methodists, sub-divided into almost as many sects as there are individuals; then the enlightened promoters of the Bible Societies and the Unitarians—the promoters of the fusion of Lutherans and Calvinists in one Evangelical community—all pursue the same end.

The object which these men have in common, to whatever religion they may ostensibly belong, is simply to overthrow all authority. Put on moral grounds, they wish *to enfranchise souls* in the same way as some of the political revolutionists who were not actuated by motives of personal ambition wished to *enfranchise the people.*

If the same elements of destruction which are now throwing society into convulsions have existed in all ages—for every age has seen immoral and ambitious men, hypocrites, men of heated imaginations, wrong motives, and wild projects—yet ours, by the single fact of the liberty of the press, possesses more than any preceding age the means of contact, seduction, and attraction whereby to act on these different classes of men.

We are certainly not alone in questioning if society can exist with the liberty of the press, a scourge unknown to the world before the latter half of the seventeenth century, and restrained until the end of the eighteenth, with scarcely any exceptions but England—a part of Europe separated from the continent by the sea, as well as by her language and by her peculiar manners.

The first principle to be followed by the monarchs, united as they are by the coincidence of their desires and opinions, should be that of maintaining the stability of political institutions against the disorganised excitement which has taken possession of men's minds; the immutability of principles against the madness of their interpretation; and respect for laws actually in force against a desire for their destruction.

The hostile faction is divided into two very distinct parties. One is that of the Levellers; the other, that of the Doctrinaires. United in times of confusion, these men are divided in times of inaction. It is for the Governments to understand and estimate them at their just value.

In the class of Levellers there are found men of strong will and determination. The Doctrinaires can count none such among their ranks. If the first are more to be feared in action, the second are more dangerous in that time of deceitful calm which precedes it; as with physical storms, so with those of social order. Given up to abstract ideas inapplicable to real wants, and generally in contradiction to those very wants, men of this class unceasingly agitate the people by their imaginary or simulated fears, and disturb Governments in order to make them deviate from the right path. The world desires to be governed by facts and according to justice, not by phrases and theories; the first need of society is to be maintained by strong authority (no authority without real strength deserves the name) and not to govern itself. In comparing the number of contests between parties in mixed Governments, and that of just complaints caused by aberrations of power in a Christian State, the comparison would not be in favour of the new doctrines. The first and greatest concern for the immense majority of every nation is the stability of the laws, and their uninterrupted action— never their change. Therefore let the Governments govern, let them maintain the groundwork of their institutions, both ancient and modern; for if it is at all times dangerous to touch them, it certainly would not now, in the general confusion, be wise to do so.

Let them announce this determination to their people, and demonstrate it by facts. Let them reduce the Doctrinaires to silence within their States, and show their contempt for them abroad. Let them not encourage by their attitude or actions the suspicion of being favourable or indifferent to error: let them not allow it to be believed that experience has lost all its rights to make way for experiments which at the least are dangerous. Let them be precise and clear in all their words, and not seek by concessions to gain over those parties who aim at the destruction of all power but their own, whom concessions will never gain over, but only further embolden in their pretensions to power.

Let them in these troublous times be more than usually cautious in attempting real ameliorations, not imperatively claimed by the needs of the moment, to the end that good itself may not turn against them—which is the case whenever a Government measure seems to be inspired by fear.

Let them not confound concessions made to parties with the good they ought to do for their people, in modifying, according to their recognised needs, such branches of the administration as require it.

Let them give minute attention to the financial state of their kingdoms, so that their people may enjoy, by the reduction of public burdens, the real, not imaginary, benefits of a state of peace.

Let them be just, but strong; beneficent, but strict.

Let them maintain religious principles in all their purity, and not allow the faith to be attacked and morality interpreted according to the *social contract* or the visions of foolish sectarians.

Let them suppress Secret Societies, that gangrene of society.

In short, let the great monarchs strengthen their union, and prove to the world that if it exists, it is beneficent, and ensures the political peace of Europe: that it is powerful only for the maintenance of tranquillity at a time when so many attacks are directed against it; that the principles which they profess are paternal and protective, menacing only the disturbers of public tranquillity.

The Governments of the second order will see in such a union the anchor of their salvation, and they will be anxious to connect themselves with it. The people will take confidence and courage, and the most profound and salutary peace which the history of any time can show will have been effected. This peace will first act on countries still in a good state, but will not be without a very decided influence on the fate of those threatened with destruction, and even assist the restoration of those which have already passed under the scourge of revolution.

To every great State determined to survive the storm there still remain many chances of salvation, and a strong union between the States on the principles we have announced will overcome the storm itself.

The Gospel of Progress:
Macaulay and Whig-Liberalism

Thomas Babington Macaulay, "Southey's Colloquies on Society," Edinburgh Review, January, 1830, pp. 538–65.

Thomas Babington Macaulay (1800–59), civil servant, historian, and politician, proved one of the most forceful spokesmen of Liberal reform. On the eve of the Reform Act of 1832, which was to herald a new middle-class age, Macaulay seized on the long and tedious *Sir Thomas More; or, Colloquies on the Progress and Prospects of Society* by the poet laureate, Robert Southey, as a point of departure for severe strictures on conservative sentimentality. Macaulay's review was slashing, neither balanced nor thoughtful. Southey posed some pointed questions about society—where it was going and why. To Macaulay, however,

Mr. Southey's political system is just what we might expect from a man who regards politics, not as matter of science, but as matter of taste and feeling. All his schemes of government have been inconsistent with themselves. In his youth he was a republican. . . . He is now a violent Ultra-Tory. Yet, while he maintains, with vehemence approaching to ferocity, all the sterner and harsher parts of the Ultra-Tory theory of government, the baser and dirtier part of that theory disgusts him. Exclusion, persecution, severe punishments for libellers and demagogues, proscriptions, massacres, civil war, if necessary, rather than any concession to a discontented people; these are the measures which he seems inclined to recommend. A severe and gloomy tyranny, crushing opposition, silencing remonstrance, drilling the minds of the people into unreasoning obedience, has in it something of grandeur which delights his imagination. But there is nothing fine in the shabby tricks and jobs of office; and Mr. Southey, accordingly, has no toleration for them. . . . he renounces the abject and paltry part of the creed of his party, without perceiving that it is also an essential part of that creed. He would have tyranny and purity together; though the most superficial observation might have shown him that there can be no tyranny without corruption.

Macaulay and men who thought like him dominated Great Britain between the first and second Reform Acts (1832–67). They were adaptable, but only within broad limits. The views of the Whig-Liberal on commercial policy, social welfare, and the role of government are set forth by Macaulay in this essay. Throughout, as Macaulay twits Southey and the "ghost" of Sir Thomas More, the tone of confidence and progress prevails. So does pride in England, the nation which historically escaped (however narrowly) the tyranny of continental absolutism. This smugness excited envy and emulation. Change within limits, due respect for established institutions, reform not revolution—these were the hallmarks of Whig-Liberalism. Two years earlier, Macaulay wrote:

We know of no great revolution which might not have been prevented by compromise early and graciously made. Firmness is a great virtue in public affairs; but it has its proper sphere. Conspiracies and insurrections in which small minorities are engaged, the outbreakings of popular violence unconnected with any extensive project or any durable principle, are best repressed by vigour and decision.

To shrink from them is to make them formidable. But no wise ruler will confound the prevailing taint with the slight local irritation. No wise ruler will treat the deeply-seated discontents of a great party, as he treats the fury of a mob which destroys mills and power-looms. The neglect of this distinction has been fatal even to governments strong in the power of the sword. The present time is indeed a time of peace and order. But it is at such a time that fools are most thoughtless and wise men most thoughtful. That the discontents which have agitated the country during the late and present reign, and which, though not always noisy, are never wholly dormant, will again break forth with aggravated symptoms, is almost as certain as that the tides and seasons will follow their appointed course. But in all the movements of the human mind which tend to great revolutions there is a crisis at which moderate concession may amend, conciliate, and preserve. Happy will it be for England if, at that crisis, her interests be confided to men for whom history has not recorded the long series of human crimes and follies in vain.

Here was the voice of the men who would make the Reform Bill of 1832, that superb constitutional expedient which conceded form but not substance. Power in England was still vested in what John Adams once termed "the rich, the well born, and the able."

SOUTHEY'S COLLOQUIES ON SOCIETY

[The opening portion of this essay has been omitted.]

It is in the same manner that Mr Southey appears to have formed his opinion of the manufacturing system. There is nothing which he hates so bitterly. It is, according to him, a system more tyrannical than that of the feudal ages,—a system of actual servitude,—a system which destroys the bodies and degrades the minds of those who are engaged in it. He expresses a hope that the competition of other nations may drive us out of the field; that our foreign trade may decline, and that we may thus enjoy a restoration of national sanity and strength. But he seems to think that the extermination of the whole manufacturing population would be a blessing, if the evil could be removed in no other way.

Mr Southey does not bring forward a single fact in support of these views, and, as it seems to us, there are facts which lead to a very different conclusion. In the first place, the poor-rate is very decidedly lower in the manufacturing than in the agricultural districts. If Mr Southey will look over the Parliamentary returns on this subject, he will find that the amount of parish relief required by the labourers in the different counties of England, is almost exactly in inverse proportion to the degree in which the manufacturing system has been introduced into those counties. . . .

As to the effect of the manufacturing system on the bodily health, we must beg leave to estimate it by a standard far too low and vulgar for a mind so imaginative as that of Mr Southey—the proportion of births and deaths. We know that, during the growth of this atrocious system—this new misery,—(we use the phrases of Mr Southey,)—this new enormity—this birth of a portentous age—this pest, which no man can approve whose heart is not seared, or whose understanding has not been darkened—there has been a great diminution of mortality—and that this diminution has been greater in the manufacturing towns than anywhere else. The mortality still is, as it always was, greater in towns than in the country. But the difference has diminished in an extraordinary degree. There is the best reason to believe, that the annual mortality of Manchester, about the middle of the last century, was one in twenty-eight. It is now reckoned at one in forty-five. In Glasgow and Leeds a similar improvement has taken place. Nay, the rate of mortality in those three great capitals of the manufacturing districts, is now considerably less than it was fifty years ago over England and Wales taken together—open country and all. We might with some plausibility maintain, that the people live longer because they are better fed, better lodged, better clothed, and better attended in sickness; and that these improvements are owing to that increase of national wealth which the manufacturing system has produced.

Much more might be said on this subject. But to what end? It is not from bills of mortality and statistical tables that Mr Southey has learned his political creed. He cannot stoop to study the history of the system which he abuses—to strike the balance between the good and evil which it has produced—to compare district with district, or generation with generation. We will give his own reason for his opinion—the only reason which he gives for it—in his own words:

We remained awhile in silence, looking upon the assemblage of dwellings below. Here, and in the adjoining hamlet of Millbeck, the effects of manufactures and of agriculture may be seen and compared. The old cottages are such as the poet and the painter equally delight in beholding. Substantially built of the native stone without mortar, dirtied with no white lime, and their long, low roofs covered with slate, if they had been raised by the magic of some indigenous Amphion's music, the materials could not have adjusted themselves more beautifully in accord with the surrounding scene; and time has still further harmonized them with weather-stains, lichens, and moss, short grasses, and short fern, and stone-plants of various kinds. The ornamented chimneys, round or square, less adorned than those which, like little turrets, crest the houses of the Portuguese peasantry; and yet not less happily suited to their place, the hedge of clipt box beneath the windows, the rose-bushes beside the door, the little patch of flower-ground, with its tall hollyhocks in front; the garden beside, the bee-hives, and the orchard with its bank of daffodils and snow-drops, the earliest and the profusest in these parts, indicate in the owners some portion of ease and leisure, some regard to neatness and comfort, some sense of natural, and innocent, and healthful enjoyment. The new cottages of the manufacturers are upon the manufacturing pattern—naked, and in a row.

How is it, said I, that every thing which is connected with manufactures presents such features of unqualified deformity? From the largest of Mammon's temples down to the poorest hovel in which his helotry are stalled, these edifices have all one character. Time will not mellow them; nature will neither clothe nor conceal them; and they will remain always as offensive to the eye as to the mind.

Here is wisdom. Here are the principles on which nations are to be governed. Rose-bushes and poor-rates, rather than steam-engines and independence. Mortality and cottages with weather-stains, rather than health and long life with edifices which time cannot mellow. We are told, that our age has invented atrocities beyond the imagination of our fathers; that society has been brought into a state, compared with which extermination would be a blessing;—and all because the dwellings of cotton-spinners are naked and rectangular. Mr Southey has found out a way, he tells us, in which the effects of manufactures and agriculture may be compared. And what is this way? To stand on a hill, to look at a cottage and a manufactory, and to see which is the prettier. Does Mr Southey think that the body of the English peasantry live, or ever lived, in substantial and ornamented cottages, with box-hedges, flower-gardens, bee-hives, and orchards? If not, what is his parallel worth? We despise those *filosofastri*, who think that they serve the cause of science by depreciating literature and the fine arts. But if any thing could excuse their narrowness of mind, it would be such a book as this. It is not strange that when one enthusiast makes the picturesque the test of political good, another should feel inclined to proscribe altogether the pleasures of taste and imagination.

Thus it is that Mr Southey reasons about matters with which he thinks himself perfectly conversant. We cannot, therefore, be surprised to find that he commits extraordinary blunders when he writes on points of which he acknowledges himself to be ignorant. He confesses that he is not versed in political economy—that he has neither liking nor aptitude for it; and he then proceeds to read the public a lecture concerning it which fully bears out his confession.

. . . .

We scarcely know at which end to begin to disentangle this knot of absurdities. . . . 'All wealth,' says he, 'was tangible and real till paper currency was introduced.' Now, was there ever, since men emerged from a state of utter barbarism, an age in which there were no debts? Is not a debt, while the solvency of the debtor is undoubted, always reckoned as part of the wealth of the creditor? Yet is it tangible and real wealth? Does it cease to be wealth, because there is the security of a written acknowledgment for it? And what else is paper currency? Did Mr Southey ever read a banknote? If he did, he would see that it is a written acknowledgment of a debt, and a promise to pay that debt. The promise may be violated—the debt may remain unpaid—those to whom it was due may suffer; but this is a risk not confined to cases of paper currency—it is a risk inseparable from the relation of debtor and creditor. Every man who sells goods for any thing but ready money, runs the risk of finding that what he considered as part of his wealth one day is nothing at all the next day. . . .

It is true, that the more readily claims of this sort are transferred from hand to hand, the more extensive will be the injury produced by a single failure. The laws of all nations sanction, in certain cases, the transfer of rights not yet reduced into possession. Mr Southey would scarcely wish, we should think, that all indorsements of bills and notes should be declared invalid. Yet even if this were done, the transfer of claims would impercept- ibly take place to a very great extent. When the baker trusts the butcher, for example, he is in fact, though not in form, trusting the butcher's cus- tomers. A man who owes large bills to tradesmen and fails to pay them, almost always produces distress through a very wide circle of people whom he never dealt with.

In short, what Mr Southey takes for a difference in kind, is only a differ- ence of form and degree. In every society men have claims on the property of others. In every society there is a possibility that some debtors may not be able to fulfil their obligations. In every society, therefore, there is wealth which is not tangible, and which may become the shadow of a shade.

Mr Southey then proceeds to a dissertation on the national debt, which he considers in a new and most consolatory light, as a clear addition to the income of the country.

'You can understand,' says Sir Thomas, 'that it constitutes a great part of the national wealth.'

'So large a part,' answers Montesinos, 'that the interest amounted, dur- ing the prosperous time of agriculture, to as much as the rental of all the land in Great Britain; and at present to the rental of all lands, all houses, and all other fixed property put together.'

The Ghost and the Laureate agree that it is very desirable that there should be so secure and advantageous a deposit for wealth as the funds afford. Sir Thomas then proceeds:

'Another and far more momentous benefit must not be overlooked; the expenditure of an annual interest, equalling, as you have stated, the present rental of all fixed property.'

'That expenditure,' quoth Montesinos, 'gives employment to half the industry in the kingdom, and feeds half the mouths. Take, indeed, the weight of the national debt from this great and complicated social ma- chine, and the wheels must stop.'

From this passage we should have been inclined to think, that Mr Southey supposes the dividends to be a free-gift periodically sent down from heaven to the fundholders, as quails and manna were sent to the Israelites; were it not that he has vouchsafed, in the following question and answer, to give the public some information which, we believe, was very little needed.

'Whence comes the interest?' says Sir Thomas.

'It is raised,' answers Montesinos, 'by taxation.'

Now, has Mr Southey ever considered what would be done with this sum if it were not paid as interest to the national creditor? If he would think over this matter for a short time, we suspect that the 'momenous bene- fit' of which he talks would appear to him to shrink strangely in amount. A fundholder, we will suppose, spends an income of five hundred pounds a-year, and his ten nearest neighbours pay fifty pounds each to the tax-gatherer, for the purpose of discharging the interest of the national debt. If the debt were wiped out—a measure, be it understood, which we by no means recommend—the fundholder would cease to spend his five hundred pounds a-year. He would no longer give employment to industry, or put food into the mouths of labourers. This Mr. Southey thinks a fearful evil. But is there no mitigating circumstance? Each of his ten neighbours has fifty pounds more than formerly. Each of them will, as it seems to our feeble understandings, employ more industry, and feed more mouths, than formerly. The sum is exactly the same. It is in different hands. But on what grounds does Mr Southey call upon us to believe that it is in the hands of men who will spend less liberally or less judiciously? He seems to think, that nobody but a fundholder can employ the poor; that if a tax is remitted, those who formerly used to pay it proceed immediately to dig holes in the earth, and bury the sum which the government had been accustomed to take; that no money can set industry in motion till it has been taken by the tax-gatherer out of one man's pocket and put into another man's. We really wish that Mr Southey would try to prove this principle, which is indeed the foundation of his whole theory of finance; for we think it right to hint to him, that our hard-hearted and unimaginative generation will expect some more satisfactory reason than the only one with which he has yet favoured it,—a similitude touching evaporation and dew.

Both the theory and the illustration, indeed, are old friends of ours. In every season of distress which we can remember, Mr Southey has been proclaiming that it is not from economy, but from increased taxation, that the country must expect relief; and he still, we find, places the undoubting faith of a political Diafoirus, in his

Resaignare, repurgare, et reclysterizare.

'A people,' he tells us, 'may be too rich, but a government cannot be so.'

'A state,' says he, 'cannot have more wealth at its command than may be employed for the general good, a liberal expenditure in national works being one of the surest means for promoting national prosperity; and the benefit being still more obvious, of an expenditure directed to the purposes of national improvement. But a people may be too rich.'

We fully admit, that a state cannot have at its command more wealth than *may be* employed for the general good. But neither can individuals, or bodies of individuals, have at their command more wealth than *may be* employed for the general good. If there be no limit to the sum which may be usefully laid out in public works and national improvement, then wealth, whether in the hands of private men or of the government, *may* always, if the possessors choose to spend it usefully, be usefully spent. The only ground, therefore, on which Mr Southey can possibly maintain that a government cannot be too rich, but that a people may be too rich, must be this, that governments are more likely to spend their money on good objects than private individuals.

But what is useful expenditure? 'A liberal expenditure in national works,' says Mr Southey, 'is one of the surest means for promoting national prosperity.' What does he mean by national prosperity? Does he mean the wealth of the state? If so, his reasoning runs thus:—The more wealth a state has the better; for the more wealth a state has, the more wealth it will have. This is surely something like that fallacy, which is ungallantly termed a lady's reason. If by national prosperity he means the wealth of the people, of how gross a contradiction is he guilty. A people, he tells us, may be too rich—a government cannot—for a government can employ its riches in · making the people richer. The wealth of the people is to be taken from them, because they have too much, and laid out in works which will yield them more.

We are really at a loss to determine whether Mr Southey's reason for recommending large taxation is that it will make the people rich, or that it will make them poor. But we are sure, that if his object is to make them rich, he takes the wrong course. There are two or three principles respecting public works, which, as an experience of vast extent proves, may be trusted in almost every case.

It scarcely ever happens, that any private man, or body of men, will invest property in a canal, a tunnel, or a bridge, but from an expectation that the outlay will be profitable to them. No work of this sort can be profitable to private speculators, unless the public be willing to pay for the use of it. The public will not pay of their own accord for what yields no profit or convenience to them. There is thus a direct and obvious connexion between the motive which induces individuals to undertake such a work, and the utility of the work.

Can we find any such connexion in the case of a public work executed by a government? If it is useful, are the individuals who rule the country richer? If it is useless, are they poorer? A public man may be solicitous for his credit: but is not he likely to gain more credit by an useless display of ostentatious architecture in a great town, than by the best road or the best canal in some remote province? The fame of public works is a much less certain test of their utility, than the amount of toll collected at them. In a corrupt age, there will be direct embezzlement. In the purest age, there will be abundance of jobbing. Never were the statesmen of any country more sensitive to public opinion, and more spotless in pecuniary transactions, than those who have of late governed England. Yet we have only to look at the buildings recently erected in London for a proof of our rule. In a bad age, the fate of the public is to be robbed. In a good age, it is much milder—merely to have the dearest and the worst of every thing.

Buildings for state purposes the state must erect. And here we think that, in general, the state ought to stop. We firmly believe, that five hundred thousand pounds subscribed by individuals for rail-roads or canals would produce more advantage to the public than five millions voted by Parliament for the same purpose. There are certain old saws about the master's eye and about every body's business, in which we place very great faith.

There is, we have said, no consistency in Mr Southey's political system. But if there be in it any leading principle, if there be any one error which diverges more widely and variously than any other, it is that of which his theory about national works is a ramification. He conceives that the business of the magistrate is, not merely to see that the persons and property of the people are secure from attack, but that he ought to be a perfect jack-of-all-trades,—architect, engineer, schoolmaster, merchant, theologian,—a Lady Bountiful in every parish,—a Paul Pry in every house, spying, eavesdropping, relieving, admonishing, spending our money for us, and choosing our opinions for us. His principle is, if we understand it rightly, that no man can do any thing so well for himself, as his rulers, be they who they may, can do it for him; that a government approaches nearer and nearer to perfection, in proportion as it interferes more and more with the habits and notions of individuals.

He seems to be fully convinced, that it is in the power of government to relieve the distresses under which the lower orders labour. Nay, he considers doubt on this subject as impious. We cannot refrain from quoting his argument on this subject. It is a perfect jewel of logic.

'Many thousands in your metropolis,' says Sir Thomas More, 'rise every morning without knowing how they are to subsist during the day; as many of them, where they are to lay their heads at night. All men, even the vicious themselves, know that wickedness leads to misery; but many, even among the good and the wise, have yet to learn that misery is almost as often the cause of wickedness.'

'There are many,' says Montesinos, 'who know this, but believe that it is not in the power of human institutions to prevent this misery. They see the effect, but regard the causes as inseparable from the conditions of human nature.'

'As surely as God is good,' replies Sir Thomas, 'so surely there is no such thing as necessary evil. For, by the religious mind, sickness, and pain, and death, are not to be accounted evils.'

Now, if sickness, pain, and death, are not evils, we cannot understand why it should be an evil that thousands should rise without knowing how they are to subsist. The only evil of hunger is, that it produces first pain, then sickness, and finally death. If it did not produce these it would be no calamity. If these are not evils, it is no calamity. We cannot conceive why it should be a greater impeachment of the Divine goodness, that some men should not be able to find food to eat, than that others should have stomachs which derive no nourishment from food when they have eaten it. Whatever physical effects want produces may also be produced by disease. Whatever salutary effects disease may produce, may also be produced by want. If poverty makes men thieves, disease and pain often sour the temper and contract the heart.

We will propose a very plain dilemma: Either physical pain is an evil, or it is not an evil. If it is an evil, then there is necessary evil in the universe: If it is not, why should the poor be delivered from it?

Mr Southey entertains as exaggerated a notion of the wisdom of governments as of their power. He speaks with the greatest disgust of the respect now paid to public opinion. That opinion is, according to him, to be distrusted and dreaded; its usurpation ought to be vigorously resisted; and the practice of yielding to it is likely to ruin the country. To maintain police is, according to him, only one of the ends of government. Its duties are patriarchal and paternal. It ought to consider the moral discipline of the people as its first object, to establish a religion, to train the whole community in that religion, and to consider all dissenters as its own enemies.

'Nothing,' says Sir Thomas, 'is more certain, than that religion is the basis upon which civil government rests; that from religion power derives its authority, laws their efficacy, and both their zeal and sanction; and it is necessary that this religion be established as for the security of the state, and for the welfare of the people, who would otherwise be moved to and fro with every wind of doctrine. A state is secure in proportion as the people are attached to its institutions; it is, therefore, the first and plainest rule of sound policy, that the people be trained up in the ways they should go. The state that neglects this prepares its own destruction; and they who train them in any other way are undermining it. Nothing in abstract science can be more certain than these positions are.'

'All of which,' answers Montesinos, 'are nevertheless denied by our professors of the arts Babblative and Scribblative; some in the audacity of evil designs, and others in the glorious assurance of impenetrable ignorance.'

The greater part of the two volumes before us is merely an amplification of these absurd paragraphs. What does Mr Southey mean by saying, that religion is demonstrably the basis of civil government? He cannot surely mean that men have no motives except those derived from religion for establishing and supporting civil government, that no temporal advantage is derived from civil government, that man would experience no temporal inconvenience from living in a state of anarchy? If he allows, as we think he must allow, that it is for the good of mankind in this world to have civil government, and that the great majority of mankind have always thought it for their good in this world to have civil government, we then have a basis for government quite distinct from religion. It is true, that the Christian religion sanctions government, as it sanctions every thing which promotes the happiness and virtue of our species. But we are at a loss to conceive in what sense religion can be said to be the basis of government, in which it is not also the basis of the practices of eating, drinking, and lighting fires in cold weather. Nothing in history is more certain than that government has existed, has received some obedience and given some protection, in times in which it derived no support from religion,—in times in which there was no religion that influenced the hearts and lives of men. . . . 'It is from religion,' says Mr Southey, 'that power derives its authority, and laws their efficacy.' From what religion does our power over the Hindoos derive its authority, or the law in virtue of which we hang Brahmins its efficacy? For thousands of years civil government has existed in almost every corner of the world,—in ages of priestcraft,—in ages of fanaticism,—in ages of Epicurean indifference,—in ages of enlightened piety. However pure or impure the faith of the people might be, whether they adored a beneficent or a malignant power, whether they thought the soul mortal or immortal, they have, as soon as they ceased to be absolute savages, found out their need of civil government, and instituted it accordingly. It is as universal as the practice of cookery. Yet, it is as certain, says Mr Southey, as any thing in abstract science, that government is founded on religion. We should like to know what notion Mr Southey has of the demonstrations of abstract science. But a vague one, we suspect.

The proof proceeds. As religion is the basis of government and as the state is secure in proportions as the people are attached to its institutions, it is therefore, says Mr Southey, the first rule of policy, that the government should train the people in the way in which they should go; and it is plain, that those who train them in any other way, are undermining the state.

Now it does not appear to us to be the first object that people should always believe in the established religion, and be attached to the established government. A religion may be false. A government may be oppressive. And whatever support government gives to false religions, or religion to oppressive governments, we consider as a clear evil.

The maxim, that governments ought to train the people in the way in which they should go, sounds well. But is there any reason for believing that a government is more likely to lead the people in the right way, than the people to fall into the right way of themselves? Have there not been governments which were blind leaders of the blind? Are there not still such governments? Can it be laid down as a general rule that the movement of political and religious truth is rather downwards from the government to the people, than upwards from the people to the government? These are questions which it is of importance to have clearly resolved. Mr Southey declaims against public opinion, which is now, he tells us, usurping supreme power. Formerly, according to him, the laws governed; now public opinion governs. What are laws but expressions of the opinion of some classes which has power over the rest of the community? By what was the world ever governed, but by the opinion of some person or persons? By what else can it ever be governed? What are all systems, religious, political, or scientific, but opinions resting on evidence more or less satisfactory? The question is not between human opinion, and some higher and more certain mode of arriving at truth, but between opinion and opinion,—between the opinion of one man and another, or of one class and another, or of one generation and another. Public opinion is not infallible; but can Mr Southey construct any institutions which shall secure to us the guidance of an infallible opinion? Can Mr Southey select any family,—any profession—any class, in short, distinguished by any plain badge from the rest of the community, whose opinion is more likely to be just than this much-abused public opinion? Would he choose the peers, for example? Or the two hundred tallest men in the country? Or the poor Knights of Windsor? Or children who are born with cawls, seventh sons of seventh sons? We cannot suppose that he would recommend popular election; for that is merely an appeal to public opinion. And to say that society ought to be governed by the opinion of the wisest and best, though true, is useless. Whose opinion is to decide, who are the wisest and best?

Mr Southey and many other respectable people seem to think that when they have once proved the moral and religious training of the people to be a most important object, it follows, of course, that it is an object which the government ought to pursue. They forget that we have to consider, not merely the goodness of the end, but also the fitness of the means. Neither in the natural nor in the political body have all members the same office. There is surely no contradiction in saying that a certain section of the community may be quite competent to protect the persons and property of the rest, yet quite unfit to direct our opinions, or to superintend our private habits.

So strong is the interest of a ruler, to protect his subjects against all depredations and outrages except his own,—so clear and simple are the means by which this end is to be effected, that men are probably better off under the worst governments in the world, than they would be in a state of anarchy. Even when the appointment of magistrates has been left to chance, as in the Italian Republics, things have gone on better than they would have done, if there had been no magistrates at all, and every man had done what seemed right in his own eyes. But we see no reason for thinking that the opinions of the magistrate are more likely to be right than those of any other man. None of the modes by which rulers are appointed,—popular election, the accident of the lot, or the accident of birth,—afford, as far as we can perceive, much security for their being wiser than any of their neighbours. The chance of their being wiser than all their neighbours together is still smaller. Now we cannot conceive how it can be laid down, that it is the duty and the right of one class to direct the opinions of another, unless it can be proved that the former class is more likely to form just opinions than the latter.

The duties of government would be, as Mr Southey says that they are, paternal, if a government were necessarily as much superior in wisdom to a people, as the most foolish father, for a time, is to the most intelligent child, and if a government loved a people as fathers generally love their children. But there is no reason to believe, that a government will either have the paternal warmth of affection or the paternal superiority of intellect. Mr Southey might as well say, that the duties of the shoemaker are paternal, and that it is an usurpation in any man not of the craft to say that his shoes are bad, and to insist on having better. The division of labour would be no blessing, if those by whom a thing is done were to pay no attention to the opinion of those for whom it is done. The shoemaker, in the Relapse, tells Lord Foppington, that his lordship is mistaken in supposing that his shoe pinches. 'It does not pinch—it cannot pinch—I know my business—and I never made a better shoe.' This is the way in which Mr Southey would have a government treat a people who usurp the privilege of thinking. Nay, the shoemaker of Vanburgh has the advantage in the comparison. He contented himself with regulating his customer's shoes, about which he knew something, and did not presume to dictate about the coat and hat. But Mr Southey would have the rulers of a country prescribe opinions to the people, not only about politics, but about matters concerning which a government has no peculiar sources of information,—concerning which any man in the streets may know as much, and think as justly, as a king,—religion and morals.

Men are never so likely to settle a question rightly, as when they discuss it freely. A government can interfere in discussion, only by making it less free than it would otherwise be. Men are most likely to form just opinions, when they have no other wish than to know the truth, and are exempt from all influence, either of hope or fear. Government, as government, can bring nothing but the influence of hopes and fears to support its doctrines. It carries on controversy, not with reasons, but with threats and bribes. If it employs reasons, it does so not in virtue of any powers which belong to it as a government. Thus, instead of a contest between argument and argument, we have a contest between argument and force. Instead of a contest in which truth, from the natural constitution of the human mind, has a decided advantage over falsehood, we have a contest, in which truth can be victorious only by accident.

And what, after all, is the security which this training gives to governments? Mr Southey would scarcely recommend, that discussion should be more effectually shackled, that public opinion should be more strictly disciplined into conformity with established institutions, than in Spain and Italy. Yet we know that the restraints which exist in Spain and Italy have not prevented atheism from spreading among the educated classes, and especially among those whose office it is to minister at the altars of God. All our readers know how, at the time of the French Revolution, priest after priest came forward to declare that his doctrine, his ministry, his whole life, had been a lie,—a mummery during which he could scarcely compose his countenance sufficiently to carry on the imposture. This was the case of a false, or at least a grossly corrupted religion. Let us take, then, the case of all others the most favourable to Mr Southey's argument. Let us take that form of religion, which he holds to be the purest, the system of the Arminian part of the Church of England. Let us take the form of government which he most admires and regrets, the government of England in the time of Charles the First. Would he wish to see a closer connexion between church and state than then existed? Would he wish for more powerful ecclesiastical tribunals? for a more zealous king? for a more active primate? Would he wish to see a more complete monopoly of public instruction given to the Established Church? Could any government do more to train the people in the way in which he would have them go? And in what did all this training end? The Report of the State of the Province of Canterbury, delivered by Laud to his Master at the close of 1639, represents the Church of England as in the highest and most palmy state. So effectually had the government pursued that policy which Mr. Southey wishes to see revived, that there was scarcely the least appearance of dissent. Most of the bishops stated that all was well among their flocks. Seven or eight persons in the diocese of Peterborough had seemed refractory to the church, but had made ample submission. In Norfolk and Suffolk all whom there had been reason to suspect had made profession of conformity, and appeared to observe it strictly. It is confessed that there was a little difficulty in bringing some of the vulgar in Suffolk to take the sacrament at the rails in the channel. This was the only open instance of non-conformity which the vigilant eye of Laud could find in all the dioceses of his twenty-one suffragans, on the very eve of a revolution, in which primate and church, and monarch and monarchy, were to perish together.

At which time would Mr Southey pronounce the constitution more secure; in 1639, when Laud presented this Report to Charles, or now, when thousands of meetings openly collect millions of dissenters, when designs against the tithes are openly avowed, when books attacking not only the Establishment, but the first principles of Christianity, are openly sold in the streets? The signs of discontent, he tells us, are stronger in England now than in France when the States-General met; and hence he would have us infer that a revolution like that of France may be at hand. Does he not know that the danger of states is to be estimated, not by what breaks out of the public mind, but by what stays in it? Can he conceive any thing more terrible than the situation of a government which rules without apprehension over a people of hypocrites,—which is flattered by the press, and cursed in the inner chambers—which exults in the attachment and obedience of its subjects, and knows not that those subjects are leagued against it in a freemasonry of hatred, the sign of which is every day conveyed in the glance of ten thousand eyes, the pressure of ten thousand hands, and the tone of ten thousand voices? Profound and ingenious policy! Instead of curing the disease, to remove those symptoms by which alone its nature can be known! To leave the serpent his deadly sting, and deprive him only of its warning rattle!

When the people whom Charles had so assiduously trained in the good way had rewarded his paternal care by cutting off his head, a new kind of training came into fashion. Another government arose, which, like the former, considered religion as its surest base, and the religious discipline of the people as its first duty. Sanguinary laws were enacted against libertinism; profane pictures were burned; drapery was put on indecorous statues; the theatres were shut up; fast-days were numerous; and the Parliament resolved that no person should be admitted into any public employment, unless the House shall be first satisfied of his vital godliness. We know what was the end of this training. We know that it ended in impiety, in filthy and heartless sensuality, in the dissolution of all ties of honour and morality. We know that at this very day scriptural phrases, scriptural names, perhaps some scriptural doctrines, excite disgust and ridicule, solely because they are associated with the austerity of that period.

Thus has the experiment of training the people in established forms of religion been twice tried in England on a large scale; once by Charles and Laud, and once by the Puritans. The High Tories of our time still entertain many of the feelings and opinions of Charles and Laud, though in a mitigated form; nor is it difficult to see that the heirs of the Puritans are still amongst us. It would be desirable that each of these parties should remember how little advantage or honour it formerly derived from the closest alliance with power,—that it fell by the support of rulers, and rose by their opposition,—that of the two systems, that in which the people were at any time being drilled, was always at that time the unpopular system,—that the training of the High Church ended in the reign of the Puritans, and the training of the Puritans in the reign of the harlots.

This was quite natural. Nothing is so galling and detestable to a people not broken in from the birth, as a paternal, or, in other words, a meddling government,—a government which tells them what to read, and say, and eat, and drink, and wear. Our fathers could not bear it two hundred years ago; and we are not more patient than they. Mr Southey thinks that the yoke of the church is dropping off, because it is loose. We feel convinced that it is borne only because it is easy, and that, in the instant in which an attempt is made to tighten it, it will be flung away. It will be neither the first nor the strongest yoke that has been broken asunder and trampled under foot in the day of the vengeance of England.

How far Mr Southey would have the government carry its measures for training the people in the doctrines of the church, we are unable to discover. . . .

It is clear . . . that Mr Southey would not give full and perfect toleration to infidelity. In another passage, however, he observes, with some truth, though too sweepingly, that 'any degree of intolerance short of that full extent which the Papal Church exercises where it has the power, acts upon the opinions which it is intended to suppress, like pruning upon vigorous plants; they grow the stronger for it.' These two passages, put together, would lead us to the conclusion that, in Mr Southey's opinion, the utmost severity ever employed by the Roman Catholic Church in the days of its greatest power ought to be employed against unbelievers in England; in plain words, that Carlile and his shopmen ought to be burned in Smithfield, and that every person who, when called upon, should decline to make a solemn profession of Christianity, ought to suffer the same fate. We do not, however, believe that Mr Southey would recommend such a course, though his language would, in the case of any other writer, justify us in supposing this to be his meaning. His opinions form no system at all. He never sees, at one glance, more of a question than will furnish matter for one flowing and well-turned sentence; so that it would be the height of unfairness to charge him personally with holding a doctrine, merely because that doctrine is deducible, though by the closest and most accurate reasoning, from the premises which he has laid down. We are, therefore, left completely in the dark as to Mr Southey's opinions about toleration. Immediately after censuring the government for not punishing infidels, he proceeds to discuss the question of the Catholic disabilities—now, thank God, removed—and defends them on the ground that the Catholic doctrines tend to persecution, and that the Catholics persecuted when they had power.

'They must persecute,' says he, 'if they believe their own creed, for conscience-sake; and if they do not believe it, they must persecute for policy; because it is only by intolerance that so corrupt and injurious a system can be upheld.'

That unbelievers should not be persecuted, is an instance of national depravity at which the glorified spirits stand aghast. Yet a sect of Christians is to be excluded from power, because those who formerly held the same opinions were guilty of persecution. We have said that we do not very well know what Mr Southey's opinion about toleration is. But, on the whole, we take it to be this, that everybody is to tolerate him, and that he is to tolerate nobody.

We will not be deterred by any fear of misrepresentation from expressing our hearty approbation of the mild, wise, and eminently Christian manner, in which the Church and the Government have lately acted with respect to blasphemous publications. We praise them for not having thought it necessary to encircle a religion pure, merciful, and philosophical,—a religion to the evidences of which the highest intellects have yielded,—with the defences of a false and bloody superstition. The ark of God was never taken till it was surrounded by the arms of earthly defenders. In captivity, its sanctity was sufficient to vindicate it from insult, and to lay the hostile fiend prostrate on the threshold of his own temple. The real security of Christianity is to be found in its benevolent morality, in its exquisite adaptation to the human heart, in the facility with which its scheme accommodates itself to the capacity of every human intellect, in the consolation which it bears to the house of mourning, in the light with which it brightens the great mystery of the grave. To such a system it can bring no addition of dignity or of strength, that it is part and parcel of the common law. It is not now for the first time left to rely on the force of its own evidences, and the attractions of its own beauty. Its sublime theology confounded the Grecian schools in the fair conflict of reason with reason. The bravest and wisest of the Caesars found their arms and their policy unavailing when opposed to the weapons that were not carnal, and the kingdom that was not of this world. The victory which Porphyry and Diocletian failed to gain, is not, to all appearance, reserved for any of those who have in this age directed their attacks against the last restraint of the powerful, and the last hope of the wretched. The whole history of the Christian Religion shows, that she is in far greater danger of being corrupted by the alliance of power, than of being crushed by its opposition. Those who thrust temporal sovereignty upon her, treat her as their prototypes treated her author. They bow the knee, and spit upon her; they cry Hail! and smite her on the cheek; they put a sceptre into her hand, but it is a fragile reed; they crown her, but it is with thorns; they cover with purple the wounds which their own hands have inflicted on her; and inscribe magnificent titles over the cross on which they have fixed her to perish in ignominy and pain.

The general view which Mr Southey takes of the prospects of society is very gloomy; but we comfort ourselves with the consideration that Mr Southey is no prophet. He foretold, we remember, on the very eve of the abolition of the Test and Corporation Acts, that these hateful laws were immortal, and that pious minds would long be gratified by seeing the most solemn religious rite of the Church profaned, for the purpose of upholding her political supremacy. In the book before us, he says that Catholics cannot possibly be admitted into Parliament until those whom Johnson called 'the bottomless Whigs,' come into power. While the book was in the press, the prophecy was falsified, and a Tory of the Tories, Mr Southey's own favourite hero, won and wore that noblest wreath, '*Ob cives servatos.*'

The signs of the times, Mr Southey tells us, are very threatening. His fears for the country would decidedly preponderate over his hopes, but for his firm reliance on the mercy of God. Now, as we know that God has once suffered the civilised world to be overrun by savages, and the Christian religion to be corrupted by doctrines which made it, for some ages, almost as bad as Paganism, we cannot think it inconsistent with his attributes that similar calamities should again befal mankind.

We look, however, on the state of the world, and of this kingdom in particular, with much greater satisfaction, and with better hopes. Mr Southey speaks with contempt of those who think the savage state happier than the social. On this subject, he says, Rousseau never imposed on him even in his youth. But he conceives that a community which has advanced a little way in civilisation is happier than one which has made greater progress. The Britons in the time of Caesar were happier, he suspects, than the English of the nineteenth century. On the whole, he selects the generation which preceded the Reformation as that in which the people of this country were better off than at any time before or since.

This opinion rests on nothing, as far as we can see, except his own individual associations. He is a man of letters; and a life destitute of literary pleasures seems insipid to him. He abhors the spirit of the present generation, the severity of its studies, the boldness of its enquiries, and the disdain with which it regards some old prejudices by which his own mind is held in bondage. He dislikes an utterly unenlightened age; he dislikes an investigating and reforming age. The first twenty years of the sixteenth century would have exactly suited him. They furnished just the quantity of intellectual excitement which he requires. The learned few read and wrote largely. A scholar was held in high estimation; but the rabble did not pre-

sume to think; and even the most enquiring and independent of the educated classes paid more reverence to authority, and less to reason, than is
usual in our time. This is a state of things in which Mr Southey would have
found himself quite comfortable; and, accordingly, he pronounces it the
happiest state of things ever known in the world.

The savages were wretched, says Mr Southey; but the people in the
time of Sir Thomas More were happier than either they or we. Now, we
think it quite certain that we have the advantage over the contemporaries
of Sir Thomas More, in every point in which they had any advantages
over savages.

Mr Southey does not even pretend to maintain that the people in the
sixteenth century were better lodged or clothed than at present. He seems
to admit that in these respects there has been some little improvement. It is
indeed a matter about which scarcely any doubt can exist in the most perverse mind, that the improvements of machinery have lowered the price of
manufactured articles, and have brought within the reach of the poorest
some conveniencies which Sir Thomas More or his master could not have
obtained at any price.

The labouring classes, however, were, according to Mr Southey, better
fed three hundred years ago than at present. We believe that he is completely in error on this point. The condition of servants in noble and wealthy
families, and of scholars at the Universities, must surely have been better
in those times than that of common day-labourers; and we are sure that it
was not better than that of our workhouse paupers. From the household
book of the Northumberland family, we find that in one of the greatest
establishments of the kingdom the servants lived almost entirely on salt
meat, without any bread at all. A more unwholesome diet can scarcely be
conceived. In the reign of Edward the Sixth, the state of the students at
Cambridge is described to us, on the very best authority, as most wretched.
Many of them dined on pottage made of a farthing's worth of beef with a
little salt and oatmeal, and literally nothing else. This account we have from
a contemporary master of St. Johns. Our parish poor now eat wheaten
bread. In the sixteenth century the labourer was glad to get barley, and
was often forced to content himself with poorer fare. In Harrison's introduction to Holinshed we have an account of the state of our working population in the 'golden days,' as Mr Southey calls them, of good Queen Bess.
'The gentilitie,' says he, 'commonly provide themselves sufficiently of wheat
for their own tables, whylest their household and poore neighbours in some
shires are inforced to content themselves with rice or barleie; yea, and in
time of dearth, many with bread made eyther of beanes, peason, or otes, or
of altogether, and some acornes among. I will not say that this extremity is
oft so well to be seen in time of plentie as of dearth; but if I should I could
easily bring my trial: for albeit there be much more grounde cared nowe
almost in everye place then hath beene of late yeares, yet such a price of
corne continueth in eache towne and markete, without any just cause, that

the artificer and poore labouring man is not able to reach unto it, but is driven to content himself with horse-corne; I mean beanes, peason, otes, tares, and lintelles.' We should like to see what the effect would be of putting any parish in England now on allowance of 'horse-corne.' The helotry of Mammon are not, in our day, so easily enforced to content themselves as the peasantry of that happy period, as Mr Southey considers it, which elapsed between the fall of the feudal and the rise of the commercial tyranny.

'The people,' says Mr Southey, 'are worse fed than when they were fishers.' And yet in another place he complains that they will not eat fish. 'They have contracted,' says he, 'I know not how, some obstinate prejudice against a kind of food at once wholesome and delicate, and everywhere to be obtained cheaply and in abundance, were the demand for it as general as it ought to be.' It is true that the lower orders have an obstinate prejudice against fish. But hunger has no such obstinate prejudices. If what was formerly a common diet is now eaten only in times of severe pressure, the inference is plain. The people must be fed with what they at least think better food than that of their ancestors.

The advice and medicine which the poorest labourer can now obtain, in disease or after an accident, is far superior to what Henry the Eighth could have commanded. Scarcely any part of the country is out of the reach of practitioners, who are probably not so far inferior to Sir Henry Halford as they are superior to Sir Anthony Denny. That there has been a great improvement in this respect Mr Southey allows. Indeed he could not well have denied it. 'But,' says he, 'the evils for which these sciences are the palliative, have increased since the time of the Druids, in a proportion that heavily overweighs the benefit of improved therapeutics.' We know nothing either of the diseases or the remedies of the Druids. But we are quite sure that the improvement of medicine has far more than kept pace with the increase of disease during the last three centuries. This is proved by the best possible evidence. The term of human life is decidedly longer in England than in any former age, respecting which we possess any information on which we can rely. All the rants in the world about picturesque cottages and temples of Mammon will not shake this argument. No test of the state of society can be named so decisive as that which is furnished by bills of mortality. That the lives of the people of this country have been gradually lengthening during the course of several generations, is as certain as any fact in statistics, and that the lives of men should become longer and longer, while their physical condition, during life, is becoming worse and worse, is utterly incredible.

Let our readers think over these circumstances. Let them take into the account the sweating sickness and the plague. Let them take into the account that fearful disease which first made its appearance in the generation to which Mr Southey assigns the palm of felicity, and raged through Europe with a fury at which the physician stood aghast, and before which the people were swept away by thousands. Let them consider the state of the northern counties, constantly the scene of robberies, rapes, massacres, and conflagrations. Let them add to all this the fact that seventy-two thousand persons suffered death by the hands of the executioner during the reign of Henry the Eighth, and judge between the nineteenth and the sixteenth century.

We do not say that the lower orders in England do not suffer severe hardships. But, in spite of Mr Southey's assertions, and in spite of the assertions of a class of politicians, who, differing from Mr Southey in every other point, agree with him in this, we are inclined to doubt whether they really suffer greater physical distress than the labouring classes of the most flourishing countries of the Continent.

It will scarcely be maintained that the lazzaroni who sleep under the porticos of Naples, or the beggars who besiege the convents of Spain, are in a happier situation than the English commonalty. The distress which has lately been experienced in the northern part of Germany, one of the best governed and most prosperous districts of Europe, surpasses, if we have been correctly informed, any thing which has of late years been known among us. In Norway and Sweden the peasantry are constantly compelled to mix bark with their bread, and even this expedient has not always preserved whole families and neighbourhoods from perishing together of famine. An experiment has lately been tried in the kingdom of the Netherlands, which has been cited to prove the possibility of establishing agricultural colonies on the waste-lands of England; but which proves to our minds nothing so clearly as this, that the rate of subsistence to which the labouring classes are reduced in the Netherlands is miserably low, and very far inferior to that of the English paupers. No distress which the people here have endured for centuries, approaches to that which has been felt by the French in our own time. The beginning of the year 1817, was a time of great distress in this island. But the state of the lowest classes here was luxury compared with that of the people of France. We find in Magendie's *Journal de Physiolo ge Expermentale*, a paper on a point of physiology connected with the distress of that season. It appears that the inhabitants of six departments, Aix, Jura, Doubs, Haute Saone, Vosges, and Saone et Loire, were reduced first to oatmeal and potatoes, and at last to nettles, beanstalks, and other kinds of herbage fit only for cattle; that when the next harvest enabled them to eat barley-bread, many of them died from intemperate indulgence in what they thought an exquisite repast; and that a dropsy of a peculiar description was produced by the hard fare of the year. Dead bodies were found on the roads and in the fields. A single surgeon dissected six of these, and found the stomach shrunk, and filled with unwholesome aliments which hunger had driven men to share with beasts. Such extremity of distress as this is never heard of in England, or even in Ireland. We are, on the whole, inclined to think, though we would speak with diffidence on a point on which it would be rash to pronounce a positive judgment without a much longer and closer investigation than we have bestowed upon it, that the labouring classes of this island, though they have their grievances and distresses, some produced by their own improvidence, some by the errors of their rulers, are on the whole better off as to physical comforts, than the inhabitants of any equally extensive district of the old world. On this very account, suffering is more acutely felt and more loudly bewailed here than elsewhere. We must take into the account the liberty of discussion, and the strong interest which the opponents of a ministry always have to exaggerate the extent of the public disasters. There are many parts of Europe in which the people quietly endure distress that here would shake the foundations of the state,—in which the inhabitants of a whole province turn out to eat grass with less clamour than one Spitalfields weaver would make here, if the overseers were to put him on barley-bread. In those new countries in which a civilized population has at its command a boundless extent of the richest soil, the condition of the labourer is probably happier than in any society which has lasted for many centuries. But in the old world we must confess ourselves unable to find any satisfactory record of any great nation, past or present, in which the working classes have been in a more comfortable situation than in England during the last thirty years. When this island was thinly peopled, it was barbarous. There was little capital; and that little was insecure. It is now the richest and the most highly civilized spot in the world; but the population is dense. Thus we have never known that golden age, which the lower orders in the United States are now enjoying. We have never known an age of liberty, of order, and of education, an age in which the mechanical sciences were carried to a great height, yet in which the people were not sufficiently numerous to cultivate even the most fertile valleys. But, when we compare our own condition with that of our ancestors, we think it clear that the advantages arising from the progress of civilisation have far more than counterbalanced the disadvantages arising from the progress of population. While our numbers have increased tenfold, our wealth has increased a hundred fold. Though there are so many more people to share the wealth now existing in the country than there were in the sixteenth century, it seems certain, that a greater share falls to almost every individual, than fell to the share of any of the corresponding class in the sixteenth century. The King keeps a more splendid court. The establishments of the nobles are more magnificent. The esquires are richer, the merchants are richer, the shopkeepers are richer. The serving-man, the artisan, and the husbandman, have a more copious and palatable supply of food, better clothing, and better furniture. This is no reason for tolerating abuses, or for neglecting any means of ameliorating the condition of our poorer countrymen. But it is a reason against telling them, as some of our philosophers are constantly telling them, that they are the most wretched people who ever existed on the face of the earth.

We have already adverted to Mr Southey's amusing doctrine about national wealth. A state, says he, cannot be too rich; but a people may be too rich. His reason for thinking this, is extremely curious.

A people may be too rich, because it is the tendency of the commercial, and more especially, of the manufacturing system, to collect wealth rather than to diffuse it. Where wealth is necessarily employed in any of the speculations of trade, its increase is in proportion to its amount. Great capitalists become like pikes in a fish-pond, who devour the weaker fish; and it is but too certain, that the poverty of one part of the people seems to increase in the same ratio as the riches of another. There are examples of this in history. In Portugal, when the high tide of wealth flowed in from the conquests in Africa and the East, the effect of that great influx was not more visible in the augmented splendour of the court, and the luxury of the higher ranks, than in the distress of the people.

Mr Southey's instance is not a very fortunate one. The wealth which did so little for the Portuguese was not the fruit, either of manufactures or of commerce carried on by private individuals. It was the wealth, not of the people, but of the government and its creatures, of those who, as Mr Southey thinks, can never be too rich. The fact is, that Mr Southey's proposition is opposed to all history, and to the phenomena which surround us on every side. England is the richest country in Europe, the most commercial, and the most manufacturing. Russia and Poland are the poorest countries in Europe. They have scarcely any trade, and none but the rudest manufactures. Is wealth more diffused in Russia and Poland than in England? There are individuals in Russia and Poland, whose incomes are probably equal to those of our richest countrymen. It may be doubted, whether there are not, in those countries, as many fortunes of eighty thousand a-year, as here. But are there as many fortunes of five thousand a-year, or of one thousand a-year? There are parishes in England, which contain more people of between five hundred and three thousand pounds a-year, than could be found in all the dominions of the Emperor Nicholas. The neat and commodious houses which have been built in London and its vicinity, for people of this class, within the last thirty years, would of themselves form a city larger than the capitals of some European kingdoms. And this is the state of society in which the great properties have devoured the smaller!

The cure which Mr Southey thinks that he has discovered is worthy of the sagacity which he has shown in detecting the evil. The calamities arising from the collection of wealth in the hands of a few capitalists are to be remedied by collecting it in the hands of one great capitalist, who has no conceivable motive to use it better than other capitalists,—the all-devouring state.

It is not strange that, differing so widely from Mr Southey as to the past progress of society, we should differ from him also as to its probable destiny. He thinks, that to all outward appearance, the country is hastening to destruction; but he relies firmly on the goodness of God. We do not see either the piety, or the rationality, of thus confidently expecting that the Supreme Being will interfere to disturb the common succession of causes and effects. We, too, rely on his goodness,—on his goodness as manifested, not in extraordinary interpositions, but in those general laws which it has pleased him to establish in the physical and in the moral world. We rely on the natural tendency of the human intellect to truth, and on the natural tendency of society to improvement. We know no well-authenticated instance of a people which has decidedly retrograded in civilisation and prosperity, except from the influence of violent and terrible calamities,— such as those which laid the Roman Empire in ruins, or those which, about the beginning of the sixteenth century, desolated Italy. We know of no country which, at the end of fifty years of peace and tolerably good government, has been less prosperous than at the beginning of that period. The political importance of a state may decline, as the balance of power is disturbed by the introduction of new forces. Thus the influence of Holland and of Spain is much diminished. But are Holland and Spain poorer than formerly? We doubt it. Other countries have outrun them. But we suspect that they have been positively, though not relatively, advancing. We suspect that Holland is richer than when she sent her navies up the Thames,— that Spain is richer than when a French king was brought captive to the footstool of Charles the Fifth.

History is full of the signs of this natural progress of society. We see in almost every part of the annals of mankind how the industry of individuals, struggling up against wars, taxes, famines, conflagrations, mischievous prohibitions, and more mischievous protections, creates faster than governments can squander, and repairs whatever invaders can destroy. We see the capital of nations increasing, and all the arts of life approaching nearer and nearer to perfection, in spite of the grossest corruption, and the wildest production on the part of rulers.

The present moment is one of great distress. But how small will that distress appear when we think over the history of the last forty years;—a war, compared with which, all other wars sink into insignificance;—taxation, such as the most heavily taxed people of former times could not have conceived;—a debt larger than all the public debts that ever existed in the world added together;—the food of the people studiously rendered dear;— the currency imprudently debased, and imprudently restored. Yet is the country poorer than in 1790? We fully believe that, in spite of all the misgovernment of her rulers, she has been almost constantly becoming richer and richer. Now and then there has been a stoppage, now and then a short retrogression; but as to the general tendency there can be no doubt. A single breaker may recede, but the tide is evidently coming in.

If we were to prophesy that in the year 1930, a population of fifty millions, better fed, clad, and lodged than the English of our time, will cover these islands,—that Sussex and Huntingdonshire will be wealthier than the wealthiest parts of the West-Riding of Yorkshire now are,—that cultivation, rich as that of a flower-garden, will be carried up to the very tops of Ben Nevis and Helvellyn,—that machines, constructed on principles yet undis-

covered, will be in every house,—that there will be no highways but rail-
roads, no travelling but by steam,—that our debt, vast as it seems to us, will
appear to our great-grandchildren a trifling encumbrance, which might
easily be paid off in a year or two,—many people would think us insane. We
prophesy nothing; but this we say—If any person had told the Parliament
which met in perplexity and terror after the crash in 1720, that in 1830 the
wealth of England would surpass all their wildest dreams—that the annual
revenue would equal the principal of that debt which they considered as
an intolerable burden—that for one man of L.10,000 then living, there
would be five men of L.50,000; that London would be twice as large and
twice as populous, and that nevertheless the mortality would have diminished to one-half what it then was,—that the post-office would bring more
into the exchequer than the excise and customs had brought in together
under Charles II,—that stage-coaches would run from London to York in
twenty-four hours—that men would sail without wind, and would be beginning to ride without horses—our ancestors would have given as much
credit to the prediction as they gave to Gulliver's Travels. Yet the prediction would have been true; and they would have perceived that it was not
altogether absurd; if they had considered that the country was then raising
every year a sum which would have purchased the fee-simple of the revenue of the Plantagenets—ten times what supported the government of
Elizabeth—three times what, in the time of Oliver Cromwell, had been
thought intolerably oppressive. To almost all men the state of things under
which they have been used to live seems to be the necessary state of things.
We have heard it said, that five per cent is the natural interest of money,
that twelve is the natural number of a jury, that forty shillings is the natural
qualification of a county voter. Hence it is, that though, in every age, every
body knows that up to his own time progressive improvement has been
taking place, nobody seems to reckon on any improvement during the next
generation. We cannot absolutely prove that those are in error who tell us
that society has reached a turning point—that we have seen our best days.
But so said all who came before us, and with just as much apparent reason.
'A million a-year will beggar us,' said the patriots of 1640. 'Two millions
a-year will grind the country to powder,' was the cry in 1660. 'Six millions
a-year, and a debt of fifty millions!' exclaimed Swift—'the high allies have
been the ruin of us.' 'A hundred and forty millions of debt!' said Junius—
'well may we say that we owe Lord Chatham more than we shall ever pay,
if we owe him such a load as this.' 'Two hundred and forty millions of debt!'
cried all the statesmen of 1783 in chorus—'what abilities, or what economy
on the part of a minister, can save a country so burdened?' We know that if,
since 1783, no fresh debt had been incurred, the increased resources of the
country would have enabled us to defray that burden, at which Pitt, Fox,
and Burke stood aghast—to defray it over and over again, and that with
much lighter taxation than what we have actually borne. On what prin-

ciple is it, that when we see nothing but improvement behind us, we are to expect nothing but deterioration before us?

It is not by the intermeddling of Mr Southey's idol—the omniscient and omnipotent State—but by the prudence and energy of the people, that England has hitherto been carried forward in civilisation; and it is to the same prudence and the same energy that we now look with comfort and good hope. Our rulers will best promote the improvement of the people by strictly confining themselves to their own legitimate duties—by leaving capital to find its most lucrative course, commodities their fair price, industry and intelligence their natural reward, idleness and folly their natural punishment—by maintaining peace, by defending property, by diminishing the price of law, and by observing strict economy in every department of the state. Let the Government do this—the People will assuredly do the rest.

The Flaws of Liberalism:
The Hegelian Critique

Georg Wilhelm Friedrich Hegel, "Concerning the English Reform Bill," The Philosophy of Hegel, ed. Carl J. Friedrich (New York: Random House, Inc., 1954), pp. 540–45.

Georg Wilhelm Friedrich Hegel (1770–1831) established a well-deserved reputation as a philosopher, political theorist, and historian. His influence in each was far-reaching and touched many of diverse political views. Hegel was no ivory-tower philosopher. His serious work ranged from the *Constitution of Germany* (1802) to the *System of Philosophy* (1812–16), *Fundamentals of the Philosophy of Right* (1821), and the posthumously published *Philosophy of History* (1837), but he also commented on affairs of the day in the periodical press. By the 1820's Hegel's followers elevated him from scholar and professor to a cult.

The revolutionary movements of 1830 created barely a ripple in many parts of Europe. Only in France, England, and Belgium were the results striking. Hegel was not a revolutionary. If he was not himself a conservative— and recall that the apogee of modern history in political form was his Prussian state—he certainly served his master, the King of Prussia, well during his years at the University of Berlin (1816–31). Hegel was antiutilitarian and he had grave qualms about the proposed English constitutional reform. The essay (as edited and abridged) does not concern triadic movement from thesis and antithesis to synthesis nor the realization of the absolute. It was the comment of the thinker who wrote political philosophy grounded in universal history.

CONCERNING THE ENGLISH REFORM BILL

THE PRESENT REFORM BILL before the English Parliament intends first of all to introduce justice and equity into the distribution of the share which the different classes and divisions of the people have in the election of members of Parliament, by establishing more order and symmetry in place of the present most bizarre, most deformed irregularities and inequalities. But the noble entrails, the vital principles of the constitution of Great Britain are at the same time being invaded. The more elevated views which have been expressed in the parliamentary debates shall be reviewed here. That the bill has encountered so much opposition, and the second reading only passed with one vote, cannot surprise one, since the powerful interests of the aristocracy which dominate the lower house are the very ones the bill attacks and seeks to reform.

The projected reform starts from the incontestable fact that the basis for determining the share which the several counties and communities of England should have in forming the Parliament has completely changed in the course of time. One of the most important opponents of the bill, Robert

66

Peel, admits that it may be easy to discourse upon the anomalies and the absurdity of the English constitution, and these absurdities have been in all detail presented both in Parliament and in the press.

[Here follow the familiar facts about parliamentary corruption.]

Hardly ever a similar symptom of the political rottenness of a people can be shown. Montesquieu has declared virtue, the unselfish sense of duty toward the state, to be the principle of the democratic constitution. In the English constitution, the democratic element plays an important part through the participation of the people in the election of the members of the Commons—the statesmen who have the largest share in the power of deciding upon general matters. It is a nearly general opinion among historians that when private interests and dirty monetary advantage interfere in the election of the key men of the state, such a state of affairs must be considered a precursor to the loss of political freedom, of the collapse of its constitution and of the state itself. We Germans may observe that even though the former Reich constitution was a shapeless aggregate of particular interests, it was merely the outer bond of the German states, and that political life in these states never reached the degree of absurdity in relation to appointments and elections nor even less that rottenness permeating all classes of society.

[After elaborating his sharply critical views, Hegel completes this section by pointing out that far from strengthening the monarchical element, the proposed reform is expected further to weaken it. After reviewing a number of more detailed provisions with care, Hegel returns to the problem of the distribution of governmental powers which seems to him the really crucial issue.]

The peculiar feature of England that a power which is supposed to be subordinate and the members of which decide the general affairs of the state, though without instruction, responsibility or the quality of officials, brings it about that the monarchical power and the power of government are quite distinct from each other. To the monarchical power are attributed the main branches of supreme political power, foreign relations, peace and war, command of the army and appointment of the ministers, the officers, the ambassadors, etc. But since to Parliament is given the sovereign decision over the budget (including even the civil list), that is to say the decision over all the means for making war, having an army, ambassadors, etc., and a ministry can therefore only govern, i.e., exist, if it agrees with the opinions and the will of Parliament, the share of the monarch of governmental authority is illusory rather than real, and the substance is found in Parliament.

[After recalling Siéyès' ill-fated scheme for reproducing such a system on a republican basis, Hegel remarks that the true power to govern always coincides with the power to appoint the chief ministers.]

This power we see in England to be in the hands of Parliament; if in the several monarchical constitutions . . . the formal separation of the governmental power as the executive from a strictly legislative and judicial power is enunciated. The appointment of the ministry is still the center of the contest and struggle, even if this right is unconditionally attributed to the crown, and the so-called merely legislative power has achieved victory; under the newest French constitution, too, the government found itself soon forced to establish its headquarters in the Chamber of Deputies.

To this power of government invested in Parliament is related what the enemies of the reform put forward as arguments in favor of rotten boroughs, namely, that as a result of this fact which implies that many parliamentary seats depend upon a few individuals or families, the most eminent statesmen of England have found their way into Parliament and from there into the ministry.

[Hegel admits that private friendship may well have done this; yet he suggests that this belongs to the realm of accidents in which new advantages may counterbalance the loss of these old ones.]

Connected with this is another supposed consequence of greater importance to which the Duke of Wellington has drawn attention. He does not possess the reputation of an orator, because he lacks fluent, ostentatious loquacity which entertains by the hour by which so many members of Parliament have achieved great fame as orators. His discourses, the disjointed sentences of which he is criticized for, often contain viewpoints which hit the essence of the matter. He utters the concern, lest entirely new men will replace those now charged with attending to the public interest, and he asks whether the merchants who will constitute the majority of the electorate under the new bill, are the kind of people who should choose members of Parliament for the great council of the nation which decides about domestic and foreign affairs, about agriculture, colonies and manufactures. The Duke is speaking from his knowledge of the English Parliament in which a small number of talented men who devote themselves completely to political activity and the state's interest stand above a mass of incompetent and ignorant members who possess only the lacquer of common prejudices and such education as one gathers from conversation.

[After elaborating this thought, Hegel observes:]

Where the public service is not made dependent upon conditions such as scientific studies, public examinations, practical preparation, etc., an individual must join a class and a party; it must acquire importance within this group, and will be supported by its influence. There are only rare exceptions.

A main factor of the power of this sort of cohesion—the other bonds of it like family connections, politicking, speaking at dinners, etc., the endless correspondence carried on to all parts of the world, even the joint hanging around at country estates, races, and fox hunts need not be disturbed—

namely, the disposition over many parliamentary seats, may indeed be greatly modified by the reform bill. This may well have the effect which the Duke mentions that many new individuals may take the place of those who now belong to the circle that concerns itself with the interest of the government of the state. But it may also have the advantage that the uniformity of maxims and prejudices which prevail in that class and constitute the common sense (*Verstand*) of Parliament may be disturbed.

[Hegel proceeds to develop this aspect of the matter quite fully, wisely recognizing that the new men may be often *hommes de principe* rather than *hommes d'état*. He also suggests that the distribution of power may be further changed. Not that the question of parliamentary supremacy would be at issue; for that has long been settled. But the effective power of Parliament may be exercised in a different way, since the opposition may change its character; instead of the near alikeness of the two parties, a sharper conflict may arise, and the parties may fight over other matters than who is to become minister. Alluding to the French situation, where the opposition is a matter of radical divergence of principle, more especially such abstract principles as freedom, equality, popular sovereignty and the like, Hegel points to a basic conflict or paradox:]

Obedience to law is admitted as necessary, but when demanded by the authorities who are, after all, human beings, such obedience seems to be opposed to freedom; the authority to command, and the difference between commanding and obeying is contrary to equality; a multitude of people can give itself the title of people, and with justification, for the people are this indefinite multitude; from it are distinguished the authorities and the officials, and they appear therefore to be without right, since they have stepped outside this equality and stand opposite the people which has the great advantage of being recognized as the sovereign will. These are the extreme of contradictions between which a nation is torn which has been seized by these formal categories. The members of the English Parliament and generally Englishmen have a more practical political sense and have a notion of what is involved in government and governing. Furthermore, the nature of their constitution is such that the government does not interfere in the particular spheres of social life, the administration of the counties, and towns, the affairs of church and education, and in other common concerns, such as road-building. This freer and more concrete condition of civic life may increase the probability that the formal principles of freedom will not be accepted by the class above the lower one—which latter is, however, very large in England and is most receptive to such formalism— though the opponents of the reform bill see it as threateningly near.

[Hegel concludes with a statement that if the contrary should prove to be the case, and yet the opposition not be able to prevail, they might be tempted to appeal to the people and to bring about a revolution, rather than a reform.]

The Soul of a Nation:
Mickiewicz's Poland

Adam Mickiewicz, "The Books of the Polish Nation" (1832), Konrad
Wallenrod and Other Writings, trans. Jewell Parish, Dorothea Prall
Radin, George Rapall Noyes, et al. (Berkeley: University of California
Press, 1925), pp. 133–43.

Early nineteenth-century nationalism assumed many forms. Count Széchenyi
sought to introduce classical political economy into Hungary and turn the
Magyars into English Whig country gentlemen to achieve a national revival.
Young Germany, following a more typical pattern, produced better literature
than politicians to judge by 1830 and 1848. A Pole, Adam Mickiewicz (1798–
1855), became the apostle of messianic nationalism with its dangerous overtones. This poet and torchbearer of the romantic movement to Polish literature extolled his land as the Christ among nations in the ruins of the ill-fated
national rising of 1830–31. As the resurrection of Christ was the salvation of
mankind, the rebirth of the Polish nation would prove the salvation of the
world. Roman Catholicism would become central to Polish nationalism.

Mickiewicz reached his conclusion from faith and despair. The historic
Polish nation had perished by the time he was born, a victim of overmighty
neighbors and domestic incapacity. Mickiewicz knew only Russian overlord-
ship. Born in Lithuania (a century later he might have led that national revival), he was educated at the University of Vilna. There he was a founder
and active member of the Philomathean Society, one of those literary and
patriotic student organizations regularly suppressed by the police. He lived
in Russia from 1823 to 1829 under police surveillance as an exile from Poland, writing, among other things, "Konrad Wallenrod," one of his most
famous poems and a summons for Poland's revenge on her oppressors. He
wandered in Germany and Italy during the next years and while in Rome
found a new mysticism to augment his deep religious feelings. Mickiewicz
never reached Poland during the insurrection and retired to Paris in 1832,
where he spent most of the remainder of his life. There he was one of the
most distinguished Polish exiles whose history, in both political and cultural terms, is a study in itself.

"The Books of the Polish Nation" and "The Books of the Polish Pilgrimage" (1832) were addressed to exiled Polish nationalists. Wherever they
might wander, they were still the people nominated by God. "Master Thad-
deus" (1834) was his culminating contribution to Polish nationalist literature. Nationalism showed its dangerous side in Mickiewicz's works. It no
longer implied, it categorically stated racial superiority. Russophobia might
be expected, but the messianism of this doctrine spelled danger for the
future.

THE BOOKS OF THE POLISH NATION

FROM THE BEGINNING OF THE WORLD TO THE MARTYRDOM

OF THE POLISH NATION

IN THE BEGINNING there was belief in one God, and there was freedom in the world. And there were no laws, only the will of God, and there were no lords and slaves, only patriarchs and their children.

But later the people denied the one God, and made for themselves idols, and bowed themselves down to them, and slew in their honor bloody offerings, and waged war for the honor of their idols.

Therefore God sent upon the idolators the greatest punishment, which is slavery.

And one half of the people became the slaves of the other half, although all had sprung from one Father. For they had denied that origin and had devised for themselves various Fathers; and said that he sprang from the earth, and another from the sea, and others from other things.

And when, thus warring, some were taking others into slavery, they all fell together into the slavery of the Roman Emperor.

The Roman Emperor called himself God, and proclaimed that there was no other law in the world except his will; what he approved, that was to be called virtue, and what he condemned, that was to be called sin.

And philosophers were found who strove to prove that the Emperor in so doing did well.

And the Roman Emperor had nothing under him nor over him that he must respect.

And all the earth became slaves, and there was never such slavery in the world, either before, or after; save in Russia in our days.

For even among the Turks the Sultan must respect the law of Mohamet, nor can he interpret it himself, but for that there are Turkish priests.

But in Russia, the Emperor is the head of the faith, and in what he commandeth men to believe, in that they must believe.

And it came to pass that when slavery had grown strong in the world, there came on a turning point for it; even as the solstice, the turning point of night, in the longest and darkest night, such was the turning point of slavery in the time of the Roman bondage.

At that time there came to earth Jesus Christ, the Son of God, teaching men that all are born brothers, children of one God.

And that he is the greatest among men, who serveth them and who sacrificeth himself for their good. And whosoever is better in any way, so much the more ought he to sacrifice. But Christ, being best of all, was to sacrifice his blood for them through the bitterest suffering.

So Christ taught that naught is to be held in respect on earth, neither human wisdom, nor office, nor riches, nor a crown; but that sacrificing oneself for the good of men is alone to be held in respect.

And whosoever sacrificeth himself for others shall find wisdom and riches and a crown on earth, in heaven, and everywhere.

But whosoever sacrificeth others for himself, that he may have wisdom, and office, and riches, shall find folly and wretchedness and damnation on earth, in hell, and everywhere.

And finally Christ said: "Whosoever will follow after me shall be saved, for I AM TRUTH AND JUSTICE." And when Christ taught in this manner, the judges, who judged in the name of the Roman Emperor, were terrified; and they said: "We drove out justice from the earth, and behold it returneth: let us slay it and bury it in the earth."

Then they martyred the holiest and most innocent of men, and laid him in the tomb, and they cried out: "Justice and truth are in the world no longer; who now will rise against the Roman Emperor?"

But they cried out foolishly, for they knew not that having committed the greatest sin, they had already filled up the measure of their iniquities; and their power came to an end in the time when they exulted most.

For Christ arose from the dead, and, having driven out the Emperor, set up his cross in their capital city; and at that time the lords freed their slaves and acknowledged them as brothers, and the kings, anointed in the name of God, acknowledged that the law of God was over them, and justice returned to the earth.

And all the nations that believed, whether they were Germans, or Italians, or French, or Poles, looked upon themselves as one nation, and this nation was called Christendom.

And the kings of the different nations looked upon themselves as brothers, and marched under the one sign of the cross.

And he who was a man of knightly rank rode out to war against the heathen in Asia, that he might protect the Christians in Asia and win back the sepulcher of the Savior.

And they called this war in Asia the war of the cross.

And although the Christians did not make war either for glory or for the conquest of lands or for riches, but for the deliverance of the Holy Land, yet God rewarded them for this war with glory and lands and riches and wisdom. And Europe became enlightened and set in order and enriched. And God rewarded her for that she had made a sacrifice of herself for the good of others.

And freedom spread abroad in Europe slowly but steadily and in order; from the kings freedom passed to the great lords, and, these being free, they bestowed freedom upon the nobility, and from the nobility freedom passed to the cities, and soon it would have come down to the people, and all Christendom would have been free, and all Christians, like brothers, equal with one another.

But the kings corrupted all.

For the kings became evil and Satan entered into them and they said in their hearts: "Let us take heed: lo, the people are attaining understanding and plenty, and they live uprightly, so that we cannot punish them, and the sword rusteth in our hands; but the people are attaining freedom and our power weakeneth, and as soon as they mature and become wholly free, our power will be at an end."

But the kings in so thinking thought foolishly, for if kings are the fathers of the nations, then the nations, like children, on coming of age go out from under the rod and guardianship.

And yet if the fathers are good, children grown up and wholly free deny not their fathers; nay, when their fathers' hair hath become gray they honor and love them the more.

But the kings desired to be like savage fathers dwelling in the forests, who yoke their children to carts like beasts and sell them to merchants for slaves. So the kings said: "Let us strive that the people may always be foolish, and thus not know their powers; and that they may quarrel among themselves and thus not unite with one another against us."

Then they called to the men of knightly rank: "Why do ye go to the Holy Land? It is far; fight rather one with another." And the philosophers at once strove to show that it was folly to fight for the faith.

Then the kings, renouncing Christ, made ready new gods that were idols, and set them up in the sight of the people, and bade them bow down to them and fight for them.

And so the kings made an idol for the French and called it *honor*; and this was the same idol that in pagan times was called the golden calf.

Then their king made an idol for the Spaniards, which he called *political preponderance*, or *political influence*, or power and authority, and this was the same idol that the Assyrians had worshiped under the name of Baal, and the Philistines under the name of Dagon, and the Romans under the name of Jupiter.

And then their king made an idol for the Engiish that he called *sea power and commerce*, and this was the same idol that of old was called Mammon.

And then an idol was made for the Germans that was called *Brotsinn* or *welfare*, and this was the same idol that of old had been called Moloch and Comus.

And the people bowed down to their idols.

And the king said to the French: "Arise and fight for *honor*."

So they arose and fought five hundred years.

And the English king said: "Arise and fight for Mammon."

So they arose and fought full five hundred years. And the other nations fought also, each for its own idol.

And the nations forgot that they had sprung from one Father. And the Englishman said: "My father is *ship* and my mother is *steam*." And the Frenchman said: "My father is *continent* and my mother is *bourse*." And the German said: "My father is *workshop* and my mother is *pothouse*."

And those same people who said that it was folly for the faith against the pagans, those same people fought for a scrap of paper called a treaty, fought over a seaport, over a city; like serfs who fight with clubs over the boundary of an estate which they do not possess but which their lords possess.

And those same people who said that it was folly to go to distant lands in the defense of their fellow men, those same people sailed over the sea at the bidding of their kings, and fought over a factory, over a bale of cotton, and over a sack of pepper. And the kings sold them for money into lands across the sea.

And the people became corrupt, so that from among the Germans, and the Italians, and the French, and the Spaniards, only one Christian man was to be found, a wise man and a knight. He was by birth a Genoese.

He exhorted them that they should cease fighting at home, but should rather win back the sepulcher of the Lord and Asia, which had become a desert plain, but which might be a populous and fair country in Christian hands. But all laughed at that man of Genoa and said: "He dreams, and is foolish."

Therefore that godly man departed himself for the war; but in that he was alone, and poor, he therefore wished first to discover lands where gold is produced; and after having gathered riches from there, to hire an army, and reconquer the Holy Land. But all when they heard him cried out: "He is mad."

Yet God saw his good intent, and blessed him; and that man discovered America, which became the land of freedom, a holy land. That man was called Christopher Columbus, and he was the last knight of the cross in Europe, and the last who undertook an enterprise in the name of God, and not for himself.

But in Europe meanwhile idolatry had increased. And just as the pagans worshiped at first different virtues in the form of idols, and then different vices, and then men and beasts, and then trees, stones, and different figures that they drew, so also it happened in Europe.

For the Italians devised for themselves an idol goddess, whom they called *Political Balance of Power*. And this idol the pagans of old had not known, but the Italians were the first to establish its worship among themselves, and fighting over it they became weak and foolish and fell into the hands of tyrants.

Then the kings of Europe, seeing that the worship of this goddess *Balance of Power* had exhausted the Italian nation, introduced her quickly into their kingdoms, and spread abroad her worship and bade men fight for her.

And the Prussian king drew a *circle* and said: "Lo, here is a new God." And they bowed down to this *circle* and called this worship *political rounding*.

And nations created in the image of God they bade men regard as stones and clods, and to clip them off, so that one might weigh the same as another. And the state, the fatherland, the people, they commanded men to regard as a piece of money that men clip for the sake of roundness.

And philosophers were found who praised everything that the kings had devised.

And of these false wise men, the priests of *Baal*, and of *Moloch*, and of *Balance of Power*, two were the most famous.

The first was called *Machiavelli*, which signifieth in Greek a man *desirous of war*, in that his doctrine led to continual wars, such as were among the pagan Greeks.

And the other liveth to this day, and he is called *Ancillon*, which signifieth in Latin *son of the slave woman*, in that his doctrine leadeth to slavery, such as was among the Latins.

Finally in idolatrous Europe there rose three rulers, the name of the first was *Frederick the Second* of Prussia, the name of the second was *Catherine the Second* of Russia, the name of the third was *Maria Theresa* of Austria.

And this was a Satanic trinity, contrary to the Divine Trinity, and was in the manner of a mock and a derision of all that is holy.

Frederick, whose name signifieth *friend of peace*, contrived wars and pillage throughout his whole life, and was like Satan eternally panting for war, who in derision should be called Christ, the God of peace.

And this Frederick in mockery of the ancient knightly orders, established a godless order, to which in derision he gave the watchword *suum cuique*, or render to each man what is his; and the badge of this order his servants wore, who seized upon and pillaged that which belonged to others.

And this Frederick in mockery of wisdom wrote a book which he called *Anti-Machiavelli*, or the adversary of Machiavelli, but he himself acted according to the teaching of Machiavelli.

Now *Catherine* signifieth in Greek pure, but she was the lewdest of women, and it was as though the shameless Venus had called herself a pure virgin.

And this Catherine assembled a council for the establishing of laws, that she might turn lawmaking into a mockery, for the rights of her neighbors she overthrew and destroyed.

And this Catherine proclaimed that she protected freedom of conscience or tolerance, that she might make a mock of freedom of conscience, for she forced millions of her neighbors to change their faith. And *Maria Theresa* bore the name of the most meek and immaculate Mother of the Savior, that she might make a mock of humility and holiness.

For she was a proud she-devil, and carried on war to make subject the lands of others.

And she was godless, for while praying and confessing her sins she took into slavery millions of her neighbors.

Now she had a son Joseph, who bore the name of a patriarch, the patriarch who did not permit himself to be seduced by the wife of Potiphar, and who freed from slavery his brothers who had sold him into slavery.

And this Joseph of Austria incited his own mother to evil, and his brothers, the Poles, who had defended his empire from Turkish slavery, he took into slavery.

The names of these three rulers, *Frederick*, *Catherine*, and *Maria Theresa*, were thus three blasphemies, and their lives three crimes, and their memory three maledictions.

Then this trinity, seeing that not yet were the people sufficiently foolish and corrupt, fashioned a new idol, the most abominable of all, and they called this idol *Interest*, and this idol was not known among the pagans of old.

And the nations became corrupt, so that among them was found only one man who was a patriot and a soldier.

He persuaded them that they should cease warring for *Interest*, but rather that they should protect the freedom of their neighbors; and he himself went away to war, to the land of freedom, to America. The name of this man is Lafayette. And he is the last man of the men of old in Europe in whom there still dwelleth the spirit of self-sacrifice, the remnant of the Christian spirit.

Meanwhile all nations were bowing down to *Interest*. And the kings said: "If we spread abroad the worship of this idol, then as nation fighteth with nation, so afterwards city will fight with city, and then man with man.

"And people will again become savage, and we shall again have such power as the savage kings had of old, idolators, and such as the Moorish kings and the cannibal kings now have, that they may eat their subjects."

But the Polish nation alone did not bow down to the new idol, and did not have in its language the expression for christening it in Polish, neither for christening its worshipers, whom it calls by the French word *egoists*.

The Polish nation worshiped God, knowing that he who honoreth God giveth honor to everything that is good.

The Polish nation then from the beginning to the end was true to the God of its ancestors.

Its kings and men of knightly rank never assaulted any believing nation, but defended Christendom from the pagans and barbarians who brought slavery.

And the Polish kings went to the defense of Christians in distant lands, King Wladislaw to Varna, and King Jan to Vienna, to the defense of the east and the west.

And never did their kings and men of knightly rank seize neighboring lands by force, but they received the nations into brotherhood, uniting them with themselves by the gracious gift of faith and freedom.

And God rewarded them, for a great nation, Lithuania, united itself with

Poland, as husband with wife, two souls in one body. And there was never before this such a union of nations. But hereafter there shall be.

For that union and marriage of Lithuania and Poland is the symbol of the future union of all Christian peoples in the name of faith and freedom.

And God gave unto the Polish kings and knights freedom, that all might be called brothers, both the richest and the poorest. And such freedom never was before. But hereafter there shall be.

The king and the men of knightly rank received into their brotherhood still more people; they received whole armies and whole tribes. And the number of brothers became as great as a nation, and in no nation were there so many people free and calling each other brothers as in Poland.

And finally, on the Third of May, the king and the knightly body determined to make all Poles brothers, at first the burghers and later the peasants.

And they called the brothers the nobility, because they had become noble, that is had become brothers with the Lachs, who were men free and equal.

And they wished to bring it about that every Christian in Poland should be ennobled and called a Nobleman, for a token that he should have a noble soul and always be ready to die for freedom.

Just as of old they called each man accepting the gospel a Christian, for a token that he was ready to shed his blood for Christ.

Nobility then was to be the baptism of freedom, and every one who was ready to die for freedom was to be baptized of the law and of the sword.

And finally Poland said: "Whosoever will come to me shall be free and equal, for I am FREEDOM."

But the kings when they heard of this were terrified in their hearts and said: "We banished freedom from the earth; but lo, it returneth in the person of a just nation, that doth not bow down to our idols! Come, let us slay this nation." And they plotted treachery among themselves.

And the King of Prussia came and kissed the Polish Nation and greeted it, saying: "My ally," but already he had sold it for thirty cities of Great Poland, even as Judas for thirty pieces of silver.

And the two other rulers fell upon and bound the Polish Nation. And Gaul was judge and said: "Verily I find no fault in this nation, and France my wife, a timid woman, is tormented with evil dreams; nevertheless, take for yourselves and martyr this nation." And he washed his hands.

And the ruler of France said: "We cannot ransom this innocent nation by our blood or by our money, for my blood and my money belong to me, but the blood and money of my nation belong to my nation."

And this ruler uttered the last blasphemy against Christ, for Christ taught that the blood of the Son of Man belonged to all our brother men.

And when the ruler had uttered these words, then the crosses fell from the towers of the godless capital, for the sign of Christ could no longer shine upon a people worshiping the idol *Interest*.

And this ruler was called Casimir-Périer, a Slavic first name and a Roman last name. His first name signifieth corrupter or annihilator of peace, and his last name signifieth, from the word *perire* or *périr*, destroyer or son of destruction. And these two names are anti-Christian. And they shall be alike accursed among the Slavic race and among the Roman race.

And this man rent the league of peoples as that Jewish priest rent his clothes upon hearing the voice of Christ.

And they martyred the Polish Nation and laid it in the grave, and the kings cried out: "We have slain and we have buried Freedom."

But they cried out foolishly, for in commiting the last sin they filled up the measure of their iniquities, and their power was coming to an end at the time when they exulted most.

For the Polish Nation did not die: its body lieth in the grave, but its spirit hath descended from the earth, that is from public life, to the abyss, that is to the private life who suffer slavery in their country and outside of their country, that it may see their sufferings.

But on the third day the soul shall return to the body, and the Nation shall arise and free all the peoples of Europe from slavery.

And already two days have gone by. One day passed with the first capture of Warsaw, and the second day passed with the second capture of Warsaw, and the third day shall begin, but shall not pass.

And as after the resurrection of Christ bloody offerings ceased in all the world, so after the resurrection of the Polish Nation wars shall cease in all Christendom.

Humanitarian Nationalism:
The Principle of Association

Giuseppe Mazzini, "The Holy Alliance of the Peoples," Life and Writings of Joseph Mazzini (New ed.; London: Smith, Elder, & Co., 1891), Vol. V, Autobiographical and Political, pp. 265–82.

The voice of nineteenth-century nationalism was sometimes calm, sometimes strident; it was always potent. Giuseppe Mazzini (1805–72) spoke for one form of early nineteenth-century nationalism—humane, liberal, religious. He believed in the infinite force of ideas. Italian independence and unity was only the first step toward the international brotherhood of free peoples. Mazzini was both a thinker of merit and an active, revolutionary politician. In each respect he proved a short-term failure. His reputation as a thinker grew with the passing of time and intellectual disillusionment with his pragmatic and more cynical successors. Mazzini was completely unsuccessful in practical terms. He devoted his life to agitation from early years in the Carbonari to his later years of republican struggle against the national state of Italy from Switzerland.

He hoped that men could reject utilitarianism and would defer seeking material gains and transmute their aspirations to a higher moral plane of association. This was the dream of Young Italy. Mazzini detested socialism as heartily as he despised practical politicians, yet both succeeded where he failed. He was a display piece in English exile, but his eloquence served to raise support for men he disliked. For Mazzini there were no higher moral values than liberty and equality, but his was an associative, not an individualistic concept. Only in the unity of man could true liberty and equality be realized.

Mazzini belongs to the world of 1848—a world in which everything seemed attainable. The infinite force of ideas proved a hyperbole. The "masses" to whom Mazzini appealed in the abstract remained unmoved. This latter-day Jacobin, however, displayed more talent than his critics allow in the administration of the short-lived Roman Republic, but the Republic still fell to the new Napoleon. Associated man, far from aspiring to common welfare, accepted material gains and personal advantage. But then the hopes of the prophet are rarely realized—Mussolini's Third Rome was a brutal caricature of Mazzini's dream.

THE HOLY ALLIANCE OF THE PEOPLES

(WRITTEN IN 1849)

NAPOLEON HAD FALLEN; the ascending movement of the French Revolution had ceased; Europe was wearied out by two-and-twenty years of war; the long-desired peace arrived, and they who brought it were hailed as benefactors, no matter who or what they were. The old dynasties, reconsecrated by victory, resumed their wonted sway; the new were scattered in exile, and the echo of the platoon by which Murat fell, conveyed to them the royal warning against any attempt to regain the thrones they had usurped and lost. Religion blessed the restoration; altar and throne upheld each other; the dualism of the Christian era appeared to be ended in a compact of love.

Yet, nevertheless, the conquering kings, uneasy and disturbed as if by a presentiment, gathered together in council to study new methods of protection against a tempest there were no signs to announce. Victory, which generally disjoins those who were allied during the battle, only suggested to them the necessity of a stronger bond. Jealous and suspicious each of the other, they yet hushed every quarrel and stifled all distrust, in order to combine a common force against an unknown enemy. The acts of the 9th June, 25th September, and 20th November 1815, organised this common force.

The *Holy Alliance* inaugurated its new policy in the outraged name of God. The masters of the world united against the future. The treaty of Westphalia, 177 years before, had given the force of law to a system of equilibrium, or, as diplomatists say, of *balance of power*, which allowed the weak some hope of assistance in case of oppression. Now the strong declared to the strong: *We will join together to prevent any of the weak from rebelling against the yoke we impose upon them; should any rebel, we will crush them.*

The policy of intervention against the progressive principle, of which the germ was contained in the *Holy Alliance*, was more distinctly developed and further extended in the Congress of Lubiana, May 12, 1821, which was the practical application of that of Verona. From that time forward, from the French intervention in Spain in 1823, to the intervention of three monarchies and a republic against Rome in '49—wheresoever a people has arisen and endeavoured to ameliorate its own condition—wheresoever an oppressed or dismembered nation has attempted to regain its own free action or its own frontier, the *Holy Alliance* has interfered to impede or prevent progress, and to protect the oppressors. The compact of 1815 offered a lesson to Europe which democracy has not yet understood.

The powers by whom that compact was signed foresaw the future; foresaw the new adversary, destined, as soon as Europe should have recovered from her exhaustion, to arise against their dominion—the People. The masses, terror-struck by the spectacle of nearly a million bayonets waiting upon the orders of the allied princes, understood not; but the princes understood that Napoleon had in fact fallen, not before the brute force they had brought against him, but before the potency of a popular idea; before the outburst of the spirit of nationality which he had outraged. They knew that the first act of the great catastrophe completed at Waterloo had been played by the *people* in Spain; they knew that the Spanish war of 1808, the attempts at rebellion in Calabria and other parts of Italy, and the German movement of 1813, had awakened to conscious existence and given form and substance to a spirit stirring in the peoples and revealing to them: *You are the true masters of your native soil; you are the sole interpreters of your own law of life.* And they understood how that spirit was destined to expand; how, having once dared to measure itself against Napoleon, it would not long shrink before princes his inferiors in genius and power.

The Treaty of 1815, unlike the leagues formed in '93 against the French Revolution, was directed against all Europe, and was signed in the hour of victory. It was the first acknowledgment of the power of a new and until then unheeded element, an enforced homage paid to the solidarity of the nations, to the unity of European life; it was a false and tyrannous application of a true *principle*, of that principle which is the soul of our belief, which declares the collective life of humanity. It was our part to give that principle its legitimate application, founded not upon the arbitrary privilege of a few, but upon the duty and right of all. It was the part of democracy, in opposition to the banner upon which the men of 1815 had inscribed *God and the Princes*, boldly to raise on high the banner bearing the device of *God and the People*.

II

The presentiment of the princes was verified: the *people* arose; not only in France, but in almost every country in Europe, with a power and vigour proportioned to the vastness of the aim to be achieved—an aim not merely political, but social. They rose, at first following and supporting those wealthier classes who had undertaken to fight their battle, the general battle for them; then, when deceived by their leaders, who, as soon as they had acquired their own rights, turned against them—with action more direct and demands more explicit. They dismembered their forces by wandering from programme to programme, from school to school; some of which would even have been dangerous but for their absurdity. Inexperienced and guided rather by instinct than by any settled plan,—now betrayed by over-confidence in untried leaders, now by unwarranted distrust of those really trustworthy, they fell, rose, and fell again, wasting in the pursuit of illusions powers sufficient to have made or unmade a world, and shedding enough of pure and precious blood to have founded a religion.

But errors and defeats extinguished factions, not peoples. Nations do not die; they are transformed. This prophetic agitation of the multitudes, this movement of the human race impelled by God towards a new goal, to a larger development of its faculties through association,—has continued to gain ground like a rising tide; has increased in breadth and depth from lustre to lustre, from year to year, and, come what may, our victory is certain. Neither princely alliances, nor Papal arts and persecutions can henceforth avail other than to retard or render it more bloody. It is not in human power to wrest it from us.

Our victory is certain; I declare it with the profoundest conviction, here in exile, and precisely when monarchical reaction appears most insolently secure. What matters the triumph of an hour? What matters is that by concentrating all your means of action, availing yourselves of every artifice, turning to your account those prejudices and jealousies of race which yet for a while endure, and spreading distrust, egotism and corruption, you have repulsed our forces and restored the former order of things? Can you restore men's faith in it, or think you can long maintain it by brute force alone, now that all faith in it is extinct? Compare the Italian movement of the last two years with those of twenty-eight and eighteen years ago; compare the popular insurrections of Sicily and Lombardy with the aristocratic and military movements of 1820 and 1821; the resistance of Venice, Bologna, and Rome, with the flights and capitulations of 1831. Our young Italians have learned how to die; therefore Italy will live. Through the arts of Louis Philippe you overcame the Monarchico-Constitutional insurrection of 1830; and we, the people, have answered you by the republican insurrection of 1848. You conquered, through your atrocious deception of the people, in Galicia, and we answered you by Hungary, as we shall answer you at no distant day by the Slavonian peoples. And the German movements?—And Vienna?—And the millions who lack bread?—And your Governments drained by the necessities of their rule, by corruption and espionage, by the cost of their regular armies and constant internecine strife? Threatened and undermined on every side, can you hold all Europe for ever in a state of siege?

. . . .

Terror and corruption;—the governments have tried each in vain. The two parties are unequal—God is on the side of the peoples. The march of ideas is unceasing; the doctrine of castes, and the belief in inequality, are extinguished: the Pariah has raised his head and dared to look his masters in the face without flinching: from that moment the question was decided. . . .

III

But meanwhile, although our ultimate victory is infallible, we are for the time overthrown; thousands of mothers weep over sons lost in battle, in prison, or on the scaffold; thousands of exiles wander over foreign lands, suffering the material and moral misery of poverty and discouragement; and thousands of new martyrs and new exiles will be added to these, should we once again arise without having laid to heart the lessons of the past. These lessons may be summed up in one word—Union; sincere and active union, between the sons of the same land holding the same faith, and between all the peoples of Europe striving towards the same aim.

The history of the popular movements of the last two years proves one vital *fact:* we are stronger than our oppressors upon any and every given point. In Italy, in Germany, and in Hungary, the governments, unable to resist alone, had recourse to others, and only conquered by the help of intervention.

And from this fact two consequences result:—that our work is truly the work and will of the people, and that whensoever we shall arise simultaneously upon *every* point of our sphere of action we shall conquer. Intervention will then be impossible. We are bound to oppose the league of princes by a Holy Alliance of the peoples. We are bound to *constitute* democracy.

[Mazzini proceeds to show the necessity of substituting *association*, the term of the new epoch, for *individuality*, the term of the epoch now exhausted; and to point out the importance of a greater spirit of abnegation and discipline in the Liberal party. While the independent philosophers of the Pagan world were writing books now lost, the early Christians, by association in a religious hierarchy, remodelled the world.]

.   .   .   .

In order to come to an understanding together to form our forces into one vast association, to organise European democracy into an army, in short—we have no need of a complete programme of the European future. What we do require is, that, taking such bases as have been already agreed upon as our common ground, we should found upon them a common Pact and mode of action enabling us to avail ourselves of all our forces, so as to overthrow all the obstacles that stand in the way of the progress of the peoples.

.   .   .   .

v

The first of these bases is nationality. Since the period of that uncertain and dangerous *cosmopolitanism* by which the labours of the second half of the eighteenth century were distinguished, the constant tendency of Europe to rally round and organise itself beneath the banner of nationality, has been more and more clearly defined. Nor could it be otherwise. From the time when the idea—affirmed in twenty passages of the great poem and minor works of Dante—of the progressive collective life of the human race, became, through long historical and philosophical study, the accepted belief of the greatest intellects of our century, *humanity* was recognised as the supreme aim of every effort, of every advance. And from that recognition followed the perception of the importance of the *nation*, as the intermediate term between humanity and the individual, who, if left to his solitary effort, unsustained by the collective force of the millions sharing the same language, customs, tendencies, and traditions, sinks from inability to do better, into egotism. And egotism is in fact the ultimate and disastrous result of the theories of the cosmopolists. The absurd and immoral *ubi bene ibi patria*, is the primary axiom of its founders. The idea of nationality arose at the opportune moment, to multiply the forces of the individual, and make known the means by which the labour and sacrifice of each man may be rendered efficacious and beneficial to humanity.

Without the nation there can be no humanity, even as without organisation and division there can be no expeditious and fruitful labour. Nations are the citizens of humanity, as individuals are the citizens of the nation. And as every individual lives a twofold life, inward and of relation, so do the nations. As every individual should strive to promote the power and prosperity of his nation through the exercise of his special function, so should every nation in performing its special mission, according to its special capacity, perform its part in the general work, and promote the progressive advance and prosperity of humanity.

Nationality and humanity are therefore equally sacred. To forget humanity is to suppress the *aim* of our labours; to cancel the nation is to suppress the instrument by which to achieve the aim.

. . . .

The indisputable tendency of the epoch in course of initiation is towards a reconstitution of Europe, in accordance with the different national vocations, into a certain number of states, as nearly as possible equal in population and extent. These states, which have remained divided, hostile, and jealous of one another, so long as their national banner merely represented the interest of a dynasty or caste, will gradually become more and more intimately associated through the medium of democracy. The nations will be sisters. Free and independent in the choice of the means by which they reach the common aim, and in the organisation of their internal life, they will gradually unite in a common faith and common pact, in all that regards their international life. The Europe of the peoples will be One; avoiding alike the anarchy of absolute independence and the centralisation of conquest.

VI

And we who belong to the progressive party, who believe in the progressive life of humanity, are all agreed as to these things.

We are all agreed that progress is the Providential Law, given, with the capacity of its gradual fulfilment, by God to humanity. We are all agreed that association is the means of its fulfilment—that the harmonious development of all the moral intellectual and physical faculties of mankind is the purpose of the law—we all believe that the people is the sole continuous interpreter of the law. We all declare the old authority for ever extinct. We do not admit that the government of humanity or of the nation may be entrusted to chance, privilege, or hereditary succession, in one or more individuals; we desire that the best amongst us in heart and intellect should be our guides upon our pilgrimage; we desire—in order to put an end to the antagonism between the governing and the governed—that our guides should be recognised and accepted as such by the universal voice. The republic is the logical form of democracy.

[Mazzini proceeds to show that the individual and society are equally sacred; sacred also the perpetual elements of human life and activity, the family, the fatherland, property, and religion; and sacred above all things—progress. History teaches us that all these elements of human life have been and will be gradually transformed, but not abolished; the family will become the sanctuary wherein citizens will be trained for the fatherland, even as the fatherland will train citizens for humanity. Property will be the sign of labour done, and will represent the individual in his relation to the material world. Religion, the supreme synthetic educational formula at a given epoch of the life of humanity, will form alike the impulse, sanction, and benediction of every social progress.]

At the present day—thanks to our governments—the *family* is too often a school of egotism, and *property* the sign of privilege or monopoly, while *religion* oscillates between paganism and hypocrisy.

VII

.   .   .   .

It is time that regular and constant relations should be established and directed from a single centre by men of tried energy, virtue, constancy, and faith, between the democracy of all parts of Europe and America, so as to form a link of union among all those who strive and suffer in the holy cause of liberty; all who worship the same ideal; all who accept our formula,—*One sole master, God; one sole law, progress; one sole interpreter of that law on earth, the people, with genius and virtue for its guides.*

Hitherto our democratic struggle has been a *guerrilla* war; it is time to organise the *regular army*, and begin the war of masses. Democracy can never conquer and transform Europe until it be organised in the fashion of a state or government, so as to form a primitive nucleus of the Europe of the peoples, a collective manifestation of the general idea destined to rule the future.

It is not ours to build the temple, the Pantheon of the faith we invoke. That temple will be erected by the peoples when the hour shall come; but we may, and we ought, to found a Church of Precursors.

I have long caressed the idea of the formation of a vast association, composed of a given number of sections; an association which, embracing all the various manifestations of human activity, should group and organise all the believers in a new era, and in those principles, sketched above, upon which they are already agreed, according to their different tendencies and capacity, so as to direct their labours upon a common general plan. A few men—rendered venerable by knowledge and virtue, intellect and love, and by sacrifices nobly endured for the sake of the common faith in different parts of Europe and America—would form the supreme Council of the association, and their utterances to the world would be collective and synthetic.

Others, more intimately related by community of origin with the ideas and tendencies of each separate people, would constitute a series of *national* councils, the president of each of which would, in order to secure the unity of the general conception, be a member of the supreme Council.

The supreme Council would declare the conception of the general mission of the peoples: the national councils would declare the special mission of each nation. The first would represent the *principle* in virtue of which humanity is now seeking a new synthesis, and the essential terms of its future progress; the second would represent the *application* of that principle among the various peoples, and the various means by which the nations may labour together in concord towards the realisation of the general aim.

Under the impulse and guidance given by such twofold direction, the labours of the members of the association would be organised, some in the sphere of knowledge (*scienza*), others in the practical sphere; while the national councils would decide upon the titles of the various peoples to be admitted as equals in the great federation of the nations, and transmit to each the European idea. The supreme Council would trace the new map of Europe, promote the holy alliance of the oppressed against the oppressors, and, unrestrained by the limits of any absolute system, indicate the broad paths of progress, and direct the movements of the different peoples as the different divisions of a single army.

Then, as soon as the actual discouragements were overcome, and men's minds restored to confidence, the supreme Council would initiate the Democratic Tax.

A portion of this tax, converted into an *institution of credit* for working people, would be expended upon the industrial establishments, both agricultural and of manufacture, in such a manner as practically to exemplify the morality, methods, and results of association. Another portion would be used to promote a popular press and popular education, no longer limited to the great centres of population, but distributed according to the necessities of the various localities. The remainder would be allowed to accumulate, and be held as a sacred deposit, to be applied by the association to affording fraternal help to such peoples as should arise in assertion of their rights.

The union of thought and action, two essential aspects of the human unity which are now, with serious peril to the future, disjoined, would be reconstituted, as in all great epochs of humanity it has been, in new vigour; and the multitudes, who are at present more distrustful of the *thinkers* than is generally believed, would be restored to faith and confidence in an authority neither despotic nor arbitrary, but founded upon the union of love and works.

How much of this idea may ever be verified in the democratic camp, I know not. But I know that democracy ought to verify it as far as possible, or it must long continue to drag along the path of isolated effort, leading too often to martyrdom,—glorious no doubt and useful to humanity,—but not to victory. To pretend that the majority must come to an understanding upon the *whole* programme of the future *before acting*, is to condemn ourselves to struggle against—I will not say long years of delay, for time is of little import in an enterprise like our own,—but against the impossibility of radically transforming men who are compelled to live and move in an atmosphere of egotism and corruption. We must first remove them from its mortal influence, and lead them into the fresh pure air beneath the heaven of God. We must awake them from their torpor by a sudden shock; rouse their hearts by the enthusiasm of battle; the excitement and concentration of all the faculties will kindle a jet of new and vigorous life, and the spirit of truth, which descends upon the assembled peoples, will render it fruitful.

We must act in short.

Action is to the multitudes a revelation. And in order to act to worthy purpose, since to arise without well-founded hope of success would be a grave error at the present day, we must unite.

Unite! The times are grave. The evil governments which weigh like an incubus upon the very souls of the nations, have made known their programme in Baden, Hungary, and Rome. It is: *alliance in order to oppress*. Let yours be: *alliance in order to emancipate*.

Publicly or secretly, according to the necessities of time and place, let us unite, learn to understand each other, and prepare. On the day on which we are able to say like the early Christians: *In the name of God and the people we are one*, the modern Pagans will be impotent against us; we shall have conquered the world. God will then reveal to us the path of the future.

B. *Lights to Live By*

Popularizing Economic and Social Orthodoxy

Jane Haldimand Marcet, Conversations on Political Economy *(London, 1816),* Conversations VIII–IX, pp. 115–51.

Jane Marcet (1769–1858) was one of the many overwhelming women of late Georgian and early Victorian England who did much to shape the moral and social attitudes of the Victorian age. The good queen herself did no more. Jane Marcet, however, has descended into undeserved oblivion, for she merits a high place in the history of ideas. The movement for popular education, not merely as an institution but in what we today call adult education, was a vital part of the "liberal awakening." The Society for the Diffusion of Useful Knowledge, which Thomas Love Peacock unkindly called the "steam intellect society," strove to bring political economy as well as liberal politics to the man in the streets. Jane Marcet, who had already popularized chemistry (1806—in its sixteenth edition in 1853) and would shortly undertake vegetable physiology (1829), proved equal to the task. In *Conversations on Political Economy,* Mrs. B. (our female Socrates) undertakes the education of Caroline by parading Smith, Malthus, Say, and Sismondi before her.

Mrs. Marcet admitted some problems in this undertaking. She allows

. . . that a few of the most abstruse questions and controversies in Political Economy have been entirely omitted, and that others have been stated and discussed without any positive conclusions being deduced. This is a defect unavoidably attached not only to the Author's limited knowledge, but also to the real difficulty of the science. In general, however, when a soundness of a doctrine has appeared well established, it has been stated conscientiously, without any excess of caution or reserve, and with the sole object of diffusing useful truths [pp. vii–viii].

The qualifications, as Conversations VIII–IX testify, are not evident. Jane Marcet knows what is important. She must disabuse the "intelligent young person, fluctuating between the impulse of her heart and the progress of her reason, and naturally imbued with all the prejudices and popular feelings of uninformed benevolence" of any notions that one can fly in the face of the fixed and immutable laws of political economy.

Thomas Babington Macaulay lauded Jane Marcet, feeling her to be far more important than her better known successor and imitator, Harriet Martineau. There could be no question as to Marcet's popularity. The *Conversations* ground through sixteen editions and was still in print in the 1860's. Jane Marcet never rested on her laurels. Since she had disposed of chemistry and botany, she capped political economy with *Conversations on Natural Philosophy in Which the Elements of That Science Are Familiarly Explained,* and *Adopted to the Comprehension of Young Pupils* (1819; in a 14th edition by 1872). Then to her popular *Bertha's Visit to Her Uncle in England* (1830), a fantastic potpourri of topics from natural history to moral philosophy; back to *John Hopkin's Notions on Political Economy* (1833); onward to *The Seasons* (1832), *Mary's Grammar* (1835), *Willy's Holidays, or Conversations on Different Kinds of Governments* (1836), and *Willy's Travels on the Railroad* (1847) among others. Nothing seemed to escape her popularizing pen; for example, *Mother's First Book: Reading Made Easy* (1845).

Never underestimate the Jane Marcets of this world. Orthodox views in the popular mind derive more from them than from Adam Smith, Thomas Malthus, and David Ricardo. When the earnest and aspiring, those rising through the middle class, discoursed on society, economics, or the problem of charity and benevolence, they were more apt than not to be parroting the views of Jane Marcet.

CONVERSATION VIII

On Wages and Population

MRS. B.

IN OUR LAST CONVERSATION I think we came to this conclusion, that capital is almost as beneficial to the poor as to the rich; for though the property of the one, it is by its nature destined for the maintenance of the other.

CAROLINE

It comes to the labourer in the form of wages, but as we must allow the capitalist a profit on his work, I should like very much to know what proportion that profit bears to the wages of the labourer.

MRS. B.

It varies extremely, but the wages of the labourer can never be permanently less than will afford him the means of living, otherwise he could not labour.

CAROLINE

On the other hand, they can never be equal to the whole value of the work he produces, for if his master made no profit by him he would not employ him.

MRS. B.

Such then are the two extremes of the wages of labour, but they admit of many intermediate degrees of variation. If besides furnishing subsistence for himself, the wages of the labourer would not enable him to maintain a wife and bring up a family, the class of labourers would gradually diminish, and the scarcity of hands would then raise their wages, which would enable them to live with more comfort and rear a family; but as the capitalist will always keep wages as low as he can, the labourer and his family can seldom command more than the necessaries of life.

CAROLINE

By the necessaries of life do you mean such things only as are indispensably necessary for its support?

MRS. B.

No; I mean such food, clothing, and general accommodation as the climate and custom of the country have rendered essential to the preservation of the life, health, and decent appearance of the lowest classes of the people. Fuel, for instance, and warm clothing are necessary articles in this country; but they are not so in Africa. Civilization and the progress of wealth and manufactures have greatly extended the scale of necessaries; the use of linen is now considered as necessary by all classes of people, and shoes and stockings in England, at least, almost equally so. Houses with glazed windows and a chimney are become necessaries; for if our poor were deprived of such accommodation it would very materially increase mortality amongst them. In Ireland the peasantry bring up their children in a mud cabin, the door of which answers also the purposes of window and chimney.

CAROLINE

Then would it not be better that the labouring classes here should, like the Irish, accustom themselves to hardships and inconveniencies, rather than indulge in a degree of comfortable accommodation, the privation of which in a season of distress is attended with so much misery?

MRS. B.

No; I would on the contrary wish rather to extend than contract the scale of the necessaries of life. There is more health, more cleanliness, more intellect, and more happiness developed in an English cottage than in an Irish cabin. There is more strength, vigour, and industry in an English peasant, who feeds on meat, bread, and vegetables, than in an Irish one, who subsists on potatoes alone.

CAROLINE

No doubt I would wish the lower classes every comfort which they can afford, but their wages will not always allow them such gratifications. What is it that determines the rate of wages?

MRS. B.

It depends upon the proportion which capital bears to the labouring part of the population of the country.

CAROLINE

Or, in other words, to the proportion which subsistence bears to the number of people to be maintained by it?

MRS. B.

Yes, it is this alone which regulates the rate of wages, when they are left to pursue their natural course. It is this alone which creates or destroys the demand for labour. In order to render it more clear to you, let us simplify the question by examining it on a small scale—let us suppose for instance that we have founded a colony in a desert island; that the settlers have divided the land amongst them, and cultivated it for their own subsistence, and that being both proprietors and labourers, they reap the whole reward of their industry. Thus situated, should a ship be wrecked on the coast, and some of the crew effect their escape to shore, what would ensue? They would furnish a supply of labourers, who would be dependent on the original settlers for maintenance and employment.

CAROLINE

But if those settlers have not raised a greater quantity of subsistence than is necessary for their own use, how can they maintain the new-comers? Without capital, you know, they cannot employ labourers.

MRS. B.

You are perfectly right. But it is probable that the most industrious of them will have raised somewhat more subsistence than is absolutely necessary for their own consumption. They will possess some little stock in reserve, which will enable them to maintain and employ at least a few of the shipwrecked crew. Yet as these poor destitute men will all be anxious to share in this little surplus, each will offer his labour in exchange for the smallest pittance that will support life. Thus the capital of the island being inadequate to the maintenance of its population, the competition amongst the labourers to get employment will render wages extremely low, and the capitalist will derive a high profit from the industry of his labourers. A small capital, therefore, creates but a small demand for labour.

CAROLINE

By demand for labour do you mean the demand of the poor for work, or of the capitalist for workmen?

MRS. B.

Certainly the latter. The demand for labour means the demand for labourers, by those who have the means of paying them for their work, whether it be in the form of wages, maintenance, or any other kind of remuneration.

But what will happen in our colony, when the labourers shall have richly repaid their employers by the fruits of their industry?

CAROLINE

By raising a more plentiful harvest they would of course have a more plentiful subsistence.

MRS. B.

The harvest, you must observe, belongs, not to the men who produced it, but to their masters; how therefore does it follow of course, that the labourers obtain a larger share of it?

CAROLINE

I suppose that their masters having more capital, are willing to bestow a larger proportion of it on their labourers.

MRS. B.

I believe that the capitalist will always make as high a profit as he can upon the work of his labourers; and that when his capital increases, he will chuse rather to increase the number of his workmen than the rate of their wages. But the power of employing more labourers increases the demand for labour; and this, as I shall explain to you, eventually raises the wages or reward of labour.

The capital of the settlers will probably be so much augmented by the industry of the labourers, that the difficulty will no longer consist in maintaining the new comers, but in finding employment for the new capital. The possessors of this surplus capital will be eager to procure the services of the labourers; one perhaps to build a hut, another to fence a field, a third to construct a boat, and so on. For the surplus, unless employed, will yield no profit; the competition therefore will not longer be amongst the labourers to obtain work, but amongst the masters to obtain workmen; and this will necessarily raise the price of wages, and consequently diminish the profits of the capitalist.

CAROLINE

Oh, that is very clear. If John offers a man a shilling a day to work at his house, and Thomas gives eighteen-pence to those who will build his boat, while James pays two shillings for fencing his field; wages must rise to two shillings a day: for if John and Thomas did not give as much as James, the latter would monopolize all the labourers.

MRS. B.

You see therefore that it is the additional capital produced by the labour of these men, which by increasing the demand for labour raises their wages. Thus whenever capital for the maintenance of labourers abounds, the capitalist must content himself with smaller profits, and allow his workmen a more liberal remuneration. Hence as national opulence increases, the labouring poor are more munificently rewarded, and the profits of capital diminish.

CAROLINE

Oh, that is charming! that is exactly what I wish. But, Mrs. B., if during the second year our colonists employ their labourers in building houses and fencing fields, instead of cultivating them, subsistence will again fall short, and the labourers will be reduced to their former necessitous condition; unless having one experienced such distress, they guard against it in future.

MRS. B.

That does not depend on the choice of the labourers who must do the work they are hired to perform, of whatever nature it may be. But their employers will be careful to provide for their maintenance, for they know that those who should neglect to make such a provision for their future services would be deprived of them. They cannot work without subsistence, nor will they work without an ample subsistence whilst any of the colony has it to offer them. If John therefore does not raise so great a harvest as James, he will not be able, the following year, to employ so many workmen. Each landed proprietor therefore will take care to direct the labour of his workmen towards raising the requisite subsistence, before he employs them in any other description of labour.

Now let us suppose that the shipwrecked crew had brought wives with them, and reared families: would that have affected the rate of wages?

CAROLINE

Their wages would remain the same; but as they would have to maintain their wives and children as well as themselves, they would not fare so well.

MRS. B.

And if there was not food enough for them all, the most weakly of the children would die, not precisely of hunger, but of some of those diseases which want of sufficient and proper food engenders. It is evident, therefore, that a labourer ought not to marry unless his wages are adequate to the maintenance of a family; or unless he has, like your gardener, some little provision in store to make up the deficiency.

Suppose now after several years of prosperity, that a hurricane makes such devastation amongst the crops of our colonists as to reduce the harvest to one half what it was the preceding year. What effect would this have on the wages of labour?

CAROLINE

It would of course reduce them, for the subsistence would be diminished. But in what manner the reduction would take effect I do not exactly see.

MRS. B.

In order to trace its consequences step by step, we may suppose that John, finding his capital will not maintain more than one half of the number of labourers he before employed, reluctantly discharges the other half. These poor men wander about the colony seeking for work, but instead of finding any, they meet only with companions in distress who have lost their employment for similar reasons; thus without resource they return to their masters, and intreat to be employed on lower terms. John, who had discharged these men not for want of work to give them, but for what of funds to pay them, is happy in his reduced circumstances to employ labourers at lower wages. He therefore makes a new agreement with them, and determines to discharge those whom he had originally retained in his service unless they will consent to work for him on the same terms. These men, aware of the difficulty of finding employment elsewhere, are compelled by necessity to accept the conditions, and thus wages are reduced to one half their former rate throughout the colony.

CAROLINE

It appears as evident as possible. I have only one objection to make, which is, that though this may be the case in our colony, it certainly is not so in other places. Wages, so far from being reduced, are, I believe, frequently raised during a scarcity; at least there are great complaints amongst the poor if that is not done.

MRS. B.

In countries where money is used, the reduction of wages does not take place in the manner I have described. In such countries it is unnecessary to make any change in the rate of wages, because the high price of provisions during a scarcity produces a similar effect. If you continue to pay your labourer the same wages when the articles of provision on which he subsists have doubled in price, his wages are really diminished one half, because he can procure with them only one half of what he did before the scarcity.

CAROLINE

But this is a kind of imposition upon the poor labourers, who, I suppose, are at least as ignorant as I am of political economy, and do not know that a shilling is worth more at one time than it is at another, and therefore during a scarcity continue to work at the usual rate of wages for want of knowing better.

MRS. B.

Knowledge in this instance would only teach them that they must bear with patience an unavoidable evil. The alternative, for the capitalist, when his capital is diminished, is to reduce, either the number of his labourers, or the rate of their wages—or rather, I should say, the remuneration of their labour; for the wages remain nominally the same. Now is it not more equitable to divide the maintenance amongst the whole of the labouring class, than to feed some of them amply, whilst the remainder starve?

CAROLINE

No doubt it is; but would it not, in this instance, be allowable for the legislature to interfere, and oblige the capitalist to raise the rate of wages in proportion to the rise of price of provisions, so as to afford the labourers their usual quantity of subsistence? I think the rate of wages ought to be regulated by the price of bread, as that is the principal subsistence of the poor; so as to enable them to purchase the same quantity of bread whatever its price may be.

MRS. B.

Or, in other words, that every man may eat his usual quantity of bread, however deficient the harvest is in its produce; for unless you could find means to increase the quantity of subsistence, it will avail nothing to raise the rate of wages.

CAROLINE

Very true; yet two shillings will purchase twice the quantity of bread that one will; is not that true also, Mrs. B.? and yet these truths appear incompatible.

MRS. B.

One of them must therefore be an error; two shillings would not purchase twice the quantity of bread that one did if wages were doubled, because provisions would continue to rise in price in proportion to the advance on wages.

CAROLINE

But I would prohibit the farmer from raising the price of his corn and his cattle, and then there would be no necessity for the butcher and the baker raising the price of meat and bread. It is not just that the farmer, when he has a bad crop, should throw his misfortune on the public, and be the only person who does not suffer from it; which is the case if he raises the price of his produce in proportion to its scarcity.

MRS. B.

The farmer consumes, as well as produces provisions; and as a consumer he partakes of the evil of the advance of price. If he sell his corn for twice the usual price, what he consumes at home stands him in the same value, for such is the price it would fetch at market.

But supposing it possible to prevent the rise in price during a scarcity, what consequences would ensue? Keep in mind the important point, that the harvest has yielded but half its usual product; that whilst the wages of labour and the price of provisions undergo no alteration, the labourers purchase and consume the usual quantity of food, and at the end of six months. . . .

CAROLINE

You need not finish the sentence, Mrs. B.; at the end of six months the whole stock of provisions would be consumed, and the people who excited my commiseration would be starved.

MRS. B.

This would infallibly be the case, were such a measure persevered in; but though it has often been attempted by sovereigns more benevolent than wise, to set limits to the price of provisions, the consequences soon became so formidable as to compel the legislature to put a stop to a remedy which was an ineffectual as it was pernicious. "In the year 1315 England was afflicted by a famine, grievous beyond all that ever were known before, which raised the price of provisions far above the reach of the people of middling classes. The parliament, in compassion to the general distress, ordered that all articles of food should be sold at moderate prices, which they took upon themselves to prescribe. The consequence was that all things, instead of being sold at or under the maximum price fixed by them, became dearer than before, or were entirely withheld from the market. Poultry were rarely to be seen. Butchers' meat was not to be found at all. The sheep were dying of a pestilence, and all kinds of grain were selling at most enormous prices. Early the next year the parliament, finding their mistake, left provisions to find their own price."

Thus you see that the rise in the price of provisions is the natural remedy to the evil of scarcity. It is the means of husbanding the short stock of provisions, and making it last out to the ensuing harvest. Government should never interfere, either with the price of provisions or the rate of wages; they will each find their respective level if left uncontrolled.

But to return to our colony. What effect would it produce on wages, were some contagious malady to carry off one half of the laborers?

CAROLINE

It would increase the demand for the labour of those which remained, and consequently raise their wages.

MRS. B.

We may generally state, therefore, that when the number of labourers remains the same, the rate of wages will increase with the increase of capital, and lower with the diminution of it; and that if the amount of capital remain the same, the rate of wages will fall as the number of labourers increase, and rise as the number of labourers diminish; or, as mathematicians would express it, the rate of wages varies directly as the quantity of capital, and inversely as the number of labourers.

Macpherson mentions that "a dreadful pestilence, which originated in the eastern regions, began its ravages in England in the year 1348, and is said to have carried off the greater part of the people, especially in the lower ranks of life. The surviving labourers took advantage of the demand for labour and the scarcity of hands to raise their prices. The king, Edward I., thereupon enacted the statute of labourers, which ordained that all men and women under 60 years of age, whether of free or servile condition, having no occupation or property, should serve any person of whom they should be required, and should receive only the wages which were usual before the year 1346, or in the five or six preceding years, on pain of imprisonment, the employers being also punishable for giving greater wages. Artificers were also prohibited from demanding more than the old wages; and butchers, bakers, brewers, &c. were ordered to sell their provisions at reasonable prices. The 'servants having no regard to the said ordinance, but to their ease and singular covetise,' refused to serve unless for higher wages than the law allowed them. Therefore the parliament, by another statute, fixed in the yearly and daily wages of agricultural servants, artificers, and labourers, the payment of threshing corn by the quarters, and even the price of shoes. They also forbad any person to leave the town in summer wherein he had dwelt in the winter, or to remove from one shire to another.

"Thus were the lower class debarred by laws, which in their own nature must be inefficient, from making any effort to improve their situation in life."

CAROLINE

I had always imagined that a great demand for labour was occasioned by some great work that was to be executed, such as digging a canal, making new roads, cutting through hills, &c.; but it seems that the demand for labour depends, not so much on the quantity of work to be done as on the quantity of subsistence provided for the workmen.

MRS. B.

Work to be performed is the immediate cause of the demand for labour; but however great or important is the work which a man may wish to undertake, the execution of it must always be limited by the extent of his capital; that is to say, by the funds he possesses for the maintenance or payment of his labourers. The same observation applies to the capital of a country, which is only an aggregate of the capital of individuals; it cannot employ more people than it has the means of maintaining. All the waste land capable of cultivation in the country might be called work to be done, but there can be no demand for labourers to do the work, until a sufficient quantity of subsistence has been raised to support such an additional number of labourers as would be required for that purpose. In our conversation on capital we observed, that in countries of large capital great works were undertaken, such as public buildings, bridges, iron rail-ways, canals, &c. All these things are a sign of redundance of wealth.

CAROLINE

In Ireland I understand that the wages of common labourers are much lower than in England: is it on account of the capital of that country being less adequate to the maintenance of its population?

MRS. B.

That is, no doubt, one of the principal causes of the low price of labour in that country; but there are many other causes which affect the price of labour, arising from the imperfection of its government. The Irish are far less industrious than the English. Arthur Young, in his travels through Ireland, observes that "husbandry labour is very *low priced*, and not *cheap*. Two shillings a-day in Suffolk is cheaper than sixpence a-day in Cork. If a Huron would dig for two-pence a-day, I have little doubt but that it might be dearer than the Irishmen's sixpence."

CAROLINE

But, Mrs. B., the price of labour does not only vary in different countries, but very considerably in different parts of the same country. In purchasing some cutlery a few days ago, I was shewn country and town made knives and forks, apparently the same, yet the difference in price was considerable. Upon inquiring the cause, I was informed that it was going to wages being so much higher in London than in the country.

MRS. B.

And if you had inquired the cause of the high rate of wages of London workmen, you would have heard that it was on account of their being better workmen; the ablest artificers generally resort to London, as the place where their skill will be most duly appreciated, and where their employers can best afford to reward it.

It is but just to remunerate labourers according to their ability. Your head gardener does less work than any of the men under him; yet he has the highest wages, on account of the skill and experience he has acquired. A working silversmith has on this account higher wages than a taylor or a carpenter.

But where skill is not requisite, the hardest and most disagreeable kinds of labour are best paid: this is the case with blacksmiths, iron founders, coal heavers, &c.

A consideration is also had for arts of an unwholesome, unpleasant, or dangerous nature, such as painters, miners, gunpowder makers, and a variety of other analogous employments.

CONVERSATION IX

ON WAGES AND POPULATION

Continued

CAROLINE

I HAVE BEEN REFLECTING a great deal on our last conversation, Mrs. B., and the conclusions I have drawn from it are, that the greater the capital a country possesses, the greater number of people it can maintain, and the higher the wages of labour will be.

MRS. B.

The greater the stock of subsistence, the more people may be maintained by it, no doubt; but your second inference is not at all a necessary conclusion. China is a very rich country, and yet wages are I believe no where so low. The accounts which travellers give of the miserable state of the inferior classes, are painful to hear; and their poverty is not the result of idleness, for they run about the streets with tools in their hands, begging for work.

CAROLINE

That is owing to the immense population of China; so that, though the capital of the country may be very considerable, still it is insufficient for the maintenance of all its inhabitants.

MRS. B.

You should therefore always remember that the rate of wages does not depend upon the absolute quantity of capital, but upon its quantity relative to the number of people to be maintained by it. This is a truth which, however simple, is continually lost sight of, and hence arise errors without number in political economy. If China had ten times the wealth it actually possesses, and its population were at the same time tenfold as numerous, the people would not be better fed.

America, on the other hand, is a country of very small capital, and yet wages are remarkably high there.

CAROLINE

How do you account for that? for the demand for labour, you know, can be only in proportion to the extent of capital.

MRS. B.

The capital of America, though small when compared with those of the countries of Europe, is very considerable in proportion to the number of people to be maintained by it. In America, and in all newly settled countries as yet thinly inhabited, the wages of labour are high, because capital increases with prodigious rapidity. Where land is plentiful and productive, and the labourers to cultivate it scarce, the competition amongst the landholders to obtain labourers is so great as to enable this class to raise their demands, and the higher the wages the labourer receives, the sooner he has it in his power to purchase a piece of land and become landholder himself. Thus the class of labourers is continually passing into the class of proprietors, and making room for a fresh influx of labourers, both from the rising generation and from emigrations from foreign countries.

CAROLINE

America has then the double advantage, of high wages and low price of land; no wonder that it is so thriving a country.

MRS. B.

The progress of wealth and improvement is no where so rapid, as in the settlement of a civilized people in a new country; provided they establish laws for the security of their property, they require no other incitement to industry. In the new settlements of America, where the experienced farmer with his European implements of husbandry is continually encroaching on the barren wilderness, want is almost unknown, and a state of universal prosperity prevails. We may form some judgment of the rapid increase of their capital by that of their population. The facility with which the Americans acquire a maintenance sufficient to bring up a family encourages early marriages, and gives rise to numerous families; the children are well fed; thriving, and healthy; you may imagine how small are the proportion that die in comparison to the number born, when I inform you that their population doubles itself in about 23 years!

CAROLINE

But does not such an immense increase of population reduce the rate of wages?

MRS. B.

No, because their capital increases in a still greater proportion; and as long as that is the case, wages, you know, will rise rather than fall. But what I have said relative to America refers only to the United States of that country; which have the advantage of a free government protecting the property of all classes of men. In the Spanish settlements, where the government is of a very different description, the condition of the people is far less flourishing. The population of Mexico, one of the finest provinces of Spanish America, does not double itself in less than 48 years.

CAROLINE

Yet I do not well understand why the poor should be worse off in England where there is large capital, than in America where there is a small one.

MRS. B.

Because you are again forgetting the fundamental rule which I have laid down for you, that capital must always be considered with reference to the number of people to be employed and maintained by it.

In England, and all the old established countries of Europe, the population has gradually increased till it has equalled the means of subsistence; and as Europe no longer affords the same facility for the growth of capital as a newly settled country, if the population goes on augmenting, it may exceed the means of subsistence, and in that case the wages of labour will fall instead of rising, and the condition of the poor become very miserable.

CAROLINE

But how is it possible for population to increase beyond the means of subsistence? Men cannot live without eating.

MRS. B.

No; but they may live upon a smaller portion of food than is necessary to maintain them in health and vigour; children may be born without their parents having the means of providing for them. Increase of population therefore under such circumstances cannot be permanent; its progress will be checked by distress and disease, and this I apprehend to be one of the causes of the reduced states of the poor in this country.

CAROLINE

I declare I always thought that is was very desirable to have a great population. All rich thriving countries are populous: great cities are populous; wealth, which you esteem so advantageous to a country, encourages population; and population in its turn promotes wealth, for labourers produce more than they consume. You recollect how rich our colony became by the acquisition of the labor of the ship-wrecked crew; their first arrival was attended with some inconvenience, it is true; but I should say as you do with respect to machinery, the inconvenience is small and temporary, the advantage both durable and extensive.

MRS. B.

You are quite mistaken if you imagine that I do not consider a great population as highly advantageous to a country, where there is a capital which will afford wages sufficient for a labourer to bring up his children; for population is not usually increased by the acquisition of a number of able labourers, (as was the case in our colony,) but by the birth of helpless infants who depend entirely upon their parents for subsistence. If this subsistence is not provided, the children are born merely to languish a few years in poverty, and to fall early victims to disease brought on by want and wretchedness. They can neither increase the strength, the wealth, nor the happiness of the country. On the contrary, they weaken, impoverish, and render it more miserable. They consume without reproducing, they suffer without enjoying, and they give pain and sorrow to their parents without ever reaching that age when they might reward their paternal cares. Yet such is the fate of thousands of children wherever population exceeds the means of subsistence.

CAROLINE

What a dreadful reflection this is! But you do not suppose that there are any children actually starved to death?

MRS. B.

I hope not; but the fate of those poor infants is scarcely less deplorable who perish by slow degrees for want of proper care and a sufficiency of wholesome food. A large family of young children would require the whole of a mother's care and attention; but that mother is frequently obliged to leave them to obtain by hard labour their scanty meal. Want of good nursing, of cleanliness, of fresh air, and of wholesome nourishment, engenders a great variety of diseases which either carry them off, or leave them in such a state of weakness that they fall a sacrifice to the first contagious malady which attacks them. It is to this state of debility, as well as to the want of medical advice and judicious treatment, that must be attributed the mortality occasioned by the small pox and measles amongst the lower classes of children, so much greater than in those of the upper ranks of society.

Nor are the fatal effects of an excess of population confined to children. A sick man, who might be restored to health by medical assistance and a proper diet, perishes because he can afford to obtain neither. A delicate or an infirm woman requires repose and indulgence which she cannot command. The necessaries of life vary not only with the climate and customs of a country, but with the age, sex, and infirmities of the individuals who inhabit it; and wherever these necessaries are deficient, mortality prevails.

Do you understand now why the rate of wages and the condition of the poor is better in countries which, like America, are growing rich; than in those which, like England, have long accumulated large capitals, but whose wealth is either stationary or making but slower progress?

CAROLINE

Yes; it is because when capital augments very rapidly, plenty precedes the increase of population, and labour is in great demand and well rewarded. But when wealth, however great, has long been stationary, population has risen up to the means of subsistence, or perhaps gone beyond it, so that wages fall and distress comes on.

MRS. B.

This is what I formerly alluded to when I told you that you would find that the acquisition of wealth was more advantageous to a country, as well as to an individual, than the actual possession of it.

I must read you a passage of Paley on this subject, in which he expresses himself with remarkable perspicuity.

"The ease of subsistence and the encouragement of industry depend neither upon the price of labour, nor upon the price of provisions; but upon the proportion which the one bears to the other. Now the influx of wealth into a country naturally tends to advance this proportion; that is, every fresh accession of wealth raises the price of labour, before it raises the price of provisions.

"It is not therefore the quantity of wealth collected into a country, but the continual increase of that quantity, from which the advantage arises to employment and population. It is only the accession of wealth which produces the effect; and it is only by wealth constantly flowing into, or springing up in a country, that the effect can be constant."

You must not, however, imagine that the capital of this country remains stationary; on the contrary, we are making rapid advances in wealth, though we cannot pretend to equal the progress of a newly settled country. In confirmation of this, Arthur Young observes, that wages had risen about one-third, both in England and Ireland, within the last 20 years; which proves that capital has been increasing in a greater ratio than population. But it must be observed, that it is about 30 years since he gave this account; and the severe checks which industry has received since that period throughout the greater part of Europe, from a constant state of the most expensive warfare, has, I fear, greatly retarded the progress of capital, without equally affecting that of population; but if the increase of the latter has occasionally outstripped the means of subsistence, it is no less owing to the ill-judged conduct of the upper classes than to the imprudence of the lower orders of people.

CAROLINE

You allude, I suppose, to the encouragement of early marriages amongst the poor?

MRS. B.

Yes; we observed that when a great population springs from ample means of subsistence, it is the highest blessing a country can enjoy; the children brought up in plenty, attain a healthy and vigorous manhood, with strength to defend, and industry to enrich their country. Those who have not reflected on the subject, have frequently confounded cause and effect, and have, with you, considered a great population under all circumstances as the cause of prosperity. Hence the most strenuous efforts have been made, not only by individuals, but even by the legislature, to encourage early marriages and large families, conceiving that by so doing they were promoting the happiness and prosperity of their country.

CAROLINE

This is a most unfortunate error. But when population is again reduced, the evil corrects itself; for capital being thus rendered more adequate to the maintenance of this diminished population, the wages of labour will again rise.

MRS. B.

Certainly. But it often happens that as soon as the labouring classes find their condition improved, whether by a diminution of numbers, or an augmentation of capital, which may spring up from some new source of industry, marriages again increase, a greater number of children are reared, and population once more outstrips the means of subsistence; so that the condition of the poor, after a temporary improvement, is again reduced to its former wretchedness.

CAROLINE

That is precisely what has occurred in the village near which we live. It was formerly, I have heard, but a small hamlet, the inhabitants of which gained a livelihood as farmers' labourers. Many years ago a cotton manufacture was set up in the neighbourhood, which afforded ample employment for the poor; and even the children, who were before idle, could now earn something towards their maintenance. This, during some years, had an admirable effect raising the condition of the labouring classes. I have heard my grandfather say that it was wonderful to see how rapidly the village improved, how many new cottages were built, and what numerous families they contained. But this prosperous state was not of long duration: in the course of time the village became over-stocked with labourers, and it is now sunk into a state of poverty and distress worse than that from which it had so recently emerged.

MRS. B.

You see, therefore, that this manufacture, which at first proved a blessing to the village, and might always have continued such, was, by the improvidence of the labourers, converted into an evil. If the population had not increased beyond the demand for labour, the manufacture might still have afforded them the advantages it at first produced.

CAROLINE

This then must be the cause of the misery which generally prevails amongst the poor in manufacturing towns, where it would be so natural to expect that the facility of finding work would produce comfort and plenty.

MRS. B.

And it proves that no amelioration of the condition of the poor can be permanent, unless to industry they add prudence and foresight. Were all men as considerate as your gardener, Thomas, and did they not marry till they had secured a provision for a family, or could earn a sufficiency to maintain it; in short, were children not brought into the world until there was bread to feed them, the distress which you have just been describing would be unknown, excepting in cases of unforeseen misfortunes, or unless produced by illness or vice.

CAROLINE

And is it not to these latter causes that a great part of the misery in manufacturing towns should be ascribed? I have heard it observed that skilful workmen, who could earn a livelihood by three or four days' labour in the week, would frequently spend the remainder of it in idleness and profligacy.

MRS. B.

I believe that it is much more common for great gains to act as a stimulus to industry. Like every other human quality, industry improves in proportion to the encouragement it receives, and it can have no greater encouragement and reward than high wages. It sometimes happens, it is true that workmen act in the way you mention, but such conduct is far from being common; the greater part, when their wages are liberal, keep steadily to their work, and if they are paid by the piece, are even apt to overwork themselves.

CAROLINE

That I have observed. My father lately agreed to pay a certain sum for digging a sunk fence in our pleasure-grounds; and two of the undergardeners engaged to do it after the day's work was over. I thought they would repent of their undertaking, when they came to such hard labour, after having performed their usual task; but I was astonished at their alacrity and perseverance: in the course of a week they completed the job, and received the price in addition to their usual wages. I wonder that work is not always paid by the piece, it is such an encouragement to industry.

MRS. B.

All kinds of work are not susceptible of being so paid; for instance, the care of a garden could not be divided into jobs, and the gardener be paid so much for planting trees, so much for cleaning borders, so much for mowing grass, &c. Besides I doubt whether it would be desirable that this mode of payment should be generally adopted, on account of the temptation it affords to labourers to overwork themselves; for notwithstanding all the advantages of industry, one would never wish it to be pushed to that extreme which would exhaust the strength of the labouring classes, and bring on disease and infirmity. The benefits resulting from industry are an increase of the comforts and conveniencies of life; but it would be paying too dear for these to purchase them by a sickly and premature old age.

In order to be of permanent service to the labouring classes we must not rest satisfied with encouraging industry; but we should endeavour by instruction to awaken their minds to a sense of remote consequences, as well as of immediate good, so that when they have succeeded in rendering their condition more comfortable, they may not rashly and inconsiderately increase their numbers beyond the means of subsistence.

CAROLINE

But if population be constantly kept within the limits of subsistence, would it not always remain stationary?

MRS. B.

Certainly not; if the people are industrious capital will increase; and the increase of population will follow of course, and with advantage.

CAROLINE

I now see evidently, that population should never be encouraged but where there is great plenty of subsistence and employment.

MRS. B.

And *then* it requires no encouragement. If men so often marry without having made any provision for a family, there is no danger of their not marrying when a subsistence is easily obtained; and their children will be healthy and long-lived in proportion as they are well fed, clothed, and taken care of.

Rural Nostalgia:
The Ideological Drag of the Country

William Cobbett, "Rural Ride, Down the Valley of the Avon, in Wilt-shire," Cobbett's Weekly Register, Vol. LIX, No. 12 (September 16, 1826), pp. 705–46.

One countercurrent in modern thought, so simple that it is usually ignored in spite of its persistence and importance, must be as old as recorded history. Urbanization and cosmopolitan culture weaken the spiritual and moral fiber of the community. The coming of industrialization added nothing substantial to the debate; little could be added since Virgil and Catullus. Industrialism and the ugliness of urbanization could reinforce the view that rural life was better. If the country bumpkin receives harsh treatment at the hands of his polished urban counterpart, something remains which is finer about the simple man, the simple life, the simple joys of the country. Man loses his individuality and character in the megalopolis.

Rural nostalgia found modern eloquence with William Cobbett (1763–1835). Uncompromising, wrathful, always shouting, foursquare against most of the leading ideas and forces of his age, Mr. Cobbett (he threw away unread those letters addressed to W. Cobbett, Esq.) cast himself in the image of what many men liked to believe they were. The ten-pound householders of manufacturing Oldham, newly enfranchised, twice returned him and repeatedly returned his son to the reformed House of Commons. Cities were "wens" to Cobbett; London the "great Wen." "Tax eaters," Scotch "feelosophers," "canting Methodists," filthy mills, paper money—above all, "the Thing" (which more recent angry young men call the Establishment)—corrupt and destroy humanity. Cobbett, right or wrong, is magnificent. He knew he was right and expected you to know it as well. Rarely has there been a more exciting and stubbornly wrong-headed book than his *History of the Protestant Reformation* (1824). "Peter Porcupine" was Cobbett's sometime pseudonym; never was one more appropriate.

The return to the land and a less complex life recurs as a theme in the ideas of many besides this tory-radical. It is an inherent part of utopian communitarian doctrine. It was even one of the answers offered by those defeated radicals, the Chartists. Land reform and resettlement appealed to John Stuart Mill and was part of Joseph Chamberlain's radical program. The point may be trivial, but Cobbett was, like Arthur Young (the champion of agrarian improvement a generation before), a failure as a farmer. His "cottage economy" is full of bad advice. But Cobbett was a successful journalist. He was a common man with uncommon eloquence, reaffirming the value and worth of man and the soil. The sturdy yeoman was his ideal, traditional farming his avocation, justice and human rights his creed.

RURAL RIDE

down the Valley of the Avon, in Wiltshire

"Thou shalt not muzzle the ox when he treadeth out the corn."
—*Deuteronomy*, ch. xxv. ver. 4.

Milton, Monday, 28th August.—I came off this morning on the Marlborough road about two miles, or three, and then turned off, over the downs, in a north-westerly direction, in search of the source of the Avon River, which goes down to Salisbury. I had once been at Netheravon, a village in this valley; but, I had often heard this valley described as one of the finest pieces of land in all England; I knew that there were about *thirty parish churches*, standing in a length of about *thirty miles*, and in an average width of *hardly a mile;* and, I was resolved to see a little into the *reásons* that could have induced our fathers to build all these churches, especially if, as the Scotch would have us believe, there were but a mere handful of people in England *until of late years.* . . .

In steering across the down, I came to a large farm, which a shepherd told me was Milton Hill Farm. This was upon the high land, and before I came to the edge of this *Valley of Avon*, which was my land of promise; or, at least, of great expectation; for I could not imagine that thirty churches had been built *for nothing* by the side of a brook (for it is no more during the greater part of the way) thirty miles long. The shepherd showed me the way towards Milton; and at the end of about a mile, from the top of a very high part of the down, with a steep slope towards the valley, I first saw this *Valley of Avon;* and a most beautiful sight it was! Villages, hamlets, large farms, towers, steeples, fields, meadows, orchards, and very fine timber-trees, scattered all over the valley. The shape of the thing is this: on each side *downs*, very lofty and steep in some places, and sloping miles back in other places; but, each *out-side* of the valley are downs. From the edge of the downs begin capital *arable fields*, generally of very great dimensions, and, in some places, running a mile or two back into little *cross-valleys*, formed by hills of downs. After the corn-fields come *meadows*, on each side, down to the *brook*, or *river*. The farm-houses, mansions, villages, and hamlets, are generally situated in that part of the arable land which comes nearest the meadows.

Great as my expectations had been, they were more than fulfilled. I delight in this sort of country; and I had frequently seen the vale of the *Itchen*, that of the *Bourne*, and also that of the *Teste*, in Hampshire; I had seen the vales amongst the *South Downs;* but I never before saw any thing to please me like this valley of the Avon. I sat upon my horse, and looked over Milton and Easton and Pewsey for half an hour, though I had not breakfasted. The hill was very steep. A road, going slanting down it, was still so steep, and washed so very deep, by the rains of ages, that I did not attempt to *ride* down it, and I did not like to lead my horse, the path was so narrow. So, seeing a boy with a drove of pigs, going out to the stubbles, I beckoned him to come up to me; and he came, and led my horse down for me. . . . Endless is the variety in the shape of the high lands which form this valley. Sometimes the slope is very gentle, and the arable lands go back very far. At others, the downs come out into the valley almost like piers into the sea, being very steep in their sides, as well as their ends towards the valley. They have no slope at their other ends: indeed, they have no *back ends*, but run into the main high land. There is also great variety in the *width* of the valley; great variety in the width of the meadows; but the land appears all to be of the very best; and it must be so, *for the farmers confess it.*

It seemed to me, that one way, and that not, perhaps, the least striking, of exposing the folly, the stupidity, the inanity, the presumption, the insufferable emptiness and insolence and barbarity, of those numerous wretches, who have now the audacity to propose to *transport* the people of England, upon the principle of the monster Malthus, who has furnished the unfeeling oligarchs and their toad-eaters with the pretence, that *man has a natural propensity to breed faster than food can be raised for the increase;* it seemed to me, that one way of exposing this mixture of madness and of blasphemy was, to take a look, now that the harvest is in, at the *produce*, the *mouths*, the *condition*, and *the changes that have taken place*, in a spot like this, which God has favoured with every good that he has had to bestow upon man.

From the top of the hill I was not a little surprised to see, in every part of the valley that my eye could reach, a due, a large, portion of fields of *Swedish Turnips*, all looking extremely well. I had found the turnips, of both sorts, by no means bad, from Salt Hill to Newbury; but, from Newbury through Burghclere, Highclere, Uphusband, and Tangley, I had seen but few. At and about Ludgarshall and Everley I had seen hardly any. But, when I came, this morning, to Milton Hill farm, I saw a very large field of what appeared to me to be fine Swedish Turnips. In the *valley*, however, I found them much finer, and the fields were very beautiful objects, forming, as their colour did, so great a contrast with that of the fallows and the stubbles, which latter are, this year, singularly clean and bright. . . .

SALISBURY, WEDNESDAY, 30TH AUGUST.—My ride yesterday, from Milton to this city of Salisbury, was, without any exception, the most pleasant; it brought before me the greatest number of, to me, interesting objects, and it gave rise to more interesting reflections, than I remember ever to have had brought before my eyes, or into my mind, in any one day of my life; and, therefore, this ride was, without any exception, the *most pleasant* that I ever had in my life, as far as my recollection serves me. I got a little *wet* in the middle of the day; but, I got dry again, and, I arrived here in very good time, though I went over the ACCURSED HILL (Old Sarum), and went across to Laverstroke, before I came to Salisbury.

Let us now, then, look back over this part of Wiltshire, and see whether the inhabitants ought to be *"transported"* by order of the *"Emigration Committee,"* of which we shall see and say more by-and-by. I have before described this valley *generally;* let me now speak of it a little more in detail. The farms are all large, and, generally speaking, they were always large, I dare say; because *sheep* is one of the great things here; and sheep, in a country like this, must be kept in *flocks,* to be of any profit. The sheep principally manure the land. This is to be done only by *folding;* and, to fold, you must have *a flock.* Every farm has its portion of *down, arable,* and *meadow;* and, in many places, the latter are *watered meadows,* which is a great resource where sheep are kept in flocks; because these meadows furnish grass for the suckling ewes, early in the spring; and, indeed, because they have always food in them for sheep and cattle of all sorts. These meadows have had no part of the suffering from the drought, this year. They fed the ewes and lambs in the spring, and they are now yielding a heavy crop of hay; for, I saw men mowing in them, in several places, particularly about Netheravon, thought it was raining at the time.

The turnips look pretty well all the way down the valley; but, I see very few, except *Swedish turnips.* The early common turnips very nearly all failed, I believe. But, the stubbles are beautifully bright; and the *rick-yards* tell us, that the crops are good, especially of *wheat.* This is not a country of *pease* and *beans,* nor of *oats,* except for home consumption. The crops are *wheat, barley, wool* and *lambs,* and these latter not to be sold to butchers, but to be sold, at the great fairs, to those who are going to keep them for some time, whether to breed from, or, finally to fat for the butcher. It is the *pulse* and the *oats* that appear to have failed most this year; and, therefore, this Valley has not suffered. I do not perceive that they have many *potatoes;* but, what they have of this base root seem to look well enough. It was one of the greatest villains upon earth (Sir Walter Raleigh), who (they say) first brought this root into England. He was hanged at last! What a pity, since he was to be hanged, the hanging did not take place before he became such a mischievous devil as he was in the latter two-thirds of his life!

The stack-yards down this Valley are beautiful to behold. They contain from *five* to *fifteen* banging *wheat-ricks,* besides *barley-ricks* and *hay-ricks,* and also besides the *contents of the barns,* many of which exceed *a hundred,* some *two hundred,* and I saw one at Pewsey and another at Fittleton, each of which exceeded *two hundred and fifty* feet in length. At a farm, which, in the old maps, is called *Chissenbury Priory,* I think I counted twenty-seven ricks of one sort and another, and sixteen or eighteen of them *wheat-ricks.* I could not conveniently get to the yard, without longer delay than

I wished to make; but, I could not be much out in my counting. A very fine sight this was, and it could not meet the eye without making one look round (and in vain) *to see the people who were to eat all this food;* and without making one reflect on the horrible, the unnatural, the base and infamous state, in which we must be, when projects are on foot, and are openly avowed, for *transporting* those who raise this food, *because they want to eat enough of it to keep them alive;* and when no project is on foot for *transporting* the idlers who live in luxury upon this same food; when no project is on foot for transporting pensioners, parsons, or dead-weight people!

A little while before I came to this farm-yard, I saw, *in one piece,* about *four hundred acres* of wheat-stubble, and I saw a sheep-fold, which, I thought, contained *an acre of ground,* and had in it about *four thousand sheep and lambs.* The fold was divided into three separate flocks; but the piece of ground was one and the same; and I thought it contained about an acre. At one farm, between Pewsey and Upavon, I counted more than 300 hogs in one stubble. This is certainly the most delightful farming in the world. No *ditches,* no *water-furrows,* no *drains,* hardly any *hedges,* no *dirt* and *mire,* even in the wettest seasons of the year; and though the *downs* are *naked* and *cold,* the valleys are snugness itself. They are, as to the downs, what *ah-ahs!* are, in parks or lawns. When you are going over the downs, you look *over* the valleys, as in the case of the *ah-ah;* and, if you be not acquainted with the country, your surprise, when you come to the edge of the hill, is very great. The *shelter,* in these valleys, and particularly where the downs are *steep* and *lofty* on the sides, is very complete. Then, the trees are every where *lofty.* They are generally *elms,* with some *ashes,* which delight in the soil that they find here. There are, almost always, two or three large clumps of trees in every parish, and a rookery or two (not *rag-*rookery) to every parish. By the water's edge there are *willows;* and to almost every farm, there is a fine *orchard,* the trees being, in general, very fine, and, this year, they are, in general, well loaded with fruit. So that, all taken together, it seems impossible to find a more beautiful and pleasant country than this, or to imagine any life more easy and happy than men might here lead, if they were untormented by an accursed system that takes the food from those that raise it, and gives it to those that do nothing that is useful to man.

Here the farmer has always an *abundance of straw.* His farm-yard is never without it. Cattle and horses are bedded up to their eyes. The yards are put close under the shelter of a hill, or are protected by lofty and thick-set trees. Every animal seems comfortably situated; and, in the dreariest days of winter, these are, perhaps, the happiest scenes in the world; or, rather, they would be such, if those, whose labour makes it all, trees, corn, sheep and every thing, had but *their fair share* of the produce of that labour. What share they really have of it one cannot exactly say; but, I should suppose, that every labouring *man* in this valley raises as much food as would suffice for *fifty*, or *a hundred persons*, fed like himself!

. . . .

Is there a family, even amongst those who live the hardest, in the Wen, that would not shudder at the thought of living upon what I have allowed to this family? Yet what *do labourers' families get*, compared to this? The answer to that question ought to make us shudder indeed. . . .

To what fare has this wretched and most infamous system brought them? Why, such a family as I have described is allowed to have, *at the utmost*, only about 9*s*. a week. The parish allowance is only about 7*s*. 6*d*. for the five people, including clothing, fuel, bedding and every thing! Monstrous state of things! But, let us suppose it to be *nine shillings*. Even that makes only 23*l*. 8*s*. a year, for food, drink, clothing, fuel and every thing, whereas I allow 62*l*. 6*s*. 8*d*. a year for the *bare eating and drinking;* and that is little enough. Monstrous, barbarous, horrible as this appears, we do not, however, see it in half its horrors; our indignation and rage against this infernal system is not half roused, till we see the *small number of labourers* who raise all the food and the drink, and, of course, the mere trifling portion of it that they are suffered to retain for their own use.

The parish of Milton does, as we have seen, produce food, drink, clothing, and all other things, enough for 502 families, or 2510 persons, upon *my allowance*, which is a great deal more than *three times* the present allowance, because the present allowance includes clothing, fuel, tools and every thing. Now, then, according to the "Population Return," laid before Parliament, this parish contains 500 persons; or, according to my division, *one hundred families*. So that here are but *one hundred* families to raise food and drink enough, and to raise wool and other things to pay for all other necessaries, for *five hundred* and *two* families! Aye, and five hundred and two families fed and lodged, too, *on my liberal scale*. Fed and lodged according to *the present scale*, this one hundred families raise enough to supply more, and many more, than *fifteen hundred* families; or *seven thousand five hundred* persons! And yet, *those who do the work are half-starved!* In the 100 families there are, we will suppose, 80 able working men, and as many boys, sometimes assisted by the women and stout girls. What a handful of people to raise such a quantity of food! What injustice, what a hellish system it must be, to make those who raise it *skin and bone and nakedness*, while the food and drink and wool are almost all carried away to be helped on the fundholders, pensioners, soldiers, dead-weight, and other's warms of tax-eaters! If such an operation do not need putting an end to, then the devil himself is a saint.

. . . from Wotton Rivers to Stratford Dean . . . are 9,116 persons raising food and raiment sufficient for 45,580 persons, fed and lodged according to my scale; and sufficient for 136,740 persons, according to the scale, on which the unhappy labourers of this fine valley are now fed and lodged!

And yet there is an *"Emigration Committee"* sitting to devise the means of getting *rid*, not of the *idlers*, not of the *pensioners*, not of the *dead-weight*, not of the *parsons*, (to *"relieve"* whom we have seen the poor labourers taxed to the tune of a million and a half of money) not of the soldiers; but to devise means of getting rid of *these working people*, who are grudged even the miserable morsel that they get! There is, in the men calling themselves "English country gentlemen," something superlatively base. They are, I *sincerely believe*, the most cruel, the most unfeeling, the most brutally insolent; but I *know*, I can *prove*, I can *safely take my oath*, that they are the MOST BASE of all the creatures that God ever suffered to disgrace the human shape. The base wretches know well, that the *taxes* amount to more than *sixty millions* a year, and that the *poor-rates* amount to about *seven millions;* yet, while the cowardly reptiles never utter a word against the taxes, they are incessantly railing against the poor-rates, though it is (and they know it) the taxes that make the paupers. The base wretches know well, that the sum of money given, even to the *fellows that gather* the taxes, is greater in amount than the poor-rates; the base wretches know well, that the money, given to the *dead-weight* (who ought not to have a single farthing), amounts to more than the poor receive out of the rates; the base wretches know well, that the common foot soldier now receives more pay per week (7s. 7d.), exclusive of *clothing, firing, candle,* and *lodging;* the base wretches know, that the common foot-soldier receives more *to go down his own single throat*, than the overseers and magistrates allow to a *working man, his wife,* and *three children;* the base wretches know all this well; and yet their railings are confined to *the poor* and the *poor-rates;* and it is expected, that they will, next session, urge the Parliament to pass a law to enable overseers and vestries and magistrates *to transport paupers beyond the seas!* They are base enough for this, or for any thing; but the whole system will go to the devil, long before they will get such an act passed; long before they will see perfected this consummation of their infamous tyranny.

It is manifest enough, that the *population* of this valley was, at one time, many times over what it is now; for, in the first place, what were the *twenty-nine* churches built *for?* The population of the 29 parishes is *now* but little more than *one-half* of that of the single parish of Kensington; and there are several of the churches bigger than the church at Kensington. What, then, should all these churches have been built FOR? And, besides, where did the *hands* come from? And where did the *money* come from? These twenty-nine churches would now not only hold all the inhabitants, men, women, and children, but all the household goods, and tools, and implements, of the whole of them, farmers and all, if you leave out the wagons and carts. In three instances, . . . the *church-porches* will hold all the inhabitants, even down to the bed-ridden and the babies. What then, will any man believe that these churches were built for such little knots of people? We are told about the *great superstition* of our fathers, and

of their readiness to *gratify the priests* by building altars and other religious edifices. But, we must think those priests to have been most devout
creatures indeed, if we believe, that they chose to have the money laid out
in *useless* churches, rather than have it put into their own pockets! At any
rate, we all know, that *Protestant Priests* have no whims of *this sort;* and
that they never lay out upon churches any money that they can, by any
means, get hold of.

But, suppose that we were to believe that the Priests had, in old times,
this unaccountable taste; and suppose we were to believe that a knot of
people, who might be crammed into a church-porch, were seized, and very
frequently too, with the desire of having a big church to go to; we must,
after all this, believe that this knot of people were more than *giants*, or, that
they had surprising *riches*, else we cannot believe that they had *the means*
of gratifying the strange wishes of their Priests and their own not less
strange piety and *devotion*. Even if we could believe that they thought that
they were paving their way to heaven, by building churches which were a
hundred times too large for the population, still we cannot believe, that the
building could have been effected without *bodily force;* and, where was this
force to *come from*, if the people were not more numerous than they now
are? What, again, I ask, were these twenty-nine churches stuck up, *not a
mile from each other;* what were twenty-nine churches made FOR, if the
population had been no greater than it is now?

But, in fact, you plainly see all the traces of a great ancient population.
The churches are almost all large, and built in the best manner. Many of
them are *very fine* edifices; very costly in the building; and, in the cases
where the body of the church has been altered in the repairing of it, so as to
make it smaller, the *tower*, which every where defies the hostility of time,
shows you what the church must formerly have been. This is the case in
several instances; and there are two or three of these villages which must
formerly have been *market-towns. . . .* There are now no less than *nine* of
the parishes, out of the twenty-nine, that have either *no parsonage-houses*,
or have such as are in such a state that a Parson will not, or cannot, live in
them. Three of them are without any parsonage-houses at all, and the rest
are become poor, mean, falling-down places. . . . Nothing can more clearly
show than this, that all, as far as buildings and population are concerned,
has been long upon the decline and decay. Dilapidation after dilapidation
have, at last, almost effaced even the parsonage-houses, and that too in
defiance of the law, ecclasiastical as well as civil. The *land* remains; and
the crops and the sheep come as abundantly as ever; but they are now *sent
almost wholly away*, instead of remaining, as formerly, to be, in great part,
consumed in these twenty-nine parishes.

. . . Every *parish* had its manor house, in the first place; and then there
were, down this Valley, *twenty-one others*; so that, in this distance of about
thirty-miles, there stood FIFTY MANSION HOUSES. Where are they *now*? I
believe, there are but EIGHT, that are at all worthy of the name of *mansion*

houses; and even these are but poorly kept up, and, except in two or three instances, are of no benefit to the labouring people; they employ but few persons; and, in short, do not half supply the place of *any eight* of the old mansions. All these mansions, all these parsonages, aye, and their goods and furniture, together with the clocks, the brass-kettles, the brewing-vessels, the good bedding and good clothes and good furniture, and the stock, in pigs, or in money, of the inferior classes, in this series of once populous and gay villages and hamlets; all these have been, by the accursed system of taxing and funding and paper-money, by the well-known exactions of the state, and by the not less real, though less generally understood, extortions of the *monopolies* arising out of paper-money; all these have been, by these accursed means, conveyed away, out of this Valley, to the haunts of the tax-eaters and the monopolizers. There are many of the *mansion houses*, the ruins of which you yet behold. At Milton there are two mansion houses, the walls and the *roofs* of which yet remain, but which are falling gradually to pieces, and the garden walls are crumbling down. At Enford Bennett, the Member for the county, had a large mansion-house, the *stables* of which are yet standing. In several places, I saw, still remaining, indubitable traces of an ancient manor house, namely, a *dove-cote*, or *pigeon-house*. The poor pigeons have kept possession of their heritage, from generation to generation, and so have the *rooks*, in their several rookeries, while the paper-system has swept away, or, rather, *swallowed up*, the owners of the dove-cotes and of the lofty trees, about forty families of which owners have been ousted in this one Valley, and have become dead-weight creatures, tax-gatherers, barrack-fellows, thief-takers, or, perhaps, paupers or thieves.

Senator Snip congratulated, some years ago, that preciously honourable "Collective *Wisdom*," of which he is a most worthy Member; Snip congratulated it on the *success of the late war* in *creating capital*! Snip is, you must know, a great *feelosofer* and a not less great *feenanceer*. Snip cited, as a proof of the great and glorious effects of paper-money, the *new and fine houses in London*, the *new streets and squares*, the *new roads*, new *canals* and *bridges*. Snip was not, I dare say, aware, that this same paper-money had destroyed forty mansion houses in this Vale of Avon, and had taken away all the goods, all the substance, of the little gentry and of the labouring class. Snip was not, I dare say, aware, that this same paper-money had, in this one Vale of only thirty miles long, dilapidated, and, in some cases, wholly demolished, *nine* out of *twenty-nine* even of the parsonage houses. I told Snip, at the time (1821), that paper-money could *create no valuable thing*. I begged Snip to bear this in mind. I besought all my readers, and particularly Mr. Mathias Atwood (one of the Members for *Lowther*-town), not to believe, that paper-money ever did, or ever could, CREATE any thing of any value. I besought him to look well into the matter, and assured him, that he would find, that, though paper-money could CREATE nothing of value, it was able to TRANSFER every thing of value; able to strip a little gentry; able to dilapidate even parsonage houses; able to rob gentlemen of their estates, and labourers of their Sunday-coats and their barrels of beer; able to snatch the dinner from the board of the reaper or the mower, and to convey it to the barrack-table of the Hessian or Hanoverian grenadier; able to take away the wool, that ought to give warmth to the bodies of those who rear the sheep, and put it on the backs of those who carry arms to keep the poor, half-famished shepherds in order!

I have never been able clearly to comprehend what the beastly Scotch *feelosofers* mean by their *"national wealth;"* but, as far as I can understand them, this is their meaning: that national wealth means, that which is *left* of the products of the country over and above what is *consumed,* or *used,* by those whose labour causes the products to be. This being the notion, it follows, of course, that the *fewer* poor devils you can screw the products out of, the *richer* the nation is. This is, too, the notion of Burdett, as expressed in his silly and most nasty, musty aristocratic speech of last session. What, then, is to be done with this *over-produce?* Who is to have it? Is it to go to pensioners, placemen, tax-gatherers, dead-weight people, soldiers, gendarmerie, police-people, and, in short, to whole millions *who do no work at all?* Is this a cause of *"national wealth"?* Is a nation made *rich* by taking the food and clothing from those who create them, and giving them to those who do nothing of any use? Aye, but, this *over-produce* may be given to *manufacturers,* and to those who supply the food-raisers with what they want besides food. Oh! but this is merely an *exchange* of one valuable thing for another valuable thing; it is an exchange of labour in Wiltshire for labour in Lancashire; and, upon the whole, here is no *over-production.* If the produce be *exported,* it is the same thing: it is an *exchange* of one sort of labour for another. But, *our course* is, that there is not an *exchange;* that those who labour, no matter in what way, have a large part of the fruit of their labour *taken away,* and receive nothing *in exchange.* If the over-produce of this Valley of Avon were given, by the farmers, to the weavers in Lancashire, to the iron and steel chaps of Warwickshire, and to other makers or sellers of useful things, there would come an abundance of all these useful things into this valley from Lancashire and other parts; but if, as is the case, the over-produce goes to the fundholders, the dead-weight, the soldiers, the lord and lady and master and miss pensioners and sinecure people; if the over-produce go to them; as a very great part of it does, nothing, not even the parings of one's nails, *can come back to the valley in exchange.* And, can this operation, then, add to the *"national wealth"?* It adds to the *"wealth"* of those who carry on the affairs of state; it fills their pockets, those of their relatives and dependants; it fattens all tax-eaters; but, it can give no *wealth* to the *"nation,"* which means, *the whole of the people.* National Wealth means, the *Commonwealth,* or *Commonweal;* and these mean, the general *good,* or *happiness,* of the people, and the *safety* and *honour* of *the state;* and, these are not to be secured by robbing those who labour, in order to support a large part of the community in *idleness*. Devizes is the market-town to which the corn goes from the greater part of this Valley. If, when a wagon-load of wheat goes off in the morning, the wagon came back at night loaded with cloth, salt, or something or other, *equal in value to the wheat*, except what might be necessary to leave with the shopkeeper as his profit; then, indeed, the people might see the wagon go off without tears in their eyes. But, now, they see it go *to carry away*, and to bring *next to nothing in return*.

What a *twist* a head must have before it can come to the conclusion, that the *nation* gains in *wealth* by the government being able to cause the work to be done by those who have hardly any share in the fruit of the labour! What a *twist* such a head must have! The Scotch *feelosofers*, who seem all to have been, by nature, formed for negro-drivers, have an insuperable objection to all those establishments and customs, which occasion *holidays*. They call them a *great hinderance*, a great *bar to industry*, a great *drawback from "national wealth."* I wish each of these unfeeling fellows had a spade put into his hand for ten days, only ten days, and that he were compelled to dig only just as much as one of the common labourers at Fulham. The metaphysical gentleman would, I believe, soon discover the *use of holidays*! But, *why* should men, why should *any* men, work *hard*! Why, I ask, should they work *incessantly*, if working part of the days of the week be sufficient? Why should the people at Milton, for instance, work incessantly, when they now raise food and clothing and fuel and every necessary *to maintain well five times their number*? Why should they not have some holidays? And, pray, say, thou conceited Scotch feelosofer, how the *"national wealth"* can be increased, by making these people work *incessantly*, that they may raise food and clothing, to go to feed and clothe *people who do not work at all*.

The state of this Valley seems to illustrate the infamous and really diabolical assertion of Malthus, which is, that the human kind have a NATURAL TENDENCY *to increase beyond the means of sustenance for them*. Hence all the schemes of this and the other Scotch writers for what they call *checking population*. Hence all the *beastly*, the *nasty*, the abominable writings, put forth to teach labouring people *how to avoid having children*. Now, look at this Valley of Avon. Here the people raise nearly *twenty times as much food and clothing as they consume*. They raise five times as much, even according to my scale of living. They have been doing this for many, many years. They have been doing it *for several generations*. Where, then, is their NATURAL TENDENCY *to increase beyond the means of sustenance for them*? Beyond, indeed, the means of that sustenance *which a system like this will leave them*. Say that, Sawneys, and I agree with you. Far beyond the means that the taxing and monopolizing system will leave in their hands: that is very true; for it leaves them nothing but the scale of the poor-book: they must cease to breed at all, or they must exceed, this mark; but, the *earth*, give them their fair share of its products, will always give sustenance in sufficiency to those who apply to it by skilful and diligent labour.

The villages down this Valley of Avon, and, indeed, it was the same in almost every part of this county, and in the North and West of Hampshire also, used to have great employment for the women and children in *the carding and spinning of wool for the making of broad-cloth.* This was a very general employment for the women and girls; but, it is *now wholly gone*; and this has made a vast change in the condition of the people, and in the state of property and of manners and of morals. In 1816, I wrote and published a Letter to the Luddites, the object of which was *to combat their hostility to the use of machinery.* The arguments I there made use of were general. I took the matter in the abstract. The *principles* were all correct enough; but their application *cannot be universal*; and, we have a case here before us, at this moment, which, in my opinion, shows, that the mechanic inventions, pushed to the extent that they have been, have been productive of great calamity to this country, and that they will be productive of still greater calamity; unless, indeed, it be their brilliant destiny to be the immediate cause of *putting an end to the present system.*

The greater part of manufactures consist of *clothing* and *bedding.* Now, if by using a machine, we can get our coat with less labour than we got it before, the machine is a desirable thing. But, then, mind, we must have the machine *at home* and we *ourselves* must have *the profit* of it; for, if the machine be *elsewhere*; if it be worked *by other hands*; if *other persons* have the *profit* of it; and if, in consequence of the existence of the machine, we have hands at home, who have *nothing to do*, and whom we *must keep*, then the machine is an injury to us, however advantageous it may be to those who use it, and whatever traffic it may occasion with foreign States.

Such is the case with regard to this cloth-making. The machines are at *Upton-Level, Warminster, Bradford, Westbury*, and *Trowbridge*, and here are some of the hands in the Valley of Avon. This Valley raises food and clothing; but, in order to raise them, it must have *labourers.* These are absolutely necessary; for, without them this rich and beautiful Valley becomes worth nothing except to wild animals and their pursuers. The labourers are *men* and *boys.* Women and girls occasionally; but the men and the boys are as necessary as the light of day, or as the air and the water. Now, if beastly Malthus, or any of his nasty disciples, can discover a mode of having men and boys *without having women and girls*, then, certainly, the *machine* must be a good thing; but, if this Valley *must absolutely have the women and the girls*, then the machine, by leaving them with *nothing to do*, is a mischievous thing; and a producer of most dreadful misery. What, with regard to the poor, is the great complaint now? Why, that the *single man* does not receive the same, or any thing like the same, wages as the *married* man. Aye, it is the *wife* and *girls* that are the burden; and, to be sure, a burden they must be, under a system of taxation like the present, and with *no work to do.* Therefore, whatever may be *saved* in labour by the *machine* is no benefit, but an injury to the mass of the people. For, in fact, all that the women and children earned was so much *clear addition* to what the family earns now. The greatest part of the clothing in the United States of America *is made by the farm women and girls*. They do almost the whole of it; and all that they do is done *at home*. To be sure, they might buy *cheap*; but they must buy for *less than nothing*, if it would not answer their purpose to *make* the things.

The survey of this Valley is, I think, the finest answer in the world to the "Emigration Committee" fellows, and to "Jerry Curteis (one of the Members for Sussex), who has been giving *"evidence"* before it. I shall find out, when I can get to see the *report*, what this "Emigration Committee" would be *after*! I remember, that, last winter, a young woman complained to one of the Police Justices, that the *Overseers* of some parish were going to *transport her orphan brother to Canada*, because he became chargeable to their parish! I remember also, that the Justices said, that the intention of the Overseers was *"premature"*; for that "the BILL *had not yet passed"*! This was rather an ugly story; and I do think, that we shall find, that there have been, and are, some pretty propositions before this "Committee." We shall see all about the matter, however, by-and-by; and, when we get the *transporting* project fairly before us, shall we not then loudly proclaim "the *envy* of surrounding nations and *admiration* of the world"!

But, what ignorance, impudence and insolence must those base wretches have, who propose to *transport* the labouring people, as being *too numerous*, while the produce, which is obtained by their labour, is more than sufficient for three, four, or five, or even ten times their numbers! Jerry Curteis, who has, it seems, been a famous witness on this occasion, says that the *poor-rates*, in many cases, amount to as much as the *rent*. Well; and what then, Jerry? The rent may be high enough too, and the farmer *may afford to pay them both*; for, a very large part of what you call *poor-rates* ought to be called *wages*. But, at any rate, what has all this do do with the *necessity of emigration*? To make out such necessity, you must make out that you have *more mouths than the produce of the parish will feed*? Do, then, Jerry, tell us, another time, a little about *the quantity of food* annually raised in four or five adjoining parishes; for, is it not something rather damnable, Jerry, to talk of *transporting* Englishmen, on account of the *excess of their numbers*, when the fact is notorious, that their labour produces five or ten times as much food and raiment as they and their families consume!

However, to drop Jerry, for the present, the baseness, the foul, the stinking, the carrion baseness, of the fellows that call themselves *"country gentlemen,"* is, that the wretches, while railing against the poor and the poor-rates; while affecting to believe, that the poor are wicked and lazy; while complaining that the poor, the working people, are *too numerous*, and that the country villages are too populous: the carrion baseness of these wretches, is, that, while they are thus *bold* with regard to the working and poor people, they never even whisper a word against pensioners, placemen, soldiers, parsons, fundholders, tax-gatherers, or tax-eaters! They say not a

word against the prolific *dead-weight*, to whom they GIVE A PREMIUM FOR
BREEDING, while they wait to check the population of labourers! They never
say a word about the too great populousness of the Wen; nor about that of
Liverpool, Manchester, Cheltenham, and the like! Oh! they are the most
cowardly, the very basest, the most scandalously base, reptiles that ever
were warmed into life by the rays of the sun!

In taking my leave of this beautiful vale I have to express my deep
shame, as an Englishman, at beholding the general *extreme poverty* of
those who cause this vale to produce such quantities of food and raiment.
This is, I verily believe it, the *worst used labouring people upon the face of
the earth*. Dogs and hogs and horses are treated with *more civility*; and as
to food and lodging, how gladly would the labourers change with them!
This state of things never can continue many years! *By some means or other*
there must be an end to it; and my firm belief is, that that end will be dreadful. In the mean while I see, and I see it with pleasure, that the common
people *know that they are ill used*; and that they cordially, most cordially,
hate those who ill-treat them.

During the day I crossed the river about fifteen or sixteen times; and in
such hot weather it was very pleasant to be so much amongst meadows and
water. I had been at Netheravon about eighteen years ago, where I had
seen a great quantity of hares. It is a place belonging to Mr. Hicks Beach, or
Beech, who was once a member of parliament. I found the place *altered* a
good deal; out of repair; the gates rather rotten; and (a very bad sign!) the
roof of the dog-kennel falling in! There is a church, at this village of Netheravon, large enough to hold a *thousand or two* of people, and the whole
parish contains only 350 souls, men, women and children. This Netheravon
was formerly a great lordship, and in the parish there were three considerable mansion-houses, besides the one near the church. These mansions are
all down now; and it is curious enough to see the former *walled gardens*
become *orchards*, together with other changes, all tending to prove the
gradual decay in all except what appertains merely to *the land* as a thing of
production for the distant market. But, indeed, the people and the means
of enjoyment *must go away*. They are *drawn* away by the taxes and the
paper-money. How are *twenty thousand new houses* to be, all at once,
building in the Wen, without people and food and raiment going from this
valley towards the Wen? It must be so; and this unnatural, this dilapidating,
this ruining and debasing work must go on, until that which produces it be
destroyed.

When I came down to Stratford Dean, I wanted to go across to Laverstoke, which lay to my left of Salisbury; but just on the side of the road here,
at Stratford Dean, rises the ACCURSED HILL. It is very lofty. It was originally
a hill in an irregular sort of sugar-loaf shape: but, it was so altered by the
Romans, or by somebody, that the upper three-quarter parts of the hill now,
when seen from a distance, somewhat resemble *three cheeses*, laid one
upon another; the bottom one a great deal broader than the next, and the

top one like a Stilton cheese, in proportion to a Gloucester one. I resolved to ride over this ACCURSED HILL. As I was going up a field towards it, I met a man going home from work. I asked how he *got on*. He said, very badly. I asked him what was the cause of it. He said the *hard times*. "What *times*," said I; "was there ever a finer summer, a finer harvest, and is there not an *old* wheat-rick in every farm-yard?" "Ah!" said he, "*they* make it bad for poor people, for all that." "*They?*" said I, "who is *they?*" He was silent. "Oh, no! my friend," said I, "it is not *they*: it is that ACCURSED HILL that has robbed you of the supper that you ought to find smoking on the table when you get home." I gave him the price of a pot of beer, and on I went, leaving the poor dejected assemblage of skin and bone to wonder at my words.

The hill is very steep, and I dismounted and led my horse up. Being as near to the top as I could conveniently get, I stood a little while reflecting, not so much on the changes which that hill had seen, as on the changes, the terrible changes, which, in all human probability, it had *yet to see*, and which it would have greatly *helped to produce*. It was impossible to stand on this accursed spot, without swelling with indignation against the base and plundering, and murderous sons of corruption. I have often wished, and I, speaking out loud, expressed the wish now; "May that man perish for ever and ever, who, having the power, neglects to bring to justice the perjured, the suborning, the insolent and perfidious miscreants, who openly sell their country's rights and their own souls."

From the ACCURSED HILL I went to Laverstoke, where "Jemmy Borough" (as they call him here), the Judge, lives. I have not heard much about "Jemmy" since he tried and condemned the two yound men who had wounded the game-keepers of Ashton Smith and Lord Palmerston. His Lordship (Palmerston) is, I see, making a tolerable figure in the newspapers as a *share-man*! I got into Salisbury about half-past seven o'clock, less tired than I recollect ever to have been after so long a ride; for, including my several crossings of the river and my deviations to look at churches and farm-yards, and rick-yards, I think I must have ridden nearly forty miles.

WM. COBBETT.

Character and Profits:
Owen's View

Robert Owen, "First Essay on the Formation of Character" and "Address to the Superintendants of Manufactories, . . ." (London, 1813), pp. 3–11, 29–32.

Robert Owen (1771–1858) had as little to do with politics as possible. He was a successful cotton-spinning entrepreneur and philanthropist who knew his business, understood its problems, and offered some answers. The difficulties of the age were economic and cultural and might be resolved by understanding the industrial process on the one hand, human character on the other. Owen is usually classed among the utopian socialists and generally credited with the first use of the term "socialist" meaning planned, independent communities. He distrusted democracy given the present state and character of men and was himself instinctively autocratic as good factory managers usually are. While moneyless exchanges and the perfect community on the banks of the Wabash dissolved in bankruptcy, while Owen's overambitious plan for a Grand National Consolidated Trade Union collapsed in the face of determined resistance, Owen was no impractical dreamer. He was a self-made man of the type championed by Samuel Smiles. Manchester and New Lanark testified to his business capacity. He knew the cotton industry and better understood the potential of machinery than did Friedrich Engels, for example, and Engels at least shared some of Owen's industrial experience.

Owen was not the only manager who recognized that benevolence paid dividends. Most successful firms had, in the long run, relatively salutary records. But Owen realized, as most others did not, that machinery created a new world with new possibilities—opportunities for the entrepreneur and worker, hope for the nation and humanity. Everything was a simple matter of education and economics. This is the problem set forth in *The New View of Society* (1813 seq., the first part of which is included here). From the axioms in these essays follow Owen's work on producer-consumer cooperatives in his *Report to the County of Lanark* (1821). His overplanned communities enjoyed less success than his efforts in general philanthropic reform. One error, common to many other planners, Owen never made. Moral cooperation was his goal. He never wished to force all men to develop in one way; he felt that each should have the opportunity to develop his individual skill and talent. Owen's views are not considered revolutionary today; many of his dreams are conventional goals in western society.

ESSAY FIRST

On the Formation of Character

"Any general character, from the best to the worst, from the most ignorant to the most enlightened, may be given to any community, even to the world at large, by the application of proper means; which means are to a great extent at the command and under the control of those who have influence in the affairs of men."

ACCORDING TO THE LAST RETURNS under the Population Act, the poor and working classes of Great Britain and Ireland have been found to exceed fifteen millions of persons, or nearly three-fourths of the population of the British Islands.

The characters of these persons are now permitted to be very generally formed without proper guidance or direction, and, in many cases, under circumstances which directly impel them to a course of extreme vice and misery; thus rendering them the worst and most dangerous subjects in the empire; while the far greater part of the remainder of the community are educated upon the most mistaken principles of human nature, such, indeed, as cannot fail to produce a general conduct throughout society, totally unworthy of the character of rational beings.

The first thus unhappily situated are the poor and the uneducated profligate among the working classes, who are now trained to commit crimes, for the commission of which they are afterwards punished.

The second is the remaining mass of the population, who are now instructed to believe, or at least to acknowledge, that certain principles are unerringly true, and to act as though they were grossly false; thus filling the world with folly and inconsistency, and making society, throughout all its ramifications, a scene of insincerity and counteraction.

In this state the world has continued to the present time; its evils have been and are continually increasing; they cry aloud for efficient corrective measures, which if we longer delay, general disorder must ensue.

"But," say those who have not deeply investigated the subject, "attempts to apply remedies have been often made, yet all of them have failed. The evil is now of a magnitude not to be controled; the torrent is already too strong to be stemmed; and we can only wait with fear or calm resignation, to see it carry destruction in its course, by confounding all distinctions of right and wrong."

Such is the language now held, and such are the general feelings on this most important subject.

These, however, if longer suffered to continue, must lead to the most lamentable consequences. Rather than pursue such a course, the character of legislators would be infinitely raised, if, forgetting the petty and humiliating contentions of sects and parties, they would thoroughly investigate the subject, and endeavour to arrest and overcome these mighty evils.

The chief object of these Essays is to assist and forward investigations of such vital importance to the well-being of this country, and of society in general.

The view of the subject which is about to be given has arisen from extensive experience for upwards of twenty years, during which period its truth and importance have been proved by multiplied experiments. That the writer may not be charged with precipitation or presumption, he has had the principle and its consequences examined, scrutinized, and fully canvassed, by some of the most learned, intelligent, and competent characters of the present day: who, on every principle of duty as well as of interest, if they had discovered error in either, would have exposed it;—but who, on the contrary, have fairly acknowledged their incontrovertible truth and practical importance.

Assured, therefore, that his principles are true, he proceeds with confidence, and courts the most ample and free discussion of the subject; courts it for the sake of humanity—for the sake of his fellow-creatures—millions of whom experience sufferings which, were they to be unfolded, would compel those who govern the world to exclaim—"Can these things exist and we have no knowledge of them?" But they do exist—and even the heart-rending statements which were made known to the public during the discussions upon negro-slavery, do not exhibit more afflicting scenes than those which, in various parts of the world, daily arise from the injustice of society towards itself; from the inattention of mankind to the circumstances which incessantly surround them; and from the want of a correct knowledge of human nature in those who govern and control the affairs of men.

If these circumstances did not exist to an extent almost incredible, it would be unnecessary now to contend for a principle regarding Man, which scarcely requires more than to be fairly stated to make it self-evident.

This principle is, that "*Any general character, from the best to the worst, from the most ignorant to the most enlightened, may be given to any community, even to the world at large, by the application of proper means; which means are to a great extent at the command and under the control of those who have influence in the affairs of men.*"

The principle as now stated is a broad one, and if it should be found to be true, cannot fail to give a new character to legislative proceedings, and such a character as will be most favourable to the well being of society.

That this principle is true to the utmost limit of the terms, is evident from the experience of all past ages, and from every existing fact.

Shall misery, then, most complicated and extensive, be experienced, from the prince to the peasant, throughout all the nations of the world, and shall its cause and the means of its prevention be known, and yet these means withheld? The undertaking is replete with difficulties, which can only be overcome by those who have influence in society: who, by foreseeing its important practical benefits, may be induced to contend against those difficulties; and who, when its advantages are clearly seen and strongly felt, will not suffer individual considerations to be put in competition with their attainment. Is is true, their ease and comfort may be for a time sacrificed to those prejudices; but, if they persevere, the principles on which this knowledge is founded must ultimately universally prevail.

In preparing the way for the introduction of these principles, it cannot now be necessary to enter into the detail of facts to prove that children can be trained to acquire "*any language, sentiments, belief, or any bodily habits and manners, not contrary to human nature.*"

For that this has been done, the history of every nation of which we have records, abundantly confirms; and that this is, and may be again done, the facts which exist around us and throughout all the countries in the world, prove to demonstration.

Possessing, then, the knowledge of a power so important; which, when understood, is capable of being weilded with the certainty of a law of nature, and which would gradually remove the evils which now chiefly afflict mankind, shall we permit it to remain dormant and useless, and suffer the plagues of society perpetually to exist and increase?

No: the time is now arrived when the public mind of this country, and the general state of the world, call imperatively for the introduction of this all-pervading principle, not only in theory, but into practice.

Nor can any human power now impede its rapid progress. Silence will not retard its course, and opposition will give increased celerity to its movements. The commencement of the work will, in fact, ensure its accomplishment; henceforth all the irritating angry passions, arising from ignorance of the true cause of bodily and mental character, will gradually subside, and be replaced by the most frank and conciliating confidence and goodwill.

Nor will it be possible hereafter for comparatively a few individuals, unintentionally to occasion the rest of mankind to be surrounded by circumstances which inevitably form such characters, as they afterwards deem it a duty and a right to punish even to death; and that too, while they themselves have been the instruments of forming those characters. Such proceedings not only create innumerable evils to the directing few, but essentially retard them and the great mass of society from attaining the enjoyment of a high degree of positive happiness. Instead of punishing crimes after they have permitted the human character to be formed so as to commit them, they will adopt the only means which can be adopted to prevent the existence of those crimes; means by which they may be most easily prevented.

Happily for poor traduced and degraded human nature, the principle for which we now contend, will speedily divest it of all the ridiculous and absurd mystery with which it has been hitherto enveloped by the ignorance of preceding times: and all the complicated and counteracting motives for good conduct, which have been multiplied almost to infinity, will be reduced to one single principle of action, which, by its evident operation and sufficiency, shall render this intricate system unnecessary, and ultimately supersede it in all parts of the earth. That principle is *the happiness of self clearly understood and uniformly practised; which can only be attained by conduct that must promote the happiness of the community.*

For that Power which governs and pervades the universe has evidently so formed man, that he must progressively pass from a state of ignorance to intelligence, the limits of which it is not for man himself to define; and in that progress to discover, that his individual happiness can be increased and extended only in proportion as he actively endeavours to increase and extend the happiness of all around him. The principle admits neither of exclusion nor of limitation; and such appears evidently the state of the public mind, that it will now seize and cherish this principle as the most precious boon which it has yet been allowed to attain. The errors of all opposing motives will appear in their true light, and the ignorance whence they arose will become so glaring, that even the most unenlightened will speedily reject them.

For this state of matters, and for all the gradual changes contemplated, the extraordinary events of the present times have essentially contributed to prepare the way.

Even the late Ruler of France, although immediately influenced by the most mistaken principles of ambition, has contributed to this happy result, by shaking to its foundation that mass of superstition and bigotry, which on the continent of Europe had been accumulating for ages, until it had so overpowered and depressed the human intellect, that to attempt improvement without its removal would have been most unavailing. And in the next place, by carrying the mistaken selfish principles in which mankind have been hitherto educated to the extreme in practice, he has rendered their error manifest, and left no doubt of the fallacy of the source whence they originated.

These transactions, in which millions have been immolated, or consigned to poverty and bereft of friends, will be preserved in the records of time, and impress future ages with a just estimation of the principles now about to be introduced into practice; and will thus prove perpetually useful to all succeeding generations.

For the direful effects of Napoleon's government have created the most deep-rooted disgust at notions which could produce a belief that such conduct was glorious, or calculated to increase the happiness of even the individual by whom it was pursued.

And the late discoveries and proceedings of the Rev. Dr. Bell and Mr. Joseph Lancaster, have also been preparing the way in a manner the most opposite, but yet not less effectual, by directing the public attention to the beneficial effects, on the young and unresisting mind, of even the limited education which their systems embrace.

They have already effected enough to prove that all which is now in contemplation respecting the training of youth may be accomplished without fear of disappointment. And by so doing, as the consequences of their improvements cannot be confined within the British Isles, they will for ever be ranked among the most important benefactors of the human race. But henceforward to contend for any new exclusive system will be in vain: the public mind is already too well informed, and has too far passed the possibility of retrogression, much longer to permit the continuance of any such evil.

For it is now obvious that such a system must be destructive of the happiness of the excluded, by their seeing others enjoy what they are not permitted to possess; and also that it tends, by creating opposition from the justly injured feelings of the excluded, in proportion to the extent of the exclusion, to diminish the happiness even of the privileged: the former therefore can have no rational motive for its continuance. If, however, owing to the irrational principles by which the world has been hitherto governed, individuals, or sects, or parties, shall yet by their plans of exclusive attempt to retard the amelioration of society, and prevent the introduction into PRACTICE of that truly just spirit which knows no exclusion, such facts shall yet be brought forward as cannot fail to render all their efforts vain. It will therefore be the essence of wisdom in the privileged class to co-operate sincerely and cordially with those who desire not to touch one iota of the supposed advantages which they now possess; and whose first and last wish is to increase the particular happiness of those classes, as well as the general happiness of society. A very little reflection on the part of the privileged will ensure this line of conduct; whence, without domestic revolution—without war or bloodshed—nay, without prematurely disturbing anything which exists, the world will be prepared to receive principles which are alone calculated to build up a system of happiness, and to destroy those irritable feelings which have so long afflicted society,—solely because society has hitherto been ignorant of the true means by which the most useful and valuable character may be formed.

This ignorance being removed, experience will soon teach us how to form character, individually and generally so as to give the greatest sum of happiness to the individual and to mankind.

These principles require only to be known in order to establish themselves; the outline of our future proceedings then becomes clear and defined, nor will they permit as henceforth to wander from the right path. They direct that the governing powers of all countries should establish rational plans for the education and general formation of the characters of their subjects.—*These plans must be devised to train children from their earliest infancy in good habits of every description (which will of course prevent them from acquiring those of falsehood and deception.) They must afterwards be rationally educated, and their labour be usefully directed. Such habits and education will impress them with an active and ardent desire to promote the happiness of every individual, and that without the* shadow of exception *for sect, or party, or country, or climate. They will also ensure, with the fewest possible exceptions, health, strength, and vigour of body; for the happiness of man can be erected only on the foundations of health of body and peace of mind.*

And that health of body and peace of mind may be preserved sound and entire, through youth and manhood, to old age, it becomes equally necessary that the irresistible propensities which form a part of his nature, and which now produce the endless and ever multiplying evils with which humanity is afflicted, should be so directed as to increase and not to counteract his happiness.

The knowledge however thus introduced will make it evident to the understanding, that by far the greater part of the misery with which man is encircled *may* be easily dissipated and removed; and that with *mathematical precision he may be surrounded with those circumstances which must gradually increase his happiness.*

Hereafter, when the public at large shall be satisfied that these principles *can* and *will* withstand the ordeal through which they must inevitably pass; when they shall prove themselves true to the clear comprehension and certain conviction of the unenlightened as well as the learned; and when by the irresistible power of truth, detached from falsehood, they shall establish themselves in the mind, no more to be removed but by the entire annihilation of the human intellect; then the consequent practice which they direct shall be explained, and rendered easy of adoption.

In the mean time, let no one anticipate evil, even in the slighest degree, from these principles; they are not innoxious only, but pregnant with consequences to be wished and desired beyond all others by *every* individual in society.

Some of the best intentioned among the various classes in society may still say, "All this is *very delightful and very beautiful in theory,* but *visionaries* alone can expect to see it *realized.*" To this remark only one reply *can* or *ought* to be made; *that these principle shave been carried most successfully into practice.* The present Essays, therefore, are not brought forward as mere matter of speculation, to amuse the idle visionary who *thinks* in his closet, and never *acts* in the world; but to create universal activity, pervade society with a knowledge of its true interests, and directs the public mind to the most important object to which it can be directed,—to a national proceeding for rationally forming the character of that immense mass of population, which is now allowed to be so formed as to fill the world with crimes. Shall questions of merely local and temporary interest, whose ultimate results are calculated only to withdraw pecuniary profits from one set of individuals and give them to others, engage, day after day, the attention of politicians and ministers; call forth petitions and delegates from the widely spread agricultural and commercial interests of the empire;—and shall the well-being of millions of the poor, half-naked, half-famished, untaught, and untrained, hourly increasing to a most alarming extent in these islands, not call forth *one* petition, *one* delegate or *one* rational effective legislative measure? No! for such has been our education, that we hesitate not to devote years and expend millions in the *detection* and *punishment* of crimes, and in the attainment of objects whose ultimate results are in comparison with this insignificancy itself: *and yet we have not moved one step in the true path to prevent crime, and to diminish the innumerable evils with which mankind are now afflicted.* Are these false principles of conduct in those who govern the world to influence mankind permanently?—and if not, *how,* and *when* is the change to commence?

AN ADDRESS

To the Superintendents of Manufactories, and to those Individuals Generally, who by Giving Employment to an Aggregated Population, May Easily Adopt the Means to Form the Sentiments and Manners of Such a Population

Like you, I am a manufacturer for pecuniary profit. But having for many years acted on principles the reverse in many respects of those in which you have been instructed, and having found my procedure beneficial to others and to myself, even in a pecuniary point of view, I am anxious to explain such valuable principles, that you and those under your influence may equally partake of their advantages.

In two Essays, already published, I have developed some of these principles, and in the following pages you will find still more of them explained, with some detail of their application to practice, under the peculiar local circumstances in which I undertook the direction of the New Lanark Mills and Establishment.

By those details you will find that from the commencement of my management I viewed the population, with the mechanism and every other part of the establishment, as a system composed of many parts, and which it was my duty and interest so to combine, as that every hand, as well as every spring, lever, and wheel, should effectually co-operate to produce the greatest pecuniary gain to the proprietors.

Many of you have long experienced in your manufacturing operations the advantages of substantial, well-contrived, and well-executed machinery.

Experience has also shown you the difference of the results between mechanism which is neat, clean, well arranged, and always in a high state of repair; and that which is allowed to be dirty, in disorder, without the means of preventing unnecessary friction, and which therefore becomes, and works, much out of repair.

In the first case, the whole economy and management are good; every operation proceeds with ease, order, and success. In the last, the reverse must follow, and a scene be presented of counteraction, confusion, and dissatisfaction among all the agents and instruments interested or occupied in the general process, which cannot fail to create great loss.

If then due care as to the state of your inanimate machines can produce such beneficial results, what may not be expected if you devote equal attention to your vital machines, which are far more wonderfully constructed?

When you shall acquire a right knowledge of these, of their curious mechanism, of their self-adjusting powers; when the proper mainspring shall be applied to their varied movements, you will become conscious of their real value, and you will be readily induced to turn your thoughts more frequently from your inanimate to your living machines; you will discover that the latter may be easily trained and directed to procure a large increase of pecuniary gain, while you may also derive from them high and substantial gratification.

Will you then continue to expend large sums of money to procure the best devised mechanism of wood, brass, or iron; to retain it in perfect repair; to provide the best substance for the prevention of unnecessary friction, and to save it from falling into premature decay? Will you also devote years of intense application to understand the connection of the various parts of these lifeless machines, to improve their effective powers, and to calculate with mathematical precision all their minute and combined movements? And when in these transactions you estimate time by minutes, and the money expended for the chance of increased gain by fractions, will you not afford some of your attention to consider whether a portion of your time and capital would not be more advantageously applied to improve your living machines?

From experience which cannot deceive me, I venture to assure you, that your time and money, so applied, if directed by a true knowledge of the subject, would return you, not five, ten, or fifteen per cent. for your capital so expended, but often fifty, and in many cases a hundred per cent.

I have expended much time and capital upon improvements of the living machinery; and it will soon appear that the time and money so expended in the manufactory at New Lanark, even while such improvements are in progress only, and but half their beneficial effects attained, are now producing a return exceeding fifty per cent., and will shortly create profits equal to cent. per cent. on the original capital expended in them.

Indeed, after experience of the beneficial effects, from due care and attention to the mechanical implements, it became easy to a reflecting mind to conclude at once, that at least equal advantages would arise from the application of similar care and attention to the living instruments. And when it was perceived that inanimate mechanism was greatly improved by being made firm and substantial; that it was the essence of economy to keep it neat, clean, regularly supplied with the best substance to prevent unnecessary friction, and by proper provision for the purpose, to preserve it in good repair; it was natural to conclude that the more delicate, complex, living mechanism, would be equally improved by being trained to strength and activity; and that it would also prove true economy to keep it neat and clean; to treat it with kindness, that its mental movements might not experience too much irritating friction; to endeavour by every means to make it more perfect; to supply it regularly with a sufficient quantity of wholesome food and other necessaries of life, that the body might be preserved in good working condition, and prevented from being out of repair, or falling prematurely to decay.

These anticipations are proved by experience to be just.

Since the general introduction of inanimate mechanism into British manufactories, man, with few exceptions, has been treated as a secondary and inferior machine; and far more attention has been given to perfect the raw materials of wood and metals than those of body and mind. Give but due reflection to the subject, and you will find that man, even as an instrument for the creation of wealth, may be still greatly improved.

But, my friends, a far more interesting and gratifying consideration remains. Adopt the means which ere long shall be rendered obvious to every understanding, and you may not only partially improve those living instruments, but learn how to impart to them such excellence as shall make them infinitely surpass those of the present and all former times.

Here then is an object which truly deserves your attention; and instead of devoting all your faculties to invent improved inanimate mechanism, let your thoughts be, at least in part, directed to discover how to combine the more excellent materials of body and mind, which, by a well devised experiment, will be found capable of progressive improvement.

Thus seeing with the clearness of noon-day light, thus convinced with the certainty of conviction itself, let us not perpetuate the really unnecessary evils which our present practices inflict on this large proportion of our fellow-subjects. Should your pecuniary interests somewhat suffer by adopting the line of conduct now urged, many of you are so wealthy, that the expense of founding, and continuing at your respective establishments, the institutions necessary to improve your animate machines, would not be felt. But when you may have ocular demonstration, that, instead of any pecuniary loss, a well directed attention to form the character and increase the comforts of those who are so entirely at your mercy, will essentially add to your gains, prosperity, and happiness, no reasons, except those founded on ignorance of your self-interest, can, in future, prevent you from bestowing your chief care on the living machines which you employ; and by so doing you will prevent an accumulation of human misery, of which it is now difficult to form an adequate conception.

That you may be convinced of this most valuable truth, which due reflection will show you is founded on the evidence of unerring facts, is the sincere wish of

THE AUTHOR

Utopian Socialism:
Saint-Simon and Technocracy

Claude Henri, Comte de Saint-Simon, "First Extract from the 'Organizer' (1819)," Selected Writings, ed. and trans. F. M. H. Markham (Oxford: Basil Blackwell, 1952), pp. 72–75.

The question of the regeneration of man must be as old as human social organization. Some are always dissatisfied. They challenge the existing order and postulate another, and their ideas are the food of social growth. One such was Claude Henri de Rouvroy, Comte de Saint-Simon (1760–1825). This most noble of aristocrats had a long, tangled career. He fought in the American Revolution, attempted to convince the Mexican government to build a canal from the Caribbean to the Pacific, made and squandered a fortune in confiscated French church lands during the Revolution, and finally discovered himself to be a philosopher while he was being supported by his former valet. Saint-Simon was an eccentric at best, quite mad at worst, but the influence of his ideas was pervasive. Auguste Comte drew his positivistic sociology, his secular religious ideas, and his notions of planned productive society from Saint-Simon. Marx was in Saint-Simon's debt. The redoubtable aristocrat was the titan among utopian socialists.

Saint-Simon had no use for democracy, very little for politics. The real division in the world was between les industriels ("the productive") and the social drones. The latter must go. Like Owen, Saint-Simon saw the potential of industrial development in easing the lot of man. Society must be reorganized in technocratic terms; men would be ranked by their relative importance in the productive process. The scientists, the pioneers of development, must be at the top of the pyramid, followed by engineers and technicians. The managers, particularly the bankers, would give direction to new developments. Artists and writers occupied a high position, for they were the moralists of the new society. Saint-Simon rejected the leveling tendencies of socialism. To the most productive, the greatest reward; to all who worked, adequate support.

Saint-Simon has a strikingly modern ring. Who would call him an eccentric today when he spoke of a managerial revolution in which the productive leaders of industry rather than the owners control policy? He talks of full employment in less sophisticated terms than Keynes, but both were attempting to secure the widespread distribution of purchasing power. Saint-Simon's planned economy was intended to produce an affluent society—right again. Saint-Simon's followers, who shared some of their mentor's eccentricities and developed new ones, were to be among the leaders of French financial, commercial, and industrial development. In the short or long term, whether considering theory or practice, Saint-Simon proved to be one of the most important creative thinkers of the early nineteenth century.

FIRST EXTRACT FROM THE 'ORGANIZER' (1819)

Suppose that France suddenly lost fifty of her best physicists, chemists, physiologists, mathematicians, poets, painters, sculptors, musicians, writers; fifty of her best mechanical engineers, civil and military engineers, artillery experts, architects, doctors, surgeons, apothecaries, seamen, dockmakers; fifty of her best bankers, two hundred of her best business men, two hundred of her best farmers, fifty of her best ironmasters, arms manufacturers, tanners, dyers, miners, cloth-makers, cotton manufacturers, silk-makers, linen-makers, manufacturers of hardware, of pottery and china, of crystal and glass, ship chandlers, carriers, printers, engravers, goldsmiths, and other metal-workers; her fifty best masons, carpenters, joiners, farriers, locksmiths, cutlers, smelters, and a hundred other persons of various unspecified occupations, eminent in the sciences, fine ats, and professions; making in all the three thousand leading scientists, artists, and artisans of France.*

These men are the Frenchmen who are the most essential producers, those who make the most important products, those who direct the enterprises most useful to the nation, those who contribute to its achievements in the sciences, fine arts and professions. They are in the most real sense the flower of French society; they are, above all Frenchmen, the most useful to their country, contribute most to its glory, increasing its civilization and prosperity. The nation would become a lifeless corpse as soon as it lost them. It would immediately fall into a position of inferiority compared with the nations which it now rivals, and would continue to be inferior until this loss had been replaced, until it had grown another head. It would require at least a generation for France to repair this misfortune; for men who are distinguished in work of positive ability are exceptions, and nature is not prodigal of exceptions, particularly in this species.

Let us pass on to another assumption. Suppose that France preserves all the men of genius that she possesses in the sciences, fine arts and professions, but has the misfortune to lose in the same day Monsieur the King's brother, Monseigneur le duc d'Angoulême, Monseigneur le duc de Berry, Monseigneur le duc d'Orléans, Monseigneur le duc de Bourbon, Madame la duchesse d'Angoulême, Madame la duchesse de Berry, Madame la duchesse d'Orléans, Madame la duchesse de Bourbon, and Mademoiselle de Condé. Suppose that France loses at the same time all the great officers of the royal household, all the ministers (with or without portfolio), all the councillors of state, all the chief magistrates, marshals, cardinals, archbishops, bishops, vicars-general, and canons, all the prefects and sub-prefects, all the civil servants, and judges, and, in addition, ten thousand of the richest proprietors who live in the style of nobles.

---

* Artisan usually means an ordinary workman. To avoid circumlocution, I mean by this expression all those who are concerned with material production, viz., farmers, manufacturers, merchants, bankers, and all the clerks and workmen employed by them.

This mischance would certainly distress the French, because they are kind-hearted, and could not see with indifference the sudden disappearance of such a large number of their compatriots. But this loss of thirty-thousand individuals, considered to be the most important in the State, would only grieve them for purely sentimental reasons and would result in no political evil for the State.

In the first place, it would be very easy to fill the vacancies which would be made available. There are plenty of Frenchmen who could fill the function of the King's brother as well as can Monsieur; plenty who could take the place of a Prince as appropriately as Monsiegneur le duc d'Angoulême, or Monseigneur le duc d'Orléans, or Monseigneur le duc de Bourbon. There are plenty of Frenchwomen who would be as good princesses as Madame la duchesse d'Angoulême, or Madame la duchesse de Berry, or Mesdames d'Orléans, de Bourbon, and de Condé.

The ante-chambers of the palace are full of courtiers ready to take the place of the great household officials. The army has plenty of soldiers who would be as good leaders as our present Marshals. How many clerks there are who are as good as our ministers? How many administrators who are capable of managing the affairs of the departments better thtan the existing prefects and sub-prefects? How many barristers who are as good lawyers as our judges? How many vicars as expert as our cardinals, archbishops, bishops, vicars-general, and canons? As for the ten thousand aristocratic landowners, their heirs could need no apprenticeship to do the honours of their drawing-rooms as well as they.

The prosperity of France can only exist through the effects of the progress of the sciences, fine arts and professions. The Princes, the great household officials, the Bishops, Marshals of France, prefects and idle landowners contribute nothing directly to the progress of the sciences, fine arts and professions. Far from contributing they only hinder, since they strive to prolong the supremacy existing to this day of conjectural ideas over positive science. They inevitably harm the prosperity of the nation by depriving, as they do, the scientists, artists, and artisans of the high esteem to which they are properly entitled. They are harmful because they expend their wealth in a way which is of no direct use to the sciences, fine arts, and professions: they are harmful because they are a charge on the national taxation, to the amount of three or four hundred millions under the heading of appointments, pensions, gifts, compensations, for the upkeep of their activities which are useless to the nation.

These suppositions underline the most important fact of present politics: they provide a point of view from which we can see this fact in a flash in all its extent; they show clearly, though indirectly, that our social organization is seriously defective: that men still allow themselves to be governed by violence and ruse, and that the human race (politically speaking) is still sunk in immorality.

The scientists, artists, and artisans, the only men whose work is of positive utility to society, and cost it practically nothing, are kept down by the princes and other rulers who are simply more or less incapable bureaucrats. Those who control honours and other national awards owe, in general, the supremacy they enjoy, to the accident of birth, to flattery, intrigue and other dubious methods.

Those who control public affairs share between them every year one half of the taxes, and they do not even use a third of what they do not pocket personally in a way which benefits the citizen.

These suppositions show that society is a world which is upside down.

The nation holds as a fundamental principle that the poor should be generous to the rich, and that therefore the poorer classes should daily deprive themselves of necessities in order to increase the superfluous luxury of the rich.

The most guilty men, the robbers on a grand scale, who oppress the mass of the citizens, and extract from them three or four hundred millions a year, are given the responsibility of punishing minor offences against society.

Ignorance, superstition, idleness and costly dissipation are the privilege of the leaders of society, and men of ability, hard-working and thrifty, are employed only as inferiors and instruments.

To sum up, in every sphere men of greater ability are subject to the control of men who are incapable. From the point of view of morality, the most immoral men have the responsibility of leading the citizens towards virtue; from the point of view of distributive justice, the most guilty men are appointed to punish minor delinquents.

The Political Impact of
Economic Theory

Friedrich List, The National System of Political Economy, *trans. G. A. Matile (Philadelphia: J. B. Lippincott & Co., 1856), Introduction, pp. 61–82.*

While there were considerable modifications of classical economic doctrine by the mid-nineteenth century, the principle of international free trade remained intact. A utopian socialist like Fourier, for example, also accepted the necessary beneficial effects of complete liberty in the interchange of goods throughout the *phalanstères* of the world. Politicians were more hesitant and some businessmen appalled at the prospect. *Das National System der Politischen Oekonomie* (1841–44) preached a very different doctrine. The argument of Friedrich List (1789–1846) was not at all new. Alexander Hamilton reasoned much the same way in his *Report on the Encouragement and Protection of Manufactures* (1791), a classic among American state papers. List, as a political refugee from his native Württemberg, was involved in American politics, learned protectionist doctrine and brought it back to Germany at just the right moment. The principal point List argued was true. Infant German industry could not compete on equal terms with the expanding colossus of Britain.

In his struggle with the prevailing school of economic thought, List rejected the cosmopolitanism of laissez-faire economics to weld protectionism and nationalism. Laissez-faire was attractive only to the economically established state. The nation was not a mere ethical and political association; it was an economic unit. Closer bonds of political association meant a stronger state, and economic nationalism would provide those sinews.

List had little direct influence on the formation of and policy for the Zollverein, the Prussian tariff union. He and the Prussian bureaucrats were, if anything, working in different directions. They sought state efficiency, not economic nationalism. By the time List's doctrines came under serious consideration in Germany, the tendency toward protection and economic aggression was already pronounced. When the tariff of 1879, one of the crucial decisions in nineteenth-century European history, passed the Reichstag, one wonders whether List, who committed suicide in 1846, would still have approved.

INTRODUCTION

Et la patrie et l'humanité!

No BRANCH of political economy presents a greater diversity of views between men of theory and men of practice, than that which treats of international commerce and commercial policy. There is, however, in the domain of this science no topic, which, in regard to the well-being and civilization of nations, as well as to their independence, power and duration, presents the same degree of importance. Poor, weak, and uncivilized countries have not unfrequently attained power and wealth by a judicious commercial system, whilst others have sunk from a high rank for want of such a system; nations have even lost their independence, and their political existence, because their commercial policy had not aided the development and the consolidation of their nationality.

In our day, more than at any former period, among all the questions which belong to political economy, that of international commerce has acquired a preponderant interest; for the more rapidly the genius of discovery and of industrial improvement, as well as that of social and political progress advances, the more rapidly is the distance between stationary nations and those which are progressive increased, and the greater is the peril of remaining behind. If in time past it required centuries to monopolize that important branch of industry, the manufacture of wool, some ten years have sufficed in our time to obtain ascendency in the much more considerable manufacture of cotton; and now the start of a few years may enable England to absorb all the flax industry of the continent of Europe.

At no other epoch has the world seen a manufacturing and commercial power possessing resources so immense as those in the control of the power which now holds sway, pursuing designedly a system so consistently selfish, absorbing with such untiring energy the manufacturing and commercial industry of the world, the important colonies, the domination of the seas, and subjecting so many people, as in the case of the Hindoos, to a manufacturing and commercial yoke.

Alarmed by the consequences of that policy, nay, constrained by the convulsions it has occasioned, we have seen in our century, Prussia, a continental nation, as yet imperfectly prepared for manufacturing industry, seeking her welfare in the prohibitory system so condemned by theorists. And what has been her reward? National prosperity.

On the other hand, encouraged by promises of theory, the United States of America, which had made a rapid growth under the protective system, have been induced to open their ports to the manufactures of England; and what fruits has this competition borne? A periodical visitation of commercial disaster.

Such experience is well calculated to provoke doubts of the infallibility which theory arrogated to itself, and of the absurdity it imputes to practice; to create fears lest our nationality be in danger of perishing by an error of theory, like the sick man, who by conforming to a printed prescription died of an error of the press: to arouse suspicion that this boasted theory has attained its large growth only for the Trojan-Horse purpose of concealing arms and soldiers, and inducing us to take down, with our own hands, the walls which protect us.

At least this truth is evinced: during the half century in which this great question of commercial policy has been discussed in all civilized nations, in books and in legislative halls, by the shrewdest minds, the abyss, which, since Quesnay and Smith has separated theory from practice, not only has not disappeared, but has actually grown wider every year. What kind of science is that which sheds no light upon the path which practice must follow? Is it reasonable to suppose that the professors of this science, by the mighty power of their intelligence, have everywhere become exactly acquainted with all that pertains to social life and industry, whilst the men of the world, mingling freely in all the outward concerns of life, unable to comprehend the truth discovered and brought to light by the former, have continued from generation to generation to mistake evident errors for truth? Is it not better to acknowledge that practical men, too much inclined in general to adhere to the actual, would not so long and so obstinately have resisted theory, if theory itself had not been in opposition to truth and nature.

Indeed we do not hesitate to aver that the contradiction between theory and practice in regard to commercial policy, is as much the fault of theory as of practice.

Political economy, in matters of international commerce, must draw its lessons from experience; the measures it advises must be appropriate to the wants of our times, to the special condition of each people; it must not, however, disavow the exigencies of the future nor the higher interests of the whole human race. Political economy must rest completely upon Philosophy, Policy, and History.

For the interests of the future and the welfare of men, philosophy requires a more intimate union and communion of nations, a renunciation of war so far as possible, the establishment and development of international law, transition of the *jus gentium* to a federal law, freedom of communication among nations, as well in moral as in material concerns; lastly, the union of all nations under some rule of law, or in some aspects of the subject, a universal association.

In the case of any particular people, a wise administration, with extended views, pursues special objects, seeking guarantees for independence and for duration, measures calculated to hasten progress in civilization, well-being, and power, and to improve social condition so that the body politic shall be completely and harmoniously developed in all its parts, perfect in itself, and politically independent.

History, for its part, assists in no equivocal manner in providing for the exigencies of the future, by teaching how, in every epoch, progress, material and intellectual, has kept pace with the extent of political association and commercial relations. But it justifies at the same time the exigencies of government and nationality, showing how nations have perished for not having sufficiently watched over the interests of their culture and power; how a commerce entirely free with nations more advanced has been of advantage to those still in the first phases of their development; also how those which had made some progress have been able by proper regulations in their foreign trade, to make still greater progress and to overtake those which had preceded them. History thus shows the way of reconciling the respective exigencies of philosophy and government.

But practice and theory, such as actually exhibited, take their sides, the former exclusively for the particular exigencies of nationality, the latter for the absolute requirements of cosmopolitism.

That practice, which is called by the theorists the mercantile system, commits the grave error of maintaining the universal utility and necessity of restrictions, because they have been useful and necessary in certain nations and in certain periods of their development. Its votaries fail to see that restrictions are but means, and that liberty, in its proper sense, is the end. Considering the nation by itself, and not humanity at large, the present alone, and not the future, it is exclusively political and national; it has no philosophical comprehension, no cosmopolitan tendency.

The prevailing theory, on the contrary, as it has been suggested by Quesnay, and elaborated by Adam Smith, is exclusively preoccupied with the cosmopolitan exigencies of even the most remote future. Universal association and absolute free trade, may possibly be realized centuries hence; their theory regards them as realizable now. Overlooking the necessities of the present and the idea of nationality, they lose sight of the nation, and consequently of the education of a nation with a view to its independence. In its exclusive cosmopolitism, this theory always regards the whole family of nations, the well-being of the whole race, never the nation nor national prosperity; it abhors government, it condemns experience and practice as mere routine. Not considering historical facts, except so far as they respond to its particular tendencies, it knows not or disfigures the lessons of history which are opposed to its system; it is under the necessity of denying the effects of the Act of Navigation, of the Treaty of Methuen, of the commercial policy of England in general, and of maintaining against all truth that England has arrived to wealth and power in spite of that policy and not by it.

Once fully acquainted with what is exclusive in the one or in the other of these systems, we cannot be astonished if, in spite of its grave errors, practice has not acquiesced in any reform proposed by theory; and we shall comprehend why theory has not been willing to heed the voice of history or of experience, or of government, or of any particular nation. If this vague theory has been proclaimed in all our streets and upon the house-tops, and especially among the nations of which it has most endangered the existence, it may account for the decided propensity of the age for philanthropic experiments and the study of philosophical problems.

But in the life of nations, as well as in that of individuals, there are two powerful remedies for the illusions of ideology, experience and necessity. If we mistake not, the nation which recently hoped to find their advantage in free trade with the great manufacturing and trading powers, are on the verge of important experiences.

It is merely impossible for the United States, if they persevere in their actual commercial system, to maintain even tolerable order in their national economy. There is no effective remedy but a return to the doctrine of protecting their own industry. In vain will the States of the South resist and a dominant party object: the power of events must prevail. We fear that soon or late, war will solve a question which proves a Gordian knot for legislatures. America may possibly pay a future balance with powder and lead; the prohibitions which must accompany war may remedy a defective tariff, and the conquest of Canada may for ever terminate the vast system of English contraband traffic announced by Huskisson.

Would we were mistaken! but if our prophecy should be fulfilled, the theory of free trade must be made accountable for that war. Strange irony of fate! if a theory, based upon the grand idea of an everlasting peace, should kindle war between two nations so well fitted, according to theorists, for mutual trade, it would only be comparable with that philanthropic abolition of the slave trade by which thousands of negroes were doomed to the bottom of the sea.

In the course of the fifty, or rather, of the last twenty-five years (for it is difficult to take into account the period of revolution and war), France has resorted, upon a grand scale, to the system of restriction, with its errors, its exuberances, and its exaggerations. Its success is obvious to every oberver. Theory may question it, nay, it must question it, unless it be inconsistent with itself. If it has had the boldness to assert and to persuade the world that England has become rich and powerful in spite of, and not in virtue of her commercial policy, how can it hesitate to maintain a position much easier of proof, that is, that without protection for her manufactures, France would be incomparably richer and more flourishing than she is at this moment. Although enlightened and experienced statesmen deny the correctness of this conclusion, many reputed to be well-informed and judicious, receive it for sound doctrine; and, truth to say, in France at this very hour, not a few seem to sigh for the blessings of free trade with England. It would be difficult to dispute, and upon that subject we shall go into some details hereafter, that greater activity in their commercial relations must prove in many respects an advantage to both nations. It is, however, obvious that England desires an exchange, not merely of raw materials, but rather a trade by which she may furnish a great quantity of manufactured goods of general consumption, in exchange for the agricultural products and the fancy goods of France. If the government of France is disposed to come into these views, if it is in fact yielding to them, it is certainly not anxious to let it be known. But if in the end it does adopt this English doctrine, it will only thereby furnish one more experiment towards the solution of this great question. In the actual state of things, can two great manufacturing nations, one of which has decidedly the advantage of the other as to the cost of production and in the extent of its external market, freely compete with each other in their respective home markets? And what must be the results of such a competition?

In Germany these questions have become, in consequence of the Zollverein or Customs-Union, national and practical questions. Whilst in France wine is the attraction which tempts England to seek a commercial treaty, in Germany wheat and timber furnish the temptation. Here, however, all is still hypothesis, for it cannot actually be ascertained whether the too selfish tories of England can ever be induced to make such concessions as will enable their own government to effect an arrangement with the German Customs-Union securing the admission into Great Britain of corn and timber from Germany. The Germans are, however, sufficiently advanced in commercial matters to regard as ridiculous, if not impertinent, the supposition that they would be satisfied with illusions and hopes in the place of gold and silver money. Should such concessions be made by the British Parliament, very serious questions of commercial policy would become immediately in Germany matter of public discussion. The last report of Dr. Bowring has given us a foretaste of the tactics which England would adopt in such a case. England will not regard the admission of German corn and timber as an equivalent for the exorbitant advantages which her manufactured products now enjoy in the German markets; nor as a means of preventing Germany from learning by degrees to spin her own cotton, and to import it directly for that purpose from cotton-growing countries, exchanging for it the products of her own manufactures; nor as a method of reforming the enormous disproportion existing between the importations and exportations of both countries. By no means! England regards the export to Germany of cotton-yarn as an acquired privilege; she will claim a new equivalent for her concessions, nothing less than the sacrifice of the German manufactures of cotton, wool, &c. England will offer for admission of German corn and timber into her markets a mess of pottage, as a price, not merely for the renunciation of the birth-right of the infant German industry, but as a price for strangling it in the cradle. If Dr. Bowring was not deceived during his stay in Germany, if, as we strongly surmise, he has not taken too much in earnest the Prussian courtesy which was lavished upon him, the people in those regions, where the policy of the German Customs-Union is elaborated, are still in the tracks of the cosmopolitan theory. There is, for instance, no distinction made between the exportation of manufactured and of agricultural products; they believe they are promoting national interests by developing the latter at the expense of the former; they have not yet comprehended the principle of the industrial training or education of the country as a basis for the regulation of duties; they scruple not to sacrifice to foreign competition manufactures, which, after enjoying protection for several years, and flourishing sufficiently to beget internal competition and a consequent large reduction of prices, they suffer to be destroyed, and with them the spirit of enterprise in Germany, in its germ. Every manufacture ruined by the reduction or withdrawal of protection, and especially by a governmental measure, is a dead body so exposed as to injure every living industry of the same kind. We cannot shut our eyes to such facts, let us give them rather our earnest attention; it is an evil that they have been, that they could be made public; for by shaking confidence in the permanence of needful protection, no light blow has fallen upon the industrial energy of the country. We are thus shown in what mode German manufactures may receive the deadly poison in such manner as not to reveal too distinctly the cause of their destruction. This is a sure method of attacking industry in the very sources of its life. Under this mode of attack, duties by weight (specific) would give place to duties *ad valorem*, which opens the door to English smuggling, and to frauds in the valuation of articles of general consumption having the least relative value and the greatest total bulk, being the very articles which form the basis of manufacturing industry.

The practical importance of the great question of free trade between nations is generally felt in our day, as also the necessity of investigating, with impartiality, once for all, how far theory and practice have erred on this subject, and how far any reconciliation between them is possible. It is at least needful to discuss seriously the problem of such a reconciliation.

It is not indeed with any assumed modesty, it is with the feeling of a profound mistrust of his power, that the author ventures upon this attempt; it is after resisting many years his inclination, after having hundreds of times questioned the correctness of opinions and again and again verifying them; after having frequently examined opposing opinions, and ascertained, beyond a doubt, their inaccuracy, that he determined to enter upon the solution of this problem. He believes himself free from the empty ambition of contradicting old authorities and propounding new theories. If the author had been an Englishman, he would probably never have entertained doubts of the fundamental principle of Adam Smith's theory. It was the condition of his own country which begot in him, more than twenty years since, the first doubts of the infallibility of that theory; it was the condition of his country which, since that time, determined him to develop, first in anonymous articles, then in more elaborate treatises, not anonymous, contrary opinions. At this moment, the interests of Germany alone give him the courage to publish the present work; he will however not dissemble, that a personal motive is connected with those interests; that is, the necessity in which he is placed of showing by a treatise of some extent, that he is not quite incompetent to treat of political economy.

The author will begin, as theory does not begin, by interrogating History, and deducing from it his fundamental principles; this being done, an examination of former systems will follow, and his tendency being especially practical, he will, in conclusion, furnish a sketch of the later phases of commercial policy.

For greater clearness, we give here a cursory view of the principal results of his researches and meditations:

The association of individuals for the prosecution of a common end is the most efficacious mode towards ensuring the happiness of individuals. Alone, and separated from his fellow-creatures, man is feeble and destitute. The greater the number of those who are united, the more perfect is the association, and the greater and the more perfect is the result, which is the moral and material welfare of individuals.

The highest association of individuals now realized, is that of the state, the nation; and the highest imaginable, is that of the whole human race. Just as the individual is happier in the bosom of the state than in solitude, all nations would be more prosperous if they were united together by law, by perpetual peace, and by free interchange.

Nature leads nations gradually to the highest degree of association; inviting them to commerce by variety of climate, soil, and productions; and by overflowing population, by superabundance of capital and talents, it leads them to emigration and the founding of distant colonies. International trade, by rousing activity and energy, by the new wants it creates, by the propagation among nations of new ideas and discoveries, and by the diffusion of power, is one of the mightiest instruments of civilization and one of the most powerful agencies in promoting national prosperity.

The association of nations by means of trade is even yet very imperfect, for it is interrupted, or at least weakened, by war or selfish measures on the part sometimes of one and sometimes of another nation.

A nation may by war be deprived of its independence, its wealth, its liberty, its constitution, its laws, of its own special features, of that degree of culture and national well-being to which it may have attained; it may be wholly enslaved. Nations are thus the victims of each other, and selfish policy is continually disturbing and delaying the economical development of nations.

To preserve, to develop, and to improve itself as a nation is consequently, at present, and ever must be, the principal object of a nation's efforts. There is in that nothing false or selfish; it is a reasonable tendency, agreeing perfectly with the real interests of humanity; for it leads naturally to universal association, which is an advantage to men, so far as nations have reached the same degree of culture and power, and, consequently, so far as it may be realized, by way of association or confederation.

A universal association proceeding from the overbearing influence and wealth of a single nation, based, consequently, upon the subjection and dependence of all others, would result in the annihilation of separate nationalities and national emulation; it would hurt the interests and wound the feelings of nations which deem themselves on the way to independence and the attainment of great wealth, as well as of high political importance; such an association would be only a repetition of what has already occurred in the attempt to subjugate the world, made by the Romans; an attempt that would be more successful in our days by means of manufactures and commerce, instead of, as formerly, by the sword; though either mode would restore the world to barbarism.

The civilization, political education, and power of nations depend chiefly on their economical condition; and, reciprocally, the more advanced the economy, the more civilized and powerful will be the nation, the more rapidly will its civilization and power increase, and the more will its economical culture be developed.

In the economical development of nations, it is necessary to distinguish the following principal stages: the savage state, the pastoral state, the agricultural state, the agricultural and manufacturing state, and finally, the agricultural, manufacturing, and commercial state.

It is obvious that a nation possessing an extensive territory, enriched with varied resources and a numerous population, uniting agriculture and manufactures with an external and internal trade, is beyond comparison more civilized, politically more developed, and more powerful than any merely agricultural country. But manufactures constitute the basis of external and internal trade, of navigation, of an improved agriculture, consequently of civilization and political power; and should any nation succeed in monopolizing all the manufacturing activity of the world, and in checking all other nations in their economical development by reducing them to the mere production of agricultural commodities and raw materials, and other indispensable local productions, it would undoubtedly attain to very wide, if not to universal dominion.

A nation that greatly values its independence and its safety, must make a vigorous effort to elevate itself as fast as possible, from an inferior to a higher state of civilization, uniting and perfecting as quickly as possible its own agriculture, manufactures, navigation, and commerce.

The transition from the savage to the pastoral, and from the pastoral to the agricultural state, as well as the first progress in agriculture, is very efficiently promoted by free intercourse among manufacturing and commercial nations.

The elevation of an agricultural people to the condition of countries at once agricultural, manufacturing, and commercial, can only be accomplished under the law of free trade when the various nations engaged at the time in manufacturing industry shall be in the same degree of progress and civilization; when they shall place no obstacle in the way of the economical development of each other, and not impede their respective progress by war or adverse commercial legislation.

But some of them, favored by circumstances, having distanced others in manufactures, commerce, and navigation, and having early perceived that this advanced state was the surest mode of acquiring and keeping political supremacy, have adopted and still persevere in a policy so well adapted to give them the monopoly of manufactures, of industry and of commerce, and to impede the progress of less advanced nations or those in a lower degree of culture. The measures enforced by such nations, taken as a whole, the prohibitions, the duties on imports, the maritime restrictions, premiums upon exports, &c., are called the protective system.

The anterior progress of certain nations, foreign commercial legislation and war have compelled inferior countries to look for special means of effecting their transition from the agricultural to the manufacturing stage of industry, and as far as practicable, by a system of duties, to restrain their trade with more advanced nations aiming at manufacturing monopoly.

The system of import duties is consequently not, as has been said, an invention of speculative minds; it is a natural consequence of the tendency of nations to seek for guarantees of their existence and prosperity, and to establish and increase their weight in the scale of national influence.

Such a tendency is legitimate and reasonable only so far as it renders easy, instead of retarding, the economical development of a nation; and it is not in opposition to the higher objects of society, the universal confederation of the future.

As human association ought to be considered under two points of view, that is to say, the cosmopolitan, embracing all the human race, and the political or merely national, every economy, private or public, ought to be considered under two different aspects, the individual, social and material power, by means of which riches are produced, and the interchangeable value of the products of industry.

There is, consequently, a cosmopolitan economy and a political economy, a theory of interchangeable value, and a theory of productive power. These doctrines are distinct in their essence, and require to be developed separately.

The productive power of nations is not solely dependent on the labor, the saving, the morality, and the intelligence of individuals, or on the possession of natural advantage and material capital; it is dependent also upon institutions and laws, social, political, and civil, but, above all, on the securities of their duration, their independence, and their power as nations. Individuals would be in vain laborious, economical, ingenious, enterprising, intelligent, and moral, without a national unity, without a division of labor and a co-operation of productive power. A nation cannot otherwise attain to a high degree of prosperity and power, nor maintain itself in the permanent possession of its intellectual, social, and material riches.

The principle of the division of labor has been hitherto but imperfectly understood. Industrial production depends much less on the apportioning of the various operations of a manufacture among several individuals, than on the moral and material association of those individuals for a common end.

The principle applies not only to a manufacture or to a rural industry; it extends also to every kind of national industry, agricultural, manufacturing, and commercial.

The division of labor and the combination of productive power take place in a nation when the intellectual power is applied so as to co-operate freely and efficiently with national production, when manufacturing industry and trade are equally and harmoniously developed.

A merely agricultural people in free intercourse with manufacturing and trading nations will lose a considerable part of their productive power and natural resources, which must remain idle and unemployed. Its intellectual and political culture, and its means of defence, will thus be limited. It can possess neither an important navigation, nor an extensive trade; its prosperity, as far as it results from external commerce, may be interrupted, disturbed, or annihilated by foreign legislation or by war.

On the other hand, manufacturing industry is favorable to science, art, and political progress; it promotes the general welfare, increases population, public revenue, and the power of the country; it enables the latter to extend its influence to all parts of the world, and to found colonies; it sustains fisheries and navies, mercantile and national. By it only, can agriculture rise to any high degree of efficiency and perfection.

Agriculture and manufacturing industry united in the same nation, under the same political power, live in perpetual peace; they are disturbed in their reciprocal action neither by war nor by foreign legislation; they ensure to a nation the continued development of its prosperity, civilization, and power.

Agriculture and manufacturing industry are subjected by nature to special conditions.

The countries of the temperate zone are especially fit for the development of manufacturing industry; for the temperate zone is the region of intellectual and physical effort.

If the countries of the torrid zone are little favored in reference to manufactures, they possess, on the other hand, the natural monopoly of many precious commodities which the inhabitants of the temperate climates greatly prize. The exchange of the manufactured products of the one for the commodities of the other, constitutes a division of labor and a co-operation of productive power throughout the chief commercial nations, and mainly constitutes the great international trade of the world.

A country of the torrid zone would make a very fatal mistake, should it try to become a manufacturing country. Having received no invitation to that vocation from nature, it will progress more rapidly in riches and civilization if it continues to exchange its agricultural productions for the manufactured products of the temperate zone.

It is true that tropical countries sink thus into dependence upon those of the temperate zone, but that dependence will not be without compensation if competition arises among the nations of temperate climes in their manufacturing industry in their trade with the former, and in their exercise of political power. This competition will not only ensure a full supply of manufactures at low prices, but will prevent any one nation from taking advantage by its superiority over the weaker nations of the torrid zone. There would be danger and damage in this dependence only so far as manufactures, important branches of trade, foreign commerce, and maritime power should become the monopoly of a single nation.

Nations of the temperate zone possessing extensive territory enriched with varied resources have lost one of the richest sources of prosperity, civilization and power, if they do not succeed in realizing a national division of labor and a co-operation of national productive power, as soon as they possess the necessary conditions, economical, intellectual, and social, for accomplishing it.

By economical conditions, we understand an advanced stage of agriculture, which cannot be sensibly stimulated by the export of its products; by moral conditions, a high moral culture among individuals; by social conditions, we mean legal security to citizens for their persons and properties and the free exercise of their moral and physical faculties; institutions regulating and facilitating trade, and suppressing all restraints upon industry, liberty, intelligence, and morality, as for instance, feudal institutions.

It is of the utmost concern for a nation uniting such advantages first fully to supply its own wants, its own consumption, with the products of its own manufactures; then to form direct connections progressively with the countries of the torrid zone, transmitting to them, upon its own vessels, its manufactured products, receiving in exchange their commodities.

In comparison with this exchange of the manufactured products of the temperate for the agricultural productions of the torrid zone, other international trade is of a secondary importance, if we but except the trade in a few special articles; wine, for instance.

The production of raw materials and commodities among the great nations of temperate climes has no real importance but in regard to internal trade. An uncultivated nation may at the beginning advance its agriculture by the exportation of wheat, wine, flax, hemp, and wood; but no great nation ever arrived at wealth, civilization, and power, by such policy.

It may be stated as a principle, that a nation is richer and more powerful in proportion as it exports more manufactured products, imports more raw materials, and consumes more tropical commodities.

Productions of the tropics serve to manufacturing countries of temperate climes not only as raw materials and alimentary commodiites, but also, and especially, as stimulants for agricultural and industrial labor. The nation which consumes the greatest quantity of tropical commodities will always be that of which the agricultural and manufacturing production is relatively the most considerable, and that which consumes the greatest quantity of its own products.

In the economical development of nations by means of external trade, four periods must be distinguished. In the first, agriculture is encouraged by the importantion of manufactured articles, and by the exportation of its own products; in the second manufactures begin to increase at home, whilst the importation of foreign manufactures to some extent continues; in the third, home manufactures mainly supply domestic consumption and the internal markets; finally, in the fourth, we see the exportation upon a large scale of manufactured products, and the importation of raw materials and agricultural products.

The system of import duties being considered as a mode of assisting the economical development of a nation by regulating its external trade, must constantly take as a rule the principle of the industrial education of the country.

To encourage agriculture by the aid of protective duties is vicious policy; for agriculture can be encouraged only by promoting manufacturing industry; and the exclusion of raw materials and agricultural products from abroad, has no other result than to impede the rise of national manufactures.

The economical education of a country of inferior intelligence and culture, or one thinly populated relatively to the extent and the fertility of its territory, is effected most certainly by free trade with more advanced, richer, and more industrious nations. Every commercial restriction in such a country aiming at the increase of manufactures is premature, and will prove detrimental not only to civilization in general but the progress of the nation in particular. If its intellectual, political, and economical education, under the operation of free trade, has advanced so far that the importation of foreign manufactures and the want of markets for its own products has become an obstacle to its ulterior development, then only can protective measures be justified.

A nation without extensive territory and of otherwise limited resources, which does not control the mouths of its rivers or which has not suitable boundaries, cannot resort to the protective system, or at least cannot employ it with full success. It must be first enlarged by way of conquest or negotiation.

Manufacturing industry is concerned with so many branches of science and art, it implies so much experience, practice, and adaptation, that the industrial training and education of a country can proceed but slowly. All excessive or premature protection is expiated by a diminution of national prosperity.

No commercial policy is more dangerous and reprehensible than a sudden resort to absolute prohibition of foreign products. It may, however, be justified when a country, separated from others by a long war, finds itself almost in a compulsory state of prohibitions in regard to foreign products, and under the absolute necessity of offering a high premium to the industry which will enable it to supply its own wants.

The return from such a condition must be by gradual transition from the prohibitive to the protective system, and should be effected by means of duties fixed by anticipation and decreasing gradually. On the other hand, a nation which is to pass from free trade to the protective system should commence with low duties to be afterwards raised by degrees according to a suitable scale.

Duties thus fixed by anticipation must be strictly maintained by the government; it must be careful not to diminish them before the appointed time, and equally careful to raise them if they should prove insufficient.

Duties upon imports so high as absolutely to exclude foreign competition are prejudicial to the country which adopts them; for they suppress all rivalry between domestic and foreign manufacturers, and encourage indolence among the former.

When, under the rule of suitable and progressive duties, the manufactures of a country do not thrive, it is an evidence that the country does not yet possess the conditions requisite to a manufacturing people.

Duties designed to favor an industry should never be put so low as to endanger the existence of the latter from foreign competition. It should be a rule to preserve what exists—to protect national industry in its trunk and in its roots.

Foreign competition should not have more than its share in the annual increase of consumption. Duties should be raised when foreign commodities supply the greatest part or the whole of the increased annual consumption.

A country like England, which is far in advance of all its competitors, cannot better maintain and extend its manufacturing and commercial industry than by a trade as free as possible from all restraints. For such a country, the cosmopolitan and the national principle are one and the same thing.

This explains the favor with which the most enlightened economists of England regard free trade, and the reluctance of the wise and prudent of other countries to adopt this principle in the actual state of the world.

A quarter of a century since, the prohibitive and protective system of England operated to her detriment and to the advantage of her rivals.

Nothing could be more prejudicial to England than her restrictions upon the importation of raw material and food.

Union of customs and commercial treaties are the most efficient means of facilitating national exchanges.

But treaties of commerce are legitimate and durable only when the advantages are reciprocal. They are fatal and illegitimate when they sacrifice one country to another; when one country, to purchase advantage for its agriculture, sacrifices a manufacturing industry already well advanced; such a treaty was that of Methuen, a compact in which one party took the lion's share.

The treaty concluded between England and France in 1786 was one of those leonine treaties. And all the propositions made since by England and France to other countries are of the same nature.

If protective duties enhance for a time the price of domestic manufactures, they secure afterwards lower prices by means of internal competition; for an industry that has reached its full development can safely reduce its prices far below those which were necessary to ensure its growth, and thus save to its consumers the whole expense of transportation and the whole profits of trade which are consequent upon imports of the same articles from other countries.

The loss occasioned by protective duties consists, after all, only in values; whilst the country thus acquires a power by which it is enabled to produce a great mass of values. This loss in values must be considered as the price of the industrial training of the country.

Protective duties upon manufactured products do not press heavily upon the agriculture of a country. By the development of manufacturing industry the wealth, population, consumption of agricultural products, rent, and exchangeable value of real estate are vastly increased, whilst the manufactured products consumed by farmers gradually fall in price. The gain thus realized exceeds, in the proportion of ten to one, the loss which agriculturalists incur by the transient rise of manufactured products.

Internal and external trade flourish alike under the protective system; these have no importance but among nations supplying their own wants by their own manufacturing industry, consuming their own agricultural products, and purchasing foreign raw materials and commodities with the surplus of their manufactured articles. Home and foreign trade are both insignificant in the merely agricultural countries of temperate climes, and their external commerce is usually in the hands of the manufacturing and trading nations in communication with them.

A good system of protection does not imply any monopoly in the manufacturers of a country; it only furnishes a guarantee against losses to those who devote their capital, their talents, and their exertions to new branches of industry.

There is no monopoly, because internal competition comes in the place of foreign competition, and every individual has the privilege of taking his share in the advantages offered by the country to its citizens; it is only an advantage to citizens as against foreigners, who enjoy in their own country a similar advantage.

But this protection is useful not only because it awakens the sleeping energies of a country and puts in motion its productive power, but because it attracts the productive power of foreign countries, including capital, both material and moral, and skilful masters as well as skilful men.

On the other hand, the absence of manufacturing industry in a nation long civilized, the productive powers of which cannot be sensibly excited by the export of raw materials and agricultural products and by the importation of foreign manufactures, exposes it to numerous and serious inconveniences.

The agriculture of such a country must necessarily suffer; for the surplus population, which, in a great manufacturing development, finds means of living in factories and creates a large demand for agricultural products, thus affording substantial profits to agriculture, will be reduced to the labor of the fields, and thence will follow a subdivision of farms and a small culture, both as prejudicial to the power and the civilization of a country as to its wealth.

An agricultural people consisting chiefly of proprietors of small estates can neither fill the channels of internal trade with large quantities of commodities nor furnish a large consumption for manufactured goods; in such a country every one is limited almost to his own production and his own consumption. In circumstances like these, no complete system of communications can be established, and the immense advantages which they afford are lost to the country.

Hence ensues necessarily, moral and material, individual and political weakness. The danger is aggravated when neighboring nations pursue a different policy; some making progress in every respect, others retrograding; some hoping for a brighter future, the courage and enterprise of their people being aroused; the absence of hope extinguishing by degrees in others all courage, intelligence, and enterprise.

History is not without examples of entire nations having perished, because they knew not and seized not the critical moment for the solution of the great problem of securing their moral, economical, and political independence by the establishment of manufacturing industry and the formation of a powerful class of manufacturers and tradesmen.

Protestant Evangelicalism:
The Moral Obligation of Empire

Daniel Corrie, A Sermon Preached . . . on . . . April 30, 1816, before the Church Missionary Society for Africa and the East. Being Their Sixteenth Anniversary *(London, 1816), pp. 17–19, 40–60.*

The aroused Victorian conscience proved a potent weapon. Moral revulsion with domestic conditions forced government intervention in factories and mines. The massacre of Balkan Christians helped to confuse British foreign policy. The hand of God, acting through His missionary servants, helped to inspire and direct imperial policy. Imperialism is in bad odor nowadays. Colonial expansion means bellicosity, economic exploitation, and the attempt of European and semi-European powers to remake the world in their own image. Every point in the indictment is partially true, but there was a positive side to imperialism. One part of this derived from the impact of the Protestant revival on underdeveloped countries. Evangelicals sparked the drive for the international abolition of the slave trade, crusaded against the institution of slavery, and attempted to improve—according to their lights—not only the morality but the condition of life of the natives in colonial areas. Every British government and every imperialist realized that he might have to reckon with evangelicalism mobilized in Exeter Hall at annual meetings.

Christian virtues concealed human defects. Evangelical missionaries assumed bad faith between native and colonist. True or not, this was no basis for meaningful reform if European and non-European were to live together. It was also easy for Christian benevolence and stewardship to slide into domination and exploitation. "Lesser breeds without the law" could arouse simultaneous feelings of obligation and a corrupt sense of superiority.

The Reverend Daniel Corrie (1777–1837), first bishop of Madras, was a model missionary. After his undergraduate career at Cambridge he entered holy orders in 1802. He departed for India in 1806 to assume a chaplaincy in Bengal. Corrie worked tirelessly in the northwest provinces—the Agra mission (still operating under the Church Missionary Society) and the Meerut mission being tangible tributes to his work. Corrie returned to England in 1815 to recover his health. This sermon is the heartfelt sentiment of a devoted, experienced missionary who had done much and would do more. Britons listened to him. His notions would be the subject matter of countless sermons from countless pulpits. Corrie's was more than a missionary statement; the attitudes and values of the Protestant revival are here. In 1817 Corrie returned to India to assume the senior chaplaincy at Calcutta and to play a leading role in the administration of the Church Missionary Society for twenty years. He took over the administration of the Calcutta diocese in 1823, and, when Madras and Bombay were made separate sees in 1835, he was appointed the first bishop of Madras. Through thirty years of missionary work, he never flagged in piety or zeal.

There is nothing profound in Corrie's sermon, which makes it all the more valuable. He developed no new theological position. His attitude and values, never subtle, make this document important. Against the growing secularization of the nineteenth century these qualities persisted as moral elements in the dynamics of imperialism. If Corrie's sermon is important for its statement of Protestant belief and the misunderstanding and denigration of native culture, it also represents an important part of imperial motivation.

A SERMON, &c.

ISAIAH 44:20

He feedeth on ashes: a deceived heart hath turned him aside, that he cannot deliver his soul, nor say, is there not a lie in my right hand?

THE PROVOKING NATURE of idolatry, as a sin against the only living and true God, is set forth in various parts of Scripture. In the Chapter, of which these words are a part, God, by the Prophet, sets before us a striking representation of the delusion and wretchedness of which Idolaters are the victims. Human Nature, prone as it is to depart from God, could yet scarcely be thought so utterly blinded, did not experience prove the fact, as to fall down before Stocks and Stones, and cry to the works of Men's hands, *Deliver us; for ye are our Gods!* Ignorance in the things of God, the evidence of the same fallen nature, has too long prevailed even among those who possess Divine Revelation; and has rendered them indifferent to the miseries of the millions of their race, who are sunk in error, and deluded by false Religion.

In this age of discovery, whilst so many have been engaged in philosophical researches, or stimulated to arduous enterprizes, by the hope of wealth or of fame, but few, in comparison, have been induced, after the example of their Lord, to leave their native abodes, in order to seek and to save the lost among mankind! But, blessed be God, *the darkness is passing away, and the true Light shineth* around—arguments for indifference to the spiritual necessities of our fellow-brethren of mankind, originating in infidel principles or in worldly policy, have now their true value assigned to them!

That part of the Church of Christ to which we belong, as well as other classes of Christians, is become more alive to its true character as the light of the world, which is to shew unto men the way of salvation; and is endeavouring, according to her daily prayer, that God's *ways may be known upon earth, his saving health among all nations.*

Our assembling together this day implies, that we are impressed with the duty of seeking the salvation of the Heathen. Our obligations to this duty, with the motives and encouragements to engage in it, have been ably stated, at different times from this place. The designs of the Society, in whose cause I am now engaged, have been long before the public; and the means used for attaining their high objects maturely discussed. An enlightened acquaintance with the word of God is, of itself, sufficient to give us right views on these points; and, hence, many of the most ardent, persevering, and successful advocates of Missions have been of the number of those who never witnessed the miseries of the Heathen, for whom they prayed, and whom they laboured to save.

The information gained by intercourse with some of those Heathen Nations, who are the objects of your pious solicitude, shall also be cheerfully contributed to this service: and may the attempt be accepted, to the setting forth of GOD's glory, and the salvation of immortal souls!

.   .   .   .

The prophet, in the passage connected with our text, is directed, in order to preserve the Israelites from idolatry, to declare to them the character of God, as the Redeemer who ordereth all things in Heaven and in Earth, and who pardoneth the iniquities of his people for his own name's sake; and he is encouraged with a promise that the Lord would pour out of his Spirit, and render the people willing and obedient to the message of his servant.

The instructions given to the prophet may lead us to consider the best means of accomplishing our end. They may, I think, be comprehended in these three:

The distribution of the Scriptures in the different languages of the Heathen;

The Establishment of Missions; and,

The Education of Youth.

.   .   .   .

i. The DISTRIBUTION OF THE WORD OF GOD has the promise of a divine blessing, and is sanctioned by high and very general approbation.

Without supplies of the Scripture in a language which the people can understand, no Missionary Efforts can be extensively or permanently useful. The labours of men of God, in the work of translating the Scriptures, have made the way of future Missionaries in India easy beyond what it has been in former times.

The character of God, as revealed in the Gospel of his Son, dispels at once all the absurdities of the Heathen Mythology. It *declares to them, that Unknown God, whom they ignorantly worship; i.e.* the God whom they acknowledge to be distinguished from, and superior to their idols, but of whose nature they are ignorant, is there declared to be Jehovah; Father, Son, and Holy Ghost; three persons, not in office or by a delegated power, but by a participation of the same undivided essence; "in majesty equal, in glory co-eternal."

Though the doctrine of God becoming incarnate is not new to them, yet they have no idea of a Suffering Saviour; their own Deities, when they visited this world, being represented as powerful, successful, and victorious over enemies. The doctrine of our Lord's Divinity is a great offence to the Mahomedans: but nothing would be gained with them by renouncing that article of our Faith; for they do profess to believe in Christ as a Prophet, and require a Jew to profess faith in Christ before they admit him as a proselyte to their religion. Both Hindoos and Mahomedans sacrifice animals in worship; and the Scripture doctrine of our Lord's atonement, as *the lamb slain from the foundation of the world,* serves to explain these their customs, which are otherwise unintelligible.

The Universality of the Gospel Salvation, renders it peculiarly suitable to the present state of the Eastern Nations. The Hindoos have traditions which lead them to expect, that, on the Tenth Incarnation of their God, the wicked shall be destroyed, and all mankind become one great family. Their traditions on this subject resemble, in many respects, parts of the Book of Revelation. The Mahomedans, too, relate sayings of their Prophet, which insinuate a general apostacy among his followers, after 1260 years of their aera should have elapsed. It will appear how happily such sentiments fall in with the predictions respecting the universal flow of all nations into Christ's kingdom, and how they tend to diminish the opposition of the natural mind against its propagation.

Another circumstance in the Holy Scriptures, which renders them peculiarly adapted to the state of the Eastern Nations, is the relations which they contain of the Faults of holy men. Those particulars in the histories of Noah, David, and others, which have been made the subject of so much infidel cavil in Europe, are as necessary to be insisted on for the instruction of Heathens and Mahomedans as any other parts of the Sacred Writings. The Mahomedans affirm that the different Prophets, as Abraham, Moses, David, &c. were without sin: those things morally wrong in them, not having been imputed to them as sin by God; and that, through their intercession, their respective families and followers will obtain acceptance with God. The Hindoos also depend upon their Spiritual Guides as infallible, and expect that the disciples of each will be taken to Paradise with them. But, by pointing out the faults that appeared in holy men of old, which prove them to be men of like passions with ourselves, and which brought down the divine displeasure upon them, we prove also that they needed forgiveness of sin, and were justified by faith in Him who should come into the world and to whom they all give witness.

Another favourable circumstance attending the circulation of the Holy Scriptures among the Natives of the East, is the extraordinary veneration which they pay to writings accounted sacred. Any ridiculous story is palmed by the Brahmins on the Hindoos, under the notion of its being recorded in their books. The Mahomedans profess their belief in the Law, the Psalms, and the Gospel, as divine books; though they have been taught that our copies of them are corrupted. But, by referring to the Scriptures in the original tongues, and to the Septuagint and other various translations as speaking the same language with our own copies; and especially by referring to the Jews, as the original depositaries of the Hebrew Scriptures; we prove that no ground remains for supposing ours to be corrupted.

These circumstances in the present state of the nations of India, show how well suited is the measure of circulating the Scriptures among them, to bring about their conversion to the faith of Christ. I would not be thought to suppose that these, or any other circumstances, however favourable, can dispose the heart of any one to a reception of the truth as it is in Jesus. The holiness and spirituality of Scripture Truth will always offend the natural man. But God works by means: and I have known many instances wherein the considerations which have been mentioned have led to a decided persuasion of the truth of Christianity, in both Hindoos and Mahomedans; and to an approbation of the Christian Scriptures, as containing *the words of eternal life.*

Here I may be permitted to observe, that the British and Foreign Bible Society has proved a noble auxiliary to the cause of Missions. Those who have felt and witnessed the pure unmixed blessings which it has been the means of conveying to British and Native Christians, as well as to Heathens and Mahomedans, in India, can only fear lest the zeal of its supporters should be suffered to grow cold, or its operations be obstructed.

ii. As we are indebted to MISSIONARIES for some of the most important Versions of the Scriptures, in the languages of Heathen Nations; so the circulation of those Versions cannot be carried on to any extent without their aid. And, when the scriptures have been put into the hands of such as are perishing for lack of knowledge, and some attention to their important contents has been awakened, the labours of a Missionary become more necessary than ever. Some affecting proofs of this have come under my own observation. I have known persons, who had acquired, from report or from parts of the Scriptures in circulation, some indistinct notions of Christianity, take long journeys, sometimes of several hundred miles, to obtain information from a Missionary.

Much has been excellently said respecting the Character and Qualifications of Missionaries. Allow me to set before you briefly, what a Missionary will find most worthy of his attention when he commences his work, especially in the East. An experimental knowledge of the Scriptures must be a pre-requisite in every Missionary; but, to his acquaintance with the saving truths of the Bible, should be added a thorough knowledge of Scripture Geography, of the minutest circumstances connected with the Ceremonial Law of the Israelites, and of the histories of the leading characters, sects, and countries even incidently mentioned in Scripture. Questions respecting these will be frequently asked, and ignorance on such subject will convey an idea of want of information on more essential points, and consequently lessen a Missionary's respectability and influence.

When he enters on the scene of his labours, his first attention should be given to the acquirement of the Language of the people among whom he is to dwell. And, for this end, it seems to me of great importance that a sufficient maintenance should be allowed to support Missionaries in comfort, without their having recourse to keeping schools for pay, or to any other occupation, in order to obtain a subsistence. Any economy here appears very ill-judged; as it tends greatly to defeat the end, for which a Missionary is sent out. When the mind is fatigued with teaching children, and the thoughts occupied with the care of a School Establishment, it unfits greatly for that labour and undivided attention which the acquisition of languages requires: and, though a Missionary, in such a case, may relieve the funds of the Society to which he belongs; yet I am decidedly of opinion, that it would be better, as a general rule, to send fewer Missionaries abroad, than that they should be obliged to lay out their time and strength on matters which are not the immediate purpose of their designation. Schools, which have for their object the education of Heathen or Mahomedan Children, with those of converts to Christianity, are of course not included in this observation. These Schools form a most important part of the Missionary's plans; but they must be conducted on the principle of Free Schools; and will produce, therefore, no emolument to the teacher, unless, as in Ceylon, the Government should supply a salary.

In addition to the language, a Missionary should make himself acquainted with the Manners and Customs of the people among whom he settles; with their mythology, and their modes of religious belief. These, as it respects India, are to be learned, in a great measure, from publications connected with that country; and, by acquaintance with these, he may fix on some point of great importance, which is conceded by the Natives, and convict them of error by their own statements. Much offence may be thus avoided, in attempting their conversion; so that, though the person argued with may and will in many cases be offended at finding himself convicted of error, yet no reasonable ground of personal opposition will be afforded.

But what, I apprehend, requires the whole strength of Christian principle, and calls for the daily and hourly exercise of faith, hope, and charity, is *the condescending to men of low estate*, which an intercourse with the Heathen, of necessity, requires. To hear their filthy conversation from day to day, and not to lose the feeling of its enormity; to behold their exceeding stupidity, ignorance, and folly, and yet to be content to be little in their eyes; to suffer from their deceitfulness and low arts of imposition, and yet to bear with them in order to do them good; to find the most pleasing appearances vanish as the morning cloud, and yet to labour hoping against hope—surely the Missionary has, of all men, the most need to arm himself with the mind that was in Christ Jesus, who *endured the contradiction of sinners against himself*.

iii. The EDUCATION OF YOUTH is another measure adopted by this Society for the Conversion of the Heathen.

Train up a child in the way he should go, and when he is old he will not depart from it, is the the dictate of that wisdom which is from above; and the wisdom, which is from beneath, is not backward to adopt it for the furtherance of its own purposes. History informs us that St. John instituted a school at Ephesus for the instruction of youth. And the Alexandrian School, founded by St. Mark, long continued to supply bright examples of useful learning and industrious labour in the Christian Church. The plans of education which are in progress in the world promise to be powerful workers together with God, in diffusing the knowledge of his glory throughout the earth. The labours of the venerable Dr. John in India will be long had in remembrance in this view. That unacquaintance with booklearning among the Heathen, which set him upon the excellent plan of General Schools, prevails to a great degree throughout India. The character used for keeping accounts being very different from that used in books, a very small number of those even who exercise trades, can read a printed book. But his design of a School for the Education of Schoolmasters and Teachers is of especial importance.

It seems quite extravagant to expect, that a number of teachers sufficient to instruct the millions of the East should ever be supplied from Europe. The establishment of a College for education in the Syrian Churches is one of the many favourable signs of the times in India. Christian Institutions, on the plan of those which are preparing by the Society, seem absolutely necessary to the due extension and permanency of Missionary Efforts. In the East, in particular, provision should be made in them for carrying forward promising youths from the inferior classes, and instructing them in the original languages of the Sacred Scriptures, as well as in the learned languages of their own country. By being brought, during the season of instruction, under the influence of Christian superintendance and example, an opportunity may be afforded for cultivating habits of piety and virtue. Thus fit men may be trained up for the Christian Ministry among their countrymen, and become capable of imparting to others the first principles of human, as well as of divine knowledge.

Let me again beg not to be misunderstood, as if I conceived that mere instruction and example were sufficient to form a truly Christian Character. A man must be *created anew in Christ Jesus,* or he will never walk in *good works:* but we have the promise of a blessing on Christian instruction; and I think we shall find, that the blessing is seldom withheld, where the means are duly and perseveringly persisted in, in dependance on the Spirit of God.

The good effects attending the use of these and similar means are visible, wherever time has been afforded for their influence to operate. The success attending the Protestant Missionaries in every part of India, especially in the South, is well known from the different Reports of those Missionaries which are before the public. The Addresses of many of the Native Christians in the South of India for copies of the Scriptures, published in the First Report of the Calcutta Auxiliary Bible Society, prove them to be sensible of the value of the Sacred Volume, and enlightened in their views of its contents. It has been objected, indeed, that many Natives, professing Christianity in India, differ little in conduct from the Heathen; but it will be found, that no means have been used to instruct such persons in the true principles of religion; and their condition forms, therefore, an additional argument to those which we have urged on the necessity of sending them the Scriptures, with intelligent Teachers to afford them instruction, and to institute Schools for their children.

Having thus stated my views on the Wretched Condition of the Heathen, with the Suitableness of the Means adopted for their relief, it may be expected that I should say something on the topic of National Prosperity, which has been connected with this subject. For, though many arguments opposed to the Evangelization of the East have been happily answered; yet, knowing that an objection has been urged on this ground, were I not to advert to it I might be thought rather to avoid a difficulty than fairly to meet it.

The inclination of the people toward a happier system than that which they possess, has appeared in numberless instances. Nature itself pleads against many of the enormities which we have noticed; as is manifest from the ready obedience paid to the prohibition of Government against casting children to the sharks;—the success of a benevolent individual in his endeavours to put an end to infanticide;—and the circumstance that, in one Province, during the first five years after it came under the authority of the Honourable East India Company, 15,000 female children were permitted to live, who would otherwise have been destroyed; and that, merely because it was understood by the people that the English Government disapproved of such cruelties.

It is apparent also to persons on the spot, that the popular opinion on many subjects has undergone a favourable change of late years. Their own books, which were long kept from us, are freely brought forward and discussed. Their contents being known, many of the better sort among them are ashamed to confess their belief in their literal meaning; and a tendency to deism and atheism appears in many. The Christian Scriptures translated, are received and read by multitudes; and children are sent for education wherever opportunities are afforded them. By these means, as well as by the natural influence of long familiarity with British Manners and Habits, Hindoos are found ready to offer themselves to make long voyages, and a spirit of enterprise is induced highly favourable to the progress of civilization. The honourable administration of affairs among them, and the protection and security afforded to property, are also becoming well understood.

But, though no body of men can surpass the British Servants of the Indian Government in attention to their duty, and in care to prevent abuses; yet, of necessity, the inferior offices of the several extensive departments are filled with Natives, who act on very different principles from their British Superiors, and no human vigilance can effectually prevent their oppression and injustice. Discontents unavoidably prevail on these accounts: and there is, besides, a natural dislike to the rule of Foreigners, with whom the Natives of India, can never assimilate, while each party retains its peculiar principles; and this dislike does and always will supply a pretext to the disaffected among them, for endeavouring to disturb the settled order of things; but these evils would be wholly removed by the introduction of Christian Principles among the different classes of the people; and to expect the removal of them in any other way, is contrary to experience and to sound reason.

Without the introduction, moreover, of Christian Principles among the people of India, it appears to many attentive observers on the spot, that the administration of affairs among them must become increasingly laborious and intricate. They have been delivered from the iron rod of despotism, and the privileges of British Subjects have been imparted to them: no summary punishments are permitted: appeals to superior tribunals are afforded; the clearest evidence made necessary in order to conviction; and the claims of the man of the lowest Caste equally attended to with those of the highest. This is, doubtless, as it should be; and among a people influenced by Christianity, produces the greatest possible good. But, let such as are accustomed to observe the progress of the human mind consider the natural tendency of this system among a people insensible, in a remarkable degree, to the enormity of perjury, unawed by the fears of eternal punishment, and proverbially wanting in honesty and truth.

It should be especially considered, that the opportunity afforded us, of making known to our perishing fellow-sinners the only *Name by which they can be saved*, is a talent put into our hands, of which the Most High will require a strict account. It is expressly declared, that *the nation and kingdom, that will not serve* the Messiah, *shall perish; yea, those nations shall be utterly wasted*. We cannot, therefore, better consult the prosperity of our beloved country, than by performing the duty appointed us: thus engaging on her side that God, *by whom kings reign, by whom princes rule, and nobles, even all the judges of the earth*.

On us, of the Established Church of these realms, it is peculiarly incumbent to take an active part in the work of evangelizing India. Connected as we are with the Government, we cannot stand aside without giving an unfavourable impression of the Religion of the State. The other European Nations, who, by the happy return of peace, will resume their intercourse with India, have always shown themselves friendly to Missions. Our Christian Brethren who differ from us on the subject of Church Government, though I would bear witness to the candour of many of them now labouring in those regions, cannot be expected to recommend that order of things which we receive. To what a disadvantage, then, shall we appear, as a body, in the eyes of intelligent Natives, if we do not manifest an equal earnestness, at least, with others, in seeking their good!

One other consideration, which peculiarly applies to Members of the

Established Church, is the deficiency of Ministers to supply instruction to the vast numbers of the Natives of India bearing the Christian Name, and who are *as sheep without a shepherd!* Multitudes of these have been accustomed to consider themselves connected with the Church of England, especially those of half-European descent, who have generally been baptized by Ministers of our Communion. The ignorance of the lower orders of this class, which some might urge as a motive for neglecting them, will operate as a loud call on us to afford them the instruction which they so greatly need. We owe to them the word of God, the means of grace, and the education of their offspring. They have a right to require these gifts at our hands. Their number is become too great for the attention of the regular Ministers of the Honourable East India Company; and they require, moreover, that the instruction imparted to them should be in the language of the country in which they dwell. To whom then shall they look for the heavenly boon? Have we not been too long guilty of beholding unmoved the sorrows of these our brethren? May the reproach be rolled away by prompt supplies of Teachers, Churches, and Schools; by which many may become wise themselves unto salvation, and important helpers in carrying on the work of conversion throughout the land!

Allow me, in conclusion, briefly to call your attention to my chief object in entering thus minutely into the state of the Heathen World. It is not merely to declare how far they are gone from God, but how incapable they are, in their present state, of being admitted into the Divine Presence, or of enjoying God even if admitted to behold Him. Losing sight of Divine Revelation after the first dispersions of mankind, a deceived heart hath withdrawn them more and more from God, till they have gone so far, as to *change the glory of the incorruptible God, into images made like to corruptible man, and to birds, and fourfooted beasts, and creeping things.* That traditional knowledge of God, so common in the world, leads no one to enquire further after Him; but rather serves to alarm the guilty conscience, and to set it upon framing systems of religion which may relieve it under the fears of futurity.

It is in the revelation alone, which God hath made of himself in his Son, that any fallen creature discovers encouragement to return to God, and strength to return. The Holy Spirit, by his grace applying to the heart those discoveries of God in Christ revealed in the Bible, inclines and encourages and enables the sinner, by motives and means suited to the constitution of his nature, *to turn from dumb idols,* and from the vain pursuit of the world, *to serve the living and true God, and to wait for his Son from heaven,* and thus trains him up to a capacity of heavenly happiness. The true knowledge of Christ, that which the Holy Spirit teaches by the instrumentality of the word, is the great means of Sanctification, no less than of Justification. Separate from Christ, there is not only no forgiveness of sins, but no spiritual life: without Him no holiness can exist among men.

Whatever difference of opinion may subsist among Christians on other points, on this there can be no controversy—that, *without holiness no man shall see the Lord.* The Heathens and Mahomedans are not only unholy in their practice, which may alas! be said also of many who bear the Christian Name, but they conceive of God as such an one as themselves; and all their expectations from Him are of an earthly, sensual, and sinful kind: of the Heaven of the Bible, they have no idea, nor any desire. Oh, then! with what compassion and perseverance should we labour to bring them to that *blood of sprinkling,* which not only *cleanseth from all sin,* but *purifieth the conscience from dead works to serve the living God.*

This cannot be expected from such as know not themselves the efficacy of that blood. What, then, brethren, think you of Christ? Have you discovered Him to be not only *the wisdom of God,* but *the power of God;* and that His living and life-giving word is the power of God to your own individual salvation? Have you learnt what the Apostle means, when he says, *Most gladly will I glory in my infirmities, that the power of Christ may rest upon me?* If not, I am aware that the work of evangelizing the Heathen will appear a comparatively uninteresting subject.

But, O reflect—*how shall you escape, if you neglect so great salvation!* and how will anguish fill your hearts in the Great Day, to see the sable tribes of Africa and India and America, sitting down in the kingdom of heaven, and you yourselves, at present the highly favoured children of that kingdom, shut out!

I have known the happiest effects arise to the British in India, on seeing the eagerness of Heathens and Mahomedans to obtain the Christian Scriptures; and I pray God that these occasions of meeting to consult on the furtherance of the Gospel, may have the same effect in Britain!

Finally, Brethren, *be not weary in well doing.* Discouragements have arisen, and we must still expect them to arise. Projects may fail, and faithful labourers be removed. But He, with whom is *the residue of the Spirit,* can and will carry on his own work. We have had encouraging and abundant proof of this in our own day, and in the few years during which this Society has existed. Some of its first agents, both at home and in Africa and in India, have been taken away; but have the hopes of our Society passed away with them? No! Other instruments, and in greater numbers, have been raised up, both in our own and in similar Institutions; and the period seems indeed not far distant, when *kings shall be the nursing-fathers* of the Church, and *queens her nursing-mothers. For the Lord shall arise upon Zion, and the Gentiles shall come to her light, and kings to the brightness of her rising: her sons shall come from far, and her daughters shall be nursed at her side.*

The Romantic Statement:
Organic and Irrational

Friedrich von Schlegel, The Philosophy of Life, trans. A. J. W. Morrison (London: Henry G. Bohn, 1847), Lecture I.

French cultural hegemony like French political domination came under attack at the opening of the nineteenth century. William Wordsworth and Samuel Taylor Coleridge provide a convenient date for the beginning of the romantic movement in Britain with the publication of *Lyrical Ballads* in 1798. British influence ran strongly through Europe. Byron in poetry, Scott in the novel were more influential on the continent than at home. Shakespeare, with his psychological insight and emotional characterization, was rediscovered and translated. France, too, had its claims for romantic leadership with writers like Chateaubriand, but the development and impact of romanticism ran as deeply in Germany as anyplace in Europe. From Herder and Goethe to Hegel the romantic element colored German thought; German philosophy was to conquer Europe two generations before German arms.

Friedrich von Schlegel (1772–1829) was a leading German convert from rationalism to romanticism. Beginning as a cosmopolitan *philosophe*, a classicist, and a rationalist, he reacted violently against the French Revolution. His literary, historical, and philosophic thought bore significant political overtones. Schlegel's bitterest attacks were against speculative reason which he considered the most insidious and dangerous of notions. A convert to Roman Catholicism, he settled comfortably into Metternich's circle in Vienna—the embodiment of romanticism as reaction. The irrational and mystical—what Schlegel termed elements of "organic life"—were in all ways preferable to the mechanistic, false world of rationalism. Schlegel grafted his own notions onto the thought of the historian philosopher Johann Gottlieb Fichte and the theological tenets of Friedrich Schleiermacher, giving his own work that mixture of historicity and spirituality so characteristic of German romantics.

The first lecture from *The Philosophy of Life* is Schlegel's challenge to traditional rationalism. It frames the direction and establishes the tone for his elaborate philosophic structure. The lecture transcends Schlegel's personal views; it embodies the ethos of emergent romanticism.

PHILOSOPHY OF LIFE

Lecture I

Of the Thinking Soul as the Centre of Consciousness, and of the False Procedure of Reason

"There are," says a poet as ingenious as profound, "more things in heaven and earth, than are dreamt of in our philosophy." This sentiment, which

163

Genius accidentally let drop, is in the main applicable also to the philosophy of our own day; and, with a slight modification, I shall be ready to adopt it as my own. The only change that is requisite to make it available for my purpose would be the addition—"and also between heaven and earth are there many things which are not dreamt of in our philosophy." And exactly because philosophy, for the most part, does nothing but dream—scientifically dream, it may be—therefore is it ignorant, ay, has no inkling even of much which, nevertheless, in all propriety it ought to know. It loses sight of its true object, it quits the firm ground where, standing secure, it might pursue its own avocations without let or hindrance, whenever, abandoning its own proper region, it either soars up to heaven to weave there its fine-spun webs of dialectics, and to build its metaphysical castles in the air, or else, losing itself on the earth, it violently interferes with external reality, and determines to shape the world according to its own fancy, and to reform it at will. Half-way between these two devious courses lies the true road; and the proper region of philosophy is even that spiritual inner life between heaven and earth.

On both sides, many and manifold errors were committed, even in the earlier and better days of enlightened antiquity. Plato himself, the greatest of the great thinkers of Greece, set up in his Republic the model of an ideal polity, which, in this respect, cannot bear the test of examination. His design indeed finds, in some measure, its apology in the disorders and corruption which, even in his day, had infected all the free states of Greece, whether great or small. His work too, by the highly finished style of the whole, the vivid perspicuity of its narrative, its rich profusion of pregnant ideas and noble sentiments, stands out in dignified contrast to the crude and ill-digested schemes of legislation so hastily propounded in our own day. Still, it will ever remain the weak point of this great man. One needs not to be a Plato to see how absolutely unfeasible, not to say practically absurd, are many of the propositions of this Platonic ideal. Accordingly it has ever been the fruitful occasion, not only among contemporaries, but also with posterity, of ridicule to the ignorant and censure to the wise. In this respect it cannot but excite our regret that such great and noble powers of mind should have been wasted in following a false direction, and in pursuit of an unattainable end. The oldest philosophers of Greece, on the other hand—those first bold adventurers on the wide ocean of thought, combined together the elements of things, water, or air, or fire, or atoms, or lastly the all-ruling Intellect itself, into as many different systems of the universe. If, however, each in his own way thus set forth a peculiar creed of nature, we must ever bear in mind that the popular religion, with its poetical imagery, and the fabulous mythology of antiquity, as affording not only no sufficient, but absolutely no answer to the inquiring mind, as to the essence of things, and the first cause of all, could not possibly satisfy these earlier thinkers. Consequently they might well feel tempted to find, each for himself, a way to honour nature, and to contemplate the supreme Being. Since then, however, the world has grown older by nearly twenty-five centuries, and much in the meanwhile has been accomplished by, or fallen to the share of, the human race. But when philosophy would pretend to regard this long succession of ages, and all its fruits, as suddenly erased from the records of existence, and for the sake of change would start afresh, so perilous an experiment can scarcely lead to any good result, but in all probability, and to judge from past experience, will only give rise to numberless and interminable disputes. Such an open space in thought—cleared from all the traces of an earlier existence (a smoothly polished marble tablet, as it were, like the *tabula rasa* of a recent ephemeral philosophy)— would only serve as an arena for the useless though daring ventures of unprofitable speculation, and could never form a safe basis for solid thought, or for any permanent manifestation of intellectual life.

In itself it is nothing surprising if young and inexperienced minds, occupying themselves prematurely, or in a perverted sense, with the grand ideas of God and Nature, liberty and the march of thought, should be wholly overmastered and carried away with them. It has often happened before now, and it is no new thing if youthful and ardent temperaments should either yield to the seductive temptation to make, not to say create, a new religion of their own; or else feel a deceitful impulse to censure and to change all that is already in existence, and, if possible, to reform the whole world by their newly acquired ideas.

That this twofold aberration and misuse of philosophical thought must prove universally injurious, and prejudicial both to education and the whole world, is so evident that it can scarcely be necessary to dwell upon it. Its effect has been to cause men, especially those whose minds have been formed in the great and comprehensive duties of practical life, to view the thing altogether in an evil light, although it must be confessed there is much injustice in this sweeping condemnation. In several of the great statesmen of Rome we may observe a similar contempt for Grecian philosophy as useless and unprofitable. And yet, as is happily indicated by its Greek name, this whole effort was assuredly based upon a noble conception, and, when duly regulated, a salutary principle. For in this beautiful word, according to its original acceptation, science is not regarded as already finished and mature, but is rather set forth as an object of search—of a noble curiosity and of a pure enthusiasm for great and sublime truths, while at the same time it implies the wise use of such knowledge. Merely, however, to check and to hinder the aberrations of a false philosophy, is not by itself sufficient. It is only by laying down and levelling the right road of a philosophy of life, that a thorough remedy for the evil is to be found. True philosophy, therefore, honouring that which has been given from above and that which is existent from without, must neither raise itself in hostility to the one, nor attempt to interfere violently with the other. For it is exactly when, keeping modestly within its proper limits of the inner spiritual life, it makes itself the handmaid neither of theology nor of politics, that it best asserts its true dignity and maintains its independence on its own peculiar domain. And thus, even while it abstains most scrupulously from intermeddling with the positive and actual, will it operate most powerfully on alien and remote branches of inquiry, and by teaching them to consider objects in a freer and more general light, indirectly it will exercise on them a salutary influence. Thus while it proceeds along its appointed path, it will, as it were, without effort disperse many a mist which spreads its dangerous delusion over the whole of human existence, or remove perhaps many a stone of stumbling, which offends the age and divides the minds of men in strife and discord. In this manner consequently will it most beautifully attest its healing virtue, and at the same time best fulfil its proper destination.

The object therefore of philosophy is the inner mental life (*geistige Leben*), not merely this or that individual faculty in any partial direction, but man's spiritual life with all its rich and manifold energies. With respect to form and method: the philosophy of life sets out from a single assumption —that of life, or in other words, of a consciousness to a certain degree awakened and manifoldly developed by experience—since it has for its object, and purposes to make known the entire consciousness and not merely a single phase of it. Now, such an end would be hindered rather than promoted by a highly elaborate or minutely exhaustive form and a painfully artificial method; and it is herein that the difference lies between a philosophy of life and the philosophy of the school. If philosophy be regarded merely as one part of a general scientific education, then is the instruction in method (whether under the old traditionary name of Logic or any other) the chief point to be regarded. For such a mere elementary course, passing over, or at least postponing for a while the consideration of the matter, as possessing as yet but a very remote interest for the student, and, in the default of an adequate internal experience of his own, incapable of being understood by him, concerns itself rather with the practice of methodical thought, both as necessary for the future, and as applicable to all matters. But the preliminary exercise in philosophical thinking is only the introduction to philosophy, and not philosophy itself. This school-teaching of philosophy might perhaps be rendered productive of the most excellent consequences, if only it were directed to the history of the human intellect. What could be more interesting than a history which should enter into the spirit, and distinctly embody the various systems which the inventive subtlety of the Greeks gave birth to, or which, taking a still wider range, should embrace the science of the Egyptians, and some Asiatic nations, and illustrate the no less wonderful nor less manifold systems of the Hindoos—those Greeks of the primeval world! But this, perhaps, would be to encroach upon the peculiar domain of erudition, and might, moreover, fail to furnish equal interest for all; and at any rate the history of philosophy is not philosophy itself.

Now, the distinction between the philosophy of life and the philosophy of the school will appear in very different lights according to the peculiarity of view which predominates in the several philosophical systems. That species of philosophy which revolves in the dialectical orbit of abstract ideas, according to its peculiar character presupposes and requires a well-practised talent of abstraction, perpetually ascending through higher grades to the very highest, and even then boldly venturing a step beyond. In short, as may be easily shown in the instance of modern German science, the being unintelligible is set up as a kind of essential characteristic of a true and truly scientific philosophy. I, for my part, must confess, that I feel a great distrust of that philosophy which swells in inaccessible light, where the inventor indeed asserts of himself, that he finds himself in an unattainable certainty and clearness of insight, giving us all the while to understand thereby, that he does see well enough how of all other mortals scarcely any, or perhaps, strictly speaking, no one, understands or is capable of understanding him. In all such cases it is only the false light of some internal *ignis fatuus* that produces this illusion of the unintelligible, or rather of nonsense. In this pursuit of wholly abstract and unintelligible thought, the philosophy of the school is naturally enough esteemed above every other, and regarded as pre-eminently the true science—*i.e.*, the unintelligible.

In such a system a philosophy of life means nothing more than a kind of translation of its abstruser mysteries into a more popular form, and an adaptation of them to the capacity of ordinary minds. But even such popular adaptations, though evincing no common powers of language and illustration, in spite of their apparent clearness, when closer examined, are found as unintelligible as the recondite originals. For inasmuch as the subject-matter of these abstract speculations was, from the very first, confused and unintelligible, it was consequently incapable of being made clear even by the most perspicuous of styles. But the true living philosophy has no relation or sympathy with this continuous advance up to the unintelligible heights of empty abstraction. Since the objects it treats of are none other than those which every man of a cultivated mind and in any degree accustomed to observe his own consciousness, both has and recognizes within himself, there is nothing to prevent its exposition being throughout clear, easy, and forcible. Here the relation is reversed. In such a system the philosophy of life is the chief and paramount object of interest; while the philosophy of the school, or the scientific teaching of it in the schools, however necessary and valuable in its place, is still, as compared with the whole thing itself, only secondary and subordinate. In the philosophy of life, moreover, the method adopted must also be a living one. Consequently it is not, by any means, a thing to be neglected. But still it need not to be applied with equal rigour throughout, or to appear prominently in every part, but on all occasions must be governed in these respects by what the particular end in view may demand.

A few illustrations, drawn from daily experience, will perhaps serve to explain my meaning. Generally speaking, the most important arts and pursuits of life are ultimately based on mathematics. This science furnishes them, as it were, with the method they observe; but it is not practicable, nor indeed has man the leisure, to revert on every occasion, with methodical exactness, to these elements, but, assuming the principles to be well known and admitted, he attends rather to the results essential to the end he has in view. The economical management of the smallest as well as of the largest household, rests in the end on the elementary principles of arithmetic; but what would come of it if, on every occasion, we were to go back to the simple "one-times-one" of the multiplication table, and reflected upon and sought for the proofs that the principle is really valid and can confidently be relied on in practice? In the same way the art of war is founded on geometry, but when the general arranges his troops for battle does he consult his Euclid to satisfy himself of the correctness and advantages of his position? Lastly, even the astronomer, whose vocation is pre-eminently dependent on accurate calculation, when he would make us acquainted with the phenomena of the sidereal heavens, confines himself almost entirely to them, without wearying those whom he wishes to interest, with the complicated reckonings which, however, in all probability, he was obliged himself to go through. With all these arts and pursuits of practical life, the intellectual business of thinking—of such thinking at least as is common to most men—and of communicating thought, has a sort of affinity and resemblance. For, unquestionably, it is one among the many problems of philosophy to establish a wise economy and prudent stewardship of that ever-shifting mass of incoming and outgoing thoughts which make up our intellectual estate and property. And this is the more necessary, the greater are the treasures of thought possessed by our age. For, in the highly rapid interchange of, and traffic in ideas, which is carrying on, the receipts and disbursements are not always duly balanced. There is much cause, therefore, to fear lest a thoughtless and lavish dissipation of the noblest mental endowments should become prevalent, or a false and baseless credit-system in thought spring up amidst an absolute deficiency of a solid and permanent capital safely invested in fundamental ideas and lasting truths. As for the second simile: I should, by all means, wish to gain a victory, not indeed for you, but with you, over some of the many errors and many semblances of thought, which are, however, but cheats and counterfeits which distract the minds of the present generation, disturb the harmony of life, and banish peace even from the intellectual world. And as respects the third illustration: I should indeed rejoice as having, in a great measure, attained my object, if only I shall succeed in directing your attention to some star in the higher region of intellect, which hitherto was either totally unknown, or, at least, never before fully observed.

But above all, I think it necessary to observe further, that in the same way as philosophy loses sight of its true object and appropriate matter, when either it passes into and merges in theology, or meddles with external politics, so also does it mar its proper form when it attempts to mimic the rigorous method of mathematics. In the middle of the last century scarcely was there to be found a German manual for any of the sciences that did not ape the mathematical style, and where every single position in the long array of interminable paragraphs did not conclude with the solemn act of demonstrative phraseology. But it is also well known that the philosophy which was propounded in this inappropriate form and method was crammed full of, nay, rather, was hardly anything more than a tissue of arbitrary, now forgotten, hypotheses, which have not brought the world at all nearer to the truth,—not at least to that truth which philosophy is in search of, and which is something higher than a mere example of accurate computation.

And even in the present day—although, indeed, the application is made in a very different way from formerly—German philosophy is anything but free from those algebraic formularies, in which all things, even the most opposite, admit of being comprised and blended together. But, be it as it may, this elaborate structure of mechanical demonstration can never produce a true, intrinsic, and full conviction. The method which philosophy really requires is quite different, being absolutely internal and intellectual (*gestige*). As in a correct architectural structure it is necessary that all its parts should be in unison, and such as the eye can take in easily and agreeably; so in every philosophical communication, the solid simple basis being laid, the arrangement of all the parts and the careful rejection and exclusion of all foreign matter, is the most essential point, both for internal correctness and external perspicuity. But, in truth, the matter in hand bears a far closer resemblance and affinity to natural objects which live and grow, than to any lifeless edifice of stone; to a great tree, for instance, nobly and beautifully spreading out on all sides in its many arms and branches. As such a tree strikes the hasty and passing glance, it forms a somewhat irregular and not strictly finished whole; there it stands, just as the stem has shot up from the root, and has divided itself into a certain number of branches and twigs and leaves, which livingly move backwards and forwards in the free air. But examine it more closely, and how perfect appears its whole structure! how wonderful the symmetry, how minutely regular the organization of all its parts, even of each little leaf and delicate fibre! In the same way will the ever-growing tree of human consciousness and life appear in philosophy, whenever it is not torn from its roots and stripped of its leaves by a pretended wisdom, but is vividly apprehended by a true science, and exhibited and presented to the mind in its life and its growth.

Not only, however, the arrangement of the whole, but also the connexion of the several parts of a philosophical treatise or development, is of a higher kind than any mere mechanical joining, such, for instance, as that by which two pieces of wood are nailed or glued together. If I must illustrate this connexion by a simile from animated nature, the facts of magnetism will best serve my purpose. Once magnetically excited, the iron needle comes into invisible contact and connexion with the whole globe and its opposite poles; and this magnetic clue has guided the bold circumnavigator

into new and unknown regions of the world. Now, the intrinsic vital coherence of the several thoughts of philosophy resembles this magnetic attraction; and no such rude, mechanical, and in fact mere external conjunction of thought, like that lately alluded to, can satisfy the requirements of
philosophical connexion.

But the supreme intrinsic unity of philosophical thought, or of a philosophical series of ideas, is quite different from every thing hitherto mentioned. It belongs not to nature, but to life; it is not derived from the latter
by way of figure or illustration, but is a part and constituent of it, and goes
to the very root and soil of the moral life. What I mean is, the unity of sentiment—the fixed character, remaining ever the same and true to itself—the
inner necessary sequence of the thoughts—which, in life no less than in the
system and philosophical theory, invariably makes a great and profound
impression on our minds, and commands our respect, even when it does
not carry along with it our convictions. This, however, is dependent on no
form, and no mere method can attain to it. How often, for instance, in some
famous political harangue, which perhaps the speaker, like the rhapsodist
of old, poured forth on the spur of the moment, do we at once recognize
and admire this character in the thoughts, this consistency of sentiment?
How often, on the contrary, in another composed with the most exquisite
research and strict method, and apparently a far more elaborate and finished creation of the intellect, we have only to pierce through the systematic exterior to find that it is nothing but an ill-connected and chance-
medley of conflicting assumptions and opinions taken from all quarters, and
the crude views of the author himself, devoid of all solidity, and resting
on no firm basis, without character, and wholly destitute of true intrinsic
unity?

If now, in the present course of Lectures, I shall succeed in laying before
you my subject in that clearness and distinctness which are necessary to
enable you to comprehend the whole, and while taking a survey of it, to
judge of the agreement of the several parts, you will find, I trust, no difficulty in discovering the fundamental idea and sentiment. And further, I
would venture to entreat you not to judge hastily of this sentiment from
single expressions, and least of all at the very outset, but, waiting for its
progressive development, to judge of it on the whole. Lastly, I would also
indulge a hope, that the views of an individual thinker, if perspicuously
enunciated, may, even where they fail of conviction, and though points of
difference still subsist, produce no revolting impression on your minds; but,
by exercising a healing influence on many a rankling wound in thought and
life, produce amongst us some of the fairest fruits of true philosophy.

Hitherto we have been considering, first of all, the object and proper
sphere of the philosophy of life; and secondly, its appropriate form of communication, as well as all other methods which are alien and foreign to it.
Of great and decisive importance for the whole course and further development of philosophical inquiry, is it to determine, in the next place, the

starting-point from which it ought to set out. It will not do to believe that we have found this in any axiom or postulate such as are usually placed at the head of a system. For such a purpose we must rather investigate the inmost foundation—the root out of which springs the characteristic feature of a philosophical view. Now, in the philosophy of life the whole consciousness, with all its different phases and faculties, must inevitably be taken for the foundation, the soul being considered as the centre thereof. This simple basis being once laid, it may be further developed in very different ways. For it is, I might almost say, a matter of indifference from what point in the circumference or periphery we set out in order to arrive at the centre, with the design of giving a further development to this as the foundation of the whole. But in order to illustrate this simple method of studying life from its true central point, which is intermediate between the two wrong courses already indicated, and in order to make by contrast my meaning the plainer, I would here in a few words, characterize the false starting-point from which the prevailing philosophy of a day—whether that of France in the eighteenth century or the more recent systems of Germany—has hitherto for the most part proceeded. False do I call it, both on account of the results to which it has led, and also of its own intrinsic nature. In one case as well as in the other, the starting-point was invariably some controverted point of the reason—some opposition or other to the legitimacy of the reason; under which term, however, little else generally was understood, than an opposition of the reason itself to some other principle equally valid and extensive. The principal, or rather only way which foreign philosophy took in this pursuit, was to reduce every thing to sensation as opposed to reason, and to derive every thing from it alone, so as to make the reason itself merely a secondary faculty, no original and independent power, and ultimately nothing else than a sort of chemical precipitate and residuum from the material impressions. But however much may be conceded to these, and to the external senses, and however great a share they may justly claim in the whole inner property of the thinking man, still it is evident, that the perception of these sensuous impressions, the inner coherence—in short, the unity of the consciousness in which they are collected—can never, as indeed it has often been objected on the other side, have come into the mind from without. This was not, however, the end which this doctrine had exclusively, or even principally, in view. The ultimate result to which they hoped to come by the aid of this premise, was simply the negation of the suprasensible. Whatever in any degree transcends the material impression, or sensuous experience, as well as all possible knowledge of, and faith therein, not merely in respect to a positive religion, but absolutely whatever is noble, beautiful, and great, whatever can lead the mind to, or can be referred to a something suprasensible and divine—all this, wherever it may be found, whether in life or thought, in history or in nature—aye, even in art itself, it was the ultimate object of this foreign philosophy to decry, to involve in doubt, to attack and to overthrow, and to bring down to the level of the common and material, or to plunge it into the sceptical abyss of absolute unbelief. The first step in this system was a seeming subordination of reason to sensation, as a derivative of it—a mere slough which it throws off in its transformations. Afterwards, however, the warfare against the suprasensible was waged entirely with the arms of reason itself. The reason, indeed, which supplied these weapons, was not one scientifically cultivated and morally regulated, but thoroughly sophistical and wholly perverted, which, however, put into requisition all the weapons of a brilliant but sceptical wit, and moved in the ever-varied turnings of a most ingenious and attractive style. Here, where the question was no longer the abrogation of any single dogma of positive religion, but where the opposition to the divine had become the ruling tendency of philosophy, it is not easy to refrain from characterising it as atheistical—what indeed in its inmost spirit it really was, and also historically proved itself by its results.

The other course adopted by French philosophy, in the times immediately preceding the Revolution, was to lay aside the weapons of wit, and to employ a burning eloquence as more likely to attract and to carry away minds naturally noble. It had consequently, if possible, still more fatal results than the former. The reason, as the peculiar character of man in a civilised state—so it was argued—is like civilised man himself, an artificial creation, and in its essence totally unnatural; and the savage state of nature is the only one properly adapted to man. As the means of emancipation from an artificial and corrupt civilisation, the well-known theory of the social contract was advanced. Our whole age has learned dearly enough the lesson, that this dogma, practically applied on a large scale, may indeed lead to a despotism of liberty, and to the lust of conquest, but can as little effect the re-establishment of a true civilisation as it can bring back the state of nature. It would be a work of supererogation to dwell upon the pernicious results or the intrinsic hollowness of this system. It is, however, worth while to remark, that, in this theory also, the beginning was made with an opposition to reason. Starting with a depreciation of it as an artificial state and a departure from nature, at the last it threw itself, and the whole existing frame of society, into the arms of reason, and thereby sought to gain for the latter an unlimited authority over all laws, both human and divine. A somewhat similar phenomenon may everywhere be observed, and the same course will invariably be taken when philosophy allows itself to set out with some question or impugning of the reason, and, in its exclusiveness, makes this dialectical faculty the basis of its investigations.

Modern German philosophy, wholly different from the French both in form and spirit, has, from its narrow metaphysical sphere, been of far less extensive influence; and, even if it has occasionally led to anarchy, it has been simply an anarchy of ideas. And yet, notwithstanding its different char-
been simply an anarchy of ideas. And yet, notwitstanding its different character, a similar course of inversion is noticeable in it. Beginning with a strict,

not to say absolute, limitation of the reason, and with an opposition to its assumptions, it also ended in its investiture with supreme authority—not to say in its deification. The founder [Kant] of the modern philosophy of Germany commenced his teaching with a lengthy demonstration that the reason is totally incapable of attaining to a knowledge of the suprasensible, and that by attempting it, it does but involve itself in endless disputes and difficulties. And then, on this assumed incompetency of the reason for the suprasensible was based the doctrine of the need, the necessity of faith—nay, faith itself. But this arbitrary faith appeared to have but little reliance on itself; and, when closely viewed, turned out to be the old reason, which, after being solemnly displaced from the front of the philosophical palace, was now again, slightly altered and disguised, set up behind it as a useful but humble postern. Dissatisfied with such a system, the philosophical *Me* (Ich, Ego) chose another and a new road, that of absolute science, in which it might, from the very first, do as it pleased—might bluster and fluster at will. But soon it became plain, that in this idealistic doctrine there was no room for any but a subjective reason-god devoid of all objective reality. In it the absolute Ego or Me of each individual, was substituted for and identified with the divine. Against this certainty of the "Me," therefore, there arose first of all a suspicion, and lastly the reproach of atheism. But, in truth, we ought to be extremely scrupulous in applying this term in all cases where the question does not turn on a rude denial of the truth, but rather on a highly erroneous confusion of ideas. At least, it would be well if, in such a case, we were to distinguish the imputed atheism by the epithet of scientific, in order to indicate thereby that the censure and the name apply in truth only to the error of the system, and not to the character of the author. For with such a scientific atheism, the sternest stoicism in the moral doctrine may, as indeed was actually the case here, be easily combined. Quite weary, however, of the transcendent vacuity of this ideal reason and mere dialectical reasoning, German philosophy now took a different road. It turned more to the side of nature in whose arms she threw herself in perfect admiration, thinking to find there alone life and the fulness thereof. Now, although this new philosophy of nature has borne many noble fruits of science, still even it has been haunted by that delusive phantom of the Absolute, and it is not free from liability to the reproach of a pantheistic deification of Nature. But properly and accurately speaking, it was not nature itself that was set up as the supreme object of veneration, but this same phantom of reason, which was taken as the basis and fundamental principle of nature. It was, in short, nothing but the old metaphysical one-times-one* in a somewhat novel application and more vivid form. Here, therefore, also did the system com-

---

* Schlegel is alluding to those systems which suppose a primary and original essence, which, by its successive spontaneous developments, produces every thing else out of itself. This absolute original of all things was by Schelling, after Spinosa, called *natura naturans*, while, by a phraseology which happily indicates the identity of the self-developing subject and its objective developments, the totality of the objects derived from it are termed *natura naturata*.

mence with a seeming disgust at the reason, and with a subordination of it to nature, in order to conclude with the absolute principle of the reason.

Viewed, however, as a philosophical science of nature, it has rather to answer for some occasional errors and perverse extravagances, than for any thoroughly consequent and systematic carrying out of the ingrafted error into all its parts. Moreover, a broad distinction must undoubtedly be drawn between its different advocates and promulgators. In these last days German philosophy has, in a measure at least, reverted again into the empty vacuum of *the absolute* idea. The latter, indeed, and the idol of absolute reason which is enshrined therein, is no more a mere inward conception, but is objectively understood and set up as the fundamental principle of all entity. But still, when we consider how the essence of mind is expressly made to consist in negation, and how also the spirit of negation is predominant through the whole system, a still worse substitution appears to have taken place, inasmuch as, instead of the living God, this spirit or negation, so opposed to Him, is, in erroneous abstraction, set up and made a god of. Here, therefore, as well as elsewhere, a metaphysical lie assumes the place of a divine reality.

Thus, then, do we everywhere observe a strange internal correspondence and affinity between the several aberrations of our age. Here the remotest mental extremes, which externally seem to repel each other, suddenly converge at the same point of delusive light, or rather of brilliant darkness. Instances of this correspondence startle us where we least expect to meet with them. An English poet [Byron], perhaps the greatest, certainly the most remarkable poet of our age, in his tragic delineation of the oldest fratricide, has pourtrayed the prime mover of this deed, the enemy of the human race, and the king of the bottomless pit, as the bold censurer of the divine order of things, and the head of all discontented spirits, and leader of the opposition of the whole creation. In this light he has painted him with unparalleled boldness, and with such moving and astonishing truthfulness, that all previous descriptions by the greatest poets seem but arbitrary and unreal phantoms when compared with this portrait, which was evidently a favourite sketch, for the author's secret partiality betrays itself in the skill and pains with which he has lavished on this dark figure all the magic colours of his fancy. Thus, then, in this poetic creation, the same hostile principle—the same absolute, *i. e.*, evil spirit of negation and contradiction that forms the consummation of the errors of German philosophy, notwithstanding its abstract unintelligibility—is enthroned amidst the disordered system. And so, by a strange law of "pre-established harmony," the antichristian poet and these anti-christian thinkers unexpectedly meet together at the point of a spurious sublimity. In any case, however, this last instance forms the third stage of idealistic confusion, and certainly the last grade of scientific atheism.

Now, briefly to recapitulate my own convictions and my view of the relation subsisting between the philosophy of life which I propose to set before you, and the prevalent philosophy and science of the age, the following few remarks will suffice. I honour and admire the discoveries so pregnant with important results which natural philosophy has made in our days, but especially the gigantic strides which the study of nature in France has taken; so far, at least, as they contain and have established a real and solid advance of human science; so far, too, as I am acquainted with them, and in my sphere understand them. On the other hand, I cannot but take exception to that admixture of materialism which has been infused into them by the ruling philosophical system of a previous age, which in France has still so many followers. I honour too and love German science, with its diligent and comprehensive research. Nay, I value the natural philosophy of Germany even still more than that of France, since, while it adopts the same great discoveries, it views them in a more spiritual light. As for that idealistic jargon, however, which runs parallel and is interwoven with it, on which, indeed, it was originally based, and from which even now it is anything but clear; this I cannot regard in any other light than, what it really is, an intellectual delusion of the most pernicious kind, and one which will inevitably produce the most destructive and fatal consequences on the human mind.

What has been now said will suffice for our notice of the opposing systems of philosophy. Henceforward we shall have no need to turn our looks to this side, but shall be able to give our attention solely and calmly to the development of that which I have already announced, and have now to communicate to you. Previously, however, to entering upon this subject, it seemed to me advisable, by contrasting the false starting-point with the true centre of philosophy, to set the latter before you in a clearer and distincter light.

The dialectical faculty of abstraction is naturally the predominant one, and the most completely evolved in the thinking mind. Accordingly, most thinkers have set it up as the basis of their speculations, in order to arrive the more rapidly at the desired end of an absolute science; or, if the habit of mind be more disposed that way, at an absolute *not-knowing*, and the rejection of all certainty; which, in the main, is quite as false, and, in this respect, identical with the former. But it is not sufficient to follow any such a partial course, and to start from any one side merely of the human consciousness. On the right and sure road of a complete and thorough investigation, our first duty is to study the human consciousness in its fulness and living development, in all its faculties and powers. And then, in the second place, when, by thus assuming a position in the centre, man has enabled himself to take a complete survey of the whole, he may unquestionably proceed to inquire what kind and what degree of knowledge, with such a consciousness, he is capable of attaining, both of the external world and of the suprasensible, and how far the latter is conceivable and its existence possible. Now, just as generally the soul is the principle of all life in nature, so is the thinking soul the centre of the human consciousness. But in the thinking soul is comprised the reason which distinguishes, combines, and infers, no less than the fancy which devises, invents, and suggests. Standing in the centre between the two, the thinking soul embraces both faculties. But it also forms the turning-point of transition between the understanding and the will; and, as the connecting link, fills up the gulf which otherwise would lie between and divide the two. It comprises also all sorts and degrees of conceptions, from the absolutely necessary, precisely definite, and permanently unchangeable, down to those which arise and pass away half involuntarily—from those in no degree clearly developed up to those which have been advanced to the highest clearness of the understanding—those which are witnessed with a calm indifference, and those also which excite a gentle longing or kindle a burning resolve. The thinking soul is the common storehouse where the whole of these conceptions are successively lodged. Indeed, to describe it in general terms, it is but the inner pulse of thought, corresponding to the pulsation of the blood in the living body.

This general description, it must be confessed, is very far from being an adequate explanation of the matter, and at best does but imperfectly convey our meaning. But perhaps a different line of thought, however bold and hazardous it may seem, may bring us far more simply to the point at present in view—a more accurate description, namely, of the peculiar property of the human mind, and of the characteristic feature which distinguishes man from other beings equally finite, but endowed in the same manner with consciousness. That the rational soul, or the reason, distinguishes him from the brutes, is a remark common and trite enough. But this is only one aspect of the matter: and must we always cast our looks downwards, and never upwards? What I mean is this: supposing that there are other created spirits and finite intelligences besides men, might not the comparison of their purely spiritual consciousness with man's serve, perhaps in an eminent degree, to elucidate the distinctive properties of the human consciousness in that other aspect which is too commonly neglected? I am far from intending to make this matter a subject of investigation in the present place. I take it merely as an hypothesis, warranted indeed by universal tradition, and solely as an aid to elucidate the matter in hand. Universal, however, I may well call this tradition, since, agreeing in the main with what Holy Writ asserts, the oldest and most civilised nations of antiquity (among whom I need only mention the Egyptians, and especially the Persians and the Hindoos) have admitted, as a well-established fact, the existence of such finite intelligences and created spirits, invisible indeed to man, but not altogether alien to him. And as for the Greeks and Romans, if occasionally they allude to the genius of Socrates as something strange and singular, this was only because the wise Athenian spoke of this subject in peculiar language, and referred to it more habitually than was the wont of his countrymen and contemporaries. Otherwise it was the general belief, both of Greeks and Romans, that every man has his guardian spirit of genius. Now this hypothesis being once admitted to be possible, let us inquire in what light were these ancients accustomed to regard, and what ought we to conceive of the peculiar nature of these spiritual beings in conformity with the representation of so universal a tradition?

Now, in the first place, they have always been thought of as pure spiritual beings, having no such gross terrestrial body as man has. At least if they were supposed to require and possess a body as the organ and medium of their spiritual operations, it was considered to be of a special kind; an ethereal body of light, but invisible to the human eye. But this incorporeity is little more than a negative quality. A more positive and a profounder distinction lies perhaps in this, that these pure spiritual beings are wholly free from that weakness of character, or frailty, which is so peculiar to man. That pervading internal mutability, that undecided vacillation between doing and letting alone, that reciprocation between effort and relaxation—the wide gulf between volition and execution, the thought and the carrying into effect—nothing of all this admits of being applied or transferred to these pure spiritual beings without contradicting the very idea of their essence. It is thus only, or not at all, that we can conceive of them. Coming and going like the lightning, and rapid as the light, they never grow weary of their endless activity. They need no rest except the spiritual contemplation which constitutes their essence. All their thoughts are marked with unity and identity. With them the conception is at the same time a deed, and the purpose and the execution are simultaneous. Every thing, too, in them has the stamp of eternity. This prerogative, however, has, it must be confessed, its disadvantages. When once they have deviated from the true centre, they go on for ever in their devious course.

But still all this is little more than a description of the whole idea which I have allowed myself, merely with a view of employing it as a passage to the point which is at present in question. That purpose was, on the supposition of the existence of such superior beings, accurately to indicate which of man's powers or faculties of mind and soul may rightly be attributed to them. Now, to my mind, the distinction is very strikingly suggested in the well-known sentiment of one of our famous poets. Thus he addresses man: "Thy knowledge thou sharest with superior beings;"—superior, for in the clearness of their eternal science, they undoubtedly stand far higher than men—and then he continues, "But art thou hast alone." But, now, what else is art than fancy become visible, and assuming a bodily shape or word or sound? It is, therefore, this nimble-footed, many-shaped, ever-inventive fancy, which forms the dangerous prerogative of man and cannot be ascribed to these pure spiritual beings. And as little justifiable would it be to ascribe to them that human reason, with its employment of means, and its slow processes of deduction and comparison. Instead of this, they possess the intuitive understanding, in which to see and to understand are simultaneous and identical. If, then, in an accurate sense of the terms, neither fancy nor reason belongs to them, it would further be wrong to attribute them a soul as distinct from the mind or spirit, and as being rather a passive faculty of inward productiveness and change and internal growth. Briefly to recapitulate what has been said: The existence of the brutes is simple, because in them the soul is completely mixed up and merged in the organic body, and is one with it; on the destruction of the latter it reverts to the elements, or is absorbed in the general soul of nature. Twofold, however, is the nature of created spirits, who besides this ethereal body of light are nothing but mind or spirit; but threefold is the nature of man, as consisting of spirit, soul, and body. And this triple constitution and property, this three-fold life of man, is, indeed, not in itself that pre-eminence, although it is closely connected with that superior excellence which ennobles and dis-tinguishes man from all other created beings. I allude to that prerogative by which he alone of all created beings is invested with the Divine image and likeness. This threefold principle is the simple basis of all philosophy; and the philosophical system which is constructed on such a foundation is the philosophy of life, which therefore has even "words of life." It is no idle speculation, and no unintelligible hypothesis. It is not more difficult, and needs not to be more obscure, than any other discourse on spiritual subjects; but it can and may be as easy and as clear as the reading of a writing, the observation of nature, and the study of history. For it is in truth nothing else than a simple theory of spiritual life, drawn from life itself, and the simple understanding thereof. If, however, it becomes abstract and unintelligible, this is invariably a consequence, and for the most part an infallible proof of its having fallen into error. When in thought we place before us the whole composite human individual, then, after spirit and soul, the organic body is the third constituent, or the third element out of which, in combination with the other two, the whole man consists and is com-pounded. But the structure of the organic body, its powers and laws, must be left to physical science to investigate. Philosophy is the science of con-sciousness alone; it has, therefore, primarily to occupy itself with soul and spirit or mind, and must carefully guard against transgressing its limits in any respect. But the third constituent beside mind and soul, in which these two jointly carry on their operations, needs not always, as indeed the above instance proves, to be an organic body. In other relations of life, this third, in which both are united, or which they in unison produce, may be the word, the deed, life itself, or the divine order on which both are de-pendent. These, then, are the subjects which I have proposed for consider-ation. But in order to complete this scale of life, I will further observe: triple is the nature of man, but fourfold is the human consciousness. For the spirit or mind, like the soul, divides and falls asunder, or rather is split and divided into two powers or halves—the mind, namely, into under-standing and will, the soul into reason and fancy. These are the four ex-treme points, or, if the expression be preferred, the four quarters of the inner world of consciousness. All other faculties of the soul, or powers of mind, are merely subordinate ramifications of the four principal branches; but the living centre of the whole is the thinking soul.

PART II

SCIENCE, STEAM, AND *REALPOLITIK*
1850–1914

A. *The Conflicting Spirit of Politics*

Liberalism:
The Plea of John Stuart Mill

John Stuart Mill, On Liberty (London: J. W. Parker & Son, 1859), chap. v.

John Stuart Mill (1806–73) was part of the temper of his age. He contributed to and reflected several main streams of nineteenth-century thought. Mill was first and foremost part of the Benthamite-Utilitarian tradition, although he was no slavish disciple of his father, James Mill, nor of Jeremy Bentham. John Stuart Mill tempered eighteenth-century rationalism without ever abandoning it. He blended Auguste Comte's positivism and Samuel Taylor Coleridge's sense of corporate society with the principal strain of liberal individualism. To a considerable extent Mill sought to reconcile opposite, sometimes incompatible lines of thought. The Principles of Political Economy (1848–49), for example, was an effort to square triumphant laissez-faire with the obvious and justifiable protests against its inhumanity.

On Liberty (1859) attempts to resolve the problem, still unanswered, of mass society and individual liberty. Mill's questions were pointed in an age in which franchise reform, education, and the construction of the liberal state were burning issues. They are no less topical today. This democrat—and Mill was one in the truest sense of the term—fought for franchise extension through social barriers and barriers of sex. At the same time he was aware that democracy might prove a monster. Another generation would pass in Britain before manhood suffrage was general; more than half a century before the political emancipation of women. Yet Mill recognized problems we still live with.

. . . It is not, in constitutional countries, to be apprehended, that the government, whether completely responsible to the people or not, will often attempt to control the expression of opinion, except when in doing so it makes itself the organ of the general intolerance of the public. Let us suppose, therefore, that the government is entirely at one with the people, and never thinks of exerting any power of coercion unless in agreement with what it conceives to be their voice. But I deny the right of the people to exercise such coercion, either by themselves or by their government. The power itself is illegitimate. The best government has no more title to it than the worst. It is as noxious, or more noxious, when exerted in accordance with public opinion, than when in opposition to it. If all mankind minus one were of one opinion, and only one person of the contrary opinion, mankind would be no more justified in silencing that one person, than he, if he had the power, would be justified in silencing mankind.

Individuality was precious. With democracy there always looms the threat of the tyranny of the majority, and it is not of necessity limited to opinions. Pressure for social conformity, for universality can mean the rule of collective mediocrity.

CHAPTER V

APPLICATIONS

THE PRINCIPLES asserted in these pages must be more generally admitted as the basis for discussion of details, before a consistent application of them to all the various departments of government and morals can be attempted with any prospect of advantage. The few observations I propose to make on questions of detail are designed to illustrate the principles, rather than to follow them out to their consequences. I offer, not so much applications, as specimens of application; which may serve to bring into greater clearness the meaning and limits of the two maxims which together form the entire doctrine of this Essay, and to assist the judgment in holding the balance between them, in the cases where it appears doubtful which of them is applicable to the case.

The maxims are, first, that the individual is not accountable to society for his actions, in so far as these concern the interests of no person but himself. Advice, instruction, persuasion, and avoidance by other people if thought necessary by them for their own good, are the only measures by which society can justifiably express its dislike or disapprobation of his conduct. Secondly, that for such actions as are prejudical to the interests of others, the individual is accountable, and may be said to be subjected either to social or to legal punishment, if society is of opinion that the one or the other is requisite for its protection.

In the first place, it must by no means be supposed, because damage, or probability of damage, to the interests of others, can alone justify the interference of society, that therefore it always does justify such interference. In many cases, an individual, in pursuing a legitimate object, necessarily and therefore legitimately causes pain or loss to others, or intercepts a good which they had a reasonable hope of obtaining. Such oppositions of interest between individuals often arise from bad social institutions, but are unavoidable while those institutions last; and some would be unavoidable under any institutions. Whoever succeeds in an overcrowded profession, or in a competitive examination; whoever is preferred to another in any contest for an object which both desire, reaps benefit from the loss of others, from their wasted exertion and their disappointment. But it is, by common admission, better for the general interest of mankind, that persons should pursue their objects undeterred by this sort of consequences. In other words, society admits no right, either legal or moral, in the disappointed competitors to immunity from this kind of suffering; and feels called on to interfere, only when means of success have been employed which it is contrary to the general interest to permit—namely, fraud or treachery, and force.

Again, trade is a social act. Whoever undertakes to sell any description of goods to the public, does what affects the interest of other persons, and of society in general; and thus his conduct, in principle, comes within the jurisdiction of society: accordingly, it was once held to be the duty of governments, in all cases which were considered of importance, to fix prices, and regulate the process of manufacture. But it is now recognised, though not till after a long struggle, that both the cheapness and the good quality of commodities are most effectually provided for by leaving the producers and sellers perfectly free, under the sole check of equal freedom to the buyers for supplying themselves elsewhere. This is the so-called doctrine of Free Trade, which rests on grounds different from, though equally solid with, the principle of individual liberty asserted in this Essay. Restrictions on trade, or on production for purposes of trade, are indeed restraints; and all restraint, *quâ* restraint, is an evil: but the restraints in question affect only that part of conduct which society is competent to restrain, and are wrong solely because they do not really produce the results which it is desired to produce by them. As the principle of individual liberty is not involved in the doctrine of Free Trade, so neither is it in most of the questions which arise respecting the limits of that doctrine; as, for example, what amount of public control is admissible for the prevention of fraud by adulteration; how far sanitary precautions, or arrangements to protect workpeople employed in dangerous occupations, should be enforced on employers. Such questions involve considerations of liberty, only in so far as leaving people to themselves is always better, *cæteris paribus*, than controlling them: but that they may be legitimately controlled for these ends is in principle undeniable. On the other hand, there are questions relating to interference with trade which are essentially questions of liberty; such as the Maine Law, already touched upon; the prohibition of the importation of opium into China; the restriction of the sale of poisons; all cases, in short, where the object of the interference is to make it impossible or difficult to obtain a particular commodity. These interferences are objectionable, not as infringements on the liberty of the producer or seller, but on that of the buyer.

One of these examples, that of the sale of poisons, opens a new question; the proper limits of what may be called the functions of police; how far liberty may legitimately be invaded for the prevention of crime, or of accident. It is one of the undisputed functions of government to take precautions against crime before it has been committed, as well as to detect and punish it afterwards. The preventive function of government, however, is far more liable to be abused, to the prejudice of liberty, than the punitory function; for there is hardly any part of the legitimate freedom of action of a human being which would not admit of being represented, and farily too, as increasing the facilities for some form or other of delinquency. Nevertheless, if a public authority, or even a private person, sees any one evidently preparing to commit a crime, they are not bound to look on inactive until the crime is committed, but may interfere to prevent it. If poisons were never bought or used for any purpose except the commission of murder it would be right to prohibit their manufacture and sale. They may, however, be wanted not only for innocent but for useful purposes, and restrictions cannot be imposed in the one case without operating in the other. Again, it is a proper office of public authority to guard against accidents. If either a public officer or any one else saw a person attempting to cross a bridge which had been ascertained to be unsafe, and there were no time to warn him of his danger, they might seize him and turn him back, without any real infringement of his liberty; for liberty consists in doing what one desires, and he does not desire to fall into the river. Nevertheless, when there is not a certainty, but only a danger of mischief, no one but the person himself can judge of the sufficiency of the motive which may prompt him to incur the risk: in this case, therefore (unless he is a child, or delirious, or in some state of excitement or absorption incompatible with the full use of the reflecting faculty), he ought, I conceive, to be only warned of the danger; not forcibly prevented from exposing himself to it. Similar considerations, applied to such a question as the sale of poisons, may enable us to decide which among the possible modes of regulation are or are not contrary to principle. Such a precaution, for example, as that of labelling the drug with some word expressive of its dangerous character, may be enforced without violation of liberty: the buyer cannot wish not to know that the thing he possesses has poisonous qualities. But to require in all cases the certificate of a medical practitioner would make it sometimes impossible, always expensive, to obtain the article for legitimate uses. The only mode apparent to me, in which difficulties may be thrown in the way of crime committed through this means, without any infringement worth taking into account upon the liberty of those who desire the poisonous substance for other purposes, consists in providing what, in the apt language of Bentham, is called "preappointed evidence." This provision is familiar to every one in the case of contracts. It is usual and right that the law, when a contract is entered into, should require as the condition of its enforcing performance, that certain formalities should be observed, such as signatures, attestation of witnesses, and the like, in order that in case of subsequent dispute there may be evidence to prove that the contract was really entered into, and that there was nothing in the circumstances to render it legally invalid: the effect being to throw great obstacles in the way of fictitious contracts, or contracts made in circumstances which, if known, would destroy their validity. Precautions of a similar nature might be enforced in the sale of articles adapted to be instruments of crime. The seller, for example, might be required to enter in a register the exact time of the transaction, the name and address of the buyer, the precise quality and quantity sold; to ask the purpose for which it was wanted, and record the answer he received. When there was no medical prescription, the presence of some third person might be required, to bring home the fact to the purchaser, in case there should afterwards be reason to believe that the article had been applied to criminal purposes. Such regulations would in general be no material impediment to obtaining the article, but a very considerable one to making an improper use of it without detection.

The right inherent in society, to ward off crimes against itself by antecedent precautions, suggests the obvious limitations to the maxim, that purely self-regarding misconduct cannot properly be meddled with in the way of prevention or punishment. Drunkenness, for example, in ordinary cases, is not a fit subject for legislative interference; but I should deem it perfectly legitimate that a person, who had once been convicted of any act of violence to others under the influence of drink, should be placed under a special legal restriction, personal to himself; that if he were afterwards found drunk, he should be liable to a penalty, and that if when in that state he committed another offence, the punishment to which he would be liable for that other offence should be increased in severity. The making himself drunk, in a person whom drunkenness excites to do harm to others, is a crime against others. So, again, idleness, except in a person receiving support from the public, or except when it constitutes a breach of contract, cannot without tyranny be made a subject of legal punishment; but if, either from idleness or from any other avoidable cause, a man fails to perform his legal duties to others, as for instance to support his children, it is no tyranny to force him to fulfil that obligation, by compulsory labour, if no other means are available.

Again, there are many acts which, being directly injurious only to the agents themselves, ought not to be legally interdicted, but which, if done publicly, are a violation of good manners, and coming thus within the category of offences against others, may rightly be prohibited. Of this kind are offences against decency; on which it is unnecessary to dwell, the rather as they are only connected indirectly with our subject, the objection to publicity being equally strong in the case of many actions not in themselves condemnable, nor supposed to be so.

There is another question to which an answer must be found, consistent with the principles which have been laid down. In cases of personal conduct supposed to be blamable, but which respect for liberty precludes society from preventing or punishing, because the evil directly resulting falls wholly on the agent; what the agent is free to do, ought other persons to be equally free to counsel or instigate? This question is not free from difficulty. The case of a person who solicits another to do an act is not strictly a case of self-regarding conduct. To give advice or offer inducements to any one is a social act, and may, therefore, like actions in general which affect others, be supposed amenable to social control. But a little reflection corrects the first impression, by showing that if the case is not strictly within the definition of individual liberty, yet the reasons on which the principle of individual liberty is grounded are applicable to it. If people must be allowed, in whatever concerns only themselves, to act as seems best to themselves, at their own peril, they must equally be free to consult with one another about what is fit to be so done; to exchange opinions, and give and receive suggestions. Whatever it is permitted to do, it must be permitted to advise to do. The question is doubtful only when the instigator derives a personal benefit from his advice; when he makes it his occupation, for subsistence or pecuniary gain, to promote what society and the State consider to be an evil. Then, indeed, a new element of complication is introduced; namely, the existence of classes of persons with an interest opposed to what is considered as the public weal, and whose mode of living is grounded on the counteraction of it. Ought this to be interfered with, or not? Fornication, for example, must be tolerated, and so must gambling; but should a person be free to be a pimp, or to keep a gambling-house? The case is one of those which lie on the exact boundary line between two principles, and it is not at once apparent to which of the two it properly belongs. There are arguments on both sides. On the side of toleration it may be said that the fact of following anything as an occupation, and living or profiting by the practice of it, cannot make that criminal which would otherwise be admissible; that the act should either be consistently permitted or consistently prohibited; that if the principles which we have hitherto defended are true, society has no business, *as* society, to decide anything to be wrong which concerns only the individual; that it cannot go beyond dissuasion, and that one person should be as free to persuade as another to dissuade. In opposition to this it may be contended, that although the public, or the State, are not warranted in authoritatively deciding, for purposes of repression or punishment, that such or such conduct affecting only the interests of the individual is good or bad, they are fully justified in assuming, if they regard it as bad, that its being so or not is at least a disputable question: That, this being supposed, they cannot be acting wrongly in endeavouring to exclude the influence of solicitations which are not disinterested, of instigators who cannot possibly be impartial—who have a direct personal interest on one side, and that side the one which the State believes to be wrong, and who confessedly promote it for personal objects only. There can surely, it may be urged, be nothing lost, no sacrifice of good, by so ordering matters that persons shall make their election, either wisely or foolishly, on their own prompting, as free as possible from the arts of persons who stimulate their inclinations for interested purposes of their own. Thus (it may be said) though the statutes respecting unlawful games are utterly indefensible—though all persons should be free to gamble in their own or each other's houses, or in any place of meeting established by their own subscriptions, and open only to the members and their visitors—yet public gambling-houses should not be permitted. It is true that the prohibition is never effectual, and that, whatever amount of tyrannical power may be given to the police, gambling-houses can always be maintained under other pretences; but they may be compelled to conduct their operations with a certain degree of secrecy and mystery, so that nobody knows anything about them but those who seek them; and more than this society ought not to aim at. There is considerable force in these arguments. I will not venture to decide whether they are sufficient to justify the moral anomaly of punishing the accessary, when the principal is (and must be) allowed to go free; of fining or imprisoning the procurer, but not the fornicator—the gambling-house keeper, but not the gambler. Still less ought the common operations of buying and selling to be interfered with on analogous grounds. Almost every article which is bought and sold may be used in excess, and the sellers have a pecuniary interest in encouraging that excess; but no argument can be founded on this, in favour, for instance, of the Maine Law; because the class of dealers in strong drinks, though interested in their abuse, are indispensably required for the sake of their legitimate use. The interest, however, of these dealers in promoting intemperance is a real evil, and justifies the State in imposing restrictions and requiring guarantees which, but for that justification, would be infringements of legitimate liberty.

A further question is, whether the State, while it permits, should nevertheless indirectly discourage conduct which it deems contrary to the best interests of the agent; whether, for example, it should take measures to render the means of drunkenness more costly, or add to the difficulty of procuring them by limiting the number of the places of sale. On this as on most other practical questions, many distinctions require to be made. To tax stimulants for the sole purpose of making them more difficult to be obtained, is a measure differing only in degree from their entire prohibition; and would be justifiable only if that were justifiable. Every increase of cost is a prohibition, to those whose means do not come up to the augmented price; and to those who do, it is a penalty laid on them for gratifying a particular taste. Their choice of pleasures, and their mode of expending their income, after satisfying their legal and moral obligations to the State and to individuals, are their own concern, and must rest with their own judgment. These considerations may seem at first sight to condemn the selection of stimulants as special subjects of taxation for purposes of revenue. But it must be remembered that taxation for fiscal purposes is absolutely inevitable; that in most countries it is necessary that a considerable part of that taxation should be indirect; that the State, therefore, cannot help imposing penalties, which to some persons may be prohibitory, on the use of some articles of consumption. It is hence the duty of the State to consider, in the imposition of taxes, what commodities the consumers can best spare; and *à fortiori*, to select in preference those of which it deems the use, beyond a very moderate quantity, to be positively injurious. Taxation, therefore, of stimulants, up to the point which produces the largest amount of revenue (supposing that the State needs all the revenue which it yields) is not only admissible, but to be approved of.

The question of making the sale of these commodities a more or less exclusive privilege, must be answered differently, according to the purposes to which the restriction is intended to be subservient. All places of public resort require the restraint of a police, and places of this kind peculiarly, because offences against society are especially apt to originate there. It is, therefore, fit to confine the power of selling these commodities (at least for consumption on the spot) to persons of known or vouched-for respectability of conduct; to make such regulations respecting hours of opening and closing as may be requisite for public surveillance, and to withdraw the licence if breaches of the peace repeatedly take place through the connivance or incapacity of the keeper of the house, or if it becomes a rendezvous for concocting and preparing offences against the law. Any further restriction I do not conceive to be, in principle, justifiable. The limitation in number, for instance, of beer and spirit houses, for the express purpose of rendering them more difficult of access, and diminishing the occasions of temptation, not only exposes all to an inconvenience because there are some by whom the facility would be abused, but is suited only to a state of society in which the labouring classes are avowedly treated as children or savages, and placed under an education of restraint, to fit them for future admission to the privileges of freedom. This is not the principle on which the labouring classes are professedly governed in any free country; and no person who sets due value on freedom will give his adhesion to their being so governed, unless after all efforts have been exhausted to educate them for freedom and govern them as freemen, and it has been definitely proved that they can only be governed as children. The bare statement of the alternative shows the absurdity of supposing that such efforts have been made in any case which needs be considered here. It is only because the institutions of this country are a mass of inconsistencies, that things find admittance into our practice which belong to the system of despotic, or what is called paternal, government, while the general freedom of our institutions precludes the exercise of the amount of control necessary to render the restraint of any real efficacy as a moral education.

It was pointed out in an early part of this Essay, that the liberty of the individual, in things wherein the individual is alone concerned, implies a corresponding liberty in any number of individuals to regulate by mutual agreement such things as regard them jointly, and regard no persons but themselves. This question presents no difficulty, so long as the will of all the persons implicated remains unaltered; but since that will may change, it is often necessary, even in things in which they alone are concerned, that they should enter into engagements with one another; and when they do, it is fit, as a general rule, that those engagements should be kept. Yet, in the laws, probably, of every country, this general rule has some exceptions. Not only persons are not held to engagements which violate the rights of third parties, but it is sometimes considered a sufficient reason for releasing them from an engagement, that it is injurious to themselves. In this and most other civilised countries, for example, an engagement by which a person should sell himself, or allow himself to be sold, as a slave, would be null and void; neither enforced by law nor by opinion. The ground for thus limiting his power of voluntarily disposing of his own lot in life, is apparent,

and is very clearly seen in this extreme case. The reason for not interfering, unless for the sake of others, with a person's voluntary acts, is consideration for his liberty. His voluntary choice is evidence that what he
so chooses is desirable, or at least endurable, to him, and his good is on the
whole best provided for by allowing him to take his own means of pursuing
it. But by selling himself for a slave, he abdicates his liberty; he foregoes
any future use of it beyond that single act. He therefore defeats, in his own
case, the very purpose which is the justification of allowing him to dispose
of himself. He is no longer free; but is thenceforth in a position which has
no longer the presumption in its favour, that would be afforded by his voluntarily remaining in it. The principle of freedom cannot require that he
should be free not to be free. It is not freedom to be allowed to alienate
his freedom. These reasons, the force of which is so conspicuous in this
peculiar case, are evidently of far wider application; yet a limit is everywhere set to them by the necessities of life, which continually require, not
indeed that we should resign our freedom, but that we should consent to
this and the other limitation of it. The principle, however, which demands
uncontrolled freedom of action in all that concerns only the agents themselves, requires that those who have become bound to one another, in things
which concern no third party should be able to release one another from
the engagement: and even without such voluntary release there are perhaps
no contracts or engagements, except those that relate to money or money's
worth, of which one can venture to say that there ought to be no liberty
whatever of retractation. Baron Wilhelm von Humboldt, in the excellent
essay from which I have already quoted, states it as his conviction, that
engagements which involve personal relations or services should never be
legally binding beyond a limited duration of time; and that the most important of these engagements, marriage, having the peculiarity that its
objects are frustrated unless the feelings of both the parties are in harmony
with it, should require nothing more than the declared will of either party
to dissolve it. This subject is too important, and too complicated, to be
discussed in a parenthesis, and I touch on it only so far as is necessary for
purposes of illustration. If the conciseness and generality of Baron Humboldt's dissertation had not obliged him in this instance to content himself
with enunciating his conclusion without discussing the premises, he would
doubtless have recognised that the question cannot be decided on grounds
so simple as those to which he confines himself. When a person, either by
express promise or by conduct, has encouraged another to rely upon his
continuing to act in a certain way—to build expectations and calculations,
and stake any part of his plan of life upon that supposition—a new series
of moral obligations arises on his part towards that person, which may possibly be overruled, but cannot be ignored. And again, if the relation between two contracting parties has been followed by consequences to others;
if it has placed third parties in any peculiar position, or, as in the case of
marriage, has even called third parties into existence, obligations arise on

the part of both the contracting parties towards those third persons, the fulfilment of which, or at all events the mode of fulfilment, must be greatly affected by the continuance or disruption of the relation between the original parties to the contract. It does not follow, nor can I admit, that these obligations extend to requiring the fulfilment of the contract at all costs to the happiness of the reluctant party; but they are a necessary element in the question; and even if, as Von Humboldt maintains, they ought to make no difference in the *legal* freedom of the parties to release themselves from the engagement (and I also hold that they ought not to make *much* difference), they necessarily make a great difference in the *moral* freedom. A person is bound to take all these circumstances into account before resolving on a step which may affect such important interests of others; and if he does not allow proper weight to those interests, he is morally responsible for the wrong. I have made these obvious remarks for the better illustration of the general principle of liberty, and not because they are at all needed on the particular question, which, on the contrary, is usually discussed as if the interest of children was everything, and that of grown persons nothing.

I have already observed that, owing to the absence of any recognised general principles, liberty is often granted where it should be withheld, as well as withheld where it should be granted; and one of the cases in which, in the modern European world, the sentiment of liberty is the strongest, is a case where, in my view, it is altogether misplaced. A person should be free to do as he likes in his own concerns; but he ought not to be free to do as he likes in acting for another, under the pretext that the affairs of the other are his own affairs. The State, while it respects the liberty of each in what specially regards himself, is bound to maintain a vigilant control over his exercise of any power which it allows him to possess over others. This obligation is almost entirely disregarded in the case of the family relations, a case, in its direct influence on human happiness, more important than all others taken together. The almost despotic power of husbands over wives needs not be enlarged upon here, because nothing more is needed for the complete removal of the evil than that wives should have the same rights, and should receive the protection of law in the same manner, as all other persons; and because, on this subject, the defenders of established injustice do not avail themselves of the plea of liberty, but stand forth openly as the champions of power. It is in the case of children that misapplied notions of liberty are a real obstacle to the fulfilment by the State of its duties. One would almost think that a man's children were supposed to be literally, and not metaphorically, a part of himself, so jealous is opinion of the smallest interference of law with his absolute and exclusive control over them; more jealous than of almost any interference with his own freedom of action: so much less do the generality of mankind value liberty than power. Consider, for example, the case of education. Is it not almost a self-evident axiom, that the State should require and compel the education, up to a certain standard, of every human being who is born its citizen? Yet who is there that is not afraid to recognise and assert this truth? Hardly any one indeed will deny that it is one of the most sacred duties of the parents (or, as law and usage now stand, the father), after summoning a human being into the world, to give to that being an education fitting him to perform his part well in life towards others and towards himself. But while this is unanimously declared to be the father's duty, scarcely anybody, in this country, will bear to hear of obliging him to perform it. Instead of his being required to make any exertion or sacrifice for securing education to his child, it is left to his choice to accept it or not when it is provided gratis! It still remains unrecognised, that to bring a child into existence without a fair prospect of being able, not only to provide food for its body, but instruction and training for its mind, is a moral crime, both against the unfortunate offspring and against society; and that if the parent does not fulfil this obligation, the State ought to see it fulfilled, at the charge, as far as possible, of the parent.

Were the duty of enforcing universal education once admitted there would be an end to the difficulties about what the State should teach, and how it should teach, which now convert the subject into a mere battlefield for sects and parties, causing the time and labour which should have been spent in educating to be wasted in quarrelling about education. If the government would make up its mind to require for every child a good education, it might save itself the trouble of providing one. It might leave to parents to obtain the education where and how they pleased, and content itself with helping to pay the school fees of the poorer classes of children, and defraying the entire school expenses of those who have no one else to pay for them. The objections which are urged with reason against State education do not apply to the enforcement of education by the State, but to the State's taking upon itself to direct that education; which is a totally different thing. That the whole or any large part of the education of the people should be in State hands, I go as far as any one in deprecating. All that has been said of the importance of individuality of character, and diversity in opinions and modes of conduct, involves, as of the same unspeakable importance, diversity of education. A general State education is a mere contrivance for moulding people to be exactly like one another: and as the mould in which it casts them is that which pleases the predominant power in the government, whether this be a monarch, a priesthood, an aristocracy, or the majority of the existing generation; in proportion as it is efficient and successful, it establishes a despotism over the mind, leading by natural tendency to one over the body. An education established and controlled by the State should only exist, if it exist at all, as one among many competing experiments, carried on for the purpose of example and stimulus, to keep the others up to a certain standard of excellence. Unless, indeed, when society in general is in so backward a state that it could not or would not provide for itself any proper institutions of education unless the government undertook the task: then, indeed, the government may, as the less of two great evils, take upon itself the business of schools and universities, as it may that of joint stock companies, when private enterprise, in a shape fitted for undertaking great works of industry, does not exist in the country. But in general, if the country contains a sufficient number of persons qualified to provide education under government auspices, the same persons would be able and willing to give an equally good education on the voluntary principle, under the assurance of remuneration afforded by a law rendering education compulsory, combined with State aid to those unable to defray the expense.

The instrument for enforcing the law could be no other than public examinations, extending to all children, and beginning at an early age. An age might be fixed at which every child must be examined, to ascertain if he (or she) is able to read. If a child proves unable, the father, unless he has some sufficient ground of excuse, might be subjected to a moderate fine, to be worked out, if necessary, by his labour, and the child might be put to school at his expense. Once in every year the examination should be renewed, with a gradually extending range of subjects, so as to make the universal acquisition, and what is more, retention, of a certain minimum of general knowledge virtually compulsory. Beyond that minimum there should be voluntary examinations on all subjects, at which all who come up to a certain standard of proficiency might claim a certificate. To prevent the State from exercising, through these arrangements, an improper influence over opinion, the knowledge required for passing an examination (beyond the merely instrumental parts of knowledge, such as languages and their use) should, even in the higher classes of examinations, be confined to facts and positive science exclusively. The examinations on religion, politics, or other disputed topics, should not turn on the truth or falsehood of opinions, but on the matter of fact that such and such an opinion is held, on such grounds, by such authors, or schools, or churches. Under this system, the rising generation would be no worse off in regard to all disputed truths than they are at present; they would be brought up either churchmen or dissenters as they now are, the State merely taking care that they should be instructed churchmen, or instructed dissenters. There would be nothing to hinder them from being taught religion, if their parents chose, at the same schools where they were taught other things. All attempts by the State to bias the conclusions of its citizens on disputed subjects are evil; but it may very properly offer to ascertain and certify that a person possesses the knowledge requisite to make his conclusions, on any given subject, worth attending to. A student of philosophy would be the better for being able to stand an examination both in Locke and in Kant, whichever of the two he takes up with, or even if with neither: and there is no reasonable objection to examining an atheist in the evidences of Christianity, provided he is not required to profess a belief in them. The examinations, however, in the higher branches of knowledge should, I conceive, be entirely voluntary. It would be giving too dangerous a power to governments were they allowed to exclude any one from professions, even from the profession of teacher, for alleged deficiency of qualifications: and I think, with Wilhelm von Humboldt, that degrees, or other public certificates of scientific or professional acquirements, should be given to all who present themselves for examination, and stand the test; but that such certificates should confer no advantage over competitors other than the weight which may be attached to their testimony by public opinion.

It is not in the matter of education only that misplaced notions of liberty prevent moral obligations on the part of parents from being recognised, and legal obligations from being imposed, where there are the strongest grounds for the former always, and in many cases for the latter also. The fact itself, of causing the existence of a human being, is one of the most responsible actions in the range of human life. To undertake this responsibility—to bestow a life which may be either a curse or a blessing—unless the being on whom it is to be bestowed will have at least the ordinary chances of a desirable existence, is a crime against that being. And in a country either over-peopled, or threatened with being so, to produce children, beyond a very small number, with the effect of reducing the reward of labour by their competition, is a serious offence against all who live by the remuneration of their labour. The laws which, in many countries on the Continent, forbid marriage unless the parties can show that they have the means of supporting a family, do not exceed the legitimate powers of the State: and whether such laws be expedient or not (a question mainly dependent on local circumstances and feelings), they are not objectionable as violations of liberty. Such laws are interferences of the State to prohibit a mischievous act —an act injurious to others, which ought to be a subject of reprobation, and social stigma, even when it is not deemed expedient to superadd legal punishment. Yet the current ideas of liberty, which bend so easily to real infringements of the freedom of the individual in things which concern only himself, would repel the attempt to put any restraint upon his inclinations when the consequence of their indulgence is a life or lives of wretchedness and depravity to the offspring, with manifold evils to those sufficiently within reach to be in any way affected by their actions. When we compare the strange respect of mankind for liberty, with their strange want of respect for it, we might imagine that a man had an indispensable right to do harm to others, and no right at all to please himself without giving pain to any one.

I have reserved for the last place a large class of questions respecting the limits of government interference, which, though closely connected with the subject of this Essay, do not, in strictness, belong to it. These are cases in which the reasons against interference do not turn upon the principle of liberty: the question is not about restraining the actions of individuals, but about helping them; it is asked whether the government should do, or cause to be done, something for their benefit, instead of leaving it to be done by themselves, individually or in voluntary combination.

The objections to government interference, when it is not such as to involve infringement of liberty, may be of three kinds.

The first is, when the thing to be done is likely to be better done by individuals than by the government. Speaking generally, there is no one so fit to conduct any business, or to determine how or by whom it shall be conducted, as those who are personally interested in it. This principle condemns the interferences, once so common, of the legislature, or the officers of government, with the ordinary processes of industry. But this part of the subject has been sufficiently enlarged upon by political economists, and is not particularly related to the principles of this Essay.

The second objection is more nearly allied to our subject. In many cases, though individuals may not do the particular thing so well, on the average, as the officers of government, it is nevertheless desirable that it should be done by them, rather than by the government, as a means to their own mental education—a mode of strengthening their active faculties, exercising their judgment, and giving them a familiar knowledge of the subjects with which they are thus left to deal. This is a principal, though not the sole, recommendation of jury trial (in cases not political); of free and popular local and municipal institutions; of the conduct of industrial and philanthropic enterprises by voluntary associations. These are not questions of liberty, and are connected with that subject only by remote tendencies; but they are questions of development. It belongs to a different occasion from the present to dwell on these things as parts of national education; as being, in truth, the peculiar training of a citizen, the practical part of the political education of a free people, taking them out of the narrow circle of personal and family selfishness, and accustoming them to the comprehension of joint interests, the management of joint concerns—habituating them to act from public or semi-public motives, and guide their conduct by aims which unite instead of isolating them from one another. Without these habits and powers, a free constitution can neither be worked nor preserved; as is exemplified by the too-often transitory nature of political freedom in countries where it does not rest upon a sufficient basis of local liberties. The management of purely local business by the localities, and of the great enterprises of industry by the union of those who voluntarily supply the pecuniary means, is further recommended by all the advantages which have been set forth in this Essay as belonging to individuality ity of development, and diversity of modes of action. Government operations tend to be everywhere alike. With individuals and voluntary associations, on the contrary, there are varied experiments, and endless diversity of experience. What the State can usefully do is to make itself a central depository, and active circulator and diffuser, of the experience resulting from many trials. Its business is to enable each experimentalist to benefit by the experiments of others; instead of tolerating no experiments but its own.

The third and most cogent reason for restricting the interference of government is the great evil of adding unnecessarily to its power. Every function superadded to those already exercised by the government causes its influence over hopes and fears to be more widely diffused, and converts, more and more, the active and ambitious part of the public into hangers-on of the government, or of some party which aims at becoming the government. If the roads, the railways, the banks, the insurance offices, the great joint-stock companies, the universities, and the public charities, were all of them branches of the government; if, in addition, the municipal corporations and local boards, with all that now devolves on them, became departments of the central administration; if the employés of all these different enterprises were appointed and paid by the government, and looked to the government for every rise in life; not all the freedom of the press and popular constitution of the legislature would make this or any other country free otherwise than in name. And the evil would be greater, the more efficiently and scientifically the administrative machinery was constructed—the more skilful the arrangements for obtaining the best qualified hands and hoads with which to work it. In England it has of late been proposed that all the members of the civil service of government should be selected by competitive examination, to obtain for these employments the most intelligent and instructed persons procurable; and much has been said and written for and against this proposal. One of the arguments most insisted on by its opponents is that the occupation of a permanent official servant of the State does not hold out sufficient prospects of emolument and importance to attract the highest talents, which will always be able to find a more inviting career in the professions, or in the service of companies and other public bodies. One would not have been surprised if this argument had been used by the friends of the proposition, as an answer to its principal difficulty. Coming from the opponents it is strange enough. What is urged as an objection is the safety-valve of the proposed system. If indeed all the high talent of the country *could* be drawn into the service of the government, a proposal tending to bring about that result might well inspire uneasiness. If every part of the business of society which required organised concert, or large and comprehensive views, were in the hands of the government, and if government offices were universally filled by the ablest men, all the enlarged culture and practised intelligence in the country, except the purely speculative, would be concentrated in a numerous bureaucracy, to whom alone the rest of the community would look for all things: the multitude for direction and dictation in all they had to do; the able and aspiring for personal advancement. To be admitted into the ranks of this bureaucracy, and when admitted, to rise therein, would be the sole objects of ambition. Under this *régime*, not only is the outside public ill-qualified, for want of practical experience, to criticise or check the mode of operation of the bureaucracy, but even if the accidents of despotic or the natural working of popular institutions occasionally raise to the summit a ruler or rulers of reforming inclinations, no reform can be effected which is contrary to the interest of the bureaucracy. Such is the melancholy condition of the Russian empire, as shown in the accounts of those who have had sufficient opportunity of observation. The Czar himself is powerless against the bureaucratic body; he can send any one of them to Siberia, but he cannot govern

without them, or against their will. On every decree of his they have a
tacit veto, by merely refraining from carrying it into effect. In countries of
more advanced civilisation and of a more insurrectionary spirit, the public,
accustomed to expect everything to be done for them by the State, or at
least to do nothing for themselves without asking from the State not only
leave to do it, but even how it is to be done, naturally hold the State responsible for all evil which befalls them, and when the evil exceeds their amount
of patience, they rise against the government, and make what is called a
revolution; whereupon somebody else, with or without legitimate authority
from the nation, vaults into the seat, issues his orders to the bureaucracy,
and everything goes on much as it did before; the bureaucracy being unchanged, and nobody else being capable of taking their place.

A very different spectacle is exhibited among a people accustomed to
transact their own business. In France, a large part of the people, having
been engaged in military service, many of whom have held at least the rank
of non-commissioned officers, there are in every popular insurrection several persons competent to take the lead, and improvise some tolerable plan
of action. What the French are in military affairs, the Americans are in
every kind of civil business; let them be left without a government, every
body of Americans is able to improvise one, and to carry on that or any
other public business with a sufficient amount of intelligence, order, and
decision. This is what every free people ought to be: and a people capable
of this is certain to be free; it will never let itself be enslaved by any man
or body of men because these are able to seize and pull the reins of the central administration. No bureaucracy can hope to make such a people as
this do or undergo anything that they do not like. But where everything is
done through the bureaucracy, nothing to which the bureaucracy is really
adverse can be done at all. The constitution of such countries is an organisation of the experience and practical ability of the nation into a disciplined
body for the purpose of governing the rest; and the more perfect that organisation is in itself, the more successful in drawing to itself and educating
for itself the persons of greatest capacity from all ranks of the community,
the more complete is the bondage of all, the members of the bureaucracy
included. For the governors are as much the slaves of their organisation
and discipline as the governed are of the governors. A Chinese mandarin
is as much the tool and creature of a depotism as the humblest cultivator.
An individual Jesuit is to the utmost degree of abasement the slave of his
order, though the order itself exists for the collective power and importance
of its members.

It is not, also, to be forgotten, that the absorption of all the principal
ability of the country into the governing body is fatal, sooner or later, to
the mental activity and progressiveness of the body itself. Banded together
as they are—working a system which, like all systems, necessarily proceeds
in a great measure by fixed rules—the official body are under the constant
temptation of sinking into indolent routine, or, if they now and then desert

that mill-horse round, of rushing into some half-examined crudity which has struck the fancy of some leading member of the corps; and the sole check to these closely allied, though seemingly opposite, tendencies, the only stimulus which can keep the ability of the body itself up to a high standard, is liability to the watchful criticism of equal ability outside the body. It is indispensable, therefore, that the means should exist, independently of the government, of forming such ability, and furnishing it with the opportunities and experience necessary for a correct judgment of great practical affairs. If we would possess permanently a skilful and efficient body of functionaries—above all, a body able to originate and willing to adopt improvements; if we would not have our bureaucracy degenerate into a pedantocracy, this body must not engross all the occupations which form and cultivate the faculties required for the government of mankind.

To determine the point at which evils, so formidable to human freedom and advancement, begin, or rather at which they begin to predominate over the benefits attending the collective application of the force of society, under its recognised chiefs, for the removal of the obstacles which stand in the way of its well-being; to secure as much of the advantages of centralised power and intelligence as can be had without turning into governmental channels too great a proportion of the general activity—is one of the most difficult and complicated questions in the art of government. It is, in a great measure, a question of detail, in which many and various considerations must be kept in view, and no absolute rule can be laid down. But I believe that the practical principle in which safety resides, the ideal to be kept in view, the standard by which to test all arrangements intended for overcoming the difficulty, may be conveyed in these words: the greatest dissemination of power consistent with efficiency; but the greatest possible centralisation of information, and diffusion of it from the centre. Thus, in municipal administration, there would be, as in the New England States, a very minute division among separate officers, chosen by the localities, of all business which is not better left to the persons directly interested; but besides this, there would be, in each department of local affairs, a central superintendence, forming a branch of the general government. The organ of this superintendence would concentrate, as in a focus, the variety of information and experience derived from the conduct of that branch of public business in all the localities, from everything analogous which is done in foreign countries, and from the general principles of political science. This central organ should have a right to know all that is done, and its special duty should be that of making the knowledge acquired in one place available for others. Emancipated from the petty prejudices and narrow views of a locality by its elevated position and comprehensive sphere of observation, its advice would naturally carry much authority; but its actual power, as a permanent institution, should, I conceive, be limited to compelling the local officers to obey the laws laid down for their guidance. In all things not provided for by general rules, those officers should be left to their own judgment, under responsibility to their constituents. For the violation of rules, they should be responsible to law, and the rules themselves should be laid down by the legislature; the central administrative authority only watching over their execution, and if they were not properly carried into effect, appealing, according to the nature of the case, to the tribunals to enforce the law, or to the constituencies to dismiss the functionaries who had not executed it according to its spirit. Such, in its general conception, is the central superintendence which the Poor Law Board is intended to exercise over the administrators of the Poor Rate throughout the country. Whatever powers the Board exercises beyond this limit were right and necessary in that peculiar case, for the cure of rooted habits of maladministration in matters deeply affecting not the localities merely, but the whole community; since no locality has a moral right to make itself by mismanagement a nest of pauperism, necessarily overflowing into other localities, and impairing the moral and physical condition of the whole labouring community. The powers of administrative coercion and subordinate legislation possessed by the Poor Law Board (but which, owing to the state of opinion on the subject, are very scantily exercised by them), though perfectly justifiable in a case of first-rate national interest, would be wholly out of place in the superintendence of interests purely local. But a central organ of information and instruction for all the localities would be equally valuable in all departments of administration. A government cannot have too much of the kind of activity which does not impede, but aids and stimulates, individual exertion and development. The mischief begins when, instead of calling forth the activity and powers of individuals and bodies, it substitutes its own activity for theirs; when, instead of informing, advising, and, upon occasion, denouncing, it makes them work in fetters, or bids them stand aside and does their work instead of them. The worth of a State, in the long run, is the worth of the individuals composing it; and a State which postpones the interests of *their* mental expansion and elevation to a little more of administrative skill, or of that semblance of it which practice gives, in the details of business; a State which dwarfs its men, in order that they may be more docile instruments in its hands even for beneficial purposes—will find that with small men no great thing can really be accomplished; and that the perfection of machinery to which it has sacrificed everything will in the end avail it nothing, for want of the vital power which, in order that the machine might work more smoothly, it has preferred to banish.

Freedom through Authority: German Liberalism

Heinrich von Treitschke, "Freedom," Treitschke: His Doctrines of German Destiny and of International Relations. Together with a Study of His Life and Work by Adolf Hausrath (New York and London: G. P. Putnam's Sons, 1914), pp. 302–32.

Conservative and radical critics of liberalism challenged the doctrine as political philosophy, but liberalism on the western model also had critics who numbered themselves in the "liberal" vanguard. Heinrich von Treitschke (1834–94) reflected and spoke for German liberalism in a voice quite different from that of John Stuart Mill in England. The German revolutions of 1848 proved crucial for the idea and the nation. The Frankfort Parliament of 1848 was the fruition of the liberal ideal. Lacking power, it sought to negotiate, but the German nation could not be forged by consent nor could German freedom, in the western sense, be realized by agreement. Where ideas and rhetoric failed, force was to succeed.

Treitschke was involved in the Dresden revolt of 1848 as a teenaged student. Later at the University of Bonn he followed the great liberal, Dahlmann, but he also read von Rochau's Realpolitik. Since western liberalism had impressed neither the German masses nor the traditional governing orders, liberals must come to terms with reality. Reality was summed up in a man, Bismarck, and a practical, viable German state under the king of Prussia. Treitschke dedicated himself to this new conception of national liberalism as a teacher, journalist, historian, and even as a member of the Imperial Reichstag (1871–84).

"Freedom" (and this is the revised version of 1862) is a challenge to Mill's On Liberty (1859). "The Macaulay of the Bismarckian Reich," as Treitschke has often been denominated, made some cogent points which still deserve consideration. He rejected the materialism of English utilitarians and the totalitarianism of German conservatives. Treitschke's liberalism has more in common with many twentieth-century "liberal" arguments than champions of the position might care to admit.

FREEDOM

WHEN SHALL we see the last of those timid spirits who find it needful to increase the burden of life by self-created torture, to whom every advance of the human mind is but one sign more of the decay of our race—of the approach of the Day of Judgment? The great majority of our contemporaries are again beginning, thank Heaven! to believe quite sturdily and heartily in themselves, yet we are weak enough to repeat some, at least, of the gloomy predictions of those atrabilious spirits. It has become a commonplace assumption that all-conquering culture will at last supplant national morality by a morality of mankind, and transform the world into a cosmopolitan, primitive pap. But the same law holds good of nations, as of individuals, who show less differentiation in childhood than in mature years. In other words, if a people has vitality enough to keep itself and its nationality going in the merciless race-struggle of history, every advance in civilization will certainly bring its external life in closer contact with other peoples, but it will bring into clearer relief its more refined, its deeper idiosyncrasies. We all follow the Paris fashions, we are linked with neighbouring nations by a thousand different interests; yet our feelings and ideas, so far as the French and British intellectual world is concerned, are undoubtedly more independent than they were seven hundred years ago, when the peasant all over Europe spent his life fettered by patriarchal custom, whilst the ecclesiastic in every country derived his knowledge from the same sources, and the nobility of Latin Christendom created for itself a common code of honour and morality under the walls of Jerusalem. That lively exchange of ideas between nations, on which the present generation rightly plumes itself, has never been a mere give and take.

We are fortified in this consoling knowledge when we see how the ideas of a German classic about the highest object of human thought—about freedom—have recently been developed in a very individual way by two distinguished political thinkers of France and England. When Wilhelm von Humboldt's essay on the limits of the operations of the State appeared for the first time in complete form, a few years ago, some sensation was caused by that brilliant work in Germany too. We were rejoiced to get a deeper insight into the evolution of one of our chief men. The more refined minds delightedly detected the inspiring breath of the golden age of German humanity, for it is indeed only in Schiller's nearly-related letters on the æsthetic education of the human race that the bright ideal of a beautiful humanity, which fascinated Germans during that period, has been depicted with equal eloquence and distinction. The gifted youth who had just had his first look into the self-complacent red-tapeism of Frederick William II's bureaucracy, and had turned away, chilled by its lifeless formalities, in order to live a life of aesthetic leisure at home—he was certainly to be forgiven for thinking very poorly of the State. Dalberg had asked him to write the little book—a prince who had the intention of lavishing profusely on his country all the good things of life by means of an administration that would know everything, and look after everything. The young thinker emphasized all the more keenly the fact that the State is nothing but an institution for purposes of security; that it must never again interfere, directly or indirectly, with a nation's morals or character; that a man was freest when the State was least active. We, of the present generation, know only too well that the true cause of the ruin of the old German State was that all free minds set themselves in such morbid opposition to the State that they fled from it like young Humboldt, instead of serving it like Humboldt when grown to a man, and elevating it by the nobility of their free human development. The doctrine which sees in the State merely a hindrance, a necessary evil, seems obsolete to the German of to-day. Curiously enough, though, this youthful work of Humboldt's is now being glorified by John Stuart Mill, in his book *On Liberty*, and by Edward Laboulaye in his essay *L'état et ses limites*, as a mine of political wisdom for the troubles of the present time.

Mill is a faithful son of those genuinely German middle classes of England, which, since the days of Richard II have preferentially represented our country's inner essence, its spiritual work both in good and bad respects, both by an earnest desire for truth and by a gloomy, fanatical zeal in religious belief. He has become a rich man since he discovered and recognized the most precious jewel of our people, German idealism. Speaking from that free watch-tower he utters words of reproach, bitter words, against his fellow-countrymen's confused thinking; and unfortunately, also, against the present generation, bitter words such as only the honoured national economist would dare to speak unpunished. But, like a true-born Englishman, as a pupil of Bentham, he tests Kant's ideas by the standard of the useful, the "well-comprehended, permanent" utility of course, and therein shows, in his own person, the deep abyss which will always separate the two nations' intellectual activities. He wavers between the English and German views of the world—in his book *On Liberty*, just as in his latest work, *Utilitarianism*—and finally gets out of the difficulty by attributing an ideal meaning to Bentham's purely materialistic thoughts, which brings them close to the German view. With the help of the apostle of German humanity he contrives to praise the North-American State-methods, which owe little, or nothing, to the beautiful humanity of German-Hellenic classicism. Laboulaye, on the other hand, belongs to that small school of keen-sighted Liberals, which feels the weakness of their country to reside in French centralization, and endeavours to re-awaken the germs of German civilization which are there slumbering under the Keltic-Roman régime. The talented author deals with historical facts, rather boldly than thoroughly; briefly, he is of opinion that Christianity was the first to recognize the worth and dignity of the individual. Well, then, our glorious heathen Humboldt must be a downright Christian philosopher, and with the nineteenth century, the age must be approaching when the ideas of Christianity shall be completely realized, and the individual, not the State, shall rule. The Frenchman will convince only a small group of believers among his numerous readers. Mill's book, on the other hand, has been received with the greatest applause by his fellow-countrymen. They have called it the gospel of the nineteenth century. As a fact, both works strike notes which have a mighty echo in the heart of every modern man; it is therefore instructive to investigate whether they really expound the principles of genuine freedom.

Although we have learnt to assign a deeper foundation and a richer meaning to the words of the Greek philosopher, no thinker has surpassed the interpretation of freedom which Aristotle discovered. He thinks, in his exhaustive, empirical way, that freedom embraces two things: the suitability of the citizens to live as they prefer, and the sharing of the citizens in the State-government (ruling, and at the same time, being ruled). The one-sidedness, which is the lever of all human progress brought it about that the nations have hardly ever inspired to the full conception of freedom. It is, on the contrary, well known that the Greeks preferred political freedom in a narrower sense, and readily sacrificed the free activity of the individual to a beautiful and sound existence as a community. The love of political liberty, on the part of the ancients, was certainly by no means so exclusive as is generally believed. That definition of the Greek thinker proves that they were by no means lacking in the comprehension of a life, lived after its own will and pleasure, of civic, personal freedom. Aristotle knows very well that a State-administration is even thinkable which does not include the national life, taken in sum; he expressly declares that States are particularly distinguished from each other, by the question whether everything, or nothing, or how much is shared by the citizens. At any rate, the idea was dominant in the mature State of antiquity, that the citizen is only a part of the State, that true virtue is realized only in the State. Political thinkers among the ancients, therefore, occupy themselves solely with the questions: Who shall rule in the State? and, How shall the State be protected? Only occasionally, as a slight misgiving, is the deeper question stirred: How shall the citizen be protected from the State? The ancients were assured that a power which a people exercises over itself, needs no limitation. How different are the German conceptions of freedom, which lay chief emphasis on the unlimited right of personality! In the Middle Age the State began everywhere, with an implacable combat of the State-power against the desire for independence on the part of individuals, guilds, classes, which was hostile to the State; and we Germans experienced in our own persons with what loss of power and genuine freedom the "Liberat" of the minor princes, the "freedoms of the Honourable classes" were bought. If, at length, in the course of this struggle, which in later times was gloriously settled by an absolute Monarchy, the majesty, the unity of the State was preserved, a transformation would take place in the people's ideas of freedom, and a fresh quarrel would start. No longer is the attempt made to separate the individual from a State-power, whose necessity has been understood. But there is a demand that the State-power should not be independent of the people; it should become an actual popular administration, working within established forms, and bound by the will of the majority of the citizens.

Everybody knows how immeasurably far from that goal our Fatherland still is. What Vittorio Alfieri proposed to himself as his object in life nearly a hundred years ago:

"Di far con penna ai falsi imperj offesa",

is still a difficult, toilsome task for the Germans. On the Fula, on the Leine, and probably also on the Spree, a pusillanimous German might even to-day repeat Alfieri's question: Ought a man who is steeped in the feeling of civism, to take the responsibility of bringing children into the world, under the yoke of a tyranny? Ought he to generate beings who, the more sensitive their conscience the stronger their sense of justice, are bound to suffer the more severely beneath that perversion of all ideas of honour, justice, and shame, whereby a tyranny poisons a people? What, however, Alfieri himself experienced, did not happen in the case of the peoples. When, having reached grown-up age, he published the savage pamphlet, *On Tyranny,* which he had once written in holy zeal as a youth, he was obliged himself to confess: To-day I should be wanting in the courage, or, more correctly speaking, the fury, which was requisite for the authorship of such a book. The nations to-day, regard with similar feelings the abstract hatred of tyrants of the past century. We no longer ask: "Come si debbe morire nella tirannide," but we stand with determined, invincible confidence, in the midst of the fight for political freedom, the result of which has for a long time not been in question. For the common lot of everything human has dominated this struggle too, and this time, also, the thoughts of the nations largely anticipated actual conditions. How poor in vitality, in fruitfulness, are the partisans of absolutism when confronted with the people's demand for freedom! When two mighty streams of thought dash roaring at one another, a new middle-stream quietly separates at last from the wild confusion. Nay, rather, a stream rages against a strong breakwater and makes itself a way through thousands and thousands of fissures. Everything new that this nineteenth century has provided, is the work of Liberalism. The foes of freedom are able to utter only a cool negative, or to revive the ideas of long-forgotten days so that they may seem alive again, or, finally, they borrow the weapons of their opponents. In the tribunals of our Chambers, by means of the free press, which they owe to the Liberals, by means of catchwords which they overhear from their adversaries, they are championing principles which, if put in operation, would be bound to annihilate all the freedom of the press, all Parliamentary life.

Everywhere, even in classes which fifty years ago were still closed to all political ideas, there is a calm and firm belief in the truth of those great words, which, with their deliberate definiteness, mark the boundary of a new period; belief in the words of the American Declaration of Independence: "The just powers of governments are deprived from the consent of the governed." So indisputable is this idea to modern men that even Gentz had, reluctantly, to agree with the detested protagonists of freedom, when he said that the State-power could claim sacrifices from the citizen only so long as the latter could call the State his State. And these problems of freedom are so old, so thoroughly examined in all their aspects, so near a decisive issue, that as regards most of them a conciliation and purgation of opinions has already been achieved. It was at last understood that the fight for political freedom is not a dispute between Republic and Monarchy, because the people's "ruling and at the same time being ruled," is equally realizable in both forms of the State. Only one single corollary of political freedom is, even to-day, the cause of embittered, passionate discussion. If, namely, the people's moral consciousness is in very truth the final, just foundation of the State, if in very truth the people rules according to its own will, and for its own happiness, a longing for the national isolation of the States arises of its own accord. Because it is only where the vital, unquestioning consciousness of belonging together permeates all members of the State, that the State is what ought to be, according to its nature, an organized people in unity. Thence the desire to exclude foreign elements, and, in divided nations, the impulse to get rid of the smaller of the two "fatherlands." It is not our intention to describe to how many necessary limitations this political liberty is subject. Suffice it that there is everywhere a demand for the government of the peoples in harmony with their will, it is more general and uniform than ever before in history, and will at last be as surely satisfied, as the peoples' existence is more permanent, more justified, and stronger than the life of their powerful opponents.

However, let us look things in the face, let us consider how entirely our ideas of freedom have changed in this protean fight, in which we, ourselves, are spectators and actors. We no longer meet the problems of freedom with the overbearingness, with the vague enthusiasm, of youth. Political freedom is freedom politically limited—this phrase, which was blamed as servile even a few decades ago, is to-day, admitted by everybody capable of political judgment. And how ruthlessly has harsh experience destroyed all those mad ideas which hid themselves behind the great name of Liberty! The ideas of freedom, which prevailed during the French Revolution, were a vague blend of Montesquieu's ideas and Rousseau's half-antique conception. The construction of political liberty was believed to be complete if only the legislative power were separated from the executive and the judicial, and every citizen were, on equal terms, to help in electing the deputies of the National Convention. Those demands were fulfilled, most abundantly fulfilled, and what was the end of it all? The most disgusting despotism Europe ever saw. The idolatry which our Radicals displayed all too long for the horrors of the Convention, is at last beginning to die out in the presence of the trifling reflection: If an all-mighty State-power forbids me to open my mouth, compels me to belie my faith, and guillotines me as soon as I defy such insolence, it is a matter of perfect indifference whether that tyranny is exercised by a hereditary prince or by a Convention; both the one and the other is slavery. But the fallacy in Rousseau's maxim that, where all are equal, each one obeys himself, seems, really, too obvious. It is much truer that he obeys the majority, and what is to prevent that majority from behaving quite as tyrannously as an unscrupulous monarch?

If we consider the feverish convulsions, which have shaken for seventy years the nation on the other side of the Rhine (which is, despite all, a great nation), we are ashamed to find that the French, in spite of all their enthusiasm for liberty, have only known equality, and never freedom. But equality is a shallow idea, which may as well signify an equal slavery of all, as an equal freedom of all. And it certainly means the former, when it is aspired to by a people as the sole, highest, political good. The highest conceivable degree of equality—communism—is the highest conceivable degree of serfdom, because it assumes the suppression of all natural inclinations. Assuredly, it is not an accident that the passionate impulse for equality is especially rife in that people, whose Keltic blood is ever and ever again finding pleasure in flocking, in blind subjection, round a great Caesarean figure, whether his name be Vercingetorix, Louis XIV, or Napoleon. We Germans insist too proudly on the limitless right of the individual, for us to be able to discover freedom in universal suffrage; we reflect, that even in several Ecclesiastical Orders, the Heads are chosen by universal suffrage; but who in the wide world has ever sought for freedom in a convent? Truly it is not the spirit of liberty which speaks in Lamartine's declaration, in the year 1848: "Every Frenchman is an elector, therefore, a self-ruler; no Frenchman can say to another, 'You are more a ruler than I.'" What instinct of mankind is gratified by such words? None other than the meanest of all—envy! Even Rousseau's enthusiasm for the civism of the ancients will not stand serious examination. The civic glory of Athens rested on the broad substratum of slavery, of contempt for all economic activities; whilst we moderns base our frame on respect for all men, on our acknowledgment of the nobility of labour. The most bigoted aristocrat in the modern world seems like a democrat, by comparison with that Aristotle, who coolly lays it down with horrible hardness of heart: "It is not possible for a man who lives the life of a manual labourer to practise works of virtue."

Deeper natures were impelled, long ago, by such considerations, to examine more carefully on what principles the much-envied freedom of the Britons rests. They found that in that country no all-powerful government determines the destinies of the most remote communities, but every county, however small, is administered by itself. This acknowledgment of the blessings of self-government was an extraordinary advance; for the enervating influence on the citizens of a State that looks after everything can hardly be depicted in sufficiently dark colours; it is, therefore, so uncanny, because a morbid state of the people is revealed in its full extent only in a later generation. So long as the eye of the great Frederick watch over his Prussians, a simple glance at the hero raised even small souls above their standard, his vigilance was a spur to the sluggards. But when he passed away, he left a generation without a will, accustomed—as Napoleon III boasts of his Frenchmen—to expect from the State all incitement to action, disposed to that vanity which is the opposite of real national pride, capable on occasion of breaking out in fleeting enthusiasm for the idea of State-unity, but incapable of commanding itself—incapable of the greatest task which is laid upon modern nations. Only those citizens who have learnt, by self-government, to act as statesmen in case of need are able to colonize, to spread the blessings of Western civilization among barbarians. The management of the business of the community by paid State officials, may be technically more perfect and may be better than the principle of the division of labour; yet a State which allows its citizens, of their own free-will, to look after districts and communities in honorary service, gains moral force by the self-consciousness, by the living, practical patriotism, of the citizens—forces which the sole rule of State officialdom can never evolve. Assuredly, this admission on our part was a significant deepening of our ideas of freedom, but it by no means contains the ultimate truth. For, if we inquire where this self-government of all small local districts exists, we discover with astonishment that the numerous small tribes in Turkey enjoy this blessing in a high degree. They pay their taxes; for the rest they live as they please, look after their pigs, hunt, kill each other, and find themselves quite happy with it all—until suddenly a pasha visits the tribe, and proves to the dullest understanding, by means of impalement and drowning in sacks, that the self-government of the communities is an illusion, if the highest powers of the State do not operate within fixed limits of the laws.

Thus, finally, we come to the conclusion, that political freedom is not, as the Napoleons assert, an ornament which may be set upon a perfectly constructed State like a golden cupola; it must permeate and inspire the whole State. It is a profound, comprehensive, extremely consistent system of political rights, which tolerates no gaps. There can be no Parliament without free communities, no free communities without Parliament; and neither can be permanent if the middle factors between the top of the State and the communities, namely, the various districts and departments, are not also administered by a concentration of the personal activity of independent citizens. We Germans have felt these gaps painfully for a long time, and are just now making the first modest endeavours to fill them.

Nevertheless, a State dominated by a government carried on by the majority of its people, with a Parliament, with an independent judiciary, with districts and communities which administer themselves, is, despite all, not yet free. It has to set limits to its operation; it has to admit that there are personal properties of so high and unassailable a nature that the State must never subject them to itself. Let no one sneer too presumptuously at the fundamental principles of the more recent Constitutions. In the midst of phrases and silliness, they contain the Magna Charta of personal freedom, with which the modern world will not again dispense. Free movement in religious faith, and in knowledge and in affairs generally, is the watchword of the times; in this domain it has had the greatest effect; this social freedom is developing the essence of all political desires for the great majority of men. It may be asserted that wherever the State resolved to let a branch of social activity grow unhindered, its self-control was gloriously rewarded; all the predictions of timorous pessimists fell to the ground. We have become a different nation, since we have been drawn into closer intercourse with the world and its ways. Even two generations ago, Ludwig Vincke, like the careful President he was, explained to his Westphalians how to set about building a high-road by means of a company, on the English plan. To-day, a dense net of associations of every kind is spread over German territory. We know that through his merchants, the German will, at the least, share in the noble destiny of our race, and fructify the wide world. And it is, even now, no empty dream that an act of government will presently result from that intercourse with the world, compared with whose world-embracing outlook all the activities of modern great Powers will seem like sorry provincialism—so immeasurably rich and many-sided is the essence of freedom. Therein lies the consoling certainty that it is never impossible at any time to work for the victory of freedom. For should a government temporarily succeed in undermining the people's participation in legislation, men of to-day, with their impulse for freedom, would simply throw their energies with the more violence into economic or spiritual activities, and the results in the one sphere influence the other sooner or later. Let us leave it to boys, and those nations which ever remain children, to hunt for freedom with passionate haste, like some phantom that dissolves at the touch of its pursuers. A mature people loves liberty, like its lawful wife; she is part of us, she enraptures us day by day with fresh charms.

But new, undreamed-of dangers to freedom, arise with the growth of civilization. It is not only the State-power which may be tyrannical, but also the unorganized majority of a society may subject the minds of its citizens to odious compulsion by the slow and imperceptible, yet irresistible, force of its opinion. And it is beyond doubt, that the danger of an intolerable limitation of the independent development of personality, by means of public opinion, is especially great in democratic States. For, whilst during the absence of freedom under the old régime, at least a few privileged classes were allowed, without hindrance, to develop, brillantly, their individual gifts, whether for good or for evil, the middle classes, who will determine Europe's future, are not free from a certain preference for the mediocre. They are justly proud of the fact that they are trying to drag down to their own level everything that rises above them, and to raise up to the level all those that are beneath them; and they may base their desire to be determining factors in the lives of States on a glorious title, on a great deed, which they, together with the old monarchy, have achieved, namely, on the emancipation of our lower classes. But woe to us, if this tendency to equality, which has ripened the most precious fruit in the domain of common right, goes astray in the domain of individual evolution! The middle classes hate all open, violent tyranny, but they are much inclined to nullify, by the ostracism of public opinion, everything that rises above a certain average of culture, of spiritual nobility, of audacity. The love of liberty which distinguishes them, and makes them, as such, the most capable political order, is liable to degenerate only too easily into idle complacency, into an unthinking sleepy endeavour to blink and gloss over all the contradictions of intellectual life, and to tolerate alert activity only in the sphere of material operations (of "improvement!"). We are not here giving utterance to vain hypotheses. Far from it. The yoke of public opinion presses heavier than elsewhere in the freest great States of modernity, in England and the United States. The sphere of what the community permits the citizen to think and to do as an honourable and decent being is there, incomparably narrower than with us. If you have knowledge of the memorable discussions about the Constitution at the Convention of Massachusetts, in the year 1853; if you know with what spirit and passion the doctrine was then championed, that "a citizen may certainly be the subject of a party, or an actual power (!), but never the subject of the State," you will not underrate the peril of a lapse into conditions of harsh morality and weakened rights—the danger of the social tyranny of the majority. Mill has excellently pointed this out, and therein lies the significance of his book for the present time. He investigates, quite apart from the form of government, the nature and limits of the power which society should suitably exercise over the individual. Humboldt saw danger for personal liberty only in the State; he scarcely thought that the society of beautiful and distinguished minds, which associated with him, could ever hinder the individual in the complete evolution of his personality. However, we know now, that they may be not only a "free sociability," but also a tyrannical public opinion.

In order to understand to what extent society should use its power over the individual, it is best, first of all, to throw gleefully overboard a question, over which political thinkers have unnecessarily spent many unhappy hours, namely: Is the State only a means for furthering the objects in life of the citizens? Or, is it the sole object of the citizens' well-being to bring into existence a beautiful and good collective life? Humboldt, Mill, and Laboulaye, and the collective Liberalism of the Rotteck-Welcker school, decide for the former; the ancients, as is well-known, for the latter. We think the one opinion is worth as little as the other. For the whole world admits that a relation of reciprocal rights and duties connects the State with its citizens. But reciprocity is unthinkable between entities which are related to one another simply as means and object. The State is, itself, an object, like everything living; for who can deny that the State lives quite as real a life as each of its citizens? How wonderful, that we Germans, with our provincialism, have to admonish a Frenchman and an Englishman to think more highly of the State! Mill and Laboulaye both live in mighty respected States; they take that rich blessing for granted and perceive in the State only the terrifying power which threatens the liberty of man. We Germans have had our esteem for the dignity of the State fortified by painful experience. When we are asked by strangers about our "narrower fatherland," and a scornful smile plays around the lips of the hearers at the mention of the name of Reuss, of the younger line, or Schwarzburg-Sondershausen's principality, we feel, indeed, that the State is something bigger than a means for lightening the burdens of our private lives. Its honour is ours, and he who cannot look upon his State with enthusiastic pride, his soul is lacking in one of the highest feelings of man. If, to-day, our best men are trying to build up a State for this nation, which shall deserve respect, they are inspired in their task, not only by the desire to spend their personal existence, henceforth, in greater security, but they, also, know they are fulfilling a moral duty, which is imposed upon every nation.

The State—which protected our forefathers with its justice, which they defended with their bodies; which the living are called upon to build further; and higher-developed children and children's children to inherit which, therefore, is a sacred bond between many generations—the State, I say, is an independent order, which lives according to its own laws. The views of rulers and ruled can never altogether coincide; they will, assuredly, reach the same goal in a free and mature State, but by widely divergent paths. The citizen demands from the State the highest possible measure of personal liberty, because he wants to live himself out, to develop all his powers. The State grants it, not because it wants to oblige the individual citizen; but it is considering itself, the whole. It is bound to support itself by its citizens; but in the moral world, only that which is free, which is also able to resist, supports. Thus, truly, the respect, which the State pays the individual and his liberty, gives the surest measure of its culture; but it pays that respect primarily because political freedom, which the State itself acquires, is impossible with citizens who do not, themselves, look after their most private affairs without hindrance.

This indissoluble connection between political and personal liberty, especially the essence of liberty, as of a closely-cohering system of noble rights, has not been properly understood by either Mill or Laboulaye. The former, in full enjoyment of English civic rights, silently assumes the existence of political freedom; the latter, under the oppression of Bonapartism, does not dare even to think about it. And yet personal freedom, without the political, leads to the dissolution of the State. He who sees in the State only a means for obtaining the objects in life of the citizens, must, consequentially, after the good mediaeval manner, seek freedom from the State, not freedom in the State. The modern world has outgrown that error. Still less, however, may a generation, which lives predominantly for social aims, and is able to devote only a small part of its time to the State, fall into the opposite error of the ancients. This age is called upon to resume in itself, and to further develop, the indestructible results of the labours of culture, and, likewise, of the political work of antiquity and the Middle Age. Thus it arrives at the harmonizing and yet independent conclusion, that there is a physical necessity, and a moral duty, for the State to further everything that serves the personal evolution of its citizens. And, again, there is a physical necessity, and a moral duty, for the individual to take his part in a State, and to make even personal sacrifices to it, which the maintenance of the community demand, even the sacrifice of his life. And, indeed, man is subject to this duty, not merely because it is only a citizen that he can become a complete man, but also because it is an historical ordinance that mankind build States, beautiful and good States. The historic world affords

superabundant evidence of such conditions of reciprocal rights, or reciprocal dependence; everything conditioned appears in it at the same time
as a conditioning entity. It is precisely that fact which often makes the
comprehension of things political difficult to keen, mathematical minds
which, like Mill, are fond of reaching conclusion by means of a radical law.

Mill now tries to draw the permissible limits of the operation of society
with the sentence: The interference of society with personal liberty is only
justified, when it is necessary, in order to protect the community itself, or
to hinder injury by others. We shall not contradict this saying—if only it
were not so entirely futile! How small is the effect of such abstract maxims
of natural law in an historical science! For is not the "self-protection of
the Community" historically capable of change? Is it not the duty of a
theocratic State, for the sake of self-protection, to tyrannously interfere,
even with the thoughts of its citizens? And do not those common labours,
which are "necessary for the community," which the citizen must be compelled to discharge, vary essentially according to time and place? There
is no absolute limit to the State-power, and it is the greatest merit of modern
science, that it has taught politicians to reckon only with relative ideas.
Every advance of civilization, every widening of national culture, necessarily makes the State's activity more varied. North America, too, is experiencing that truth; the State and society in the big towns there are also
being obliged to develop a manifold activity, which is not needed in a
primeval forest.

The much-vaunted voluntarism, the activity of free private associations,
is not by any means sufficient in all cases to satisfy the needs of our society.
The net of our intercourse has such small meshes, that a thousand collisions
between rights and interests necessarily occur; it is the duty of the State in
both instances to intervene conciliatingly as an impartial power. In the
same way there exist in every highly-civilized nation, big private powers
which actually exclude free competition; the State has to restrain their
selfishness, even if they do not injure any rights of third parties. The English Parliament some years ago ordered the railway companies, not only to
attend to the safety of the passengers, but also to allow a certain number of
so-called Parliamentary trains, to run at the usual rates for all classes of
carriages. Nobody can say that there is an exceeding of the sensible limits
of the State-power in this law, which makes travelling possible for the
lower classes. But if you see in the State merely an institution for safety,
you can defend the measure only by means of very artificial and uncon-
vincing argument. For who has a right to demand that he should be carried
from A to B for three shillings? The railway company has certainly no
monopoly by law, and it is free to anyone to construct a parallel line! No, the
modern State cannot do without an extensive positive activity for the
people's benefit. In every nation there are spiritual and material properties,
without which the State cannot exist. A constitutional State assumes a high
average of national culture; it may never leave it to the pleasure of parents,

whether they want to give their children the most needful education; it requires compulsory education. The sphere of these benefits, which are requisite for the community's existence, is inevitably widened by the growth of civilization. Who would seriously propose to shut up the precious art institutions in our States? We old cultured nations shall certainly not relapse into the crude conception which sees a luxury in art; it is like our daily bread to us. In point of fact, the demand for the extremest limitation of State-activity is the more loudly urged in theory to-day, the more it is contradicted by practice, even in free countries. The school of Tocqueville, Laboulaye, Charles Dollfus, grew up in combat with an all-embracing State-power which wanted, not to guide, but to replace society, under the Second Empire; a school which goes beyond its mark, and discerns in the State simply an obstacle, an oppressing force. Even Mill is dominated by the opinion that the greater the power of the State, the smaller the freedom. The State however is not the citizen's foe. England is free, and yet the English police have a very great discretionary power and is bound to have it; it is enough if a citizen may make any official answerable in a law-court.

Luckily, another historical law is operating in opposition to the increasing growth of State-power. In proportion as the citizens become riper for self-government, the State is under obligation, nay, is physically obliged, to operate in a more varied way so far as comprehensiveness is concerned, but more moderately so far as method is concerned. If the immature State was a guarantee for individual branches of national activity, the guardianship of the highly-developed State embraces the sum total of national life, but it operates as far as possible, only as a force that spurs on, instructs, clears away impediments. A mature people must therefore demand these things of the State for the assurance of its personal liberty: The most fruitful outcome of the metaphysical fights for freedom during the past century, namely, the truth that the citizen must never be utilized by the State merely as a means, should be recognized as a true fundamental principle. Next: all activity on the part of the government is beneficial which brings forth, furthers, purifies, the individual activity of the citizens; all government activity which suppresses the activity of individuals is evil. For the whole dignity of the State rests ultimately on the personal worth of its citizens, and that State is the most moral, which combines the powers of the citizens for the purpose of accomplishing the greatest number of works beneficial to the society, and yet permits each one, honestly and independently, to pursue his personal development untouched by compulsion on the part of the State and public opinion. Thus we agree with Mill and Laboulaye in the final result: in the desire for the highest possible degree of personal liberty, although we do not share their view of the State as an obstacle to freedom.

And what significance do these reflections on personal liberty possess for us? The presentiment of a great and decisive movement is permeating the world, and imposing on every nation the question, what value it puts on personal freedom, on the personal independence of its citizens. We Germans in particular cannot evade the question; we, whose whole future rests, not on the established power of all our States, but on the personal thoroughness of our people. The historical facts are dominant, that only a nation which is imbued with a strong sense of personal freedom can win and keep political freedom, and that the well-being or real personal freedom is only possible under the protection of political freedom, since despotism, in whatever shape it may appear, is able to give rein only to the lower passions, to commerce, and commonplace ambition.

The most precious and especial possession of our nation, which will yet constitute the German State a new phenomenon in political history, is the Germans' invincible love of personal freedom. Many will smile at this, and put the bitter question: Where are the fruits of this love? And indeed we redden as we confront that stately line of legislative measures which the Anglo-Saxon race has passed for its personal freedom. Mill is far from deifying our nation; as has been said of him with some justice, he inwardly feels his near kinship with the German genius, but he is afraid of the weaknesses of our temperament, he deliberately avoids penetrating too deeply into German literature, and holds to French novels. And the same man confesses that in no country except Germany alone, are people capable of understanding and aspiring to the highest and purest personal liberty, the all-sided evolution of the human spirit!

Our science is the freest on earth; it tolerates no compulsion, either from without or within; it aims at the truth, nothing but the truth, without any prejudice. The opinionativeness of our learned men became a by-word, yet it goes very well together with a frank acknowledgment of an adversary's scientific importance. A free mind, which goes its own way, and not the well-worn way of the schools, and reaches important results, may, with certainty, finally count upon cordial agreement. The most stupid police tutelage did not succeed in breaking down the Germans' ardour for personal idiosyncrasy. It is a conviction, which has taken firm root in the lowest strata of our nation, that in all questions of conscience every man must decide for himself alone. In the tiniest States, which would entirely distort the character of any other people, the ideal of free human development is preached to the youth, namely, the fearless seeking after truth, the evolution of character from within outwards, the harmonious growth of all human gifts. And, as freedom and toleration necessarily go hand in hand, nowhere is the tolerance of different opinions so much at home as with us; we learned it in the hard school of those religious wars, which this nation fought for the salvation of the whole of humanity. Ours, too, is the noblest blessing of inward freedom: beautiful moderation. The most daring thoughts about the highest problems which trouble mankind are uttered by Germans. Human respect for everything human became second nature to the German.

Let nobody believe that the free scientific activity of the Germans is a welcome lightning conductor to the existing State authorities. All intellectual gains, of which a nation can be proud, influence the State-life as one pledge more for its political greatness. We are slowly proceeding from intellectual to political work, as Germany's recent history clearly shows, and we may expect with certainty that the independent courage of German learned men in the search for truth will react on the whole nation. Inclination, and capacity for self-government are abundant among us. Towns like Berlin and Leipzig are at least on level terms with the great English communities in the excellence of their administration, in the common feeling dominating their inhabitants. And how much natural talent and inclination for genuine personal liberty dwell in our Fourth Estate is revealed more clearly every year in the trade unions.

The last and supreme requisite of personal freedom is that the State and public opinion must allow the individual to develop in his individual character, both in thought and in act. What Mill announces to his fellow-countrymen as a new thing, has long been common property in Germany, namely Humboldt's doctrine of the "individuality of capacity and culture," of the "highest and harmonious evolution of all capacities," which thrives by means of freedom and multiplicity of situations, that unique combination of the Platonic sense of beauty and Kant's severity, which marks the zenith of German humanity.

Radicalism and Social Welfare:
British Collectivism

Joseph Chamberlain, "Speech at Hull, August 5, 1885," The Radical Platform (Edinburgh: Morrison & Gibb, 1885), pp. 1–13.

The Great Depression of 1873–95, while far from an unrelieved collapse, reinforced growing criticism of liberal values. Socialist alternatives were gaining adherents in western Europe. Even the conservative Otto von Bismarck opted for social insurance. The ethics of personal initiative were no longer blandly accepted. Reform and social adjustment could be a concession or it would be coerced from the governing classes. In Britain there was a long tradition of radicalism pressing forward within the liberal political framework. Joseph Chamberlain (1836–1914) was among the leaders in the demand for a complete reshaping of Liberal doctrine. Mill and Smiles were insufficient. As Lord Mayor of Birmingham, Chamberlain pioneered "gas and water socialism"—placing basic utilities under municipal ownership—creating a model for other British cities. The radicalism of this wealthy industrialist was a product of his social consciousness and of political necessity. He recognized the potential power of social doctrine and was shrewd enough to realize that the power of socialism as a mass movement rested not on ideas and doctrine but on economic and social maladjustment. Chamberlain believed that it was possible to retain leadership in political life by coming to realistic terms with the times. He proved his point on the local scale as the ascendancy of his family in Birmingham politics, regardless of party affiliation, demonstrates.

To contemporaries Joseph Chamberlain—monocle, orchid in the lapel, and all—was preaching class war and revolution. He could, to be sure, advocate fundamental land reform with impunity, for it was the Conservative not the Liberal party which counted upon the support of the landed interests. Equitable taxation and free education across the board in secular schools were other matters. But for the longevity of William Ewart Gladstone, a democrat but a Liberal of the anticollectivist school idealized by the public for the moral figure he was, Joe Chamberlain might have succeeded. He might have reshaped the Liberal party (with himself as its leader) and delayed the rise of a working-class party. Gladstone's obsession with Irish home rule and his resistance to social change led the radical Joseph Chamberlain to break away to the Conservative party. There he was able to indulge himself in imperialism and economic protectionism. Chamberlain, however, never completely abandoned his early-day radicalism. He advocated a Bismarckian program of social insurance, and he succeeded—with both imperialism and social reform—in retaining a large measure of working-class support for the continued rule of the established social order.

SPEECH AT HULL

Mr. Chamberlain, who was received on rising with loud and prolonged cheering, said:—

Mr. Chairman, Ladies, and Gentlemen,—I thank you very sincerely for the warmth and cordiality of your greeting on the occasion of this my first political visit to Hull, and I venture to hope that the enthusiasm which distinguishes this meeting is characteristic of the spirit of Liberals throughout this and the neighbouring constituencies, and that at the next election you will all do your part to promote the cause and the principles with which this ancient borough has been generally identified.

. . . .

In the Liberal army there must be pioneers to clear the way, and there must be men who watch the rear. Some may always be in advance; others may occasionally lag behind; but the only thing we have a right to demand is that no one shall stand still, and that all shall be willing to follow the main line of Liberal progress to which the whole party are committed. I do not conceal from you my own opinion that the pace will be a little faster in the future than it has been in the past. Everywhere the reforms to which the resolution has made reference are casting their shadows before; everywhere in the country I see a quickening of political life; everywhere there is discussion and hope and expectation. Gentlemen, it will be dangerous to disappoint that hope. It will be impossible to stifle that discussion; and if there are any people who imagine that the enfranchisement of two millions of citizens can have taken place, and that these men intend to make no use of the privilege which has been conferred upon them, they will have a rude awakening. They are not wise men, believe me—they are not the true friends of the institutions of this country, who will not bring impartial minds to the consideration of the new problems that are calling for solution.

I am not altogether surprised, under these circumstances, that there has recently been a demand in some quarters that the leaders of the two great parties should frame a definite programme; that they should discard empty platitudes and generalities, and put a clear issue before the electors. I can say for myself personally that I have done my best in that direction; and although in the speeches I have recently made I have expressly disclaimed any right to speak for the party as a whole, I have been soundly rated for my presumption in daring to speak at all, and I have been solemnly excommunicated by some of the great authorities who claim a monopoly of the orthodox Liberal faith and doctrine. Gentlemen, I am not discouraged, I am not repentant. I am told that if I pursue this course I shall break up the party, and that I shall altogether destroy any chance which I might otherwise have had of office. I do not believe it. But if it were true, I say that I care little for party, and nothing at all for office, except so far as these things may be made instrumental in promoting the objects which I publicly avowed when I first entered Parliament, and which I will prosecute as long as I remain in public life. The Liberal party has always seemed to me the great agency of progress and reform, and by the changes which have recently taken place it has secured a vantage ground which I myself had hardly dared to anticipate. I had looked forward with hope to the future, but I had not supposed in my time so great a change could have been successfully effected.

But now that my wildest expectations have been surpassed, I am not willing to be silent as to the uses to which, I believe, the people ought to put the new power and the privileges which have been conferred upon them. I have always had a deep conviction that when the people came to govern themselves, and when the clamour of vested interests and class privileges was overborne by the powerful voice of the whole nation, that then the social evils which disgrace our civilisation, and the wrongs which have cried vainly for redress, would at last find a hearing and a remedy. And if that be not so, it will be no longer statesmen or Governments that you will have to blame. It will not be the fault of parties or of individuals— it will be the apathy or the ignorance, the indifference or the folly, of the people themselves, which alone can hinder their progress and their prosperity.

One of the speakers has said, and said truly, that this is a critical time— it is the turning-point in our political history, and if the people are content with the old formulae, and with the watchwords which satisfied a limited electorate, then, I think, some of us might have been better employed than we were when we joined the agitation of last autumn, and the enfranchisement of two millions of men will have been a barren and an unprofitable business. We shall have perfected the machinery, but we shall have done nothing at all to improve the manufacture.

I do not want you to think that I suggest to you that legislation can accomplish all that we desire, and, above all, I would not lead you into wild and revolutionary projects which would upset unnecessarily the existing order of things. But, on the other hand, I want you not to accept as final or as perfect, arrangements under which hundreds of thousands, nay millions, of your fellow-countrymen are subjected to untold privations and misery, with the evidence all around them of accumulated wealth and unbounded luxury. The extremes of wealth and of poverty are alike the sources of great temptation. I believe that the great evil with which we have to deal is the excessive inequality in the distribution of riches. Ignorance, intemperance, immorality, and disease—these things are all inter-dependent and closely connected; and although they are often the cause of poverty they are still more frequently the consequence of destitution; and if we can do anything to raise the whole condition of the poor in this country, to elevate the masses of the people, and give them means of enjoyment and recreation, to afford to them opportunities of improvement, we should do more for the prosperity, aye, and for the morality of this country than anything we can do by laws, however stringent, for the prevention of excess or the punishment of crime.

I want you to make this the first object in the Liberal programme for the reformed Parliament. It is not our duty, it is not our wish, to pull down and abase the rich, although I do not think that the excessive aggregation of wealth in a few hands is any advantage to anybody. But our object is to elevate the poor, to raise the general condition of the people.

The other day I was present at a meeting when a labourer was called upon suddenly to speak. He got up and in his rude dialect, without any rhetorical flourish, said something to this effect—he said, 'Neighbours and friends, you have known me for forty years. I have lived among you and worked among you. I am not a drunkard. I am a steady man. I am an industrious man. I am not a spending man. I have worked and laboured for forty years. It has been a weary task, and I ain't any forwarder now than I was when I begun! What is the reason of that? What is the remedy?"

Gentlemen, believe me, the question of the poor labourer cannot be put aside. Our ideal, I think, should be that in this rich country, where everything seems to be in profusion, an honest, a decent, and an industrious man should be able to earn a livelihood for himself and his family, should have access to some means of self-improvement and enjoyment, and should be able to lay aside something for sickness and old age. It that unreasonable? Is it impossible? It is a condition of things which already exists under the British rule in certain communities, and in certain favoured districts of the country. It exists in the Channel Islands, under a different system of legislation to that from which we suffer. It exists in England on the estates of Lord Tollemache, and of some other great and generous landlords, and in villages scattered here and there throughout the country. Why should it be impossible for modern statesmanship to secure for the whole of the United Kingdom the advantages which, by a different system of law and custom, the Channel Islands have been able to secure for their population, and which certain generous and wise landlords have been able to provide for the benefit of those who are dependent upon them?

Let us consider what are the practical means by which we can accomplish such an object. I am not a Communist, although some people will have it that I am. Considering the difference in the character and the capacity of men, I do not believe that there can ever be an absolute equality of conditions, and I think that nothing would be more undesirable than that we should remove the stimulous to industry and thrift and exertion which is afforded by the security given to every man in the enjoyment of the fruits of his own individual exertions. I am opposed to confiscation in every shape or form, because I believe that it would destroy that security and lessen that stimulus. But, on the other hand, I am in favour of accompanying the protection which is afforded to property with a large and stringent interpretation of the obligations of property. It seems to me that there are three main directions in which we may seek for help in the task which I think we ought to set to ourselves.

In the first place, I look for great results from the development of local government amongst us. The experience of the great towns is very encouraging in this respect. By their wise and liberal use of the powers entrusted to them they have in the majority of cases protected the health of the community; they have provided means of recreation and enjoyment and instruction, and they have done a great deal to equalize social advantages, and to secure for all the members of the community the enjoyments which, without their aid and assistance, would have been monopolized by the rich alone.

You have in connection with the great municipal corporations, hospitals, schools, museums, free libraries, art galleries, baths, parks. All these things which a generation ago could only have been obtained by the well-to-do are now, in many large towns, placed at the service of every citizen by the action of the municipalities. I desire that this opportunity should be afforded to the whole country, and I think that, having regard to what has been done in the past, we may show great confidence in the work of popular representative bodies, and be contented to extend their functions and increase their powers and authority.

Closely connected with this subject there is another question which I think of urgent importance. I have spoken of education. I think the time has come when education ought to be free. I have always held that the exaction of fees in our primary schools was unjust and uneconomical, and prejudicial to the best interests of eduction. It is a system which long ago has been abolished in the United States. It has recently disappeared in France; it does not exist in the majority of Continental countries, or in the majority of the self-governing colonies of the British Empire; and I hope that working men will insist that in this country also the system shall cease, which is only defended in deference to false and pedantic notions of political economy, and to the supposed interest of denominational schools. Just consider for a moment the objections to this system. Look, in the first place, at the heavy burdens which it inflicts on the teachers. Their time is too valuable to be taken up in the collection of pence and in the preparation of the voluminous returns which the present system demands. Then it tends to irregularity of attendance. Poor people who cannot find the pence at the beginning of the week, keep their children away until, perhaps, they are forced to send them under the pressure of the compulsory law, and in that way what ought to be a boon, and what ought to be recognised as such by the whole population, becomes an irritating and exacting obligation. I believe that nothing has done more to tend to the unpopularity of our educational system than the exaction of these miserable fees. Then it is uneconomical, because the cost of collection is in excessive proportion to the amount collected; and it is unjust, because it lays upon the shoulders of the poor man a burden which is proportioned, not to his means, but to his necessities and his wants. Well, what is to be said in its favour? If you have paid any attention to the subject, you will find that the chief argument is that it is necessary in order to secure the independence of the parents. There are two answers which strike one at once to such an argument. In the first place, the fees only pay for one-fourth of the education—the independence of the parents has been three-fourths destroyed already.

Is it worth while to protect this small fraction at the cost of the efficiency of the schools themselves? But, I think, there is a better answer than that. Why should working men feel themselves degraded, or their independence gone, if they send their children to free schools, to which every one contributes his share, either through the local rates or through the imperial taxation, any more than he does when he uses the free libraries, which I wish you had in Hull, or the free roads or the free bridges, or any other of the benefits of civilisation, which are provided by the whole community at the cost of every member of the community? I do not attach much importance to these arguments. I think little of the arguments, and I think still less of them because of the quarter from whence they come. Who are the people who are so anxious for the independence of the working classes? The nobility, the gentry, the professors, the editors of newspapers—every one who has owed more or less to free education, by scholarships, or other endowments, in connection with our public schools or universities, and to the cost of which they have not contributed a single farthing. Let them look at home; let them take care of their own independence before they look after yours. I hope that one of the first acts of the new Parliament will be to see that this anomaly shall cease, and that education, suited to the capacity of every child, which is the indispensable instrument for any progress in life, shall be conferred on all, for the benefit of all at the cost of all.

In the second place, we have to consider the question of taxation. Now I have been criticised a good deal for saying that the rich pay too little and the poor pay too much. Well, I have given the matter further and careful consideration, and I maintain the statement. On the occasion of previous speeches I have endeavoured to compare the proportion of taxation paid by families in the different classes, and I admit that that may fairly be objected to, because the condition of families vary so much that, unless you take them over a large area, you might make a mistake. I will take, however, a few statistics bearing upon the whole of the country and upon the different classes of the poulation. I take for my purpose the year 1883–84, because that was a year of normal expenditure, although it included a grant of £1,000,000 for the Afghan War, and very large naval and military expenditure. In that year the revenue was £87,200,000. From that I deduct £21,800,000, as being the product of the Post Office and telegraph service, and also some other sources of taxation, which it is impossible to distribute between different classes. Well, that leaves £65,400,000 as the sum with which we have to deal. Now I have assumed that the upper and middle classes pay the whole of the assessed taxes, the whole of the land tax, the whole of the income tax, the whole of the death duties, the whole of the wine duties, the whole of the game licences, and some other small taxes. I have assumed that they pay one-third of the duties on spirits, beer, and tobacco, and three-fifths of the duty upon tea and coffee. I think you will agree with me that I have made a very liberal estimate of what the upper and middle classes pay. In the first place, I believe I ought to have excluded the land tax. It is not a tax in the proper sense of the word, but it is a State rent, and a very inadequate one. Then I do not believe that the consumption by the upper and middle classes of dutiable articles is anything like so great as I have taken it at, and I suppose that working men occasionally receive a legacy, although I am afraid not so often as I could wish. But still, taking the calculation upon the basis I have stated, I find that the upper and middle classes pay £38,200,000 on an income which has been reckoned by Professor Leoni Levi at £750,000,000. That is, upon the whole of this amount they pay a little more than 5 per cent. The working classes pay £27,200,000 upon an income estimated by the same authority at £520,000,000, so that they also pay a little over 5 per cent. But that does not exhaust the considerations you have to take into account. All political economists are agreed that the true principle of taxation is equality of sacrifice, and it is perfectly absurd to talk of 'equality of sacrifice' when a great duke with £300,000 or £400,000 a year, or a capitalist with £10,000 a year, pays in the same proportion as a working man with twenty shillings a week. You must deduct, at least, from the incomes of these working classes what is absolutely necessary for existence. Mr. Giffen, the most eminent of living statisticians, has calculated that £12 a head ought to be deducted on this ground, and if you will make that correction you will get then the net result of the whole matter. Twenty-six and a half millions of working people have between them incomes available for taxation of £203,000,000. Upon that the taxation which they pay amounts to 13½ per cent. On the other hand, nine and a half millions, belonging to the upper and middle classes, have an income available for taxation of £639,000,000, upon which the taxation which they actually pay amounts to 6 per cent, so that, to put the matter in another way, at the present time the working classes are paying upon their available incomes more than double the rate which is paid by the upper and the middle classes. Now, in my opinion, there is only one way in which this injustice can properly be remedied, and that is by some scheme of graduated taxation—of taxation which increases in proportion to the amount of the property taxed. It need not necessarily be a graduated income tax. It might be more convenient to levy it in the shape of a graduated death tax or house tax. I care nothing at all about the method— all I want to bring before you, for your earnest and serious consideration, is the principle of such taxation. I have been told by Mr. Goschen, and by other persons, that in making a proposition of this kind I am flying in the face of the greatest master of modern finance—the late Prime Minister. Well, if so, it is a very singular thing that Mr. Goschen is so ready to quote Mr. Gladstone against me, although he does not pay much attention to his opinion in other matters. But I think that Mr. Goschen is entirely wrong. I am not aware, and I have some authority for what I am saying, that Mr. Gladstone has ever expressed an opinion against the principle of graduated taxation. He has spoken very strongly against what is called 'differential taxation,' which means taxation varied according to the character of the income, but I believe he has never opposed graduated taxation—that is, taxation varied according to the amount of the property taxed. It is a principle which has the high authority of Mr. Pitt, who proposed it in the last century in the House of Commons. It was adopted in the United States of America at the time of the Civil War. It was adopted in France at the time of the first Republic. It was proposed by Prince Bismarck the other day in the German Reichstag, and it is at the present moment in force in some of the Swiss cantons, and in a somewhat varied form in some of the Australian colonies, where land is taxed according to the number of acres held. In my opinion it is the only principle of taxation fair and just to all classes of the community.

Now I will go on to what is the last, but also the most important, of the reforms to which I wish to call your attention, and that is the reform of the land laws. This is a question which lies at the root of the whole matter that we have been discussing. Agriculture is the greatest of all our industries. When it is depressed every employment follows suit, and when work is scant in the counties and the wages are low the agricultural labourers are driven into the towns to compete with you for employment and to reduce the rate of your remuneration. Anything which could bring about a revival of prosperity in agriculture, anything which would increase the production of the land and give better prospects to the agricultural labourer, would do an immense deal towards raising the general condition of the whole country, and would procure a market for our manufacturers for surpassing any that can possibly be expected from foreign countries, and even from our own colonies. The evils of the present land system are apparent to everybody. They are greater than accompany the land system of any other country in the world. Our laws and practice seem to have been designed over a long course of years in order to build up and maintain vast estates, until at the present moment something less than 1000 persons hold one-third of the land of the United Kingdom. In the meantime the rights of property have been so much extended that the rights of the community have almost altogether disappeared, and it is hardly too much to say that the prosperity and the comfort and the liberties of a great proportion of the population have been laid at the feet of a small number of proprietors, who 'neither toil nor spin.' The soil of every country originally belonged to its inhabitants, and if it has been thought expedient to create private ownership in place of common rights, at least that private ownership must be considered as a trust, and subject to the conditions of a trust. Land must be owned so as to give the greatest employment to the largest number of persons and so as to secure the greatest possible return in the produce of the soil. The land was not created—and it must not be used as a mere machine for exacting the highest possible rent from the cultivators of the soil—for the benefit of those who own it. I have not time for anything like an exhaustive treatment of this vast subject. What I should like to do to-night is to give you two illustrations of our present system, and then lay before you, for your consideration, some practical suggestions for reform.

The other day, in company with my friend Mr. Saunders, and by his invitation, I paid a short visit to a beautiful part of the county of Wilts. The county of Wilts at the present time is represented by four Tory members in Parliament, but I shall be surprised if, at the next election, four Radicals do not take their place. There is plenty of reason for some kind of change. In the part that I visited there are thousands of acres of fertile land lying waste, growing only couch grass, because the owner will not let his land at a rent which would induce cultivation—will not give a lease which will give some security of tenure; and as a consequence, the population is diminishing, and the little traders in the villages find their customers departing from them. Everywhere I saw cottages which at one time sheltered industrious families, and which now are closed and have fallen into disrepair. Meantime, the labourers who remain are insufficient for the proper cultivation of the land, and they eke out their miserable wages of 10s. or 12s. a week, and in some cases of only 9s. a week, by the help of allotments, which they rent at three or four times the rate which is paid by the farmers in the immediate neighbourhood. One and all of these men whom I saw told me they could live a happy and comfortable life if they could get a little land at a fair and reasonable rent—only a little of the land which was lying idle to satisfy the caprice of its proprietor. But in the same district I saw other properties well cared for indeed, over which, within the memory of man, the villagers could roam undisturbed, and which are now fenced in and hemetically closed against all intruders. I was told that in some cases the owners, not content with their abundance, have taken from the poor the roadside land which used to be free,—the odd corners where the children used to play. They have stopped up the public footpaths, and exercised with the utmost stringency all the rights which the law affords to them. And as if to make the case complete, I found there that a great endowment which was left for the poor of the parish and the immediate neighbourhood, and which might now be used to promote their happiness and comfort, is, the greater part of it, to be diverted under a scheme of the Charity Commissioners in order to create a school of secondary education for the middle classes in the neighbouring county town. (A voice—'They tried it here.') I hope they failed. They have tried it in big towns, and there, where there is energy, and organization, and influence, and Parliamentary power, they may fail. But they try it in country villages—they have been trying it all over the country,—and again and again, as I declared in my place in the House of Commons, the poor have been robbed of the endowments which were intended for their benefit. I hear sometimes that the agricultural labourers are very stupid and unintelligent; that they will not know what use to make of the vote which has been given to them. I can only say, if I may judge from the Wiltshire labourers I saw the other day, that they are, at all events, aware of the injustice to which they have been subjected, and of the wrongs which have been inflicted upon them; that they are aware of their responsibilities, and will not rest until, with the co-operation of their fellow-labourers in the towns, they have reformed or abolished a system which condemns them to lives of hopeless and unremitting toil, and which refuses to them the opportunities of improvement and advancement.

The other case that I wanted to mention was that of the crofters and cottars of the Highlands of Scotland. These men, many of them, are direct descendants of the clans which formerly owned the land. They had their chieftains, who were the guardians of their rights and property, for whom they fought, whom they served; they shed their blood to preserve their authority and rank and dignity; but in the course of time the idea of guardianship and trusteeship disappeared. The idea of private ownership came up. Rent was asked in lieu of service, and with rent crept in the notion of private property, and now in most cases—in many cases, at all events—the chiefs have disappeared; they have sold the land to which they had no equitable right—they have sold it to strangers, who are now the landlords and landowners of the soil which once belonged to the whole of the people. The crofters and cottars have been rack-rented. They have been evicted from their holdings to make way for sheep farms and deer forests—sometimes under circumstances of the most brutal cruelty and oppression. They have beeen charged rent on their improvements; their pastures on the hillsides have been taken from them; they have been reduced to misery and degradation. I have been in these parts, and I know something of the people of whom I am speaking. I believe a finer race does not exist within the four corners of the United Kingdom. In spite of all their disadvantages, physically they are a splendid race of men, whom any country might be proud to claim amongst its defenders, and in morality they yield to no other part of the population. Well, what is the reason for the treatment to which they have been subjected? It is said the sheep farms and deer forests produce a larger return than the crofters could afford to pay. That may be so; but seeing that a great deal is paid to absentee landlords I do not see that the country benefits much by it. But, in any case, I say the land was not made for rent alone, and that the test of any system is how many families live in happiness and comfort on the soil, and not the amount of money which finds its way into the pockets of the landlords. Tried by this test, the system has failed. The population of the Highlands has diminished and is still diminishing, and the condition of the people is going from bad to worse. It is time that a remedy was found. You know that the Bill which was introduced by the late Government for the purpose of dealing in some sort of fashion with this subject has been dropped by the present Government. They have time for a good deal. They have time to provide for the interests of the landlords of Ireland at the expense of the British tax-payer. They have no time to give to the claims of the Highlanders in Scotland. Well, they have dropped the Bill. I am not certain that it is very much to be regretted. It was the best Bill we could bring in with any chance of its being passed in the present Parliament, but I shall be surprised, if, in the reformed Parliament, this matter is not raised again and subjected to more drastic treatment than could be expected from a limited representation.

Now I come to the practical proposals that I want to submit to you. I am in favour of free trade in land. That includes the registration of title, the cheapening of transfer, the abolition of settlements and entails, and of the custom of primogeniture in cases of intestacy. Upon all that, I think, we are pretty well agreed. It would do something. It would tend no doubt to the dispersion of those great estates. It would bring more landed property into the market, but I do not think it would do much for the labourers of Wiltshire or for the crofters of the Highland of Scotland. We must go further if we want to go to the root of the matter.

Well, what can we do for the farmer? If we want to revive agriculture the farmer must become prosperous. The farmer is a difficult man to serve. He is not in this country, I am afraid, a very wise man. (A voice—'Let him go to America.') I doubt whether he is not wise enough for that. But he re- mains in this country, and he chooses to confide his interests to the land- lords who represent him in Parliament, which is very much like, in the words of a homely proverb, 'setting the cat to guard the cream.' The English farmer pursues a 'will-o'-the-wisp' in the shape of protection, and he excites himself very much about the relief of local taxation. Well, he must be a very foolish person to imagine that the people of this country will ever again submit to the terrors of the 'small loaf,' and he must be a very sanguine man who imagines that any relief of local taxation will make much difference to the local rates. But even if the farmer could get all he desired in those two respects, that would not benefit him one single iota, though it might enable his landlord to extract a higher rent. There is only one thing that can benefit the farmer, and that is a fair rent, fixed by an impartial tri- bunal, with the right of free sale of the goodwill of his undertaking just the same as any other trader. He would be required, of course, to provide a fit and proper person, and his landlord might object if the person provided was not satisfactory in character or means. Subject to that, the farmer should have the same liberty of sale which in enjoyed by other persons. I am told that the farmers do not care about 'fair rent' or 'free sale.' All that I can say is, that so long as that is their position they are not likely to get it. Nobody will impose upon them a benefit that they do not want, and that was only conferred on Irish tenants after many years of bitter and almost savage agitation.

But when we come to the labourers the task is easier. They know what they want, which is the first condition for getting it. They want that facilities shall be afforded to them for having decent cottages and fair allotments at reasonable rents and with security of tenure. Why should they not have it? Who would be injured if they did have it? The produce of the land would be increased, the respectability and character of the labourers would be raised, the happiness of their families would be secured. Who would be injured? For my part, I confess I see no injustice at all in the case of great landlords, many of whom have driven the labourers off their properties, and have pulled down their cottages, partly in order to escape responsibilities in connection with them, partly in order to throw the land into immense farms, and partly for other reasons—I see no objection in such cases as these to compelling these landlords to repair the wrong they have done. I do not see why you should not enforce upon them the duty of providing in every case a sufficient number of decent cottages, with land attached, for all the men who are required for the cultivation of the particular estate. I would leave the supervision of this duty to the local authority, and in order to meet every case which may arise I would give to local authorities power to acquire land on their own behalf and to let it out in allotments for labourers and small farms. I believe that this would meet the cases to which I have called your attention. Where the landlord will not do his duty to the land the local authority would have power to step in and restore it to production. In the case of the Highlands the local authority would be able to acquire pasture land which is absolutely necessary for the livelihood of the crofters. All these things could be done, and only one other condition is absolutely necessary, and that is that when the local authority acquires land for this or any other public purpose, it should not be called upon to pay an extravagant or unnatural price; that it should be able to obtain it at the fair market value—at the value which the willing purchaser would pay to the willing seller, without any addition for compulsory sale. I believe that if these additional powers were conferred upon local authorities, if these additional obligations were enforced upon landlords, that, at all events, so far as the labourers are concerned, the land difficulty will disappear. Then, I would go a step further, and I would revise the taxation upon land. I would equalize the death-duties, as the Government recently proposed to do. To that extent, at all events, I would invade the sanctity of landed property, and in addition I would tax all unoccupied and sporting land at its full value. I believe that that would put an end to much of the abuse of which we now complain. And, lastly, gentlement, I would insist upon the restitution of the property of the community where it has been wrongfully appropriated. I would insist upon the restitution of the endowments which have been diverted to improper uses, of enclosures which have been illegally made, of rights which have been improperly disregarded and ignored. I cannot allow that there should be a prescription for such arbitrary acts as these, or why a man should be able to allege a long enjoyment of the profits of wrongdoing as a reason for immunity and a bar to all redress on the part of the people who have suffered. I do not pretend that this constitutes an exhaustive programme. It is perhaps enough for tonight. If objection is taken to it in any quarter, I ask my opponents, what are their proposals? If they have an alternative which is more effective than the suggestions I have made, I have no pride in the matter, and I will gladly accept it; but something must be done. We have been suffering from a depression in trade unexampled in its intensity and duration. The privations which it has imposed have been borne with resignation and courage by those upon whose shoulders they have most heavily fallen, but these men have a right to demand that the depression shall not be intensified or fostered by bad legislation, and that there shall be no obstacle or hindrance to the fullest development of the resources of the country. The sanctity of private property is no doubt, an important principle, but the public good is a greater and higher object than any private interest, and the comfort and the happiness of the people and the prosperity of the country must not be sacrificed to the exaggerated claim of a privileged class who are now the exclusive possessors of the great gift of the Almighty to the human race.

The Cultural Spirit of the Super-State: Pan-Slavism

Fyodor Dostoevsky, Introduction to "Pushkin: a Speech Delivered on 8th June 1880 at the Meeting of the Society of Lovers of Russian Literature," Pages from the Journal of an Author, trans. S. Koteliansky and J. Middleton Murray (Edinburgh: T. and A. Constable, s.d.), pp. 33–46.

Nationalist ideology presumed superiority. Thought soared over artificial frontiers to embrace a wider, mystical, racial communion of fellow souls. This development of "pan-" nationalism was pronounced in areas having an ill-defined national history. Thus Pan-Germanism, solemnly organized into committees and chapters in 1891, proved a dangerous, emotional way of flexing new-found muscles. Pan-Slavism, whatever its vague antecedents, can be traced directly from the Slav Congress held in Prague in June 1848 under the leadership of František Palacký. The Slav Congress proposed that the Habsburg Empire endorse semi-independent, federated slavic states and thus save itself from German, Italian, and Hungarian nationalist pressure. Nicholas Danilevsky argued that all Slavs were brothers in *Russia and Europe* (1865–67) and that Russia, as the great center of the Slavic peoples, would lead in their emancipation and regeneration.

Quite apart from the matter of the reality of Slavic brotherhood, this was sheer Russian imperialism. Pan-Slavism gave Russian nationalism a mystic character and mission. One who believed in the unique soul and mission of Russia was the great novelist, Fyodor Dostoevsky (1821–81). He had vision and insight. No man penetrated more deeply into the tortured mind of the revolutionary, and thus he is still not quite respectable in many circles of the Soviet Union. Dostoevsky's speech on Pushkin in 1880 was "an event," even if he publicly denied it. His own introduction speaks for itself.

PUSHKIN

A Word of Explanation Concerning the Speech on Pushkin Published Below

My speech upon Pushkin and his significance, printed below, which forms the chief matter of this number of *The Journal of an Author* (the only number published in 1880), was delivered on the 8th of June of this year in the presence of a numerous audience at the grand meeting of the Society of Lovers of Russian Literature, and made a considerable impression. Ivan Sergueyevich Aksakov, who there said of himself that all people considered him the leader of the Slavophiles, declared from the chair that my speech was 'an event.' I do not refer to this now to boast, but to say just this: if my speech is an event, then it is an event from one and only one point of view, which I will proceed to expound. That is the reason of this foreword. In my speech I endeavoured to emphasise only these four aspects of the value of Pushkin to Russia.

1. Pushkin with his profound insight, his genius, and his purely Russian heart, was the first to detect and exhibit the chief symptom of the sickness of our intellectual society, uprooted from the soil and raised above the people. He exhibited and set in relief before us our negative type, the disturbed and unsatisfied man, who can believe neither in his own country nor in its powers, who finally denies Russia and himself (that is, his own society, his own intellectual stratum, raised from our native soil), who does not want to work with others, and who suffers sincerely. Aleko and Onyegin were the fathers of a host of their similars in our literature. After them came the Pechorins, Tchichikovs, Rudins, and Lavrezkys, Bolkonskys (in Tolstoi's *War and Peace*) and many others who by the mere fact of their appearance bore witness to the truth of the idea originally enunciated by Pushkin. All honour and glory to him, to his mighty mind and genius, who discovered the most sore disease of the society which had grown up amongst us after Peter's great reform. To his skilful diagnosis we owe our knowledge and realisation of our disease, and it was he who first gave us consolation, for he gave us also the great hope that the disease is not mortal, but that Russian society could be cured, regenerated, and revived if it were bathed in the truth of the people, because

2. He was the first—the first indeed: none was before him—to give us artistic types of Russian moral beauty, which had sprung directly out of the Russian soul, which had its home in the truth of the people, in our very soil—these types did Pushkin trace out. To which bear witness Tatiana, a perfectly Russian woman, who guarded herself from the monstrous lie; historical types, for instance the Monk and others in *Boris Godunov*; realistic types, as in *The Captain's Daughter*, and many other figures which appear in his poems, his stories, his memories, and even in his account of the riot at Pougachov. But what must be chiefly emphasised is that all these types of the positive beauty of the Russian and the Russian soul are wholly drawn from the spirit of the people. Now the whole truth must be said: not in our present civilsation, not in the so-called European culture (which, by the way, never existed with us), not in the monstrosities of European ideas and forms only outwardly assimilated, did Pushkin discover this beauty, but he found it in the *spirit of the people alone.* Thus, I repeat, having revealed the disease, he gave us also a great hope. 'Believe in the spirit of the people, expect salvation from it alone, and you will be saved.' It is impossible not to come to this conclusion, when one has really gone deep into Pushkin.

3. The third aspect of Pushkin's significance which I wish to emphasise, is that most peculiar and characteristic trait of his artistic genius, one never met before—his capacity for universal sympathy, and for the most complete reincarnation in the genius of other nations, a reincarnation almost perfect. I said in my 'Speech' that there had been mighty world-geniuses in Europe: a Shakespeare, a Cervantes, a Schiller, but in none of them do we find this capacity—save in Pushkin alone. Not the sympathy only is

here in point, but the astonishing completeness of the reincarnation. This capacity of course I could not help emphasising as the most characteristic peculiarity of his genius, which belongs to him alone of all the artists of the world, by which he differs from them all. I did not say it to belittle European geniuses so great as Shakespeare and Schiller: only a fool could draw a conclusion so foolish from my words. The universal comprehensibility and unfathomable depth of the types of Aryan man created by Shakespeare meet with no scepticism in me. And had Shakespeare created Othello really a Venetian Moor, and not an Englishman, he would only have added a halo of local, national peculiarity to his creation. But the universal significance of the type would have been the same, for in an Italian too he would have expressed what he wanted to say with the same power. I repeat, I did not want to diminish from the universal significance of a Shakespeare and a Schiller when I pointed out Pushkin's wonderful faculty for reincarnating himself in the genius of foreign nations: I only wanted to point out the great and prophetical indication for us in this faculty and its perfection, because

4. This faculty is a completely Russian faculty, a national faculty. Pushkin only shares it with the whole Russian people; but as a perfect artist, he most perfectly expresses this faculty, in his sphere at least, in the sphere of his art. Our people does truly contain within its soul this tendency to universal sympathy and reconciliation; it has already given voice to it more than once in the two centuries since Peter's reforms. As I pointed out this capacity of our people I could not help showing that in this very fact is the great consolation of our future, our great, perhaps our greatest, hope, shining for us ahead. Above all, I showed that our aspiration after Europe, in spite of all its infatuations and extremes, was not only right and necessary in its *basis*, but also popular; it fully coincided with the aspirations of the national spirit itself, and was without doubt ultimately a higher purpose also. In my very short speech I naturally could not develop my idea fully, but what I said at least seems to me clear. And people should not be indignant with me for saying: 'Perhaps our poor country will at the end say the new word to the world.' It is ridiculous to assert that we must complete our economic, scientific, and social development, before we can dream of saying 'new words' to such perfect organisms as the states of Europe. Indeed, I emphasise it in my 'Speech,' that I make no attempt to compare Russia with the western nations in the matter of economic or scientific renown. I say only that the Russian soul, the genius of the Russian people, is perhaps among all nations the most capable of upholding the ideal of a universal union of mankind, of brotherly love, of the calm conception which forgives contrasts, allows for and excuses the unlike, and softens all contradictions. This is not an economical, but a *moral* trait; and can any one deny that it is present in the Russian people? Can any one say that the Russian nation is only an inert mass, doomed to serve, only economically, the prosperity and development of the European *intelligentsia* which has lifted itself above the people; that the mass of the people in itself contains only a

dead inertia, from which nothing can be expected, nor any hopes be formed? Alas, many people assert this, but I dared to proclaim something different. I repeat, I naturally could not prove 'this fancy of mine,' as I myself called it, circumstantially and fully; neither could I help pointing it out. To assert that our poor untidy country cannot harbour such lofty aspirations until it has become economically and socially the equal of the West, is simply absurd. In their fundamental substance at least the moral treasures of the spirit do not depend upon economical power. Our poor untidy land, save for its upper classes, is as one single man. The eighty millions of her population represent a spiritual union whose like cannot be found anywhere in Europe, and because of this alone, it is impossible to say that the land is untidy, it is strictly impossible to say even that it is poor. On the other hand, in Europe—this Europe where so many treasures have been amassed—the whole social foundation of every European nation is undermined, and perhaps will crumble away to-morrow, leaving no trace behind, and in its place will arise something radically new and utterly unlike that which was before. And all the treasures which Europe has amassed will not save her from her fall, for 'in the twinkling of an eye all riches too will be destroyed.' To this social order, infected and rotten indeed, our people is being pointed as to an ideal to which they must aspire, and only when they have reached it, should they dare to whisper their word to Europe. But we assert that it is possible to contain and cherish the power of a loving spirit of universal union even in our present economic poverty, and in poverty still greater than this. It can be preserved and cherished even in such poverty as there was after the Tartar invasion, or after the disasters of the 'Troublous Age' when Russia was saved solely by her national spirit of unity. Finally, if it is indeed required, in order to love mankind and preserve within ourselves a soul for universal unity; in order to have within ourselves the capacity not to hate foreign nations because they are not like us; in order to have the desire not to let our national feeling grow so strong that we should aim at getting everything and the other nations be only so many lemons to be squeezed—there are nations of this spirit in Europe!—if to obtain all this, it is necessary, I repeat, that we should first become a rich nation and adapt the European social order to ourselves, then must we still slavishly imitate that European order which may crumble to pieces in Europe to-morrow? Will the Russian organism even now not be suffered to develop nationally by its own organic strength, but must it necessarily lose its individuality in a servile imitation of Europe? What is then to be done with the Russian organism? Do these gentlemen understand what an organism is? And they still talk of natural sciences. 'The people will not suffer that,' said a friend of mine on an occasion two years ago to a vehement Westernist. 'Then the people should be destroyed!' was the quiet and majestic answer. And he was not a person of no importance, but one of the leaders of our intellectuals. The story is true.

In these four aspects I showed Pushkin's significance for us, and my

'Speech' made an impression. It did not make an impression by its merits—
I emphasise this—nor by any talent in its exposition (wherein I agree with
all my opponents, and do not boast), but by its sincerity, and I will even
say by some irresistible power in the facts displayed notwithstanding its
brevity and incompleteness. But wherein lay 'the event,' as Ivan Sergueyevich Aksakov put it? In that the Slavophiles, or the Russian party so-called
—we have a Russian party!—made an immense, and perhaps final step towards reconciliation with the Westernists, for the Slavophiles fully recognised the validity of the Westernist aspiration after Europe, the validity
even of their most extreme enthusiasms ad conclusions, and explained this
validity by our purely Russian and national aspiration, which coincides
with the national spirit itself. They explained the enthusiasms by historical
necessity, by historical destiny, so that in the whole sum-total (if that sum-
total is ever reckoned) it will appear that the Westernists have served the
Russian land and spirit as much as all those purely Russian men who have
sincerely loved their native land and hitherto perhaps too jealously guarded
her from all the infatuations of 'Russian foreigners.' It was finally declared
that all the friction between the two parties and all their unpleasant quarrels
had been due to a misunderstanding. This perhaps might have been an
event, for the representatives of the Slavophiles present fully agreed with
the conclusions of my speech when it was ended. And I declare now—as I
declared in my 'Speech' also—that the honour of this new step (for even a
sincere desire for reconciliation is an honour), that the merit of this new
word, if you will, belongs not to me alone, but to the whole Slavophile
movement, to the whole spirit and tendency of our 'party,' that this was
always clear to those who impartially examined the movement, and that
the idea which I expressed had more than once been, if not expressed, at
least indicated by the Slavophiles. My part was only to seize the opportune
moment. Now this is the conclusion: if the Western is to accept our reasoning and agree with it, then of course all the misunderstandings between
both parties will be removed, and the Westernists and the Slavophiles will
have nothing to quarrel about, since, as Ivan Sergueyevich put it, 'from this
day forward everything has been cleared up.' Naturally, from this point of
view my 'Speech' would have been an event. But, alas! the word 'event'
was uttered in a moment of sincere enthusiasm by one side, but whether it
will be accepted by the other side and not remain merely an ideal—that is
another question. Together with the Slavophiles who embraced me and
shook me by the hand on the platform as soon as I had finished my speech,
there came up to me Westernists also, the leading representatives of the
movement who occupy the principal rôles in it, above all at the present
time. They pressed my hand with the same sincere and fervent enthusiasm
as the Slavophiles, spoke of my speech as the work of genius, and repeated
the word over and over again. But I am afraid, genuinely afraid, that this
word was pronounced in the first rush of enthusiasm. Oh, I am not afraid
that they will recant their opinion that my speech was the work of genius.

I myself know that it was not, I was not at all deceived by the praise, so that from my whole heart I shall forgive them their disappointment in my genius. But it may happen that the Westernists, upon reflections, will say— mark well that I am not writing of those who pressed by hand, but of the Westernists in general—'Ah,' they will perhaps say (you hear; no more 'perhaps')—'Ah, you've agreed at last, after so much dispute and discussion, that our aspiration after Europe was justified and normal, you have acknowledged that there was truth on our side as well, and you have lowered your flag. Well, we accept your acknowledgment good-heartedly, and hasten to assure you that it is not at all bad on your part. At least it shows a certain intelligence in you, which indeed we never denied, with the exception perhaps of our stupidest members, from whom we have neither the will nor the power to be responsible, but . . .' Here you see another 'but' appears, and it must be explained immediately. 'The point is that your thesis and conclusion that in our enthusiasms we, as it were, coincided with the national spirit and were mysteriously guided by it—that proposition is still more than doubtful to us, and so an agreement between us once more becomes impossible. Please understand that we were guided by Europe, by her science, and by Peter's reforms, but not by the spirit of the people at all, for we neither met nor scented this spirit on our way: on the contrary, we left it behind and ran away from it as soon as we could. From the very outset we went our way independently, and did not in the least follow some instinct or other which is leading the Russian people to universal sympathy and the unification of mankind—to all that you have just talked so much about. In the Russian people, for the time has come to speak perfectly frankly, we see, as before, only an inert mass, from which we have nothing to learn, which, on the contrary, hinders Russia's development towards something better, and must be wholly recreated and remade—if it is impossible organically, then mechanically at least—by simply making them obey us once for all. And to obtain this obedience we must adopt the social order just as it is in European countries, which we were discussing just now. Strictly speaking, our nation is poor and untidy, as it always has been, and can have neither individuality nor ideal. The whole history of our people is absurd, from which you have deduced the devil knows what, while we alone have looked at it soberly. It is necessary that a people like ours should have no history, and that what it has in the shape of a history should be utterly forgotten by it in disgust. Only an intellectual society must have a history, and this society the people must serve, and only serve, with its labour and powers.

'Don't worry and don't shout! We don't want to enslave our people when we talk of making it obey, of course not. Please don't rush to such conclusions. We are humane, we are Europeans, you know that as well as we. On the contrary, we intend to develop our people gradually, in due order, and to crown our edifice by raising up the people to ourselves and by remaking its nationality into something different which will appear when its development is complete. We will lay the foundations of education and begin whence we ourselves started, with the renunciation of all the past, and with the damnation to which the people must itself deliver up its past. The moment we have taught one of the people to read and write, we shall immeditely make him scent the delights of Europe, we will seduce him with Europe, by the refinement of European life, of European customs, clothes, drinks, dances—in a word, we will make him ashamed of his bast shoes and his kvass, ashamed of his old songs, and though there are many excellent, musical songs among them, we will make him sing vaudeville, no matter how furious you may be. In brief, for the good purpose, by any and every means, we will first work on the weak springs of his character, just as it has been in our case, and then the people will be ours. He will be ashamed of his past and will curse it. He who curses his past—is ours!—that is our formula. We will apply it to the full when we begin to raise up the people to ourselves. And if the people prove itself incapable of enlightenment, then "remove the people." For then it will be clearly shown that our people is only a worthless and barbarous horde, only to be made to obey. For what else is there to be done? Truth exists in the intellectuals and in Europe alone, and therefore though you have eighty million people—you seem to boast of it—all these millions must first serve this European truth, since there is not and cannot be another truth. You won't frighten us with your millions. That is our permanent conclusion, though you have it now in its nakedness. We abide by it. We cannot accept your conclusions and talk together, for instance, about such a strange thing as the *Pravoslavié* [the idea of the Orthodox Faith] and its so-called particular significance. We hope at least that you will not expect it of us, above all at a time when the last word of Europe and European Science is an enlightened and humane atheism, and we can but follow Europe.

'Therefore—well—we agree to accept with certain limitations that half of your speech in which you pay us compliments: yes, we will do you this kindness. As for the other half which refers to you and those "principles" of yours, please forgive us, but we cannot accept it.'

Such is the sad conclusion possible. I repeat, not only would I not venture to put this conclusion into the mouths of the Westernists who pressed my hand, but not even into the mouths of a very great number of the most enlightened among them, Russian workers and perfect Russians, and, in spite of their theories, respectable and esteemed Russian citizens. But the mass, the great mass of those who have been uprooted, the outcasts, your Westernists, the average, the men in the street, through which the ideal is being dragged—all these rank and file of 'the tendency,' as many as the sand of the sea, will say something of the kind, perhaps have already said it. (Concerning religion, for instance, one paper has already said, wtih its peculiar wit, that the aim of the Slavophiles is to rebaptize all Europe into orthodoxy.) But let us throw off gloomy thoughts and place our hope in the leaders of Europeanism. If they will accept only one half of our conclusions and our hopes in them, then honour and glory to them, and we shall meet them with full hearts. If they accept only one half, and acknowledge the independence and the individuality of the Russian spirit, the justification of its being, and its humane tendency to universal unity, even then there will be nothing left to quarrel about, at least nothing of fundamental importance. Then my 'Speech' would really serve for the foundation of a new event—not the 'Speech' itself, I repeat for the last time, (it is not worthy of such a name), but the solemn celebration of the mighty Pushkin, which was the occasion of our union—a union now of all sincere and enlightened Russians for the great purpose of the future.

Racialism and Nationalism: A German Definition

Heinrich von Treitschke, "Races, Tribes, and Nations," Politics, trans. Blanche Dugdale and Torben de Bille (London: Constable and Co. Ltd., 1916), Vol. I, pp. 270–302.

Heinrich Gotthard von Treitschke (1834–96) has already been considered as the voice of conforming German liberalism—the *désenchanté* of 1848 who had come to terms with what Henry James called "the bitch Goddess Success." Treitschke was a success. His crowning work was the *History of Germany in the Nineteenth Century*, which made his fame when the first volume appeared in 1879. The argument is often advanced that the Treitschke was hysterically militant because he, the son of a general, was physically disqualified for military service. Certainly the songwriters on the home front almost invariably have a more aggressive attitude than the soldiers in the front lines. Treitschke had already written his *Vaterländische Gedichte* in 1857 and now could beat the nationalist drum from his university chair in Berlin.

Treitschke cast his eye on Germany's place in the world and on what that place should be. Needless to say, it was not large enough. Germany was the dominant power in Europe; Europe dominated most of the world; therefore it followed that Germany must seize her rightful position. This was dangerous doctrine resting upon a racial rationale for nationalism. Germany was the true Aryan state, the master nation. From the pen of this liberal— Treitschke always counted himself one—flowed language worthy of Houston Stewart Chamberlain or Edouard Drumont. But then nationalism and its concomitant imperialism everywhere assumed this foggy character. The will of Cecil Rhodes is not dissimilar, nor the messianic Pan-Slavism of Dostoevsky.

VIII

RACES, TRIBES, AND NATIONS

WE TURN NOW from the simplest forms of State-membership, the family and the clan, to consider nationalities, races, and tribes. I have made use of the word "nationality" because in science it is impossible to form clear conceptions without employing such foreign terms. The strength of the German language shows itself precisely in its ability to assimilate so many of them. We will not allow ourselves to be abused for this pride of our nation in its costmopolitanism in the best sense of the word, which gives us power to take for ourselves in the undying parts of the speech of other peoples. Any one who is capable of thinking historically will realize how completely such words as *Majestät* and *gravitätisch* have become part of the German language. The word *gravitätisch* has been so skilfully assimilated that already the very spirit of the seventeeenth century seems to breathe through its syllables. Our speech, as the poet says, has not only passed through the oak forests of primeval Germany, but also through the palaces of princes, and yet it remains to-day what it always was. It has absorbed certain elements, and again rejected others, nor should we always accept the treasures of foreign speech which it has drawn unto itself. The word "nation" will be used by preference in the political sense. The meaning attached to it in ordinary speech is in any case extremely capricious; if we wish to express clearly that we desire to convey the idea of a common blood, we must use the expression "nationality." Everybody knows what is meant by "the right of nationality," and it is in this sense that we shall use the term.

It is quite clear that difference of descent was not brought about by the State, but existed before it. But it is no less clear that the State must try to penetrate with the same speech and culture all those whom it unites. We cannot repeat too often that political science requires nowadays an unprejudiced historical judgment before all else. It must finally tear itself free from the abstractions of Natural Right and the resultant revolutionary political doctrines, which sought after principles rather than forces in the current of historical life. The dominating idea was always that fixed written principles ruled historical existence, and that living facts had to shape themselves by them. Such hollow abstractions must be finally destroyed.

The one which chiefly occupies the minds of the present day is the so-called principle of nationality. The reason is not difficult to grasp. We are still under the influence of the reaction against the Napoleonic world-empire. It was perfectly natural that this attempt should arouse the consciousness of nationality to an energy which had never been felt before. Both Italy and Germany offered the imposing spectacle of two great peoples rising to the attainment of a political unity. We see the same forces working where they are in opposition to ourselves. The law of historical ingratitude still holds good; often, indeed, has it operated in Germany! We displayed it ourselves towards the Romans, and now the sub-German peoples, who are our debtors for the whole of their civilization, are showing it towards us. In the sixteenth century the Scandinavian nations began to work for their independence; now we see the same process going on in the south-east. All the races in Austria have to thank us Germans for their culture, yet now we see the weapons, with which we have ourselves supplied them, turned against the power of Germany.

Thus our century is filled with national antagonisms, and it is not surprising therefore that there should have been talk of setting up a principle of nationality. If we keep our vision clear from the confusions of Napoleonic phraseology, we see that there are two strong forces working in history; firstly, the tendency of every State to amalgamate its population in speech and manners into one single mould, and secondly, the impulse of every vigorous nationality to construct a State of its own. It is obvious that we have here two divergent forces, which generally oppose and struggle against each other. We have next to discover what settlement they arrive at. That the conceptions of Nation and State should merge into one is the tendency of all great nations, but history shows us how far this is from being actually put into practice. The superiority of Western culture arises from the fact that Western Europe has larger compact ethnological masses, while the East is the classic soil for the fragments of nations. This alone would be enough to make it very difficult for the Oriental State to attain to any inward unity. It must content itself with external administration and the exaction by the ruling race of tribute and submission. Russia and Austria are in this respect countries of transition between East and West; the ethnographical conditions in these empires are already more Oriental than European, and hence comes the exotic character of the whole life of the State.

Thus we see two great forces which may either work in harmony or in discord with one another. Furthermore, it is clear that the idea of nationality is the more active, and itself forms part of the current of history. Almighty God did not separate the nations into glass cases as if they were botanical specimens, and we can see for ourselves how history has moulded them all. Nationality is no permanent thing; there are great nations whose original character and native genius have never quite been lost, but we can trace how it has mingled with other streams. The Greeks and the Germans are instances of two primitive peoples whose own peculiar genius has never been subdued; even the iron strength of the Roman Empire was powerless against them. It was easy enough to establish military colonies on German soil, but to Romanize the Germans was an impossibility. When our forefathers marched as conquerors into Rome, however, the ethnographical process was reversed: the superior civilization revenged itself upon the victors. The Lombards retained their German speech comparatively long, the Ostrogoths never discarded it, but their Empire was shorterlived. In far the greater number of the other German States established on Roman soil we see the conquerors adopting pretty quickly the language and customs of the more highly civilized vanquished race. The Visigoths became Spaniards, the Burgundians Gauls.

In addition to this we find some periods in history filled with the cosmopolitan spirit, while others display as strong a tendency towards national cleavage. At times some common intellectual movement stirs all nations to such an extent that national antagonisms withdraw into the background. The epoch of the Reformation was one of these; at that time the struggle for religious truth took such hold upon men's hearts that in every nation the alien co-religionists drew together against their kindred who were enemies of their faith. History in its fruitfulness will somewhere and some day produce the same phenomena again.

It is safe to assert that the energy of national feeling works differently in the different nations. Some there are in whom narrowness of outlook is innate. This applies most particularly to the insular nations, and as we think to the English. The Germans are their very anti-type, far the greater number of them being naturally cosmopolitan. Our people are for ever struggling with themselves; they have at length so overcome their perpetual assimilation of foreign elements as to find time to think of themselves. This peculiarity of the German nature should be described by the word *selbstlos* (self-less), a term whose meaning has been so thoughtlessly abused by our journalists.

Thus manifold have been the conflicting influences of the various living forces of history in national questions. When we examine these complicated conditions more closely we find first of all a great antagonism of races among human kind. We need not dwell here upon those newly discovered by our geography. No doubt the Berbers of Northern Africa, the Australian Aborigine, and the Malays are specific races, but the historian need only concern himself with the broad divisions of white, black, red, and yellow. The yellow race has never achieved political liberty, for their States have always been despotic and unfree. In the same way the artistic faculty has always been denied to the Mongols, in spite of that sense of comfort which we may admire among the Chinese, if we are soft and effeminate enough to wish to. The black races have always been servants, and looked down upon by all the others, nor has any negro State ever raised itself to a level of real civilization. Physical strength and endurance are such marked characteristics in the negro that he is employed inevitably to serve the ends of a will and intelligence higher than his own. The red race of North America, although now fallen into decay, once possessed a remarkable talent for State building. The old States of Peru knew no liberty indeed, but they had brought administration to an uncommon pitch of perfection, and had a postal service and a police force such as did not exist in Spain at the time of the conquest of South America. The red and yellow races spring from a common stock. Opposed to them stands the white race, which falls into two classes, the Aryan and the Semitic peoples.

These divisions are tremendously wide and deep. If we start from the supposition of the descent of all mankind from a single pair, and if we are still so fully persuaded of the equality of all men in the eyes of God, the differentiation of the various species must lie in an immeasurably distant past. But it is well known that when Nature has once carried out such a differentiation she will not tolerate any attempt to go back upon it. She revenges herself for any mixture of species by making the higher type give way before the lower. Even as by the interbreeding of a horse and a donkey a creature is produced which possesses the qualities of the less noble animal, so it is with human beings. The Mulatto is a nigger in all but his paler skin; that he is aware of it is shown by his consorting with other blacks. The same applies to mongrels. A physical disgust subsists between whites and blacks —the white cannot endure the presence of negroes in a confined space. The American States are obliged to run compartments for negroes only upon their railways, because their proximity is intolerable to those of a differeent race. If the character of a State is to be absolutely determined by the difference of races within it, it is quite certain that political freedom in the proper sense of the word is impossible, for a practical equality can never exist between beings which Nature has created unequal. In North America, even after slavery was abolished, the number of negroes who actually held posts under the State has always been of the smallest. The difference of capacities is so great that this will undoubtedly always be the case, but since the black population is in a minority, freedom is still possible. It is different in such countries as Hindustan, where the whole character of the State is modified by the juxtaposition of different races. Here a free Constitution is not practicable, for the subjects of the State can only feel themselves as belonging to a race which has, as it happens, been subjugated by a foreign power. Thus the contrast between races will always persist, and need not be deplored, for the world would be unbearably uninteresting if they were all alike.

These great racial antagonisms are crippling to the State; the differences of nationality within one race are more easily smoothed over. But how is nationality to be exactly defined? The question is difficult to answer; in some cases a whole sequence of historical facts must be taken into consideration before we can decide what really constitutes a nationality, for a single proof may not suffice. Speech is the most relatively certain sign, but not absolutely, for the Irish are most assuredly not Englishmen, although they speak English. There are besides nations of wanderers, such as the Jews, for whom the language they speak has no inward meaning, but is merely the convenient method of expression. A certain number of European Jews have, as a matter of fact, succeeded in really adopting the nationality of the people among whom they live, and in becoming truly Germans, Frenchmen, or Englishmen. Every one will recognize Benjamin Disraeli as an Englishman through and through, even in certain externals, and the history of our own literature affords instances of some Jews whose characteristics are essentially German. This is pre-eminently true of Moses Mendelssohn, but it is equally certain that in Berlin, and eastwards from that city, there are many Jews who are inwardly real Orientals, in spite of the language they speak.

While admitting the existence of such essentially homeless peoples, we must also not forget that it is possible for single groups to outgrow the characteristics of their old national community in the course of their political and social development.

This applies to the German-Swiss, and in a still higher degree to the French-Swiss. The dwellers on the Lake of Geneva are of the same blood as the people of Franche-Comté, but the whole tone of their life is so totally different from the superficiality of the essentially French nature that we have to label them French-Swiss, not French out and out. The same thing may be said, though less absolutely, of the German-Swiss.

We can follow the process of this growth away from the old cradles of their nationality, particularly clearly in the people of the Netherlands. They are of low-German stock, such as Saxons and Westphalians, but already throughout the Middle Ages they led a separate existence; then followed the division within the Hanseatic League between the eastern region and the Flemish cities of the west; and finally the great War of Religion in which Germany failed to stand by her daughter nation. The Dutch developed their dialect quite consciously into an independent language. For a time, and until the middle of the eighteenth century, the literature of the Netherlands was cosmopolitan and classical. Leyden was the headquarters of the Latin culture which dominated the world. Gradually, however, they began to cultivate their mother tongue, and to-day Dutch has as much ceased to be a dialect of German as has Portuguese of Spanish. Its grammatical construction has departed widely from ours, for it has adhered to the logical Latin syntax. What is it that gives this language its irresistibly comic touch? It is nothing but a sailor's dialect, framed to express the lowest and most ordinary ideas; therefore when it would raise itself to convey the conceptions of the highest education it is forced to employ expressions whose original meaning was perfectly trivial. This is a most instructive instance of how a nationality may become transformed, for it is unmistakable that the modern Dutch are Germans no longer.

So it is possible for a tribe to outgrow its ancient community, and it is also possible for this nationality to develop a fresh expansive impetus of its own.

Put this question to yourselves—What is Germany, in the historic sense, and where used her boundaries to be? The whole idea of what constitutes our country has altered. About one-third of the territories which we call Germany to-day were first won for her five or six hundred yeas ago. The marvel is that in spite of this there is no mistaking what the German spirit is. The real German is absolutely not to be confounded with any other people, although the frontiers of Germany have undergone so many changes in history.

Thus it is impossible to expound the facts of history genealogically as if it were a family tree. We must rather say that even nationalities are subject to the currents of historical life, and it is equally instructive and difficult for the historian to trace out these ethnographical fluctuations. Sometimes he seems to meet with a miracle. Think of England and see how Anglo-Saxons and Normans became one nation after a furious national struggle. We can see the completed process, and imagine, from our knowledge of indivdual instances, how this fusion of races comes to pass. The normal condition, however, is that the unity of the State should be based on nationality. The legal bond must at the same time be felt to be a natural one, arising automatically out of a blood-relationship either real or imaginary (for on this point nations labour under the most extraordinary delusions). Almost all great nations, like the Athenians, call themselves autochthonous, and boast, nearly always without cause, of the purity of their blood. Yet it is just the State-constructing nations, like the Romans and the English, who are of the most strongly mixed race. The Arabs and the Indians are of very pure blood, but no one can say that they have been peculiarly successful State-builders; their strength lies in quite other directions.

When we consider the ways of Germany we find that the inhabitants of large parts of Hesse, of Hanoverian Lower Saxony, as well as East Fries-land, Westphalia, and perhaps Northern Thuringia also, are of quite un-mixed Germanic blood. We can recognize this even at the present day. Wherever the girls carry their burdens on their heads we may be mathe-matically certain that there the Romans have been, but never when the load is carried on the back or in the hands. No one, however, would try to maintain that the creative political strength of Germany resided in these unmixed Germanic stocks. The real champions and pioneers of civilization in Germany in the Middle Ages were the South Germans, who have a Celtic strain, and in modern times the North Germans, who are partly Slav. The same applies to Piedmont in Italy. In France, pure Celtic blood is now found nowhere except in Brittany. The Bretons have always been a valiant little people; they furnish the best soldiers in the French Army, since the loss of Alsace. It is, however, a country of bigotry; the people lead a calm, idyllic existence, but the constructive political gift could never be ascribed to them.

In the powerful mill through which a nation is ground when it mingles with another, the softer sides of the character are easily destroyed, but the power of the will is fortified. So it is; and to that you must add that there is no such thing as a purely national history, for the process of give and take and the influence of cosmopolitan forces will always almost entirely form the basis of historic life. On the other hand, all true heroism, whether in literature or politics, must be national if it is not to be powerless in the moral sense. When we take both these great contradictions together we see that there is nothing to be gained from barren talk about a right of nationality. Every State has the right to allow the nations it contains to amalgamate, and, on the other hand, every nationality will feel the impulse to make itself politically independent.

It is clear that these two tendencies must of necessity lead to manifold contradictions in an old world where national divisions cannot be very sharply defined, and it is also obvious that national unity is the most con-servative foundation for a State, for it contains the outward conditions for preservation of peace. Aristotle observes that peoples of different races incline to unrest until they have inwardly amalgamated.

When several nations are united under one State, the simplest relation-ship is that the one which wields the authority should also be the superior in civilization. Matters can then develop comparatively peacefully, and when the blending is complete it is felt to have been inevitable, although it can never be accomplished without endless misery for the subjugated race. The most remarkable fusion took place after this fashion in the colonies of North-East Germany. It was the murder of a people; that cannot be denied, but after the amalgamation was complete it became a blessing.

What could the Prussians have contributed to history? The Germans were so infinitely their superiors that to be Germanized was for them as great a good fortune as it was for the Wends.

Even where the intermixture under these conditions is not completely succesful, an alien nationality may still be entrusted with certain rights of its own, if it deserves them. We pursued this policy with Posen, when it was made into a Grand-Duchy and received a banner of its own. But how were we repaid? By continual fresh treasons on the part of the Poles; by constantly recurring revolts. Thus the State was forced to treat this province simply as a province, and to revoke the promises made to it. The great Bismarckian system set us at last upon the right road in Posen, and under him we were on the point of Germanizing education. Now on the contrary we are permitting German Catholic children to be given instruction in Polish, under the name of private lessons. The whole point of the conflict is that Protestantism and Germanism are there held to be synonymous, and that an attempt is being made to infuse Polish sympathies into the German Catholics. To proffer the schools in order that German children may receive private lessons in Polish is a shocking piece of folly. Prince Bismarck disposed of it very summarily. His policy was the natural policy of a great State, conscious of itself.

We Germans to-day are in evil case. The time has come, as we have seen already, when the sub-German peoples are beginning to awake to consciousness of themselves. Up to a certain point this is justified. It is undeniable that Peter the Great's innovating methods with the Russians were arbitrary. For a Russian who holds his nationality superior to the German, the reaction apparent to-day is easily comprehensible.

Every nation over-estimates itself. Without this feeling of itself it would also lack the consciousness of being a community; as Fichte truly said, "a nation cannot dispense with arrogance." The same is true of the little nations; the less they have to show for it, the more pride they feel.

The Germanic element in the Baltic Provinces had fenced itself about with various territorial privileges, even as the Poles in Posen have had their separate rights; but the Germans in Livonia have never damaged theirs by rebellion, nor has the Czar ever had more loyal subjects anywhere than they. Nay, more, these German Baltic provinces were not only innocuous to the Czar's dominion, but were invaluable to the civilization of the Russian Empire. They have produced a veritable legion of men who have done remarkable service to the State, both in the civil and military spheres. Russia has a thousand motives, therefore, for preserving the Germanic element in this region, especially because it is in nowise propagandist. Now, however, the ancient, aristocratic Provincial Constitution has been withdrawn, and an effort is being made to force the German population down into the democratic welter of despotic Russia, for a democratic despotism is the truly fundamental characteristic of the Russian Empire. This attempt to de-Germanize a German country, whose vicinty has never brought anything but benefit to Russia, can only be described as barbarous. If these dwellers in the Baltic provinces were not Germans, and as such upholders of the superior civilization, if they had not deserved so much at the hands of the State, the Russian Government would be less to blame for many an unscrupulous act perpetrated upon them.

There are other cases of amalgamation between nations in which the strength of the dominant people does not show itself in what we call culture, but rather in a certain kind of conventional dexterity. Upon this reposed the superiority of the Romans when they subdued the tribes of Italy. They were not only the exponents of a firm political administration, but they also possessed a peculiar power of receptivity for a higher civilization, which the Etruscans lacked. For the very reason that they did not themselves possess many of the higher gifts of civilization, the Romans were capable of absorbing the culture of the Hellenes. Thus it came about that the want of intellectual depth in the Roman spirit became in itself a uniting bond.

This fortunate circumstance of the dominating nationality being at the same time the bringer or the spreader of a superior civilization does not, however, always occur. Sometimes the very reverse is the case, and then, as we have seen, civilization takes its revenge for its political subjection. The political victors adopt the language of the vanquished. We observe, in the migration of races, how the strong German races gradually became imbued with Roman civilization, and soon became proud of having assimilated it to themselves. Such an intermingling of speech and customs gives rise to many transitional phenomena; Jacob Grimm refers to them again and again. When words and institutions are transferred from one nation to another, the form is first changed, while the substance remains unaltered. The Latin root of such words as *regieren, spazieren* persists, but the inflection takes on the German form. Similarly the English language later adopted a quantity of French words, but gave them the German inflection. The same thing applies to institutions. In the case of the adoption of a foreign law, the form or application of it is first converted, while in essentials it remains for long the same.

In all this we perceive the tremendous importance of form, most especially in the history of national civilization. Even when two peoples come into peaceful contact with one another, both sides begin inevitably to try to mould the speech of the other. Here certain homely influences come into play. In German we speak correctly of the "mother-tongue," not the "father-tongue," for the child does in fact learn its speech from its mother; in the same way the processes of national amalgamation depend more upon the women than the men. The fact that women are more appreciative of beauty of form than men are, explains in many cases the reason why, when two equally great nations meet, that one prevails which has the superiority in its outward forms. Let us examine for a moment how the German element has lost ground in the South Tyrol. In the sixteenth century Trent was still half a German town, now it is completely Italianized; the foreigners have advanced step by step in the last few hundred years. The causes of their progress are economic, for this was the very home of a particularly sturdy Germanic stock. Upon one side we find the burly forms of the red-jerkined countrymen of Andreas Hofer. Over against these men, who were so avid of present enjoyment, we have the shrewd, thrifty, niggardly Italian. He bought out one German peasant proprietor after another, and thus the language frontier drew constantly back towards the north. The second, perhaps still more important, influence at work is that of forms. Italian civilization is not indeed higher than our own, but it is older. In the days when we were still savages, they had long been a civilized nation. This ancient culture makes itself felt in the manner of their social intercourse, and in the urbanity of their character; they are essentially city-dwellers in their good points as well as their bad ones. The feminine temperament is particularly accessible to the outward superiority of these thoroughly cultivated courteous manners, and in mixed marriages it is easy enough to understand how the German woman takes the Italian characteristics of her husband, while the reverse is seldom or never the case.

We are bound to say that the Latin races have done much to further the processes of national amalgamation, for the very reason that they content themselves, after the fashion of the Romans, with a stereotyped ideal.

There is absolutely no centrifugal element in Italy and France. In Dalmatia the Italianizing force has reached such a point that it is necessary to pierce below the universal crust of Italian culture before we discover that the bulk of the population is Slavonic. The towns in Istria are all upon the model of their old mistress, Venice. This capacity of the Romans for imposing their nationality upon others is less inherent in the Germans. The German temperament is deeper; it strives to mould men's characters according to its own ideas; a far more difficult task, and therefore much oftener unsuccessful. Hence the many centrifugal forces in German States. England herself, despite the anglicizing of the language, has never yet succeeded in inwardly coercing the Emerald Isle.

In Germany, as a whole, the centrifugal elements are still unendingly various. One reason is the long-standing discord within the German race itself, which has naturally impeded the subjugation of other nationalities. Nevertheless the internal contrasts between dispositions are much less with us than with other civilized nations. We have no such divisions as exist between the Provençal and the Flemish northern Frenchman (who is, properly speaking, a North German), or between the Sicilian and the Piedmontese. As a matter of fact, some of our different races who live far distant from each other get on very well together. The Schleswig-Holsteiners and the Swabians have always been good friends, and a very large number of marriages take place between the inhabitants of Electoral Saxony and the East Prussians. Both stocks are combative in the highest degree, but their differences do not conflict. On the other hand, some tribes living side by side display the strongest dislike for one another. Who does not know the antagonism between the Rhinelander and the Westphalian, the Bavarian and the Swabian, etc.? It all goes to prove, however, what a strong bond of inward unity our people possess. Long ago the Romans reported, when they found Germans first in the Balkan Peninsula and then again in Gaul, that here was a people who had no State and no over-lord, and yet one was so like another as to be indistinguishable.

Greeks and Germans, perhaps the two noblest nations in the world's history, have also been the most cosmopolitan. Out of the Hellenism of Greece sprang the cosmopolitan Hellenism of Alexander the Great, and later the Byzantine civilization; from Teutonism went forth all the "Romanic" States; while the Romans, precisely because they had little either in their hearts or heads, displayed national energy in a marked degree. Roman unity was primarily made up of outward forms. It was founded first upon discipline and the argument of the corporal's cane. Their very language is formed to express their policy—soul-less, but with a wonderful intellectual power which makes it an indispensable part of the equipment of an educated man. Nevertheless how long it was before Rome developed a literature, and when it came it was Greek in spirit, though written with Latin words. But a whole nation submitted to these forms, and in a long period of communal life evolved a strength of national instinct which we Germans cannot too greatly envy.

We continue to be the people which has the least power of national resistance. This is even the case in our relations with our Polish neighbours, and here again a great deal depends upon the women. Observe how marriages are contracted in this region; in Posen it is the rule that the wife is Polish, the husband German. This is a peculiar phenomenon: two nations who mutually detest each other are yet found intermarrying. The Germans and the Wends did the same, although their hatred for each other was so deep-seated. Now Germans marry Poles, but the mother takes care to remain Polish, and so it goes on.

The attitude of the Church is important in these processes of amalgamation. The Catholic Church is always on the side of the language of the inferior civilization. They love the dialect of the people better than the speech of the educated, for they find more support among the former; hence it comes that the clericals on our Eastern frontier are out-and-out Polish in sympathies. In Belgium they take the Flemish part, for there the French are the Freemasons.

Thus manifold are the influences which co-operate in the intermixture of different nations. The normal thing is for one of them gradually to succeed in obtaining the dominion over the other; then a State language comes into being, and certain separate rights can be agreed upon, such as are in accordance with the political resources of a frontier province.

Cases can arise, however, where the absorption of one race by the other is not possible, and these lead to very complicated political conditions. It is remarkable in how many different ways the problem can be solved, and we often find in history that the same circumstances lead to diametrically opposite results. A World-Empire may be constructed by the absolute ruling will of a Caesar, or by a loosely-knit form of association, as in North America. Thus, too, a State in which the nationalities are mixed can be most easily ruled in one of two totally contrasting ways; either by a federative Republic, in which very little business is transacted in common, as in Switzerland (where neighbours can live in peace and amity in spite of the difference of nationality), or by means of a strong despotic Government. In Switzerland we find three nations politically united, each of them living on the borders of their own mother-country, and so comfortably situated upon the whole that its natural power of attraction is not a disturbing factor. In German and French Switzerland there is no one who wishes to be either German or French, and it is only in the Ticino Canton that the Italian feeling is perceptible. There is no room in the new Cantonal Constitution for any yearnings towards the great neighbouring nationalities.

The other form of Government by which the coexistence of several nations within one State can be made bearable is a wise Despotism, which keeps them all in a lethargy. It is a singular fact that these national questions become more dangerous in proportion as the Government, which was originally despotic, assumes the forms of freeedom. A people, as a whole, can never possess the patience of a single ruler; in national questions it cannot stand neutral. In this matter the history of Denmark is endlessly instructive. The old Denmark ruled its various German territories quite peacefully; no one in Holstein had any thoughts about national antagonisms at the beginning of the nineteenth century. The Court at Copenhagen was German in culture, the German language prevailed, and most of the officials, even the highest, such as Counts Bernstorff, Schimmelmann, etc., were of the Holstein nobility; therefore the Holsteiners had no cause to feel themselves affronted. But with the Constitutional forms there came a change, and since a nationality cannot be forbearing, the Danes began to misuse their greater numbers in order to annihilate the Germans.

It therefore remains true for such mixed States that, when they have not the power to organize themselves quite loosely, freer forms of government are dangerous. Austria has learnt this by experience since the founding of her Parliament. Old Austria, like the Ottoman Empire, pursued a very skilful policy towards her various races on the principle of *divide et impera*. Charles V. is a typical figure for a ruler of this kind. Of Brabantian origin, educated in Castile, he became more and more of a Spaniard as life went on, but in Germany it was only quite gradually that he came to be regarded as a foreigner. It was one of his great gifts as a ruler to be able to assume the position of a sort of demi-god without appearing to any one of his subject peoples in the light of a stranger. Where that can be achieved, the *divide et impera* system can be very successfully applied, by playing off one nation against another. In this way Charles tried to use his Spaniards for the destruction of the turbulent Germans. Our gorge rises at the spectacle of the House of Hapsburg inciting the Magyar against the German, and then the Slav against the Magyar.

Conditions such as these prevent the States in which they prevail from possessing a civilization of their own in the highest human sense of the word. For good or for evil, he who would be ruler must either oppress the individual nations or else attempt to pit them against each other. No better instance can be found than the history of the Ottoman Empire. The rulership of the Turks in their great days is worthy of all admiration, but it was unproductive from beginning to end. Go to Hungary, which they governed for 180 years, and what traces of this long dominion do you find to-day? Nothing but the tomb of the Father of Roses, the Prophet of Mohammed; that is absolutely all. They only understood how to make their Government secure for the time being, but that they could do in masterly fashion. Their power of turning the weakness of the Giaours to good account compels our admiration. There, in a corner of the Bosphorus lies Lampsacos, where Aphrodite bore her turbulent son; there, too, is Lesbos, home of incestuous love; here all the vices were first cradled. Well did the Turks know how to avail themselves of the material which lay ready to their hand, by allowing the Greeks to tear one another to pieces. They possessed the gift of sowing discord and ruling through it, in the highest degree.

When the Constitution is freer, and the people is made up of several nationalities, the problems of Government become more and more difficult, and give rise to a multitude of experiments such as we have seen attempted by the Emperor Francis Joseph of Austria. History has never produced any other monarch like Francis Joseph; he has tried almost every conceivable political system, and therefore the confusion which has ensued is indescribable. There is no doubt that the partition of Austria is simply a recurrence to old historical conditions. Its organizer was Maria Theresa, but she was not its originator, for the Dual Monarchy is as old as the Crown of Stephen. The already existent form was settled by Maria Theresa on the fixed basis, by which the Hungarian Kingdom was left under its old Constitution, while the Cisleithan territories were gathered up under the administration of the Austrian Imperial Chancery, thus following out the trend of Austrian history.

With the awakening of national feeling the national conditions in Hungary became more and more difficult to manage, and the Magyar aristocracy, who were always the dominant party in the State, obtained so great a mastery that the position of the other nationalities was often unendurable. Every State must have one official language, in which to transact the business of Parliament. In the Cisleithan Parliament German is the only tongue which everybody understands. Therefore the old Empire rightly chose Latin for the language of the State. Its common use injured no one's feelings, and it was in consequence particularly well adapted for practical ends. It was a thoroughly bad and ridiculous dog-Latin which was spoken, but it kept the peace between the nations. Then in the nine-teenth century began the stormy Magyar movement, and Magyar was made the official language. Here lay a source of deadly offence for the Germans, who there possess a language of literature and culture. Moreover, Magyar is very difficult to learn, as its grammar is on the principle of agglutination, not of inflection; totally different in its genius from our own. This speech of a minority was thus imposed upon the other nations, and so it all went on. It is only quite recently that signs of a change have begun to manifest themselves, in the Magyar nobility beginning to come to a better understanding with the worthy Saxon peasantry. The danger which threatens from the Vlaks is working here as a uniting force. In other respects the arrangements in Hungary are still very unreasonable in many ways, and the compulsory language is used in a ridiculous manner. On the rail-ways the time-tables are all made out in Magyar, but if you mention the Magyar name for the place at the booking-office you are asked in German what it means; the official does not recognize these artificially made-up names.

We have, in addition, to reckon with the peculiar characteristics of the Germans in Hungary. There are only two regions there where the German element has maintained itself worthily and courageously; the beautiful Saxon province of Transylvania, which cherishes so touching an affection for us that it is always sad to think how powerless we are to help the poor little people. German civilization is so strong among them, however, that we may allow ourselves to hope that it will some day make its own way. The same applies to the Protestant Germans in Croatia. The remainder, almost all of them Catholics, are the saddest examples of the Germanic race which are anywhere to be found. Such a depth of national degradition is positively horrible to behold, and it is disgraceful also, since the Germans used always to be the champions of material and intellectual civilization in Hungary. Ofen is as good a German town as Berlin, except for a few Magyars who live there; and now it has become Buda-Pesth; so named because it lies opposite a preponderatingly Jewish town with Magyar char-acteristics, and must needs be called after it. In the same way the German theatre too has gradually disappeared.

On the other side the so-called Cisleithanians, gathered of necessity un-der the control of the Imperial Parliament, are also suffering from passionate national antagonisms. Besides this, nothing could be more unfortunate than the geographical circumstances, because to the Danube territory proper is added on the one hand Dalmatia, on the other Galicia, both far-distant provinces with which the Danube lands have nothing whatever to do. The Poles have been the wisest; they sit firm in the Imperial Parlia-ment, and generally give the casting vote. All this introduces incalculable factors into the situation, and it is impossible to forecast even the immediate future. Federalistic experiments are not likely to be tried again. The State which has acquiesced in the Dual System will not undertake them any more in its western territories. One other plan might still be feasible. The edge might be to some extent taken off the racial enmities, if an *itio in partes* were assured to all the nationalities. If no party were permitted to overrule the other in educational legislation, etc., but the Crown be made the final arbiter, elections might lose their bitterness, and internal harmony be better secured. So great, however, is the hashness of national feeling that no one feels any desire to smooth it over.

In the immediate future, then, it will still be Austria's destiny to be torn with internal struggles. Moreover, there is the sad fact that even in Cisleithania Teutonism still goes upon a broken wing. The fine German culture of Vienna in the Middle Ages has long since vanished. In the eighteenth century music was the only form of creative art in which Austria excelled, and music does not influence national character as poetry does. In more recent times there has been more approximation to the German spirit, but on the other hand Austrian Germanism has been unspeakably corrupted by Semitism. It is clear that in such a country an experimental and make-shift policy is unavoidable.

The Jews play a quite abnormal part in this singular whirlpool of national antagonisms. Once on a time, when they were still a nation, they made for themselves a lasting place in history by their maintenance of a pure monotheism; but soon the exodus began, and we find them scatttered over the face of the earth. Semitic is their great religious genius, which, however, contains no propagandist tendency, and finds its antithesis in their trading instinct developed into the wildest passion. This outstanding feature of Jewish character, added to an overweening racial conceit and a deadly hatred of everything Christian, explains the quite unique position which Judaism has occupied in all periods of history. In plain words, the Jews have always been "an element of national decomposition"; they have always helped in the disintegration of nations. Trade recognizes no frontiers, and it is not necessary to demonstrate how one group of the great capitalists of Europe are formed in an international association to promote their own interests at the expense of their smaller colleagues and the landowners.

On the other hand, the Jews marry so strictly among themselves that they never amalgamate with an alien people. In history they appear to belong to them all, but in spite of this the majority of them keep their innate characteristics unimpaired, and wear the foreign nationality like a garment. Hence the well-known fact that the only art in which the modern Jew shows real genius is the art of the theatre. Imitative faculty, without any inward originating power, has always been a strong point of Jewish literature. Great poet as Heine was—and he was one of the few Jews who really knew the German language—we see when we compare him with Goethe, or even with Chamisso and others, how they are the originators, he the imitator.

This nation whose qualities are so contradictory has three times played an essential rôle in history. Firstly, in the Empire of Alexander the Great, when Greek genius expanded into Hellenism. Then the Jews were not only the merchants of the world, but they were also the uniting element in intellectual life. This was the time when Greek culture proper was falling into decay, and those schools of philosophy were arising in Alexandria, whose teaching was a mixture of Jewish and Greek thought, and prepared the way for the great Christian idea. Once again did the Jews play a like part in the Empire of Rome. Caesar designedly favoured them, and rightly so, for he ruled the world. The nations united under one sway must cease to feel themselves nations, and for this end no means could be better adapted than the influence of the homeless Jews. Therefore, here again they took their place in history. Next we come to the time when the young States of the Germans began to rise upon the ruins of the Roman Empire. In order to find their bearings in this unfamiliar civilization and finance, the Germanic farmers required some helpers conversant with the use of a currency. In the early Middle Ages the Jews controlled the trade of the world. This explains why they were then treated with so much more friendliness than was the case later. Theodoric the Ostrogoth could not dispense with his Jews, and long after his day Louis the Debonnair was an acknowledged philo-Semite, although even so he was unable to extricate himself from his embarrassments.

Presently, however, the Jews ceased to be indispensable, for the Aryan races learnt how to manage their own finance themselves. It then became apparent what a dangerous disintegrating force lurked in this people who were able to assume the mask of any other nationality. Fair-minded Jews must themselves admit that after a nation has become conscious of its own personality there is no place left for the cosmopolitanism of the Semites; we can find no use for an international Judaism in the world to-day. We must speak plainly upon this point, undeterred by the abuse which the Jewish press pours upon what is a simple historical truth. It is indisputable that the Jews can only continue to hold a place if they will make up their minds to become Englishmen, Frenchmen, or Germans, as the case may be, and provisionally consent to merge their old memories into those of the nation to which they belong politically. This is the perfectly just and reasonable demand which we Western races must make of them; no people can concede a double nationality to the Jews.

The considerations in this matter are extremely complicated, because we have no certain standard by which we can ascertain the extent to which the Jews have spread themselves among the alien nationality. Baptism alone is no guide. There are unbaptized Jews who are good Germans—I have known some myself—and there are others who are not, although they have been baptized; the legal aspect of the question is therefore a difficult one. If legislation were to treat the Jews simply as sojourners in the country, allowing them to ply civil trades, but withholding political and magisterial rights, it would be an injustice because it would not fulfil the purpose for which it was designed. A baptized Christian cannot be legally regarded as a

Jew. I can see only one means by which the end can be attained, and that is to arouse an energy of national pride, so real that it becomes a second nature to repel involuntarily everything which is foreign to the Germanic nature. This principle must be carried into everything; it must apply to our visits to the theatre and to the music-hall as much as to the reading of the newspapers. Whenever he finds his life sullied by the filth of Judaism the German must turn from it, and learn to speak the truth boldly about it. The party of compromise must bear the blame for any unsavoury wave of anti-Semitism which may arise.

Self-Portrait of an Imperialist: Rhodes and South Africa

Cecil Rhodes, "Speech at Port Elizabeth, September 17, 1898" and "Speech at Cape Town, October 25, 1898," Cecil Rhodes: His Political Life and Speeches, ed. "Vindex" [F. Verschoyle] (London: Chapman and Hall, 1900), pp. 609–13, 614–16, 620–21, 628–30.

Method and madness animated the European imperial orgy of the late nineteenth century. Crude economic gain which Hobson, Lenin, and Rosa Luxemburg were to emphasize played its part. So did Christian and secular humanitarianism. But the amorphic and mystical quest for glory for its own sake meant as much as, if not more than, any other element. An empire was needed, as Bethmann-Hollweg put it when asked why German naval expansion, "for the general purpose of imperial greatness." All three factors moved Cecil Rhodes (1853–1902)—a man with a mission. Rhodes sought wealth, and he found it. He dreamed of a mystic bond of human brotherhood aspiring to the highest ideals, and he endowed it. He set himself the task of completing an inland Suez Canal—a British Africa from the Cape to Cairo—and he just missed.

At the ripe age of twenty-four Rhodes drafted his first will on September 19, 1877, bequeathing his then nonexistent fortune, according to the first clause

To and for the establishment, promotion and development of a Secret Society, the true aim and object whereof shall be for the extension of British rule throughout the world, the perfecting of a system of emigration from the United Kingdom, and of colonisation by British subjects of all lands where the means of livelihood are attainable by energy, labour and enterprise, and especially the occupation by British settlers of the entire Continent of Africa, the Holy Land, the Valley of the Euphrates, the Islands of Cyprus and Candia, the whole of South America, the Islands of the Pacific not heretofore possessed by Great Britain, the whole of the Maylay Archipelago, the seaboard of China and Japan, the ultimate recovery of the United States of America as an integral part of the British Empire, the inauguration of a system of Colonial representation in the Imperial Parliament which may tend to weld together the disjointed members of the Empire and, finally, the foundation of so great a Power as to render wars impossible and promote the best interests of humanity.

Later versions of Rhodes's will—he drafted them in 1882, 1888, 1891, and 1893—were scarcely less grandiose. Notice that Rhodes did not conceive of empire in a narrow sense. He championed the maximum of self-government to such a degree that he contributed handsomely to the Irish Nationalist party. The federal union of self-governing components on a higher cultural plane would guarantee the domination of the world by the best in the Anglo-Saxon tradition.

Rhodes used politics—as prime minister of the Cape Colony and through his influence and friendship with imperialists in Britain—and the power of business (through companies he controlled) to reach his goal. The gold discoveries in the Transvaal in 1886 complicated Rhodes's task. While gold gave credence to arguments about economic imperialism, Rhodes wanted the Boer republics regardless of their economic potential. Rhodes had his Dutch counterpart. Paul Kruger, President of the Transvaal and leader of the anti-British element, had his own expansionist notions. Rhodes, frustrated, attempted to overthrow Kruger by combining an "internal revolt" with an invasion by his Rhodesian company troopers in 1895. The disaster of Jameson's Raid ruined Rhodes politically. He had alienated his wide Cape Boer support.

The two speeches included here were made during the election of 1898. Kruger had been re-elected President of the Transvaal, and war semed imminent. Rhodes and his Progressive party attempted a political comeback on the eve of fighting. If Rhodes could not recover what he had so recklessly thrown away, he clung to his dream, and it animated others.

SPEECH AT PORT ELIZABETH
September 17, 1898

A GREAT DEAL has been said as to my position, and I can tell you in a few words that I am not going away from the country to which I owe so much. I am going to fight for the principles that your party has adopted, in whatever position I may be. I have a lot of work to do yet. If you will only think of it, we are getting on very nicely with our telegraph through the continent. You may say, "What has that to do with us?" I say everything. Your cable rates will be reduced by half. They have already been reduced owing to fear of the new line, and it is drawing on us. As you know, Sir Herbert Kitchener only started the other day, and we can fancy we see them marching to-night towards Khartoum. We are coming up from the South, and we are going to join him as sure as I am standing here. That is not in the interests only of an imaginative idea; it is in the interests of this country, and . . . what was attempted by Alexander, Cambyses, and Napoleon we practical people are going to finish. That is something better for me to do than to retire to a hermit's cell, the destination devoutly wished for me by the Independents to-day. And I am going to make the railway to Tanganyika, and that is going to benefit you. You will send up the goods, and we will bring down the millions of labourers and distribute them amongst the mines. At Tanganyika they labour for 2d. a day, and that reminds me of the last time I visited Egypt, when I went to a place below Cairo. In a chat I had with the man in charge of large works he said, "I don't know what is going to happen to us; we can't go on with these irrigation works. Would you believe it, we are paying labour 3d. a day." I said, "I don't know what is coming to Egypt." With such a supply of labour we can work many of those mines which are not payable to-day on account of the heavy charges for labour. This, I may remark, is being used against me by some of the natives. They say Mr. Rhodes is going to make us work for 2d. a day.

Now, the only way we can gain this advantage of cheap labour is by extension of the railway lines. You do not know what you have missed. When I went to Beira I was in trouble, and I had been up a great deal. The proposition was, we must have a railway, and in my daily walks through the veldt I discussed the problem—Beira to Bulawayo or Mafeking to Bulawayo? I had the money. On the one hand the distance was 600 miles, and on the other 1250 miles. I decided for Port Elizabeth and the South. I do not say that because there is an election before you, but because it was the thought which came. What decided me was not your vote, not your ideas, but I had made my plans as a youngster that I would have the Cape as the basis for the development of Africa. If I had decided on the Beira route, all connection with the South was over. Look at the map. There are other ports to consider. Strong reasons might be advanced towards an opposite course, but I had made up my mind, and my idea was to develop South Africa from the south. If we get our money for Tanganyika—and of course we will get it— I propose that the line from Salisbury should be extended and join our line farther in on the Zambesi, so as not to be in competition. It is one of the greatest mistakes for a man to work competing railways; he cannot afford the competition, and will probably be working at a loss. I propose to let the Beira line join farther north, so as not to interfere with the relations of the South.

There is the work of the telegraph to do; there is the work of the railway to do; and there is another very big question—an approaching question— the question of union, of South African federation. That federation is very close. By federation I mean that the native question, the laws, and the railways should be together. Local questions should be dealt with by the local States. The solution does not rest with me; it is being discussed to-night. If we could look to-night into the various camps thousands of miles away we would see strong men returning from their mines. They are discussing the richness of their mines. On them depends federation. If that country is rich, the prize of Africa will be the North. If you will not have it, Natal will federate to-morrow; and I can state here that if I am driven away by a Bond Ministry under Hofmeyr management I shall turn my thoughts to Natal. I am determined to have union. Some people may say, "But how about the Transvaal, between the Colony, Natal, and the North?" I do not consider the Transvaal; I am thinking of the next twenty-five years, when the new population must have their proper position. If we get Natal the other States must fall in. Now, you are beginning to follow my thought. The question is, Will the Cape, by its own conduct, be left out in the cold? The people in the North are not going to have any feeling for a State in the South which is not necessary to them, and which is dominated by the tactics of the Bond. Assume that a Bond Ministry gets the power. In your responsible position I talk to you boldly. I must speak out boldly. I see the danger that is coming. My North is all right. No human being could have better prospects. Eight hundred thousand square miles with a loyal people. You might fairly say, "Why don't you go there?" I will tell you why. I am determined not to leave the South till I see that you are clear of the risk of being dominated by Krugerism. And my picture would not be a complete one if the future held a union of States in the North and the Cape was left out in the cold. Last year we took £600,000 worth of goods, and the bulk of these goods came through Port Elizabeth. I have arranged the railways to the North so that whatever trade we have in the North will have to come through this port. You will admit that East London cannot deal with our trade because that is not the nearest route, and Cape Town is too remote. I have sketched the extension of the line, and, having spent £2,000,000 on the Mafeking-Bulawayo line, I would not be a business man to put another line into competition with it. I wish to earn dividends on that line, so as to get guarantees from Her Majesty to go on to Tanganyika. Thus you will see that it is essentially in the interests of the port to support no Independents. Now I have put to you practically why I cannot retire from public life. My telegraph will go to the dogs, and my railway will not go to Tanganyika, and the efforts of my public life for the union of South Africa would be done with. I believe, therefore, in dealing with people whose confidence I think I possess, rather than in retiring to the position of meditation which my dearest friends suggest for me. Apart from chaff, I think you can see with these objects before me why I should not retire. It would be paltry on my part, having the opportunity to forward them better, perhaps, than any other man in South Africa, were I to propose to retire. I hope you are with me in the ideas that I have sketched to you to-night, that you will see the whole thing as a picture—a picture that can be worked out; but it can only be worked out if you are thoroughly with me in that idea. Do not spoil the whole thing, when one looks for co-operation, by sending down an Independent. I am not saying this personally, but do not send down to Parliament an Independent whose whole mind is antagonistic to these thoughts. Send down those who will loyally work with these thoughts. The North is asking from you nothing. The North is my thought. Co-operation is my thought—Federalism and the Union of South Africa.

SPEECH AT CAPE TOWN
October 25, 1898

There is no one to fight to-night. Now, gentlemen, the last time I met a Capt Town audience was during the Council elections, when we had a great fight, and we won. I met you in the hall close by, and we had a very successful meeting, and I felt that our case had your support. Since then, as far as I am personally concerned, there has been a good deal of work. I had to go home to get my Charter right, and I came back, and we fought another election, and in spite of having no organisation, and in spite of being taken by surprise, we had a tie. And a tie on what question? On the question of the proper representation of the people, because you must remember that the greater covers the less. If you get proper representation of the people, you will get those measures which you, as Progressive people, desire. If we don't have proper representation, we shall not get those measures, and therefore we have to do everything in our power to get a proper Redistribution. Bill. Well, the speaker before me told you exactly what the position is, but I will even bore you by labouring the point again. You have a hundred and eight thousand voters in the country. Eighty per cent. voting would be eighty-six thousand. When I say eighty per cent. voting, I mean to say that if you made a careful calculation, and eighty-six thousand had recorded their votes, you would have fifty thousand votes, and the people who are in charge of this country thirty-six thousand. Well, that is a most anomalous condition. That is a most extraordinary position. But what do those people do who are in power? After they had declared that they would give you a Redistribution Bill; after getting into power and finding that they were in a hopeless minority, so far as the people were concerned, they say they will give no redistribution at all. They wish to keep us in a position which I call an application of Krugerism.

I will tell you what I mean by Krugerism. As you know, in the Transvaal the whole of the wealth, the greater portion of the population, practically the whole of the intelligence, is not represented at all, but they are lived upon by foreigners and an ignorant minority. Now, in this country they desire to apply Krugerism in this way. They are perfectly aware that the votes of the majority are for the party of progress, and they say, "We will not allow you to be fairly represented, we will evade it in every possible way, and allow the government of the country to be carried on by a minority, and we will prevent any fair redistribution, so as to prevent the majority having a voice." This is really Krugerism again in a minor form, and that is what we are fighting. And shall we win? Well, it will depend upon ourselves. Yes, if we keep united in the Cape Parliament, we shall win. But there are always some weak-kneed ones. There are always a number of those who have immense rectitude, who are always finding reasons for not voting with the Progressive party. At present we are united, but I cannot help throwing back my thoughts to last session, where there was a third party. . . . What occurred last session? We had a bill for the better representation of the people, on which hung the whole issue of Africa, and we should have won it.

    •   •   •   •   •   •   •   •   •   •   •   •   •   •   •

. . . You must remember the whole of the issues of Africa are before you now. You are in an exceedingly pleasant and happy position, in so far as politics are concerned. A hundred years hence the whole of the races and relations of this country will be settled, and you have to assist. We have developed this new state in the North. We are just considering closer relations with Natal. We know the Republics must change on account of the enormous influx of Europeans. I know I have to be awfully careful about the Republics, so as not to hurt any one's feelings. But still we know that these two states are to change very rapidly, and it rests with the Colony at the base, it rests with us here, as to what will be the relations with the other states in South Africa. But when you think that, in addition to that, in the north of Africa the whole thing is changed by the conquest of Khartoum, and that what appeared to be imaginative madness five years ago is absolutely practicable now. And when we know absolutely that we are going to join—I know for myself and the state I represent that we shall join—the matter is beyond dispute. It is the agreement of all. Only the other day, I heard that the telegraph was nearly into Nyassa, that it will be completed to Tanganyika by the end of the year, and then I have only six hundred miles to Uganda, and we know that Kitchener is at Sobat. You see, it is a very little distance, and what you feel is that you will take a part in the whole work. And then we are opposed by this non-Progressive party who hate any expansion, because they think that it means their annihilation. We must remember that it is not the Dutch people, for this non-Progressive party consists of just a few. It is Camp Street; it is Pretoria. It is not the people, it is not the Dutch people. It is a little coterie who hate expansion, and who wish to keep in their own narrow groove of misrepresentation and libel to maintain their position. Not having the decision to face the people, and not having the courage to face Parliament, they have to do it by subterranean alleys. Gentlemen, we are not fighting the Dutch people, but the coterie, and I believe we shall succeed—and we shall succeed through this expansion that is going on, and which you all share in the satisfaction of working for. As I said just now, you believe now we are going to join from north to south. You hope you will share in that. You believe now thoroughly in federation in South Africa, in the union of the neighbouring states. Now, these are all principles of the Progressive party.

.　.　.　.　.　.　.　.　.　.　.　.　.　.　.　.

　I am afraid I have tired you, gentlemen, but I have been pointing out to you the need of your Redistribution Bill, the deeper reason of those terrible wranglings that have been going on in Parliament during the last few days, and the scope of the Progressive party, and the object that lies behind it; and I have been showing that the reason why I am anxious for a change is that I am afraid to see a party or ministers in power, whose only politics are that they wish for my head on a charger, and who are therefore most antagonistic to the state which has been created in the North. I will do everything I possibly can for their removal and for a change, because having commenced my life in the Cape Colony, owing to the Cape Colony all my work and my position, it is natural that I should continue to hold that thought of a big scheme of the federal union of Africa. I know that you have placed in power a party whose whole thought is against the union of Africa, who wish for separation in the same way that Kruger desired separation, because separation means their own combination. Under union the gentleman of Camp Street must disappear, under union the President of the Transvaal must disappear. Our whole politics, whether Bond or Progressive, are subordinate to the ambition of these two men.

　Now, we are on the other side. We cannot win—and when I say we, I mean the Progressives—unless we have a majority in Parliament, and that majority is due to us upon our votes. The Cape Colony is different from the Transvaal. The Transvaal is an oligarchy, but in the Cape Colony we have adopted representation by the people, and therefore we should have representation proportionate to our votes. We must have the representation which is due to us on our numbers. We are fifty thousand against thirty-six thousand. We have equality of numbers in the House, and we are told that we are not entitled even to the members that we have got, and that they all got in by corruption, bribery, and immorality, unrighteousness, and impurity. That is what we are told; but we say this, Give us representation proportionate to our votes. This is an English colony. We are entitled to representation on the basis of the franchise passed by our people. Give us a fair representation, and that, gentlemen, is the whole question; and if the people support us earnestly, and if we don't become separated by the ideas of rectitude which end in pecuniary emoluments, if we do not separate and if we fight as one party, we shall win. We shall get a Progressive majority: we shall get the Progressives in power, Progressives representing the Dutch as well as the English. When we are in power, during the next five years we shall prove whether that new state, Rhodesia, is of great value or otherwise. If of value, we shall federate, and we shall join with Natal; and we shall deal gently with the other states, so as not to excite their indignation. We shall not relax our efforts, until by our civilisation and the efforts of our people we reach the shores of the Mediterranean.

Imperialism:
An Economic View

*John Atkinson Hobson, Imperialism (2d ed.; London: George Allen &
Unwin, 1905), Introduction, pp. 1-11; and chap. vii, pp. 356-68.*

The champions of imperialism were legion and not wholly simple-minded.
Critics were many, but they tended increasingly to come from antinationalist
ranks, particularly Socialist theorists. John Atkinson Hobson (1858–1940), a
radical but no Socialist, framed so strong an argument against imperialism
in 1902 that no analysis could be made without taking his views into account.
Lenin and Rosa Luxemburg were in his debt for their critiques. Hobson's
argument was fortified by British and foreign doubts as to the merits of imperialism after the debauch of the Boer War.

Hobson based his case primarily, although not exclusively, upon economic necessity. He had already elaborated a theory of underconsumption
derived from the great classical economist, Thomas Robert Malthus, and
later further refined by John Maynard Keynes. Cycles of prosperity and depression intensified in the late nineteenth century and raised question as to
the "abnormality" of depression in the minds of economists and laymen
alike. One answer was a glut of savings. As a corollary to this theory, Hobson developed his argument about imperialism in economic terms. While
including older critiques of imperialism ascribing it to a primitive lust for
power and jobs for the chldren of the ruling classes, Hobson considered imperialism primarily as the search for protected investments overseas. The
gold of the Transvaal was the primary cause of the Boer War.

Hobson argued that imperialism does not pay, that the empire cost more
than it returned. The effort to cope with the vagaries of domestic overproduction and surplus capital through overseas expansion was morally corrupting and economically unsound. Lenin and Luxemburg were so tantalized
by the possibilities that they argued that imperialism was the final and necessary extension of capitalism. Just as Hobson's theory of underconsumption
was inadequate of itself, so his theory of imperialism left too many factors
out of account. But to this non-Marxist goes credit for the formulation of the
"Marxist view" of imperialism (Marx had none), and to this radical, credit
for stating in ringing terms the moral revulsion of many to nineteenth-century empire-building.

IMPERIALISM: A STUDY
NATIONALISM AND IMPERIALISM

AMID THE WELTER of vague political abstractions to lay one's finger accurately upon any "ism" so as to pin it down and mark it out by definition
seems impossible. Where meanings shift so quickly and so subtly, not only
following changes of thought, but often manipulated artificaly by political
practitioners so as to obscure, expand, or distort, it is idle to demand the

same rigour as is expected in the exact sciences. A certain broad consistency in its relations to other kindred terms is the nearest approach to definition which such a term as Imperialism admits. Nationalism, internationalism, colonialism, its three closest congeners, are equally elusive, equally shifty, and the changeful overlapping of all four demands the closest vigilance of students of modern politics.

During the nineteenth century the struggle towards nationalism, or establishment of political union on a basis of nationality, was a dominant factor alike in dynastic movements and as an inner motive in the life of masses of population. That struggle, in external politics, sometimes took a disruptive form, as in the case of Greece, Servia, Roumania, and Bulgaria breaking from Ottoman rule, and the detachment of North Italy from her unnatural alliance with the Austrian Empire. In other cases it was a unifying or a centralising force, enlarging the area of nationality, as in the case of Italy and the Pan-Slavist movement in Russia. Sometimes nationality was taken as a basis of federation of States, as in United Germany and in North America.

It is true that the forces making for political union sometimes went further, making for federal union of diverse nationalities, as in the cases of Austria-Hungary, Norway and Sweden, and the Swiss Federation. But the general tendency was towards welding into large strong national unities the loosely related States and provinces with shifting attachments and alliances which covered large areas of Europe since the break-up of the Empire. This was the most definite achievement of the nineteenth century. The force of nationality, operating in this work, is quite as visible in the failures to achieve political freedom as in the successes; and the struggles of Irish, Poles, Finns, Hungarians, and Czechs to resist the forcible subjection to or alliance with stronger neighbours brought out in its full vigour the powerful sentiment of nationality.

The middle of the century was especially distinguished by a series of definitely "nationalist" revivals, some of which found important interpretation in dynastic changes, while others were crushed or collapsed. Holland, Poland, Belgium, Norway, the Balkans, formed a vast arena for these struggles of national forces.

The close of the third quarter of the century saw Europe fairly settled into large national States or federations of States, though in the nature of the case there can be no finality, and Italy continued to look to Trieste, as Germany still looks to Austria, for the fulfilment of her manifest destiny.

This passion and the dynastic forms it helped to mould and animate are largely attributable to to the fierce prolonged resistance which peoples, both great and small, were called on to maintain against the imperial designs of Napoleon. The national spirit of England was roused by the tenseness of the struggle to a self-consciousness it had never experienced since "the spacious days of great Elizabeth." Jena made Prussia into a great nation; the Moscow campaign brought Russia into the field of European nationalities as a factor in politics, opening her for the first time to the full tide of Western ideas and influences.

Turning from this territorial and dynastic nationalism to the spirit of racial, linguistic, and economic solidarity which has been the underlying motive, we find a still more remarkable movement. Local particularism on the one hand, vague cosmopolitanism upon the other, yielded to a ferment of nationalist sentiment, manifesting itself among the weaker peoples not merely in a sturdy and heroic resistance against political absorption or territorial nationalism, but in a passionate revival of decaying customs, language, literature and art; while it bred in more dominant peoples strange ambitions of national "destiny" and an attendant spirit of Chauvinism.

The true nature and limits of nationality have never been better stated than by J. S. Mill.

"A portion of mankind may be said to constitute a nation if they are united among themselves by common sympathies which do not exist between them and others. This feeling of nationality may have been generated by various causes. Sometimes it is the effect of identity of race and descent. Community of language and community of religion greatly contribute to it. Geographical limits are one of the causes. But the strongest of all is identity of political antecedents, the possession of a national history and consequent community of recollections, collective pride and humiliation, pleasure and regret, connected with the same incidents in the past."

It is a debasement of this genuine nationalism, by attempts to overflow its natural banks and absorb the near or distant territory of reluctant and unassimilable peoples, that marks the passage from nationalism to a spurious colonialism on the one hand, Imperialism on the other.

Colonialism, where it consists in the migration of part of a nation to vacate or sparsely peopled foreign lands, the emigrants carrying with them full rights of citizenship in the mother country, or else establishing local self-government in close conformity with her institutions and under her final control, may be considered a genuine expansion of nationality, a territorial enlargement of the stock, language and institutions of the nation. Few colonies in history have, however, long remained in this condition when they have been remote from the mother country. Either they have severed the connexion and set up for themselves as separate nationalities, or they have been kept in complete political bondage so far as all major processes of government are concerned, a condition to which the term Imperialism is at least as appropriate as colonialism. The only form of distant colony which can be regarded as a clear expansion of nationalism is the self-governing British colony in Australasia and Canada, and even in these cases local conditions may generate a separate nationalism based on a strong consolidation of colonial interests and sentiments alien from and conflicting with those of the mother nation. In other "self-governing" colonies, as in Cape Colony and Natal, where the majority of whites are not descended from British settlers, and where the presence of subject or "inferior" races in vastly preponderating numbers, and alien climatic and other natural conditions, mark out a civilization distinct from that of the "mother country," the conflict between the colonial and the imperial ideas has long been present in the forefront of the consciousness of politicians. When Lord Rosmead spoke of the permanent presence of the imperial factor as "simply an absurdity," and Mr. Rhodes spoke of its "elimination," they were championing a "colonialism" which is more certain in the course of time to develop by inner growth into a separate "nationalism" than in the case of the Australasian and Canadian colonies, because of the wider divergence, alike of interests and radical conditions of life, from the mother nation. Our other colonies are plainly representative of the spirit of Imperialism rather than of colonialism. No considerable proportion of the population consists of British settlers living with their families in conformity with the social and political customs and laws of their native land: in most instances they form a small minority wielding political or economic sway over a majority of alien and subject people, themselves under the despotic political control of the Imperial Government or its local nominees. This, the normal condition of a British colony, was well-nigh universal in the colonies of other European countries. The "colonies" which France and Germany established in Africa and Asia were in no real sense plantations of French and German national life beyond the seas; nowhere, not even in Algeria, did they represent true European civilization; their political and economic structure of society is wholly alien from that of the mother country.

Colonialism, in its best sense, is a natural overflow of nationality; its test is the power of colonists to transplant the civilization they represent to the new natural and social environment in which they find themselves. We must not be misled by names; the "colonial" party in Germany and France is identical in general aim and method with the "imperialist" party in England, and the latter is the truer title. Professor Seeley well marked the nature of Imperialism. "When a State advances beyond the limits of nationality its power becomes precarious and artificial. This is the condition of most empires, and it is the condition of our own. When a nation extends itself into other territories the chances are that it cannot destroy or completely drive out, even if it succeeds in conquering, them. When this happens it has a great and permanent difficulty to contend with, for the subject or rival nationalities cannot be properly assimilated, and remain as a permanent cause of weakness and danger."

The novelty of recent Imperialism regarded as a policy consists chiefly in its adoption by several nations. The notion of a number of competing empires is essentially modern. The root idea of empire in the ancient and mediaeval world was that of a federation of States, under a hegemony, covering in general terms the entire known recognized world, such as was held by Rome under the so-called *pax Romana*. When Roman citizens, with full civic rights, were found all over the explored world, in Africa and Asia, as well as in Gaul and Britain, Imperialism contained a genuine element of internationalism. With the fall of Rome this conception of a single empire wielding political authority over the civilized world did not disappear. On the contrary, it survived all the fluctuations of the Holy Roman Empire. Even after the definite split between the Eastern and Western sections had taken place at the close of the fourth century, the theory of a single State, divided for administrative purposes, survived. Beneath every cleavage or antagonism, and notwithstanding the severance of many independent kingdoms and provinces, this ideal unity of the empire lived. It formed the conscious avowed ideal of Charlemagne, though as a practical ambition confined to Western Europe. Rudolph of Habsburg not merely revived the idea, but laboured to realize it through Central Europe, while his descendant Charles V gave a very real meaning to the term by gathering under the unity of his imperial rule the territories of Austria, Germany, Spain, the Netherlands, Sicily, and Naples. In later ages this dream of a European Empire animated the policy of Peter the Great, Catherine, and Napoleon. Nor is it impossible that Kaiser Wilhelm II held a vision of such a world-power.

Political philosophers in many ages, Vico, Machiavelli, Dante, Kant, have speculated on an empire as the only feasible security for peace, a hierarchy of States conforming on the larger scale to the feudal order within the single State.

Thus empire was identified with internationalism, though not always based on a conception of equality of nations. The break-up of the Central European Empire, with the weakening of nationalities that followed, evoked a new modern sentiment of internationalism which, through the eighteenth century, was a flickering inspiration in the intellectual circles of European States. "The eve of the French Revolution found every wise man in Europe—Lessing, Kant, Goethe, Rousseau, Lavater, Condorcet, Priestley, Gibbon, Franklin—more of a citizen of the world than of any particular country. Goethe confessed that he did not know what patriotism was, and was glad to be without it. Cultured men of all countries were at home in polite society everywhere. Kant was immensely more interested in the events of Paris than in the life of Prussia. Italy and Germany were geographical expressions; those countries were filled with small States in which there was no political life, but in which there was much interest in the general progress of culture. The Revolution itself was at bottom also human and cosmopolitan. It is, as Lamartine said, 'a date in the human mind,' and it is because of that fact that all the carping of critics like Taine cannot prevent us from seeing that the character of the men who led the great movements of the Revolution can never obliterate the momentous nature of the Titanic strife. The soldiers of the Revolution who, barefooted and ragged, drove the insolent reactionaries from the soil of France were fighting not merely for some national cause, but for a cause dimly per-

ceived to be the cause of general mankind. With all its crudities and im-
perfections, the idea of the Revolution was that of a conceived body of
Right in which all men should share."

This early flower of humane cosmosopitanism was destined to wither before the powerful revival of nationalism which marked the next century.
Even in the narrow circles of the cultured classes it easily passed from a
noble and a passionate ideal to become a vapid sentimentalism, and after
the brief flare of 1848 among the continental populace had been extinguished, little remained but a dim smouldering of the embers. Even the
Socialism which upon the continent retains a measure of the spirit of internationalism is so tightly confined within the national limits, in its struggle
with bureaucracy and capitalism, that "the international" expresses little
more than a holy aspiration and has little opportunity of putting into
practice the genuine sentiments of brotherhood which its prophets have
always preached.

Thus the triumph of nationalism seem to have crushed the rising hope
of internationalism. Yet it would appear that there is no essential antagonism between them. A true strong internationalism in form or spirit would
rather imply the existence of powerful self-respecting nationalities which
seek union on the basis of common national needs and interests. Such a
historical development would be far more conformable to laws of social
growth than the rise of anarchic cosmopolitanism from individual units
amid the decadence of national life.

Nationalism is a plain highway to internationalism, and if it manifests
divergence we may well suspect a perversion of its nature and its purpose.
Such a perversion is Imperialism, in which nations trespassing beyond the
limits of facile assimilation transform the wholesome stimulative rivalry of
varied national types into the cut-throat struggle of competing empires.

Not only does aggressive Imperialism defeat the movement towards
internationalism by fostering animosities among competing empires: its attack upon the liberties and the existence of weaker or lower races stimulates
in them a corresponding excess of national self-consciousness. A nationalism
that bristles with resentment and is all astrain with the passion of self- defence is only less perverted from its natural genius that the nationalism
which glows with the animus of greed and self-aggrandisement at the expense of others. From this aspect aggressive Imperialism is an artificial
stimulation of nationalism in peoples too foreign to be absorbed and too
compact to be permanently crushed. We welded Africanderdom into just
such a strong dangerous nationalism, and we joined with other nations in
creating a resentful nationalism until then unknown in China. The injury to
nationalism in both cases consists in converting a cohesive, pacific internal
force into an exclusive, hostile force, a perversion of the true power and use
of nationality. The worst and most certain result is the retardation of internationalism. The older nationalism was primarily an inclusive sentiment;
its natural relation to the same sentiment in another people was lack of

sympathy, not open hostility; there was no inherent antagonism to prevent nationalities from growing and thriving side by side. Such in the main was the nationalism of the earlier nineteenth century, and the politicians of Free Trade had some foundation for their dream of a quick growth of effective, informal internationalism by peaceful, profitable intercommunication of goods and ideas among nations recognizing a just harmony of interests in free peoples.

The overflow of nationalism into imperial channels quenched all such hopes. While co-existent nationalities are capable of mutual aid involving no direct antagonism of interests, co-existent empires following each its own imperial career of territorial and industrial aggrandisement are natural necessary enemies. The full nature of this antagonism on its economic side is not intelligible without a close analysis of those conditions of modern capitalist production which compel an even keener "fight for markets," but the political antagonism is obvious.

The scramble for Africa and Asia virtually recast the policy of all European nations, evoked alliances which cross all natural lines of sympathy and historical association, drove every continental nation to consume an ever-growing share of its material and human resources upon military and naval equipment, drew the great new power of the United States from its isolation into the full tide of competition; and, by the multitude, the magnitude, and the suddenness of the issues it had thrown on to the stage of politics, became a constant agent of menace and of perturbation to the peace and progress of mankind. The new policy exercised the most notable and formidable influence upon the conscious statecraft of the nations which indulge in it. While producing for popular consumption doctrines of national destiny and imperial missions of civilization, contradictory in their true import, but subsidiary to one another as supports of popular Imperialism, it evoked a calculating, greedy type of Machiavellianism, entitled "real-politik" in Germany, where it was made, which remodelled the whole art of diplomacy and erected national aggrandisement without pity or scruple as the conscious motive force of foreign policy. Earth hunger and the scramble for markets were responsible for the openly avowed repudiation of treaty obligations which Germany, Russia, and England had not scrupled to defend. The sliding scale of diplomatic language, hinterland, sphere of interest, sphere of influence, paramountcy, suzerainty, protectorate, veiled or open, leading up to acts of forcible seizure or annexation which sometimes continue to be hidden under "lease," "rectification of frontier," "concession," and the like, was the invention and expression of this cynical spirit of Imperialism. While Germany and Russia were perhaps more open in their professed adoption of the material gain of their country as the sole criterion of public conduct, other nations were not slow to accept the standard. Though the conduct of nations in dealing with one another has commonly been determined at all times by selfish and shortsighted considerations, the conscious, deliberate adoption of this standard at an age when the intercourse of nations and their interdependence for all essentials of human life grow ever closer, is a retrograde step fraught with grave perils to the cause of civilization.

CHAPTER VII

THE OUTCOME

I

IF IMPERIALISM may no longer be regarded as a blind inevitable destiny, is it certain that imperial expansion as a deliberately chosen line of public policy can be stopped?

We have seen that it is motived, not by the interests of the nation as a whole, but by those of certain classes, who impose the policy upon the nation for their own advantage. The amalgam of economic and political forces which exercise this pressure has been submitted to close analysis. But will the detection of this confederacy of vicious forces destroy or any wise abate their operative power? For this power is a natural outcome of an unsound theory in our foreign policy. Put into plain language, the theory is this, that any British subject choosing, for his own private pleasure or profit, to venture his person or his property in the territory of a foreign State can call upon this nation to protect or avenge him in case he or his property is injured either by the Government or by any inhabitant of this foreign State. Now this is a perilous doctrine. It places the entire military, political, and financial resources of this nation at the beck and call of any missionary society which considers it has a peculiar duty to attack the religious sentiments or observances of some savage people, or of some reckless explorer who chooses just those spots of earth known to be inhabited by hostile peoples ignorant of British power; the speculative trader or the mining prospector gravitates naturally towards dangerous and unexplored countries, where the gains of a successful venture will be quick and large. All these men, missionaries, travellers, sportsmen, scientists, traders, in no proper sense the accredited representatives of this country, but actuated by private personal motives, are at liberty to call upon the British nation to spend millions of money and thousands of lives to defend them against risks which the nation has not sanctioned. It is only right to add that unscrupulous statesmen have deliberately utilized these insidious methods of encroachment, seizing upon every alleged outrage inflicted on these private adventurers or marauders as a pretext for a punitive expedition which results in the British flag waving over some new tract of territory. Thus the most reckless and irresponsible individual members of our nation are permitted to direct our foreign policy. Now that we have some four hundred million British subjects, any one of whom in theory or in practice may call upon the British arms to extricate him from the results of his private folly, the prospects of a genuine *pax Britannica* are not particularly bright.

But these sporadic risks, grave though they have sometimes proved, are insignificant when compared with the dangers associated with modern methods of international capitalism and finance. It is not long since industry was virtually restricted by political boundaries, the economic intercourse of nations being almost wholly confined to commercial exchanges of goods. The recent habit of investing capital in a foreign country has now grown to such an extent that the well-to-do and politically powerful classes in Great Britain to-day derive a large and ever larger proportion of their incomes from capital invested outside the British Empire. This growing stake of our wealthy classes in countries over which they have no political control is a revolutionary force in modern politics; it means a constantly growing tendency to use their political power as citizens of this State to interfere with the political condition of those States where they have an industrial stake.

The essentially illicit nature of this use of the public resources of the nation to safeguard and improve private investments should be clearly recognized. If I put my savings in a home investment, I take into consideration all the chances and changes to which the business is liable, including the possibilities of political changes of tariff, taxation, or industrial legislation which may affect its profits. In the case of such investment, I am quite aware that I have no right to call upon the public to protect me from loss of depreciation of my capital due to any of these causes. The political conditions of my country are taken into calculation at the time of my investment. If I invest in consols [government bonds], I fully recognize that no right of political interference with foreign policy affecting my investment is accorded to me in virtue of my interest as a fund-holder. But, if I invest either in the public funds or in some private industrial venture in a foreign country for the benefit of my private purse, getting specially favourable terms to cover risks arising from the political insecurity of the country or the deficiencies of its Government, I am entitled to call upon my Government to use its political and military force to secure me against those very risks which I have already discounted in the terms of my investment. Can anything be more palpably unfair?

It may be said that no such claim of the individual investor upon State aid is admitted. But while the theory may not have been openly avowed, recent history shows a growth of consistent practice based upon its tacit acceptance. I need not retrace the clear chain of evidence, consisting chiefly of the admissions of the mining capitalists, by which this claim to use public resources for their private profit has been enforced by the financiers who seduced our Government and people into our latest and most costly exploit. This is but the clearest and most dramatic instance of the operation of the world-wide forces of international finance. These forces are commonly described as capitalistic, but the gravest danger arises not from genuine industrial investments in foreign lands, but from the handling of stocks and shares based upon these investments by financiers.

Those who own a genuine stake in the natural resources or the industry of a foreign land have at least some substantial interest in the peace and good government of that land; but the stock speculator has no such stake: his interest lies in the oscillations of paper values, which require fluctuation and insecurity of political conditions as their instrument.

As these forms of international investment and finance are wider spread and better organized for economic and political purposes, these demands for political and military interference with foreign countries, on the ground of protecting the property of British subjects, will be more frequent and more effective; the demands of investors will commonly be backed by personal grievances of British outlanders, and we shall be drawn into a series of interferences with foreign Governments, which, if we can conduct them successfully, will lead to annexation of territory as the only security for the lives and property of our subjects.

That this policy marks a straight road to ruin there can be no doubt. But how to stop it? What principle of safety can we lay down? Only one—an absolute repudiation of the right of British subjects to call upon their Government to protect their persons or property from injuries or dangers incurred on their private initiative. This principle is just and expedient. If we send an emissary on a public mission into a foreign country, let us support and protect him by our public purse and arms; if a private person, or a company of private persons, place their lives or property in a foreign land, seeking their own ends, let them clearly understand that they do so at their own risk, and that the State will not act for their protection.

If so complete a reversal of our consistent policy be regarded as a counsel of perfection involving a definite abandonment of domiciliary, trading, and other rights secured by existing treaties or conventions with foreign States, upon the observance of which we are entitled to insist, let us at any rate lay down two plain rules of policy. First, never to sanction any interference on the part of our foreign representatives on general grounds of foreign misgovernment outside the strict limits of our treaty rights, submitting interpretation of such treaty rights to arbitration. Secondly, if in any case armed force is applied to secure the observance of these treaty rights, to confine such force to the attainment of the specific object which justifies its use.

II

Analysis of Imperialism, with its natural supports, militarism, oligarchy, bureaucracy, protection, concentration of capital and violent trade fluctuations, has marked it out as the supreme danger of modern national States. The power of the imperialist forces within the nation to use the national resources for their private gain, by operating the instrument of the State, can only be overthrown by the establishment of a genuine democrary, the direction of public policy by the people for the people through representatives over whom they exercise a real control. Whether this or any other nation is yet competent for such a democracy may well be a matter of grave doubt, but until and unless the external policy of a nation is "broad-based upon a people's will" there appears little hope of remedy. The scare of a great recent war may for a brief time check the confidence of these conspirators against the commonwealth, and cause them to hold their hands, but the financial forces freshly generated will demand new outlets, and will utilize the same political alliances and the same social, religious, and philanthropic supports in their pressure for new enterprises. The circumstances of each new imperialist exploit differ from those of all preceding ones: whatever ingenuity is requisite for the perversion of the public intelligence, or the inflammation of the public sentiment, will be forthcoming.

Imperialism is only beginning to realize its full recources, and to develop into a fine art the management of nations: the broad bestowal of a franchise, wielded by a people whose education has reached the stage of an uncritical ability to read printed matter, favours immensely the designs of keen business politicians, who, by controlling the press, the schools, and where necessary the churches, impose Imperialism upon the masses under the attractive guise of sensational patriotism.

The chief economic source of Imperialism has been found in the inequality of industrial opportunities by which a favoured class accumulates superfluous elements of income which, in their search for profitable investments, press ever farther afield: the influence on State policy of these investors and their financial managers secures a national alliance of other vested interests which are threatened by movements of social reform: the adoption of Imperialism thus serves the double purpose of securing private material benefits for favoured classes of investors and traders at the public cost, while sustaining the general cause of conservatism by diverting public energy and interest from domestic agitation to external employment.

The ability of a nation to shake off this dangerous usurpation of its power, and to employ the national resources in the national interest, depends upon the education of a national intelligence and a national will, which shall make democracy a political and economic reality. To term Imperialism a national policy is an impudent falsehood: the interests of the nation are opposed to every act of this expansive policy. Every enlargement of Great Britain in the tropics is a distinct enfeeblement of true British nationalism. Indeed, Imperialism is commended in some quarters for this very reason, that by breaking the narrow bounds of nationalities it facilitates and forwards internationalism. There are even those who favour or condone the forcible suppression of small nationalities by larger ones under the impulse of Imperialism, because they imagine that this is the natural approach to a world-federation and eternal peace. A falser view of political evolution it is difficult to conceive. If there is one condition precedent to effective internationalism or to the establishment of any reliable relations between States, it is the exsitence of strong, secure, well-developed, and responsible nations. Internationalism can never be subserved by the suppression or forcible absorption of nations; for these practices react disastrously upon the springs of internationalism, on the one hand setting nations on their armed defence and stifling the amicable approaches between them, on the other debilitating the larger nations through excessive corpulence and indigestion. The hope of a coming internationalism enjoins above all else the maintenance and natural growth of independent nationalities, for without such there could be no gradual evolution of internationalism, but only a series of unsuccessful attempts at a chaotic and unstable cosmopolitanism. An individualism is essential to any sane form of national socialism, so nationalism is essential to internationalism: no organic conception of world-politics can be framed on any other supposition.

Just in proportion as the substitution of true national governments for the existing oligarchies or sham democracies becomes possible will the apparent conflicts of national interests disappear, and the fundamental cooperation upon which nineteenth-century Free Trade prematurely relied manifest itself. The present class government means the severance or antagonism of nations, because each ruling class can only keep and use its rule by forcing the antagonisms of foreign policy: intelligent democracies would perceive their identity of interest, and would ensure it by their amicable policy. The genuine forces of internationalism, thus liberated, would first display themselves as economic forces, securing more effective international co-operation for postal, telegraphic, railway, and other transport services, for monetary exchange and for common standards of measurement of various kinds, and for the improved intercommunication of persons, goods, and information. Related and subsidiary to these purposes would come a growth of machinery of courts and congresses, at first informal and private, but gradually taking shape in more definite and more public machinery: the common interests of the arts and sciences would everywhere be weaving an elaborate network of intellectual internationalism, and both economic and intellectual community of needs and interests would contribute to the natural growth of such political solidarity as was required to maintain this real community.

It is thus, and only thus, that the existing false antagonisms of nations, with their wastes and perils and their retardation of the general course of civilization, can be resolved. To substitue for this peaceful discovery and expression of common interests a federal policy proceeding upon directly selfish political and military interests, the idea which animates an Anglo-Saxon alliance or a Pan-Teutonic empire, is deliberately to choose a longer, more difficult, and far more hazardous road to internationalism. The economic bond is far stronger and more reliable as a basis of growing internationalism than the so-called racial bond or a political alliance construced on some short-sighted computation of a balance of power. It is, of course, quite possible that a Pan-Slav, Pan-Teutonic, Pan-British, or Pan-Latin alliance might, if the federation were kept sufficiently voluntary and elastic, contribute to the wider course of internationalism. But the frankly military purpose commonly assigned for such alliances bodes ill for such assistance. It is far more likely that such alliances would be formed in the interests of the "imperialist" classes of the contracting nations, in order the more effectively to exploit the joint national resources.

We have foreshadowed the possibility of even a larger alliance of Western States, a European federation of great Powers which, so far from forwarding the cause of world-civilization, might introduce the gigantic peril of a Western parasitism, a group of advanced industrial nations, whose upper classes drew vast tribute from Asia and Africa, with which they supported great tame masses of retainers, no longer engaged in the staple industries of agriculture and manufacture, but kept in the performance of personal or minor industrial services under the control of a new financial aristocracy. Let those who would scout such a theory as undeserving of consideration examine the economic and social condition of districts in Southern England to-day which are already reduced to this condition, and reflect upon the vast extension of such a system which might be rendered feasible by the subjection of China to the economic control of similar groups of financiers, investors, and political and business officials, draining the greatest potential reservoir of profit the world has ever known, in order to consume it in Europe. The situation is far too complex, the play of world-forces far too incalculable, to render this or any other single interpretation of the future very probable: but the influences which govern the Imperialism of Western Europe to-day are moving in this direction, and, unless counteracted or diverted, make towards some such consummation.

If the ruling classes of the Western nations could realize their interests in such a combination (and each year sees capitalism more obviously international), and if China were unable to develop powers of forcible resistance, the opportunity of a parasitic Imperialism which should reproduce upon a vaster scale many of the main features of the latter Roman Empire visibly presents itself.

Whether we regard Imperialism upon this larger scale or as confined to the policy of Great Britain, we find much that is closely analogous to the Imperialism of Rome.

The rise of a money-loaning aristocracy in Rome, composed of keen, unscrupulous men from many nations, who filled the high offices of States with their creatures, political "bosses" or military adventurers, who had come to the front as usurers, publicans, or chiefs of police in the provinces, was the most distinctive feature of later imperial Rome. This class was continually recruited from returned officials and colonial millionaires. The large incomes drawn in private official plunder, public tribute, usury and official incomes from the provinces had the following reactions upon Italy. Italians were no longer wanted for working the land or for manufactures, or even for military service. "The later campaigns on the Rhine and the Danube," it is pointed out, "were really slave-hunts on a gigantic scale."

The Italian farmers, at first drawn from rural into military life, soon found themselves permanently ousted from agriculture by the serf labour of the *latifundia*, and they and their families were sucked into the dregs of town life, to be subsisted as a pauper population upon public charity. A mercenary colonial army came more and more to displace the home forces. The parasitic city life, with its lowered vitality and the growing infrequency of marriage, to which Gibbon draws attention, rapidly impaired the physique of the native population of Italy, and Rome subsisted more and more upon immigration of raw vigour from Gaul and Germany. The necessity of maintaining powerful mercenary armies to hold the provinces heightened continually the peril, already manifest in the last years of the Republic, arising from the political ambitions of great proconsuls conspiring with a moneyed interest at Rome against the Commonwealth. As time went on, this moneyed oligarchy became an hereditary aristocracy, and withdrew from military and civil service, relying more and more upon hired foreigners: themselves sapped by luxury and idleness and tainting by mixed servitude and licence the Roman populace, they so enfeebled the State as to destroy the physical and moral vitality required to hold in check and under government the vast repositary of forces in the exploited Empire. The direct cause of Rome's decay and fall is expressed politically by the term "over-centralization," which conveys in brief the real essence of Imperialism as distinguished from national growth on the one hand and colonialism upon the other. Parasitism, practised through taxation and usury, involved a constantly increasing centralization of the instruments of government, and a growing strain upon this government, as the prey became more impoverished by the drain and showed signs of restiveness. "The evolution of this centralized society was as logical as every other work of nature. When force reached the stage where it expressed itself exclusively through money, the governing class ceased to be chosen because they were valiant or eloquent, artistic, learned or devout, and were selected solely because they had the faculty of acquiring and keeping wealth. As long as the weak retained enough vitality to produce something which could be absorbed, this oligarchy was invariable; and, for very many years after the native peasantry of Gaul and Italy had perished from the land, new blood, injected from more tenacious races, kept the dying civilization alive. The weakness of the moneyed class lay in this very power, for they not only killed the producer but in the strength of their acquisitiveness they failed to propagate themselves."

This is the largest, plainest instance history presents of the social parasitic process by which a moneyed interest within the State, usurping the reins of government, makes for imperial expansion in order to fasten economic suckers into foreign bodies so as to drain them of their wealth in order to support domestic luxury. The new Imperialism differs in no vital point from this old example. The element of political tribute is now absent or quite subsidiary, and the crudest forms of slavery have disappeared: some elements of more genuine and disinterested government serve to qualify and mask the distinctively parasitic nature of the later sort. But nature is not mocked: the laws which, operative throughout nature, doom the parasite to atrophy, decay, and final extinction, are not evaded by nations any more than by individual organisms. The greater complexity of the modern process, the endeavour to escape the parasitic reaction by rendering some real but quite unequal and inadequate services to "the host," may retard but cannot finally avert the natural consequences of living upon others. The claim that an imperial State forcibly subjugating other peoples and their lands does so for the purpose of rendering services to the conquered equal to those which she exacts is notoriously false: she neither intends equivalent services nor is capable of rendering them, and the pretence that such benefits to the governed form a leading motive or result of Imperialism implies a degree of moral or intellectual obliquity so grave as itself to form a new peril for any nation fostering so false a notion of the nature of its conduct. "Let the motive be in the deed, not in the event," says a Persion proverb.

Imperialism is a depraved choice of national life, imposed by self-seeking interests which appeal to the lusts of quantitative acquisitiveness and of forceful domination surviving in a nation from early centuries of animal struggle for existence. Its adoption as a policy implies a deliberate renunciation of that cultivation of the higher inner qualities which for a nation as for an individual constitutes the ascendency of reason over brute impulse. It is the besetting sin of all successful States, and its penalty is unalterable in the order of nature.

B. *The World of Facts and Its Challengers*

The Ethics of Capitalism

Samuel Smiles, Self Help *(New ed.; New York: Harper & Bros., 1861),
chap. x, pp. 290–313.*

Technological progress was a salient fact in nineteenth-century history. No
man could speak for the many facets of industrial capitalism and its impact,
but Samuel Smiles (1812–1904) voiced its confidence and moral earnestness.
Self Help (1859) was more than a set of platitudes; it sprang from the basic
ethics of entrepreneurial society. Translated into dozens of languages, including Japanese and several Indian tongues, *Self Help* stood as a monument
to social mobility and social aspiration. Smiles spoke to the man on the rise.
Countless imitators down to the present have warmed over the maxims of
Self Help, although they always seem to come out in perverted form. Your
own home, savings, a carriage, servants are tangible symbols of intangible
virtue.

Smiles's "individuality" probably held better in Britain than anywhere
else in Europe, but with the coming of combinations, trusts, and cartels, the
rhetoric of individuality became even more important as myth than it had
been as fact. You, too, can succeed. Anything is possible for the virtuous
and industrious. Smiles is the evangelical religious impulse secularized as a
code of values at the apex of which stands "respectability." It is a short
but significant step from John Wesley's sermon, "The Use of Money"—
itself a document of cardinal importance in understanding the evangelical
impulse—to Samuel Smiles.

Smiles teaches by precept and example. His message is never elusive or
subtle.

"Heaven helps those who help themselves" is a well-tried maxim, embodying in
a small compass the results of vast human experience. The spirit of self-help is the
root of all genuine growth in the individual; and exhibited in the lives of many,
it constitutes the true source of national vigour and strength. Help from without
is often enfeebling in its effects, but help from within invariably invigorates.
Whatever is done *for* men or classes, to a certain extent takes away the stimulus
and necessity of doing for themselves; and where men are subject to over-guid-
ance and over-government, the inevitable tendency is to render them comparatively helpless.

Smiles was more perceptive than Marx in a sense, for *Self Help* never
appealed to the crude test of financial success. The entrepreneur seeks to
make money, and he makes the most he can the best way he can. Nothing
could be more simple. Smiles, however, appeals to pride and status, showing
how these most important human aspirations can be found in the humdrum
aspects of life.

The greatest results in life are usually obtained by simple means, and the exercise
of ordinary qualities. The common life of every day, with its cares, necessities,

and duties, affords ample opportunity for acquiring experience of the best kind; and its most beaten paths provide the true worker with abundant scope for effort and room for self-improvement. The road of human welfare lies along the old highway of steadfast well-doing; and they who are the most persistent and work in the truest spirit, will usually be the most successful.

And how strong the appeal to pride! English civilization, as Smiles portrayed it, was obviously the best in the world, and it rested foursquare on the virtues he preached.

The career of industry which the nation has pursued, has also proved its best education. As steady application to work is the healthiest training for every individual, so is it the best discipline of a state. Honourable industry travels the same road with duty; and Providence has closely linked both with happiness. The gods, says the poet, have placed labour and toil on the way leading to the Elysian fields. Certain it is that no bread eaten by man is so sweet as that earned by his own labour, whether bodily or mental. By labour the earth has been subdued, and man redeemed from barbarism; nor has a single step in civilisation been made without it. Labour is not only a necessity and a duty, but a blessing: only the idler feels it to be a curse. The duty of work is written on the thews and muscles of the limbs, the mechanism of the hand, the nerves and lobes of the brain—the sum of whose healthy action is satisfaction and enjoyment. In the school of labour is taught the best practical wisdom; nor is a life of manual employment, as we shall hereafter find, incompatible with high mental culture.

Here, then, is Samuel Smiles, the apostle of mid-Victorian social ethics. The following chapter, "Money—Its Use and Abuse," did not have to be accurate. The world was full of social critics railing against the heartlessness and cynicism of industrial society. Smiles is not silly. Many of his most banal observations are, after all, quite true. In this chapter he considers problems, still very much with us, in terms that the entrepreneurs of the modern world hoped and still hope are true.

CHAPTER X

MONEY—ITS USE AND ABUSE.

> "Not for to hide it in a hedge,
> Nor for a train attendant,
> But for the glorious privilege
> Of being independent."—*Burns*

> "Neither a borrower nor a lender be:
> For loan oft loses both itself and friend;
> And borrowing dulls the edge of husbandry."—*Shakespeare*

> Never treat money affairs with levity—Money is character.
> —*Sir E. L. Bulwer Lytton*

How a man uses money—makes it, saves it, and spends it—is perhaps one of the best tests of practical wisdom. Although money ought by no means to be regarded as a chief end of man's life, neither is it a trifling matter, to be held in philosophic contempt, representing as it does to so large an extent, the means of physical comfort and social well-being. Indeed, some of the finest qualities of human nature are intimately related to the right use of money; such as generosity, honesty, justice, and self-sacrifice; as well as the practical virtues of economy and providence. On the other hand, there are their counterparts of avarice, fraud, injustice, and selfishness, as displayed by the inordinate lovers of gain; and the vices of thriftlessness, extravagance, and improvidence, on the part of those who misuse and abuse the means entrusted to them. "So that," as is wisely observed by Henry Taylor in his thoughtful 'Notes from Life,' "a right measure and manner in getting, saving, spending, giving, taking, lending, borrowing, and bequeathing, would almost argue a perfect man."

Comfort in worldly circumstances is a condition which every man is justified in striving to attain by all worthy means. It secures that physical satisfaction, which is necessary for the culture of the better part of his nature; and enables him to provide for those of his own household, without which, says the Apostle, a man is "worse than an infidel." Nor ought the duty to be any the less indifferent to us, that the respect which our fellow-men entertain for us in no slight degree depends upon the manner in which we exercise the opportunities which present themselves for our honourable advancement in life. The very effort required to be made to succeed in life with this object, is of itself an education; stimulating a man's sense of self-respect, bringing out his practical qualities, and disciplining him in the exercise of patience, perseverance, and such like virtues. The provident and careful man must necessarily be a thoughtful man, for he lives not merely for the present, but with provident forecast makes arrangements for the future. He must also be a temperate man, and exercise the virtue of self-denial, than which nothing is so much calculated to give strength to the character. John Sterling says truly, that "the worst education which teaches self-denial, is better than the best which teaches everything else, and not that." The Romans rightly employed the same word (virtus) to designate courage, which is in a physical sense what the other is in a moral; the higest virtue of all being victory over ourselves.

Hence the lesson of self-denial—the sacrificing of a present gratification for a future good—is one of the last that is learnt. Those classes which work the hardest might naturally be expected to value the most the money which they earn. Yet the readiness with which so many are accustomed to eat up and drink up their earnings as they go, renders them to a great extent helpless and dependent upon the frugal. There are large numbers of persons among us who, though enjoying sufficient means of comfort and independence, are often found to be barely a day's march ahead of actual want when a time of pressure occurs; and hence a great cause of social helplessness and suffering. On one occasion a deputation waited on Lord John Russell, respecting the taxation levied on the working classes of the country, when the noble lord took the opportunity of remarking, "You may rely upon it that the Government of this country durst not tax the working classes to anything like the extent to which they tax themselves in their expenditure upon intoxicating drinks alone!" Of all great public questions, there is perhaps none more important than this,—no great work of reform calling more loudly for labourers. But it must be admitted that "self-denial and self-help" would make a poor rallying cry for the hustings; and it is to be feared that the patriotism of this day has but little regard for such common things as indivdual economy and providence, although it is by the practice of such virtues only that the genuine independence of the industrial classes is to be secured. "Prudence, frugality, and good management," said Samuel Drew, the philosophical shoemaker, "are excellent artists for mending bad times: they occupy but little room in any dwelling, but would furnish a more effectual remedy for the evils of life than any Reform Bill that ever passed the Houses of Parliament." Socrates said, "Let him that would move the world move first himself." Or as the old rhyme runs—

> "If every one would see
> To his own reformation.
> How very easily
> You might reform a nation."

It is, however, generally felt to be a far easier thing to reform the Church and the State than to reform the least of our own bad habits; and in such matters it is usually found more agreeable to our tastes, as it certainly is the common practice, to begin with our neighbours rather than with ourselves.

Any class of men that lives from hand to mouth will ever be an inferior class. They will necessarily remain impotent and helpless, hanging on to the skirts of society, the sport of times and seasons. Having no respect for themselves, they will fail in securing the respect of others. In commercial crises, such men must inevitably go to the wall. Wanting that husbanded power which a store of savings, no matter how small, invariably gives them, they will be at every man's mercy, and, if possessed of right feelings, they cannot but regard with fear and trembling the future possible fate of their wives and children. "The world," once said Mr. Cobden to the working men of Huddersfield, "has always been divided into two classes,—those who have saved, and those who have spent—the thrifty and the extravagant. The building of all the houses, the mills, the bridges, and the ships, and the accomplishment of all other great works which have rendered man civilized and happy, has been done by the savers, the thrifty; and those who have wasted their resources have always been their slaves. It has been the law of nature and of Providence that this should be so; and I were an impostor if I promised any class that they would advance themselves if they were improvident, thoughtless, and idle."

Equally sound was the advice given by Mr. Bright to an assembly of working men at Rochdale, in 1847, when, after expressing his belief that, "so far as honesty was concerned, it was to be found in pretty equal amount among all classes," she used the following words:—"There is only one way that is safe for any man, or any number of men, by which they can maintain their present position if it be a good one, or raise themselves above it if it be a bad one,—that is, by the practice of the virtues of industry, frugality, temperance, and honesty. There is no royal road by which men can raise themselves from a position which they feel to be uncomfortable and unsatisfactory, as regards their mental or physical condition, except by the practice of those virtues by which they find numbers amongst them are continually advancing and bettering themselves."

There is no reason why the condition of the average workman should not be a useful, honourable, respectable, and happy one. The whole body of the working classes might, (with few exceptions) be as frugal, virtuous, well-informed, and well-conditioned as many individuals of the same class have already made themselves. What some men are, all without difficulty might be. Employ the same means, and the same results will follow. That there should be a class of men who live by their daily labour in every state is the ordinance of God, and doubtless is a wise and righteous one; but that this class should be otherwise than frugal, contented, intelligent, and happy, is not the design of Providence, but springs solely from the weakness, self-indulgence, and perverseness of man himself. The healthy spirit of self-help created amongst working people would more than any other measure serve to raise them as a class, and this, not by pulling down others, but by levelling them up to a higher and still advancing standard of religion, intelligence, and virtue. "All moral philosophy," says Montaigne, "is as applicable to a common and private life as to the most splendid. Every man carries the entire form of the human condition within him."

When a man casts his glance forward, he will find that the three chief temporal contingencies for which he has to provide are want of employment, sickness, and death. The two first he may escape, but the last is inevitable. It is, however, the duty of the prudent man so to live, and so to arrange, that the pressure of suffering, in event of either contingency occurring, shall be mitigated to as great an extent as possible, not only to himself, but also to those who are dependent upon him for their comfort and subsistence. Viewed in this light the honest earning and the frugal use of money are of the greatest importance. Rightly earned, it is the representative of patient industry and untiring effort, of temptation resisted, and hope rewarded; and rightly used, it affords indications of prudence, fore-thought and self-denial—the true basis of manly character. Though money represents a crowd of objects without any real worth or utility, it also represents many things of great value; not only food, clothing, and household satisfaction, but personal self-respect and independence. Thus a store of savings is to the working man as a barricade against want; it secures him a footing, and enables him to wait, it may be in cheerfulness and hope, until better days come round. The very endeavour to gain a firmer position in the world has a certain dignity in it, and tends to make a man stronger and better. At all events it gives him greater freedom of action, and enables him to husband his strength for future effort.

But the man who is always hovering on the verge of want is in a state not far removed from that of slavery. He is in no sense his own master, but is in constant peril of falling under the bondage of others, and accepting the terms which they dictate to him. He cannot help being in a measure, servile, for he dares not look the world boldly in the face; and in adverse times he must look either to alms or the poor's rates. If work fails him altogether, he has not the means of moving to another field of employment; he is fixed to his parish like a limpet to its rock, and can neither migrate nor emigrate.

To secure independence, the practice of simple economy is all that is necessary. Economy requires neither superior courage nor eminent virtue; it is satisfied with ordinary energy, and the capacity of average minds. Economy, at bottom, is but the spirit of order applied in the administration of domestic affairs: it means management, regularity, prudence, and the avoidance of waste. The spirit of economy was expressed by our Divine Master in the words 'Gather up the fragments that remain, so that nothing may be lost.' His omnipotence did not disdain the small things of life; and even while revealing His infinite power to the multitude, he taught the pregnant lesson of carefulness of which all stand so much in need.

Economy also means the power of resisting present gratification for the purpose of securing a future good, and in this light it represents the ascendancy of reason over the animal instincts. It is altogether different from penuriousness: for it is economy that can always best afford to be generous. It does not make money an idol but regards it as a useful agent. As Dean Swift observes, "we must carry money in the head, not in the heart." Economy may be styled the daughter of Prudence, the sister of Temperance, and the mother of Liberty. It is evidently conservative—conservative of character, of domestic happiness, and social well-being. It is, in short, the exhibition of self-help in one of its best forms.

Francis Horner's father gave him this advice on entering life:—"Whilst I wish you to be comfortable in every respect, I cannot too strongly inculcate economy. It is a necessary virtue to all; and however the shallow part of mankind may despise it, it certainly leads to independence, which is a grand object to every man of a high spirit." Burns' lines, quoted at the head of this chapter, contain the right idea; but unhappily his strain of song was higher than his practice; his ideal better than his habit. When laid on his death-bed he wrote to a friend, "Alas! Clarke, I begin to feel the worst. Burns' poor widow, and half a dozen of his dear little ones helpless orphans; —there I am weak as a woman's tear. Enough of this;—'tis half my disease."

Every man ought so to contrive as to live within his means. This parctice is of the very essence of honesty. For if a man do not manage honestly to live within his own means, he must necessarily be living dishonestly upon the means of somebody else. Those who are careless about personal expenditure, and consider merely their own gratification, without regard for the comfort of others, generally find out the real uses of money when it is too late. Though by nature generous, these thriftless persons are often driven in the end to do very shabby things. They waste their money as they do their time; draw bills upon the future; anticipate their earnings; and are thus under the necessity of dragging after them a load of debts and obligations which seriously affect their action as free and independent men.

It was a maxim of Lord Bacon, that when it was necessary to economize, it was better to look after petty savings than to descend to petty gettings. The loose cash which many persons throw away uselessly, and worse, would often form a basis of fortune and independence for life. These wasters are their own worst enemies, though generally found amongst the ranks of those who rail at the injustice of "the world." But if a man will not be his own friend, how can he expect that others will? Orderly men of moderate means have always something left in their pockets to help others; whereas your prodigal and careless fellows who spend all never find an opportunity for helping anybody. It is poor economy, however, to be a scrub. Narrow-mindedness in living and in dealing is generally short-sighted, and leads to failure. The penny soul, it is said, never came to twopence. Generosity and liberality, like honesty, prove the best policy after all. Though Jenkinson, in the 'Vicar of Wakefield,' cheated his kind-hearted neighbor Flamborough in one way or another every year, "Flamborough," said he, "has been regularly growing in riches, while I have come to poverty and a gaol." And practical life abounds in cases of brilliant results from a course of generous and honest policy.

The proverb says that "an empty bag cannot stand upright;" neither can a man who is in debt. It is also difficult for a man who is in debt to be truthful; hence it is said that lying rides on debt's back. The debtor has to frame excuses to his creditor for postponing payment of the money he owes him; and probably also to contrive falsehoods. It is easy enough for a man who will exercise a healthy resolution, to avoid incurring the first obligation; but the facility with which that has been incurred often becomes a temptation to a second; and very soon the unfortunate borrower becomes so entangled that no late exertion of industry can set him freee. The first step in debt is like the first step in falsehood; almost involving the necessity of proceeding in the same course, debt following debt, as lie follows lie. Haydon, the painter, dated his decline from the day on which he first borrowed money. He realized the truth of the proverb, "Who goes a-borrowing, goes a-sorrowing." The significant entry in his diary is: "Here began debt and obligation, out of which I have never been and never shall be extricated as long as I live." His Autobiography shows but too painfully how embarrassment in money matters produces poignant distress of mind, utter incapacity for work, and constantly recurring humiliations. The written advice which he gave to a youth when entering the navy was as follows: "Never purchase any enjoyment if it cannot be procured without borrowing of others. Never borrow money: it is degrading. I do not say never lend, but never lend if by lending you render yourself unable to pay what you owe; but under any circumstances never borrow." Fichte, the poor student, refused to accept even presents from his still poorer parents.

Dr. Johnson held that early debt is ruin. His words on the subject are weighty, and worthy of being held in remembrance. "Do not," said he, "accustom yourself to consider debt only as an inconvenience; you will find it a calamity. Poverty takes away so many means of doing good, and produces so much inability to resist evil, both natural and moral, that it is by all virtuous means to be avoided. . . . Let it be your first care, then, not to be in any man's debt. Resolve not to be poor; whatever you have spend less. Poverty is a great enemy to human happiness; it certainly destroys liberty, and it makes some virtues impracticable and others extremely difficult. Frugality is not only the basis of quiet, but of beneficence. No man can help others that wants help himself; we must have enough before we have to spare."

It is the bounden duty of every men to look his affairs in the face, and to keep an account of his incomings and outgoings in money matters. The exercise of a little simple arithmetic in this way will be found of great value. Prudence requires that we shall pitch our scale of living a degreee below our means, rather than up to them; but this can only be done by carrying out faithfully a plan of living by which both ends may be made to meet. John Locke strongly advised this course: "Nothing," said he "is likelier to keep a man within compass than having constantly before his eyes the state of his affairs in a regular course of account." The Duke of Wellington kept an accurate detailed account of all the monies received and expended by him. "I make a point," said he to Mr. Gleig, "of paying my own bills, and I advise every one to do the same; formerly I used to trust a confidential servant to pay them, but I was cured of that folly by receiving one morning, to my great surprise, duns of a year or two's standing. The fellow had speculated with my money, and left my bills unpaid." Talking of debt his remark was, "It makes a slave of a man. I have often known what it was to be in want of money, but I never got into debt." Washington was as particular as Wellington was, in matters of business detail; and it is a remarkable fact, that he did not disdain to scrutinize the smallest outgoings of his household—determined as he was to live honestly within his means—even while holding the high office of President of the American Union.

Admiral Jervis, Earl St. Vincent, has told the story of his early struggles, and, amongst other things, of his determination to keep out of debt. "My father had a very large family," said he, "with limited means. He gave me twenty pounds at starting, and that was all he ever gave me. After I had been a considerable time at the station [at sea], I drew for twenty more, but the bill came back protested. I was mortified at this rebuke, and made a promise, which I have ever kept, that I would never draw another bill without a certainty of its being paid. I immediately changed my mode of living, quitted my mess, lived alone, and took up the ship's allowance, which I found quite sufficient; washed and mended my own clothes; made a pair of trousers out of the ticking of my bed; and having by these means saved as much money as would redeem my honour, I took up my bill, and from that time to this I have taken care to keep within my means." Jervis for six years endured pinching privation, but preserved his integrity, studied his profession with success, and gradually and steadily rose by merit and bravery to the highest rank.

Mr. Hume hit the mark when he once stated in the House of Commons— though his words were followed by "laughter"—that the tone of living in England is altogether too high. Middle-class people are too apt to live up to their incomes, if not beyond them: affecting a degree of "style" which is most unhealthy in its effects upon society at large. There is an ambition to bring up boys as gentlemen, or rather "genteel" men; though the result frequently is, only to make them gents. They acquire a taste for dress, style, luxuries, and amusements, which can never form any solid foundation for manly or gentlemanly character; and the result is, that we have a vast number of gingerbread young gentry thrown upon the world, who remind one of the abandoned hulls sometimes picked up at sea, with only a monkey on board.

There is a dreadful ambition abroad for being "genteel." We keep up appearances, too often at the expense of honesty; and, though we may not be rich, yet we must seem to be so. We must be "respectable," though only in the meanest sense—in mere vulgar outward show. We have not the courage to go patiently onward in the condition of life in which it has pleased God to call us; but must needs live in some fashionable state to which we ridiculously please to call ourselves, and all to gratify the vanity of that unsubstantial genteel world of which we form a part. There is a constant struggle and pressure for front seats in the social amphitheatre; in the midst of which all noble self-denying resolve is trodden down, and many fine natures are inevitably crushed to death. What waste, what misery, what bankruptcy, come from all this ambition to dazzle others with the glare of apparent worldly success, we need not describe. The mischievous results show themselves in a thousand ways—in the rank frauds committed by men who dare to be dishonest, but do not dare to seem poor; and in the desperate dashes at fortune, in which the pity is not so much for those who fail, as for the hundreds of innocent families who are so often involved in their ruin.

The late Sir Charles Napier, in taking leave of his command in India, did a bold and honest thing in publishing his strong protest, embodied in his last General Order to the officers of the Indian army, against the "fast" life led by so many young officers in that service, involving them in ignominious obligations. Sir Charles strongly urged, in that famous document—what had almost been lost sight of—that "honesty is inseparable from the character of a thorough-bred gentleman;" and that "to drink unpaid-for champagne and unpaid-for beer, and to ride unpaid-for horses, is to be a cheat, and not a gentleman." Men who lived beyond their means and were summoned, often by their own servants, before Courts of Requests for debts contracted in extravagant living, might be officers by virtue of their commissions, but they were not gentlemen. The habit of being constantly in debt, the Commander-in-chief held, made men grow callous to the proper feelings of a gentleman. It was not enough that an officer should be able to fight: that any bull-dog could do. But did he hold his word inviolate?—did he pay his debts? These were among the points of honour which, he insisted, illuminated the true gentleman's and soldier's career. As Bayard was of old, so would Sir Charles Napier have all British officers to be. He knew them to be "without fear," but he would also have them "without reproach." There are, however, many gallant young fellows, both in India and at home, capable of mounting a breach on an emergency amidst belching fire, and of performing the most desperate deeds of valour, who nevertheless cannot or will not exercise the moral courage necessary to enable them to resist a petty temptation presented to their senses. They cannot utter their valiant "No," or "I can't afford it," to the invitations of pleasure and self-enjoyment; and they are found ready to brave death rather than the ridicule of their companions.

The young man, as he passes through life, advances through a long line of tempters ranged on either side of him; and the inevitable effect of yielding, is degradation in a greater or a less degree. Contact with them tends insensibly to draw away from him some portion of the divine electric element with which his nature is charged; and his only mode of resisting them is to utter and to act out his "no" manfully and resolutely. He must decide at once, not waiting to deliberate and balance reasons; for the youth, like "the woman who deliberates, is lost." Many deliberate, without deciding; but "not to resolve, *is* to resolve." A perfect knowledge of man is in the prayer, "Lead us not into temptation." But temptation will come to try the young man's strength; and once yielded to, the power to resist grows weaker and weaker. Yield once, and a portion of virtue has gone. Resist manfully, and the first decision will give strength for life; repeated, it will become a habit. It is in the outworks of the habits formed in early life that the real strength of the defence must lie; for it has beeen wisely ordained, that the machinery of moral existence should be carried on principally through the medium of the habits, so as to save the wear and tear of the great principles within. It is good habits, which insinuate themselves into the thousand inconsiderable acts of life, that really constitute by far the greater part of man's moral conduct.

Hugh Miller has told how, by an act of youthful decision, he saved himself from one of the strong temptations so peculiar to a life of toil. When employed as a mason, it was usual for his fellow-workmen to have an occasional treat of drink, and one day two glasses of whisky fell to his share, which he swallowed. When he reached home he found, on opening his favourite book—'Bacon's Essays'—that the letters danced before his eyes, and that he could no longer master the sense. "The condition," he says, "into which I had brought myself was, I felt, one of degradation. I had sunk, by my own act, for the time, to a lower level of intelligence than that on which it was my privilege to be placed; and though the state could have been no very favourable one for forming a resolution, I in that hour determined that I should never again sacrifice my capacity of intellectual enjoyment to a drinking usage; and, with God's help, I was enabled to hold by the determination." It is such decisions as this that often form the turning-points in a man's life, and furnish the foundation of his future character. And this rock, on which Hugh Miller might have been wrecked, if he had not at the right moment put forth his moral strength to strike away from it, is one that youth and manhood alike need to be constantly on their guard against. It is about one of the worst and most deadly, as well as extravagant, temptations, which lie in the way of youth. Sir Walter Scott used to say that "of all vices drinking is the most incompatible with greatness." Not only so, but it is incompatible with economy, decency, health, and honest living. When a youth cannot restrain, he must abstain. Dr. Johnson's case is the case of many. He said, referring to his own habits, "Sir, I can abstain; but I can't be moderate."

But to wrestle vigorously and successfully with any vicious habit, we must not merely be satisfied with contending on the low ground of wordly prudence, though that is of use, but take stand upon a higher moral elevation. Mechanical aids, such as pledges, may be of service to some, but the great thing is to set up a high standard of thinking and acting, and endeavour to strengthen and purify the principles as well as to reform the habits. For this purpose a youth must study himself, watch his steps, and compare his thoughts and acts with his rule. The more knowledge of himself he gains, the more humble will he be, and perhaps the less confident in his own strength. But the discipline will be always found most valuable which is acquired by resisting small present gratifications to secure a prospective greater and higher one. It is the noblest work in self-education,—for

> "Real glory
> Springs from the silent conquest of ourselves,
> And without that the conqueror is nought
> But the first slave."

Many popular books have been written for the purpose of communicating to the public the grand secret of making money. But there is no secret whatever about it, as the proverbs of every nation abundantly testify. "Take care of the pennies and the pounds will take care of themselves." "Diligence is the mother of good luck." "No pains no gains." "No sweat so sweet." "Work and thou shalt have." "The world is his who has patience and industry." "Better go to bed supperless than rise in debt." Such are specimens of the proverbial philosophy, embodying the hoarded experience of many generations, as to the best means of thriving in the world. They were current in people's mouths long before books were invented; and like other popular proverbs they were the first codes of popular morals. Moreover they have stood the test of time, and the experience of every day still bears witness to their accuracy, force, and soundness. The proverbs of Solomon are full of wisdom as to the force of industry, and the use and abuse of money:—"He that is slothful in work is brother to him that is a great waster." "Go to the ant thou sluggard; consider her ways and be wise." Poverty, says the preacher, shall come upon the idler, "as one that travelleth, and want as an armed man;" but of the industrious and upright, "the hand of the diligent maketh rich." "The drunkard and the glutton shall come to poverty; and drowsiness shall clothe a man with rags." "Seest thou a man diligent in his business? he shall stand before kings." But above all, "It is better to get wisdom than gold; for wisdom is better than rubies, and all the things that may be desired are not to be compared to it."

Simple industry and thrift will go far towards making any person of ordinary working faculty comparatively independent in his means. Even a working man may be so, provided he will carefully husband his resources, and watch the little outlets of useless expenditure. A penny is a very small matter, yet the comfort of thousands of families depends upon the proper spending and saving of pennies. If a man allows the little pennies, the results of his hard work, to slip out of his fingers—some to the beershop, some this way and some that—he will find that his life is little raised above one of mere animal drudgery. On the other hand, if he take care of the pennies —putting some weekly into a benefit society or an insurance fund, others into a savings' bank, and confiding the rest to his wife to be carefully laid out, with a view to the comfortable maintenance and education of his family —he will soon find that this attention to small matters will abundantly repay him, in increasing means, growing comfort at home, and a mind comparatively free from fears as to the future. And if a working man have high ambition and possess richness in spirit,—a kind of wealth which far transcends all mere worldly possessions—he may not only help himself, but be a profitable helper of others in his path through life. That this is no impossible thing even for a common labourer in a workshop, may be illustrated by the remarkable career of Thomas Wright of Manchester, who not only attempted but succeeded in the reclamation of many criminals while working for weekly wages in a foundry.

Accident first directed Thomas Wright's attention to the difficulty encountered by liberated convicts in returning to habits of honest industry. His mind was shortly possessed by the subject; and to remedy the evil became the purpose of his life. Though he worked from six in the morning till six at night, still there were leisure minutes that he could call his own— more especially his Sundays—and these he employed in the service of convicted criminals; a class then far more neglected than they are now. But a few minutes a day, well employed, can effect a great deal; and it will scarcely be credited, that in ten years this working man, by steadfastly holding to his purpose, succeeded in rescuing not fewer than three hundred felons from continuance in a life of villany! He came to be regarded as the moral physician of the Manchester Old Bailey; and where the Chaplain and all others failed, Thomas Wright often succeeded. Children he thus restored reformed to their parents; sons and daughters otherwise lost, to their homes; and many a returned convict did he contrive to settle down to honest and industrious pursuits. The task was by no means easy. It required money, time, energy, prudence, and above all, character, and the confidence which character invariably inspires. The most remarkable circumstance was that Wright relieved many of these poor outcasts out of the comparatively small wages earned by him at foundry work. He did all this on an income which did not average, during his working career, 100*l.* per annum; and yet, while he was able to bestow substantial aid on criminals, to whom he owed no more than the service of kindness which every human being owes to another, he also maintained his family in comfort, and was, by frugality and carefulness, enabled to lay by a store of savings against his approaching old age. Every week he apportioned his income with deliberate care; so much for the indispensable necessaries of food and clothing, so much for the landlord, so much for the schoolmaster, so much for the poor and needy; and the lines of distribution were resolutely observed. By such means did this humble workman pursue his great work, with the results we have so briefly described. Indeed, his career affords one of the most remarkable and striking illustrations of the force of purpose in a man, of the might of small means carefully and sedulously applied, and, above all, of the power which an energetic and upright character invariably exercises upon the lives and conduct of others.

There is no discredit, but honour, in every right walk of industry, whether it be in tilling the ground, making tools, weaving fabrics, or selling the products behind a counter. A youth may handle a yard-stick, or measure a piece of ribbon; and there will be no discredit in doing so, unless he allows his mind to have no higher range than the stick and ribbon; to be as short as the one, and as narrow as the other. "Let not those blush who *have,*" said Fuller, but those who *have not* a lawful calling." And Bishop Hall said, "Sweet is the destiny of all trades, whether of the brow or of the mind." Men who have raised themselves from a humble calling, need not be ashamed, but rather ought to be proud of the difficulties they have surmounted. An American President, when asked what was his coat-of-arms, remembering that he had been a hewer of wood in his youth, replied, "A pair of shirt sleeves." A French doctor once taunted Flechier, Bishop of Nismes, who had been a tallow-chandler in his youth, with the meanness of his origin, to which Flechier replied, "If you had been born in the same condition that I was, you would still have been but a maker of candles."

Nothing is more common than energy in money-making, quite independent of any higher object than its accumulation. A man who devotes himself to this pursuit, body and soul, can scarcely fail to become rich. Very little brains will do: spend less than you earn; add guinea to guinea; scrape and save; and the pile of gold will gradually rise. Osterwald the Parisian banker, began life a poor man. He was accustomed every evening to drink a pint of beer for supper at a tavern which he visited, during which he collected and pocketed all the corks that he could lay his hands on. In eight years he had collected as many corks as sold for eight louis d'ors. With that sum he laid the foundations of his fortune—gained mostly by stock-jobbing; leaving at his death some three millions of francs. John Foster has cited a striking illustration of what this kind of determination will do in money-making. A young man who ran through his patrimony, spending it in profligacy, was at length reduced to utter want and despair. He rushed out of his house intending to put an end to his life, and stopped on arriving at an eminence overlooking what were once his estates. He sat down, ruminated for a time, and rose with the determination that he would recover them. He returned to the streets, saw a load of coals which had been shot out of a cart on to the pavement before a house, offered to carry them in, and was employed. He thus earned a few pence, requested some meat and drink as a gratuity, which was given him, and the pennies were laid by. Pursuing this menial labour, he earned and saved more pennies; accumulated sufficient to enable him to purchase some cattle, the value of which he understood, and these he sold to advantage. He proceeded by degrees to undertake larger transactions, until at length he became rich. The result was, that he more than recovered his possessions, and died an inveterate miser. When he was buried, mere earth went to earth. With a nobler spirit, the same determination might have enabled such a man to be a benefactor to others as well as to himself. But the life and its end in this case were alike sordid.

To provide for others and for our own comfort and independence in old age, is honourable, and greatly to be commended; but to hoard for mere wealth's sake is the characteristic of the narrow-souled and the miserly. It is against the growth of this habit of inordinate saving that the wise man needs most carefully to guard himself: else, what in youth was simple economy, may in old age grow into avarice, and what was a duty in the one case, may become a vice in the other. It is the *love* of money—not money itself—which is "the root of evil,"—a love which narrows and contracts the soul, and closes it against generous life and action. Hence, Sir Walter Scott makes one of his characters declare that "the penny siller slew more souls than the naked sword slew bodies." It is one of the defects of business too exclusively followed, that it insensibly tends to a mechanism of character. The business man gets into a rut, and often does not look beyond it. If he lives for himself only, he becomes apt to regard other human beings only in so far as they minister to his ends. Take a leaf from such men's ledger and you have their life.

Worldly success, measured by the accumulation of money, is no doubt a very dazzling thing; and all men are naturally more or less the admirers of worldly success. But though men of persevering, sharp, dexterous, and unscrupulous habits, ever on the watch to push opportunities, may and do "get on" in the world, yet it is quite possible that they may not possess the slightest elevation of character, nor a particle of real goodness. He who recognizes no higher logic than that of the shilling, may become a very rich man, and yet remain all the while an exceedingly poor creature. For riches are no proof whatever of moral worth; and their glitter often serves only to draw attention to the worthlessness of their possessor, as the light of the glowworm reveals the grub.

The manner in which many allow themselves to be sacrificed to their love of wealth reminds one of the cupidity of the monkey—that caricature of our species. In Algiers, the Kabyle peasant attaches a gourd, well fixed, to a tree, and places within it some rice. The gourd has an opening merely sufficient to admit the monkey's paw. The creature comes to the tree by night, inserts his paw, and grasps his booty. He tries to draw it back, but it is clenched, and he has not the wisdom to unclench it. So there he stands till morning, when he is caught, looking as foolish as may be, though with the prize in his grasp. The moral of this little story is capable of a very extensive application in life.

The power of money is on the whole over-estimated. The greatest things which have been done for the world have not been accomplished by rich men, or by subscription lists, but by men generally of small pecuniary means. Christianity has propagated over half the world by men of the poorest class; and the greatest thinkers, discoverers, inventors, and artists, have been men of moderate wealth, many of them little raised above the condition of manual labourers in point of wordly circumstances. And it will always be so. Riches are oftener an impediment that a stimulus to action; and in many cases they are quite as much a misfortune as a blessing. The youth who inherits wealth is apt to have life made too easy for him, and he soon grows sated with it, because he has nothing left to desire. Having no special object to struggle for, he finds time hang heavy on his hands; he remains morally and spiritually asleep; and his position in society is often no higher than that of a polypus over which the tide floats.

> "His only labour is to kill the time,
> And labour dire it is, and weary woe."

Yet the rich man, inspired by a right spirit, will spurn idleness as unmanly; and if he bethink himself of the responsibilities which attach to the possession of wealth and property he will feel even a higher call to work than men of humbler lot. This, however, must be admitted to be by no means the practice of life. The golden mean of Agur's perfect prayer is, perhaps, the best lot of all, did we but know it: "Give me neither poverty nor riches; feed me with food convenient for me." The late Joseph Brotherton, M. P., left a fine motto to be recorded upon his monument in the Peel Park at Manchester,—the declaration in his case being strictly true: "My riches consisted not in the greatness of my possessions, but in the smallness of my wants." He rose from the humblest station, that of a factory boy, to an eminent position of usefulness, by the simple exercise of homely honesty, industry, punctuality, and self-denial. Down to the close of his life, when not attending Parliament, he did duty as minister in a small chapel in Manchester to which he was attached; and in all things he made it appear, to those who knew him in private life, that the glory he sought was *not* "to be seen of men," or to excite their praise, but to earn the consciousness of discharging the every-day duties of life, down to the smallest and humblest of them, in an honest, upright, truthful, and loving spirit.

"Respectability," in its best sense, is good. The respectable man is one worthy of regard, literally worth turning to look at. But the respectability that consists in merely keeping up appearances is not worth looking at in any sense. Far better and more respectable is the good poor man than the bad rich one—better the humble silent man than the agreeable well-appointed rogue who keeps his gig. A well balanced and well-stored mind, a life full of useful purpose, whatever the position occupied in it may be, is of far greater importance than average worldly respectability. The highest object of life we take to be, to form a manly character, and to work out the best development possible, of body and spirit—of mind, conscience, heart, and soul. This is the end: all else ought to be regarded but as the means. Accordingly, that is not the most successful life in which a man gets the most pleasure, the most money, the most power or place, honour or fame; but that in which a man gets the most manhood, and performs the greatest amount of useful work and of human duty. Money is power after its sort, it is true; but intelligence, public spirit, and moral virtue, are powers too, and far nobler ones. "Let others plead for pensions," wrote Lord Collingwood to a friend; "I can be rich without money, by endeavouring to be superior to everything poor. I would have my services to my country unstained by any interested motive; and old Scott and I can go on in our cabbage-garden without much greater expense than formerly." On another occasion he said, "I have motives for my conduct which I would not give in exchange for a hundred pensions."

The making of a fortune may no doubt enable some people to "enter society," as it is called; but to be esteemed there, they must possess qualities of mind, manners, or heart, else they are merely rich people, nothing more. There are men "in society" now, as rich as Croesus, who have no consideration extended towards them, and elicit no respect. For why? They are but as money-bags: their only power is in their till. The men of mark in society —the guides and rulers of opinion—the really successful and useful men— are not necessarily rich men; but men of sterling character, of disciplined experience, and of moral excellence. Even the poor man, like Thomas Wright, though he possess but little of this world's goods, may, in the enjoyment of a cultivated nature, of opportunities used and not abused, of a life spent to the best of his means and ability, look down, without the slightest feeling of envy, upon the person of mere worldly success, the man of money-bags and acres.

Marxism:
An Economic and Social Statement

Karl Marx, "Wage Labour and Capital" (1849), with Introduction by Friedrich Engels (1891), in Marx and Engels, Selected Works (Moscow: Foreign Languages Publishing House, 1955), Vol. I, pp. 70–105.

Karl Marx (1818–83) and his collaborator, Friedrich Engels (1820–95) played the dual role of thinkers and activists. Their success in the first should not obscure their importance in the second. History, economics, sociology, and ethics were grist for their prolific mill. From the 1840's, however, practical agitation was their principal concern. Both came from middle-class backgrounds. Engels' experience in his father's Manchester business gave him the opportunity to write his classic *Condition of the Working Class in England* in 1844 as well as to participate in and be disillusioned by the Chartist movement, the English democratic movement seeking universal manhood suffrage and constitutional reforms as the means to cure social and economic ills. Marx trained for an academic career at Bonn and the University of Berlin. With no hope of securing a fitting professorial appointment, Marx turned to journalism and popular agitation. In 1843 he carried Hegelian dialectic and Feuerbach's materialism with him into Parisian exile. Utopian socialist and anarchist doctrine now augmented Marx's notions of Ricardian economics. Within two years, now in Brussels, he had developed the principal lines of his thought. Marx met Engels in 1844, beginning a fruitful, lifelong partnership.

"Wage Labour and Capital" was a series of lectures delivered by Marx in December, 1847. It was first published in his newspaper, the *Neue Rheinische Zeitung* in April, 1849. The tract is a brief polemic, a cogent statement of his position like that in *The Communist Manifesto* (1848). "Wage Labour and Capital" lacks the more sophisticated analysis of *Das Kapital*, *The Critique of Political Economy*, or *Wages, Price and Profit*, but the statement succinctly sets forth in popular language a theoretical analysis fundamentally unchanged. The edition here given is that prefaced and edited by Engels in 1891. His introduction to this May Day piece states the modest doctrinal changes—principally the substitution of "labour power" for "labour," a change of some importance.

Karl Marx

WAGE LABOUR AND CAPITAL

Introduction by Frederick Engels

THE FOLLOWING WORK appeared as a series of leading articles in the *Neue Rheinische Zeitung* from April 4, 1849 onwards. It is based on the lectures delived by Marx in 1847 at the German Workers' Society in Brussels. The work as printed remained a fragment; the words at the end of No. 269: "To be continued," remained unfulfilled in consequence of the events which just then came crowding one after another: the invasion of Hungary by the Russians, the insurrections in Dresden, Iserlohn, Elberfeld, the Palatinate and Baden, which led to the suppression of the newspaper itself (May 19, 1849). The manuscript of the continuation was not found among Marx's papers after his death.

Wage Labour and Capital has appeared in a number of editions as a separate publication in pamphlet form, the last being in 1884, by the Swiss Co-operative Press, Hottingen-Zurich. The editions hitherto published retained the exact wording of the original. The present new edition, however, is to be circulated in not less than 10,000 copies as a propaganda pamphlet, and so the question could not but force itself upon me whether under these circumstances Marx himself would have approved of an unaltered reproduction of the original.

In the forties, Marx had not yet finished his critique of political economy. This took place only towards the end of the fifties. Consequently, his works which appeared before the first part of *A Contribution to the Critique of Political Economy* (1859) differ in some points from those written after 1859, and contain expressions and whole sentences which, from the point of view of the later works, appear unfortunate and even incorrect. Now, it is self-evident that in ordinary editions intended for the general public this earlier point of view also has its place, as a part of the intellectual development of the author, and that both author and public have an indisputable right to the unaltered reproduction of these older works. And I should not have dreamed of altering a word of them.

It is another thing when the new edition is intended practically exclusively for propaganda among workers. In such a case Marx would certainly have brought the old presentation dating from 1849 into harmony with his new point of view. And I feel certain of acting as he would have done in understanding *for this edition* the few alterations and additions which are required in order to attain this object in all essential points. I therefore tell the reader beforehand: this is not the pamphlet as Marx wrote it in 1849 but approximately as he would have written it in 1891. The actual text, moreover, is circulated in so many copies that this will suffice until I am able to reprint it again, unaltered, in a later complete edition.

My alterations all turn on one point. According to the original, the worker sells his *labour* to the capitalist for wages: according to the present text he sells his labour *power*. And for this alteration I owe an explanation. I owe it to the workers in order that they may see it is not a case here of mere juggling with words, but rather of one of the most important points in the whole of political economy. I owe it to the bourgeois, so that they can convince themselves how vastly superior the uneducated workers, for whom one can easily make comprehensible the most difficult economic analyses, are to our supercilious "educated people" to whom such intricate questions remain insoluble their whole life long.

Classical political economy took over from industrial practice the current conception of the manufacturer, that he buys and pays for the *labour* of his workers. This conception had been quite adequate for the business needs, the book-keeping and price calculations of the manufacturer. But, naively transferred to political economy, it produced there really wondrous errors and confusions.

Economics observes the fact that the prices of all commodities, among them also the price of the commodity that it calls "labour," are continually changing; that they rise and fall as the result of the most varied circumstances, which often bear no relation whatever to the production of the commodities themselves, so that prices seem, as a rule, to be determined by pure chance. As soon, then, as political economy made its appearance as a science, one of its first tasks was to seek the law which was concealed behind this chance apparently governing the prices of commodities, and which, in reality, governed this very chance. Within the prices of commodities, continually fluctuating and oscillating, now upwards and now downwards, political economy sought for the firm central point around which these fluctuations and oscillations turned. In a word, it started from the *prices* of commodities in order to look for the *value* of the commodities as the law controlling prices, the value by which all fluctuations in price are to be explained and to which finally they are all to be ascribed.

Classical economics then found that the value of a commodity is determined by the labour contained in it, requisite for its production. With this explanation it contented itself. And we also can pause here for the time being. I will only remind the reader, in order to avoid misunderstandings, that this explanation has nowadays become totally inadequate. Marx was the first thoroughly to investigate the value-creating quality of labour and he discovered in so doing that not all labour apparently, or even really, necessary for the production of a commodity adds to it under all circumstances a magnitude of value which corresponds to the quantity of labour expended. If therefore today we say offhandedly with economists like Ricardo that the value of a commodity is determined by the labour necessary for its production, we always in so doing imply the reservations made by Marx. This suffices here; more is to be found in Marx's *A Contribution to the Critique of Political Economy*, 1859, and the first volume of *Capital*.

But as soon as the economists applied this determination of value by labour to the commodity "labour," they fell into one contradiction after another. How is the value of "labour" determined? By the necessary labour contained in it. But how much labour is contained in the labour of a worker for a day, a week, a month, a year? The labour of a day, a week, a month, a year. If labour is the measure of all values, then indeed we can express the "value of labour" only in labour. But we know absolutely nothing about the value of an hour of labour, if we only know that it is equal to an hour of labour. This brings us not a hair's breadth nearer the goal; we keep on moving in a circle.

Classical economics, therefore, tried another tack. It said: The value of a commodity is equal to its cost of production. But what is the cost of production of labour? In order to answer this question, the economists have to tamper a little with logic. Instead of investigating the cost of production of labour itself, which unfortunately cannot be ascertained, they proceed to investigate the cost of production of the *worker*. And this can be ascertained. It varies with time and circumstance, but for a given state of society, a given locality and a given branch of production, it too is given, at least within fairly narrow limits. We live today under the domination of capitalist production, in which a large, even-increasing class of the population can live only if it works for the owners of the means of production—the tools, machines, raw materials and means of subsistence—in return for wages. On the basis of this mode of production, the cost of production of the worker consists of that quantity of the means of subsistence—or their price in money—which, on the average, is necessary to make him capable of working, keep him capable of working, and to replace him, after his departure by reason of old age, sickness or death, with a new worker—that is to say, to propagate the working class in the necessary numbers. Let us assume that the money price of these means of subsistence averages three marks a day.

Our worker, therefore, receives a wage of three marks a day from the capitalist who employs him. For this, the capitalist makes him work, say, twelve hours a day, calculating roughly as follows:

Let us assume that our worker—a machinist—has to make a part of a machine which he can complete in one day. The raw material—iron and brass in the necessary previously prepared form—costs twenty marks. The consumption of coal by the steam engine, and the wear and tear of this same engine, of the lathe and the other tools which our worker uses represent for one day, and reckoned by his share of their use, a value of one mark. The wage for one day, according to our assumption, is three marks. This makes twenty-four marks in all for our machine part. But the capitalist calculates that he will obtain, on an average, twenty-seven marks from his customers in return, or three marks more than his outlay.

Whence came the three marks pocketed by the capitalist? According to the assertion of classical economics, commodities are, on the average, sold at their values, that is, at prices corresponding to the amount of necessary labour contained in them. The average price of our machine part—twenty-seven marks—would thus be equal to its value, that is, equal to the labour embodied in it. But of these twenty-seven marks, twenty-one marks were values already present before our machinist began work. Twenty marks were contained in the raw materials, one mark in the coal consumed during the work, or in the machines and tools which were used in the process and which were diminished in their efficiency by the value of this sum. There remain six marks which have been added to the value of the raw material. But according to the assumption of our economists themselves, these six marks can only arise from the labour added to the raw material by our worker. His twelve hours' labour has thus created a new value of six marks. The value of his twelve hours' labour would, therefore, be equal to six marks. And thus we would at last have discovered what the "value of labour" is.

"Hold on there!" cries our machinist. "Six marks? But I have received only three marks! My capitalist swears by all that is holy that the value of my twelve hours' labour is only three marks, and if I demand six he laughs at me. How do you make that out?"

If previously we got into a vicious circle with our value of labour, we are now properly caught in an insoluble contradiction. We looked for the value of labour and we have found more than we can use. For the worker, the value of the twelve hours' labour is three marks, for the capitalist it is six marks, of which he pays three to the worker as wages and pockets three for himself. Thus labour would have not one but two values and very different values into the bargain!

The contradiction becomes still more absurd as soon as we reduce to labour time the values expressed in money. During the twelve hours' labour a new value of six marks is created. Hence, in six hours three marks—the sum which the worker receives for twelve hours' labour. For twelve hours' labour the worker receives as an equivalent value the product of six hours' labour. Either, therefore, labour has two values, of which one is double the size of the other, or twelve equals six! In both cases we get pure nonsense.

Turn and twist as we will, we cannot get out of this contrdiction, as long as we speak of the purchase and sale of labour and of the value of labour. And this also happened to the economists. The last offshoot of classical economics, the Ricardian school, was wrecked mainly by the insolubility of this contradiction. Classical economics had got into a blind alley. The man who found the way out of this blind alley was Karl Marx.

What the economists had regarded as the cost of production of "labour" was the cost of production not of labour but of the living worker himself. And what this worker sold to the capitalist was not his labour. "As soon as his labour actually begins," says Marx, "it has already ceased to belong to him; it can therefore no longer be sold by him." At the most, he might sell his *future* labour, that is, undertake to perform a certain amount of work in a definite time. In so doing, however, he does not sell labour (which would first have to be performed) but puts his labour power at the disposal of the capitalist for a definite time (in the case of time-work) or for the purpose of a definite output (in the case of piece-work) in return for a definite payment: he hires out, or sells, his *labour power*. But this labour power is intergrown with his person and inseparable from it. Its cost of production, therefore, coincides with his cost of production; what the economists called the cost of production of labour is really the cost of production of the worker and therewith of his labour power. And so we can go back from the cost of production of labour power to the *value* of labour power and determine the amount of socially necessary labour requisite for the production of labour power of a particular quality, as Marx has done in the chapter on the buying and selling of labour power. (*Kapital*, Band IV, 3.)

Now what happens after the worker has sold his labour power to the capitalist, that is, placed it at the disposal of the latter in return for a wage —day wage or piece wage—agreed upon beforehand? The capitalist takes the worker into his workshop or factory, where all the things necessary for work—raw materials, auxiliary materials (coal, dyes, etc.), tools, machines —are already to be found. Here the worker begins to drudge. His daily wage may be, as above, three marks—and in this connection is does not make any difference whether he earns it as day wage or piece wage. Here also we again assume that in twelve hours the worker by his labour adds a new value of six marks to the raw materials used up, which new value the capitalist realizes on the sale of the finished piece of work. Out of this he pays the worker his three marks; the other three marks he keeps for himself. If, now, the worker creates a value of six marks in twelve hours, then in six hours he creates a value of three marks. He has, therefore, already repaid the capitalist the counter-value of the three marks contained in his wages when he has worked six hours for him. After six hours' labour they are both quits, neither owes the other a pfennig.

"Hold on there!" the capitalist now cries. "I have hired the worker for a whole day, for twelve hours. Six hours, however, are only half a day. So go right on working until the other six hours are up—only then shall we be quits!" And, in fact, the worker has to comply with his contract "voluntarily" entered into, according to which he has pledged himself to work twelve whole hours for a labour product which costs six hours of labour.

It is just the same with piece wages. Let us assume that our worker makes twelve items of a commodity in twelve hours. Each of these costs two marks in raw materials and depreciation and is sold at two and a half marks. Then the capitalist, on the same assumptions as before, will give the worker twenty-five pfennigs per item; that makes three marks for twelve items, to earn which the worker needs twelve hours. The capitalist receives thirty marks for the twelve items; deduct twenty-four marks for raw materials and depreciation and there remain six marks, of which he pays three marks to the worker in wages and pockets three marks. It is just as above. Here, too, the worker works six hours for himself, that is, for replacement of his wages (half an hour in each of the twelve hours) and six hours for the capitalist.

The difficulty over which the best economists came to grief, so long as they started out from the value of "labour," vanishes as soon as we start out from the value of "labour *power*" instead. In our present-day capitalist society, labour power is a commodity, a commodity like any other, and yet quite a peculiar commodity. It has, namely, the peculiar property of being a value-creating power, a source of value, and, indeed, with suitable treatment a source of more value than it itself possesses. With the present state of production, human labour power not only produces in one day a greater value than it itself possesses and costs; with every new scientific discovery, with every new technical invention, this surplus of its daily product over its daily cost increases, and therefore that portion of the labour day in which the worker works to produce the replacement of his day's wage decreases; consequently, on the other hand, that portion of the labour day in which he has to *make a present* of his labour to the capitalist without being paid for it increases.

And this is the economic constitution of the whole of our present-day society: it is the working class alone which produces all values. For value is only another expression for labour, that expression whereby in our present-day capitalist society is designated the amount of socially necessary labour contained in a particular commodity. These values produced by the workers do not, however, belong to the workers. They belong to the owners of the raw materials, machines, tools and the reserve funds which allow these owners to buy the labour power of the working class. From the whole mass of products produced by it, the working class, therefore, receives back only a part for itself. And as we have just seen, the other part, which the capitalist class keeps for itself and at most has to divide with the class of landowners, becomes larger with every new discovery and invention, while the part falling to the share of the working class (reckoned per head) either increases only very slowly and inconsiderably or not at all, and under certain circumstances may even fall.

But these discoveries and inventions which supersede each other at an ever-increasing rate, this productivity of human labour which rises day by day to an extent previously unheard of, finally gives rise to a conflict in which the present-day capitalist economy must perish. On the one hand are immeasurable riches and a superfluity of products which the purchasers cannot cope with: on the other hand, the great mass of society proletarianized, turned into wage-workers, and precisely for that reason made incapable of appropriating for themselves this superfluity of products. The division of society into a small, excessively rich class and a large, propertyless class of wage-workers results in a society suffocating from its own superfluity, while the great majority of its members is scarcely, or even not at all, protected from extreme want. This state of affairs becomes daily more absurd and—more unnecessary. It *must* be abolished, it *can* be abolished. A new social order is possible in which the present class differences will have disappeared and in which—perhaps after a short transitional period involving some privation, but at any rate of great value morally—through the planned utilization and extension of the already existing enormous productive forces of all members of society, and with uniform obligation to work, the means for existence, for enjoying life, for the development and employment of all bodily and mental faculties will be available in an equal measure and in ever-increasing fulness. And that the workers are becoming more and more determined to win this new social order will be demonstrated on both sides of the ocean by May the First, tomorrow, and by Sunday, May 3.

FREDERICK ENGELS

London, April 30, 1891

WAGE LABOUR AND CAPITAL

I

FROM VARIOUS QUARTERS we have been reproached with not having presented the *economic relations* which constitute the material foundation of the present class struggles and national struggles. We have designedly touched upon these relations only where they directly forced themselves to the front in political conflicts.

The point was, above all, to trace the class struggle in current history, and to prove empirically by means of the historical material already at hand and which is being newly created daily, that, with the subjugation of the working class that February and March had wrought, its opponents were simultaneously defeated—the bourgeosis republicans in France and the bourgeois and peasant classes which were fighting feudal absolutism throughout the continent of Europe; that the victory of the "honest republic" in France was at the same time the downfall of the nations that had responded to the February Revolution by heroic wars of independence; finally, that Europe, with the defeat of the revolutionary workers, had relapsed into its old double slavery, the *Anglo-Russian* slavery. The June struggle in Paris, the fall of Vienna, the tragicomedy of Berlin's November 1848, the desperate exertions of Poland, Italy and Hungary, the starving of Ireland into submission—these were the chief factors which characterized the European class struggle between bourgeoisie and working class and by means of which we proved that every revolutionary upheaval, however remote from the class struggle its goal may appear to be, must fail until the revolutionary working class is victorious, that every social reform remains a utopia until the proletarian revolution and the feudalistic counter-revolution measure swords in a *world war*. In our presentation, as in reality, *Belgium* and *Switzerland* were tragicomic genre-pictures akin to caricature in the great historical tableau, the one being the model state of the bourgeois monarchy, the other the model state of the bourgeois republic, both of them states which imagine themselves to be as independent of the class struggle as of the European revolution.

Now, after our readers have seen the class struggle develop in colossal political forms in 1848, the time has come to real more closely with the economic relations themselves on which the existence of the bourgeoisie and its class rule, as well as the slavery of the workers, are founded.

We shall present in three large sections: 1) the relation of *wage labour to capital*, the slavery of the worker, the domination of the capitalist; 2)

*the inevitable destruction of the middle bourgeois classes and of the so-
called peasant estate under the present system;* 3) *the commercial subjugation and exploitation of the bourgeois classes of the various European nations* by the despot of the world market—*England.*

We shall try to make our presentation as simple and popular as possible
and shall not presuppose even the most elementary notions of political
economy. We wish to be understood by the workers. Moreover, the most
remarkable ignorance and confusion of ideas prevails in Germany in regard
to the simplest economic relations, from the accredited defenders of the
existing state of things down to the *socialist miracle workers* and the *unrecognized political geniuses* in which fragmented Germany is even richer
than in sovereign princes.

Now, therefore, for the first question: *What are wages? How are they
determined?*

If workers were asked: "How much are your wages?" one would reply:
"I get a mark a day from my employer"; another, "I get two marks," and so
on. According to the different trades to which they belong, they would
mention different sums of money which they receive from their respective
employers for the performance of a particular piece of work, for example,
weaving a yard of linen or type-setting a printed sheet. In spite of the
variety of their statements, they would all agree on one point: wages are
the sum of money paid by the capitalist for a particular labour time or for a
particular output of labour.

The capitalist, it seems, therefore, *buys* their labour with money. They
sell him their labour for money. But this is merely the appearance. In reality
what they sell to the capitalist for money is their labour *power.* The capitalist buys this labour power for a day, a week, a month, etc. And after he
has bought it, he uses it by having the workers work for the stipulated time.
For the same sum with which the capitalist has bought their labour power,
for example, two marks, he could have bought two pounds of sugar or a
definite amount of any other commodity. The two marks, with which he
bought two pounds of sugar, are the *price* of the two pounds of sugar. The
two marks, with which he bought twelve hours' use of labour power, are the
price of twelve hours' labour. Labour power, therefore, is a commodity,
neither more nor less than sugar. The former is measured by the clock, the
latter by the scales.

The workers exchange their commodity, labour power, for the commodity of the capitalist, for money, and this exchange takes place in a
definite ratio. So much money for so long a use of labour power. For twelve
hours' weaving, two marks. And do not the two marks represent all the
other commodities which I can buy for two marks? In fact, therefore, the
worker has exchanged his commodity, labour power, for other commodities
of all kinds and that in a definite ratio. By giving him two marks, the
capitalist has given him so much meat, so much clothing, so much fuel,
light, etc., in exchange for his day's labour. Accordingly, the two marks ex-

press the ratio in which labour power is exchanged for other commodities, the *exchange value* of his labour power. The exchange value of a commodity, reckoned in *money*, is what is called its *price. Wages* are only a special name for the price of labour power, commonly called the *price of labour*, for the price of this peculiar commodity which has no other repository than human flesh and blood.

Let us take any worker, say, a weaver. The capitalist supplies him with the loom and yarn. The weaver sets to work and the yarn is converted into linen. The capitalist takes possession of the linen and sells it, say, for twenty marks. Now are the wages of the weaver a *share* in the linen, in the twenty marks, in the product of his labour? By no means. Long before the linen is sold, perhaps long before its weaving is finished, the weaver has received his wages. The capitalist, therefore, does not pay these wages with the money which he will obtain from the linen, but with money already in reserve. Just as the loom and the yarn are not the product of the weaver to whom they are supplied by his employer, so likewise with the commodities which the weaver receives in exchange for his commodity, labour power. It was possible that his employer found no purchaser at all for his linen. It was possible that he did not get even the amount of the wages by its sale. It is possible that he sells it very profitably in comparison with the weaver's wages. All that has nothing to do with the weaver. The capitalist buys the labour power of the weaver with a part of his available wealth, of his capital, just as he has bought the raw material—the yarn—and the instrument of labour—the loom—with another part of his wealth. After he has made these purchases, and these purchases include the labour power necessary for the production of linen, he produces only with the *raw materials and instruments of labour belonging to him.* For the latter include now, true enough, our good weaver as well, who has as little share in the product or the price of the product as the loom has.

Wages are, therfore, not the worker's share in the commodity produced by him. Wages are the part of already existing commodities with which the capitalist buys for himself a definite amount of productive labour power.

Labour power is, therefore, a commodity which its possessor, the wageworker, sells to capital. Why does he sell it? In order to live.

But the exercise of labour power, labour, is the worker's own life-activity, the manifestation of his own life. And this *life-activity* he sells to another person in order to secure the necessary *means of subsistence.* Thus his lifeactivity is for him only a means to enable him to exist. He works in order to live. He does not even reckon labour as part of his life, it is rather a sacrifice of his life. It is a commodity which he has made over to another. Hence, also, the product of his activity is not the object of his activity. What he produces for himself is not the silk that he weaves, not the gold that he draws from the mine, not the palace that he builds. What he produces for himself is *wages*, and silk, gold, palace resolve themselves for him into a definite quantity of the means of subsistence, perhaps into a cotton jacket, some copper coins and a lodging in a cellar. And the worker, who for twelve hours weaves, spins, drills, turns, builds, shovels, breaks stones, carries loads, etc.—does he consider this twelve hours' weaving, spinning, drilling, turning, building, shovelling, stone breaking as a manifestation of his life, as life? On the contrary, life begins for him where this activity ceases, at table, in the public house, in bed. The twelve hours' labour, on the other hand, has no meaning for him as weaving, spinning, drilling, etc. but as *earnings*, which bring him to the table, to the public house, into bed. If the silk worm were to spin in order to continue its existence as a caterpillar, it would be a complete wage-worker. Labour power was not always a *commodity*. Labour was not always wage labour, that is, *free labour*. The *slave* did not sell his labour power to the slave owner, any more than the ox sells its services to the peasant. The slave, together with his labour power, is sold once and for all to his owner. He is a commodity which can pass from the hand of one owner to that of another. He is *himself* a commodity, but the labour power is not *his* commodity. The *serf* sells only a part of his labour power. He does not receive a wage from the owner of the land; rather the owner of the land receives a tribute from him.

The serf belongs to the land and turns over to the owner of the land the fruits thereof. The *free labourer*, on the other hand, sells himself and, indeed, sells himself piecemeal. He sells at auction eight, ten, twelve, fifteen hours of his life, day after day, to the highest bidder, to the owner of the raw materials, instruments of labour and means of subsistence, that is, to the capitalist. The worker belongs neither to an owner nor to the land, but eight, ten, twelve, fifteen hours of his daily life belong to him who buys them. The worker leaves the capitalist to whom he hires himself whenever he likes, and the capitalist discharges him whenever he thinks fit, as soon as he no longer gets any profit out of him, or not the anticipated profit. But the worker, whose sole source of livelihood is the sale of his labour power, cannot leave the *whole class of purchasers, that is, the capitalist class,* without renouncing his existence. He belongs not to this or that capitalist but to the *capitalist class,* and moreover, it is his business to dispose of himself, that is, to find a purchaser within this capitalist class.

Now, before going more closely into the relation between capital and wage labour, we shall present briefly the most general relations which come into consideration in the determination of wages.

Wages, as we have seen, are the *price* of a definite commodity, of labour power. Wages are, therefore, determined by the same laws that determine the price of every other commodity. The question, therefore, is, *how is the price of a commodity determined?*

II

By what is the *price* of a commodity determined?

By competition between buyers and sellers, by the relation of inquiry to delivery, of demand to supply. Competition, by which the price of a commodity is determined, is *three-sided.*

The same commodity is offered by various sellers. With goods of the same quality, the one who sells most cheaply is certain of driving the others out of the field and securing the greatest sale for himself. Thus, the sellers mutually contend among themselves for sales, for the market. Each of them desires to sell, to sell as much as possible and, if possible, to sell alone, to the exclusion of the other sellers. Hence, one sells cheaper than another. Consequently, *competition* takes place *among the sellers*, which *depresses* the price of the *commodities* offered by them.

But *competition* also takes place *among the buyers*, which in its turn *causes* the commodities offered to *rise* in price.

Finally, *competition* occurs *between buyers and sellers;* the former desire to buy as cheaply as possible, the latter to sell as dearly as possible. The result of this competition between buyers and sellers will depend upon how the two above-mentioned sides of the competition are related, that is, whether the competition is stronger in the army of buyers or in the army of sellers. Industry leads two armies into the field against each other, each of which again carries on a battle within its own ranks, among its own troops. The army whose troops beat each other up the least gains the victory over the opposing host.

Let us suppose there are 100 bales of cotton on the market and at the same time buyers for 1,000 bales of cotton. In this case, therefore, the demand is ten times as great as the supply. Competition will be very strong among the buyers, each of whom desires to get one, and if possible all, of the hundred bales for himself. This example is no arbitrary assumption. We have experienced periods of cotton crop failure in the history of the trade, when a few capitalists in alliance have tried to buy, not one hundred bales, but all the cotton stocks of the world. Hence, in the example mentioned, one buyer will seek to drive the other from the field by offering a relatively higher price per bale of cotton. The cotton sellers, who see that the troops of the enemy army are engaged in the most violent struggle among themselves and that the sale of all their hundred bales is absolutely certain, will take good care not to fall out among themselves and depress the price of cotton at the moment when their adversaries are competing with one another to force it up. Thus, peace suddenly descends on the army of the sellers. They stand facing the buyers as one man, fold their arms philosophically, and there would be no bounds to their demands were it not that the offers of even the most persistent and eager buyers have very definite limits.

If, therefore, the supply of a commodity is lower than the demand for it, then only slight competition, or none at all, takes place among the sellers. In the same proportion as this competition decreases, competition increases among the buyers. The result is a more or less considerable rise in commodity prices.

It is well known that the reverse case with a reverse result occurs more frequently. Considerable surplus of supply over demand; desperate competition among the sellers; lack of buyers; disposal of goods at ridiculously low prices.

But what is the meaning of a rise, a fall in prices; what is the meaning of high price, low price? A grain of sand is high when examined through a microscope, and a tower is low when compared with a mountain. And if price is determined by the relation between supply and demand, what determines the relation between supply and demand?

Let us turn to the first bourgeois we meet. He will not reflect for an instant but, like another Alexander the Great, will cut this metaphysical knot with the multiplication table. If the production of the goods which I sell has cost me 100 marks, he will tell us, and if I get 110 marks from the sale of these goods, within the year of course—then that is sound, honest, legitimate profit. But if I get in exchange 120 or 130 marks, that is a high profit; and if I get as much as 200 marks, that would be an extraordinary, an enormous profit. What, therefore, serves the bourgeois as his *measure* of profit? The *cost of production* of his commodity. If he receives in exchange for this commodity an amount of other commodities which it has cost less to produce, he has lost. If he receives in exchange for his commodity an amount of other commodities the production of which has cost more, he has gained. And he calculates the rise or fall of the profit according to the degree in which the exchange value of his commodity stands above or below zero—the *cost of production*.

We have thus seen how the changing relation of supply and demand causes now a rise and now a fall of prices, now high, now low prices. If the price of a commodity rises considerably because of inadequate supply or disproportionate increase of the demand, the price of some other commodity must necessarily have fallen proportionately, for the price of a commodity only expresses in money the ratio in which other commodities are given in exchange for it. If, for example, the price of a yard of sik material rises from five marks to six marks, the price of silver in relation to silk material has fallen and likewise the prices of all other commodities that have remained at their old prices have fallen in relation to the silk. One has to give a larger amount of them in exchange to get the same amount of silks. What will be the consequence of the rising price of a commodity? A mass of capital will be thrown into that flourishing branch of industry and this influx of capital into the domain of the favoured industry will continue until it yields the ordinary profits or, rather, until the price of its products, through overproduction, sinks below the cost of production.

Conversely, if the price of a commodity falls below its cost of production, capital will be withdrawn from the production of this commodity. Except in the case of a branch of industry which has become obsolete and must, therefore, perish, the production of such a commodity, that is, its supply, will go on decreasing owing to this flight of capital until it corresponds to the demand, and consequently its price is again on a level with its cost of production or, rather, until the supply has sunk below the demand, that is, until its price rises again above its cost of production, *for the current price of a commodity is always either above or below its cost of production.*

We see how capital continually migrates in and out, out of the domain of one industry into that of another. High prices bring too great an immigration and low prices too great an emigration.

We could show from another point of view how not only supply but also demand is determined by the cost of production. But this would take us too far away from our subject.

We have just seen how the fluctuations of supply and demand continually bring the price of a commodity back to the cost of production. *The real price of a commodity, it is true, is always above or below its cost of production; but rise and fall reciprocally balance each other*, so that within a certain period of time taking the ebb and flow of the industry together, commodities are exchanged for one another in accordance with their cost of production, their price, therefore, being determined by their cost of production.

This determination of price by cost of production is not to be understood in the sense of the economists. The economists say that the *average price* of commodities is equal to the cost of production; that this is a *law*. The anarchical movement, in which rise is compensated by fall and fall by rise, is regarded by them as chance. With just as much right one could regard the fluctuations as the law and the determination by the cost of production as chance, as has actually been done by other economists. But it is solely these fluctuations, which, looked at more closely, bring with them the most fearful devastations and, like earthquakes, cause bourgeois society to tremble to its foundations—it is solely in the course of these fluctuations that prices are determined by the cost of production. The total movement of this disorder is its order. In the course of this industrial anarchy, in this movement in a circle, competition compensates, so to speak, for one excess by means of another.

We see, therefore, that the price of a commodity is determined by its cost of production in such manner that the periods in which the price of this commodity rises above its cost of production are compensated by the periods in which it sinks below the cost of production, and vice versa. This does not hold good, of course, for separate, particular industrial products but only for the whole branch of industry. Consequently, it also does not hold good for the individual industrialist but only for the whole class of industrialists.

The determination of price by the cost of production is equivalent to the determination of price by the labour time necessary for the manufacture of a commodity, for the cost of production consists of 1) raw materials and depreciation of instruments, that is, of industrial products the production of which has cost a certain amount of labour days and which, therefore, represent a certain amount of labour time, and 2) of direct labour, the measure of which is, precisely, time.

Now, the same general laws that regulate the price of commodities in general of course also regulate *wages*, the *price of labour*.

Wages will rise and fall according to the relation of supply and demand, according to the turn taken by the competition between the buyers of labour power, the capitalists, and the sellers of labour power, the workers. The fluctuations in wages correspond in general to the fluctuations in prices of commodities. *Within these fluctuations, however, the price of labour will be determined by the cost of production, by the labour time necessary to produce this commodity—labour power.*

What, then, is the cost of production of labour power?

It is the cost required for maintaining the worker as a worker and of developing him into a worker.

The less the period of training, therefore, that any work requires the smaller is the cost of production of the worker and the lower is the price of his labour, his wages. In those branches of industry in which hardly any period of apprenticeship is required and where the mere bodily existence of the worker suffices, the cost necessary for his production is almost confined to the commodities necessary for keeping him alive and capable of working. The *price of his labour* will, therefore, be determined by the *price of the necessary means of subsistence.*

Another consideration, however, also comes in. The manufacturer in calculating his cost of production and, accordingly, the price of the products, takes into account the wear and tear of the instruments of labour. If, for example, a machine costs him 1,000 marks and wears out in ten years, he adds 100 marks annually to the price of the commodities so as to be able to replace the worn-out machine by a new one at the end of ten years. In the same way, in calculating the cost of production of simple labour power, there must be included the cost of reproduction, whereby the race of workers is enabled to multiply and to replace worn-out workers by new ones. Thus the depreciation of the worker is taken into account in the same way as the depreciation of the machine.

The cost of production of simple labour power, therefore, amounts to the *cost of existence and reproduction of the worker.* The price of this cost of existence and reproduction constitutes wages. Wages so determined are called the *wage minimum.* This wage minimum, like the determination of the price of commodities by the cost of production in general, does not hold good for the *single individual* but for the *species.* Individual workers, millions of workers, do not get enough to be able to exist and reproduce themselves; *but the wages of the whole working class* level down, within their fluctuations, to this minimum.

Now that we have arrived at an understanding of the most general laws which regulate wages like the price of any other commodity, we can go into our subject more specifically.

III

Capital consists of raw materials, instruments of labour and means of subsistence of all kinds, which are utilized in order to produce new raw materials, new instruments of labour and new means of subsistence. All these component parts of capital are creations of labour, products of labour, *accumulated labour*. Accumulated labour which serves as a means of new production is capital.

So say the economists.

What is a Negro slave? A man of the black race. The one explanation is as good as the other.

A Negro is a Negro. He only becomes a slave in certain relations. A cotton-spinning jenny is a machine for spinning cotton. It becomes *capital* only in certain relations. Torn from these relationships it is no more capital than gold in itself is *money* or sugar the price of sugar.

In production, men not only act on nature but also on one another. They produce only by co-operating in a certain way and mutually exchanging their activities. In order to produce, they enter into definite connections and relations with one another and only within these social connections and relations does their action on nature, does production, take place.

These social relations into which the producers enter with one another, the conditions under which they exchange their activities and participate in the whole act of production, will naturally vary according to the character of the means of production. With the invention of a new instrument of warfare, firearms, the whole internal organization of the army necessarily changed; the relationships within which individuals can constitute an army and act as an army were transformed and the relations of different armies to one another also changed.

Thus the social relations within which individuals produce, *the social relations of production, change, are transformed, with the change and development of the material means of production, the productive forces. The relations of production in their totality constitute what are called the social relations, society, and specifically, a society at a definite stage of historical development*, a society with a peculiar, distinctive character. *Ancient* society, *feudal* society, *bourgeois* society are such totalities of production relations, each of which at the same time denotes a special stage of development in the history of mankind.

Capital, also, is a social relation of production. *It is a bourgeois production relation*, a production relation of bourgeois society. Are not the means of subsistence, the instruments of labour, the raw materials of which capital consists, produced and accumulated under given social conditions, in definite social relations? Are they not utilized for new production under given social conditions, in definite social relations? And is it not just this definite social character which turns the products serving for new production into *capital?*

Capital consists not only of means of subsistence, instruments of labour and raw materials, not only of material products; it consists just as much of *exchange values*. All the products of which it consists are *commodities*. Capital is, therefore, not only a sum of material products; it is a sum of commodities, of exchange values, *of social magnitudes*.

Capital remains the same, whether we put cotton in place of wool, rice in place of wheat or steamships in place of railways, provided only that the cotton, the rice, the steamships—the body of capital—have the same exchange value, the same price as the wool, the wheat, the railways in which it was previously incorporated. The body of capital can change continually without the capital suffering the slightest alteration.

But while all capital is a sum of commodities, that is, of exchange values, not every sum of commodities, of exchange values, is capital.

Every sum of exchange values is an exchange value. Every separate exchange value is a sum of exchange values. For instance, a house that is worth 1,000 marks is an exchange value of 1,000 marks. A piece of paper worth a pfennig is a sum of exchange values of one-hundred hundredths of a pfennig. Products which are exchangeable for others are *commodities*. The particular ratio in which they are exchangeable constitutes their *exchange value* or, expressed in money, their *price*. The quantity of these products can change nothing in their quality of being *commodities* or representing an *excange value* or having a definite *price*. Whether a tree is large or small it is a tree. Whether we exchange iron for other products in ounces or in hundredweights, does this make any difference in its character as commodity, as exchange value? It is a commodity of greater or lesser value, of higher or lower price, depending upon the quantity.

How, then, does any amount of commodities, of exchange value, become capital?

By maintaining and multiplying itself as an independent social *power,* that is, as the power *of a portion of society,* by means of its *exchange for direct, living labour power.* The existence of a class which possesses nothing but its capacity to labour is a necessary prerequisite of capital.

It is only the domination of accumulated, past, materialized labour over direct, living labour that turns accumulated labour into capital.

Capital does not consist in accumulated labour serving living labour as a means for new production. It consists in living labour serving accumulated labour as a means for maintaining and multiplying the exchange value of the latter.

What takes place in the exchange between capitalist and wage-worker?

The worker receives means of subsistence in exchange for his labour power, but the capitalist receives in exchange for his means of subsistence labour, the productive activity of the worker, the creative power whereby the worker not only replaces what he consumes but *gives to the accumulated labour a greater value than it previously possessed.* The worker receives a part of the available means of subsistence from the capitalist. For what purpose do these means of subsistence serve him? For immediate consumption. As soon, however, as I consume the means of subsistence, they are irretrievably lost to me unless I use the time during which I am kept alive by them in order to produce new means of subsistence, in order during consumption to create by my labour new values in place of the values which perish in being consumed. But it is just this noble reproductive power that the worker surrenders to the capitalist in exchange for means of subsistence received. He has, therefore, lost it for himself.

Let us take an example: a tenant farmer gives his day labourer five silver groschen a day. For these five silver groschen the labourer works all day on the farmer's field and thus secures him a return of ten silver groschen. The farmer not only gets the value replaced that he had to give the day labourer; he doubles it. He has therefore employed, consumed, the five silver groschen that he gave to the labourer in a fruitful, productive manner. He has bought with the five silver groschen just that labour and power of the labourer which produces agricultural products of double value and makes ten silver groschen out of five. The day labourer, on the other hand, receives in place of his productive power, the effect of which he has bargained away to the farmer, five silver groschen, which he exchanges for means of subsistence, and these he consumes with greater or less rapidity. The five silver groschen have, therefore, been consumed in a double way, *reproductively* for capital, for they have been exchanged for labour power[1] which produced ten silver groschen, *unproductively* for the worker, for they have been exchanged for means of subsistence which have disappeared forever and the value of which he can only recover by repeating the same exchange with the farmer. *Thus capital presupposes wage labour; wage labour presupposes capital. They reciprocally condition the existence of each other; they reciprocally bring forth each other.*

Does a worker in a cotton factory produce merely cotton textiles? No, he produces capital. He produces values which serve afresh to command his labour and by means of it to create new values.

Capital can only increase by exchanging itself for labour power, by calling wage labour to life. The labour power of the wage-worker can only be exchanged for capital by increasing capital, by strengthening the power whose slave it is. *Hence, increase of capital is increase of the proletariat, that is, of the working class.*

The interests of the capitalist and those of the worker are, therefore, *one and the same*, assert the bourgeois and their economists. Indeed! The worker perishes if capital does not employ him. Capital perishes if it does not exploit labour power, and in order to exploit it, it must buy it. The faster capital intended for production, productive capital, increases, the more, therefore, industry prospers, the more the bourgeoisie enriches itself and the better business is, the more workers does the capitalist need, the more dearly does the worker sell himself.

The indispensable condition for a tolerable situation of the worker *is, therefore, the fastest possible growth of productive capital.*

But what is the growth of productive capital? Growth of the power of accumulated labour over living labour. Growth of the domination of the bourgeoisie over the working class. If wage labour produces the wealth of

[1] The term "labour power" was not added here by Engels but had already been in the text Marx published in the *Neue Rheinische Zeitung.*—*Ed.*

others that rules over it, the power that is hostile to it, capital, then the means of employment, that is, the means of subsistence, flow back to it from this hostile power, on condition that it makes itself afresh into a part of capital, into the lever which hurls capital anew into an accelerated movement of growth.

To say that the interests of capital and those of the workers are one and the same is only to say that capital and wage labour are two sides of one and the same relation. The one conditions the other, just as usurer and squanderer condition each other.

As long as the wage-worker is a wage-worker his lot depends upon capital. That is the much-vaunted community of interests between worker and capitalist.

IV

If capital grows, the mass of wage labour grows, the number of wage-workers grows; in a word, the domination of capital extends over a greater number of individuals. Let us assume the most favourable case: when productive capital grows, the demand for labour grows; consequently, the price of labour, wages, goes up.

A house may be large or small; as long as the surrounding houses are equally small it satisfies all social demands for a dwelling. But let a palace arise beside the little house, and it shrinks from a little house to a hut. The little house shows now that its owner has only very slight or no demands to make; and however high it may shoot up in the course of civilization, if the neighbouring palace grows to an equal or even greater extent, the occupant of the relatively small house will feel more and more uncomfortable, dissatisfied and cramped within its four walls.

A noticeable increase in wages presupposes a rapid growth of productive capital. The rapid growth of productive capital brings about an equally rapid growth of wealth, luxury, social wants, social enjoyments. Thus, although the enjoyments of the worker have risen, the social satisfaction that they give has fallen in comparison with the increased enjoyments of the capitalist, which are inaccessible to the worker, in comparison with the state of development of society in general. Our desires and pleasures spring from society; we measure them, therefore, by society and not by the objects which serve for their satisfaction. Because they are of a social nature, they are of a relative nature.

In general, wages are determined not only by the amount of commodities for which I can exchange them. They embody various relations.

What the workers receive for their labour power is, in the first place, a definite sum of money. Are wages determined only by this money price?

In the sixteenth century, the gold and silver circulating in Europe increased as a result of the discovery of richer and more easily worked mines in America. Hence, the value of gold and silver fell in relation to other commodities. The workers received the same amount of coined silver for their labour power as before. The money price of their labour remained the same, and yet their wages had fallen, for in exchange for the same quantity of silver they received a smaller amount of other commodities. This was one of the circumstances which furthered the growth of capital and the rise of the bourgeoisie in the sixteenth century.

Let us take another case. In the winter of 1847, as a result of a crop failure, the most indispensable means of subsistence, cereals, meat, butter, cheese, etc., rose considerably in price. Assume that the workers received the same sum of money for their labour power as before. Had not their wages fallen? Of course. For the same money they received less bread, meat, etc., in exchange. Their wages had fallen, not because the value of silver had diminished, but because the value of the means of subsistence had increased.

Assume, finally, that the money price of labour remains the same while all agricultural and manufactured goods have fallen in price owing to the employment of new machinery, a favourable season, etc. For the same money the workers can now buy more commodities of all kinds. Their wages, therefore, have risen, just because the money value of their wages has not changed.

Thus, the money price of labour, nominal wages, do not coincide with real wages, that is, with the sum of commodities which is actually given in exchange for the wages. If, therefore, we speak of a rise or fall of wages, we must keep in mind not only the money price of labour, the nominal wages.

But neither nominal wages, that is, the sum of money for which the worker sells himself to the capitalist, nor real wages, that is, the sum of commodities which he can buy for this money, exhaust the relations contained in wages.

Wages are, above all, also determined by their relation to the gain, to the profit of the capitalist—comparative, relative wages.

Real wages express the price of labour in relation to the price of other commodities; relative wages, on the other hand, express the share of direct labour in the new value it has created in relation to the share which falls to accumulated labour, to capital.

We said above, . . . "Wages are not the worker's share in the commodity produced by him. Wages are the part of already existing commodities with which the capitalist buys for himself a definite amount of productive labour power." But the capitalist must replace these wages out of the price at which he sells the product produced by the worker; he must replace it in such a way that there remains to him, as a rule, a surplus over the cost of production expended by him, a profit. For the capitalist, the selling price of the commodities produced by the worker is divided into three parts: *first*, replacement of the price of the raw materials advanced by him together with replacement of the depreciation of the tools, machinery and other means of labour also advanced by him; *secondly,* the replacement of the wages advanced by him, and *thirdly,* the surplus left over, the capitalist's profit. While the first part only replaces *previously existing values,* it is clear that both the replacement of the wages and also the surplus profit of the capitalist are, on the whole, taken from the *new value created by the worker's labour* and added to the raw materials. And *in this sense,* in order to compare them with one another, we can regard both wages and profit as shares in the product of the worker.

Real wages may remain the same, they may even rise, and yet relative wages may fall. Let us suppose, for example, that all means of subsistence have gone down in price by two-thirds while wages per day have only fallen by one-third, that is to say, for example, from three marks to two marks. Although the worker can command a greater amount of commodities with these two marks than he previously could with three marks, yet his wages have gone down in relation to the profit of the capitalist. The profit of the capitalist (for example, the manufacturer) has increased by one mark; that is, for a smaller sum of exchange values which he pays to the worker, the latter must produce a greater amount of exchange values than before. The share of capital relative to the share of labour has risen. The division of social wealth between capital and labour has become still more unequal. With the same capital, the capitalist commands a greater quantity of labour. The power of the capitalist class over the working class has grown, the social position of the worker has deteriorated, has been depressed one step further below that of the capitalist.

What, then, is the general law which determines the rise and fall of wages and profit in their reciprocal relation?

They stand in inverse ratio to each other. Capital's share, profit, rises in the same proportion as labour's share, wages, falls, and vice versa. Profit rises to the extent that wages fall; it falls to the extent that wages rise.

The objection will, perhaps, be made that the capitalist can profit by a favourable exchange of his products with other capitalists, by increase of the demand for his commodities, whether as a result of the opening of new markets, or as a result of a momentarily increased demand in the old markets, etc.; that the capitalist's profit can, therefore, increase by overreaching other capitalists, independently of the rise and fall of wages, of the exchange value of labour power; or that the capitalist's profit may also rise owing to the improvement of the instruments of labour, a new application of natural forces, etc.

First of all, it will have to be admitted that the result remains the same, although it is brought about in reverse fashion. True, the profit has not risen because wages have fallen, but wages have fallen because the profit has risen. With the same amount of other people's labour, the capitalist has acquired a greater amount of exchange values, without having paid more for the labour on that account; that is, therefore, labour is paid less in proportion to the net profit which it yields the capitalist.

In addition, we recall that, in spite of the fluctuations in prices of commodities, the average price of every commodity, the ratio in which it is exchanged for other commodities, is determined by its *cost of production.* Hence the overreachings within the capitalist class necessarily balance one another. The improvement of machinery, new application of natural forces in the service of production, enable a larger amount of products to be created in a given period of time with the same amount of labour and capital, but not by any means a larger amount of exchange values. If, by the use of the spinning jenny, I can turn out twice as much yarn in an hour as before its invention, say, one hundred pounds instead of fifty, then in the long run I will receive for these hundred pounds no more commodities in exchange than formerly for the fifty pounds, because the cost of production has fallen by one-half, or because I can deliver double the product at the same cost.

Finally, in whatever proportion the capitalist class, the bourgeoisie, whether of one country or of the whole world market, shares the net profit of production within itself, the total amount of this net profit always consists only of the amount by which, on the whole, accumulated labour has been increased by direct labour. This total amount grows, therefore, in the proportion in which labour augments capital, that is, in the proportion in which profit rises in comparison with wages.

We see, therefore, that even if we remain *within the relation of capital and wage labour, the interests of capital and the interests of wage labour are diametrically opposed.*

A rapid increase of capital is equivalent to a rapid increase of profit. Profit can only increase rapidly if the price of labour, if relative wages, decrease just as rapidly. Relative wages can fall although real wages rise simultaneously with nominal wages, with the money value of labour, if they do not rise, however, in the same proportion as profit. If, for instance, in times when business is good, wages rise by five per cent, profit on the other hand by thirty per cent, then the comparative, the relative wages, have not *increased* but *decreased.*

Thus if the income of the worker increases with the rapid growth of capital, the social gulf that separates the worker from the capitalist increases at the same time, and the power of capital over labour, the dependence of labour on capital, likewise increases at the same time.

To say that the worker has an interest in the rapid growth of capital is only to say that the more rapidly the worker increases the wealth of others, the richer will be the crumbs that fall to him, the greater is the number of workers that can be employed and called into existence, the more can the mass of slaves dependent on capital be increased.

We have thus seen that:

Even the *most favourable situation* for the working class, the *most rapid possible growth of capital,* however much it may improve the material existence of the worker, does not remove the antagonism between his interests and the interests of the bourgeoisie, the interests of the capitalists. *Profit and wages* remain as before in *inverse proportion.*

If capital is growing rapidly, wages may rise; the profit of capital rises incomparably more rapidly. The material position of the worker has improved, but at the cost of his social position. The social gulf that divides him from the capitalist has widened.

Finally:

To say that the most favourable condition for wage labour is the most rapid possible growth of productive capital is only to say that the more rapidly the working class increases and enlarges the power that is hostile to it, the wealth that does not belong to it and that rules over it, the more favourable will be the conditions under which it is allowed to labour anew at increasing bourgeois wealth, at enlarging the power of capital, content with forging for itself the golden chains by which the bourgeoisie drags it in its train.

v

Are *growth of productive capital and rise of wages* really so inseparably connected as the bourgeois economists maintain? We must not take their word for it. We must not even believe them when they say that the fatter capital is, the better will its slave be fed. The bourgeoisie is too enlightened, it calculates too well, to share the prejudices of the feudal lord who makes a display by the brilliance of his retinue. The conditions of existence of the bourgeoisie compel it to calculate.

We must, therefore, examine more closely:

How does the growth of productive capital affect wages?

If, on the whole, the productive capital of bourgeois society grows, a *more manifold* accumulation of labour takes place. The capitals increase in number and extent. The *numerical increase* of the capitals increases the *competition between the capitalists.* The *increasing extent* of the capitals provides the means for *bringing more powerful labour armies with more gigantic instruments of war into the industrial battlefield.*

One capitalist can drive another from the field and capture his capital only by selling more cheaply. In order to be able to sell more cheaply without ruining himself, he must produce more cheaply, that it, raise the productive power of labour as much as possible. But the productive power of labour is raised, above all, by *a greater division of labour,* by a more universal introduction and continual improvement of *machinery.* The greater the labour army among whom labour is divided, the more gigantic the scale on which machinery is introduced, the more does the cost of production proportionately decrease, the more fruitful is labour. Hence, a general rivalry arises among the capitalists to increase the division of labour and machinery and to exploit them on the greatest possible scale.

If, now, by a greater division of labour, by the utilization of new machines and their improvement, by more profitable and extensive exploitation of natural forces, one capitalist has found the means of producing with the same amount of labour or of accumulated labour a greater amount of products, of commodities, than his competitors, if he can, for example, produce a whole yard of linen in the same labour time in which his competitors weave half a yard, how will this capitalist operate?

He could continue to sell half a yard of linen at the old market price; this would, however, be no means of driving his opponents from the field and of enlarging his own sales. But in the same measure in which his production has expanded, his need to sell has also increased. The more powerful and costly means of production that he has called into life *enable* him, indeed, to sell his commodities more cheaply, they *compel* him, however, at the same time *to sell more commodities,* to conquer a much *larger* market for his commodities; consequently, our capitalist will sell his half yard of linen more cheaply than his competitors.

The capitalist will not, however, sell a whole yard as cheaply as his competitors sell half a yard, although the production of the whole yard does not cost him more than the half yard costs the others. Otherwise he would not gain anything extra but only get back the cost of production by the exchange. His possibly greater income would be derived from the fact of having set a larger capital into motion, but not from having made more of his capital than the others. Moreover, he attains the object he wishes to attain, if he puts the price of his goods only a small percentage lower than that of his competitors. He drives them from the field, he wrests from them at least a part of their sales, by *underselling* them. And, finally, it will be remembered that the current price always stands *above or below the cost of production,* according to whether the sale of the commodity occurs in a favourable or unfavourable industrial season. The percentage at which the capitalist who has employed new and more fruitful means of production sells above his real cost of production will vary, depending upon whether the market price of a yard of linen stands below or above its hitherto customary cost of production.

However, the *privileged position* of our capitalist is not of long duration; other competing capitalists introduce the same machines, the same division of labour, introduce them on the same or on a larger scale, and this introduction will become so general that the price of linen *is reduced* not only *below its old,* but *below its new cost of production.*

The capitalists find themselves, therefore, in the same position relative to one another as *before* the introduction of the new means of production, and if they are able to supply by these means double the production at the same price, they are *now* forced to supply the double product *below* the old price. On the basis of this new cost of production, the same game begins again. More division of labour, more machinery, enlarged scale of exploitation of machinery and division of labour. And again competition brings the same counter-action against this result.

We see how in this way the mode of production and the means of production are continually transformed, revolutionized, *how the division of labour is necessarily followed by greater division of labour, the application of machinery by still greater application of machinery, work on a large scale by work on a still larger scale.*

This is the law which again and again throws bourgeois production out of its old course and which compels capital to intensify the productive forces of labour, *because it* has intensified them, it, the law which gives capital no rest and continually whispers in its ear: "Go on! Go on!"

This law is none other than that which, within the fluctuations of trade periods, necessarily *levels out* the price of a commodity to its *cost of production.*

However powerful the means of production which a capitalist brings into the field, competition will make these means of production universal and from the moment when it has made them universal, the only result of the greater fruitfulness of his capital is that he must now supply *for the same price* ten, twenty, a hundred times as much as before. But, as he must sell perhaps a thousand times as much as before in order to outweight the lower selling price by the greater amount of the product sold, because a more extensive sale is now necessary, not only in order to make more profit but in order to replace the cost of production—the instrument of production itself, as we have seen, becomes more and more expensive—and because this mass sale becomes a question of life and death not only for him but also for his rivals, the old struggle begins again *all the more violently the more fruitful the already discovered means of production are. The division of labour and the application of machinery, therefore, will go on anew on an incomparably greater scale.*

Whatever the power of the means of production employed may be, competition seeks to rob capital of the golden fruits of this power by bringing the price of the commodities back to the cost of production, by thus making cheaper production—the supply of ever greater amounts of products for the same total price—an imperative law to the same extent as production can be cheapened, that is, as more can be produced with the same amount of labour. Thus the capitalist would have won nothing by his own exertions but the obligation to supply more in the same labour time, in a word, *more difficult conditions for the augmentation of the value of his capital.* While, therefore, competition continually pursues him with its law of the cost of production and every weapon that he forges against his rivals recoils against himself, the capitalist continually tries to get the better of competition by incessantly introducing new machines, more expensive, it is true, but producing more cheaply, and new division of labour in place of the old, and by not waiting until competition has rendered the new ones obsolete.

If now we picture to ourselves this feverish simultaneous agitation on the *whole world market,* it will be comprehensible how the growth, accumulation and concentration of capital results in an uninterrupted division of labour, and in the application of new and the perfecting of old machinery precipitately and on an ever more gigantic scale.

But how do these circumstances, which are inseparable from the growth of productive capital, affect the determination of wages?

The greater *division of labour* enables *one* worker to do the work of five, ten or twenty; it therefore multiplies competition among the workers five-fold, tenfold and twentyfold. The workers do not only compete by one selling himself cheaper than another; they compete by *one* doing the work of five, ten, twenty; and the *division of labour,* introduced by capital and continually increased, compels the workers to compete among themselves in this way.

Further, as the *division of labour* increases, labour *is simplified.* The special skill of the worker becomes worthless. He becomes transformed into a simple, monotonous productive force that does not have to use intense bodily or intellectual faculties. His labour becomes a labour that anyone can perform. Hence, competitors crowd upon him on all sides, and besides we remind the reader that the more simple and easily learned the labour is, the lower the cost of production needed to master it, the lower do wages sink, for, like the price of every other commodity, they are determined by the cost of production.

Therefore, as labour becomes more unsatisfying, more repulsive, competition increases and wages decrease. The worker tries to keep up the amount of his wages by working more, whether by working longer hours or by producing more in one hour. Driven by want, therefore, he still further increases the evil effects of the division of labour. The result is that *the more he works the less wages he receives,* and for the simple reason that he competes to that extent with his fellow workers, hence makes them into so many competitors who offer themselves on just the same bad terms as he does himself, and that, therefore, in the last resort he *competes with himself, with himself as a member of the working class.*

Machinery brings about the same results on a much greater scale, by replacing skilled workers by unskilled, men by women, adults by children. It brings about the same results, where it is newly introduced, by throwing the hand workers on to the streets in masses, and, where it is developed, improved and replaced by more productive machinery, by discharging workers in smaller batches. We have portrayed above, in a hasty sketch, the industrial war of the capitalists among themselves; *this was has the peculiarity that its battles are won less by recruiting than by discharging the army of labour. The generals, the capitalists, compete with one another as to who can discharge most soldiers of industry.*

The economists tell us, it is true, that the workers rendered superfluous by machinery find *new* branches of employment.

They dare not assert directly that the same workers who are discharged find places in the new branches of labour. The facts cry out too loudly against this lie. They really only assert that new means of employment will open up for *other component sections of the working class*, for instance, for the portion of the young generation of workers that was ready to enter the branch of industry which has gone under. That is, of course, a great consolation for the disinherited workers. The worshipful capitalists will never want for fresh exploitable flesh and blood, and will let the dead bury their dead. This is a consolation which the bourgeois give themselves rather than one which they give the workers. If the whole class of wage-workers were to be abolished owing to machinery, how dreadful that would be for capital which, without wage labour, ceases to be capital!

Let us suppose, however, that those directly driven out of their jobs by machinery, and the entire section of the new generation that was already on the watch for this employment, *find a new occupation*. Does any one imagine that it will be as highly paid as that which has been lost? *That would contradict all the laws of economics*. We have seen how modern industry always brings with it the substitution of a more simple, subordinate occupation for the more complex and higher one.

How, then, could a mass of workers who have been thrown out of one branch of industry owing to machinery find refuge in another, unless the latter *is lower, worse paid*?

The workers who work in the manufacture of machinery itself have been cited as an exception. As soon as more machinery is demanded and used in industry, it is said, there must necessarily be an increase of machines, consequently of the manufacture of machines, and consequently of the employment of workers in the manufacture of machines; and the workers engaged in this branch of industry are claimed to be skilled, even educated workers.

Since the year 1840 this assertion, which even before was only half true, has lost all semblance of truth because ever more versatile machines have been employed in the manufacture of machinery, no more and no less than in the manufacture of cotton yarn, and the workers employed in the machine factories, confronted by highly elaborate machines, can only play the part of highly unelaborate machines.

But in place of the man who has been discharged owing to the machine, the factory employs maybe *three* children and *one* woman. And did not the man's wages have to suffice for the three children and a woman? Did not the minimum of wages have to suffice to maintain and to propagate the race? What, then, does this favourite bourgeois phrase prove? Nothing more than that now four times as many workers' lives are used up in order to gain a livelihood for *one* worker's family.

Let us sum up: *The more productive capital grows, the more the division of labour and the application of machinery expands. The more the division of labour and the application of machinery expands, the more competition among the workers expands and the more their wages contract.*

In addition, the working class gains recruits from the *higher strata of society* also; a mass of petty industrialists and small rentiers are hurled down into its ranks and have nothing better to do than urgently stretch out their arms alongside those of the workers. Thus the forest of uplifted arms demanding work becomes ever thicker, while the arms themselves become ever thinner.

That the small industrialist cannot survive in a contest one of the first conditions of which is to produce on an ever greater scale, that is, precisely to be a large and not a small industrialist, is self-evident.

That the interest on capital decreases in the same measure as the mass and number of capitals increase, as capital grows; that, therefore, the small rentier can no longer live on his interest but must throw himself into industry, and, consequently, help to swell the ranks of the small industrialists and thereby of candidates for the proletariat—all this surely requires no further explanation.

Finally, as the capitalists are compelled, by the movement described above, to exploit the already existing gigantic means of production on a larger scale and to set in motion all the mainsprings of credit to this end, there is a corresponding increase in industrial earthquakes, in which the trading world can only maintain itself by sacrificing a part of wealth, of products and even of productive forces to the gods of the nether world—in a word, *crises* increase. They become more frequent and more violent, if only because, as the mass of production, and consequently the need for extended markets, grows, the world market becomes more and more contracted, fewer and fewer new markets remain available for exploitation, since every preceding crisis has subjected to world trade a market hitherto unconquered or only superficially exploited. But capital does not *live* only on labour. A lord, at once aristocratic and barbarous, it drags with it into the grave the corpses of its slaves, whole hecatombs of workers who perish in the crises. Thus we see: *if capital grows rapidly, competition among the workers grows incomparably more rapidly, that is, the means of employment, the means of subsistence, of the working class decrease proportionately so much the more, and, nevertheless, the rapid growth of capital is the most favourable condition for wage labour.*

Anarchism:
Kropotkin's Answer

Peter Alexeivich Kropotkin, "The Scientific Bases of Anarchy," Nineteenth Century, *Volume XXI (February, 1887), pp. 238–52.*

Anarchism was the extreme nineteenth-century challenge to social, economic, and political organization. It has antecedents in communitarian ideology and twentieth-century legatees like syndicalism and parties bearing the title but hardly the program. Anarchism really lived and died, save as an intellectual eccentricity, between the French Revolution and World War I. While the first great spokesmen of the idea were west Europeans (William Godwin and Pierre Joseph Proudhon—some might argue for Babeuf and Buonarotti), the most eloquent and popular anarchists were two Russian aristocrats, Michael Bakunin and Prince Peter Kropotkin. Both were shaped and molded by their Russian inheritance; both were inconsistent to a greater or lesser degree; and both made their greatest impact in western Europe, particularly Latin Europe.

Peter Kropotkin (1842–1921) forcefully stated the anarchist case. A successful geographer and sometime court attendant, his cause was humanity. Authority in all forms limited and warped human development. Man, Kropotkin felt, develops through mutual aid and sympathy to realize true liberty. The economic system is hopelessly corrupt, but the abiding evil is not capitalism; it is the state. Socialism offers no cure, for it strengthens, not weakens, state authority. Once the state were destroyed, Kropotkin believed, the way would be clear and relatively quick to a free, pacific society of men. Kropotkin hated war but never criticized necessary violence, particularly the assassination of tyrants. When confronted by the fact of World War I, he supported the allies, fearing the consequences of the triumph of German militarism as the greater of two evils.

Kropotkin's critique of the state underscores and expands the warnings of John Stuart Mill and is more topical today than when it was written. *Mutual Aid* (1902) was his cogent statement of proper human evolution; *Fields, Factories, Workshops* (1899) an eloquent summary of his anarchist position; and *The Conquest of Bread* (1906) perhaps the most comprehensive treatment of anarchist economics. *Memoirs of a Revolutionist* (1899) brought him a wide, respectable reading audience and accounts to a considerable extent for his lasting popularity among educated west Europeans and Americans. There is a difference between popularity and acceptance, although it may be too subtle for the author to understand. Kropotkin wrote most of his pamphlets and tracts in English or French, was best received in Latin- and English-speaking countries (although he enjoyed surprising popularity in Japan and much in Scandinavia and Weimar Germany), and ranked among Russian revolutionary heroes by force of his personality rather than his ideas.

THE SCIENTIFIC BASES OF ANARCHY

ANARCHY (*àv-àρχὴ*), the No-Government system of Socialism, has a double origin. It is an outgrowth of the two great movements of thought in the economical and the political fields which characterise our century, and especially its second part. In common with all Socialists, the anarchists hold that the private ownership of land, capital, and machinery has had its time; that it is condemned to disappear; and that all requisites for production must, and will, become the common property of society, and be managed in common by the producers of wealth. And, in common with the most advanced representatives of political Radicalism, they maintain that the ideal of the political organisation of society is a condition of things where the functions of government are reduced to a minimum, and the individual recovers his full liberty of initiative and action for satisfying, by means of free groups and federations—freely constituted—all the infinitely varied needs of the human being. As regards Socialism, most of the anarchists arrive at its ultimate conclusion, that is, at a complete negation of the wage-system and at communism. And with reference to political organisation, by giving a further development to the above-mentioned part of the Radical programme, they arrive at the conclusion that the ultimate aim of society is the reduction of the functions of government to *nil*—this is, to a society without government, to An-archy. The anarchists maintain, moreover, that such being the ideal of social and political organisation, they must not remit it to future centuries, but that only those changes in our social organisation which are in accordance with the above double ideal, and constitute an approach to it, will have a chance of life and be beneficial for the commonwealth.

As to the method followed by the anarchist thinker, it differs to a great extent from that followed by the Utopists. The anarchist thinker does not resort to metaphysical conceptions (like the 'natural rights,' the 'duties of the State,' and so on) for establishing what are, in his opinion, the best conditions for realising the greatest happiness of humanity. He follows, on the contrary, the course traced by the modern philosophy of evolution—without entering, however, the slippery route of mere analogies so often resorted to by Herbert Spencer. He studies human society as it is now and was in the past; and, without either endowing men altogether, or separate individuals, with superior qualities which they do not possess, he merely considers society as an aggregation of organisms trying to find out the best ways of combining the wants of the individual with those of co-operation for the welfare of the species. He studies society and tries to discover its *tendencies*, past and present, its growing needs, intellectual and economical; and in his ideal he merely points out in which direction evolution goes. He distinguishes between the real wants and tendencies of human aggregations and the accidents (want of knowledge, migrations, wars, conquests) which prevented these tendencies from being satisfied, or temporarily paralysed them. And he concludes that the two most prominent, although often unconscious, tendencies throughout our history were: a tendency towards integrating our labour for the production of all riches in common, so as finally to render it impossible to discriminate the part of the common production due to the separate individual; and a tendency towards the fullest freedom of the individual for the prosecution of all aims, beneficial both for himself and for society at large. The ideal of the anarchist is thus a mere summing-up of what he considers to be the next phase of evolution. It is no longer a matter of faith; it is a matter for scientific discussion.

In fact, one of the leading features of our century is the growth of Socialism and the rapid spreading of Socialist views among the working classes. How could it be otherwise? We have witnessed during the last seventy years an unparalleled sudden increase of our powers of production, resulting in an accumulation of wealth which has outstripped the most sanguine expectations. But, owing to our wage system, this increase of wealth—due to the combined efforts of men of science, of managers, and workmen as well—has resulted only in an unprevented accumulation of wealth in the hands of the owners of capital; while an increase of misery for the great numbers, and an insecurity of life for all, have been the lot of the workmen. The unskilled labourers, in continuous search for labour, are falling into an unheard-of destitution; and even the best paid artisans and skilled workmen, who undoubtedly are living now a more comfortable life than before, labour under the permanent menace of being thrown, in their turn, into the same conditions as the unskilled paupers, in consequence of some of the continuous and unavoidable fluctuations of industry and caprices of capital. The chasm between the moden millionaire who squanders the produce of human labour in a gorgeous and vain luxury, and the pauper reduced to a miserable and insecure existence, is thus growing more and more, so as to break the very unity of society—the harmony of its life—and to endanger the progress of its further development. At the same time, the working classes are the less inclined patiently to endure this division of society into two classes, as they themselves become more and more conscious of the wealth-producing power of modern industry, of the part played by labour in the production of wealth, and of their own capacities of organisation. In proportion as all classes of the community take a more lively part in public affairs, and knowledge spreads among the masses, their longing for equality becomes stronger, and their demands of social reorganisation become louder and louder: they can be ignored no more. The worker claims his share in the riches he produces; he claims his share in the management of production; and he claims not only some additional well-being, but also his full rights in the higher enjoyments of science and art. These claims, which formerly were uttered only by the social reformer, begin now to be made by a daily growing minority of those who work in the factory or till the acre; and they so conform with our feelings of justice, that they find support in a daily growing minority amidst the privileged class themselves. Socialism becomes thus *the* idea of the nineteenth century; and neither coercion nor pseudo-reforms can stop its further growth.

Much hope of improvement was laid, of course, in the extension of political rights to the working classes. But these concessions, unsupported as they were by corresponding changes in the economical relations, proved delusory. They did not materially improve the conditions of the great bulk of the workmen. Therefore, the watchword of Socialism is: 'Economical freedom, as the only secure basis for political freedom.' And as long as the present wage system, with all its bad consequences, remains unaltered, the Socialist watchword will continue to inspire the workmen. Socialism will continue to grow until it has realised its programme.

Side by side with this great movement of thought in economical matters, a like movement was going on with regard to political rights, political organisation, and the functions of government. Government was submitted to the same criticism as Capital. While most of the Radicals saw in universal suffrage and republican institutions the last word of political wisdom, a further step was made by the few. The very functions of government and the State, as also their relations to the individual, were submitted to a sharper and deeper criticism. Representative government having been experimented on a wider field than before, its defects became more and more prominent. It became obvious that these defects are not merely accidental, but inherent to the system itself. Parliament and its executive proved to be unable to attend to all the numberless affairs of the community and to conciliate the varied and often opposite interests of the separate parts of a State. Election proved unable to find out the men who might represent a nation, and manage, otherwise than in a party spirit, the affairs they are compelled to legislate upon. These defects became so striking that the very principles of the representative system were criticised and their justness doubted. Again, the dangers of a centralised government became still more conspicuous when the Socialists came to the front and asked for a further increase of the powers of government by entrusting it with the management of the immense field covered now by the economical relations between individuals. The question was asked, whether a government, entrusted with the management of industry and trade, would not become a permanent danger for liberty and peace, and whether it even would be able to be a good manager?

The Socialists of the earlier part of this century did not fully realise the immense difficulties of the problem. Convinced as they were of the necessity of economical reforms, most of them took no notice of the need of freedom for the individual; and we have had social reformers ready to submit society to any kind of theocracy, dictatorship, or even Caesarism, in order to obtain reforms in a Socialist sense. Therefore we saw, in this country and also on the Continent, the division of men of advanced opinions into political Radicals and Socialists—the former looking with distrust on the latter, as they saw in them a danger for the political liberties which have been won by the civilised nations after a long series of struggles. And even now, when the Socialists all over Europe are becoming political parties, and profess the democratic faith, there remains among most impartial men a well-founded fear of the *Volksstaat* or 'popular State' being as great a danger for liberty as any form of autocracy, if its government be entrusted with the management of all the social organisation, including the production and distribution of wealth.

The evolution of the last forty years prepared, however, the way for showing the necessity and possibility of a higher form of social organisation which might guarantee economical freedom without reducing the individual to the *rôle* of a slave to the State. The origins of government were carefully studied, and all metaphysical conceptions as to its divine or 'social contract' derivation having been laid aside, it appeared that it is among us of a relatively modern origin, and that its powers grew precisely in proportion as the division of society into the privileged and unprivileged classes was growing in the course of ages. Representative government was also reduced to its real value—that of an instrument which has rendered services in the struggle against autocracy, but not an ideal of free political organisation. As to the system of philosophy which saw in the State (the *Kultur-Staat*) a leader to progress, it was more and more shaken as it became evident that progress is the more effective when it is not checked by State interference. It thus became obvious that a further advance in social life does not lie in the direction of a further concentration of power and regulative functions in the hands of a governing body, but in the direction of decentralisation, both territorial and functional—in a subdivision of public functions with respect both to their sphere of action and to the character of the functions; it is in the abandonment to the initiative of freely constituted groups of all those functions which are now considered as the functions of government.

This current of thought found its expression not merely in literature, but also, to a limited extent, in life. The uprise of the Paris Commune, followed by that of the Commune of Cartagena—a movement of which the historical bearing seems to have been quite overlooked in this country—opened a new page of history. If we analyse not only this movement in itself, but also the impression it left in the minds and the tendencies which were manifested during the communal revolution, we must recognise in it an indication showing that in the future human agglomerations which are more advanced in their social development will try to start an independent life; and that they will endeavour to convert the more backward parts of a nation by example, instead of imposing their opinions by law and force, or submitting themselves to the majority-rule, which always is a mediocrity-rule. At the same time the failure of representative government within the Commune itself proved that self-government and self-administration must be carried on further than in a mere territorial sense; to be effective they must be carried on also with regard to the various functions of life within the free community; a merely territorial limitation of the sphere of action of government will not do—representative government being as deficient in a city as it is in a nation. Life gave thus a further point in favour of the no-government theory, and a new impulse to anarchist thought.

Anarchists recognise the justice of both the just-mentioned tendencies towards economical and political freedom, and see in them two different manifestations of the very same need of equality which constitutes the very essence of all struggles mentioned by history. Therefore, in common with all Socialists, the anarchist says to the political reformer: 'No substantial reform in the sense of political equality, and no limitation of the powers of government, can be made as long as society is divided into two hostile camps, and the labourer remains, economically speaking, a serf to his employer.' But to the Popular State Socialist we say also: 'You cannot modify the existing conditions of property without deeply modifying at the same time the political organisation. You must limit the powers of government and renounce Parliamentary rule. To each new economical phasis of life corresponds a new political phasis. Absolute monarchy—that is, Court-rule—corresponded to the system of serfdom. Representative government corresponds to Capital-rule. Both, however, are class-rule. But in a society where the distinction betweeen capitalist and labourer has disappeared, there is no need of such a government; it would be an anachronism, a nuisance. Free workers would require a free organisation, and this cannot have another basis than free agreement and free co-operation, without sacrificing the autonomy of the individual to the all-pervading interference of the State. The no-capitalist system implies the no-government system.'

Meaning thus the emancipation of man from the oppressive powers of capitalist and government as well, the system of anarchy becomes a synthesis of the two powerful currents of thought which characterise our century.

In arriving at these conclusions anarchy proves to be in accordance with the conclusions arrived at by the philosophy of evolution. By bringing to light the plasticity of organisation, the philosophy of evolution has shown the admirable adaptivity of organisms to their conditions of life, and the ensuing development of such faculties as render more complete both the adaptations of the aggregates to their surroundings and those of each of the constituent parts of the aggregate to the needs of free co-operation. It familiarised us with the circumstance that throughout organic nature the capacities for life in common are growing in proportion as the integration of organisms into compound aggregates becomes more and more complete; and it enforced thus the opinion already expressed by social moralists as to the perfectibility of human nature. It has shown us that, in the long run of the struggle for existence, 'the fittest' will prove to be those who combine intellectual knowledge with the knowledge necessary for the production of wealth, and not those who are now the richest because they, or their ancestors, have been momentarily the strongest. By showing that the 'struggle for existence' must be conceived, not merely in its restricted sense of a struggle between individuals for the means of subsistence, but in its wider sense of adaptation of all individuals of the species to the best conditions for the survival of the species, as well as for the greatest possible sum of life and happiness for each and all, it permitted us to deduce the laws of moral science from the social needs and habits of mankind. It showed us the infinitesimal part played by positive law in moral evolution, and the immense part played by the natural growth of altruistic feelings, which develop as soon as the conditions of life favour their growth. It thus enforced the opinion of social reformers as to the necessity of modifying the conditions of life for improving man, instead of trying to improve human nature by moral teachings while life works in an opposite direction. Finally, by studying human society from the biological point of view, it came to the conclusions arrived at by anarchists from the study of history and present tendencies, as to further progress being in the line of socialisation of wealth and integrated labour, combined with the fullest possible freedom of the individual.

It is not a mere coincidence that Herbert Spencer, whom we may consider as a pretty fair expounder of the philosophy of evolution, has been brought to conclude, with regard to political organisation, that 'that form of society towards which we are progressing' is 'one in which *government* will be reduced to the smallest amount possible, and *freedom* increased to the greatest amount possible.' When he opposes in these words the conclusions of his synthetic philosophy to those of Auguste Comte, he arrives at very nearly the same conclusion as Proudhon and Bakunin. More than that, the very methods of argumentation and the illustrations resorted to by Herbert Spencer (daily supply of food, post-office, and so on) are the same which we find in the writings of the anarchists. The channels of thought were the same, although both were unaware of each other's endeavours.

Again, when Mr. Spencer so powerfully, and even not without a touch of passion, argues (in his Appendix to the third edition of the *Data of Ethics*) that human societies are marching towards a state when a further identification of altruism with egoism will be made 'in the sense that personal gratification will come from the gratification of others;' when he says that 'we are shown, undeniably, that it is a perfectly possible thing for organisms to become so adjusted to the requirements of their lives, that energy expended for the general welfare may not only be adequate to check energy expended for the individual welfare, but may come to subordinate it so far as to leave individual welfare no greater part than is necessary for maintenance of individual life'—provided the conditions for such relations between the individual and the community be maintained—he derives from the study of nature the very same conclusions which the forerunners of anarchy, Fourier and Robert Owen, derived from a study of human character.

When we see further Mr. Bain so forcibly elaborating the theory of moral habits, and the French philosopher, M. Guyau, publishing his remarkable work on *Morality without Obligation or Sanction;* when J. S. Mill so sharply criticises representative government, and when he discusses the problem of liberty, although failing to establish its necessary conditions; when Sir John Lubbock prosecutes his admirable studies on animal societies, and Mr. Morgan applies scientific methods of investigation to the philosophy of history—when, in short, every year, by bringing some new arguments to the philosophy of evolution, adds at the same time some new arguments to the theory of anarchy—we must recognise that this last, although differing as to its starting-points, follows the same sound methods of scientific investigation. Our confidence in its conclusions is still more increased. The difference between anarchists and the just-named philosophers may be immense as to the presumed speed of evolution, and as to the conduct which one ought to assume as soon as he has had an insight into the aims todwards which society is marching. No attempt, however, has been made scientifically to determine the ratio of evolution, nor have the chief elements of the problem (the state of mind of the masses) been taken into account by the evolutionist philosophers. As to bringing one's action into accordance with his philosophical conceptions, we know that, unhappily, intellect and will are too often separated by a chasm not to be filled by mere philosophical speculations, however deep and elaborate.

There is, however, between the just-named philosophers and the anarchists a wide difference on one point of primordial importance. This difference is the stranger as it arises on a point which might be discussed figures in hand, and which constitutes the very basis of all further deductions, as it belongs to what biological sociology would describe as the physiology of nutrition.

There is, in fact, a widely spread fallacy, maintained by Mr. Spencer and many others, as to the causes of the misery which we see round about us. It was affirmed forty years ago, and it is affirmed now by Mr. Spencer and his followers, that misery in civilised society is due to our insufficient production, or rather to the circumstance that 'population presses upon the means of subsistence.' It would be of no use to inquire into the origin of such a misrepresentation of facts, which might be easily verified. It may have its origin in inherited misconceptions which have nothing to do with the philosophy of evolution. But to be maintained and advocated by philosophers, there must be, in the conceptions of these philosophers, some confusion as to the different aspects of the struggle for existence. Sufficient importance is not given to the difference between the struggle which goes on among organisms which do *not* co-operate for providing the means of subsistence, and those which *do* so. In this last case again there must be some confusion between those aggregates whose members find their means of subsistence in the ready produce of the vegetable and animal kingdom, and those whose members artificially grow their means of subsistence and whose members artificially grow their means of subsistence and are enabled to increase (to a yet unknown amount) the productivity of each spot of the surface of the globe. Hunters who hunt, each of them for his own sake, and hunters who unite into societies for hunting, stand quite differently with regard to the means of subsistence. But the difference is still greater between the hunters who take their means of subsistence as they are in nature, and civilised men who grow their food and produce all requisites for a comfortable life by machinery. In this last case—the stock of potential energy in nature being little short of infinite in comparison with the present population of the globe—the means of availing ourselves of the stock of energy are increased and perfected precisely in proportion to the density of population and to the previously accumulated stock of technical knowledge; so that for human beings who are in possession of scientific knowledge, and co-operate for the artificial production of the means of subsistence and comfort, the law is quite the reverse to that of Malthus. The accumulation of means of subsistence and comfort is going on at a much speedier rate than the increase of population. The only conclusion which we can deduce from the laws of evolution and of multiplication of effects is that the available amount of means of subsistence increases at a rate which increases itself in proportion as population becomes denser—unless it be artificially (and temporarily) checked by some defects of social organisation. As to our *powers* of production (our potential production), they increase at a still speedier rate; in proportion as scientific knowledge grows, the means for spreading it are rendered easier, and inventive genius is stimulated by all previous inventions.

If the fallacy as to the pressure of population on the means of subsistence could be maintained a hundred years ago, it can be maintained no more, since we have witnessed the effects of science on industry, and the enormous increase of our productive powers during the last hundred years. We know, in fact, that while the growth of population of England has been from 16½ millions in 1844 to 26¾ millions in 1883, showing thus an increase of 62 per cent., the growth of national wealth (as testified by schedule A of the Income Tax Act) has increased at a twice speedier rate; it has grown from 221 to 507½ millions—that is, by 130 per ment. And we know that the same increase of wealth has taken place in France, where population remains almost stationary, and that it has gone on at a still speedier rate in the United States, where population is increasing every year by immigration.

But the figures just mentioned, while showing the real increase of production, give only a faint idea of what our production might be under a more reasonable economical organisation. We know well that the owners of capital, while trying to produce more wares with fewer 'hands,' are also continually endeavouring to limit the production, in order to sell at higher prices. When the benefits of a concern are going down, the owner of the capital limits the production, or totally suspends it, and prefers to engage his capital in foreign loans or shares of Patagonian gold-mines. Just now there are plenty of pitmen in England who ask nothing better than to be permitted to extract coal and supply with cheap fuel the households where children are shivering before empty chimneys. There are thousands of weavers who ask for nothing better than to weave stuffs in order to replace the Whitechapel rugs with linen. And so in all branches of industry. How can we talk about a want of means of subsistence when 246 blasting furnaces and thousands of factories lie idle in Great Britain alone; and when there are, just now, thousands of men who would consider themselves happy if they were permitted to transform (under the guidance of experienced men) the heavy clay of Middlesex into a rich soil, and to cover with rich cornfields and orchards the acres of meadow-land which now yield only a few pounds' worth of hay? But they are prevented from doing so by owners of the land, of the weaving factory, and of the coal-mine, because capital finds it more advantageous to supply the Khedive with harems and the Russian Government with 'strategic railways' and Krupp guns. Of course the maintenance of harems *pays*: it gives ten or fifteen per cent. on the capital, while the extraction of coal does not pay—that is, it brings three or five per cent.,—and that is a sufficient reason for limiting the production and permitting would-be economists to indulge in reproaches to the working classes as to their too rapid multiplication!

Here we have instances of a direct and conscious limitation of production, due to the circumstance that these few have the right of disposing of them at their will, without caring about the interests of the community. But there is also the indirect and unconscious limitation of production—that which results from squandering the produce of human labour in luxury, instead of applying it to a further increase of production.

This last even cannot be estimated in figures, but a walk through the rich shops of any city and a glance at the manner in which money is squandered now, can give an approximate idea of this indirect limitation. When a rich man spends a thousand pounds for his stables, he squanders five to six thousand days of human labour, which might be used, under a better social organisation, for supplying with comfortable homes those who are compelled to live now in dens. And when a lady spends a hundred pounds for her dress, we cannot but say that she squanders, at least, two years of human labour, which, again under a better organisation, might have supplied a hundred women with decent dresses, and much more if applied to a further improvement of the instruments of production. Preachers thunder against luxury, because it is shameful to squander money for feeding and sheltering hounds and horses, when thousands live in the East End on sixpence a day, and other thousands have not even their miserable sixpence every day. But the economist sees more than that in our modern luxury: when millions of days of labour are spent every year for the satisfaction of the stupid vanity of the rich, he says that so many millions of workers have been diverted from the manufacture of those useful instruments which would permit us to decuple and centuple our present production of means of subsistence and of requisites for comfort.

In short, if we take into account both the real and the potential increase of our wealth, and consider both the direct and indirect limitation of production, which are unavoidable under our present economical system, we must recognise that the supposed 'pressure of population on the means of subsistence' is a mere fallacy, repeated, like many other fallacies, without even taking the trouble of submitting it to a moment's criticism. The causes of the present social disease must be sought elsewhere.

Let us take a civilised country. The forest have been cleared, the swamps drained. Thousands of roads and railways intersect it in all directions; the rivers have been rendered navigable, and the seaports are of easy access. Canals connect the seas. The rocks have been pierced by deep shafts; thousands of manufacturers cover the land. Science has taught men how to use the energy of nature for the satisfaction of his needs. Cities have slowly grown in the long run of ages, and treasures of science and art are accumulated in these centres of civilisation. But—who has made all these marvels?

The combined efforts of scores of generations have contributed towards the achievement of these results. The forests have been cleared centuries ago; millions of men have spent years and years of labour in draining the swamps, in tracing the roads, in building the railways. Other millions have built the cities and created the civilisation we boast of. Thousands of inventors, mostly unknown, mostly dying in poverty and neglect, have elaborated the machinery in which Man admires his genius. Thousands of writers, philosophers and men of science, supported by many thousands of compositors, printers, and other labourers whose name is legion, have contributed in elaborating and spreading knowledge, in dissipating errors, in creating the atmosphere of scientific thought, without which the marvels of our century never would have been brought to life. The genius of a Mayer and a Grove, the patient work of a Joule, surely have done more for giving a new start to modern industry than all the capitalists of the world; but these men of genius themselves are, in their turn, the children of industry: thousands of engines had to transform heat into mechanical force, and mechanical force into sound, light, and electricity—and they had to do so years long, every day, under the eyes of humanity—before some of our contemporaries proclaimed the mechanical origin of heat and the correlation of physical forces, and before we ourselves became prepared to listen to them and understand their teachings. Who knows for how many decades we should continue to be ignorant of this theory which now revolutionises industry, were it not for the inventive powers and skill of those unknown workers who have improved the steam-engine, who brought all its parts to perfection, so as to make steam more manageable than a horse, and to render the use of the engine nearly universal? But the same is true with regard to each smallest part of our machinery. In each machine, however simple, we may read a whole history—a long history of sleepless nights, of delusions and joys, of partial inventions and partial improvements which brought it to its present state. Nay, nearly each new machine is a synthesis, a result of thousands of partial inventions made, not only in one special department of machinery, but in all departments of the wide field of mechanics.

Our cities, connected by roads and brought into easy communication with all peopled parts of the globe, are the growth of centuries; and each house in these cities, each factory, each shop, derives its value, its very *raison d'être*, from the fact that it is situated on a spot of the globe where thousands or millions have gathered together. Every smallest part of the immense whole which we call the wealth of civilised nations derives its value precisely from being a part of this whole. What would be the value of an immense London shop or storehouse were it not situated precisely in London, which has become the gathering spot for five millions of human beings? And what the value of our coal-pits, our manufactures, our ship-building yards, were it not for the immense traffic which goes on across the seas, for the railways which transport mountains of merchandise, for the cities which number their inhabitants by millions? Who is, then, the individual who has the right to step forward and, laying his hands on the smallest part of this immense whole, to say, '*I* have produced this; it belongs to *me*'? And how can we discriminate, in this immense interwoven whole, the part which the isolated individual may appropriate to himself with the slightest approach to justice? Houses and streets, canals and railways, machines and works of art, all these have been created by the combined efforts of generations past and present, of men living on these islands and men living thousands of miles away.

But it happened in the long run of ages that everything which permits men futher to increase their production, or even to continue it, has been appropriated by the few. The land, which derives its value precisely from its being necessary for an ever-increasing population, belongs to the few, who may prevent the community from cultivating it. The coal-pits, which represent the labour of generations, and which also derive their value from the wants of the manufactures and railroads, from the immense trade carried on and the density of population (what is the value of coal-layers in Transbaikalia?), belong again to the few, who have even the right of stopping the extraction of coal if they choose to give another use to their capital. The lace-weaving machine, which represents, in its present state of perfection, the work of three generations of Lancashire weavers, belongs again to the few; and if the grandsons of the very same weaver who invented the first lace-weaving machine claim their rights of bringing one of these machines into motion, they will be told 'Hands off! this machine does not belong to you!' The railroads, which mostly would be useless heaps of iron if Great Britain had not its present dense population, its industry, trade, and traffic, belong again to the few—to a few shareholders, who may even not know where the railway is situated which brings them a yearly income larger than that of a mediaeval king; and if the children of those people who died by thousands in digging the tunnels would gather and go—a ragged and starving crowd—to ask bread or work from the shareholders, they would be met with bayonets and bullets.

Who is the sophist who will dare to say that such an organisation is just?

But what is unjust cannot be beneficial for mankind; and *it is not*. In consequence of this monstrous organisation, the son of a workman, when he is able to work, finds no acre to till, no machine to set in motion, unless he agrees to sell his labour for a sum inferior to its real value. His father and grandfather have contributed in draining the field, or erecting the factory, to the full extent of their capacities—and nobody can do more than that— but he comes into the world more destitute than a savage. If he resorts to agriculture, he will be permitted to cultivate a plot of land, but on the condition that he gives up one quarter of his crop to the landlord. If he resorts to industry, he will be permitted to work, but on the condition that out of the thirty shillings he has produced, ten shillings or more will be pocketed by the owner of the machine. We cry against the feudal baron who did not permit anyone to settle on his land otherwise than on payment of one quarter of the crops to the lord of the manor; but we continue to do as they did—we extend their system. The forms have changed, but the essence has remained the same. And the workman is compelled to accept the feudal conditions which we call 'free contract,' because nowhere will he find better conditions. Everything has been appropriated by somebody; he *must* accept the bargain, or starve.

Owing to this circumstance our production takes a wrong turn. It takes no care of the needs of the community; its only aim is to increase the benefits of the capitalist. Therefore—the continuous fluctuations of industry, the crises periodically coming nearly every ten years, and throwing out of employment several hundred thousand men who are brought to complete misery, whose children grow up in the gutter, ready to become inmates of the prison and workhouse. The workmen being unable to purchase with their wages the riches they are producing, industry must search for markets elsewhere, amidst the middle classes of other nations. It must find markets in the East, in Africa, anywhere; it must increase, by trade, the number of its serfs in Egypt, in India, in the Congo. But everywhere it finds competitors in other nations which rapidly enter into the same line of industrial development. And wars, continuous wars, must be fought for the supremacy on the world-market—wars for the possession of the East, wars for getting possession of the seas, wars for having the right of imposing heavy duties on foreign merchandise. The thunder of guns never ceases in Europe; whole generations are slaughtered; and we spend in armaments the third of the revenue of our States—a revenue raised, the poor know with what difficulties.

Education is the privilege of the few. Not because we can find no teachers, not because the workman's son and daughter are less able to receive instruction, but because one can receive no reasonable instruction when at the age of fifteen he descends into the mine, or goes selling newspapers in the streets. Society becomes divided into two hostile camps; and no freedom is possible under such conditions. While the Radical asks for a further extension of liberty, the statesman answers him that a further extension of liberty would bring about an uprising of the paupers; and those political liberties which have cost so dear are replaced by coercion, by exceptional laws, by military rule.

And finally, the injustice of our repartition of wealth exercises the most deplorable effect on our morality. Our principles of morality say: 'Love your neighbour as yourself'; but let a child follow this principle and take off his coat to give it to the shivering pauper, and his mother will tell him that he must never understand the moral principles in their right sense. If he lives according to them, he will go barefoot, without alleviating the misery round about him! Morality is good on the lips, not in deeds. Our preachers say, 'Who works, prays,' and everybody endeavours to make others work for himself. They say, 'Never lie!' and politics is a big lie. And we accustom ourselves and our children to live under this double-facedness morality, which is hypocrisy, and to conciliate our double-facedness by sophistry. Hypocrisy and sophistry become the very basis of our life. But society cannot live under such a morality. It cannot last so: it must, it will, be changed.

The question is thus no more a mere question of bread. It covers the whole field of human activity. But it has at its bottom a question of social economy, and we conclude: The means of production and of satisfaction of all needs of society, having been created by the common efforts of all, must be at the disposal of all. The private appropriation of requisites for production is neither just nor beneficial. All must be placed on the same footing as producers and consumers of wealth. That would be the only way for society to step out of the bad conditions which have been created by centuries of wars and oppression. That would be the only guarantee for further progress in a direction of equality and freedom, which always were the real, although unspoken goal of humanity.

The Flight from Laissez-faire

Edwin Ernest Williams, Made in Germany (4th ed.; London: W. Heinemann, 1896), pp. 7–13, 161–75.

An economic national revival was one product of the Great Depression (1873–95). Significant tariffs appeared in Russia, France, Germany, and the United States. At the same time the United States and Germany threatened Britain's international economic predominance. Economic nationalism rose as a corollary to political nationalism. British suspicions and hostility were directed much more against Germany than the United States. The economic rivalry by itself would not have produced British Germanophobia; rather it compounded a problem of a shattered stereotype. The British had looked on the Germans as "little cousins" and were rudely awakened by the Franco-Prussian war (1870–71) and the character of the new German Reich. German political and economic success led to the bumptious behavior of the once-patronized *nouveau riche*.

The tangible symbol of growing German economic strength and its inroads into British life came with the Act of 1887 requiring that all imported commodities to Britain be labeled by country of origin. "Made in Germany" became frighteningly common. Edwin Ernest Williams, an economist and polemicist, turned the label into a brilliantly effective title for a powerful book. *Made in Germany* (1896) was a skilful demand for protection or at least reciprocity. Like his book, *The Foreigner in the Farmyard*, it struck a response in the public. Williams was instrumental in the conversion of Joseph Chamberlain to the cause of tariff reform in 1903. The short-term results proved politically disastrous to the British Conservative party, for free trade was still a canon of British self-confidence.

Williams recognized the fact that much of Britain's economic difficulty should be laid at the door of British industrialists and businessmen. They were too content with past success to think of present problems and future crises. *Made in Germany*, however, was more than a treatise in political economy; it was a political polemic which challenged the liberal attitude and outlook.

MADE IN GERMANY

As It Was

THERE WAS A TIME when our industrial Empire was unchallenged. It was England which first emerged from the Small-Industry stage. She produced the Industrial Revolution about the middle of the last century, and well-nigh until the middle of this she developed her multitude of mills, and factories, and mines, and warehouses, undisturbed by war at home, and profiting by wars abroad. The great struggles which drained the energies of the Continental nations, sealed her industrial supremacy, and made her absolute mistress of the world-market. Thanks to them, she became the Universal Provider. English machinery, English pottery, English hardware, guns, and cutlery, English rails and bridge-work, English manufactures of well-nigh every kind formed the material of civilisation all over the globe. She covered the dry land with a network of railways, and the seas were alive with her own ships freighted with her own merchandise. Between 1793 and 1815 the value of her exports had risen from £17,000,000 to £58,000,000. Her industrial dominion was immense, unquestioned, unprecedented in the history of the human race; and not unnaturally we have come to regard her rule as eternal. But careless self-confidence makes not for Empire. While she was throwing wide her gates to the world at large, her sisters were building barriers of protection against her; and behind those barriers, and aided often by State subventions, during the middle and later years of the century, they have developed industries of their own. Of course, this was to a certain extent inevitable. England could not hope for an eternal monopoly of the world's manufactures; and industrial growths abroad do not of necessity sound the knell of her greatness. But she must discriminate in her equanimity. And most certainly she must discriminate against Germany. For Germany has entered into a deliberate and deadly rivalry with her, and is battling with might and main for the extinction of her supremacy.

In estimating England's industrial position, regard must also be had to her function as the world's middleman. Not only is she a manufacturer for other peoples: she is likewise their agent for distribution. There is scarce a nation—certainly not one of any importance—which does not come to England to buy goods sent in for sale from elsewhere. She sells those nations hams from her Colonies, coffee from Arabia, gloves from France, currants from Greece, cotton from America—in fact it would be hard to name an article produced abroad which is not on sale in those universal market-places, the Mersey and the Thames. In this retail business, also, the Germans are setting themselves to beat us; and South Americans are already buying their Irish linen through Hamburg houses. If there be an advance in this form of competition on the part of Germany, we shall lose the little benefit accruing from the German export trade; for in all other respects it is wholly baneful to us.

The German Revolution

Up to a couple of decades ago, Germany was an agricultural State. Her manufactures were few and unimportant; her industrial capital was small; her export trade was too insignificant to merit the attention of the official statistician; she imported largely for her own consumption. Now she has changed all that. Her youth has crowded into English houses, has wormed its way into English manufacturing secrets, and has enriched her establishments with the knowledge thus purloined. She has educated her people in a fashion which has made it in some branches of industry the superior, and in most the equal of the English. Her capitalists have been content with a simple style, which has enabled them to dispense with big immediate profits, and to feed their capital. They have toiled at their desks, and made their sons do likewise; they have kept a strict controlling hand on all the strings of their businesses; they have obtained State aid in several ways—as special rates to shipping ports; they have insinuated themselves into every part of the world—civilised, barbarian, savage—learning the languages, and patiently studying the wants and tastes of the several peoples. Not content with reaping the advantages of British colonisation—this was accomplished with alarming facility—Germany has "protected" the simple savage floats on the breezes of the South Sea Islands, and droops in the thick air of the African littoral. Her diplomats have negotiated innumerable commercial treaties. The population of her cities has been increasing in a manner not unworthy of England in the Thirties and Forties. Like England, too, she is draining her rural dstricts for the massing of her children in huge factory towns. Her yards (as well as those of England) too, are ringing with the sound of hammers upon ships being builded for the transport of German merchandise. Her agents and travellers swarm through Russia, and wherever else there is a chance of trade on any terms—are even supplying the foreigner with German goods *at a loss*, that they may achieve their purpose in the end. In a word, an industrial development, unparalleled, save in England a century ago, is now her portion. A gigantic commercial State is arising to menace our prosperity, and contend with us for the trade of the world. It is true that this mad rush towards industrialism does not meet with universal approval; and the Agrarian Party is energetic in its denunciation of the ruin wrought thereby to German as an agricultural State. But its protests have nothing availed it yet, nor are ever likely to avail it anything.

Made in Germany

The phrase is fluent in the mouth: how universally appropriate it is, probably no one who has not made a special study of the matter is aware. Take observations, Gentle Reader, in your own surroundings: the mental exercise is recommended as an antidote to that form of self-sufficiency which our candid friends regard as indigenous to the British climate. Your investigations will work out somewhat in this fashion. You will find that the material of some of your own clothes was probably woven in Germany. Still more probable is it that some of your wife's garments are German importations; while it is practically beyond a doubt that the magnificent mantles and jackets wherein her maids array themselves on their Sundays out are German-made and German-sold, for only so could they be done at the figure. Your governess's *fiancé* is a clerk in the City; but he also was made in Germany. The toys, and the dolls, and the fairy books which your children maltreat in the nursery are made in Germany: nay, the material of your favourite (patriotic) newspaper had the same birthplace as like as not. Roam the house over, and the fateful mark will greet you at every turn, from the piano in your drawing-room to the mug on your kitchen dresser, blazoned though it be with the legend, *A present from Margate*. Descend to your domestic depths, and you shall find your very drain-pipes German made. You pick out of the grate the paper wrappings from a book consignment, and they also are "Made in Germany." You stuff them into the fire, and reflect that the poker in your hand was forged in Germany. As you rise from your hearthrug you knock over an ornament on your mantel-piece; picking up the pieces you read, on the bit that formed the base, "Manufactured in Germany." And you jot your dismal reflections down with a pencil that was made in Germany. At midnight your wife comes home from an opera which was made in Germany, has been here enacted by singers and conductor and players made in Germany, with the aid of instruments and sheets of music made in Germany. You go to bed, and glare wrathfully at a text on the wall; it is illuminated with an English village church, and it was "Printed in Germany." If you are imaginative and dyspeptic, you drop off to sleep only to a dream that St. Peter (with a duly stamped halo round his head and a bunch of keys from the Rhineland) has refused you admission into Paradise, because you bear not the Mark of the Beast upon your forehead, and are not of German make. But you console yourself with the thought that it was only a Bierhaus Paradise any way; and you are awakened in the morning by the sonorous brass of a German band.

Is the picture exaggerated? Bear with me, while I tabulate a few figures from the Official Returns of Her Majesty's Custom House, where, at any rate, fancy and exaggeration have no play. In '95 Germany sent us linen manufacturers to the value of £91,257; cotton manufactures to the value of £536,471; embroidery and needlework to the value of £11,309; leather gloves to the value of £27,934 (six times the amount imported six years earlier); and woollen manufactures to the value of £1,016,694. Despite the exceeding cheapness of toys, the value of German-made playthings for English nurseries amounted, in '95, to £459,944. In the same year she sent us books to the value of £37,218, and paper to the value of £586,835. For musical instruments we paid her as much as £563,018; for china and earthenware £216,876; for prints, engravings, and photographs, £111,825. This recital of the moneys which *in one year* have come out of John Bull's pocket for the purchase of his German-made household goods is, I submit disproof enough of any charge of alarmism. For these articles, it must be remembered, are not like oranges and guano. They are not products which we must either import or lack:—*they all belong to the category of English manufactures*, the most important of them, indeed, being articles in the preparation of which Great Britain is held pre-eminent. The total value of manufactured goods imported into the United Kingdom by Germany rose from £16,629,987 in '83 to £21,632,614 in '93: an increase of 30.08 per cent.

A few figures more. I said that a little while since Germany was a large importer of manufactures needed for her own consumption. Take as a first example, the iron and steel industries. In '78 the make of pig-iron in Germany was 2,147,000 tons; in '95 it was 5,788,000 tons. German made in '78

492,512 tons of steel; in '94 3,617,000 tons. Her import and export statistics tell the same tale. In '80 her iron exports only totalled 1,301,000 tons; in '94 they stood at 2,008,000 tons. (In the same period England's exports of iron had decreased.) In the matter of cottons Germany exported 14,666,100 kilogs. in '83; in '93, 33,350,800 kilogs., an increase of more than 127 per cent. (England's increase in the same period was only about 2½ per cent.) Shippng returns are a pretty sure test of commercial prosperity: it is therefore significant that in '93 the total tonnage of the sea-going ships which touched at Hamburg for the first time left Liverpool behind, and in '94 Hamburg cut her record of the year before.

   •   •   •   •   •   •   •   •   •   •   •   •   •   •   •

In General

I might go on for many pages setting out the superior powers of self-help which the Germans possess, and owing to which they steal our markets. But I think I have indicated in this, or in those earlier chapters dealing with specific industries, the main features. Push and adaptability account for most; but one or two other qualities must be recorded. There is the great principle of Show. It might be imagined that, with our railway stations, our hoardings, our journals, our programmes, our fields and our bathing-machines smeared with advertisements of every ware known to civilisation, English traders can have little to reproach themselves withal on the score of pushing their merchandise into the public gaze. Yet, though the hoarding of bewildering ugliness is unknown in German streets, it is a fact that German manufacturers have somewhat to teach the English. I have spoken more than once of the curious reluctance to exhibit at international shows which has afflicted English manufacturers of late. They say that, by taking part in these exhibitions, they do but provide the foreigner with the opportunity for displaying his imitative skill. This argument is merely fallacious. The Germans are always well to the front at such exhibitions, and their trade is growing, their success, indeed, being ascribed by themselves in no small measure to this very fact. Englishmen should explain how they expect to sell their wares at all except by bringing them before the public. They should, to be consistent, refrain from advertising altogether.

At the same time English manufacturers are not entirely foolish in their dread of this faculty of imitativeness which the German possesses in a remarkable degree. Indeed, a list of the factors in German success would be lacking in an important item were it omitted. Seeing how many inventions have England for birthplace, it is obvious that the present proportions of German industry can only have been attained by a careful imitation of those inventions. It was thus the Germans got their start. They have come, and they still come, to England in large numbers for the very purpose; and, whenever they have deemed it expedient, they have engaged English managers and artisans to go to Germany, and work in the factories there.

But it is significant that the German inventive genius, which in the past was somewhat backward, is now developing at a rate which bids fair soon to place the German beyond the need of English models. One special cause of complaint against him is that his imitations are inferior to the models, though (apart from fraud) his copy is often sufficiently like the British original to deceive the purchaser, and where it is of cheaper workmanship, and can therefore be sold at a lower price, the English maker is heavily handicapped. But it must not be forgotten that the German imitation is not as a rule inferior in all respects. In the matter of artistic finish it is often— one may say, as a rule—decidedly better. In many kinds of manufacture such superiority is vital: in most it is an integral factor. So artistry must be added to the list of those accomplishments which tell.

So, too, must the greatest steadiness of the German worker. Ask your tailor whether he would rather employ an Englishman or a German? and why? His answer will be conclusive. In that view, however, it is a matter concerning the English workmen only, and so beside my present inquiry. But the greater steadiness of the German is also effective in another way, which is pertinent to my purpose:—the cost of running a factory is less when the men are regular. Engines have to be tended and fed, and the wear and tear of machinery goes on, whether sixty men or six hundred turn up on Monday morning. Of the fact that work in German factories does progress more steadily than in English there is no doubt whatever in the minds of those who have made observations in both countries.

Lastly, let me reiterate that the great cause of German success is an alert progressiveness, contrasting brilliantly, with the conservative stupor of ourselves. It is all very well to run an old-established business; but you must diligently and continuously be striving to bring its methods up to date. And this is what English manufacturers fail to recognise. There are plenty of exceptions, of course—chiefly amongst houses which have their reputations to make, though here and there are firms of established repute with men of foresight ready to break with orthodox tradition whenever they can find a better way. But the mass of English manufacturers and traders clings to the faith of its fathers; still thinks "We have never done so" a model sentence in commercial correspondence; still believes that what was good enough of old is good enough yet; ignores the constant change of condition, which renders the nature and wants of the market as variable as the weather. German houses reflect the exact opposite of this attitude. They are all for progress and the eager and intelligent study of changing fashions and changing needs. They are ready at all times to make a new departure, if thereby they may save but a single small market.

    .   .   .   .

These are the reasons why Germany beats us. The list has been a long one; yet I could not well have made it shorter, without leaving out items any one of which is capable of accounting for much of England's failure.

What we Must Do to be Saved

Is, shortly, the opposite of what we are doing now. This final chapter may therefore be brief. As matter of fact and dismal reflection, much of the harm wrought is irreparable: the German Industrial State is a fact, and there is no human probability of its being crushed. Much, too, may for the present be set down as almost irreparable, for the remedy could only come by revolution in the English State or in the English mind and habit. But much else is remediable—some of it easily remediable.

Fair Trade

This is one of the revolutionary changes, the most revolutionary indeed of all, and, in the present state of general opinion, one almost shrinks from reference to it. Yet there is now visible in the public mind a movement which makes discussion less appalling than it was. And in any case, as the question must be faced, it is well to give it a foremost place.

A consideration of the facts forces the conviction that England's Free Trade policy, existing side by side with Protection in Germany, has been responsible in no small degree for the strides which Germany has made at England's expense. What then? Our fiscal policy requires to be reviewed if not recast. The conclusion is inevitable.

It is a bold saying, I know, and one which will make me many enemies. It is a view, too, which, with an Englishman's hereditary Free-Trade instinct, I have struggled against. But the struggle has availed me nothing. Those of my critics who, when the earlier portions of this book were appearing in serial form, assailed my work as being a piece of Protectionist Agitation (notwithstanding my disclaimer at starting) have misunderstood my position. My object, as I stated, was to make a diagnosis in a scientific spirit, and from that diagnosis to arrive at such remedies as might be. Most reluctantly have I been convinced that one cause of the disease afflicting the Industrial Body Politic is the pursuit of a Free Trade which is no Free Trade at all. Cobden anticipated that the cheapening of food resulting from the abolition of the Corn Laws would encourage English manufacture by diminishing the cost of living to the English worker. Free Trade, it was admitted, might hurt English agriculture; but it was maintained, it could not but be of great service to English manufacture. How the alternative has been realised will be patent to those who have followed my statement of the under-selling of English goods both in England and abroad.

Let us face the position. England is being flooded with foreign manufactures, which come here duty free, and which are sold at a price made artificially low by the Protective Tariffs of other Governments. Under these Tariffs English goods have their cost raised in their passage through foreign ports, and in neutral markets also they are at a disadvantage with the goods of foreign rivals, whose Protected home-markets permit reductions on Export Prices, which under normal conditions would be quite unremunerative.

Are we then to adopt an autonomous Protective Tariff? By no means: the time has gone by for that; just as surely as it has not yet come for the inauguration of complete Free Trade. A middle course is possible, and it is that middle course which I am here advocating, at whatever cost to popularity. Germany herself, under the Caprivi Administration, is a good illustration of it in practice. The motto is simply *quid pro quo. To the extent to which a foreign country shuts out our goods from her markets, to that extent should we penalise her goods in our markets.*

Then, *we must federate the Empire*, in the most practical way—the way of commerce. At the present we are losing our grip of our own colonies and dependencies, which are steadily falling into the hands of the German. German goods enter India and Canada and Australia and the Cape on equal terms with English goods; both pay duties, German no more than English. Surely this can be rectified? The existing treaties between England and Belgium and Germany must be got rid of—Lord Salisbury has said they should never have been entered into—and our colonies must learn to be filial. We protect them with our Flag; our gigantic Navy is largely for the purpose of safe-guarding them. But we pay all the cost; they, in return think they have done their duty by the mother-country, when they have sung the National Anthem at their banquets. *They must discriminate in their Tariffs, and admit English products on more favourable terms than those of other nations.* We might in return discriminate between their produce and foreign produce entering England: Canadian and Austrialian Wheat, for example, might come free; Wheat from the United States and Germany and Russia being penalized with a ten per cent. Tariff. So we might become a great Industrial Empire.

Of course the carrying out of the reform would not be unattended by difficulties, but they are not insuperable; while the benefits would be immense.

A year or two ago such a suggestion would have been classed with Utopian dreams. Fair-Traders were commonly laughed at; to-day Fair Trade in the form of Commercial Federation is within the range of practical politics.

Subsidised Transport

This is an exceedingly difficult question. German success is in part due to the low transport charges paid on German merchandise; that lowness is the result of the State subsidy system which prevails in Germany. Shall we follow suit? To do so would be to take on a form of Protection: though that consideration should not in itself be fatal to the proposal. The question to decide is,—Would the British tax-payer consent to pay the piper? The payment would have to be a heavy one; for the discrepancy between English and Continental railway rates is big, especially on goods destined for export, and equalisation would be a costly business. The thing is feasible, of course, and its benefits to English manufacture would be undoubted and great. Moreover, it is almost the only way of effecting any large reduction in English railway rates, and it will be hard work to screw much more out of the companies. But it is a form of Protection which no Government would venture on with a light heart. Yet ours would have a certain sort of precedent for granting this aid if it were so minded: the Treasury is offering a million sterling to help light railways and agriculture, and the principle is much the same in the case of ordinary railways and manufacture. But there is another method of checkmating our rival. The English Government once proposed to tax bounty-fed German sugar to the extent of the bounty. *All German manufactures carried at specially low export rates on German State lines should be penalised at English ports to the exten of the bounty.* It would be a most excellent reform; and it would be most welcome. The German Government, for example, would soon tire of letting Silesian coal-owners send their coal at ruinously low rates to Baltic ports for shipment to England, when it found that England calculated the amount it gave, and added an equal sum to the cost of the coal on landing in England.

Commercial Consuls

Under this heading in the previous chapter I called attention to the greater usefulness of the German Consular Service. Here, at any rate, we are outside the region of controversy, and no one can refuse to follow me on the plea that I am leading him astray from the sacred principles in which he has been reared. There are no drawbacks to the institution of improvements here, nor is the path of reform beset with difficulties. *Our commercial attachés must be increased in number.* Three for the whole of Europe is a mere absurdity. Every Legation should have one as a matter of course. And *our Consular System must be overhauled.* There must be no poorly paid Vice-Consuls at industrial centres. Properly and well-trained men must represent our commerce in all important towns throughout the world, and they must be remunerated on a fit and proper scale. They should regard it as their chief business, the pushing of English trade, and the assisting of English traders, both personally and by the collection and dissemination of knowledge as to changing fashions and wants and conditions of market. *The Consular Bureau should be a commercial barometer for the use of English manufacturers and merchants.*

Here is one useful remedy which may be applied immediately; without raising any controversy; without treading on any corns; without very much trouble to State Departments concerned; without much expense, relatively to the sums which the State spends in other directions; but with the certainty of doing *something*—probably something substantial—towards checking the ebb of our commercial prosperity.

Technical Education

*We must give our people a sound practical and theoretical acquaintance
with the industries in which they are to work.* There are [those] who place
the lack of Technical Education in England in the forefront of her failure,
and they are men whose opinion is worth heeding. I endeavoured in the
previous chapter to give an idea of the way the German educates. We must
take example by him. We have already Technical Education of a kind in
England, and Mr. Ritchie estimates that we spend four millions a year upon
it; but it is insignificant and half-hearted. The Technical Instruction Act of
1889, giving local authorities power to supply, or aid in the supply of technical instruction, is a move in the right direction; the Local Taxation
(Customs and Excise) Act, 1890, under which a sum, amounting in one
year ('94–'5) to £744,000, is given to English County Councils and County
Boroughs for technical education, is another: though some of these local
bodies, to their shame, diverted £144,000 of this sum to the relief of their
rates last year. But more, very much more, needs to be done. It is no use
to boggle at the expense. You grumble at your children's school bills: but
you pay them, knowing the schools to be necessary; and you must pay the
national bill, for the nation's education is also necessary. See to it that the
money is rightly expended; but make up your minds to spend it. We increase our naval armaments to keep pace with the development of foreign
powers; it is just as wise and necessary a policy to increase our educational
armaments, so that our industrial army shall not fall below the standard of
Germany's. As a fact, it has fallen very far below. We have now to make up
lee-way, and the best endeavours of statesmen and educational experts
should be devoted to the task. There is none more pressing.

The advocacy of this policy needs no further argument; but in case that
among my readers there remain any yet unconvinced—any who, in spite
of the lesson spread out before them, still rely on the position that England
got on very well in the past without technical schools—let me remind these
unbelievers that the conditions of to-day are entirely changed. We got our
supremacy from a number of political and other causes, which I alluded to
in my first chapter. Those causes no longer operate. We have now to defend
our position against the most determined and the best equipped foes; and
for this warfare the best possible training is needed.

This is not the place for a detailed discussion of the improvements and
new departures which we require; but there is one suggestion I desire to
put forward. The Technical Instruction Act provides for instruction in the
principles of science and art applicable to industries, and in the application
of special branches of science and art to specific industries; but it forbids
teaching the practice of an industry. This is wrong. The one ought to be
done, but the other ought not to be left undone. The apprenticeship system
is disappearing, and practical instruction in an industry must be provided.
The actual trade must be taught. Here and there, it is true, despite the Act,

actual trades are being taught, and with the money provided by the Act. For example, at Luton instruction under the Act is now being given in the practice of the local straw-plaiting industry, which had got into a moribund condition; the effects so far have been most satisfactory, and are reviving the trade. In other words, the Act attempts to draw a distinction, which would be foolish if it could be put into practice, and though in several towns it is wisely ignored, it is objectionable, and should be got rid of.

Let me make one other suggestion. Why cannot Technical Instruction be commenced in Board Schools? There seems no convincing reason why Elementary Education should be merely literary; while there seems every reason why it should be combined with healthy and interesting training in manual industry and artistic craftmanship. The time-limit blocks the way at present to much reform; and the age at which children of the poorer classes are taken away from school should be raised. But in the meantime many hours might be saved by compressing the less necessary parts of the school curriculum. Learning the names of Canaanitish chiefs and the like gymnastics of the mind might with advantage make room for elementary instruction in some useful or beautiful craft.

Individual Enterprise

But let me again reiterate that help from the State is not enough. Fair Trade, Commercial Consuls, Technical Colleges—good and necessary as they are—will not avail to stem the inroad of the German, unless our manufacturers and merchants brace themselves for exertions more strenuous and better directed, and a more forward and spirited policy generally, than have been the rule with them for many years.

They must be more studious of the tastes and wishes of their customers. Evidence on this head is accumulating daily; scarce a British Consul's report but emphasises the paramount need of English manufacturers paying more regard to the desires of those with whom they do, or would do, business.

They must send out travellers who know the language of the country which they are to canvass.

They must cease to scorn the small order. Witnesses to the folly of contemning orders derisively described by English houses as "mere retail business" are numerous. The manufacturers usually awake to the fatal results which follow this policy of pinchbeck magnificence when the trade has gone.

They must pay more heed to the merits of careful packing and the like details of well-conducted commerce.

Yet more important: *They must have an up-to-date equipment in their workshops.* Much of the disaster which has overtaken our Iron and Steel Trades is attributed to the better machinery of the Continental ironmasters. Much of the havoc wrought in our Chemical trades is due to parsimony in equipment.

They must adopt the Metric System of Weights and Measures, for their Export Business at any rate. It is difficult to refer to this subject without exhibiting impatience. Statesmen approve the reform in their speeches; Chambers of Commerce resolve that it is a necessity; the Decimal System forms part of the Board School repertory: no one has a word to say against its adoption. Yet our traders persist—knowing it to be to their own hurt—in the antiquated and clumsy table of Weights and Measures used by our forefathers before international commerce was born. Also, *whatever the system of money and measures in vogue in a country in which Englishmen purpose to trade, they must conform to that system,* or be prepared to see the puzzled native transfer his orders to the accommodating German.

They must be more artistic. It is well enough—it is very well—to be thorough and substantial, but articles for sale must take the eye of the purchaser, and English goods are very often inferior to German in this respect. The defect must be remedied: it is hard to believe that elegance is beyond the reach of English designers and craftsmen. If our people will only recognise the importance of graceful form, pleasing design, and artistic finish, and cultivate the necessary skill, they can repair the deficiency, in a great measure. Any way, the experiment is worth trying. Arts and Crafts Exhibition should not be regarded as the property of Mr. John Burns's "aesthetic dawdlers."

They must practise the Imitatice Art. Englishmen have done this in the past—witness the foreign names of many English manufactures: "holland," to take one example: which indicate an originally foreign industry captured by our own people. But the Germans have shown themselves even better and more thorough masters of the art, as Englishmen know to their cost. Englishmen must practise it more sedulously.

They must advertise more boldly. The fear of exhibitions is a craven fear, and must be overcome. Just now, particularly, when English goods are being supplanted by German, our manufacturers, when their manufactures are worthy of praise, should take advantage of any chance that may offer of putting them before the public side by side with the German equivalent. Foreigners who want to imitate English wares can secure the necessary specimens; they are not confined to looking at them through a glass case.

Labour Troubles must be avoided. English manufacturers should recognise that it is necessary for their servents to enjoy decent conditions of life. Well paid workers—other things being equal—are the best workers, and a raising of wages or a shortening of hours is often a profitable investment. It is poor policy on the part of the masters to risk or throw away trade for the sake of a few pence. And the men on their part should be careful how they foster disputes; the rules of a trade-union should not be rigid in non-essentials, but should emulate the elasticity of the market and the changing conditions of industry. Trade-unionism is a beneficent power, when it is wielded with descretion. One often observes signs of a lack in this regard.

Lastly, *Englishmen must be more progressive.* They must not rest on their reputation; they must be ever alert and watchful, ready to take instant and full advantage of new discoveries, ready to accommodate themselves to the continual changes in the wants of the peoples of all nations. Let the fate of the Dyeing Trade serve for a common warning.

.   .   .   .

Are these counsels of perfection? They are counsels, nevertheless, which are, every one of them necessary to salvation. Every one of them is followed in Germany, and I decline to believe that England's industrial character has so deteriorated that she is unable, an she will, to pull herself up to the German standard of conduct. *Her unique position as unchallenged mistress of the Industrial World is gone, and is not likely to be regained.* But some of the departed glory may yet be restored to her. At least let us see to it that she fares no worse.

Anarcho-Syndicalism:
The Challenge of Sorel

Georges Sorel, "Letter to Daniel Halévy," Reflections on Violence, trans. T. E. Hulme [New York: Peter Smith, 1941], pp. 1–42.

While revisionist Socialists like Eduard Bernstein domesticated the revolutionary ideology of Socialist doctrine in an effort to adapt social democracy to the realities of the modern liberal state, others restated and extended the challenge to the western political, social, and economic order. One was Nicolai Lenin; another was Georges Sorel. The two share much in ideological terms—more than either might have chosen to admit. They were to become the foundations of the mass doctrines of the twentieth century. Fascist ideologues potted Sorel. Lenin and Trotsky found their heir in Stalin and modern communism.

Georges Sorel (1847–1922) was an engineer and civil servant. His doctrine has much of the flavor of Saint-Simon before him; both, after all, were social engineers. The reformation of mankind could never be realized through tinkering and amendment; it required a total moral, economic, and social revolution. Sorel was a humanist, but there was nothing humane in this humanitarian cynic's creed.

Morality is not doomed to perish because the motive forces behind it will change; it is not destined to become a mere collection of precepts as long as it can still vivify itself by an alliance with an enthusiasm capable of conquering all the obstacles, prejudices, and the need of immediate enjoyment, which oppose its progress.

· · · · · · · · · · · ·

There is only one force which can produce to-day that enthusiasm without whose co-operation no morality is possible, and that is the force resulting from the propaganda in favour of a general strike (constantly rejuvenated by the feelings roused by proletarian violence) produces an entirely epic state of mind, and at the same time bends all the energies of the mind to that condition necessary to the realisation of a workshop carried on by free men, eagerly seeking the betterment of the industry; we have thus recognized that there are great resemblances between the sentiments aroused by the idea of the general strike and those which are necessary to bring about a continued progress in methods of production. We have then the right to maintain that the modern world possesses that prime mover which is necessary to the creation of the ethics of the producers. [p. 294]

On one point, if on no other, Sorel demonstrated his grasp of reality. He underscored the vital role of myth as an animating force in history, and then proceeded to erect the general strike as the greatest myth of all. As with so many other turn-of-the-century thinkers, Sorel's strength lay in his incisive criticism of a decadent bourgeois order and of the half-answers to the pressing problems of the age.

INTRODUCTION

Letter to Daniel Halévy

My dear Halévy—I should doubtless have left these studies buried in the bound volumes of a review if some friends, whose judgment I value, had not thought that it would be a good thing to bring them before the notice of a wider public, as they serve to make better known one of the most singular social phenomena that history records. But it seemed to me that it would be necessary to give this public some additional explanations, since I cannot often expect to find judges as indulgent as you have been.

When I published, in the *Mouvement Socialiste*, the articles which are now collected in this volume, I did not write with the intention of composing a book: I simply wrote down my reflections as they came into my mind. I knew that the subscribers to that review would have no difficulty in following me, since they were already familiar with the theories, which for some years my friends and I had developed in its pages. But I am convinced that the readers of this book, on the contrary, will be very bewildered if I do not submit a kind of defence which will enable them to consider things from my own habitual point of view. In the course of our conversations, you have sometimes made remarks which fitted so well into the system of my own ideas that they often led me to investigate certain questions more thoroughly. I am sure that the reflections which I here submit to you, and which you have provoked, will be very useful to those who wish to read this book with profit.

There are perhaps few studies in which the defects of my method of writing are more evident; I have been frequently reproached for not respecting the rules of the art of writing, to which all our contemporaries submit, and for thus inconveniencing my readers by the disorder of my explanations. I have tried to render the text clearer by numerous corrections of detail, but I have not been able to make the disorder disapper. I do not wish to defend myself by pleading the example of great writers who have been blamed for not knowing how to compose Arthur Chuquet, speaking of J. J. Rousseau, said: "His writings lack harmony, order, and that connection of the parts which constitutes a unity." The defects of illustrious men do not justify the faults of the obscure, and I think that it is better to explain frankly the origin of this incorrigible vice in my writings.

It is only recently that the rules of the art of writing have imposed themselves in a really imperative way; contemporary authors appear to have accepted them readily, because they wished to please a hurried and often very inattentive public, and one which is desirous above all of avoiding any personal investigation. These rules were first applied by the people who manufacture scholastic books. Since the aim of education has been to make the pupils absorb an enormous amount of information, it has been necessary to put into their hands manuals suitable to this extra rapid instruction;

everything has had to be presented in a form so clear, so logically arranged, and so calculated to dispel doubt, that in the end the beginner comes to believe that science is much simpler than our fathers supposed. In this way the mind is very richly furnished in a very little time, but it is not furnished with implements which facilitate individual effort. These methods have been imitated by political publicists and by the people who attempt to popularise knowledge. Seeing these rules of the art of writing so widely adopted, people who reflect little have ended by believing that they were based on the nature of things themselves.

I am neither a professor, a populariser of knowledge, nor a candidate for party leadership. I am a self-taught man exhibiting to other people the notebooks which have served for my own instruction. That is why the rules of the art of writing have never interested me very much.

During twenty years I worked to deliver myself from what I retained of my education; I read books, not so much to learn as to efface from my memory the ideas which had been thrust upon it. It is only during the last fifteen years that I have really worked for the purpose of learning; but I have never found any one to teach me what I wanted to know. I have had to be my own master, and in a way to educate myself. I make notes in which I formulate my thoughts as they arise; I return three or four times to the same question, adding corrections which amplify the original, and some-times even transform it from top to bottom; I only stop when I have ex-hausted the reserve of ideas stirred up by recent reading. This work is very difficult for me; that is why I like to take as my subject the discussion of a book by a good author: I can then arrange my thoughts more easily than when I am left to my own unaided efforts.

You will remember what Bergson has written about the impersonal, the socialised, the *ready-made,* all of which contains a lesson for students who need knowledge for practical life. A student has more confidence in the formulas which he is taught, and consequently retains them more easily, when he believes that they are accepted by the great majority; in this way all metaphysical preoccupations are removed from his mind and he is to feel no need for a personal conception of things; he often comes to look on the absence of any inventive spirit as a superiority.

My own method of work is entirely opposed to this; for I put before my readers the working of a mental effort which is continually endeavouring to break through the bonds of what has been previously constructed for common use, in order to discover that which is truly personal and individ-ual. The only things I find it worth while entering in my notebooks are those which I have not met elsewhere; I readily skip the transitions be-tween these things, because they nearly always come under the heading of commonplaces.

The communication of thought is always very difficult for any one who has strong metaphysical preoccupations; he thinks that speech will spoil the most fundamental parts of his thought, those which are very near to the motive power of the mind, those which appear so natural to him that he never seeks to express them. A reader has great difficulty in grasping the thought of an inventor, because he can only attain it by finding again the path traversed by the latter. Verbal communication is much easier than written communication, because words act on the feelings in a mysterious way and easily establish a current of sympathy between people; it is for this reason that an orator is able to produce conviction by arguments which do not seem very comprehensible to any one reading the speech later. You know how useful it is to have heard Bergson if one wants to recognise clearly the tendencies of his doctrine and to understand his books rightly. When one has followed his courses of lectures for some time one becomes familiar with the order of his ideas and gets one's bearings more easily amidst the novelties of his philosophy.

The defects of my manner of writing prevent me getting access to a wide public; but I think that we ought to be content with the place that nature and circumstances have assigned to each of us, without desiring to force our natural talent. There is a necessary division of functions in the world; it is a good thing that some are content to work, simply that they may submit their reflections to a few studious people, whilst others love to address the great mass of busy humanity. All things considered, I do not think that mine is the worst lot, for I am not exposed to the danger of becoming my own disciple, as has happened to the greatest philosophers when they have endeavoured to give a perfectly symmetrical form to the intuitions they brought into the world. You will certainly not have forgotten the smiling disdain with which Bergson has spoken of this infirmity of genius. So little am I capable of becoming my own disciple that I am unable to take up an old work of mine again with the idea of stating it better, or even of completing it; it is easy enough for me to add corrections and to annotate it, but I have many times vainly tried to think the past over again.

Much more, then, am I prevented from ever becoming the founder of a school; but is that really a great misfortune? Disciples have nearly always exercised a pernicious influence on the thought of him they called their master, and who has often believed himself obliged to follow them. There is no doubt that his transformation by young enthusiasts into the leader of a party was real disaster for Marx; he would have done much more useful work if he had not been the slave of the Marxists.

People have often laughed at Hegel's belief—that humanity, since its origins, had worked to give birth to the Hegelian philosophy, and that with that philosophy Spirit had at last completed its development. Similar illusions are found to a certain extent in all founders of schools; disciples expect their master to close the era of doubt by giving final solutions to all problems. I have no aptitude for a task of that kind. Every time that I have approached a question, I have found that my enquiries ended by giving rise to new problems, and the farther I pushed my investigations the more disquieting these new problems became. But philosophy is after all per-

haps only the recognition of the abysses which lie on each side of the foot-
path that the vulgar follow with the serenity of somnambulists.

It is my ambition to be able occasionally to stir up personal research.
There is probably in the mind of every man, hidden under the ashes, a
quickening fire, and the greater the number of ready-made doctrines the
mind has received blindly the more is this fire threatened with extinction;
the awakener is the man who stirs the ashes and thus makes the flames leap
up. I do not think that I am praising myself without cause when I say that
I have sometimes succeeded in liberating the spirit of invention in my
readers; and it is the spirit of invention which it is above all necessary to
stir up in the world. It is better to have obtained this result than to have
gained the banal approbation of people who repeat formulas and enslave
their own thought in the disputes of the schools.

I

My *Reflections on Violence* have irritated many people on account of
the pessimistic conception on which the whole of the study rests; but I
know that you do not share this impression; you have brilliantly shown in
your *Histoire de quatre ans* that you despise the deceptive hopes with
which the weak solace themselves. We can then talk pessimism freely to
each other, and I am happy to have a correspondent who does not revolt
against a doctrine without which nothing very great has been accomplished in this world. I have felt for some time that Greek philosophy did
not produce any great moral result, simply because it was, as a rule, very
optimistic. Socrates was at times optimistic to an almost unbearable degree.

The aversion of most of our contemporaries from every pessimistic conception is doubtless derived, to a great extent, from our system of education.
The Jesuits, who created nearly everything that the University still continues to teach, were optimists because they had to combat the pessimism
which dominated Protestant theories, and because they popularised the
ideas of the Renaissance; the Renaissance interpreted antiquity by means
of the philosophers, and consequently misunderstood the masterpieces of
tragic art so completely that our contemporaries have had considerable
difficulty in rediscovering their pessimistic significance.

At the beginning of the nineteenth century, there was such a concert of
groaning that pessimism became odious. Poets, who were not, as a matter
of fact, much to be pitied, professed to be victims of fate, of human wickedness, and still more of the stupidity of a world which had not been able to
distract them; they eagerly assumed the attitudes of a Prometheus called
upon to dethrone jealous gods, and with a pride equal to that of the fierce
Nimrod of Victor Hugo (whose arrows, hurled at the sky, fell back stained
with blood), they imagined that their verses inflicted deadly wounds on the
established powers who dared to refuse to bow down before them. The
prophets of the Jews never dreamed of so much destruction to avenge their
Jehovah as these literary people dreamed of to satisfy their vanity. When

this fashion for imprecations had passed, sensible men began to ask themselves if all this display of pretended pessimism had not been the result of a certain want of mental balance.

The immense successes obtained by industrial civilisation has created the belief that, in the near future, happiness will be produced automatically for everybody. "The present century," writes Hartmann, "has for the last forty years only entered the third period of illusion. In the enthusiasm and enchantment of its hopes, it rushes towards the realisation of the promise of a new age of gold. Providence takes care that the anticipations of the isolated thinker do not disarrange the course of history by prematurely gaining too many adherents." He thinks that for this reason his readers will have some difficulty in accepting his criticism of the illusion of future happiness. The leaders of the contemporary world are pushed towards optimism by economic forces.

So little are we prepared to understand pessimism, that we generally employ the word quite incorrectly: we call pessimists people who are in reality only disillusioned optimists. When we meet a man who, having been unfortunate in his enterprises, deceived in his most legitimate ambitions, humiliated in his affections, expresses his griefs in the form of a violent revolt against the duplicity of his associates, the stupidity of society, or the blindness of destiny, we are disposed to look upon him as a pessimist; whereas we ought nearly always to regard him as a disheartened optimist who has not had the courage to start afresh, and who is unable to understand why so many misfortunes have befallen him, contrary to what he supposes to be the general law governing the production of happiness.

The optimist in politics is an inconstant and even dangerous man, because he takes no account of the great difficulties presented by his projects; these projects seem to him to possess a force of their own, which tends to bring about their realisation all the more easily as they are in his opinion, destined to produce the happiest results. He frequently thinks that small reforms in the political constitution, and, above all, in the personnel of the government, will be sufficient to direct social development in such a way as to mitigate those evils of the contemporary world which seem so harsh to the sensitive mind. As soon as his friends come into power, he declares that it is necessary to let things alone for a little, not to hurry too much, and to learn how to be content with whatever their own benevolent intentions prompt them to do. It is not always self-interest that suggests these expressions of satisfaction, as people have often believed; self-interest is strongly aided by vanity and by the illusions of philosophy. The optimist passes with remarkable facility from revolutionary anger to the most ridiculous social pacificism.

If he possesses an exalted temperament, and if unhappily he finds himself armed with great power, permitting him to realise the ideal he has fashioned, the optimist may lead his country into the worst disasters. He is not long in finding out that social transformations are not brought about with the ease that he has counted on; he then supposes that this is the fault of his contemporaries, instead of explaining what actually happens by historical necessities; he is tempted to get rid of people whose obstinacy seems to him to be so dangerous to the happiness of all. During the Terror, the men who spilt most blood were precisely those who had the greatest desire to let their social equals enjoy the golden age they had dreamt of, and who had the most sympathy with human wretchedness: optimists, idealists, and sensitive men, the greater desire they had for universal happiness the more inexorable they showed themselves.

Pessimism is quite a different thing from the caricatures of it which are usually presented to us; it is a philosophy of conduct rather than a theory of the world; it considers the *march towards deliverance* as narrowly conditioned, on the one hand, by the experimental knowledge that we have acquired from the obstacles which oppose themselves to the satisfaction of our imaginations (or, if we like, by the feeling of social determinism), and, on the other, by a profound conviction of our natural weakness. These two aspects of pessimism should never be separated, although, as a rule, scarcely any attention is paid to their close connection.

1. The conception of pessimism springs from the fact that literary historians have been very much struck with the complaints made by the great poets of antiquity on the subject of the griefs which constantly threaten mankind. There are few people who have not, at one time or another, experienced a piece of good fortune; but we are surrounded by malevolent forces always ready to spring out on us from some ambuscade and overwhelm us. Hence the very real sufferings which arouse the sympathy of nearly all men, even of those who have been more favourably treated by fortune; so that the literature of grief has always had a certain success throughout the whole course of history. But a study of this kind of literature would give us a very imperfect idea of pessimism. It may be laid down as a general rule, that in order to understand a doctrine it is not sufficient to study it in an abstract manner, nor even as it occurs in isolated people: it is necessary to find out how it has been manifested in historical groups; it is for this reason that I am here led to add the two elements that were mentioned earlier.

2. The pessimist regards social conditions as forming a system bound together by an iron law which cannot be evaded, so that the system is given, as it were, in one block, and cannot disappear except in a catastrophe which involves the whole. If this theory is admitted, it then becomes absurd to make certain wicked men responsible for the evils from which society suffers; the pessimist is not subject to the sanguinary follies of the optimist, infatuated by the unexpected obstacles that his projects meet with; he does not dream of bringing about the happiness of future generations by slaughtering existing egoists.

3. The most fundamental element of pessimism is its method of conceiving the path towards deliverance. A man would not go very far in the

examination either of the laws of their own wretchedness or of fate, which so much shock the ingenuousness of our pride, if he were not borne up by the hope of putting an end to these tyrannies by an effort, to be attempted with the help of a whole band of companions. The Christians would not have discussed original sin so much if they had not felt the necessity of justifying the deliverance (which was to result from the death of Jesus) by supposing that this sacrifice had been rendered necessary by a frightful crime, which could be imputed to humanity. If the people of the West were much more occupied with original sin than those of the East, it was not solely, as Taine thought, owing to the influence of Roman law, but also because the Latins, having a more elevated conception of the imperial majesty than the Greeks, regarded the sacrifice of the Son of God as having realised an extraordinarily marvellous deliverance; from this proceeded the necessity of intensifying human wretchedness and of destiny.

It seems to me that the optimism of the Greek philosophers depended to a great extent on economic reasons; it probably arose in the rich and commercial urban populations who were able to regard the universe as an immense shop full of excellent things with which they could satisfy their greed. I imagine that Greek pessimism sprang from poor warlike tribes living in the mountains, who were filled with an enormous aristocratic pride, but whose material conditions were correspondingly poor; their poets charmed them by praising their ancestors and made them look forward to triumphal expeditions conducted by superhuman heroes; they explained their present wretchedness to them by relating catastrophes in which semi-divine former chiefs had succumbed to fate or the jealousy of the gods; the courage of the warriors might for the moment be unable to accomplish anything, but it would not always be so; the tribe must remain faithful to the old customs in order to be ready for great and victorious expeditions, which might very well take place in the near future.

Oriental asceticism has often been considered the most remarkable manifestation of pessimism; Hartmann is certainly right when he regards it as having only the value of an anticipation, which was useful since it reminded men how much there is that is illusory in vulgar riches; he was wrong, however, in saying that asceticism taught men that the "destined end to all their efforts" was the annihilation of will, for in the course of history deliverance has taken quite other forms than this.

In primitive Christianity we find a fully developed and completely armed pessimism: man is condemned to slavery from his birth—Satan is the prince of the world—the Christian, already regenerate by baptism, can render himself capable of obtaining the resurrection of the body by means of the Eucharist; he awaits the glorious second coming of Christ, who will destroy the rule of Satan and call his comrades in the fight to the heavenly Jerusalem. The Christian life of that time was dominated by the necessity of membership in the holy army which was constantly exposed to the ambuscades set by the accomplices of Satan; this conception produced many heroic acts, engendered a courageous propaganda, and was the cause of considerable moral progress. The deliverance did not take place, but we know by innumerable testimonies from that time what great things the march towards deliverance can bring about.

Sixteenth-century Calvinism presents a spectacle which is perhaps even more instructive; but we must be careful not to confuse it, as many authors have done, with contemporary Protestantism; these two doctrines are the antipodes of each other. I cannot understand how Hartmann came to say that Protestantism "is a halting place in the journey of true Christianity," and that it "allied itself with the renaissance of ancient paganism." These judgments only apply to recent Protestantism, which has abandoned its own principles in order to adopt those of the Renaissance. Pessimism, which formed no part of the current ideas which characterised the Renaissance, has never been so strongly affirmed as it was by the Reformers. The dogmas of sin and predestination which correspond to the two first aspects of pessimism, the wretchedness of the human species, and social determinism, were pushed to their most extreme consequences. Deliverance was conceived under a very different form to that which had been given it by primitive Christianity; Protestants organised themselves into a military force wherever possible; they made expeditions into Catholic countries, expelled the priests, introduced the reformed cult, and promulgated laws of proscription against papists. They no longer borrowed from the apocalypses the idea of a great final catastrophe, of which the brothers-in-arms who had for so long defended themselves against the attacks of Satan would only be spectators; the Protestants, nourished on the reading of the Old Testament, wished to imitate the exploits of the conquerors of the Holy Land; they took the offensive, and wished to establish the kingdom of God by force. In each locality they conquered the Calvinists brought about a real catastrophic revolution, which changed everything from top to bottom.

Calvinism was finally conquered by the Renaissance; it was full of theological prejudices derived from medieval traditions, and there came a time when it feared to be thought too far behind the times; it wished to be on the level of modern culture, and it finished by becoming simply a lax Christianity.[1] To-day very few people suspect what the reformers of the sixteenth century meant by "free examination"; the Protestants of to-day apply the same method to the Bible that philologists apply to any profane text; Calvin's exegesis has been replaced by the criticisms of the humanists.

The annalist who contents himself with recording facts is tempted to regard the conception of deliverance as a dream or an error, but the true historian considers things from a different point of view; whenever he endeavours to find out what has been the influence of the Calvinist spirit on

---

[1] If Socialism comes to grief it will evidently be in the same way, because it will have been alarmed at its own barbarity.

morals, law, or literature, he is always driven back to a consideration of the way in which former Protestant thought was dominated by the conception of the path to deliverance. The experience of this great epoch shows quite clearly that in this warlike excitement which accompanies this *will-to-deliverance* the courageous man finds a satisfaction which is sufficient to keep up his ardour. I am convinced that in the history of that time you might find excellent illustrations of the idea that you once expressed to me —that the Wandering Jew may be taken as a symbol of the highest aspiration of mankind, condemned as it is to march for ever without knowing rest.

II

My theses have shocked many people who are, to a certain extent, under the influence of the ideas of natural justice implanted in us by our education; very few educated men have been able to free themselves from these ideas. While the philosophy of natural justice is in perfect agreement with that of force (understanding this word in the special meaning that I have given it in Chapters IV. and V.), it cannot be reconciled with my conception of the historical function of violence. The scholastic doctrines of natural right contain nothing but this simple tautology—what is just is good, and what is unjust is bad; as if in enunciating such a doctrine we did not implicitly admit that the just must adapt itself to the natural order of events. It was for a reason of this kind that the economists for a long time asserted that the conditions created under the capitalist regime of competition are perfectly just, because they result from the *natural course* of things; and inversely the makers of Utopias have always claimed that the actual state of the world was *not natural enough*; they have wished, consequently, to paint a picture of a society naturally better regulated and therefore juster.

I cannot deny myself the pleasure of quoting some of Pascal's *Pensées* which terribly embarrassed his contemporaries, and which have only been understood in our day. Pascal had considerable difficulty in freeing himself from the ideas of natural justice which he found in the philosophers; he abandoned them because he did not think them sufficiently imbued with Christianity. "I have passed a great part of my life believing that there was justice, and in this I was not mistaken, for there is justice *according as God has willed to reveal it to us*. But I did not take it so, and this is where I made a mistake, for I believed that our justice was essentially just, and that I possessed means by which I could know this and judge of it" (fragment 375 of the Braunschvieg edition). "Doubtless there are natural laws; but this good reason once corrupted, has corrupted all" (fragment 294); "*Veri juris.* We have it no longer" (fragment 297).

Moreover, mere observation showed Pascal the absurdity of the theory of natural right; if this theory was correct, we ought to find laws which are universally admitted; but actions which we regard as criminal have at other times been regarded as virtuous. "Three degrees of latitude nearer the Pole reverse all jurisprudence, a meridian decides what is truth; fundamental laws change after a few years of possession, right has its epochs, the entry of Saturn into the constellation of the Lion marks to us the origin of such and such a crime. A strange justice that is bounded by a river! Truth on this side of the Pyrenees becomes error on the other. . . . We must, it is said, get back to the natural and fundamental laws of the State, which an unjust custom has abolished. This is a game certain to result in the loss of all; nothing will be just on the balance" (fragment 294; cf. fragment 379).

As it is thus impossible for us to reason about justice, we ought to appeal to custom; and Pascal often falls back on this precept (fragments 294, 297, 299, 309, 312). He goes still further and shows how justice is practically dependent on force: "Justice is subject to dispute; might is easily recognised and is not disputed. Thus it is not possible to attribute might to justice, because might has often contradicted justice, and said that it itself was just. And thus not being able to make what was just strong, what was strong has been made just" (fragment 298; cf. fragments 302, 303, 306, 307, 311).

This criticism of natural right has not the perfect clearness that we could give it at the present day, because we know now that it is in economics we must seek for a type of force that has attained absolutely uncontrolled development, and can thus be identified naturally with right, whilst Pascal under the one heading confuses together all the manifestations of force.

Pascal was vividly impressed by the charges that the conception of justice has experienced in the course of time, and these changes still continue to embarrass philosophers exceedingly. A well-organized social system is destroyed by a revolution and is replaced by another system, which in its turn is considered to be perfectly just; so that what was just before now becomes unjust. Any amount of sophisms have been produced to show that force has been placed at the service of justice during revolutions; these arguments have been many times shown to be absurd. But the public is so accustomed to believe in natural rights that it cannot make up its mind to abandon them.

There is hardly anything, not execpting even war, that people have not tried to bring inside the scope of natural right; they compare war to a process in which one nation reclaims a right which a malevolent neighbour refuses to recognise. Our fathers readily acknowledged that God decided battles in favour of those who had justice on their side; the vanquished were to be treated as an unsuccessful litigant: they must pay the costs of the war and give guarantees to the victor in order that the latter might enjoy their restored rights in peace. At the present time there are plenty of people who propose that international conflicts should be submitted to arbitration; this would only be a secularisation of the ancient mythology.[2]

The people who believe in natural right are not always implacable

---

[2] I cannot succeed in finding the idea of international arbitration in fragment 296 of Pascal, where several people claim to have discovered it; in this paragraph Pascal simply points out the ridiculous aspect of the claim made in his time by every belligerent—to condemn the conduct of his adversary in the name of justice,

enemies of civil struggles, and certainly not of tumultuous rioting; that has been sufficiently shown in the course of the Dreyfus question. When the force of the State was in the hands of their adversaries, they acknowledged, naturally enough, that it was being employed to violate justice, and they then proved that one might with a good conscience "step out of the region of legality in order to enter that of justice" (to borrow a phrase of the Bonapartists); when they could not overthrow the government, they tried at least to intimidate it. But when they attacked the people who for the time being controlled the force of the State, they did not at all desire to suppress that force, for they wished to utilise it some day for their own profit; all the revolutionary disturbances of the nineteenth century have ended in reinforcing the power of the State.

Proletarian violence entirely changes the aspect of all the conflicts in which it intervenes, since it disowns the force organised by the middle class, and claims to suppress the State which serves as its central nucleus. Under such conditions, it is no longer possible to argue about the primordial rights of man. That is why our parliamentary socialists, who spring from the middle classes and who know nothing outside the ideology of the State, are so bewildered when they are confronted with working-class violence. They cannot apply to it the commonplaces which generally serve them when they speak about force, and they look with terror on movements which may result in the ruin of the institutions by which they live. If revolutionary syndicalism triumphs, there will be no more brilliant speeches on immanent Justice, and the parliamentary regime, so dear to the intellectuals, will be finished with—it is the abomination of desolation! We must not be astonished, then, that they speak about violence with so much anger.

Giving evidence on June 5, 1907, before the Cours d'Assises de la Seine, in the Bousquet-Levy case, Jaurès said, "I have no superstitious belief in legality, it has already received too many blows; but I always advise workmen to have recourse to legal means, *for violence is the sign of temporary weakness.*" This is clearly a reminiscence of the Dreyfus question. Jaurès remembered that his friends were obliged to have recourse to revolutionary manifestations, and it is easy to understand that, as a result of this affair, he had not retained very great respect for legality. He probably likened the present position of the syndicalists to the former position of the Dreyfusards; for the moment they are weak, but they are destined ultimately to have the force of the State at their own disposal; they would then be very imprudent to destroy by violence a force which is destined to become theirs. He may even regret at times that the State has been so severely shaken by the Dreyfus agitation, just as Gambetta regretted that the administration had lost its former prestige and discipline.

One of the most elegant of Republican ministers has made a specialty of high-sounding phrases directed against the upholders of violence. Viviani charms deputies, senators, and the employés assembled to admire his excellency on his official tours, by telling them that violence is the caricature, or rather "the fallen and degenerate daughter," of force. After boasting that he has, by a magnificent gesture, extinguished the lamps of Heaven, he assumes the attitudes of a matador, at whose feet a furious bull has fallen.

If I were more vain about my literary efforts than I am, I should like to imagine that he was thinking of me when he said in the Senate, on November 16, 1906, that "one must not mistake a fanatic for a party, nor rash statements for a system of doctrine." There is only one pleasure greater than that of being appreciated by intelligent people, and that is the pleasure of not being understood by blunderheads, who are only capable of expressing in a kind of jargon what serves them in the place of thought. But I have every reason to suppose that, in the brilliant set which surrounds this *charlatan,* there is not one who has ever heard of the *Mouvement Socialiste.* It is quite within the comprehension of Viviani and his companions in the Cabinet that people may attempt an insurrection when they feel themselves solidly organised enough to take over the State; but working-class violence which has no such aim, seems to them only folly and an odious caricature of revolution. Do what you like, but don't kill the goose.

III

In the course of this study one thing has always been present in my mind, which seeemed to me so evident that I did not think it worth while to lay much stress on it—the men who are participating in a great social movement always picture their coming action as a battle in which their cause is certain to triumph. These constructions, knowledge of which is so important for historians, I propose to call myths; the syndicalist "general strike" and Marx's catastrophic revolution are such myths. As remarkable examples of such myths, I have given those which were constructed by primitive Christianity, by the Reformation, by the Revolution and by the followers of Mazzini. I now wish to show that we should not attempt to analyse such groups of images in the way that we analyse a thing into its elements, but that they must be taken as a whole, as historical forces, and that we should be especially careful not to make any comparison between accomplished fact and the picture people had formed for themselves before action.

I could have given one more example which is perhaps still more striking: Catholics have never been discouraged even in the hardest trials, because they have always pictured the history of the Church as a series of battles between Satan and the hierarchy supported by Christ; every new difficulty which arises is only an episode in a war which must finally end in the victory of Catholicism.

At the beginning of the nineteenth century the revolutionary persecutions revived this myth of the struggle with Satan, which inspired so many of the eloquent pages in Joseph de Maistre; this rejuvenation explains to a large extent the religious renascence which took place at that epoch. If

Catholicism is in danger at the present time, it is to a great extent owing to the fact that the myth of the Church militant tends to disappear. Ecclesiastical literature has greatly contributed to rendering it ridiculous; thus in 1872, a Belgian writer recommended a revival of exorcisms, as they seemed to him an efficacious means of combating the revolutionaries. Many educated Catholics are horrified when they discover that the ideas of Joseph de Maistre have helped to encourage the ignorance of the clergy, which did not attempt to acquire an adequate knowledge of a science which it held to be accursed; to these educated Catholics the myth of the struggle with Satan then appears dangerous, and they point out its ridiculous aspects; but they do not in the least understand its historical bearing. The gentle, sceptical, and, above all, pacific, habits of the present generation are, moreover, unfavourable to its continued existence; and the enemies of the Church loudly proclaim that they do not wish to return to a regime of persecution which might restore their former power to warlike images.

In employing the term myth I believed that I had made a happy choice, because I thus put myself in a position to refuse any discussion whatever with the people who wish to submit the idea of a general strike to a detailed criticism, and who accumulate objections against its practical possibility. It appears, on the contrary, that I had made a most unfortunate choice, for while some told me that myths were only suitable to a primitive state of society, others imagined that I thought the modern world might be moved by illusions analogous in nature to those which Renan thought might usefully replace religion. But there has been a worse misunderstanding than this even, for it has been asserted that my theory of myths was only a kind of lawyer's plea, a falsification of the real opinions of the revolutionaries, the *sophistry of an intellectual*.

If this were true, I should have been exactly fortunate, for I have always tried to escape the influence of that intellectualist philosophy, which seems to me a great hindrance to the historian who allows himself to be dominated by it. The contradiction that exists between this philosophy and the true understanding of events has often struck the readers of Renan. Renan is continually wavering betweeen his own intuition, which was nearly always admirable, and a philosophy which cannot touch history without falling into platitudes; but, alas, he too often believed himself bound to think in accordance with the *scientific opinions* of his day.

The intellectualist philosophy finds itself unable to explain phenomena like the following—the sacrifice of his life which the soldier of Napoleon made in order to have the honour of taking part in "immortal deeds" and of living in the glory of France, knowing all the time that "he would always be a poor man"; then, again, the extraordinary virtues shown by the Romans who resigned themselves to a frightful inequality and who suffered so much to conquer the world; "the belief in glory (which was) a value without equal," created by Greece, and as a result of which "a selection was made from the swarming masses of humanity, life acquired an incentive and there was a recompense here for those who had pursued the good and the beautiful." The intellectualist philosophy, far from being able to explain these things, leads, on the contrary, to an admiration for the fifty-first chapter of Jeremiah, "the lofty though profoundly sad feeling with which the peaceful man contemplates these falls of empires, and the pity excited in the heart of the wise man by the spectacle of the nations *labouring for vanity*, victims of the arrogance of the few." Greece, according to Renan, did not experience anything of that kind, and I do not think that we need complain about that. Moreover, he himself praises the Romans for not having acted in accordance with the conceptions of the Jewish thinker. "They laboured, they wore themselves out for nothing, said the Jewish thinker—yes, doubtless, but those are the virtues that history rewards."

Religions constitute a very troublesome problem for the intellectualists, for they can neither regard them as being without historical importance nor can they explain them. Renan, for example, has written some very strange sentences on this subject. "Religion is a necessary imposture. Even the most obvious ways of throwing dust in people's eyes cannot be neglected when you are dealing with a race as stupid as the human species, a race created for error, which, when it does admit the truth, never does so for the right reasons. It is necessary then to give it the wrong ones."

Comparing Giordano Bruno, who "allowed himself to be burnt at Champ-de-Flore" with Galileo, who submitted to the Holy See, Renan sides with the second because, according to him, the scientist need not bring anything to support his discoveries beyond good arguments. He considered that the Italian philosopher wished to supplement his inadequate proofs by his sacrifice, and he puts forward this scornful maxim: "A man suffers martyrdom only for the sake of things about which he is not certain." Renan here confuses *conviction*, which must have been very powerful in Bruno's case, with that particular kind of *certitude* about the accepted theories of science, which instruction ultimately produces; it would be difficult to give a more misleading idea of the forces which really move men.

The whole of this philosophy can be summed up in the following phrase of Renan's: "Human affairs are always an approximation lacking gravity and precision"; and as a matter of fact, for an intellectualist, what lacks precision must also lack gravity. But in Renan the conscientious historian was never entirely asleep, and he at once adds as a corrective: "To have realised this truth is a great result obtained by philosophy; but it is an abdication of any active rôle. The future lies in the hands of those who are not disillusioned." From this we may conclude that the intellectualist philosophy is entirely unable to explain the great movements of history.

The intellectualist philosophy would have vainly endeavoured to convince the ardent Catholics, who for so long struggled successfully against the revolutionary traditions, that the myth of the Church militant was not in harmony with the scientific theories formulated by the most learned

authors according to the best rules of criticism; it would never have succeeded in persuading them. It would not have been possible to shake the
faith that these men had in the promises made to the Church by any argument; and so long as this faith remained, the myth was, in their eyes, incontestable. Similarly, the objections urged by philosophy against the
revolutionary myths would have made an impression only on those men
who were anxious to find a pretext for abandoning any active rôle, for
remaining revolutionary in words only.

I can understand the fear that this myth of the general strike inspires in
many *worthy progressives*,[3] on account of its character of *infinity*;[4] the
world of to-day is very much inclined to return to the opinions of the ancients and to subordinate ethics to the smooth working of public affairs,
which results in a definition of virtue as the golden mean; as long as socialism remains a *doctrine expressed only in words*, it is very easy to deflect it
towards this doctrine of the golden mean; but this transformation is manifestly impossible when the myth of the "general strike" is introduced, as
this implies an absolute revolution. You know as well as I do that all that
is best in the modern mind is derived from this "torment of the infinite";
you are not one of those people who look upon the tricks by means of which
readers can be deceived by words, as happy discoveries. That is why you
will not condemn me for having attached great worth to a myth which
gives to socialism such high moral value and such great sincerity. It is because the theory of myths tends to produce such fine results that so many
seek to dispute it.

IV

The mind of man is so constituted that it cannot remain content with the
mere observation of facts, but always attempts to penetrate into the inner
reason of things. I therefore ask myself whether it might not be desirable
to study this theory of myths more thoroughly, utilising the enlightenment
we owe to the Bergsonian philosophy. The attempt I am about to submit
to you is doubtless very imperfect, but I think that it has been planned in
accordance with the only method which can possibly throw light on the
problem. In the first place, we should notice that the discussions of the
moralists hardly ever come into contact with what is truly fundamental in
our individuality. As a rule, they simply try to appraise our already com-

---

[3] Translator's Note.—In French, "*braves gens.*" Sorel is using the words ironically
to indicate those naïve, philanthropically disposed people who believe that they have
discovered the solution to the problem of social reform—whose attitude, however, is
often complicated by a good deal of hypocrisy, they being frequently rapacious when
their own personal interests are at stake.

[4] Parties, as a rule, *define* the reforms that they wish to bring about; but the general
strike has a character of *infinity*, because it puts on one side all discussions of definite
reforms and confronts men with a catastrophe. People who pride themselves on their
practical wisdom are very much upset by such a conception, which puts forward no
definite project of future social organisation.

pleted acts with the help of the moral valuations formulated in advance by society, for the different types of action commonest in contemporary life. They say that in this way they are determining motives; but these motives are of the same nature as those which jurists take account of in criminal justice; they are merely social valuations of facts known to everybody. Many philosophers, especially the ancients, have believed that all values could be deduced from utility, and if any social valuation does exist, it is surely this latter,—theologians estimate transgressions by the place they occupy on the road which, according to average human experience, leads to mortal sin; they are thus able to ascertain the degreee of viciousness of any given sin,—while the moderns usually teach that we act after having established a particular maxim (which is, as it were, an abstraction or generalisation of our projected conduct), and justify this maxim by deducing it (more or less sophistically) from general principles which are, to a certain extent, analogous to the Declaration of the Rights of Man; and, as a matter of fact, this theory was probably inspired by the admiration excited by the Bill of Rights placed at the head of each American constitution.

We are all so extremely concerned in knowing what the world thinks of us that, sooner or later, considerations analogous to those the moralists speak of do pass through our mind; as a result of this the moralists have been able to imagine that they have really made an appeal to experience for the purpose of finding out what exists at the bottom of the creative conscience, when, as a matter of fact, all they have done is to consider already accomplished acts from the point of view of its social effects.

Bergson asks us, on the contrary, to consider the inner depths of the mind and what happens there during a creative moment. "There are," he says, "two different selves, one of which is, as it were, the external projection of the other, its spatial and, so to speak, social representation. We reach the former by deep introspection, which leads us to grasp our inner states as living things, constantly *becoming*, as states not amenable to measure. . . . But the moments at which we thus grasp ourselves are rare, and that is just why we are rarely free. The greater part of our time we live outside ourselves, hardly perceiving anything of ourselves but our own ghost, a colourless shadow. . . . Hence we live for the external world rather than for ourselves; we speak rather than think; we are acted rather than act ourselves. To act freely is to recover possession of oneself, and to get back into pure duration."

In order to acquire a real understanding of this psychology we must "carry ourselves back in thought to those moments of our life, when we made some serious decision, moments unique of their kind, which will never be repeated—any more than the past phases in the history of a nation will ever come back again." It is very evident that we enjoy this liberty pre-eminently when we are making an effort to create a new individuality in ourselves, thus endeavouring to break the bonds of habit which enclose us. It might at first be supposed that it would be sufficient to say that, at such moments, we are dominated by an overwhelming emotion; but everybody now recognises that movement is the essence of emotional life, and it is, then, in terms of movement that we must speak of creative consciousness.

It seems to me that this psychology of the deeper life must be represented in the following way. We must abandon the idea that the soul can be compared to something moving, which, obeying a more or less mechanical law, is impelled in the direction of certain given motive forces. To say that we are acting, implies that we are creating an imaginary world placed ahead of the present world and composed of movements which depend entirely on us. In this way our freeedom becomes perfectly intelligible. Starting from a study of these artificial constructions which embrace everything that interests us, several philosophers, inspired by Bergsonian doctrines, have been led to formulate a rather startling theory. Edouard Le Roy, for example, says: "Our real body is the entire universe in as far as it is experienced by us. And what common sense more strictly calls our body is only the region of least unconsciousness and greatest liberty in this greater body, the part which we most directly control and by means of which we are able to act on the rest." But we must not, as this subtle philosopher constantly does, confuse a passing state of our willing activity with the stable affirmations of science.[5]

These artificial worlds generally disappear from our minds without leaving any trace in our memory; but when the masses are deeply moved it then becomes possible to trace the outlines of the kind of representation which constitutes a social myth.

This belief in "glory" which Renan praised so much quickly fades away into rhapsodies when it is not supported by myths; these myths have varied greatly in different epochs: the citizen of the Greek republics, the Roman legionary, the soldier of the wars of Liberty, and the artist of the Renaissance did not picture their conception of glory by the help of the same set of images. Renan complained that "the faith in glory" is compromised by the *limited historical outlook* more or less prevalent at the present day. "Very few," he said, "act with a view to immortal fame. . . . Every one wants to enjoy his own glory; they eat it in the green blade and do not gather the sheaves after death." In my opinion, this limited historical outlook is, on the contrary, not a cause but a consequence; it results from the weakening of the heroic myths which had such great popularity at the beginning of the nineteenth century; the belief in "glory" perished and a limited historic outlook became predominant at the time when these myths vanished.

As long as there are no myths accepted by the masses, one may go on talking of revolts indefinitely, without ever provoking any revolutionary

---

[5] It is easy to see here how the sophism creeps in; the *universe experienced by us* may be either the real world in which we live or the world invented by us for action.

movement; this is what gives such importance to the general strike and renders it so odious to socialists who are afraid of a revolution; they do all they can to shake the confidence felt by the workers in the preparations they are making for the revolution; and in order to succeed in this they cast ridicule on the idea of the general strike—the only idea that could have any value as a motive force. One of the chief means employed by them is to represent it as a Utopia; this is easy enough, because there are very few myths which are perfectly free from any Utopian element.

The revolutionary myths which exist at the present time are almost free from any such mixture; by means of them it is possible to understand the activity, the feelings and the ideas of the masses preparing themselves to enter on a decisive struggle; the myths are not descriptions of things, but expressions of a determination to act. A Utopia is, on the contrary, an intellectual product; it is the work of theorists who, after observing and discussing the known facts, seek to establish a model to which they can compare existing society in order to estimate the amount of good and evil it contains. It is a combination of imaginary institutions having sufficient analogies to real institutions for the jurist to be able to reason about them; it is a construction which can be taken to pieces, and certain parts of it have been shaped in such a way that they can (with a few alterations by way of adjustment) be fitted into approaching legislation. Whilst contemporary myths lead men to prepare themselves for a combat which will destroy the existing state of things, the effect of Utopias has always been to direct men's minds towards reforms which can be brought about by patching up the existing system; it is not surprising, then, that so many makers of Utopias were able to develop into able statesmen when they had acquired a greater experience of political life. A myth cannot be refuted, since it is, at bottom, identical with the convictions of a group, being the expression of these convictions in the language of movement; and it is, in consequence, unanalysable into parts which could be placed on the plane of historical descriptions. A Utopia, on the contrary, can be discussed like any other social constitution; the spontaneous movements it presupposes can be compared with the movements actually observed in the course of history, and we can in this way evaluate its verisimilitude; it is possible to refute Utopias by showing that the economic system on which they have been made to rest is incompatible with the necessary conditions of modern production.

Liberal political economy is one of the best examples of a Utopia that could be given. A state of society was imagined which could contain only the types produced by commerce, and which would exist under the law of the fullest competition; it is recognised to-day that this kind of ideal society would be as difficult to realise as that of Plato; but several great statesmen of modern times have owed their fame to the efforts they made to introduce something of this ideal of commercial liberty into industrial legislation.

We have here a Utopia free from any mixture of myth; the history of French democracy, however, presents a very remarkable combination of

Utopias and myths. The theories that inspired the authors of our first constitutions are regarded to-day as extremely chimerical; indeed, people are often loth to concede them the value which they have been so long recognised to possess—that of an ideal on which legislators, magistrates, and administrators should constantly fix their eyes, in order to secure for men a little more justice. With these Utopias were mixed up the myths which represented the struggle against the ancient regime; so long as the myths survived, all the refutations of liberal Utopias could produce no result; the myth safeguarded the Utopia with which it was mixed.

For a long time Socialism was scarcely anything but a Utopia; the Marxists were right in claiming for their master the honour of bringing about a change in this state of things; Socialism has now become the preparation of the masses employed in great industries for the suppression of the State and property; and it is no longer necessary, therefore, to discuss how men must organise themselves in order to enjoy future happiness; everything is reduced to the *revolutionary apprenticeship* of the proletariat. Unfortunately Marx was not acquainted with facts which have now become familiar to us; we know better than he did what strikes are, because we have been able to observe economic conflicts of considerable extent and duration; the myth of the "general strike" has become popular, and is now firmly established in the minds of the workers; we possess ideas about violence that it would have been difficult for him to have formed; we can then complete his doctrine, instead of making commentaries on his text, as his unfortunate disciples have done for so long.

In this way Utopias tend to disappear completely from Socialism; Socialism has no longer any need to concern itself with the organisation of industry since capitalism does that. I think, moreover, that I have shown that the general strike corresponds to a kind of feeling which is so closely related to those which are necessary to promote production in any very progressive state of industry, that a revolutionary apprenticeship may at the same time be considered as an apprenticeship which will enable the workmen to occupy a high rank among the best workmen of his own trade.

People who are living in this world of "myths," are secure from all refutation; this has led many to assert that Socialism is a kind of religion. For a long time people have been struck by the fact that religious convictions are unaffected by criticism, and from that they have concluded that everything which claims to be beyond science must be a religion. It has been observed also that Christianity tends at the present day to be less a system of dogmas than a Christian life, *i.e.* a moral reform penetrating to the roots of one's being; consequently, a new analogy has been discovered between religion and the revolutionary Socialism which aims at the apprenticeship, preparation, and even reconstruction of the individual,—a gigantic task. But Bergson has taught us that it is not only religion which occupies the profounder region of our mental life; revolutionary myths have their place there equally with religion. The arguments which Yves Guyot urges against Socialism on the ground that it is a religion, seem to me, then, to be founded on an imperfect acquaintance with the new psychology.

Renan was very surprised to discover that Socialists are beyond discouragement. "After each abortive experiment they recommence their work: the solution is not yet found, but it will be. The idea that no solution exists never occurs to them, and in this lies their strength." The explanation given by Renan is superficial; it regards Socialism as a Utopia, that is, as a thing which can be compared to observed realities; if this were true, it would be scarcely possible to understand how confidence can survive so many failures. But by the side of the Utopias there have always been myths capable of urging on the workers to revolt. For a long time these myths were founded on the legends of the Revolution, and they preserved all their value as long as these legends remained unshaken. To-day the confidence of the Socialists is greater than ever since the myth of the general strike dominates all the truly working-class movement. No failure proves anything against Socialism since the latter has become a work of preparation (for revolution); if they are checked, it merely proves that the apprenticeship has been insufficient; they must set to work again with more courage, persistence, and confidence than before; their experience of labour has taught workmen that it is by means of patient apprenticeship that a man may become a true comrade, and it is also the only way of becoming a true revolutionary.[6]

v

The works of my friends have been treated with great contempt by the Socialists who mix in politics, but at the same time with much sympathy by people who do not concern themselves with parliamentary affairs. We cannot be suspected of seeking to carry on a kind of *intellectual industry*, and we protest every time people profess to confuse us with the intellectuals, who do, as a matter of fact, make the exploitation of thought their profession. The old stagers of democracy cannot understand why people should take so much trouble unless they secretly aim at the leadership of the working classes. However, we could not act in any other way.

The man who has constructed a Utopia designed to make mankind happy is inclined to look upon the invention as his own personal property; he believes that no one is in a better position than he is to apply his system. He thinks it very unreasonable that his writings do not procure him some post in the government. But we, on the contrary, have invented nothing at all, and even assert that nothing can be invented; we have limited ourselves to defining the historical bearing of the notion of a general strike. We have tried to show that a new culture might spring from the struggle of the revolutionary trades unions against the employers and the State; our greatest

---

[6] It is extremely important to notice the analogy between the revolutionary state of mind and that which corresponds to the *morale* of the producers. I have indicated some remarkable resemblances at the end of these reflections, but there are many more analogies to be pointed out.

claim to originality consists in our having maintained that the proletariat
can emancipate itself without being compelled to seek the guidance of that
section of the middle classes which concerns itself professionally with matters of the intellect. We have thus been led to regard as essential in contemporary phenomena what was before regarded as accessory, and what
is indeed really educative for a revolutionary proletariat that is serving its
apprenticeship in struggle. It would be impossible for us to exercise any
direct influence on such a work of formation.

We may play a useful part if we limit ourselves to attacking middle-class
thought in such a way as to put the proletariat on its guard against an invasion of ideas and customs from the hostile class.

Men who have received an elementary education are generally imbued
with a certain reverence for print as such, and they readily attribute genius
to the people who attract the attention of the literary world to any great
extent; they imagine that they must have a great deal to learn from authors
whose names are so often mentioned with praise in the newspapers; they
listen with singular respect to the commentaries that these literary prize-
winners present to them. It is not easy to fight against these prejudices, but
it is very useful work; we regard this task as being absolutely of the first
importance, and we can carry it to a profitable conclusion without ever
attempting to direct the working-class movement. The proletariat must be
preserved from the experience of the Germans who conquered the Roman
Empire; the latter were ashamed of being barbarians, and put themselves
to school with the rhetoricians of the Latin decadence; they had no reason
to congratulate themselves for having wished to be civilised.

In the course of my career I have touched on many subjects which might
be considered to be outside the proper range of a Socialist writer. I have
endeavoured to show that the science whose marvellous results the middle
class constantly boasts of is not as infallible as those who live by its exploitation would have us believe; and that a study of the phenomena of the
Socialist world would often furnish philosophers with an enlightenment
which they do not find in the works of the learned. I do not believe, then,
that I am labouring in vain, for in this way I help to ruin the prestige of
middle-class culture, a prestige which up to now has been opposed to the
complete development of the principle of the "class war."

In the last chapter of my book, I have said that art is an anticipation of
the kind of work that ought to be carried on in a highly productive state of
society. It seems that this observation has been very much misunderstood
by some of my critics, who have been under the impression that I wished
to propose as the socialist solution—an aesthetic education of the proletariat under the tutelage of modern artists. This would have been a singular paradox on my part, for the art that we possess to-day is a *residue* left
to us by an aristocratic society, a residue which has, moreover, been greatly
corrupted by the middle class. According to the most enlightened minds,
it is greatly to be desired that contemporary art could renew itself by a
more intimate contact with craftsmen; academic art has used up the great-

est geniuses without succeeding in producing anything which equals what has been given us by generations of craftsmen. I had in view something altogether different from such an imitation when I spoke of an anticipation. I wished to show how one found in art (practised by its best representatives, and, above all, in its best periods) analogies which make it easier for us to understand what the qualities of the workers of the future would be. Moreover, so little did I think of asking the *École des Beaux-Arts* to provide a teaching suitable to the proletariat, that I based the *morale* of the producers not on an aesthetic education transmitted by the middle class, but on the feelings developed by the struggles of the workers against their masters.

These observations lead us to recognise the enormous differences which exists between the *new school* and the anarchism which flourished twenty years ago in Paris. The middle class itself had much less admiration for its literary men and its artists than the anarchists of that time felt for them; their enthusiasm for the celebrities of a day often surpassed that felt by disciples for the greatest masters of the past. We neeed not then be astonished that by a kind of compensation the novelists and the poets thus adulated have shown a sympathy for the anarchists which has often astonished people who do not know what a force vanity is in the artistic world.

Intellectually, then, this kind of anarchism was *entirely middle class*, and the Guesdistes attacked it for this reason. They said that their adversaries, while proclaiming themselves the irreconcilable enemies of the past, were themselves the servile pupils of this cursed past; they observed, moreover, that the most eloquent dissertations on revolt could produce nothing, and that literature cannot change the course of history. The anarchists replied by showing that their adversaries had entered on a road which could not lead to the revolution they announced; by taking part in political debates, Socialists, they said, will become merely reformers of a more or less radical type, and will lose the sense of their revolutionary formulas. Experience has quickly shown that the anarchists were right in this view, and that in entering into middle-class institutions, revolutionaries have been transformed by adopting the spirit of these institutions. All the deputies agree that there is very little difference between a middle-class representative and a representative of the proletariat.

Many anarchists, tired at last of continually reading the same grandiloquent maledictions hurled at the capitalist system, set themselves to find a way which would lead them to acts which were really revolutionary. They became members of syndicates which, thanks to violent strikes, realised, to a certain extent, the social war they had so often heard spoken of. Historians will one of the humanists; like the Reformation, revolutionary syndicalism may prove abortive, if it loses, as did the latter, the sense of its own originality; it is this which gives such great interest to inquiries on proletarian violence.

July 15th, 1907.

The Spirit of the Republic: Péguy and France

Charles Péguy, Notre Jeunesse, in Oeuvres en Prose, ed. Marcel Pé-guy (Paris: Librairie Gallimard, 1957), pp. 506–16, 540–44, 590–603, 614–15, 640–42, 643–45. I am indebted to George A. Kelly of Harvard University for the translation.

Fin de siècle has become synonymous with cultural disillusionment. Jaded, vulgar, perverse, obsessively self-conscious—these are conventional adjectives to describe much of the literature and thought of the turn of the century. Political reformers appealed to the masses for a high mission, and the masses reponded by pursuing material comforts and endorsing the emotional drive of nationalism and imperialism. Mass education produced literacy but not discrimination in culture and taste. The intellectual found himself more isolated than ever or swept along in the popular tide. Charles Péguy (1873–1914) might have been among those contributing to disenchantment were it not for his faith—faith in man, in France, and in Christianity. Joan of Arc, also animated by visions and mystique, haunted this poet from Orléans. His greatest literary work concerns her, first in his militantly atheistic, socialist phase and then again in his last, deeply Catholic, fervently nationalist years. Péguy was a man of belief, not a doctrinaire. Joan of Arc was a better subject for him than Kant, on whom he wrote his graduate thesis. For his times Péguy was always a distinguished minority of one. He even resisted the blandishments of cosmopolitan Paris in which he spent most of his life. He remained the inspired provincial, sophisticated but in tune with the peasant roots of the nation. France, the republic, had a soul, and Péguy slashed through the trivialities of life in search of the pure, animating spirit.

Notre Jeunesse, written in 1910, appeared in Péguy's Cahiers de la Quinzaine and was published as a unit only in 1916. It is specifically a piece of French history, for the subject matter is the Dreyfus case and its aftermath. "The Affair"—no other cause is so honored in France—was crucial in the evolution of the nation. It divided and remade France. Péguy presumes the familiarity of the reader with the facts and with French history. You are expected to know that Bernard Lazare was the brilliant young Jewish writer commissioned by the Dreyfus family to prepare and publish a defense; that Maurice Barrès was the literary champion of the French right [military, religious, and political]; that the triumph of French arms in the revolutionary and Napoleonic wars began at Valmy and ended at Hougoumont; that "restauration" meant much more to the historically minded Frenchman than mere royal restoration; and even that de Joinville was one of the great medieval French chroniclers and biographer of St. Louis.

Péguy, ironically, often regretted that he lived in a period of history, not an epoch. He was wrong and may have known it. Péguy is an epic figure for the quality of his thought and the incisiveness of his criticism. He mirrored the finest in the French tradition and died, as he would have wished, leading troops at the battle of the Marne.

NOTRE JEUNESSE

WE ARE THE LAST, almost too late. After us, another age begins, a very different world, the world of those who no longer believe in anything, who are quit of glory and pride.

After us begins the world we have named and will not desist from naming the modern world. The world depending on cleverness. The world of the experts and the up-to-date, the wise, those who have nothing to learn and no more room to grow. The world of those who can no longer be taught anything. The world of those who depend on their cleverness. The world of those who are not half-wits and imbeciles—like us. That is: the world of those who believe in nothing, not even in atheism, who dedicate and sacrifice themselves to nothing. In other words: the world of those who are vainglorious about having no mystique. Let there be no mistake and let no one therefore be glad about it, whatever side he belongs to. The movement *against republicanism* in France shares its roots with the movement *against Christianity*. Together they form a deep, single and solitary movement of demystification. It is from this single deep movement, this solitary movement, that our people no longer believes in the Republic or in God; it no longer wishes to lead the republican or the Christian life—it has had enough. You could almost say that it no longer wishes to believe in idols or in the true God. This same incredulity, a single incredulity pertaining to idols and God alike, pertains to the false gods and true God together, the antique gods, the new God, the old gods and the Christian God. A single sterility dries up the city on earth and Christianity, the political city and the Christian city, the city of men and the city of God. This we can call modern sterility. Let no one rejoice, then, seeing misfortune befall his enemy, his adversary, his neighbor. For all are beset with *the same* misfortune, *the same* sterility. As I have written so often in these *cahiers*, even in the days when nobody read them, the argument is not really between the Republic and the Monarchy, the Republic and the Kingdom, especially if you look on them as political forms, as two political forms; it is not only or precisely between the old French regime and the new—the modern world is opposed not only to the old French regime, it opposes and contradicts all the former cultures at once, all the old regimes together, all the old citadels together, everything that is culture or a citadel. In fact this is the first time in the world's history that a whole world lives and prospers, and *appears* to prosper *against all culture*.

Mark my words carefully. I don't say it will last forever. The human race has seen plenty of others. But when all is said and done, this is what we have now.

And so here we are.

We have even very compelling reasons to hope that this won't last long. But we are in an extremely bad position. Historically, we are situated at a critical point, a point of discretion, a point of discrimination. We find ourselves midway between the generations who have the republican mystique and those who have none of it, between those who keep it still and those who have lost it. Thus we are believed by no one, no matter which side; in equal measure, by neither of them. The old republicans don't want to believe that there are no more young republicans. The young people don't want to believe that there have been old republicans.

We are neither fish nor fowl. So nobody wants to believe us, neither the ones nor the others. Both say we are wrong. When we tell the old republicans to watch out because we have no successors, they shrug their shoulders. They think somebody will always come along. And when we say to the young people: Watch out, don't speak so lightly of the Republic—it hasn't always been the preserve of the politicians, it has a mystique behind it and within it, it has behind it a past full of glory and honor, and still more important, closer to the heart of the matter, a past of good lineage and heroism and perhaps sainthood—when we tell the young people this, they show us mild contempt and treat us like old fogeys.

They take us for maniacs.

I repeat that I am not saying this will always be. The deepest reasons, the most serious indications persuade us of the contrary and compel us to think that the next generation, two generations from us, soon to be the offspring of our own children, will be a mystical generation at last. Our race has too much blood in its veins to rest more than the stretch of a generation in ashes and musty criticism. It is too full of life not to reimmerse itself in the organic after a generation.

Everything leads us to believe that the two mystiques, the republican and the Christian, will blossom again at the same time. And do this from the same impetus, a single deep stimulation, just as they disappeared together (for the time being), just as they wiped themselves out in unison. But what I say holds good for the present, for the whole present time. And in the space of a generation many things can happen.

Misfortunes can happen.

This is our sorry situation. We are sorry, puny, a frail membrane. It's as if we were pressed, stretched out flat between all the prior generations and the fecund source of generations to come. This is the chief reason for our puniness, for the shrinkage of our position. We have the ungrateful and puny task, the little job, the meager duty to see that through us messages are passed, to make sure that the ones receive the others' messages, to keep them all alerted, to inform them about each other. And so we are generally spat upon by all. This is the common lot of anyone who tries to speak a little bit of truth.

We have, as if by accident, the mission to see that through us messages are passed between people who have absolutely no wish to communicate. We have the mission to inform people who have absolutely no wish to be informed.

That is our ungrateful situation.

So we turn back again to our elders; yet we can say and do nothing, we can only repeat to these earlier republicans: take care. You don't suspect, you can't imagine how little you are followed, how true it is that we are the last, how dangerously your regime is being eaten away from the inside and upward from its base. You hang on above, naturally, you grasp the pinnacle. But each new year, each passing year loosens you a notch, shaves your pinnacle more narrow, shakier, more solitary, hollows it more from beneath. Already ten, fifteen, and close to twenty years' classes of young people have failed to renew you at the base.

You hold fast to the point, you grasp the pinnacle, the top, but it's only a position which time has acquired for you and can refuse you—like a geographical, historical, temporal, temporary, chronological, chronographical situation. The situation is no more than a situation. It has nothing to do with being an organic situation. It is not that situation one finds at the point, at the tip of the bud which organically, vegetally, masters the tree and draws the whole tree to it. The way it has passed the whole tree shall pass.

I am shocked to see and note the simple fact that our elders have no wish to see even the plain evidence, what you need only take the trouble to glance at: how alienated our young people have become from all that was real thought and republican mystique. It's especially and lastingly obvious that thoughts which for us were real thoughts have become ideas for them, what were for us and our fathers instinct, heritage, and thoughts have become mere propositions for them, what we saw as organic has become for them merely logical.

Thoughts, instincts, heritages, habits which for us were very natural, unquestionable things from which one drew life, which were the essence of life, and about which, consequently, one didn't have to think; things more than legitimate, more than unarguable—in fact, unreasoned things—have become the thing that is worst of all: theses, historical theses, hypothesis; I mean what is least solid, least actual. The scraps of theses. When a regime, once organic and alive, becomes logical and historical, that regime is in the dust.

Today we have to prove and demonstrate the Republic. While it was still living no one had to prove it.

We lived by it. But when a regime must be demonstrated in ease and comfort and victory, this is because it is hollow, it is in the dust.

Today the Republic is a thesis accepted by the young people. Accepted, rejected, indifferently: what does it matter? Proved, refuted. What does matter, what is serious, what counts is not that it be supported or upheld, more or less indifferently; it's that it should be a mere thesis.

I mean that we should have to uphold or support it.

When a regime is a thesis among others (so many others), it is in the dust. A regime which stands upright and lives is not a thesis.

What difference does it make? The politicians, the professionals tells us.

What's it to us? The politicians answer, what have we to do with it? Our prefects are very good. And so, what's it to us? Things are going fine. We are no longer republicans, it's true, but we know how to govern. We even know how to govern much better than when we were republicans, they say. Or rather, when we were republicans we didn't know how to at all. Now, they add modestly, now we know a little. We have forgotten the Republic, but we have learned to govern. Look at the elections. They are just wonderful. They are always wonderful. They will be more wonderful. They will be still more wonderful because we are running them. And because we are beginning to know how to run them. The Right has lost a million votes. We could just as easily have made them lose fifty and a half million. But we are circumspect. The government makes the elections, the elections make the government. It's a loan paid back. The government makes the voters. The voters make the government. The government makes the deputies. The deputies make the government. Everyone has good manners. The people look on. The country is requested to pay. The government makes the legislature, the legislature makes the government. Not at all a vicious circle, as you might think. Not vicious in the least. It's just a plain circle, a perfect circle, a closed circle. All circles are closed. Otherwise they wouldn't be circles. This isn't exactly what our founders had in mind. But our founders wouldn't have had the knack of getting on so well. And, after all, you can't just keep founding things all the time. That would be exhausting. The proof that this thing is lasting, that it's sticking, is that already it has lasted forty years. It could go on forty centuries. The first forty years are the hardest. Then you get used to it. The country and regime don't need you, they don't need mystics or a mystique or their own mystique. That would be rather embarrassing. For such a great journey. What is needed is good policy, in other words a policy leaving no doubt that it is for and by the government.

They are mistaken. These politicians are mistaken. From the height of this Republic forty centuries are not looking down on them. If the Republic has worked for forty years, this is because everything has worked. If the Republic is solid in France, this isn't because the Republic is solid in France but because everything everywhere is solid. In modern history, though not in all history, modern peoples have experienced great waves of crisis, usually begun in France (1789–1815, 1830, 1848), that cause everything to tremble, from one end of the world to the other. And there are plateaus, more or less long, there are passages of calm, smooth seas, that leave everything unruffled for a time more or less long. There are *epochs* and there are *periods*. We are in a period. If the Republic is stable, this is not because it's the Republic (this Republic). It's not because of its own special virtue; it is because it is, because we are in a period of stability. That the Republic has lasted proves the endurance of the Republic no more than the duration of the neighboring monarchies proves that Monarchy will last. This endurance doesn't prove that they are durable, but that they began durably and are in a durable period. They are contemporaneous, drenched in the same time, in the same bath of endurance. They bathe in the same period. They belong to the same age. That's all that can be proved.

Thus when the republicans argue from the fact that the Republic has lasted in order to pronounce and propose and establish and derive the proposition that it is lasting, when they argue from the fact that it has lasted forty years in order to infer and conclude and propose that it has been durable for forty years and more, that it was at least durable for forty years, that it was valid and *advantageous* for at least forty years, then it seems they are pleading the evidence itself. And yet they are making a plea that, in principle, exceeds their prerogative. For in the Republic that endures it is not the Republic itself enduring. It is the endurance. It isn't the Republic that endures in itself, as self. It isn't the regime enduring in it. It is the time enduring. Its own time, it own age. And that which endures in it is the only thing that does. It is the calm of a certain period of humanity, a certain period of history, a certain period, a certain historical plateau.

Thus when the republicans attribute the endurance of the Republic to the strength of the regime, to some certain virtue of the Republic, they are guilty of overreaching their credit and morale, on their own and on the Republic's behalf. But, on the other hand, when the reactionaries and monarchists show us and, with a customary complacence that is equivalent and contrary, represent to us, in the guise of an argument, the solidity, tranquillity and endurance of the neighboring monarchies (and even, in a way, their prosperity—though here, in a way, they are sometimes nearer the truth), they reason, on their part, not only in an exactly similar way but by using the same argument. They are guilty of the same expectancy contrary but the same, an expectancy, a usurpation, a perversion, an imposition, an excess of symmetrical, antithetical, homothetical credit: the same expectancy, the same usurpation, the same perversion, the same imposition, the same excess of credit.

When the republicans attribute the endurance of the Republic to the Republic (the republicans, the people, the citizens), to stability, to tranquillity, to solidity, they attribute to the Republic a quality belonging not to it but to the time through which it moves. When the monarchists attribute their endurance to the neighboring monarchies (monarchs, monarchists, peoples, subjects), to their stability, tranquillity, solidity, endurance, they attribute to those monarchies a quality belonging not to them but to the time through which they move. The same time, which is everbody's time. And this stairway with a double central spiral, this symmetry, this homothetical antithesis of situations, this similarity of attributions should not surprise us. Republicans and monarchists, republican rulers and monarchist theorists follow the same reasoning, are guilty of the same attribution—contrary, complementary, homothetical attributions—the same false attribution because both types have the same conception, both are intellectual, both together and separately, together and in opposition are politicians, believing that politics makes sense, speaking the language of politics, lo-cated and moving on the political plane. They believe in regimes, and that a regime can bring or not bringe peace and war, strength and virtue, sickness and health, the stability, endurance and tranquillity of a people. The strength of a race. It's as if one were to believe that the châteaux of the Loire caused or didn't cause earthquakes.

We believe instead (as opposed to each of the two and both together) that there are forces and realities that go infinitely deeper, and that it is the peoples, instead, who create the strength and weakness of regimes; much less that regimes are responsible for the strength and weakness of peoples.

We believe that together both of them neither see nor wish to see these forces, these realities that go infinitely deeper.

If the Republic and the neighboring monarchies enjoy the same tranquillity, the same endurance, it's because they are drenched in the same bath, in the same period, that they are crossing the same plateau together. It's because, in reality, they lead the same life, follow the same diet. Here the republicans and the monarchists use the same reasoning against each other, thus yoking their arguments together. On the contrary, we others, using completely different premises, descending to a completely different level, trying to arrive at completely different profundities, we believe it is the peoples who make regimes, war and peace, strength and weakness, the sickness and health of regimes.

The republicans and monarchists together construct arguments, and these arguments turn out to be linked, joined, complementary, and inseparable.

Turning then to the young people, turning elsewhere, in another direction, we can but say to them: watch out. You take us for old fools. All right. But watch out. When you speak lightly, when you treat the Republic as lightly as you do, you not only run the risk of being unjust (which perhaps doesn't matter in your system—at least you say so—but which amounts to quite a lot in our system and in our ideas), but, what is more, you risk being foolish, even in terms of your system and ideas. I permit myself here the use of your system and its terms. You forget, you fail to recognize that there has been a republican mystique; but forgetting and ignoring it won't make it go away. Men died for freedom just as they died for faith. Today, these elections strike you as a grotesque formality, a universal lie, everywhere rigged. And you have the right to say so. But men have lived, countless men, heroes, martyrs, I will even say saints— and when I say "saints" it may be that I know what I'm talking about—countless men have lived heroically and with saintliness, men have suffered, men have died, a whole people has lived so that the very last imbecile today should have the right to enjoy this rigged formality. The birth of this event was terrible, ponderous, and fearful. It was not always as grotesque as it has become. And peoples around us, entire peoples, whole races labor over the same painful childbirth, labor and struggle to obtain that ludicrous formality. These elections are ludicrous. But there was a time . . . a heroic time when the sick and the dying had themselves carried in chairs *to place their ballots in the voting box.*

Place one's ballot in the box, that expression strikes you today as the last word in grotesque. It was procured by a century of heroism. Not empty heroism, or mere literary heroism. But by a century of the most incontestable, the most authentic—I will even say, the most French—heroism. These elections are ludicrous. But there is one that was not. There was that great partition of the world, the modern world's great election between the old Regime and the Revolution. And there was a sacred run-off . . . There was that little run-off that began at the mill of Valmy and scarcely ended on the heights of Hougoumont. Anyway, that ended like all political questions with a kind of compromise, a disproportionate settlement between the two parties who were there.

These elections are ludicrous. But the heroism and sanctity by which and through which it was possible to obtain these ludicrous results, *temporally* ludicrous results, is the sum of all that is greatest and holiest in the world, all that is finest. You hold the temporal degradation of these results, our results, against us. But just have a look. Look at your own results. You always talk to us of republican degradation. But isn't the degradation of mystique in politics our common law?

You speak to us of republican degradation or, to put it more accurately, the degradation of the republican mystique in republican politics. Haven't there been and aren't there still other degradations? Everything begins in mystique and ends in politics. Everything begins with *mystique*, with a mystique, its own mystique, and ends with *some kind* of politics. We would agree that the question is an important one. The real question and interest, however, is not that a certain type of politics prevails over this or that other type. Neither is it of knowing which will prevail over all the others. The essential interest and question is that in each order, in each system, *a mystique should not be devoured by the politics to which it has given birth.*

Neither the essential nor the interest nor the question is that this or that sort of politics should triumph, but that in each order and in each system the mystique belonging to it should not be devoured by the politics that is its offspring.

In other words, if the republicans prevail over the royalists or the royalists over the republicans, this may matter and obviously does matter; but the importance is exceedingly paltry, the interest is nothing by comparison with whether the republicans remain republicans, or with whether they were in the first place.

And I shall add, in complement but not just for the sake of symmetry: whether the royalists are and remain royalists. For that is perhaps what they are not doing at this moment, at the very moment when they believe they are doing it the most.

. . . .

Politics derides mystique, and yet feeds on it.

For the politicians make up their losses, or think to, by saying they are practical and we are not. Here they deceive themselves, and they deceive others. No, we will not even grant them that much. It is the mystics who are practical and the politicians who are not. We are the practical ones, the ones *who do something*, while they, *who do nothing*, are not. It is we who gather and they who despoil. It is we who build and inaugurate; they who demolish. It is we who nourish and they who feed from us. It is we who create works and men, peoples and generations. And it is they who bring them to ruin.

Even the little that they are is our doing. Even our doing is the wretchedness, vanity, emptiness, infirmity, frivolity, baseness, the nothing that they are. There's no reason, then, why they should scrutinize us like inspectors (as they scrutinize themselves). There's no reason for them to examine and judge us, passing us in review and inspecting us. For them to demand an accounting from us would be truly ridiculous. The only right they have in our regard is to keep silent and allow us to forget them. Hopefully they will use it liberally.

My claim is that the whole mystical body of Dreyfusism has remained intact. What difference does it make if the politicians have betrayed that mystique? That is only what one expects of them.

Afterward you will tell me that neither the staffs nor the committees nor the leagues partook of that mystique, then. Naturally they didn't. You wouldn't even have wished them to. What does the whole League of the Rights of Man, and even of the Citizen, matter, what does it stand for, as compared to a conscience, as compared to a mystique? What does a policy, what do a hundred policies matter, when a mystique is at stake? Thoroughly detestable that they are, they are nothing without us, they are still and always in our debt. Every mystique is the creditor of some sort of politics.

Even their detestation comes from us, is our work, our parasite.

You will add that even the victim himself had nothing to do with his mystique. With his own mystique. That became quite clear. We would have died for Dreyfus. Dreyfus is not in the least dead for Dreyfus. But the rule is that the victim should not be party to the mystique of his own case.

This is the triumph of human weakness, the crowning of our vanity, the highest evidence; the finest effort, the masterpiece, the culminating, supreme and most exalted demonstration of our infirmity.

It had to be that way so that the masterpiece of our wretchedness could be completed, so that all the bitterness could be drunk, so that the coronation of gratitude could be authentic.

So that it might be complete. So that all deception might be dissipated.

The Dreyfus affair, Dreyfusism, its mystique, the mysticism of Dreyfus was a culmination, a culminating intersection of at least three mysticisms—Jewish, Christian, and French. And I shall show that these three mysticisms didn't rip each other to pieces, they didn't beat each other black and blue; instead they converged to meet and to intersect, in a meeting and intersection probably unique in the world's history.

I can affirm that all the Dreyfus mystics have remained mystics and

Dreyfusards, that their hands have stayed pure. I know this; I have kept a list of them in the *cahiers*. I mean that all there were of mystics, faithful, believers in Dreyfusism have taken refuge and been collected in the *cahiers* from the time they took up the fight and for always, guided by a sure instinct, the deepest of instincts, as if in the single dwelling which had preserved meaning and tradition, the repository, sacred to us and perhaps to history, of the mystique of Dreyfus. Such was the first layer, the first group of our friends and subscribers. Already many are dead. All the living have remained invariably loyal to us. Or rather it was this first layer, this first group, all that was mystical and loyal and convinced in Dreyfusism, who were, who became not only our friends and subscribers but our very *cahiers*, the form and content of our *cahiers*. I may say it, then. Men who hold their peace, the only ones who matter, the silent, the only ones who count, the quiet ones, the only ones who will count, all these mystics have never varied, never shifted. All the humble people, which is to say, us. I had another proof of it during the last Easter holiday and at Pentecost, when so many friends and subscribers from outside of Paris, especially schoolteachers, paid us the kindness of a visit to our office. They are just as they were and what they were: men such as they were ten years ago, twelve, fifteen years ago. And I, too, dare say that they found me the man of ten, twelve, fifteen years ago. Perhaps this is not as easy.

Only the words of those who hold their peace matter.

Here is what was the heart and the strength of Dreyfusism. This heart, this center, this strength has stayed intact.

That very loyalty that our friends and subscribers showed us for fifteen years, through so many trials and hardships, so much distress, through and in spite of all the political shamefulness—this unsullied friendship, this loyalty from another age, this ancient and antiquated loyalty from another time, this friendship, the loyalty unique in the modern world—can only be explained as the loyalty and friendship of a mystical order. It repays us for our own mystique with a highly mystical loyalty.

He didn't die for himself; but there were some who died for him. This makes and consecrates and sanctions a mystique.

Others died for him.

He didn't ruin himself on his own behalf. He will ruin himself for no other being. But many ruined themselves for him. On his behalf many sacrificed their career, their daily bread, their life itself, the daily bread of their wives and children. For him many cast themselves into an inexpliable wretchedness. This makes and consecrates and sanctions a mystique.

Wretchedness—the only incurable ill.

Others ruined themselves, made a temporal sacrifice for him.

The greatest of all, Bernard-Lazare, no matter what people have said or, the more they were cowards, allowed to be said, lived for him, died for him, died thinking of him.

The greatest irony is that this mystique which our friends not only misinterpreted but failed to recognize (by *friends*, I mean the word in the sense of politics and political battles—our political friends, our politicians, our parasites) was suspected by our opponents. M. Barrès has very correctly noted on several occasions that Dreyfusism was a religious movement. He even wrote, quite a while ago, that it was regrettable if this religious force should be lost. Well, we are at least able to reassure him on that point. This religious force shall not be lost. To the necessary rebuilding, to the restitutions and *restorations* (we dare to say it) that lie ahead we come with head high, proud and brimming with our past; buffeted by all those trials, forged by our very hardships. To the restorations that lie ahead we come with full memory, full heart, and our hands full and undefiled.

As for myself, if for almost fifteen years (counting everything), disposing of few resources, disposing of little strength of any kind and little talent, amid every sort of difficulties and countless misfortunes, I was able to hold out, to keep on with this work, to persevere in it, in this ceaseless undertaking, it must be that I am dedicated to these *cahiers*, to this institution, to this work of a dedication, a liaison of a mystical order.

· · · · · · · · · · · · · · · ·

Our own socialism, our earlier socialism, I hardly need say, was not in the least anti-French, antipatriotic, or *anti*national. It was essentially, rigorously, thoroughly *inter*national. Theoretically, it was not in the least antinationalist. It was thoroughly internationalist. Far from weakening or slighting the people, it exalted and improved it. Far from enfeebling or weakening or slighting the nation, it exalted and improved it. Our thesis was the opposite, and remains so, that, instead, it is the bourgeoisie, bourgeoisism, bourgeois capitalism, bourgeois and capitalist sabotage that is obliterating nation and people. Believe us when we say that our former socialism and what today passes by that name had nothing in common. Here again, politics has done its work; nowhere more than here has politics destroyed and denatured mystique. By politics, I mean the politics of the politicians, the professionals, the politicos, the parliamentary politicians. But, more than that undoubtedly, through invention, intervention, interposing of sabotage, which is a political invention just like the vote—*more than the vote*, worse, I mean more political, more deeply political— more than that undoubtedly, we have the professional antipoliticians, the antipoliticos, the labor leaders, the antiparliamentary antipoliticians. We thought then and continue to think—fifteen years ago everybody thought like us and with us, or affected to think with us—that on this very point and principle there wasn't the shadow of hesitation or dispute. The evidence shows clearly that the bourgeois and capitalists started the whole thing. I mean the bourgeois and capitalists ceased to perform their social duty, before the workers neglected theirs, long before. There is no doubt that the sabotage from above came long before the sabotage from below, that the bourgeois and capitalist sabotage came earlier, much earlier, than

the workers' sabotage; that the bourgeois and capitalists lost their affection
for bourgeois and capitalist duty long before the workers lost the taste for
their own. It is in that precise order, starting with the bourgeois and capitalists, that there came about that general distaste for work which is the
deepest thorn in the flesh of the modern world. Since that is how it is in
our modern world, it serves no purpose, as our labor union politicos have
done, to invent and add labor turbulence to bourgeois turbulence, labor
sabotage to bourgeois and capitalist sabotage. Our socialism, on the contrary, was purposeful; it was essentially and, moreover, officially a general
theory, a doctrine, a general method, a philosophy for the organization and
reorganization of labor, for its *restoration*. Our socialism was essentially
and, moreover, officially a restoration, even a general restoration, a universal restoration. No one formerly contested this. But for fifteen years the
politicians have fallen in line. The two-faced politicians, the politicos and
the antipoliticos. The politicians have turned a deaf ear. But what we
needed was a general restoration, a total restoration, a universal restoration
beginning with the working-class world. We needed total restoration based
on a preliminary restoration of the working-class world, on a preliminary
total restoration of that world. What we needed then—and no one contested it, on the contrary, everyone taught it and announced it—was a
general housecleaning of the working-class world, a repair, a molecular
and organic housecleaning, and beginning with that a progressive housecleaning of the whole community. Already it had become a system of
morals, that general method and philosophy of producers which would
find in the moralist and philosopher Sorel its highest and most definitive
expression. This is the way it had to be.

And there was no possibility that it could have been anything else. Put
it this way: for the philosopher, for any philosophizing man our socialism
was nothing less than a religion of temporal salvation. And it remains the
same today. We were seeking nothing less than the temporal salvation of
humanity through the housecleaning of the working-class world, through
the rectification of work and the world of work, through the restoration of
work and the dignity of work, through a housecleaning, an organic and
molecular repair of the world of work, and through it the whole economic
and industrial world. We speak of what is called the industrial world, as
opposed to the intellectual and political worlds, the scholarly and parliamentary worlds, of what is called *economy*; the morals of the producers;
industrial morality; the world of producers; the economic world; the working-class world; the economic and industrial (the organic and molecular)
structure; what is called industry, the industrial regime; what is called the
regime of industrial production. Opposed to this, the intellectual and political worlds, the scholarly and parliamentary worlds go together. By restoring industrial morality, by rectifying the industrial workshop we hoped
and sought for nothing less than the temporal salvation of humanity. Only
those will deride us who do not care to see that Christianity itself, which is

the religion of eternal salvation, is besmirched by that mire, the mire of evil economic and industrial morality; that of its own efforts it won't escape, that without an economic and industrial revolution, it will not extricate itself; that, finally, there is no place of damnation better built, better laid out, better equipped—let us say, there is no place of damnation better adapted than the modern workshop.

They don't want to see that this is where all the Church's real troubles come from, all its real, deep, and common troubles. From the fact that, despite a few so-called working-class works, in the disguise of a few so-called working-class works and a few so-called Catholic workers, the workshop is closed to it and it to the workshop. From the fact that, itself experiencing a modernization, it has become in the modern world almost uniquely the religion of the rich and no longer, in a social sense, the communion of the faithful. All the weakness—perhaps we should say the growing weakness—of the Church in the modern world is not, as people think, because Science has raised so-called invincible systems against Religion, not because Science has unearthed and discovered seemingly triumphant arguments and reasons against Religion, but because what is left today of the Christian social world is profoundly lacking in charity. None of these arguments and systems and pseudoscientific constructions would weigh much or mean much, if there were but an ounce of charity. All these brainstorms would have little impact if Christendom had remained a communion, if Christianity had stayed a religion of the heart. That's one of the reasons why the moderns understand nothing about the true and real Christianity, its true and real history, what it really was. (And how many Christians, on this very point, too, have not themselves become "modern"?). They believe, when they are sincere—some are—they believe that Christianity was always modern, in other words, that it was always the way they see it in the modern world, where there is no longer a Christendom in the previous sense. And so, in the modern world everything is modern, no matter what, and it is probably the cleverest thing that modernism and modernity have done, making Christianity itself modern—in so many ways, almost all ways —as well as the Church and what part of Christendom has lingered on. Thus, when there is an eclipse, everything is in shadow. Everything passing through an age of humanity, through an epoch into a period, into a zone, everything set down in a place, in a time, in a world, everything placed in a temporal situation in a temporal world receives its tint and bears its shadow. We have heard a lot of noise about a certain intellectual modernism which is not even a heresy, but rather a sort of modern intellectual poverty—dregs, a residue, silt from the bottom of the vat, the bottom of the tub, the bottom of the barrel, a modern intellectual impoverishment for the use of the modern representatives of the former great heresies. This poverty would have committed no destruction, it would have been no more than laughable, if its ways had not been prepared in the form of this great modernism of the heart, this serious-minded, so serious-minded, modernism of charity. If its ways had not been prepared by this modernism of the heart and of charity. This is why the modern Church, the Church in the modern world of Christendom, is no longer the people. What it was once, it is no longer. This is why it is no longer a people in the social sense, an immense people, an immense race; this is why Christianity is no longer a social religion of deep insight, a religion of the common people, the religion of the whole people, temporal and eternal, rooted in the very greatest temporal profundities, the religion of a race, of a whole temporal race, a whole eternal race. This is why, socially, it is only a religion of the bourgeois and the rich, a kind of upper religion for the upper classes of society and the nation, a wretched sort of eminent religion for supposedly eminent persons. Consequently, it is everything that is most superficial and, still, most official, least profound, least actual; everything that is most poorly and wretchedly formal; above all, everything that is most contrary to its own institution: to holiness, to poverty, to the very most formal form of its institution. To the virtue, the spirit and letter of its institution, its own institution. Just take a look at the most ordinary passage from the Gospels.

Just take a look at what we might call, collectively, the Gospel.

It is this poverty, this spiritual meanness and temporal wealth which has done everything to bring about the evil. It is this modernism of the heart, this modernism of charity which has led to the bankruptcy and exhaustion of vigor in the Church, in Christianity, and in Christendom itself; which has brought about the degradation of mystique in politics.

Today I observe a lot of commotion made over the fact that since the separation of Church and State, Catholicism and Christianity being no longer the official state religion, the Church is thereby free. In a way, this is right. The Church's position is obviously very different, entirely different under the new regime. Never under the new regime will we get bishops as bad as the bishops under the concordat. But neither shall we exaggerate. We must not hide the fact that in ceasing to create the official state religion, the Church has not ceased to create the official religion of the state bourgeoisie. It has relinquished its political prerogatives, but it has scarcely lost those charges of social servitude to which its official position laid it open. That is why there isn't any triumph to celebrate. That is why the workshop is closed to it and it to the workshop. It creates and becomes the official religion, the formal religion of the rich. That is what, obscurely or formally, but very definitely, the common people feel. That is what they see. And so it is nothing, and that is why. Especially, it is nothing of what it once was, and it has become everything most contrary to itself, everything most contrary to its own institution. And it will never go back into the workshop, never go among the people, unless it, too, like everybody and everything, *bears the charges* of an economic and social revolution, an industrial revolution, and—to say it plain—a *temporal* revolution for *eternal* salvation. Such is, eternally, temporally (by the eternal temporal and the temporal eternal), the mysterious subjection of the eternal itself to the temporal.

Such, in fact, is the inscription of the eternal in the temporal. The costs must be borne: the economic, social, industrial, and *temporal costs*. Nothing can be held back: not even the eternal, not even the spiritual, not even the inner life. That is why our socialism wasn't so stupid; that's why it was deeply Christian.

That's why, when you set the old Christendom before their eyes, when you put them face to face with what used to be the reality of a Christain parish, a French parish at the beginning of the fifteenth century, in a time when there use to be French parishes, when you show them and make them see what Christendom was in its reality, in a time when there was a Christendom, and what a great saint was—she who was perhaps greatest of all—in the time when there was such a thing as sainthood, in the time when there was such a thing as *charity*, in the time when men and women could be saints, part of a whole Christian people, a whole Christian world, a whole people, a whole world made up of saints and sinners: as soon as you do that, some of our modern Catholics, modern without knowing it, but deeply modern to the marrow of their bones, unsuspectingly intellectual and proud not to be, but all the same profoundly intellectual to the marrow of their bones, bourgeois and the sons of bourgeois, stockholders and sons of stockholders, government pensioners, state pensioners, functionaries, pensioners depending on others, other citizens, other voters, other tax-payers, who have taken the ingenious precaution of having the becomingly modest insurance of their daily bread added to the Great Book of Public Debt—thus provided for, some of these contemporary Catholics, when faced with a sudden revelation of the old, ancient, and bygone Christendom, hasten to fill the air with cries, as if their modesty had been affronted. If the need arose, they would deny Joinville as being too coarse, too close to the people. Or the *sire* of Joinville. Perhaps they would even deny Saint Louis as being too much king of France.

We have to bear the temporal charges. In other words, nobody, be it the Church or any spiritual power, can escape short of a temporal revolution, an economic revolution, a social revolution. Short of paying for that. In order not to pay, not to bear the charges, a singular agreement has been struck, a singular collusion has been made, joining the Church and the intellectuals in league. This would be funny, laughable even, if it were not also deeply sorrowful. This agreement, this collusion consists of shifting and misplacing the argument, the very grounds of the argument. The object of the argument. To keep the modernism of the heart, the modernism of charity, hidden in a corner in order to thrust forward with false value and in false light, to thrust forward in full relief and full view the whole surface of intellectual modernism, the machinery of intellectual modernism, its solemn, glorious machinery. This was everybody gains: for this no longer costs anything, it no longer costs any economic, industrial, social, and temporal revolution. And our bourgeois and capitalists of both camps, both confessions, clericals and radicals, radical clericals and clerical radicals, intellectuals and clergy, intellectual clergy and clerical intellectuals want nothing so much as this: *not to pay.* Not to bear the charges. Not to bear the charges. Not to let go of the purse strings. Pardon me this coarse expression, but one is needed in this coarse situation. Wondrous agreement, collusion of wonders. Everybody gets what he wants. Not only does it cost nobody anything, but also, above and beyond this, there is the glory which naturally only comes to those who deserve it. Everyone discovers an advantage, even for us. Once more the two contrary parties are of a single mind, they have found a way to make their mutual interest falsify not only the argument dividing or seeming to divide them but also the grounds of the argument, shifting it so that it will be most profitable to them and cost them both the least—driven as they are by the sole consideration of their temporal interests. This operation consists of subduing and keeping in shadow that frightening modernism of the heart, while placing intellectual modernism in a unique and paramount position, in attributing everything that happens to the sham omnipotence, the frightening—supposedly frightening —power of intellectual modernism. What a shift, a substitution, a transfer, a transportation, a wondrous transposition. A displacement brought to perfection. The intellectuals are enthralled. *Look here,* they exclaim, *how powerful we are. We really have the brains. We have found such extraordinary rationalizations and arguments that by these arguments alone we have shaken the faith. The proof of this is that the parish priests are saying it.* And the priests in unison and the good clerical bourgeois, supposedly Catholic, presumably Christian, oblivious of the anathemas against the rich, the terrifying injunctions against money with which the Gospels are saturated, mellow in their peace of the heart, in their social peace, all our good bourgeois exclaim: *All that, too,* they exclaim, *all that is the fault of those damned professors who discovered such extraordinary arguments and rationalizations. The proof of it is that we, the parish priests, say that it is.* All well and good. Not only is everybody in the Republic, but everybody is happy. The pocketbooks stay in the pockets, and the money stays in the pocketbooks. No one touches the pocketbook. That's what counts. But truly I say again, none of these arguments would carry weight if there were an ounce of charity.

The clerical bourgeois world affects to believe that rationalizations and cerebral modernism have a unique importance: they relieve us of the expense of an industrial and economic revolution.

Since that was our socialism—it couldn't have been any secret then, there could have been no doubt about it—obviously it neither threatened nor could threaten the legitimate rights of nations. Since it was and was undertaking a general housecleaning, and thereby a housecleaning of nationalism and of the nation itself, it served and protected the most essential interests and most legitimate rights of peoples. Their most sacred interests and rights. It alone was doing so. Not by violating or reducing nations and peoples, not by perverting them, attacking them, destroying them, com-

pelling them, twisting them; but, on the contrary, by working to exchange
—in substitution, in organic and molecular replacement—for a closed
court, an anarchic competition of frantic and angry peoples, a healthy
forest, a forest bursting with prosperous peoples, a whole people of flourishing peoples. Peoples rising in their sap, in their essence, in the strict integrity of their vegetal lineage, free of the crushing burden of economic
servitudes, liberated from the organic and molecular corruption of evil
industrial morality. No, it wasn't by eliminating nations and peoples.
Rather, it was by founding them, stabilizing them at last, letting them be
born and letting them grow. By *letting* them. From the time when we
started we had the certainty, which we still have, that the world suffers
infinitely more from bourgeois and capitalist sabotage than from the
workers' sabotage. Not only did bourgeois and capitalist sabotage set the
whole thing off, but swiftly it became almost total. And, if I may say, it
entered the bourgeois world just as naturally as you please. But it is very
far from penetrating so totally and deeply into the working-class world.
And this is a very difficult thing. It didn't, by a long shot, take hereditary
root there. Contrary to what people generally think, what the writers, publicists, and sociologists—bourgeois intellectuals, all of them—believe in
common, the sabotage in the working-class world doesn't come from the
depths of the working-class world, it doesn't come from the workers' own
world. It has nothing to do with the workers. It is fundamentally bourgeois.
It doesn't come from below by a filtering upward of the working-class silt,
the working-class muddy bottom. It comes from above. And socialism alone
can avoid this contamination. Bourgeois sabotage, itself alone, descends in
horizontal layers into the working-class world and progressively contam-
inates it. It isn't the working-class world that arouses its own vices. The
working-class world is gradually acquiring a bourgeois consciousness. But
contrary to what people think, the sabotage is not innate, it isn't born in
the working-class world. It is learned there. It is taught there, dogmatically
and intellectually, like a foreign invention. It is a bourgeois invention, a
political invention, parliamentary and in essence intellectual, which penetrates by contamination and intellectualist teaching, from above, into the
working-class world. There it meets resistances which it had never encountered in the bourgeois world. It has won no battles, taken no cities. In
the working-class world it is, to put it briefly, artificial. There it collides
with unexpected resistances, resistances that go incredibly deep, that age-
old love of work which used to enrich the laborer's heart. The bourgeois
and capitalist world is almost completely, or completely, devoted to pleasure. But you can still find a very large number of workers, and not just the
older ones, who still *love* work.

Since that was our Socialism, it clearly was and was undertaking a housecleaning of nation and people, a still unfulfilled shoring up, a prosperity, a
flourishing, a ripening. It was very far from plotting and conjuring the
downfall of these things. Already we had the certainty—we still have it—
that such a people as would be first to set out on this road, having the honor

and courage and, in a sense, the cleverness to do it, would gain such
strength, such organic and molecular, constitutional and histological prosperity, such reinforcement and growth, such rectification in all aspects of
its strength, that not only would it march in the vanguard of peoples, but
evermore have nothing to fear, in present and future, either from its economic, industrial and commercial competitors or from its military ones.

But the rise of bourgeois consciousness through sabotage follows a path
exactly the opposite of what we wanted to take. And have others take. We
wanted a housecleaning of the working-class world, expanding progressively to clean out the bourgeois world, and thus the whole society, the
whole community. But it happened the other way, it came about that a
demoralization of the bourgeois world, in economic and industrial matters
and all other matters, in the order of work and all other orders, descending
progressively, demoralized the working-class world, and thus all society,
the whole community. Far from adding or wishing to add disorder to disorder, we wanted to install and restore an order both new and ancient;
new and bygone, not in the least modern; an order of labor and industry,
a workers' order, an economic, temporal, industrial order; and through the
rising contamination of that order, so to say, regulate the disorder itself.
But by a descending contamination, disorder itself wrought havoc with
order; it disorganized the organization of the organism. And we have the
right to say that this disorder, this bad example, came about as a kind of
intellectual foreign matter introduced into the working-class world, an
operation with as artificial a significance as might have been, for example,
that other invention of the People's Universities.

It would be an error to think that only good and the striving after good
and morality are artificial. Especially in a race like ours, evil and the striving after evil, the striving for debasement and contamination can just as
easily be artificial. Q.E.D.

I know how much these efforts in instruction and moralization, these
People's Universities and all other universities and efforts, as much as anyone I know how much these bourgeois, intellectual efforts, distilled from
above on the working-class world, were factitious, empty, vain, and hollow;
how they gave nothing and could give nothing. How artificial and superficial they were. But what I can say is that, opposed to these, the lessons of
sabotage were also bourgeois and intellectual lessons: they were also lessons given and received; offered and accepted; taught and learned. Lessons and apprenticeships. They proved more, carried further, penetrated
more successfully and much more deeply, because evil always penetrates
more easily than good—what I mean to say, what never gets said, what I
am anxious to say, what needs to be said is that these, too, were lessons of
the same type, filtering downward from the same place, the same world.
They were just as bourgeois, intellectual, and artificial. They may have
been a little less superficial because evil is always less superficial than good.
Basically, they were just as alien to the working-class world.

They were lessons of the same kind. Given what the working-class world was, it was an error to think that evil was natural to it and that, through a sort of disgrace, good alone was artificial.

And so in this modern world which strains, without exception, toward money and is strained by money, the contamination of the Christian world in its straining after money forces it to sacrifice its faith and morals to the maintenance of economic and social peace.

There, precisely, we find that modernism of the heart, that modernism of charity, that *modernism of morals.*

There are two categories of rich people: the rich *atheists*, who, being rich, understand nothing about religion. So they have set to work on the history of *religions*, and they excel at it (besides, we have to give them credit for having taken every precaution against creating a history of *the religion*). It is they who have invented the sciences of religion;

and the rich *devout*, who, being rich, understand nothing about Christianity. And so they profess it.

Such is—you have to see and judge it—the terrifying modernism of the modern world; its terrible, wretched efficacy. It has succeeded in breaching, has modernized and breached Christendom. It has made Christianity itself maggoty and rotten in its charity and morals.

Need I say, in retrospect, need I note and point out how our socialism was in the pure French tradition, the French ancestry and lineage. The rectification and clarification of the world has always been the French destination and vocation, the prime French duty. The rectification of what is ailing, the clarification of what is inchoate, the ordering of what is disorder, the organization of what is crude. Must we point out how precisely this socialism based on generosity, how this illustrious generosity, this full and pure generosity was in the French tradition; more even than in the French tradition, profoundly in the French genius. In the sap and blood of the race. A generosity at once plentiful and sober, generous and yet informed, full and pure, fecund and clean, full and discriminating, plentiful without nonsense, informed without sterility. Finally, a heroism full and sober, gay and discreet, a heroism none other than French.

.   .   .   .

We were heroes. Let's say this very simply, because I am quite sure that no one will say it for us. And this is precisely how and why we were heroes. Everywhere in the world in which we moved and were completing the years of our apprenticeship, everywhere in the atmosphere where we moved and worked and were still growing up and completing our education, the question before us, during the two or three years of that rising curve, was not in the slightest that of knowing whether *in reality* Dreyfus was innocent or guilty. It was whether one would have the courage to recognize and declare his innocence. To show his innocence. To know whether we would have that double courage. There was, in the first place, the first courage, that rough outer courage, not easy to come by, that public, social courage of showing him innocent before the world, in the eyes of the public, of recommending him to the public, glorifying him, recommending him publicly, declaring publicly on his behalf, testifying for him publicly. Of risking, putting everything one had on him, a whole wretchedly earned currency, a whole poor and wretched currency, a whole little people's currency of poverty and wretchedness; all one's time, life and career; all health, body and soul; the ruin of the body, every ruin, the bursting of the heart, the uprooting of families, the breaking of close relations, the evasion of others' glances, reprobation silent or angry, or both, isolation, every kind of quarantine; the rupture of twenty-year friendships, friendships begun as far back as we can remember. All social life, all the life of the heart, everything. Then, in the second place, that second courage, still harder to come by, the inner courage, the secret courage of making one's own inner confession that he was innocent. Of renouncing all tranquillity for this man.

Renouncing not only the peace of the community and the peace of the hearth, not only the peace of the family and the members of the family. But, finally, the peace of the heart.

The most cherished possession, the only possession.

The courage of entering into the kingdom of an incurable anxiety for this man.

The kingdom of a bitterness that shall never heal.

. . . .

Not only were we heroes but basically the Dreyfus affair can be explained only by that need for heroism which seizes this people, this race, periodically—by a need for heroism which seized us then, a whole generation of us. So it is with these great movements, these great trials of a whole people, just like those other great trials called wars. Or rather, peoples have but one kind of great temporal trial, which is war; these great trials of the present are themselves wars. In all these great trials and great annals, an internal strength, the violence of eruption, makes historical matter much more than the matter makes and imposes the experience. When a great war —a great revolution, this kind of war—breaks out, it is because a great people, a great race, is seeking release, because it has had enough—enough of peace. It is always because a great mass feels a violent need, a vast and deep need, the mysterious need for a great movement. If our people and race, the French masses, had felt like having a great war forty years ago, then that wretched and unhappy war of 1870, ill-prepared and ill-met as it was, would have become a great war like others, and March 1871 would only have signaled its beginning. Great history—I mean great history like the Wars of the Revolution and the Empire—can be explained in no other way than a grasping of need, a very deep need of glory, war, and history that at a given moment seizes a whole people and race, driving them to erupt and explode. A mysterious need for a sort of historical fecundity. A mysterious need to inscribe a great history in eternal history. Any other explanation is vain, reasonable, rational, sterile, unreal. Similarly, our

Dreyfus affair can be explained only by this same need, the need for heroism that seized a whole generation—our generation—a need for war,
soldierly war and soldierly glory, a need for sacrifice to the point of martyrdom, very likely a need for sainthood. What our opponents couldn't see
except through their own optic, what they could grasp only hollowly, what
our own chiefs always forgot, was how much like an army we marched.
How such hope and enterprise could be shattered without obtaining or
leaving a historical epitaph is what I tried to explain and portray *to our
friends and subscribers* in a *cahier* of just about a year ago. If we were once
again an army of lions led by asses, this is because we took our cue from
the purest French tradition.

We have been great, indeed very great. Today, those of whom I speak,
we—we are people who earn our living poorly, wretchedly, piteously. But
it is hard to understand why the poor Jews still keep their distances, earning their living by a sweep of the hand, suffering no ill or at least less ill in
earning their living that we do. Perhaps this could be said: if they contribute somewhat to each other's welfare—though less than is thought and
said, for sometimes they quarrel and betray one another—they must, on
the other hand, endure an anti-Semitism renewed and increasing. What I
do understand is that we, Jews and Christians together, poor Jews and poor
Christians, earn our living as we can, generally badly, in this hell of a life,
this bitch of a modern society.

.   .   .   .

Here is the real situation in people's attitudes that we were up against
for a long time: they didn't say or believe that Dreyfus was guilty, but they
did believe and say that, whether he was innocent or guilty, one shouldn't
be disturbed and get all upset; for a man, a single man, one shouldn't *compromise* or risk the life and salvation of a people, the immense salvation of
a whole people. By this was meant: its *temporal* salvation. But it so happened that our Christian mystique coincided so perfectly, so precisely with
our French mystique, with the patriotic mystique contained in the mystique
of Dreyfus, that obviously—as I shall say and write in my confessions—we
took no less a view of the situation than to claim it involved *the eternal
salvation of France.* What were we really saying? Everything was against
us, wisdom and law, I mean human wisdom and human law. What we
were doing bordered on madness or sainthood, qualities which, interpreted by human wisdom and human opinion, have so many resemblances,
so many secret contacts. Well, we went against wisdom, against the law.
Against human wisdom and human law. What were we really saying? The
others were saying: A people, a whole people, in an enormous collection of
interests, of highly legitimate rights. Highly sacred ones. Thousands and
millions of lives depend on this, in the present, in the past—in the future—
thousands, millions, hundreds of millions of lives go to make it up, in present, past, and future (millions of memories), and by the play of history, the
accumulation history makes in its storehouse of incalculable interests.

Legitimate, sacred, incalculable rights. A whole people of men and families; a whole people of legitimate rights and interests; a whole people of lives; a whole people of memories; a whole history; a whole push and pull —all the past, all the future, all the promise of a people and its ancestors; all that is inestimable, incalculable, of infinite worth because unique, happening only one time, never recreating itself again, because it is a unique and wondrous achievement; a people—notably and namely this people— of unique worth; this old people: no people has the right—a people's primary and strict duty is not to place all that in jeopardy, not to place itself in jeopardy for any man, whoever he may be, whatever legitimate interests or rights he may possess, even those that are sacred. No people ever has that right. You don't bring to ruin a whole community; a community cannot be brought to ruin for a single citizen. This was the true language of undeviating civic honor and of wisdom—it was wisdom, the ancient wisdom. This was the language of reason. Seen thus, it was obvious that Dreyfus should consecrate himself to France; not only for the tranquillity of France but for its very salvation, which he was placing in danger. And if he didn't want to consecrate himself, others had the duty to do it for him. And what were we saying? We were saying that a single injustice, a single crime, a single illegality, especially if it is officialy recorded and confirmed, a single injury to humanity and justice and righteousness, especially if it is universally, legally, nationally, conveniently acquiesced in—a single crime shatters and is enough to shatter the whole social fabric, the whole social contract; a single breach of duty, a single dishonor is enough to ruin and dishonor a whole people. It is a speck of gangrene that corrupts the whole body. We are not only defending our own honor. Not only the honor of our whole people in the present, but the historical honor of our people, all the historical honor of our whole race, the honor of our sires and of our children. And the more of a past we have and the more memory, the more we have a responsibility, and the more also we ought to defend that responsibility. The more past we have behind us, the more we must defend it and keep it pure. *I will give my blood back pure as I received it.* That was the rule and honor and thrust of Corneille, the old Corneillian thrust. It was also the rule, honor, and thrust of Christianity. A single blemish stains a whole family. It also stains a whole people. A single speck spots the honor of a whole family. That single speck can also spot the honor of a whole people. A people cannot pass off an injury that works on it and tries it, it cannot remain so solemnly and fatally burdened with a crime. A people's honor is indivisible.

C. Science, Faith, and Man

The Nineteenth Century Challenged: The Syllabus of Errors

Pius IX, Syllabus Errorum: *The Syllabus of the Principal Errors of Our Time* . . . *(December 8, 1864), in William Ewart Gladstone,* The Vatican Decrees in Their Bearing on Civil Allegiance: a Political Expostulation *(New York: Harper & Bros., 1875), pp. 109–29.*

One of the tragedies of the nineteenth century derived from the determination of most of the Roman Catholic Church hierarchy to judge political doctrines out of their historical context. Little regard was given to their real content and meaning; rather, they were considered in traditional scholastic terms. The strain between advanced political doctrine and Church polity was pronounced before the French Revolution. Afterward anticlericalism became a facet of liberalism in Catholic as well as Protestant countries. Those who sought a *rapprochement* between faith and the age—and one was badly needed given the impact of science, historical scholarship, and the revolutionary improvement in material conditions—were forced instead to choose between them. Distinguished Catholic thinkers despaired, Protestants and secularists rejoiced in the promulgation of the *Syllabus of Errors* in 1864. Pius IX (1792–1878), who had briefly toyed with moderation, shuddered at the revolutions of 1848 as the product of the age and denounced "modernism."

The *Syllabus*, fittingly framed in medieval invective and negative form, rejected religious toleration, demanded control of science and culture, and denounced, point by point, every major force of the nineteenth century. Reinforced in 1870 with the promulgation of the dogma of papal infallibility, the Catholic Church challenged the age. If the Church was institutionally strengtened and centralized, the political implications were dangerous. Almost a generation would pass from the *Syllabus* to *Rerum Novarum* (1891) before the Roman Catholic Church began to come to terms with vital social forces. Far more gradually still did the Church adjust its political alignment with reactionary causes.

SYLLABUS ERRORUM

[THE PAPAL SYLLABUS OF ERRORS. A.D. 1864.]

The Syllabus of the principal errors of our time, which are stigmatized in the Consistorial Allocutions, Encyclicals, and other Apostolical Letters of our Most Holy Father, Pope Pius IX.

§ I.—PANTHEISM, NATURALISM, AND ABSOLUTE RATIONALISM.

1. THERE EXISTS no supreme, most wise, and most provident divine being distinct from the universe, and God is none other than nature, and is there-

fore subject to change. In effect, God is produced in man and in the world, and all things are God, and have the very substance of God. God is therefore one and the same thing with the world, and thence spirit is the same thing with matter, necessity with liberty, true with false, good with evil, justice with injustice.

2. All action of God upon man and the world is to be denied.

3. Human reason, without any regard to God, is the sole arbiter of truth and falsehood, of good and evil; it is its own law to itself, and suffices by its natural force to secure the welfare of men and of nations.

4. All the truths of religion are derived from the native strength of human reason; whence reason is the master rule by which man can and ought to arrive at the knowledge of all truths of every kind.

5. Divine revelation is imperfect, and, therefore, subject to a continual and indefinite progress, which corresponds with the progress of human reason.

6. Christian faith contradicts human reason, and divine revelation not only does not benefit, but even injures the perfection of man.

7. The prophecies and miracles set forth and narrated in the Sacred Scriptures are the fictions of poets; and the mysteries of the Christian faith are the result of philosophical investigations. In the books of both Testaments there are contained mythical inventions, and Jesus Christ is himself a mythical fiction.

§ II.—MODERN RATIONALISM.

8. As human reason is placed on a level with religion, so theological matters must be treated in the same manner as philosophical ones.

9. All the dogmas of the Christian religion are, without exception, the object of scientific knowledge or philosophy, and human reason, instructed solely by history, is able, by its own natural strength and principles, to arrive at the true knowledge of even the most abstruse dogmas: provided such dogmas be proposed as subject-matter for human reason.

10. As a philosopher is one thing, and philosophy is another, so it is the right and duty of the philosopher to submit to the authority which he shall have recognized as true; but philosophy neither can nor ought to submit to any authority.

11. The Church not only ought never to animadvert upon philosophy, but ought to tolerate the errors of philosophy, leaving to philosophy the care of their correction.

12. The decrees of the Apostolic See and of the Roman Congregations fetter the free progress of science.

13. The method and principles by which the old scholastic doctors cultivated theology are no longer suitable to the demands of the age and the progress in science.

14. Philosophy must be treated of without any account being taken of supernatural revelation.

§ III.—INDIFFERENCE, LATITUDINARIANISM.

15. Every man is free to embrace and profess the religion he shall believe true, guided by the light of reason.

16. Men may in any religion find the way of eternal salvation, and obtain eternal salvation.

17. We may entertain at least a well-founded hope for the eternal salvation of all those who are in no manner in the true Church of Christ.

18. Protestantism is nothing more than another form of the same true Christian religion, in which it is possible to be equally pleasing to God as in the Catholic Church.

§ IV.—SOCIALISM, COMMUNISM, SECRET SOCIETIES, BIBLICAL SOCIETIES, CLERICO-LIBERAL SOCIETIES.

§ V.—ERRORS CONCERNING THE CHURCH AND HER RIGHTS.

19. The Church is not a true, and perfect, and entirely free society, nor does she enjoy peculiar and perpetual rights conferred upon her by her Divine Founder, but it appears to the civil power to define what are the rights and limits with which the Church may exercise authority.

20. The ecclesiastical power must not exercise its authority without the permission and assent of the civil government.

21. The Church has not the power of defining dogmatically that the religion of the Catholic Church is the only true religion.

22. The obligation which binds Catholic teachers and authors applies only to those things which are proposed for universal belief as dogmas of the faith, by the infalible judgment of the Church.

23. The Roman Pontiffs and oecumenical Councils have exceeded the limits of their power, have usurped the rights of princes, and have even committed errors in defining matters of faith and morals.

24. The Church has not the power of availing herself of force, or any direct or indirect temporal power.

25. In addition to the authority inherent in the Episcopate, a further and temporal power is granted to it by the civil authority, either expressly or tacitly, which power is on that account also revocable by the civil authority whenever it pleases.

26. The Church has not the innate and legitimate right of acquisition and possession.

27. The ministers of the Church, and the Roman Pontiff, ought to be absolutely excluded from all charge and dominion over temporal affairs.

28. Bishops have not the right of promulgating even their apostolical letters, without the permission of the government.

29. Dispensations granted by the Roman Pontiff must be considered null, unless they have been asked for by the civil government.

30. The immunity of the Church and of ecclesiastical persons derives its origin from civil law.

31. Ecclesiastical courts for temporal causes, of the clergy, whether civil or criminal, ought by all means to be abolished, either without the concurrence and against the protest of the Holy See.

32. The personal immunity exonerating the clergy from military service may be abolished, without violation either of natural right or of equity. Its abolition is called for by civil progress, especially in a community constituted upon principles of liberal government.

33. It does not appertain exclusively to ecclesiastical jurisdiction, by any right, proper and inherent, to direct the teaching of theological subjects.

34. The teaching of those who compare the sovereign Pontiff to a free sovereign acting in the universal Church is a doctrine which prevailed in the middle ages.

35. There would be no obstacle to the sentence of a general council, or the act of all the universal peoples, transferring the pontifical sovereignty from the Bishop and City of Rome to some other bishopric and some other city.

36. The definition of a national council does not admit of any subsequent discussion, and the civil power can regard as settled an affair decided by such national council.

37. National churches can be established, after being withdrawn and plainly separated from the authority of the Roman Pontiff.

38. Roman Pontiffs have, by their too arbitrary conduct, contributed to the division of the Church into eastern and western.

§ VI.—ERRORS ABOUT CIVIL SOCIETY, CONSIDERED BOTH IN ITSELF

AND IN ITS RELATION TO THE CHURCH.

39. The commonwealth is the origin and source of all rights, and possesses rights which are not circumscribed by any limits.

40. The teaching of the Catholic Church is opposed to the well-being and interests of society.

41. The civil power, even when exercised by an unbelieving sovereign, possesses an indirect and negative power over religious affairs. It therefore possesses not only the right called that of *exequatur,* but that of the (so-called) *appellatio ab abusu.*

42. In the case of conflicting laws between the two powers, the civil law ought to prevail.

43. The civil power has a right to break, and to declare and render null, the conventions (commonly called *Concordats*) concluded with the Apostolic See, relative to the use of rights appertaining to the ecclesiastical immunity, without the consent of the Holy See, and even contrary to its protest.

44. The civil authority may interfere in matters relating to religion, morality, and spiritual government. Hence it has control over the instructions for the guidance of consciences issued, conformably with their mission, by the pastors of the Church. Further, it possesses power to decree, in the matter of administering the divine sacraments, as to the dispositions necessary for their reception.

45. The entire direction of public schools, in which the youth of Christian states are educated, except (to a certain extent) in the case of episcopal seminaries, may and must appertain to the civil power, and belond to it so far that no other authority whatsoever shall be recognized as having any right to interfere in the discipline of the schools, the arrangement of the studies, the taking of degrees, or the choice and approval of the teachers.

46. Much more, even in clerical seminaries, the method of study to be adopted is subject to the civil authority.

47. The best theory of civil society requires that popular schools open to the children of all classes, and, generally, all public institutes intended for instruction in letters and philosophy, and for conducting the education of the young, should be freed from all ecclesiastical authority, government, and interference, and should be fully subject to the civil and political power, in conformity with the will of rulers and the prevalent opinions of the age.

48. This system of instructing youth, which consists in separating it from the Catholic faith and from the power of the Church, and in teaching exclusively, or at least primarily, the knowledge of natural things and the earthly ends of social life alone, may be approved by Catholics.

49. The civil power has the right to prevent ministers of religion, and the faithful, from communicating freely and mutually with each other, and with the Roman Pontiff.

50. The secular authority possesses, as inherent in itself, the right of presenting bishops, and may require of them that they take possession of their dioceses before having received canonical institution and the apostolic letters from the Holy See.

51. And, further, the secular government has the right of deposing bishops from their pastoral functions, and it is not bound to obey the Roman Pontiff in those things which relate to episcopal sees and the institution of bishops.

52. The government has of itself the right to alter the age prescribed by the Church for the religious profession, both of men and women; and it may enjoin upon all religious establishments to admit no person to take solemn vows without its permission.

53. The laws for the protection of religious establishments, and securing their rights and duties, ought to be abolished: nay, more, the civil government may lend its assistance to all who desire to quit the religious life they have undertaken, and break their vows. The government may also suppress religious orders, collegiate churches, and simple benefices,

even those belonging to private patronage, and submit their goods and revenues to the administration and disposal of the civil power.

54. Kings and princes are not only exempt from the jurisdiction of the Church, but are superior to the Church, in litigated questions of jurisdiction.

55. The Church ought to be separated from the State, and the State from the Church.

§ VII.—ERRORS CONCERNING NATURAL AND CHRISTIAN ETHICS.

56. Moral laws do not stand in need of the divine sanction, and there is no necessity that human laws should be conformable to the law of nature, and receive their sanction from God.

57. Knowledge of philosophical things and morals, and also civil laws, may and must depart from divine and ecclesiastical authority.

58. No other forces are to be recognized than those which reside in matter; and all moral teaching and moral excellence ought to be made to consist in the accumulation and increase of riches by every possible means, and in the enjoyment of pleasure.

59. Right consists in the material fact, and all human duties are but vain words, and all human acts have the force of right.

60. Authority is nothing else but the result of numerical superiority and material force.

61. An unjust act, being successful, inflicts no injury upon the sanctity of right.

62. The principle of *non-intervention*, as it is called, ought to be proclaimed and adhered to.

63. It is allowable to refuse obedience to legitimate princes: nay, more, to rise in insurrection against them.

64. The violation of a solemn oath, even every wicked and flagitious action repugnant to the eternal law, is not only blamable, but quite lawful, and worthy of the highest praise, when done for the love of country.

§ VIII.—THE ERRORS CONCERNING CHRISTIAN MARRIAGE.

65. It can not be by any means tolerated, to maintain that Christ has raised marriage to the dignity of a sacrament.

66. The sacrament of marriage is only an adjunct of the contract, and separable from it, and the sacrament itself consists in the nuptial benediction alone.

67. By the law of nature, the marriage tie is not indissoluble, and in many cases divorce, properly so called, may be pronounced by the civil authority.

68. The Church has not the power of laying down what are diriment impediments to marriage. The civil authority does possess such a power, and can do away with existing impediments to marriage.

69. The Church only commenced in later ages to bring in diriment

impediments, and then availing herself of a right not her own, but borrowed from the civil power.

70. The canons of the Council of Trent, which pronounce censure of anathema against those who deny to the Church the right of laying down what are diriment impediments, either are not dogmatic, or must be understood as referring only to such borrowed power.

71. The form of solemnizing marriage prescribed by the said Council, under penalty of nullity, does not bind in cases where the civil law has appointed another form, and where it decrees that this new form shall effectuate a valid marriage.

72. Boniface VIII. is the first who declared that the vow of chastity pronounced at ordination annuls nuptials.

73. A merely civil contract may, among Christians, constitute a true marriage; and it is false, either that the marriage contract between Christians is always a sacrament, or that the contract is null if the sacrament be excluded.

74. Matrimonial causes and espousals belong by their very nature to civil jurisdiction.

§ IX.—ERRORS REGARDING THE CIVIL POWER OF THE SOVEREIGN PONTIFF.

75. The children of the Christian and Catholic Church are not agreed upon the compatibility of the temporal with the spiritual power.

76. The abolition of the temporal power, of which the Apostolic See is possessed, would contribute in the greatest degree to the liberty and prosperity of the Church.

§ X.—ERRORS HAVING REFERENCE TO MODERN LIBERALISM.

78. In the present day, it is no longer expedient that the Catholic religion shall be held as the only religion of the State, to the exclusion of all other modes of worship.

78. Whence it has been wisely provided by law, in some countries called Catholic, that persons coming to reside therein shall enjoy the public exercise of their own worship.

79. Moreover, it is false that the civil liberty of every mode of worship, and the full power given to all of overtly and publicly manifesting their opinions and their ideas, of all kinds whatsoever, conduce more easily to corrupt the morals and minds of the people, and to the propagation of the pest of indifferentism.

80. The Roman Pontiff can and ought to reconcile himself to, and agree with, progress, liberalism, and civilization as lately introduced.

Catholics and Social Change: Leo XIII and Rerum Novarum

Leo XIII, Rerum Novarum: *Encyclical Letter (May 15, 1891) on the Condition of the Working Classes, in* The Pope and the People *(New York: Catholic Truth Society, 1931), pp. 133–68.*

The reaction of the Roman Catholic Church to the new world of the nineteenth century was alternately one of hope and despair. Influential Catholic clergymen and laymen attempted to avoid too obvious an identification of Catholic faith and political reaction. Lamennais sought to swing the Church away from the dying cause of divine right only to be rebuked by the encyclical *Mirari vos* (1832). Given the political obscurantism of the *Syllabus of Errors* buttressed by the declaration of papal infallibility in 1870, the Church appeared to be totally alienated from the age.

The accession of Pope Leo XIII (1810–1903) in 1878 initiated a far more constructive era. Leo XIII confirmed the *Syllabus* (the political position of the Church changed but slowly even through the first half of the twentieth century) and eloquently set forth a neo-Thomist statement of faith and political theory in *Inscrutabili Dei Consilio* (1878) and *Immortale Dei* (1885). These encyclicals challenged materialism and secular dogmas. The Church never accepted the enlightenment's cult of man. *Rerum Novarum* was an effort to reach beyond liberal or socialist doctrine. The economic crises and social upheaval of the late nineteenth century demanded a reasoned statement of a tenable position. Survival of the Catholic Church demanded that it come to terms with the industrial world. *Rerum Novarum* offered an alternative. No form of atheistic "improvement" or revolutionary doctrine could solve the problems of man. He must understand the true meaning of Christian Commonwealth.

RERUM NOVARUM

THE CONDITION OF THE WORKING CLASSES

Encyclical Letter of Leo XIII, May 15, 1891

THAT THE SPIRIT of revolutionary change, which has long been disturbing the nations of the world, should have passed beyond the sphere of politics and made its influence felt in the cognate sphere of practical economics is not surpising. The elements of the conflict now raging are unmistakable, in the vast expansion of industrial pursuits and marvellous discoveries of science; in the changed relations between masters and workmen; in the enormous fortunes of some few individuals, and the utter poverty of the masses; in the increased self-reliance and closer mutual combination of the working classes; as also, finally, in the prevailing moral degeneracy. The momentous gravity of the state of things now obtaining fills every mind with painful apprehension; wise men are discussing it; practical men are proposing schemes; popular meetings, legislatures, and rulers of nations are all busied with it—and actually there is no question which has taken a deeper hold on the public mind.

Therefore, Venerable Brethren, as on former occasions when it seemed opportune to refute false teaching, We have addressed you in the interests of the Church and of the common weal, and have issued Letters bearing on "Political Power," "Human Liberty," "The Christian Constitution of the State," and like matters, so have we thought it expedient now to speak on the Condition of the Working Classes. It is a subject on which We have already touched more than once, incidentally. But in the present Letter, the responsibility of the Apostolic office urges Us to treat the question of set purpose and in detail, in order that no misapprehension may exist as to the principles which truth and justice dictate for its settlement. The discussion is not easy, nor is it void of danger. It is no easy matter to define the relative rights and mutual duties of the rich and of the poor, of Capital and of Labour. And the danger lies in this, that crafty agitators are intent on making use of these differences of opinion to pervert men's judgments and to stir up the people to revolt.

Causes of Social Problem

In any case we clearly see, and on this there is general agreement, that some opportune remedy must be found quickly for the misery and wretchedness pressing so unjustily on the majority of the working class: for the ancient working-men's guilds were abolished in the last century, and no other protective organization took their place. Public institutions and the laws set aside the ancient religion. Hence by degrees it has come to pass that working-men have been surrendered, isolated and helpless, to the hardheartedness of employers and the greed of unchecked competition. The mischief has been increased by rapacious usury, which, although more than once condemned by the Church, is nevertheless, under a different guise, but with the like injustice, still practised by covetous and grasping men. To this must be added that the hiring of labour and the conduct of trade are concentrated in the hands of comparatively few; so that a small number of very rich men have been able to lay upon the teeming masses of the labouring poor a yoke little better than that of slavery itself.

The Socialist Solution

To remedy these wrongs the Socialists, working on the poor man's envy of the rich, are striving to do away with private property, and contend that individual possessions should become the common property of all, to be administered by the State or by municipal bodies. They hold that by thus transferring property from private individuals to the community, the present mischievous state of things will be set to rights, inasmuch as each citizen will then get his fair share of whatever there is to enjoy. But their contentions are so clearly powerless to end the controversy that were they carried into effect the working-man himself would be among the first to suffer. They are moreover emphatically unjust, because they would rob the lawful possessor, distort the functions of the State, and create utter confusion in the community.

The Worker would Suffer

It is surely undeniable that, when a man engages in remunerative labour, the impelling reason and motive of his work is to obtain property, and thereafter to hold it as his very own. If one man hires out to another his strength or skill, he does so for the purpose of receiving in return what is necessary for maintenance and education; he therefore expressly intends to acquire a right full and real, not only to the remuneration, but also to the disposal of such remuneration, just as he pleases. Thus, if he lives sparingly, saves money, and, for greater security, invests his savings in land, the land, in such case, is only his wages under another form; and, consequently, a working-man's little estate thus purchased should be as completely at his full disposal as are the wages he receives for his labour. But it is precisely in such power of disposal that ownership obtains, whether the property consist of land or chattels. Socialisits, therefore, by endeavouring to transfer the possessions of individuals to the community at large, strike at the interests of every wage-earner, since they would deprive him of the liberty of disposing of his wages, and thereby of all hope and possibility of increasing his resources and of bettering his condition in life.

The Right to own Private Property a Natural Right

What is of far greater moment, however, is the fact that the remedy they propose is manifestly against justice. For every man has by nature the right to possess property as his own. This is one of the chief points of distinction between man and the animal creation, for the brute has no power of self-direction, but is governed by two main instincts, which keep his powers on the alert, impel him to develop them in a fitting manner, and stimulate and determine him to action without any power of choice. One of these instincts is self-preservation, the other the propagation of the species. Both can attain their purpose by means of things which lie within range; beyond their verge the brute creation cannot go, for they are moved to action by their senses only, and in the special direction which these suggest. But with man it is wholly different. He possesses, on the one hand, the full perfection of the animal being, and hence enjoys, at least as much as the rest of the animal kind, the fruition of things material. But animal nature, however perfect, is far from representing the human being in its completeness, and is in truth but humanity's humble handmaid, made to serve and to obey. It is the mind, or reason, which is the predominant element in us who are human creatures; it is this which renders a human being human, and distinguishes him essentially from the brute. And on this very account—that man alone among the animal creation is endowed with reason—it must be within his right to possess things not merely for temporary and momentary use, as other living things do, but to have and to hold them in stable and permanent possession; he must have not only things that perish in the use, but those also which, though they have been reduced into use, continue for further use in after time.

The Right to Private Property proved from the Nature of Man

This becomes still more clearly evident if man's nature be considered a little more deeply. For man, fathoming by his faculty of reason matters without number, linking the future with the present, and being master of his own acts, guides his ways under the eternal law and the power of God, whose Providence governs all things. Wherefore it is in his power to exercise his choice not only as to matters that regard his present welfare, but also about those which he deems may be for his advantage in time yet to come. Hence man not only should possess the fruits of the earth, but also the very soil, inasmuch as from the produce of the earth he has to lay by provision for the future. Man's needs do not die out, but for ever recur; although satisfied to-day, they demand fresh supplies for to-morrow. Nature accordingly must have given to man a source that is stable and remaining always with him from which he might look to draw continual supplies. And this stable condition of things he finds solely in the earth and its fruits.

In what Sense God has given the Earth to All

There is no need to bring in the State. Man precedes the State, and possesses, prior to the formation of any State, the right of providing for the sustenance of his body. The fact that God has given the earth for the use and enjoyment of the whole human race can in no way be a bar to the owning of private property. For God has granted the earth to mankind in general, not in the sense that all without distinction can deal with it as they like, but rather that no part of it was assigned to any one in particular, and that the limits of private possession have been left to be fixed by man's own industry, and by the laws of individual races. Moreover, the earth, even though apportioned among private owners, ceases not thereby to minister to the needs of all, inasmuch as there is no one who does not sustain life from what the land produces. Those who do not possess the soil, contribute their labour; hence it may truly be said that all human subsistence is derived either from labour on one's own land, or from some toil, some calling which is paid for either in the produce of the land itself, or in that which is exchanged for what the land brings forth.

Here, again, we have further proof that private ownership is in accordance with the law of nature. Truly, that which is required for the preservation of life, and for life's well-being, is produced in great abundance from the soil, but not until man has brought it into cultivation and expended upon it his solicitude and skill. Now, when man thus turns the activity of his mind and the strength of his body towards procuring the fruits of nature, by such act he makes his own that portion of nature's field which he cultivates— that portion on which he leaves, as it were, the impress of his individuality; and it cannot but be just that he should possess that portion as his very own, and have a right to hold it without any one being justified in violating that right.

Refutation of False Opinions

So strong and convincing are these arguments, that it seems amazing that some should not be setting up anew certain obsolete opinions in opposition to what is here laid down. They assert that it is right for private persons to have the use of the soil and its various fruits, but that it is unjust for any one to possess outright either the land on which he has built, or the estate which he has brought under cultivation. But those who deny these rights do not perceive that they are defrauding man of what his own labour has produced. For the soil which is tilled and cultivated with toil and skill utterly changes its condition; it was wild before, now it is fruitful; was barren, but now brings forth in abundance. That which has thus altered and improved the land becomes so truly part of itself as to be in great measure indistinguishable and inseparable from it. Is it just that the fruit of a man's own sweat and labour should be possessed and enjoyed by any one else? As effects follow their cause, so is it just and right that the results of labour should belong to those who have bestowed their labour.

Private Property in accord with the Natural and Divine Law

With reason, then, the common opinion of mankind, little affected by the few dissentients who have contended for the opposite view, has found in the careful study of nature, and in the laws of nature, the foundations of the division of property, and the practice of all ages has consecrated the principle of private ownership, as being pre-eminently in conformity with human nature, and as conducing in the most unmistakable manner to the peace and tranquillity of human existence. The same principle is confirmed and enforced by the civil laws—laws which, so long as they are just, derive from the law of nature their binding force. The authority of the Divine Law adds its sanction, forbidding us in severest terms even to covet that which is another's:—*Thou shalt not covet thy neighbour's wife; nor his house, nor his field, nor his man-servant, nor his maid-servant, nor his ox, nor his ass, nor anything that is his.*

The Family a True Society

The rights here spoken of, belonging to each individual man, are seen in much stronger light when considered in relation to man's social and domestic obligations. In choosing a state of life, it is indisputable that all are at full liberty to follow the counsel of Jesus Christ as to observing virginity, or to bind themselves by the marriage tie. No human law can abolish the natural and orignal right of marriage, nor in any way limit the chief and principal purpose of marriage, ordained by God's authority from the beginning: *Increase and multiply.* Hence we have the family; the "society" of a man's house—a society very small, one must admit, but none the less a true society, and one older than any State. Consequently it has rights and duties peculiar to itself which are quite independent of the State.

The Right to Private Property proved from the Family

That right to property, therefore, which has been proved to belong naturally to individual persons, must in like wise belong to a man in his capacity of head of a family; nay, that right is all the more valid in proportion as human personality in the life of the family takes various forms. For it is a most sacred law of nature that a father should provide food and all necessaries for those whom he has begotten; and, similarly, it is natural that he should wish that his children, who carry on, so to speak, and continue his personality, should be by him provided with all that is needful to enable them to keep themselves decently from want and misery amid the uncertainties of this mortal life. Now in no other way can a father effect this except by the ownership of productive property, which he can transmit to his children by inheritance. A family, no less than a State, is, as We have said, a true society, governed by an authority peculiar to itself, that is to say, by the authority of the father. Provided, therefore, the limits which are prescribed by the very purposes for which it exists be not transgressed, the family has at least equal rights with the State in the choice and pursuit of the things needful to its preservation and its just liberty.

The Rights of the Family

We say, at least equal rights; for inasmuch as the domestic household is antecedent, as well in idea as in fact, to the gathering of men into a community, the family must necessarily have rights and duties which are prior to those of the community, and founded more immediately in nature. If the citizens of a State—in other words the families—on entering into association and fellowship, were to experience at the hands of the State hindrance instead of help, and were to find their rights attacked instead of being upheld, that association (viz., the State) would rightly be an object of detestation, rather than of desire.

The Duty of the State towards the Family

The contention, then, that the civil government should at its option intrude into and exercise intimate control over the family and the household, is a great and pernicious error. True, if a family finds itself in exceeding distress, utterly deprived of the counsel of friends, and without any prospect of extricating itself, it is right that extreme necessity be met by public aid, since each family is a part of the commonwealth. In like manner, if within the precincts of the household there occur grave disturbance of mutual rights, public authority should intervene to force each party to yield to the other its proper due; for this is not to deprive citizens of their rights, but justly and properly to safeguard and strengthen them. But the rulers of the State must go no further: here nature bids them stop. Paternal authority can be neither abolished nor absorbed by the State; for it has the same source as human life itself. "The child belongs to the father," and is, as it were, the continuation of the father's personality; and, speaking strictly, the child takes its place in civil society, not of its own right, but in its quality as member of the family in which it is born. And for the very reason that "the child belongs to the father," it is, as St. Thomas of Aquin says, "before it attains the use of free will, under the power and the charge of its parents." The Socialists, therefore, in setting aside the parent and setting up a State supervision, act *against natural justice*, and break into pieces the stability of all family life.

Undue State Interference Mischievous

And not only is such interference unjust, but it is quite certain to harass and worry all classes of citizens, and subject them to odious and intolerable bondage. It would throw open the door to envy, to mutual invective, and to discord; the sources of wealth themselves would run dry, for no one would have any interest in exerting his talents or his industry; and that ideal equality about which they entertain pleasant dreams would be in reality the levelling down of all to a like condition of misery and degradation.

Hence it is clear that the main tenet of Socialism, community of goods, must be utterly rejected, since it only injures those whom it would seem meant to benefit, is directly contrary to the natural rights of mankind, and would introduce confusion and disorder into the commonweal. The first and most fundamental principle, therefore, if one would undertake to alleviate the condition of the masses, must be the inviolability of private property. This being established, we proceed to show where the remedy sought for must be found.

No Practical Solution without Religion and the Church

We approach the subject with confidence, and in the exercise of the rights which manifestly appertain to Us, for no practical solution of this question will be found apart from the intervention of Religion and of the Church. It is We who are the chief guardian of Religion and the chief dispenser of what pertains to the Church: and by keeping silence we would seem to neglect the duty incumbent on us. Doubtless this most serious question demands the attention and the efforts of others besides ourselves— to wit, of the rulers of States, of employers of labour, of the wealthy, aye, of the working classes themselves, for whom We are pleading. But We affirm without hesitation that all the striving of men will be vain if they leave out the Church. It is the Church that insists, on the authority of the Gospel, upon those teachings whereby the conflict can be brought to an end, or rendered, at least, far less bitter; the Church uses her efforts not only to enlighten the mind, but to direct by her precepts the life and conduct of each and all; the Church improves and betters the condition of the working-man by means of numerous organizations; does her best to enlist the services of all classes in discussing and endeavouring to further in the most practical way, the interests of the working classes; and considers that for this purpose recourse should be had, in due measure and degree, to the intervention of the law and of State authority.

Inequalities are inevitable

It must be first of all recognized that the condition of things inherent in human affairs must be borne with, for it is impossible to reduce civil society to one dead level. Socialists may in that intent do their utmost, but all striving against nature is in vain. There naturally exist among mankind manifold differences of the most important kind; people differ in capacity, skill, health, strength; and unequal fortune is a necessary result of unequal condition. Such inequality is far from being disadvantageous either to individuals or to the community. Social and public life can only be maintained by means of varous kinds of capacity for business and the playing of many parts; and each man, as a rule, chooses the part which suits his own peculiar domestic condition. As regards bodily labour, even had man never fallen from *the state of innocence*, he would not have remained wholly unoccupied; but that which would then have been his free choice and his delight, became afterwards compulsory, and the painful expiation for his disobedience. *Cursed be the earth in thy work; in thy labour thou shalt eat of it all the days of thy life.*

To Suffer and Endure is the lot of Men

In like manner, the other pains and hardships of life will have no end or cessation on earth; for the consequences of sin are bitter and hard to bear, and they must accompany man so long as life lasts. To suffer and to endure, therefore, is the lot of humanity; let them strive as they may, no strength and no artifice will ever succeed in banishing from human life the ills and troubles which beset it. If any there are who pretend differently—who hold out to a hard-pressed people the boon of freedom from pain and trouble, an undisturbed repose, and constant enjoyment—they delude the people and impose upon them, and their lying promises will only one day bring forth evils worse than the present. Nothing is more useful that to look upon the world as it really is—and at the same time to seek elsewhere, as we have said, for the solace to its troubles.

Class War Wrong. Duties of Working-man and Employer

The great mistake made in regard to the matter now under consideration, is to take up with the notion that class is naturally hostile to class, and that the wealthy and the working men are intended by nature to live in mutual conflict. So irrational and so false is this view, that the direct contrary is the truth. Just as the symmetry of the human frame is the result of the suitable arrangement of the different parts of the body, so in a State is it ordained by nature that these two classes should dwell in harmony and agreement, so as to maintain the balance of the body politic. Each needs the other: Capital cannot do without Labour, nor Labour without Capital. Mutual agreement results in the beauty of good order; while perpetual conflict necessarily produces confusion and savage barbarity. Now, in preventing such strife as this, and in uprooting it, the efficacy of Christian institutions is marvellous and manifold. First of all, there is no intermediary more powerful than Religion (whereof the Church is the interpreter and guardian) in drawing the rich and the working class together, by reminding each of its duties to the other, and especially of the obligations of justice. Thus Religion teaches the labourer and the artisan to carry out honestly and fairly all equitable agreements freely entered into; never to injure the property, nor to outrage the person, of an employer; never to resort to violence in defending their own cause, nor to engage in riot or disorder; and to have nothing to do with men of evil pinciples, who work upon the people with artful promises of great results, and excite foolish hopes which usually end in useless regrets and grievous loss. Religion teaches the wealthy owner and the employer that their work-people are not to be accounted their bondsmen; that in every man they must respect his dignity and worth as a man and as a Christian; that labour for wages is not a thing to be ashamed of, if we lend ear to right reason and to Christian philosophy, but is to a man's credit, enabling him to earn his living in an honourable way; and that it is shameful and inhuman to treat men like chattels to make money by, or to look upon them merely as so much muscle or physical strenght. Again the Church teaches that, in dealing with the working man religion and the good of his soul must be kept in mind. Hence the employer is bound to see that the worker has time for his religious duties; that he be not exposed to corrupting influences and dangerous occasions; and that he be not led away to neglect his home and family, or to squander his earnings. Furthermore, the employer must never tax his work-people beyond their strength, or employ them in work unsuited to their sex or age. His great and principal duty is to give every one what is just. Doubtless before deciding whether wages are fair, many things have to be considered; but wealthy owners and all masters of labour should be mindful of this—that to exercise pressure upon the indigent and the destitute for the sake of gain, and to gather one's profit out of the need of another, is condemned by all laws, human and devine. To defraud any one of wages that are his due is a crime which cries to the avenging anger of Heaven. *Behold, the hire of the labourers . . . which by fraud has been kept back by you, crieth; and the cry of them hath entered into the ears of the Lord of Sabaoth.* Lastly, the rich must religiously refrain from cutting down the workmen's earnings, whether by force, by fraud, or by usurious dealing; and with all the greater reason because the labouring man is, as a rule, weak and unprotected, and because his slender means should in proportion to their scantiness be accounted sacred.

Were these precepts carefully obeyed and followed out, would they not be sufficient of themselves to keep under all strife and all its causes?

The Church teaches the True Value of Things

But the Church, with Jesus Christ as her Master and Guide, aims higher still. She lays down precepts yet more perfect, and tries to bind class to class in friendliness and good feeling. The things of earth cannot be understood or valued aright without taking into consideration the life to come, the life that will know no death. Exclude the idea of futurity, and forthwith the very notion of what is good and right would perish; nay, the whole scheme of the universe would become a dark and unfathomable mystery. The great truth which we learn from Nature herself is also the grand Christian dogma on which Religion rests as on its foundation—that when we have given up this present life, then shall we really begin to live. God has not created for us the perishable and transitory things of earth, but for things heavenly and everlasting; He has given us this world as a place of exile, and not as our abiding-place. As for riches and the other things which men call good and desirable, whether we have them in abundance, or are lacking in them—so far as eternal happiness is concerned—it makes no difference, the only important thing is to use them aright. Jesus Christ, when He redeemed us with *plentiful redemption,* took not away the pains and sorrows which in such large proportion are woven together in the web of our mortal life. He transformed them into motives of virtue and occasions of merit: and no man can hope for eternal reward unless he follow in the blood-stained footprints of his Saviour. *If we suffer with Him, we shall also reign with Him.* Christ's labours and sufferings, accepted of His own free will, have marvellously sweetened all suffering and all labour. And not only by His example, but by His grace and by the hope held forth of everlasting recompense, has He made pain and grief more easy to endure; *for that which is at present momentary and light of our tribulation, worketh for us above measure exceedingly an eternal weight of glory.*

The Right Use of Money. Almsgiving

Therefore those whom fortune favours are warned that riches do not bring freedom from sorrow and are of no avail for eternal happiness, but rather are obstacles; that the rich should tremble at the threatenings of Jesus Christ—threatenings so unwonted in the mouth of our Lord—and that a most strict account must be given to the Supreme Judge for all we possess. The chief and most excellent rule for the right use of money is one which the heathen philosophers hinted at, but which the Church has traced out clearly, and has not only made known to men's minds, but has impressed upon their lives. It rests on the principle that it is one thing to have a right to the possession of money, and another to have a right to use money as one wills. Private ownership, as we have seen, is the natural right of man; and to exercise that right, especially as members of society, is not only lawful, but absolutely necessary. "It is lawful," says St. Thomas of Aquin, "for a man to hold private property; and it is also necessary for the carrying on of human existence." But if the question be asked, How must one's possessions be used? the Church replies without hesitation in the words of the same holy Doctor: "Man should not consider his material possessions as his own, but as common to all, so as to share them without hesitation when others are in need. Whence the Apostle saith, Command the rich of this world . . . to offer with no stint, to apportion largely." True, no one is commanded to distribute to others that which is required for his own needs and those of his household; nor even to give away what is reasonably required to keep up becomingly his condition in life; "for no one ought to live other than becomingly." But when what necessity demands has been supplied, and one's standing fairly taken thought for, it becomes a duty to give the indigent out of what remains over. *Of that which remaineth, give alms.* It is a duty, not of justice (save in extreme cases), but of Christian charity—a duty not enforced by human law. But the laws and judgments of men must yield place to the laws and judgments of Christ the true God, who in many ways urges on His followers the practice of almsgiving—*It is more blessed to give than to receive;* and who will count a kindness done or refused to the poor as done or refused to Himself—*As long as you did it to one of My least brethren you did it to Me.* To sum up then what has been said:—Whoever has received from the Divine bounty a large share of temporal blessings, whether they be external and material, or gifts of the mind, has received them for the purpose of using them for the perfecting of his own nature, and, at the same time, that he may employ them, as the steward of God's Providence, for the benefit of others. "He that hath a talent," says St. Gregory the Great, "let him see that he hide it not; he that hath abundance, let him quicken himself to mercy and generosity; he that hath art and skill, let him do his best to share the use and the utility thereof with his neighbour."

Poverty and Work not Things to be ashamed of

As for those who possess not the gifts of fortune, they are taught by the Church that in God's sight poverty is no disgrace, and that there is nothing to be ashamed of in earning their bread by labour. This is enforced by what we see in Christ Himself, who, *whereas He was rich, for our sakes became poor;* and who, being the Son of God, and God Himself, chose to seem and to be considered the son of a carpenter—nay, did not disdain to spend a great part of His life as a carpenter Himself. *Is not this the carpenter, the son of Mary?*

The True Worth of Man

From contemplation of this Divine model, it is more easy to understand that the true worth and nobility of man lie in his moral qualities, that is, in virtue; that virtue is moreover the common inheritance of men, equally within the reach of high and low, rich and poor; and that virtue, and virtue alone, whenever found, will be followed by the rewards of everlasting happiness. Nay, God Himself seems to incline rather to those who suffer misfortune; for Jesus Christ calls the poor "blessed"; He lovingly invites those in labour and grief to come to Him for solace, and He displays the tenderest charity towards the lowly and the oppressed. These reflections cannot fail to keep down the pride of the well-to-do, and to give heart to the unfortunate; to move the former to be generous and the latter to be moderate in their desires. Thus the separation which pride would set up tends to disappear, nor will it be difficult to make rich and poor join hands in friendly concord.

But, if Christian precepts prevail, the respective classes will not only be united in the bonds of friendship, but also in those of brotherly love. For they will understand and feel that all men are children of the same common Father, who is God; that all have alike the same last end, which is God Himself, who alone can make either men or angels absolutely and perfectly happy; that each and all are redeemed and made sons of God, by Jesus Christ, *the first-born among many brethren;* that the blessings of nature and the gifts of grace belong to the whole human race in common, and that from none except the unworthy is withheld the inheritance of the Kingdom of Heaven. *If sons, heirs also; heirs indeed of God, and co-heirs with Christ.*

Such is the scheme of duties and of rights which is shown forth to the world by the Gospel. Would it not seem that, were Society penetrated with ideas like these, strife must quickly cease?

The Social Action of the Church

But the Church, not content with pointing out the remedy, also applies it. For the Church does her utmost to teach and to train men, and to educate them; and by the intermediary of her bishops and clergy diffuses her salutary teachings far and wide. She strives to influence the mind the heart so that all may willingly yield themselves to be formed and guided by the commandments of God. It is precisely in this fundamental and momentous matter, on which everything depends, that the Church possesses a power peculiarly her own. The agencies which she employs are given to her by Jesus Christ Himself for the very purpose of reaching the hearts of men, and derive their efficiency from God. They alone can reach the innermost heart and conscience, and bring men to act from a motive of duty, to control their passions and appetites, to love God and their fellow-men with a love that is outstanding and of the highest degree and to break down courageously every barrier which blocks the way to virtue.

The Witness of History

On this subject we need but recall for one moment the examples recorded in history. Of these facts there cannot be any shadow of doubt: for instance, that civil society was renovated in every part by the teachings of Christianity; that in the strength of that renewal the human race was lifted up to better things—nay, that it was brought back from death to life, and to so excellent a life that nothing more perfect had been known before, or will come to be known in the ages that have yet to be. Of this beneficent transformation, Jesus Christ was at once the first Cause and the final End; as from Him all came, so to Him was all to be brought back. For when the human race, by the light of the Gospel message, came to know the grand mystery of the Incarnation of the Word and the redemption of man, at once the life of Jesus Christ, God and Man, pervaded every race and nation, and interpenetrated them with His faith, His precepts, and His laws. And if Society is to be healed now, in no other way can it be healed save by a return to Christian life and Christian institutions. When a society is perishing, the wholesome advice to give to those who would restore it is to call it to the principles from which it sprang; for the purpose and perfection of an association is to aim at and to attain that for which it was formed; and its efforts should be put in motion and inspired by the end and object which orignally gave it being. Hence to fall away from its primal constitution implies disease: to go back to it, recovery. And this may be asserted with utmost truth both of the State in general and of that body of its citizens—by far the great majority—who get their living by their labour.

The Church not concerned with the Soul alone

Neither must it be supposed that the solicitude of the Church is so preoccupied with the spiritual concerns of her children as to neglect their temporal and earthly interests. Her desire is that the poor, for example, should rise above poverty and wretchedness, and better their condition in life; and for this she makes a strong endeavour. By the very fact that she calls men to virtue and forms them to its practice, she promotes this in no slight degree. Christian morality, when adequately and completely practised, leads of itself to temporal prosperity, for it merits the blessing of that God who is the source of all blessings; it powerfully restrains the greed of possession and the thirst for pleasure—twin plagues, which too often make a man who is void of self-restraint miserable in the midst of abundance; it makes men supply for the lack of means through economy, teaching them to be content with frugal living, and further, keeping them out of the reach of those vices which devour not small incomes merely, but large fortunes, and dissipate many a goodly inheritance.

The Church's Care of the Poor

The Church, moreover, intervenes directly in behalf of the poor, by setting on foot and maintaining many associations which she knows to be efficient for the relief of poverty. Herein again she has always succeeded so well as to have even extorted the praise of her enemies. Such was the ardour of brotherly love among the earliest Christians that numbers of those who were in better circumstances despoiled themselves of their possessions in order to relieve their brethren; whence *neither was there any one needy among them.* To the order of deacons, instituted in that very intent, was committed by the Apostles the charge of the daily doles; and the Apostle Paul, though burdened with the solicitude of all the churches, hesitated not to undertake laborious journeys in order to carry the alms of the faithful to the poorer Christians. Tertullian calls these contributions, given voluntarily by Christians in their assemblies, deposits of piety; because, to cite his own words, they were employed "in feeding the needy, in burying them, in the support of youths and maidens destitute of means and deprived of their parents, in the care of the aged, and the relief of the shipwrecked."

Thus by degrees came into existence the patrimony which the Church has guarded with religious care as the inheritance of the poor. Nay, to spare them the shame of begging, the common Mother of rich and poor has exerted herself to gather together funds for the support of the needy. The Church has aroused everywhere the heroism of charity, and has established congregations of religious and many other useful institutions for help and mercy, so that hardly any kind of suffering could exist which was not afforded relief. At the present day many there are who, like the heathen of old, seek to blame and condemn the Church for such eminent charity. They would substitute in its stead a system of relief organized by the State. But no human expedients will ever make up for the devotedness and self-sacrifice of Christian charity. Charity, as a virtue, pertains to the Church; for virtue it is not, unless it be drawn from the Sacred Heart of Jesus Christ; and whosoever turns his back on the Church cannot be near to Christ.

It cannot, however, be doubted that to attain the purpose we are treating of, not only the Church, but all human agencies must concur. All who are concerned in the matter should be of one mind and according to their ability act together. It is with this, as with the Providence that governs the world; the results of causes do not usually take place save where all the causes co-operate.

It is sufficient, therefore, to inquire what part the State should play in the work of remedy and relief.

The Social Action of the State

By the State we here understand, not the particular form of government prevailing in this or that nation, but the State as rightly apprehended; that is to say, any government conformable in its institutions to right reason and natural law, and to those dictates of the Divine wisdom which we have expounded in the Encyclical on "The Christian Constitution of the State."

The foremost duty, therefore, of the rulers of the State should be to make sure that the laws and institutions, the general character and administration of the commonwealth, shall be such as of themselves to realize public well being and private prosperity. This is the proper scope of wise statesmanship and is the work of the heads of the State. Now a State chiefly prospers and thrives through moral rule, well-regulated family life, respect for religion and justice, the moderation and fair imposing of public taxes, the progress of the arts and of trade, the abundant yield of the land—through everything, in fact, which makes the citizens better and happier. Hereby, then, it lies in the power of a ruler to benefit every class in the State, and amongst the rest to promote to the utmost the interests of the poor; and this in virtue of his office, and without being open to any suspicion of undue interference—since it is the province of the State to consult the common good. And the more that is done for the benefit of the working classes by the general laws of the country, the less need will there be to seek for special means to relieve them.

The Interests of All to be Safeguarded

There is another and deeper consideration which must not be lost sight of. As regards the State, the interests of all, whether high or low, are equal. The working classes are by nature members of the State equally with the rich: they are real living parts which make up through the family the body of the State; and it need hardly be said that they are in every State very largely in the majority. It would be irrational to neglect one portion of the citizens and favour another; and therefore the public administration must duly and solicitously provide for the welfare and the comfort of the working classes; otherwise that law of justice will be violated which ordains that each man shall have his due. To cite the wise words of St. Thomas of Aquin: "As the part and the whole are in a certain sense identical, so that what belongs to the whole in a sense belongs to the part." Among the many and grave duties of rulers who would do their best for the people, the first and chief is to act with strict justice—with that justice which is called by the Schoolmen *distributive*—towards each and every class alike.

The Duty of the State towards the Working Class

But although all citizens, without exception, can and ought to contribute to that common good in which individuals share so advantageously to themselves, yet it should not be supposed that all can contribute in the like way and to the same extent. No matter what changes may occur in forms of government, there will ever be differences and inequalities of condition in the State. Society cannot exist or be conceived of without them. Some there must be who devote themselves to the work of the commonwealth, who make the laws or administer justice, or whose advice and authority govern the nation in times of peace, and defend it in war. Such men clearly occupy the foremost place in the State, and should be held in highest estimation, for their work concerns most nearly and effectively the general interests of the community. Those who labour at a trade or calling do not promote the general welfare in such measure as this; but they benefit the nation, if less directly, in a most important manner. We have insisted, it is true, that, since the end of Society is to make men better, the chief good that Society can possess is Virtue. Nevertheless, it is the business of all well-constituted States to seee to the provision of those material and external helps *the use of which is necessary to virtuous action.* Now for the provision of such commodities, the labour of the working class—the exercise of their skill, and the employment of their strength, in the cultivation of the land, and in the workshops of trade—is especially responsible and quite indispensable. Indeed, their co-operation is in this respect so important that it may be truly said that it is only by the labour of working-men that States grow rich. Justice, therefore, demands that the interests of the working classes should be carefully watched over by the administration, so that they who contribute so largely to the advantage of the community may themselves share in the benefits which they create—that being housed, clothed, and bodily fit, they may find their life less hard and more endurable. It follows that whatever shall appear to prove conducive to the well-being of those who work should obtain favourable consideration. There is no fear that solicitude of this kind will be harmful to any interest: on the contrary, it will be to the advantage of all; for it cannot but be good for the common wealth to shield from misery those on whom it so largely depends for the things that it needs.

We have said that the State must not absorb the indivdual or the family; both should be allowed free and untrammelled action so far as is consistent with the common good and the interests of others. Rulers should, nevertheless, anxiously safeguard the community and all its members; the community, because the conservation thereof is so emphatically the business of the supreme power, that the safety of the commonwealth is not only the first law, but it is a government's whole reason of existence; and the members, because both philosophy and the Gospel concur in laying down that the object of the government of the State should be, not the advantage of the ruler, but the benefit of those over whom he is placed. As the power to rule comes from God, and is, as it were, a participation in His, the highest of all sovereignties, it should be exercised as the power of God is exercised— with a fatherly solicitude which not only guides the whole, but reaches also to details.

When the State should interfere

Whenever the general interest or any particular class suffers, or is threatened with harm, which can in no other way be met or prevented, the public authority must step in to deal with it. Now, it is to the interest of the State, as well as of the individual, that peace and good order should be main-

tained; that family life should be carried on in accordance with God's laws
and those of nature; that Religon should be reverenced and obeyed; that a
high standard of morality should prevail, both in public and private life;
that justice should be held sacred and that no one should injure another
with impunity; that the members of the commonwealth should grow up to
man's estate strong and robust, and capable, if need be, of guarding and
defending their country. If by a strike, or other combination of workmen,
there should be imminent danger of disturbance to the public peace; or if
circumstances were such as that among the working class the ties of family
life were relaxed; if Religon were found to suffer through the workers not
having time and opportunity afforded them to practise its duties; if in
workshops and factories there were danger to morals through the mixing
of the sexes or from other harmful occasions of evil; or if employers laid
burdens upon their workmen which were unjust, or degraded them with
conditions repugnant to their dignity as human beings; finally, if health
were endangered by excessive labour, or by work unsuited to sex or age—in
such cases, there can be no question but that, within certain limits, it would
be right to invoke the aid and authority of the law. The limits must be determined by the nature of the occasion which calls for the law's interference—
the principle being that the law must not undertake more, nor proceed
further, than is required for the remedy of the evil or the removal of
the mischief.

The Poor have a Special Claim on the State

Rights must be religiously respected wherever they exist; and it is the
duty of the public authority to prevent and to punish injury, and to protect
every one in the possession of his own. Still, when there is question of defending the rights of individuals, the poor and badly-off have a claim to
especial consideration. The richer class have many ways of shielding themselves, and stand less in need of help from the State; whereas the mass of
the poor have no resources of their own to fall back upon, and must chiefly
depend upon the assistance of the State. And it is for this reason that wage-
earners, since they mostly belong to that class, should be specially cared
for and protected by the Government.

Private Property to be Safeguarded

Here, however, it is expedient to bring under special notice certain
matters of moment. The chief thing is the duty of safeguarding private
property by legal enactment and protection. Most of all it is essential, where
the passion of greeed is so strong, to keep the people within the line of duty;
for if all may justly strive to better their conditon, neither justice nor the
common good allows any individual to seize upon that which belongs to
another, or, under the futile and shallow pretext of equality, to lay violent
hands on other people's possessions. Most true it is that by far the larger

part of the workers prefer to better themselves by honest labour rather than by doing any wrong to others. But there are not a few who are imbued with evil principles and eager for revolutionary change, whose main purpose is to stir up disorder and incite their fellows to acts of violence. The authority of the State should intervene to put restraint upon such fire-brands, to save the working classes from being led astray by their manoeuvres, and to protect lawful owners from spoliation.

Strikes, their Causes and Effects

When work-people have recourse to a strike, it is frequently because the hours of labour are too long, or the work too hard, or because they consider their wages insufficient. The grave inconvenience of this not uncommon occurrence should be obviated by public remedial measures; for such paralyzing of labour not only affects the masters and their work-people alike, but is extremely injurious to trade and to the general interests of the public; moreover, on such occasions, violence and disorder are generally not far distant, and thus it frequently happens that the public peace is imperilled. The laws should forestall and prevent such troubles from arising; they should lend their influence and authority to the removal in good time of the causes which lead to conflicts between employers and employed.

The Spiritual Interests of the Working-man to be Safeguarded

The working-man too has interests in which he should be protected by the State; and first of all, there are the interests of his soul. Life on earth, however good and desirable in itself, is not the final purpose for which man is created; it is only the way and the means to that attainment of truth and that love of goodness in which the full life of the soul consists. It is the soul which is made after the image and likeness of God; it is in the soul that the sovereignty resides in virtue whereof man is commanded to rule the creatures below him and to use all the earth and the ocean for his profit and advantage. *Fill the earth and subdue it; and rule over the fishes of the sea, and the fowls of the air, and all living creatures that move upon the earth.* In this respect all men are equal; there is here no difference between rich and poor, master and servant, ruler and ruled, *for the same is Lord over all.* No man may with impunity outrage that human dignity which God Himself treats *with great reverence,* nor stand in the way of that higher life which is the preparation of the eternal life of heaven. Nay, more; no man has in this matter power over himself. To consent to any treatment which is calculated to defeat the end and purpose of his being is beyond his right; he cannot give up his soul to servitude; for it is not man's own rights which are here in question, but the rights of God, the most sacred and inviolable of rights.

From this follows the obligation of the cessation from work and labour on Sundays and certain holy days. The rest from labour is not to be understood as mere giving way to idleness; much less must it be an occasion for spending money and for vicious indulgence, as many would have it to be; but it should be rest from labour, hallowed by religion. Rest (combined with religious observances) disposes man to forget for a while the business of his everyday life, to turn his thoughts to things heavenly, and to the worship which he so strictly owes to the Eternal Godhead. It is this, above all, which is the reason and motive of Sunday rest; a rest sanctioned by God's great law of the Ancient Covenant—*Remember thou keep holy the Sabbath day,* and taught the world by His own mysterious "rest" after the creation of man: *He rested on the seventh day from all His work which He had done.*

The State and the Regulation of Work

If We turn now to things external and material, the first thing of all to secure is to save unfortunate working people from the cruelty of men of greed, who use human beings as mere instruments for money-making. It is neither just nor human so to grind men down with excessive labour as to stupefy their minds and wear out their bodies. Man's powers, like his general nature, are limited, and beyond these limits he cannot go. His strength is developed and increased by use and exercise, but only on condition of due intermission and proper rest. Daily labour, therefore, should be so regulated as not to be protracted over longer hours than strength admits. How many and how long the intervals of rest should be, must depend on the nature of the work, on circumstances of time and place, and on the health and strength of the workman. Those who work in mines and quarries, and extract coal, stone, and metals from the bowels of the earth, should have shorter hours in proportion as their labour is more severe and trying to health. Then, again, the season of the year should be taken into account; for not unfrequently a kind of labour is easy at one time which at another is intolerable or exceedingly difficult. Finally, work which is quite suitable for a strong man cannot rightly be required from a woman or a child. And, in regard to children, great care should be taken not to place them in workshops and factories until their bodies and minds are sufficiently developed. For just as very rough weather destroys the buds of spring, so does too early an experience of life's hard toil blight the young promise of a child's faculties, and render any true education impossible. Women, again, are not suited for certain occupations; a woman is by nature fitted for home-work, and it is that which is best adapted at once to preserve her modesty and to promote the good bringing-up of children and the well-being of the family. As a general principle it may be laid down that a workman ought to have leisure and rest proportionate to the wear and tear of his strength; for waste of strength must be repaired by cessation from hard work.

In all agreements between masters and work-people there is always the condition expressed or understood that there should be allowed proper rest for soul and body. To agree in any other sense would be against what is right and just; for it can never be just or right to require on the one side, or

to promise on the other, the giving up of those duties which a man owes to
his God and to himself.

The Living Wage

We now approach a subject of great importance, and one in respect of
which, if extremes are to be avoided, right notions are absolutely necessary.
Wages, as we are told, are regulated by free consent, and therefore the
employer, when he pays what was agreed upon, has done his part and
seemingly is not called upon to do anything beyond. The only way, it is said,
in which injustice might occur would be if the master refused to pay the
whole of the wages, or if the workman should not complete the work undertaken; in such cases the State should intervene, to see that each obtains his
due: but not under any other circumstances.

To this kind of argument a fair-minded man will not easily or entirely
assent: it is not complete, for there are important considerations which it
leaves out of account altogether. To labour is to exert oneself for the sake
of procuring what is necessary for the various purposes of life, and chief
of all for self-preservation. *In the sweat of thy face thou shalt eat bread.*
Hence a man's labour necessarily bears two notes or characters. First of all,
it is *personal,* inasmuch as the force which acts is bound up with the personality and is the exclusive property of him who acts, and, further, was given
to him for his advantage. Secondly, man's labour is *necessary;* for without
the result of labour a man cannot live; and self-preservation is a law of nature, which it is wrong to disobey. Now, were we to consider labour merely
in so far as it is *personal,* doubtless it would be whatsoever; for in the same
way as he is free to work or not, so is he free to accept a small wage or even
none at all. But our conclusion must be very different if together with the
personal element in a man's work we consider the fact that work is also
necessary for him to live: these two aspects of his work are separable in
thought, but not in reality. The preservation of life is the bounden duty of
one and all, and to be wanting therein is a crime. It necessarily follows that
each one has a natural right to procure what is required in order to live; and
the poor can procure that in no other way than by what they earn through
their work.

A Just Wage

Let the working man and the employer make free agreements, and in
particular let them agree freely as to the wages; nevertheless, there underlies a dictate of natural justice more imperious and ancient than any bargain between man and man, namely, that wages ought not to be insufficient
to support a frugal and well-behaved wage-earner. If through necessity
or fear of a worse evil the workman accept harder conditions because an
employer or contractor will afford him no better, he is made the victim of
force and injustice. In these and similar questions, however—such as, for
example, the hours of labour in different trades, the sanitary precautions

to be observed in factories and workshops, &c.—in order to supersede undue interference on the part of the State, especially as circumstances, times and localities differ so widely, it is advisable that recourse be had to Societies or Boards such as We shall mention presently, or to some other mode of safeguarding the interests of the wage-earners; the State being appealed to, should circumstances require, for its sanction and protection.

Owning Property to be encouraged

If a workman's wages be sufficient to enable him comfortably to support himself, his wife, and his children, he will find it easy, if he be a sensible man, to practise thrift; and he will not fail, by cutting down expenses, to put by some little savings and thus secure a modest source of income. Nature itself would urge him to this. We have seen that this great labour question cannot be solved save by assuming as a principle that private ownership must be held sacred and inviolable. The law, therefore, should favour ownership, and its policy should be to induce as many as possible of the people to become owners.

The Good Results of Ownership

Many excellent results will follow from this; and first of all, property will certainly become more equitably divided. For the result of civil change and revolution has been to divide society into two widely differing castes. On the one side there is the party which holds power because it holds wealth; which has in its grasp the whole of labour and trade; which manipulates for its own benefit and its own purposes all the sources of supply, and which is even represented in the councils of the State itself. On the other side there is the needy and powerless multitude, sick and sore in spirit and every ready for disturbance. If working people can be encouraged to look forward to obtaining a share in the land, the consequence will be that the gulf between vast wealth and sheer poverty will be bridged over, and the respective classes will be brought nearer to one another. A further consequence will result in the greater abundance of the fruits of the earth. Men always work harder and more readily when they work on that which belongs to them; nay, they learn to love the very soil that yields in response to the labour of their hands, not only food to eat, but an abundance of good things for themselves and those that are dear to them. That such a spirit of willing labour would add to the produce of the earth and to the wealth of the community is self-evident. And a third advantage would spring from this: men would cling to the country in which they were born; for no one would exchange his country for a foreign land if his own afforded him the means of living a decent and happy life. These three important benefit's, however, can be reckoned on only provided that a man's means be not drained and exhausted by excessive taxation. The right to possess private property is derived from nature, not from man; and the State has the right to control its use in the interests of the public good alone, but by no means to absorb it altogether. The State would therefore be unjust and cruel if under the name of taxation it were to deprive the private owner of more than is fair.

The Benefit of Helpful Organizations

In the last place—employers and workmen may of themselves effect much in the matter we are treating, by means of such associations and organizations as afford opportune aid to those who are in distress, and which draw the two classes more closely together. Among these may be enumerated societies for mutual help; various benevolent foundations established by private persons to provide for the workman, and for his widow or his orphans, in case of sudden calamity, in sickness, and in the event of death; and institutions for the welfare of boys and girls, young people and those more advanced in years.

Trade Unions

The most important of all are Working-men's Unions; for these virtually include all the rest. History attests what excellent results were brought about by the Artificers' Guilds of olden times. They were the means of affording not only many advantages to the workmen, but in no small degree of promoting the advancement of art, as numerous monuments remain to bear witness. Such Unions should be suited to the requirements of this our age—an age of wider education, of different habits, and of far more numerous requirements in daily life. It is gratifying to know that there are actually in existence not a few associations of this nature, consisting either of workmen alone, or of workmen and employers together; but it were greatly to be desired that they should become more numerous and more efficient. We have spoken of them more than once; yet it will be well to explain here how notably they are needed, to show that they exist of their own right, and what should be their organization and their mode of action.

The consciousness of his own weakness urges man to call in aid from without. We read in the pages of Holy Writ: *It is better that two should be together than one; for they have the advantage of their society. If one fall he shall be supported by the other. Woe to him that is alone, for when he falleth he hath none to life him up.* And further: *A brother that is helped by his brother is like a strong city.* It is this natural impulse which binds men together in civil society; and it is likewise this which leads them to join together in associations which are, it is true, lesser and not independent societies, but, nevertheless, real societies.

The Right to form Associations

These lesser societies and the society which constitutes the State differ in many respects, because their immediate purpose and aim is different. Civil society exists for the common good, and hence is concerned with the interests of all in general, albeit with individual interests also in their due place and degree. It is therefore called a *public* society, because by its agency, as St. Thomas of Aquin says, "Men establish relations in common with one another in the setting up of a commonwealth." But societies which are formed in the bosom of the State are styled *private*, and rightly so, since their immediate purpose is the private advantage of the associates. "Now a private society," says St. Thomas again, "is one which is formed for the purpose of carrying out private objects; as when two or three enter into partnership with the view of trading in common." Private societies, then, although they exist within the State, and are severally part of the State, cannot nevertheless be absolutely, and as such prohibted by the State. For to enter into a "society" of this kind is the natural right of man; and the State is bound to protect natural rights, not to destroy them; and if it forbid its citizens to form associations, it contradicts the very principle of its own existence; for both they and it exist in virtue of the like principle, namely, the natural tendency of man to dwell in society.

There are occasions, doubtless, when it is fitting that the law should intervene to prevent associations; as when men join together for purposes which are evidently bad, unlawful, or dangerous to the State. In such cases public authority may justly forbid the formation of associations, and may dissolve them if they already exist. But every precaution should be taken not to violate the rights of individuals and not to impose unreasonable regulations under pretense of public benefit. For laws only bind when they are in accordance with right reason, and hence with the eternal law of God.

The Rights of Associations in the Church

And here we are reminded of the confraternities, societies, and religious orders which have arisen by the Church's authority and the piety of Christian men. The annals of every nation down to our own days bear witness to what they have accomplished for the human race. It is indisputable that on grounds of reason alone such associations, being perfectly blameless in their objects, possess the sanction of the law of nature. In their religious aspect, they claim rightly to be responsible to the Church alone. The rulers of the State accordingly have no rights over them, nor can they claim any share in their control; on the contrary, it is the duty of the State to respect and cherish them, and, if need be, to defend them from attack. It is notorious that a very different course has been followed, more especially in our own times. In many places the State authorities have laid violent hands on these communities, and committed manifold injustice against them; it has placed them under control of the civil law, taken away their rights as corporate bodies, and despoiled them of their property. In such property the Church had her rights, each member of the body had his or her rights, and these were also the rights of those who had founded or endowed these communities for a definite purpose, and, furthermore, of those for whose benefit and assistance they had their being. Therefore We cannot refrain from complaining of such spoliation as unjust and fraught with evil results; and with all the more reason do We complain because, at the very time when the law proclaims that association is free to all, We see that Catholic societies, however peaceful and useful, are hampered in every way, whereas the utmost liberty is conceded to individuals whose purposes are at once hurtful to Religion and dangerous to the State.

Dangers of Some Associations

Associations of every kind, and especially those of working-men, are now far more common than heretofore. As regards many of these there is no need at present to inquire whence they spring, what are their objects, or what the means they employ. There is a good deal of evidence, however, which goes to prove that many of these societies are in the hands of secret leaders, and are managed on principles ill-according with Christianity and the public well-being; and that they do their utmost to get within their grasp the whole field of labour, and force working-men either to join them or to starve. Under these circumstances Christian working-men must do one of two things: either join associations in which their religion will be exposed to peril, or form associations among themselves—unite their forces and shake off courageously the yoke of so unrighteous and intolerable an oppression. No one who does not wish to expose man's chief good to extreme risk will for a moment hesitate to say that the second alternative should by all means be adopted.

Catholic Action praised

Those Catholics are worthy of all praise—and they are not a few—who, understanding what the times require, have striven, by various undertakings and endeavours, to better the condition of the working-class by rightful means. They have taken up the cause of the working-man, and have spared no efforts to better the condition both of families and individuals; to infuse a spirit of equity into the mutual relations of employers and employed; to keep before the eyes of both classes the precepts of duty and the laws of the Gospel—that Gospel which, by inculcating self-restraint, keeps men within the bounds of moderation, and tends to establish harmony among the divergent interests and the various classes which compose the State. It is with such ends in view that we see men of eminence meeting together for discussion, for the promotion of concerted action, and for practical work. Others, again, strive to unite working-men of various grades into associations, help them with their advice and means, and enable them to obtain fitting and profitable employment. The bishops, on their part, bestow their ready good-will and support; and with their approval and guidance many members of the clergy, both secular and regular, labour assiduously in behalf of the spiritual and mental interests of the members of such associations. And there are not wanting Catholics blessed with affluence, who have, as it were, cast in their lot with the wage-earners, and who have spent large sums in founding and widely spreading benefit and insurance societies, by means of which the working-man may without difficulty acquire through his labour not only many present advantages, but also the certainty of honourable support in days to come. How greatly such manifold and earnest activity has benefited the community at large is too well known to require Us to dwell upon it. We find therein grounds for most cheering hope in the future, provided always that the associations We have described continue to grow and spread, and are well and wisely administered. The State should watch over these societies of citizens banded together in accordance with their rights; but it should not thrust itself into their peculiar concerns and their organization; for things move and live by the spirit inspiring them, and may be killed by the rough grasp of a hand from without.

The Marks of a Good Association

In order that an association may be carried on with unity of purpose and harmony of action, its administration and government should be firm and wise. All such societies, being free to exist, have the further right to adopt such rules and organization as may best conduce to the attainment of their respective objects. We do not judge it possible to enter into minute particulars touching the subject of organization: this must depend on national character, on practice and experience, on the nature and aim of the work to be done, on the scope of the various trades and employments, and on other circumstances of fact and of time:—all of which should be carefully considered.

Duties of Associations

To sum up, then, We may lay it down as a general and lasting law, that working-men's associations should be so organized and governed as to furnish the best and most suitable means for attaining what is aimed at, that is to say, for helping each individual member to better his condition to the utmost in body, soul, and property. It is clear that they must pay special and chief attention to the duties of religion and morality, and that social betterment should have this chiefly in view; otherwise they would lose wholly their special character, and end by becoming little better than those societies which take no account whatever of Religion. What advantage can it be to a working-man to obtain by means of a society material well-being, if he endangers his soul for lack of spiritual food? *What doth it profit a man, if he gain the whole world and suffer the loss of his own soul?* This, as our Lord teaches, is the mark or character that distinguishes the Christian from the heathen. *After all these things do the heathen seek. . . . Seek ye first the Kingdom of God and His justice: and all these things shall be added unto you.* Let our associations, then, look first and before all things to God; let religious instruction have therein the foremost place, each one being carefully taught what is his duty to God, what he has to believe, what to hope for, and how he is to work out his salvation: and let all be warned and strengthened with special care against wrong principles and false teaching. Let the working-man be urged and led to the worship of God, to the earnest practice of religion, and among other things, to the keeping holy of Sundays and holy days. Let him learn to reverence and love holy Church, the common mother of us all; and hence to obey the precepts of the Church, and to frequent the sacraments, since they are the means ordained by God for obtaining forgiveness of sin and for leading a holy life.

Activities of Associations

The foundations of the organization being thus laid in religion, We next proceed to make clear the relations of the members one to another, in order that they may live together in concord and go forward prosperously and with good results. The offices and charges of the society should be apportioned for the good of the society itself, and in such mode that difference in degree or standing should not interfere with unanimity and good-will. It is most important that office-bearers be appointed with due prudence and discretion, and each one's charge carefully mapped out, in order that no member may suffer harm. The common funds must be administered with strict honesty, in such a way that a member may receive assistance in proportion to his necessities. The rights and duties of the employers, as compared with the rights and duties of the employed, ought to be the subject of careful consideration. Should it happen that either a master or a workman believes himself injured, nothing would be more desirable than that a committee should be appointed composed of reliable and capable members of the association, whose duty would be, conformably with the rules of the association, to settle the dispute. Among the several purposes of a society, one should be to try to arrange for a continuous supply of work at all times and seasons; as well as to create a fund out of which the members may be effectually helped in their needs, not only in the cases of accident, but also in sickness, old age, and distress.

Social Benefits

Such rules and regulations, if willingly obeyed by all, will sufficiently ensure the well-being of the less well-to-do; whilst such mutual associations among Catholics are certain to be productive in no small degree of prosperity to the State. It is not rash to conjecture the future from the past. Age gives way to age, but the events of one century are wonderfully like those of another; for they are directed by the Providence of God, who overrules the course of history in accordance with His purposes in creating the race of man. We are told that it was cast as a reproach on the Christians in the early ages of the Church that the greater number among them had to live by begging or by labour. Yet, destitute though they were of wealth and influence, they ended by winning over to their side the favour of the rich and the good-will of the powerful. They showed themselves industrious, hard-working, assiduous, and peaceful, ruled by justice, and, above all, bound together in brotherly love. In presence of such mode of life and such exemple, prejudice gave way, the tongue of malevolence was silenced, and the lying legends of ancient superstition little by little yielded to Christian truth.

At the time being, the condition of the working-classes is the pressing question of the hour; and nothing can be of higher interest to all classes of the State than that it should be rightly and reasonably settled. But it will be easy for Christian working-men to solve it aright if they will form associations, choose wise guides, and follow on the path which with so much advantage to themselves and the commonweal was trodden by their fathers before them. Prejudice, it is true, is mighty, and so is the greed of money; but if the sense of what is just and rightful be not deliberately stifled, their fellow-citizens are sure to be won over to a kindly feeling towards men whom they see to be in earnest as regards their work and who prefer so unmistakably right dealing to mere lucre, and the sacredness of duty to every other consideration.

Advantages to lax or lapsed Catholic workers

And further great advantage would result from the state of things We are describing; there would exist so much more ground for hope, and likelihood even, of recalling to a sense of their duty those working-men who have either given up their faith altogether, or whose lives are at variance with its precepts. Such men feel in most cases that they have been fooled by empty promises and deceived by false pretexts. They cannot but perceive that their grasping employers too often treat them with great inhumanity and hardly care for them outside the profit their labour brings; and if they belong to any union, it is probably one in which there exists, instead of charity and love, that intestine strife which ever accompanies poverty when unresigned and unsustained by religion. Broken in spirit and worn down in body, how many of them would gladly free themselves from such galling bondage! But human respect, or the dread of starvation, makes them tremble to take the step. To such as these, Catholic associations are of incalculable service, by helping them out of their difficulties, inviting them to companionship and receiving the returning wanderers to a haven where they may securely find repose.

Summary and Conclusion

We have now laid before you, Venerable Brethren, both who are the persons, and what are the means whereby this most arduous question must be solved. Every one should put his hand to the work which falls to his share, and that at once and straightway, lest the evil which is already so great become through delay absolutely beyond remedy. Those who rule the State should avail themselves of the laws and institutions of the country; masters and wealthy owners must be mindful of their duty; the working class, whose interests are at stake, should make every lawful and proper effort; and since religion alone, as We said at the beginning, can avail to destroy the evil at its root, all men should rest persuaded that the main thing needful is to return to real Christianity, apart from which all the plans and devices of the wisest will prove of little avail.

In regard to the Church, her co-operation will never be found lacking, be the time or the occasion what it may; and she will intervene with all the greater effect in proportion as her liberty of action is the more unfettered. Let this be carefully taken to heart by those whose office it is to safeguard the public welfare. Every minister of holy religion must bring to the struggle the full energy of his mind and all his power of endurance. Moved by your authority, Venerable Brethren, and quickened by your example, they should never cease to urge upon men of every class, upon the high-placed as well as the lowly, the Gospel doctrines of Christian life; by every means in their power they must strive to secure the good of the people; and above all must earnestly cherish in themselves, and try to arouse in others, charity, the mistress and the queen of virtues. For the happy results we all long for must be chiefly brought about by the plenteous outpouring of charity; of that true Christian charity which is the fulfilling of the whole Gospel law, which is always ready to sacrifice itself for others' sake, and is man's surest antidote against worldly pride and immoderate love of self; that charity whose office is described and whose Godlike features are outlined by the Apostle St. Paul in these words: *Charity is patient, is kind, . . . seeketh not her own, . . . suffereth all things, . . . endureth all things.*

The Challenge to Religion:
Renan and History

Joseph Ernest Renan, "Preface," Studies of Religious History (London: William Heinemann, 1893), pp. xi–xxxi.

An easy if incorrect equation has often been drawn in which nineteenth-century scientific advances are set in direct ratio to the erosion of religious faith. Few read Lyell or Chambers or Darwin, glanced up from the last page, and found themselves bereft of belief. The impact of science was considerable; astronomy, geology, and biology rocked traditional Christian cosmogony. But religious doubt, as more than one historian has emphasized, derived just as often from ethics where Magian morality did not square with nineteenth-century humanitarianism. Equally serious were the harsh blows of historical scholarship to literal interpretation of scripture. Protestants, lacking an institution for historic revisionism, were particularly sensitive. D. F. Strauss fired the opening salvo with *Leben Jesu*, a bombardment continued by the Tübingen school. Strauss was soon translated into French and English where it and subsequent works found a wide, disturbed public. Whether in Robertson Smith's scathing article on the Bible in the ninth edition of the *Encyclopaedia Britannica* or the more scholarly *History of Dogma* by Adolf von Harnack, scientific, social scientific, and humanitarian research and popularization tore the fabric of faith.

Ernest Renan (1823–92), a scholarly orientalist, historian, and critic, offered nothing new or unique in his *Vie de Jesus*, but the authorities of Napoleon III found it necessary to suppress his recently founded university chair. Renan's positivist explanations were not a product of militant atheism. He had no desire to destroy belief. Renan was a scholar in search of the truth—a cardinal nineteenth-century virtue—and Renan pursued the truth as he saw it regardless of where it might lead. This preface to a series of his collected essays (from which some introductory matter has been omitted) reflects his pain at unreasoned and unscholarly attacks. But the issue ran deeper than scholarship. Where was man to turn, in what would he believe once his traditional cosmogony had been destroyed?

PREFACE

THE FRAGMENTS which compose the present volume all relate to the history of religions, and will be found to embrace the principal forms with which religious sentiment has been clothed in ancient times, in the Middle Ages, and in modern days. These subjects have for me an attraction which I cannot conceal, and which I know not how to resist. Religion is certainly the highest and most interesting of the manifestations of human nature. Among all kinds of poetry, it is the one that best reaches the end essential to art, which is to raise man above the vulgar life and awaken in him the sense of his celestial origin. No part of the great instincts of the heart shows itself with better evidence. Even when one adopts in particular, the teaching of

425

any of the great religious systems, they divide themselves, or they divide the world; from the whole of these systems results one fact, which constitutes to my mind the most consolatory guarantee of a mysterious future, where the race and the individual will find again their works and the fruit of their sacrifices.

A grave difficulty, I know, attaches to these studies, and causes timid people to impute to the authors that they occupy themselves with tendencies and objects to which they are strangers. The essence of all religions is to exact absolute belief, and consequently to place themselves above common right, and to deny to the impartial historian all competence when he seeks to judge them. Religions, in effect, in order to sustain the pretension of being beyond reproach, are obliged to have recourse to a particular system of philosophic history, founded upon the belief of a miraculous intervention of the Deity in human affairs—an intervention made solely for their profit. Religions otherwise are not able to dispose freely of their past; the past must bend to the necessities of the present, and furnish a foundation for institutions more evidently brought about by the course of time. The critic, on the contrary, whose rule is to follow only sight, and fair deduction, without any political after-thought; the critic, whose first principle is that the miracle has no part in the course of human affairs, any more than in the series of natural facts; the critic, who begins by proclaiming that everything in history is capable of human explanation, even when that explanation escapes us by reason of insufficient teaching, would evidently not agree with the schools of theology, who employ a method opposed to his, and follow it with a different purpose. Susceptible, like all powers attributed to a divine source, religions naturally regard the expression, however respectful, of a difference of opinion as hostility, and look upon those as enemies, who place before themselves the most simple duties of reason.

This unfortunate misunderstanding, which will endure eternally between the critical spirit and the habitual doctrines imposed all of a piece, ought it to obstruct the human mind in the track of free research? We think not. Firstly, human nature never consents to mutilate itself; however one may conceive, perhaps, that reason consents to its own sacrifice, if it finds itself in the face of a doctrine which is unique, and adopted by all mankind. But one set of systems claims the absolute truth, which all can possess at the same time; any one of these systems, showing a title by which it says it can reduce to nothing the pretensions of the others, the abdication of the critic will contribute nothing towards giving the world the benefit, so desirable, of peace and unanimity. In default of a conflict between religions and criticism, religions fight among themselves for the supremacy. If all the religions were reduced to a single one, the different fractions of that religion would each curse the other; and even supposing that all the sects came to recognise a sort of catholicity, the internal dissensions— twenty times more active and more hateful than those which separate

religions and rival Churches—would serve to supply the eternal need
which individual thought has to create, according to its fancy, the divine
world. What are we to conclude from this? That in suppressing criticism
we shall not suppress the cause, but we shall suppress perhaps the only
judge who can clear up the difficulty. The right which each religion insists
on as absolute truth is a perfectly respectable right, which no one ought to
dream of contesting; but it does not exclude a parallel right in other religions, nor the right of the critic, who regards himself as outside the sects.
The duty of civil society is to maintain itself in the face of all these contradictory rights, without seeking to reconcile them. That would be to
attempt the impossible, and, without permitting them to be absorbed,
nullify, which could not be done without detriment to the general interests
of civilisation. It is as well to remark, that in effect the critic, in exercising,
with regard to the history of religions, the right which belongs to him, does
not encroach, so that one might complain, I do not say only from the point
of view as to equality of rights (that is too clear, since religious controversialists daily permit themselves to deliver against independent science
attacks full of violence), but even in making concessions as large as possible to propriety and the majesty of established worship. Religion, at the
same time that it reaches in its height the pure heaven of the ideal, stands
for its base upon the unstable ground of human affairs, and participates in
things which are fleeting and defective. Every work of which men furnish
the matter being but a compromise between the opposing necessities which
make up this transitory life, necessarily provides matter for the critic, and
one has said nothing against an institution so much that one is limited to
this inoffensive remark, that she has not completely escaped from the fragile
nature which belongs to all structures here below. Religion must be of one
manner, and not of another: that condition, essential to all existence, implies
a limit—something excluded, a defect. Art, which, like religion, aspires to
render the infinite under finite forms, does it renounce its mission because
it knows of no image to represent the ideal? Does it not disappear in the
vague and the intangible, whenever it would be as boundless in its
forms as it is in its conceptions?

Religion, in the same way, only exists on the condition of its being a decided opinion, a fixed idea, very clear, very finite, and consequently very
much liable to criticism. The narrow and peculiar side of each religion,
which constitutes its weakness, constitutes also its strength; for men are
drawn together by their narrow thoughts rather than by their enlarged
ideas. It would be a small matter to have shown that every religious form
is enormously disproportionate to its divine object, if one did not hasten to
add that it could not be otherwise, and that every symbol must appear
insufficient and coarse when compared with the extreme delicacy of the
truths which it represents. The glory of religion is precisely this: it provides
a programme beyond human power for one to pursue the realisation with

boldness, and to nobly make the attempt to give a determinate form to the infinite aspirations of the heart of man.

Eternal and sacred in their spirit, religions cannot be equally so in their forms and history; they would be mutilated in their fairest parts if they were obliged to regard the dogmatic exigency which does not permit the sects to own to their weak sides. What do I say? It should be suppressed; for the unreasonableness of different sects being contradictory, it would follow, in order that no one should be hurt, we ought to keep silence on the principal part of human development. In political affairs every government similarly affirms its right in an absolute manner, but no government has on that account forbidden history; at least those States which have carried superstition to this point have found in their moral deterioration, that they have brought about their own punishment. Spain offers a striking example of intellectual decay, traceable to the exaggeration of respect shown by the political to the religious order. On the contrary, the breadth of mind and intelligence which distinguish the Catholics of Germany, are owing still more to the constant contact with the Protestant critic than to the superiority of the Germanic race in all that pertains to the wise cultivation of the mind.

I protest once for all against the false interpretation which will be given to my works if the different essays upon the history of religions which I have published, or which I may in future publish, are taken as polemical works. Considered as polemical works, these essays (and I am the first to recognise the fact) are very unskilfully prepared. Polemics require a degree of strategy to which I am a stranger: one ought to know how to select the weak side of one's adversary; to keep there, and never to touch upon any uncertain question; to keep every concession—that is to say, to renounce that which constitutes the very essence of the scientific spirit. Such is not my method. The fundamental question upon which religious discussion ought to turn—that is to say, the question of the fact of revelation and of the supernatural—I never touch;[1] not but that these questions may not be existentialism. Every aspirant to the status of intellectual finds comfort in solved for me with complete certainty, but because the discussion of such questions is not scientific, or rather because independent science supposes them to have been previously settled. Certainly if I should pursue an end, whether of polemics or of proselytism, this would be a leading fault: it would be to bring upon the ground of delicate and obscure problems a question to be dealt with on much more evidence in the common terms which controversialists and apologists usually lay down. Far from regretting these advantages which I have given as against myself, I rejoice at it, if it will convince theologians that my writings are of another order to theirs;

---

[1] Some passages of the article entitled *The Critical Historians of Jesus* are an exception to what I have said here, because this article was composed at a time when my manner of treating questions of religious history was not fixed as it is now.

that they are the pure researches of erudition, assailable, as such, where one endeavours to apply those principles of criticism, equally to the Jewish religion as to the Christian, which one observes in the other branches of history and philology. As to the discussion of questions properly theological, I never enter upon it any more than MM. Burnouf, Creuzer, Guigniaut, and other critical historians of the religions of antiquity, who do not consider themselves obliged to undertake the refutation or the apology of the worships on which they employ themselves. The history of humanity is to me a vast entirety, where everything is unequal and diverse, but where all is of the same order, arises out of the same causes, and obeys the same laws. These laws I search out with no other intention than to discover the exact shade or degree of that which is. Nothing will make me exchange a part so obscure, but productive to science, for the part of controversialist—an easy part in this, that it gains for the writer an assured favour from those who believe in the duty of opposing war to war. This polemic, of which I am far from disputing the necessity, but which is neither to my taste nor my ability, satisfied Voltaire. One cannot be at the same time a good controversialist and a good historian. Voltaire, if weak as a scholar— Voltaire, who seems to us so destitute of the sentiment of antiquity, to us who are educated according to a better method—Voltaire is twenty times victorious over adversaries still more unprovided with critical power than he is himself. The new edition which is in preparation of the works of this great man will satisfy the need which seems to exist for an answer to the invasions of theology—an answer evil in itself, but useful to those who engage in the contest; an answer much behind-hand to a science equally behind-hand. Let us do better; we all possess the love of truth and great curiosity. Let us leave debating to those who are pleased with it; let us work for the small number of those who march in the great line of the human spirit. Popularity, as I know, gives the preference to writers who, instead of pursuing the highest form of truth, apply themselves to combat the opinions of their times; but by a just return they have no value when the opinions they have combated have ceased to exist.

Those who refuted magic and judicial astrology in the sixteenth and seventeenth centuries have rendered to reason an immense service, and yet, notwithstanding, their writings are unknown at the present day—their victory has caused them to be forgotten. On the contrary, the names of Scaliger, Bochart, Bayle, Richard Simon—whose works are, however, obsolete upon many points of detail—will remain inscribed for ever among those of the great promoters of human knowledge.

The regrettable but necessary difference of opinion which will always exist upon the history of a religion between the partisans of that religion and disinterested science, ought not, then, to give occasion to accuse science of anti-religious proselytism. That if in a moment of passing impulse, a man devoted to critical research evinces something of the desire of St. Paul, *"Cupio omnes fieri qualis et ego sum,"* there is a sentiment which effaces itself before a truer judgment of the limits and common range of the human spirit. Each person makes of religion a shelter to his measure and according to his needs. To dare to place hands upon this particular work of the faculties of each person is dangerous and rash, for no one has a right to penetrate deep enough into the conscience of another to distinguish the accessory from the principal. In seeking to extirpate beliefs which may be thought superfluous, one risks the injury of the organs essential to religious life and morality. Propagandism is out of its element when it undertakes high scientific culture or philosophy, and the most excellent intellectual discipline imposed upon persons who have not been prepared for it, cannot but have an evil effect. The duty of the learned man, then, is to express with frankness the result of his study, without seeking to trouble the conscience of persons who have not been called to the same life as himself, but also without regarding the interested motives and pretended proprieties which so often assume the expression of truth.

There is, moreover, a way by which the most austere critc, if he has some philosophy, can sympathise with those who have not the right to be as tolerant as he is. He knows that with exalted beliefs disagreement almost always changes itself into anathema: if anathema excites repugnance, the motive which directs it induces respect, and thus the critic comes to understand, and almost to love, the anger he inspires.

This anger, indeed, taking for granted a certain pettiness of spirit, comes from an excellent source, the vivacity of religious sentiment. The worst penalty which man pays in order to arrive at a life of reflection atones for his exceptional position, and is without doubt when he finds himself isolated thus from the great family of the religious where the better souls of the world are found, and dreams that the persons with whom he would like best to be in moral communion are those who think they ought perforce to regard him as perverse. He ought to be well sure of himself, so as not to be troubled when the women and children join their hands and say, "Believe like us!" We may console ourselves by thinking that this schism between the simple and the cultivated, is a fatal law belonging to the state through which we are passing, and that there is a higher region for lofty souls in which we shall often meet, without doubting, those who have anathematised us, the ideal city seen by the Seer of the Apocalypse, where thronged a crowd none could count, of every tribe, every nation, every tongue, shouting with one voice the symbol in which they all met, "Holy, holy, holy is he who is, who has been, and who will be!"

The word *religion* being that under which, as it is here recapitulated in the eyes of the majority, the life of the spirit is comprised, a coarser materialism can only assail in its essence this happily eternal need of our nature. Nothing but our defective mode of speaking could confound with irreligion the refusal to adhere to such and such a creed professing to be as a revelation. The man who takes life seriously and employs his activity to a generous purpose, he is the religious man; the frivolous, superficial man, without any high morality, he is the impious man. Those who adore something are brothers, or certainly less hostile than those who obey only their own interests, and pretend, with material enjoyment, to have a right understanding of the divine instincts of the heart of man. The worst policy which religious passions can pursue is to seek in lightness or indifference, an ally against the dissenters, who seek the truth in good faith and according to the particular need of their soul.

For the great majority of mankind, the established religion provides all that is required towards the worship of the ideal. To suppress or weaken among the private classes, with their other means of education, this great and unique remembrance of nobleness, is to degrade human nature, and to take away the essential sign, which distinguishes it from the animal. The popular conscience, in its grand and high spontaneity, only attaches itself to the spirit, and not distinguishing the dross from the gold, sanctifies the most imperfect symbol. Religion is always true in the belief of the people; for the people, not being theologians, and hardly entering into the details of dogma, only take that which is true; I would say, the breath and the high-flown inspiration. In this sense the philosopher is much nearer in understanding with the man simple of heart than with the half-educated man who carries into religious matters a kind of left-handed reflection. How charming to see in cottages and in vulgar houses, where utility crushes everything, ideal figures, images which represent nothing real!

How delightful for the man bowed down by six days' toil, to come on the seventh and rest upon his knees and contemplate the lofty columns, the vaulted roof, the arches, the altar, to hear and appreciate the hymns, to listen to words, moral and consolatory! The nourishment which science, art, the elevating exercise of all his faculties, furnishes to the educated man, religion alone undertakes to supply to the illiterate. This elementary education, naturally brought to consider itself superior, has often the effect, I know, of dwarfing the minds confined by it. But the greater part of those dwarfed by religion are already small before they take to it; narrow and limited by religion, they would probably have been wicked without it. Intellectual elevation will always be the lot of the few: provided that the few should develop freely, they would hardly trouble themselves with the manner in which the remainder approached the sublimity of God. Whatever there may be scanty or even dangerous in an established dogma, it does not exist for the people who have no vocation to be critical; for see, why superstitions which are displeasing to the educated man have a charm for the common people. The simple faith is the true one, and I admit that I should be inconsolable if I knew that my writings would ever cause offence to one of those simple souls who worship so well in spirit. But they are protected by their ignorance: the dogmas which are assailed not being for them the object of positive assertion, no difficulty occurs to them; it is the privilege of pure sentiment to be invulnerable and to play with poisons without being hurt.

The lofty separation, sometimes the reproach of philosophy, established between men in relation to their religious capacities, is not in reality an injury to the majority nor an act of pride. Science, it is true, is not made for all: it presupposes a long intellectual education, years of study, mental ability, of which but few men are capable. But for all that, it does not exclude the ideal: the simple man finds in his spontaneous instincts full compensation for that which he wants on the side of reflection. Even then no one will believe that great intellectual cultivation, when it does not exclude religious sentiment, is superior to simple faith. What is one to conclude? Inequality, at the bottom more painful to the privileged than to the inferior, is the fault of Nature. Mary has the better part; Martha may be blamed for it. The theological formula here preserves its perfect truth: all have sufficient grace to attain their salvation, but all are not called to the same degree of blessedness. Every man has his right to the ideal; but it would be falsifying evidence to pretend that all can equally participate in the worship of the perfect.

This distinction in religion, understood in its general sense, and the particular forms that history shows us succeeding one another with divers fortunes and divers merits, are essential to its maintenance. Far from seeking to weaken religious sentiment, I would help in some things, to elevate and purify it. It seems to me, indeed, that a consolatory result arises from the independent study of religion, which serves to calm the soul and furnish the foundation of a happy life. The result is, that religion, being an integral part of human nature, is true in its essence, and above particular forms of worship it is necessarily affected with the same defects which belong to the times and the country to which it belongs; such is religion—an evident sign that man has a superior destiny.

Thus it is demonstrated that religion always has been and always will be that which inspires more love and hatred: thus it is demonstrated that man, by an invincible effort, raises himself to the conception and to the worship of the perfect; is not this the best proof of the divine spirit which is in us, and which answers by its aspirations to a transcendent ideal? In my eyes, I confess it is not the most comforting thought; and it is here we ought to pronounce the word of certainty that there is not any particular dogma or any philosophical or theological formula, but what may be challenged. The infinite should not be shut up in a system. How will the human spirit lay hold of it? how will it translate the word, the essence of which is ineffable? But this same impotence of language and of reason to exhaust the idea which we form of the divine world, is it not the greatest mark of adoration, the most significant act of faith? Far from leading us to a negation, the philosophical history of religion shows us the constant faith of humanity in a celestial principle and a supreme order, and thus brings us to faith; not that faith which materialises its object in coarse symbols, but that faith which believes in the ideal without the need of belief in the supernatural, and which, following the thought of St. Augustine, sees the divinity better in the immutable order of things than in derogations from the eternal order.

Some facts which pass under our eyes, and will count in the history of the human mind, confirm me in this method, at once respectful and free, of knowing how to distinguish the form which passes away, from the spirit which remains for ever. Some allowances, indeed, should be made for the seriousness and depth of the religious reaction which we have witnessed—a reaction, like all movements of opinion, very often made to serve as a pretext for inferior estimates and weaknesses; but we cannot deny that they hide a true event of moral order. If this reaction manifests itself almost everywhere under the form of conversion to Catholicism, it arises less from Catholicism itself than from the religious sentiment.

Catholicism being the most characteristic, and, if I dare say so, the most religious of religions, all religious reaction slightly tends necessarily to its profit. Let us say, however, that Catholicism, for the majority of those who return to it, is less the vast and minute mass of beliefs which fill the volumes of a treatise on theology, than religion in its general acceptation. Among the neophytes who attach themselves to it with most zeal, there are few who consider seriously the dogmas they embrace; when these dogmas are exhibited to them under a strict form, they decline them, or they extenuate them by complaisant explanations: almost all are heretics without knowing it. What brings them to the Church is the eternal instinct which induces man to adopt a religious belief, an instinct so imperious that it will not allow him to rest in doubt, but makes him accept, without examination, the faith which he finds ready-made. The eighteenth century, which had the mission of clearing the field of the human mind from a crowd of obstacles with which it had become encumbered during the course of ages, carried on the work of demolition with an ardour which may be taken as the fulfilment of conscientious duty. Scepticism and impiety (or rather, the appearance of scepticism and impiety, for at bottom few ages have proceeded in their work with as much conviction and religious devotion) please him in themselves, and he enjoys a kind of content at having acquitted himself of a task which might otherwise have cost him many tears to accomplish. But the generation following, having returned to the inner life, has found in it the need of belief, and to be in communion of faith with other souls, no longer appreciates the joy of the first, and rather than remain in a state of negation which has become intolerable, has tried to take up again the very doctrines which their fathers had exploded. When we know no longer how to knock down churches we restore them, and we imitate the ancients; for we can let religious originality go, but we cannot let go religion. Who has not stopped, when exploring our ancient cities, before those gigantic monuments of former faith, which alone claim notice in the midst of the level of modern vulgarity? Everything is restored round about; the cathedral alone remains, a little degraded from its pre-eminence by the hand of man, but deeply rooted in the soil. It is so far true that in the fact of religious creation, the ages are brought to refuse the privilege they accord so freely to remote times; it is so far true also that rational science being, by its nature, the lot of the few, cannot, in the actual state of society, press upon the belief of the world with any decided weight.

We may understand now what distance separates the controversialist, who aspires to change existing religious forms, from the learned man who only proposes a speculative end, without any direct reference to the order of contemporaneous facts. Strangers to the causes which produce these abrupt varieties of opinion, which belong rightfully to the circle of men of the world, but which ought not to extend beyond the learned, they are not obliged to perform acts of faith according to the caprices of fashion, nor condemn themselves to silence because they have not brought their studies to bear upon ideas which such parties think most suitable to their views at the time. The government of affairs here below belongs, in fact, to other forces than science and reason; the thinker believes himself to have but a small right to the direction of affairs in his planet, and, satisfied with the share allotted to him, he accepts his impotence without regret. A spectator in the universe, he knows that the world only belongs to him as a subject of study, and that the part of reformer requires almost always in those who undertake it, defects and qualities which he does not possess.

Let us keep, then, each of the elements in their place, though often contradictory, yet without which the development of humanity remains incomplete. Let us leave the religions to proclaim themselves unassailable, since without that they will not obtain from their adherents the respect of which they are in need; but do not let us compel science to pass under the censure of a power which has nothing scientific about it. Do not let us confound legend with history; but let us not endeavour to get rid of legend, since that is the form in which the faith of humanity is necessarily clothed. Humanity is not composed of the learned and the philologist. She deceives herself frequently, or, we should rather say, she deceives herself of necessity, upon questions of facts and persons: she often renders homage and bestows sympathy in the wrong place; more often still she exaggerates the position of individuals, and heaps on the heads of her favourites, merits which belong to the entire generation; but to see the truth of all this, one ought to have a delicacy of mind and a knowledge which is utterly wanting in her. But she does not deceive herself on the particular object of her worship: that which she adores is really adorable; for what she adores in characters, what she has idealised, are the goodness and beauty she has put there. It may be affirmed that if a new religious phenomenon were to appear, the myth would find its place in the timid disposition which characterises our age of reflection. Whatever care may be taken at first to repress everything which emanates from the purest rationalism, the second generation would doubtless be less puritanical than the first, and the third less still. Thus we should introduce successive complications where the great imaginative instincts of humanity would give themselves full scope, and then the critic would again find, at the end of several ages, that he would have to undertake his work of analysis and research.

Persons more influenced towards sentiment than towards science, and more richly endowed for action than for thought, understand with difficulty (I know it) the opportunity of like researches, and receive them generally with displeasure. This is a respectable sentiment, which we ought to be slow to blame. To those who entertain it I would venture to advise not to read works composed from the point of view of the modern critic; these writings can only provoke, as far as they are concerned, disagreeable feelings, and even the trouble that they feel in reading them proves that such reading is not good for them. The good spirit (or rather that which we so term), which keeps from the little minds the points necessarily for good, is essential to the government of this world; a ship without ballast, carrying showy sails, is as ill fitted for the voyage as a hulk without sails and heavily laden. The incapacity of Germany in the field of action, is it not the consequence of the incomparable gifts with which nature has endowed her for intellectual speculation? The practical man cannot have the breadth of mind of the man devoted to thought: on his side, the thinker, if he wishes to take part in worldly affairs, is bound by a crowd of compromise which weakens and destroys his originality. Here, as in all things, good government of the human mind involves liberty. I wish people would leave these peaceable and inoffensive researches to be pursued in the obscurity which suits them. Science would be very rash if it should aspire to change opinion; her proceedings interest only the few. Repulsive and without attraction, with what means could she resist so much power as retains the world, doubtless by the better right? We only ask for liberty; with liberty souls will divide themselves, and each one chose spontaneously the view, which for it, is the truth.

I do not overlook the misunderstanding to which I am liable every time I touch upon matters which are the objects of belief to a certain number of men; but the delicate exercise of thought would be interested with if I were obliged to consider the contrary meaning which preoccupied minds could conceive in reading what they do not understand. Persons, but little familiar with intellectual matters, often imagine that they give themselves an air of profound wisdom in falsifying and exaggerating opinions at the expense of those who wish to have the merit of moderation. For these persons writers should be classed in distinct categories; by their favour one is pantheistic or atheistic without knowing it; they create schools by their own private authority, and one often learns from them with surprise, that one has been brought up by masters whom one did not know. Men of the world willingly believe themselves possessed of the attribute of good sense in summing up with some absurd terms, and who contradict of themselves the great theses of science and genius. Strauss has thus become a lunatic,

who has denied the existence of Jesus; Wolf is a fool, who has denied
Homer; Hegel a mad fellow, who has said that yes is equal to no; and if I
might be permitted to say here, that so far from denying the existence of
Jesus, Strauss admits it, and admits it in every page of his book; that Wolf
only denies the artificial composition of the Iliad and the Odyssey; that
Hegel has not wished in his boldest formula anything more than to mark
the relative and partial character of all our affirmations, I shall pass for a
disciple of Strauss, whom I have strenuously opposed; of Wolf, whom I
have never considered; of Hegel, whose loftiness of mind I admire, but
with whom I have few points in common. The inconvenience of this kind
of thing is unavoidable. The discernment of fine points will always be the
lot of the few; but this few, when they undertake works of the spirit, are
the only persons whose suffrage one ought to seek.

Among the objections which I foresee, is one to which I ought to make
some answer beforehand. I should regret if, in enunciating certain ideas
contrary to the opinions generally received in France, it should be considered that I ought to have made a greater display of demonstration. But
this defect is inseparable from the very nature of the fragments which compose the present volume. The question here is not as to memorandum
specially collected, in which erudition and philology have full scope, but as
to articles written for reviews and newspapers without any more scientific
preparation than was necessary for their insertion, whether such ought to
find a place. If we consult the works of which I have taken account, or those
which I have cited on contested points, we shall find proofs which I could
not set out at large, and which I should have had but little time to add elsewhere. Critical works destined for reviews would become impossible if in
rendering an account of a book we were compelled to set up again the
scaffolding which had been made use of by the author in constructing the
edifice. In another series of works of a more technical character, my "General History of the Semitic Languages" in particular, I have endeavoured
to treat under the more special form, some of the questions which I could
not have dealt with here in a general way. I hope that what may now appear gratuitous in the views I present to the public will appear some day
in their full light and conformably to the plan of study I have laid down.
After I have finished the history of the Semitic languages I may be permitted to contribute something towards clearing up the history of the
Semitic religions and the origins of Christianity. I shall not then spare any
of the details which the nature of the collected works forbids me now to
give.

I had at first resolved to answer here the recent criticisms which, by
distortions of fact, mixed with strange reasoning, rather than by their own
value, seemed to require rectification. But the attack regulates the defence,
and it would have been difficult for me to answer sophism and subtlety
without being myself somewhat fastidious and subtle. The silence which I
have kept until now, which has enabled my adversaries to triumph as for a

victory, I desire still to keep. However, I am ready to receive with gratitude; to discuss, and adopt, if need be, any observations truly scientific which may be addressed to me. Moreover, I shall be firm in resisting the declamations of the sectarian spirit, and avoiding at any price those pitiable debates which too often make learning ridiculous in substituting personal questions for pure researches after truth. If it be thought that by injuries, by falsified citations, anonymous denials which none dare avow, equivocations skilfully calculated to delude people unacquainted with science, I shall be hindered in the object of research and reflection on which I am engaged, they deceive themselves. These researches have always had for me a supreme interest; they will remain, under a form more and more enlarged, the principal object of my curiosity. If I was, like many others, the slave of my desire, if self-interest or vanity guided me in the conduct of my works, they would by such means doubtless succeed in making me abandon my studies, which are generally recompensed by injury. But desiring nothing, if this is not to do good, not demanding for study other reward than itself, I venture to affirm that no human motive has the power to make me say one word more or less than I have resolved to say. The liberty of which I have need, being that of science, it ought not to be wanting; if the seventeenth century had its Holland, it is difficult that, in the diminution of souls of our day, we cannot find a corner of the world where we can think at our ease. Nothing, consequently, will make me deviate from the plan I have laid down, and which seems to me to be the line of duty: inflexible research after truth, according to the measure of my strength, by all the means of legitimate investigation which are at the disposal of the human mind; firm and frank expression of the results which seem to me probable or certain, without any after-thought of application and all expedient formulas; open to the correction which the criticism of competent persons or the progress of science may bring to bear upon me. The attacks of ignorance as well as fanaticism afflict me, without moving me when I think they are sincere. In the case where I cannot consider them as such, I hope to arrive by familiarity to the time when they will not even trouble me.

Christian Humanism: Newman and Education

John Henry Newman, "Discourse V: Knowledge Its Own End," The Idea of a University Defined and Illustrated . . . (New ed.; London: Longmans, Green and Co., 1893), pp. 99–123.

John Henry, Cardinal Newman (1801–90) was among the most distinguished and at the same time most suspect religious thinkers of the nineteenth century. The Oxford Movement, a dispute about the catholicity or protestantism of the Anglican Church, haunted England in the 1830's and '40's. It was romantic, mysterious, yet vigorous—a heated debate over issues of deep concern to the age. Newman and the ablest leaders of the movement deserted Anglicanism, rejecting protestantism and the Erastianism of the liberal age. Newman was first of all an antiliberal. He despised utilitarianism and materialism. Newman was not immune to "the age of improvement," but he was concerned with the depth of "progress." What sort of man must society produce? What is the role of education in this development?

As rector of Dublin Catholic University (1854–58), Newman was directly concerned with the elevation of the Catholic upper classes to the poise, sophistication, and capacity to lead that he found in the English Protestant upper classes. That, coming from a recent convert, was suspect among the Irish bishops. Newman was talking, as G. M. Young put it, about the "form of mind," not the "quality of mind." He transcended the question of the material utility of education—which still leads to raised eyebrows a century after the lectures were delivered—to point out that cultivation is worth more than knowledge or skills.

The preceding four discourses are theological—a statement of Newman's credentials to address a Catholic audience. Some measure of this remains in Discourse V and marks Newman as the heir of Erasmus. The question of education, of the meaning and content of a university, remains timeless.

DISCOURSE V

KNOWLEDGE ITS OWN END

A UNIVERSITY may be considered with reference either to its Students or to its Studies; and the principle, that all Knowledge is a whole and the separate Sciences parts of one, which I have hitherto been using in behalf of its studies, is equally important when we direct our attention to its students. Now then I turn to the students, and shall consider the education which, by virtue of this principle, a University will give them; and thus I shall be introduced, Gentlemen, to the second question, which I proposed to discuss, viz, whether and in what sense its teaching, viewed relatively to the taught, carries the attribute of Utility along with it.

1

I have said that all branches of knowledge are connected together, because the subject-matter of knowledge is intimately united in itself, as being the acts and the work of the Creator. Hence it is that the Sciences, into which our knowledge may be said to be cast, have multiplied bearings one on another, and an internal sympathy, and admit, or rather demand, comparison and adjustment. They complete, correct, balance each other. This consideration, if well-founded, must be taken into account, not only as regards the attainment of truth, which is their common end, but as regards the influence which they exercise upon those whose education consists in the study of them. I have said already, that to give undue prominence to one is to be unjust to another; to neglect or supersede these is to divert those from their proper object. It is to unsettle the boundary lines between science and science, to disturb their action, to destroy the harmony which binds them together. Such a proceeding will have a corresponding effect when introduced into a place of education. There is no science but tells a different tale, when viewed as a portion of a whole, from what it is likely to suggest when taken by itself, without the safeguard, as I may call it, of others.

Let me make use of an illustration. In the combination of colours, very different effects are produced by a difference in their selection and juxtaposition; red, green, and white, change their shades, according to the contrast to which they are submitted. And, in like manner, the drift and meaning of a branch of knowledge varies with the company in which it is introduced to the student. If his reading is confined simply to one subject, however such division of labour may favour the advancement of a particular pursuit, a point into which I do not here enter, certainly it has a tendency to contract his mind. If it is incorporated with others, it depends on those others as to the kind of influence which it exerts upon him. Thus the Classics, which in England are the means of refining the taste, have in France subserved the spread of revolutionary and deistical doctrines. In Metaphysics, again, Butler's Analogy of Religion, which has had so much to do with the conversion to the Catholic faith of members of the University of Oxford, appeared to Pitt and others, who had received a different training, to operate only in the direction of infidelity. And so again, Watson, Bishop of Llandaff, as I think he tells us in the narrative of his life, felt the science of Mathematics to indispose the mind to religious belief, while others see in its investigations the best parallel, and thereby defence, of the Christian Mysteries. In like manner, I suppose, Arcesilas would not have handled logic as Aristotle, nor Aristotle have criticized poets as Plato; yet reasoning and poetry are subject to scientific rules.

It is a great point then to enlarge the range of studies which a University professes, even for the sake of the students; and, though they cannot pursue every subject which is open to them, they will be the gainers by living among those and under those who represent the whole circle. This I conceive to be the advantage of a seat of universal learning, considered as a place of education. An assemblage of learned men, zealous for their own sciences, and rivals of each other, are brought, by familiar intercourse and for the sake of intellectual peace, to adjust together the claims and relations of their respective subjects of investigation. They learn to respect, to consult, to aid each other. Thus is created a pure and clear atmosphere of thought, which the student also breathes, though in his own case he only pursues a few sciences out of the multitude. He profits by an intellectual tradition, which is independent of particular teachers, which guides him in his choice of subjects, and duly interprets for him those which he chooses. He apprehends the great outlines of knowledge, the principles on which it rests, the scale of its parts, its lights and its shades, its great points and its little, as he otherwise cannot apprehend them. Hence it is that his education is called "Liberal." A habit of mind is formed which lasts through life, of which the attributes are, freedom, equitableness, calmness, moderation, and wisdom; or what in a former Discourse I have ventured to call a philosophical habit. This then I would assign as the special fruit of the education furnished at a University, as contrasted with other places of teaching or modes of teaching. This is the main purpose of a University in its treatment of its students.

And now the question is asked me, What is the *use* of it? and my answer will constitute the main subject of the Discourses which are to follow.

2

Cautious and practical thinkers, I say, will ask of me, what, after all, is the gain of this Philosophy, of which I make such account, and from which I promise so much. Even supposing it to enable us to exercise the degree of trust exactly due to every science respectively, and to estimate precisely the value of every truth which is anywhere to be found, how are we better for this master view of things, which I have been extolling? Does it not reverse the principle of the division of labour? will practical objects be obtained better or worse by its cultivation? to what then does it lead? where does it end? what does it do? how does it profit? what does it promise? Particular sciences are respectively the basis of definite arts, which carry on to results tangible and beneficial the truths which are the subjects of the knowledge attained; what is the Art of this science of sciences? what is the fruit of such a Philosophy? what are we proposing to effect, what inducements do we hold out to the Catholic community, when we set about the enterprise of founding a University?

I am asked what is the end of University Education, and of the Liberal or Philosophical Knowledge which I conceived it to impart: I answer, that what I have already said has been sufficient to show that it has a very tangible, real, and sufficient end, though the end cannot be divided from that knowledge itself. Knowledge is capable of being its own end. Such is the constitution of the human mind, that any kind of knowledge, if it be really such, is its own reward. And if this is true of all knowledge, it is true also of that special Philosophy, which I have made to consist in a comprehensive view of truth in all its branches, of the relations of science to science, of their mutual bearings, and their respective values. What the worth of such an acquirement is, compared with other objects which we seek,—wealth or power of honour or the conveniences and comforts of life, I do not profess here to discuss; but I would maintain, and mean to show, that it is an object, in its own nature so really and undeniably good, as to be the compensation of a great deal of thought in the compassing, and a great deal of trouble in the attaining.

Now, when I say that Knowledge is, not merely a means to something beyond it, or the preliminary of certain arts into which it naturally resolves, but an end sufficient to rest in and to pursue for its own sake, surely I am uttering no paradox, for I am stating what is both intelligible in itself, and has ever been the common judgment of philosophers and the ordinary feeling of mankind. I am saying what at least the public opinion of this day ought to be slow to deny, considering how much we have heard of late years, in opposition to Religion, of entertaining, curious, and various knowledge. I am but saying what whole volumes have been written to illustrate, viz., by a "selection from the records of Philosophy, Literature, and Art, in all ages and countries, of a body of examples, to show how the most unpropitious circumstances have been unable to conquer an ardent desire for the acquisition of knowledge." That further advantages accrue to us and redound to others by its possession, over and above what it is in itself, I am very far indeed from denying; but, independent of these, we are satisfying a direct need of our nature in its very acquisition; and, whereas our nature, unlike that of the inferior creation, does not at once reach its perfection, but depends, in order to it, on a number of external aids and appliances, Knowledge, as one of the principal of these, is valuable for what its very presence in us does for us after the manner of a habit, even though it be turned to no further account, nor subserve any direct end.

3

Hence it is that Cicero, in enumerating the various heads of mental excellence, lays down the pursuit of Knowledge for its own sake, as the first of them. "This pertains most of all to human nature," he says, "for we are all of us drawn to the pursuit of Knowledge; in which to excel we consider excellent, whereas to mistake, to err, to be ignorant, to be deceived, is both an evil and a disgrace." And he considers Knowledge the very first object to which we are attracted, after the supply of our physical wants. After the calls and duties of our animal existence, as they may be termed, as regards ourselves, our family, and our neighbours, follows, he tells us, "the search after truth. Accordingly, as soon as we escape from the pressure of necessary cares, forthwith we desire to see, to hear, and to learn; and consider the knowledge of what is hidden or is wonderful a condition of our happiness."

This passage, though it is but one of many similar passages in a multitude of authors, I take for the very reason that it is so familiarly known to us; and I wish you to observe, Gentlemen, how distinctly it separates the pursuit of Knowledge from those ulterior objects to which certainly it can be made to conduce, and which are, I suppose, solely contemplated by the persons who would ask of me the use of a University or Liberal Education. So far from dreaming of the cultivation of Knowledge directly and mainly in order to our physical comfort and enjoyment, for the sake of life and person, of health, of the conjugal and family union, of the social tie and civil security, the great Orator implies, that it is only after our physical and political needs are supplied, and when we are "free from necessary duties and cares," that we are in a condition for "desiring to see, to hear, and to learn." Nor does he contemplate in the least degree the reflex or subsequent action of Knowledge, when acquired, upon those material goods which we set out by securing before we seek it; on the contrary, he expressly denies its bearing upon social life altogether, strange as such a procedure is to those who live after the rise of the Baconian philosophy, and he cautions us against such a cultivation of it as will interfere with our duties to our fellow-creatures. "All these methods," he says, "are engaged in the investigation of truth; by the pursuit of which to be carried off from public occupations is a transgression of duty. For the praise of virtue lies altogether in action; yet intermissions often occur, and then we recur to such pursuits; not to say that the incessant activity of the mind is vigorous enough to carry us on in the pursuit of knowledge, even without any exertion of our own." The idea of benefiting society by means of "the pursuit of science and knowledge" did not enter at all into the motives which he would assign for their cultivation.

This was the ground of the opposition which the elder Cato made to the introduction of Greek Philosophy among his countrymen, when Carneades and his companions, on occasion of their embassy, were charming the Roman youth with their eloquent expositions of it. The fit representative of a practical people, Cato estimated every thing by what it produced; whereas the Pursuit of Knowledge promised nothing beyond Knowledge itself. He despised that refinement or enlargement of mind of which he had no experience.

4

Things, which can bear to be cut off from everything else and yet persist in living, must have life in themselves; pursuits, which issue in nothing, and still maintain their ground for ages, which are regarded as admirable, though they have not as yet proved themselves to be useful, must have their sufficient end in themselves, whatever it turn out to be. And we are brought to the same conclusion by considering the force of the epithet, by which the knowledge under consideration is popularly designated. It is common to speak of "*liberal* knowledge," of the "*liberal* arts and studies," and of a "*liberal* education," as the especial characteristic or property of a

University and of a gentleman; what is really meant by the word? Now, first, in its grammatical sense it is opposed to *servile;* and by "servile work" is understood, as our catechisms inform us, bodily labour, mechanical employment, and the like, in which the mind has little or no part. Parallel to such servile works are those arts, if they deserve the name, of which the poet speaks, which owe their origin and their method to hazard, not to skill; as, for instance, the practice and operations of an empiric. As far as this contrast may be considered as a guide into the meaning of the word, liberal education and liberal pursuits are exercises of mind, of reason, of reflection.

But we want something more for its explanation, for there are bodily exercises which are liberal, and mental exercises which are not so. For instance, in ancient times the practitioners in medicine were commonly slaves; yet it was an art as intellectual in its nature, in spite of the pretence, fraud, and quackery with which it might then, as now, be debased, as it was heavenly in its aim. And so in like manner, we contrast a liberal education with a commercial education or a professional; yet no one can deny that commerce and the professions afford scope for the highest and most diversified powers of mind. There is then a great variety of intellectual exercises, which are not technically called "liberal;" on the other hand, I say, there are exercises of the body which do receive that appellation. Such, for instance, was the palaestra, in ancient times; such the Olympic games, in which strength and dexterity of body as well as of mind gained the prize. In Xenophon we read of the young Persian nobility being taught to ride on horseback and to speak the truth; both being among the accomplishments of a gentleman. War, too, however rough a profession, has even been accounted liberal, unless in cases when it becomes heroic, which would introduce us to another subject.

Now comparing these instances together, we shall have no difficulty in determining the principle of this apparent variation in the application of the term which I am examining. Manly games, or games of skill, or military prowess, though bodily, are, it seems, accounted liberal; on the other hand, what is merely professional, though highly intellectual, nay, though liberal in comparison of trade and manual labour, is not simply called liberal, and mercantile occupations are not liberal at all. Why this distinction? because that alone is liberal knowledge, which stands on its own pretensions, which is independent of sequel, expects no complement, refuses to be *informed* (as it is called) by any end, or absorbed into any are, in order duly to present itself to our contemplation. The most ordinary pursuits have this specific character, if they are self-sufficient and complete; the highest lose it, when they minister to something beyond them. It is absurd to balance, in point of worth and importance, a treatise on reducing fractures with a game of cricket or a fox-chase; yet of the two the bodily exercise has that quality which we call "liberal," and the intellectual has it not. And so of the learned professions altogether, considered merely as professions; although one of them be the most popularly beneficial, and another the most politically important, and the third the most intimately divine of all human pursuits, yet the very greatness of their end, the health of the body, or of the commonwealth, or of the soul, diminishes, not increases, their claim to the appellation "liberal," and that still more, if they are cut down to the strict exigencies of that end. If, for instance, Theology, instead of being cultivated as a contemplation, be limited to the purposes of the pulpit or be represented by the catechism, it loses,—not its usefulness, not its divine character, not its meritoriousness (rather it gains a claim upon these titles by such charitable condescension),—but it does lose the particular attribute which I am illustrating; just as a face worn by tears and fasting loses its beauty, or a labourer's hand loses its delicateness;—for Theology thus exercised is not simple knowledge, but rather is an art of a businss making use of Theology. And thus it appears that even what is supernatural need not be liberal, nor need a hero be a gentleman, for the plain reason that one idea is not another idea. And in like manner the Baconian Philosophy, by using its physical sciences in the service of man, does thereby transfer them from the order of Liberal Pursuits to, I do not say the inferior, but the distinct class of the Useful. And, to take a different instance, hence again, as is evident, whenever personal gain is the motive, still more distinctive an effect has it upon the character of a given pursuit; thus racing, which was a liberal exercise in Greece, forfeits its rank in times like these, so far as it is made the occasion of gambling.

All that I have been now saying is summed up in a few characteristic words of the great Philosopher. "Of possessions," he says, "those rather are useful, which bear fruit; those *liberal, which tend to enjoyment*. By fruitful, I mean, which yield revenue; by enjoyable, where *nothing accrues of consequence beyond the using.*"

5

Do not suppose, that in thus appealing to the ancients, I am throwing back the world two thousand years, and fettering Philosophy with the reasonings of paganism. While the world lasts, will Aristotle's doctrine on these matters last, for he is the oracle of nature and of truth. While we are men, we cannot help, to a great extent, being Aristotelians, for the great Master does but analyze the thoughts, feelings, views, and opinions of human kind. He has told us the meaning of our own words and ideas, before we were born. In many subject-matters, to think correctly, is to think like Aristotle, and we are his disciples whether we will or no, though we may not know it. Now, as to the particular instance before us, the word "liberal" as applied to Knowledge and Education, expresses a specific idea, which ever has been, and ever will be, while the nature of man is the same, just as the idea of the Beautiful is specific, or of the Sublime, or of the Ridiculous, or of the Sordid. It is in the world now, it was in the world then; and, as in the case of the dogmas of faith, it is illustrated by a continuous historical tradition, and never was out of the world, from the time it came into it.

There have indeed been differences of opinion from time to time, as to what pursuits and what arts came under that idea, but such differences are but an additional evidence of it reality. That idea must have a substance in it, which has maintained its ground amid these conflicts and changes, which has ever served as a standard to measure things withal, which has passed from mind to mind unchanged, when there was so much to colour, so much to influence any notion or thought whatever, which was not founded in our very nature. Were it a mere generalization, it would have varied with the subjects from which it was generalized; but though its subjects vary with the age, it varies not itself. The palaestra may seem a liberal exercise to Lycurgus, and illiberal to Seneca; coach-driving and prize-fighting may be recognized in Elis, and be condemned in England; music may be despicable in the eyes of certain moderns, and be in the highest place with Aristotle and Plato,—(and the case is the same in the particular application of the idea of Beauty, or of Goodness, or of Moral Virtue, there is a difference of tastes, a difference of judgments)—still these variations imply, instead of discrediting, the archetypal idea, which is but a previous hypothesis or condition, by means of which issue is joined between contending opinions, and without which there would be nothing to dispute about.

I consider, then, that I am chargeable with no paradox, when I speak of a Knowledge which is its own end, when I call it liberal knowledge, or a gentleman's knowledge, when I educate for it, and make it the scope of a University. And still less am I incurring such a charge, when I make this acquisition consist, not in Knowledge in a vague and ordinary sense, but in that Knowledge which I have especially called Philosophy or, in an extended sense of the word, Science; for whatever claims Knowledge has to be considered as a good, these it has in a higher degree when it is viewed not vaguely, not popularly, but precisely and transcendently as Philosophy. Knowledge, I say, is then especially liberal, or sufficient for itself, apart from every external and ulterior object, when and so far as it is philosophical, and this I proceed to show.

6

Now bear with me, Gentlemen, if what I am about to say, has at first sight a fanciful appearance. Philosophy, then, or Science, is related to Knowledge in this way:—Knowledge is called by the name of Science or Philosophy, when it is acted upon, informed, or if I may use a strong figure, impregnated by Reason. Reason is the principle of that intrinsic fecundity of Knowledge, which, to those who possess it, is its especial value, and which dispenses with the necessity of their looking abroad for any end to rest upon external to itself. Knowledge, indeed, when thus exalted into a scientific form, is also power; not only is it excellent in itself, but whatever such excellence may be, it is something more, it has a result beyond itself. Doubtless; but that is a further consideration, with which I am not concerned. I only say that, prior to its being a power, it is a good; that it is, not only an instrument, but an end. I know well it may resolve itself into an art, and terminate in a mechanical process, and in tangible fruit; but it also may fall back upon that Reason which informs it, and resolve itself into Philosophy. In one case it is called Useful Knowledge, in the other Liberal. The same person may cultivate it in both ways at once; but this again is a matter foreign to my subject; here I do but say that there are two ways of using Knowledge, and in matter of fact those who use it in one way are not likely to use it in the other, or at least in a very limited measure. You see, then, here are two methods of Education; the end of the one is to be philosophical, of the other to be mechanical; the one rises towards general ideas, the other is exhausted upon what is particular and external. Let me not be thought to deny the necessity, or to decry the benefit, of such attention to what is particular and practical, as belongs to the useful or mechanical arts; life could not go on without them; we owe our daily welfare to them; their exercise is the duty of the many, and we owe to the many a debt of gratitude for fulfilling that duty. I only say that Knowledge, in proportion as it tends more and more to be particular, ceases to be Knowledge. It is a question whether Knowledge can in any proper sense be predicated of the brute creation; without pretending to metaphysical exactness of phraseology, which would be unsuitable to an occasion like this, I say, it seems to me improper to call that passive sensation, or perception of things, which brutes seem to possess, by the name of Knowledge. When I speak of Knowledge, I mean something intellectual, something which grasps what it perceives through the senses; something which takes a view of things; which sees more than the senses convey; which reasons upon what it sees, and while it sees; which invests it with an idea. It expresses itself, not in a mere enunciation, but by an enthymeme: it is of the nature of science from the first, and in this consists its dignity. The principle of real dignity in Knowledge, its worth, its desirableness, considered irrespectively of its results, is this germ within it of a scientific or a philosophical process. This is how it comes to be an end in itself; this is why it admits of being called Liberal. Not to know the relative disposition of things is the state of slaves or children; to have mapped out the Universe is the boast, or at least the ambition, of Philosophy.

   Moreover, such knowledge is not a mere extrinsic or accidental advantage which is ours to-day and another's to-morrow, which may be got up from a book, and easily forgotten again, which we can command or communicate at our pleasure, which we can borrow for the occasion, carry about in our hand, and take into the market; it is an acquired illumination, it is a habit, a personal possession, and an inward endowment. And this is the reason, why it is more correct, as well as more usual, to speak of a University as a place of education, than of instruction, though, when knowledge is concerned, instruction would at first sight have seemed the more appropriate word. We are instructed, for instance, in manual exercises, in the fine and useful arts, in trades, and in ways of business; for these are methods, which have little or no effect upon the mind itself, are contained in rules committed to memory, to tradition, or to use, and bear upon an end external to themselves. But education is a higher word; it implies an action upon our mental nature, and the formation of a character; it is something individual and permanent, and is commonly spoken of in connexion with religion and virtue. When, then, we speak of the communication of Knowledge as being Education, we thereby really imply that that Knowledge is a state or condition of mind; and since cultivation of mind is surely worth seeking for its own sake, we the thus brought once more to the conclusion, which the word "Liberal" and the word "Philosophy" have already suggested, that there is a Knowledge, which is desirable, though nothing come of it, as being of itself a treasure, and a sufficient remuneration of years of labour.

7

This, then, is the answer which I am prepared to give to the question with which I opened this Discourse. Before going on to speak of the object of the Church in taking up Philosophy, and the uses to which she puts it, I am prepared to maintain that Philosophy is its own end, and, as I conceive, I have now begun the proof of it. I am prepared to maintain that there is a knowledge worth possessing for what it is, and not merely for what it does; and what minutes remain to me to-day I shall devote to the removal of some portion of the indistinctness and confusion with which the subject may in some minds be surrounded.

It may be objected then, that, when we profess to seek Knowledge for some end or other beyond itself, whatever it be, we speak intelligibly; but that, whatever men may have said, however obstinately the idea may have kept its ground from age to age, still it is simply unmeaning to say that we seek Knowledge for its own sake, and for nothing else; for that it ever leads to something beyond itself, which therefore is its end, and the cause why it is desirable;—moreover, that this end is twofold, either of this world or of the next; that all knowledge is cultivated either for secular objects or for eternal; that if it is directed to secular objects, it is called Useful Knowledge, if to eternal, Religious or Christian Knowledge;—in consequence, that if, as I have allowed, this Liberal Knowledge does not benefit the body or estate, it ought to benefit the soul; but if the fact be really so, that it is neither a physical or a secular good on the one hand, nor a moral good on the other, it cannot be a good at all, and is not worth the trouble which is necessary for its acquisition.

And then I may be reminded that the professors of this Liberal or Philosophical Knowledge have themselves, in every age, recognized this exposition of the matter, and have submitted to the issue in which it terminates; for they have ever been attempting to make men virtuous; or, if not, at least have assumed that refinement of mind was virtue, and that they themselves were the virtuous portion of mankind. This they have professed on the one hand; and on the other, they have utterly failed in their professions, so as ever to make themselves a proverb among men, and a laughing-stock both to the grave and the dissipated portion of mankind, in consequence of them. Thus they have furnished against themselves both the ground and the means of their own exposure, without any trouble at all to any one else. In a word, from the time that Athens was the University of the world, what has Philosophy taught men, but to promise without practising, and to aspire without attaining? What has the deep and lofty thought of its disciples ended in but eloquent words? Nay, what has its teaching ever meditated, when it was boldest in its remedies for human ill, beyond charming us to sleep by its lessons, that we might feel nothing at all? like some melodious air, or rather like those strong and transporting perfumes, which at first spread their sweetness over every thing they touch, but in a little while do but offend in proportion as they once pleased us. Did Philosophy support Cicero under the disfavour of the fickle populace, or nerve Seneca to oppose an imperial tyrant? It abandoned Brutus, as he sorrowfully confessed, in his greatest need, and it forced Cato, as his panegyrist strangely boasts, into the false position of defying heaven. How few can be counted among its professors, who, like Polemo, were thereby converted from a profligate course, or like Anaxagoras, thought the world well lost in exchange for its possession? The philosopher in Rasselas taught a superhuman doctrine, and then succumbed without an effort to a trial of human affection.

"He discoursed," we are told, "with great energy on the government of the passions. His look was venerable (his action graceful, his pronunciation clear, and his diction elegant. He showed, with great strength of sentiment and variety of illustration, that human nature is degraded and debased, when the lower faculties predominate over the higher. He communicated the various precepts given, from time to time, for the conquest of passion, and displayed the happiness of those who had obtained the important victory, after which man is no longer the slave of fear, nor the fool of hope. . . . He enumerated many examples of heroes immoveable by pain or pleasure, who looked with indifference on those modes or accidents to which the vulgar give the names of good and evil."

Rasselas in a few days found the philosopher in a room half darkened, with his eyes misty, and his face pale. "Sir," said he, "you have come at a time when all human friendship is useless; what I suffer cannot be remedied, what I have lost cannot be supplied. My daughter, my only daughter, from whose tenderness I expected all the comforts of my age, died last night of a fever." "Sir," said the prince, "mortality is an event by which a wise man can never be surprised; we know that death is always near, and it should therefore always be expected." "Young man," answered the philosopher, "you speak like one who has never felt the pangs of separation." "Have you, then, forgot the precept," said Rasselas, "which you so powerfully enforced? . . . consider that external things are naturally variable, but truth and reason are always the same." "What comfort," said the mourner, "can truth and reason afford me? Of what effect are they now, but to tell me that my daughter will not be restored?"

8

Better, far better, to make no professions, you will say, than to cheat others with what we are not, and to scandalize them with what we are. The sensualist, or the man of the world, at any rate is not the victim of fine words, but pursues a reality and gains it. The Philosophy of Utility, you will say, Gentlemen, has at least done its work; and I grant it,—it aimed low, but it has fulfilled its aim. If that man of great intellect who has been its Prophet in the conduct of life played false to his own professions, he was not bound by his philosophy to be true to his friend or faithful in his trust. Moral virtue was not the line in which he undertook to instruct men; and though, as the poet calls him, he were the "meanest" of mankind, he was so in what may be called his private capacity and without any prejudice to the theory of induction. He had a right to be so, if he chose, for any thing that the Idols of the den or the theatre had to say to the contrary. His mission was the increase of physical enjoyment and social comfort; and most wonderfully, most awfully has he fulfilled his conception and his design. Almost day by day have we fresh and fresh shoots, and buds, and blossoms, which are to ripen into fruit, on that magical tree of Knowledge which he planted, and to which none of us perhaps, except the very poor, but owes, if not his present life, at least his daily food, his health, and general well-being. He was the divinely provided minister of temporal benefits to all of us so great, that, whatever I am forced to think of him as a man, I have not the heart, from mere gratitude, to speak of him severely. And, in spite of the tendencies of his philosophy, which are, as we see at this day, to depreciate, or to trample on Theology, he has himself, in his writings, gone out of his way, as if with a prophetic misgiving of those tendencies, to insist on it as the instrument of that beneficent Father, who, when He came on earth in visible form, took on Him first and most prominently the office of assuaging the bodily wounds of human nature. And truly, like the old mediciner in the tale, "he sat diligently at his work, and hummed, with cheerful countenance, a pious song;" and then in turn "went out singing into the meadows so gaily, that those who had seen him from afar might well have thought it was a youth gathering flowers for his beloved, instead of an old physician gathering healing herbs in the morning dew."

Alas, that men, in the action of life or in their heart of hearts, are not what they seem to be in their moments of excitement, or in their trances or intoxications of genius,—so good, so noble, so serene! Alas, that Bacon too in his own way should after all be but the fellow of those heathen philosophers who in their disadvantages had some excuse for their inconsistency, and who surprise us rather in what they did say than in what they did not do! Alas, that he too, like Socrates or Seneca, must be stripped of his holy-day coat, which looks so fair, and should be but a mockery amid his most majestic gravity of phrase; and, for all his vast abilities, should, in the little-ness of his own moral being, but typify the intellectual narrowness of his school! However, granting all this, heroism after all was not his philosophy: —I cannot deny he has abundantly achieved what he proposed. His is simply a Method whereby bodily discomforts and temporal wants are to be most effectually removed from the greatest number; and already, before it has shown any signs of exhaustion, the gifts of nature, in their most artificial shapes and luxurious profusion and diversity, from all quarters of the earth, are, it is undeniable, by its means brought even to our doors, and we rejoice in them.

9

Useful Knowledge then, I grant, has done its work; and Liberal Knowledge as certainly has not done its work,—that is, supposing, as the objectors assume, its direct end, like Religious Knowledge, is to make men better; but this I will not for an instant allow, and, unless I allow it, those objectors have said nothing to the purpose. I admit, rather I maintain, what they have been urging, for I consider Knowledge to have its end in itself. For all its friends, or its enemies, may say, I insist upon it, that it is as real a mistake to burden it with virtue or religion as with the mechanical arts. Its direct business is not to steel the soul against temptation or to console it in affliction, any more than to set the loom in motion, or to direct the steam carriage; be it ever so much the means or the condition of both material and moral advancement, still, taken by and in itself, it as little mends our hearts as it improves our temporal circumstances. And if its eulogists claim for it such a power, they commit the very same kind of encroachment on a province not their own as the political economist who should maintain that his science educated him for casuistry or diplomacy. Knowledge is one thing, virtue is another; good sense is not conscience, refinement is not humility, nor is largeness and justness of view faith. Philosophy, however enlightened, however profound, gives no command over the passions, no influential motives, no vivifying principles. Liberal Education makes not the Christian, not the Catholic, but the gentleman. It is well to be a gentlemen, it is well to have a cultivated intellect, a delicate taste, a candid, equitable, dispassionate mind, a noble and courteous bearing in the conduct of life;—these are the connatural qualities of a large knowledge; they are the objects of a University; I am advocating, I shall illustrate and insist upon them; but still, I repeat, they are no guarantee for sanctity or even for conscientiousness, they may attach to the man of the world, to the profligate, to the heartless,—pleasant, alas, and attractive as he shows when decked out in them. Taken by themselves, they do but seem to be what they are not; they look like virtue at a distance, but they are detected by close observers, and on the long run; and hence it is that they are popularly accused of pretence and hypocrisy, not, I repeat, from their own fault, but because their professors and their admirers persist in taking them for what they are not, and are officious in arrogating for them a praise to which they have no claim. Quarry the granite rock with razors, or moor the vessel with a thread of silk;

then may you hope with such keen and delicate instruments as human knowledge and human reason to contend against those giants, the passion and the pride of man.

Surely we are not driven to theories of this kind, in order to vindicate the value and dignity of Liberal Knowledge. Surely the real grounds on which its pretensions rest are not so very subtle or abstruse, so very strange or improbable. Surely it is very intelligible to say, and that is what I say here, that Liberal Education, viewed in itself, is simply the cultivation of the intellect, as such, and its object is nothing more or less than intellectual excellence. Every thing has its own perfection, be it higher or lower in the scale of things; and the perfection of one is not the perfection of another. Things animate, inanimate, visible, invisble, all are good in their kind, and have a *best* of themselves, which is an object of pursuit. Why do you take such pains with your garden or your park? You see to your walks and turf and shrubberies; to your trees and drives; not as if you meant to make an orchard of the one, or corn or pasture land of the other, but because there is a special beauty in all that is goodly in wood, water, plain, and slope, brought all together by art into one shape, and grouped into one whole. Your cities are beautiful, your palaces, your public buildings, your territorial mansions, your churches; and their beauty leads to nothing beyond itself. There is a physical beauty and a moral: there is a beauty of person, there is a beauty of our moral being, which is natural virtue; and in like manner there is a beauty, there is a perfection, of the intellect. There is an ideal perfection in these various subject-matters, towards which individual instances are seen to rise, and which are the standards for all instances whatever. The Greek divinities and demigods, as the statuary has moulded them, with their symmetry of figure, and their high forehead and their regular features, are the perfection of physical beauty. The heroes, of whom history tells, Alexander, or Caesar, or Scipio, or Saladin, are the representatives of that magnanimity or self-mastery which is the greatness of human nature. Christianity too has its heroes, and in the supernatural order, and we call them Saints. The artist puts before him beauty of feature and form; the poet, beauty of mind; the preacher, the beauty of grace: then intellect too, I repeat, has its beauty, and it has those who aim at it. To open the mind, to correct it, to refine it, to enable it to know, and to digest, master, rule, and use its knowledge, to give it power over its own faculties, application, flexibility, method, critical exactness, sagacity, resource, address, eloquent expression, is an object as intelligible (for here we are inquiring, not what the object of a Liberal Education is worth, nor what use the Church makes of it, but what it is in itself), I say, an object as intelligible as the cultivation of virtue, while, at the same time, it is absolutely distinct from it.

10

This indeed is but a temporal object, and a transitory possession; but so are other things in themselves which we make much of and pursue. The moralist will tell us that man, in all his functions, is but a flower which blossoms and fades, except so far as a higher principle breathes upon him, and makes him and what he is immortal. Body and mind are carried on into an eternal state of being by the gifts of Divine Munificence; but at first they do but fail in a failing world; and if the powers of intellect decay, the powers of the body have decayed before them, and, as an Hospital or an Almshouse, though its end be ephemeral, may be sanctified to the service of religion, so surely may a University, even were it nothing more than I have as yet described it. We attain to heaven by using this world well, though it is to pass away; we perfect our nature, not by undoing it, but by adding to it what is more than nature, and directing it towards aims higher than its own.

To Shape the Modern Mind:
Huxley and Liberal Education

Thomas Henry Huxley, "A Liberal Education; and Where to Find It,"
The Collected Essays of Thomas Henry Huxley (New York: D. Apple-
ton & Co., 1897), Vol. III, Science and Education, pp. 76–100.

Thomas Henry Huxley (1825–95), renowned as "Darwin's Bulldog," was himself a distinguished scientist and educator. He was more than a publicist and popularizer of natural selection or an anticlerical controversialist (in the broadest sense of the term). Huxley had reservations about the adequacy of Darwin's hypotheses and was a severe critic of the efforts to translate natural selection into social and political philosophy.

The antagonism between science and religion, about which we hear so much, appears to me to be purely factitious—fabricated, on the one hand, by short-sighted religious people who confound a certain branch of science, theology, with religion; and, on the other, by equally short-sighted scientific people who forget that science takes for its province only that which is susceptible of clear intellectual comprehension; and that, outside the boundaries of that province, they must be content with imagination, with hope, and with ignorance. [T. H. Huxley, "The Interpreters of Genesis and the Interpreters of Nature," Essays upon Some Controverted Questions (New York, 1892), p. 72.]

Huxley was a liberal reformer and the most ethical of humanists. He distrusted speculative philosophy, believing that materialism and spirituality were equal absurdities. Neither could be demonstrated; each was dangerous.

The antagonism of science is not to religion, but to the heathen survivals and the bad philosophy under which religion herself is often well-nigh crushed. And, for my part, I trust that this antagonism will never cease; but that, to the end of time, true science will continue to fulfill one of her most beneficent functions, that of relieving men from the burden of false science which is imposed upon them in the name of religion. [Ibid., p. 73.]

A savage controversialist, Huxley never tired of puncturing inflated self-confidence nor of challenging complacency. A stream of gentlemanly invective runs through his lectures, essays, and autobiography. Many of his attacks were as unbecoming as the banality he assailed, but the criticism—and it was made—would not impress him. Huxley believed that everyone must understand these matters. Agreement was less important than awareness. Being primarily concerned with modern ethics, Huxley reached conclusions strikingly similar to those of Nietzsche but lacking Nietzsche's despair. Man could understand; education will serve the function of intellectual and social regeneration.

"A Liberal Education; and Where to Find It" is addressed to the specific problem of educational reform. The burning issue of the day in Britain, this question continued to haunt the liberal state. Who should be educated? why? how? The impact of science on nineteenth-century thought and culture can be considered many ways; not the least important of them is that raised by Huxley.

IV

A LIBERAL EDUCATION; AND WHERE TO FIND IT

[1868]

The business which the South London Working Men's College has under-taken is a great work; indeed, I might say, that Education, with which that college proposes to grapple, is the greatest work of all those which lie ready to a man's hand just at present.

And, at length, this fact is becoming generally recognised. You cannot go anywhere without hearing a buzz of more or less confused and contra-dictory talk on this subject—nor can you fail to notice that, in one point at any rate, there is a very decided advance upon like discussions in former days. Nobody outside the agricultural interest now dares to say that educa-tion is a bad thing. If any representative of the once large and powerful party, which, in former days, proclaimed this opinion, still exists in a semi-fossil state, he keeps his thoughts to himself. In fact, there is a chorus of voices, almost distressing in their harmony, raised in favour of the doctrine that education is the great panacea for human troubles, and that, if the country is not shortly to go to the dogs, everybody must be educated.

The politicians tells us, "You must educate the masses because they are going to be masters." The clergy join in the cry for education, for they affirm that the people are drifting away from church and chapel into the broadest infidelity. The manufacturers and the capitalists swell the chorus lustily. They declare that ignorance makes bad workmen; that England will soon be unable to turn out cotton goods, or steam engines, cheaper than other people; and then, Ichabod! Ichabod! the glory will be departed from us. And a few voices are lifted up in favour of the doctrine that the masses should be educated because they are men and women with unlimited ca-pacities of being, doing, and suffering, and that it is as true now, as ever it was, that the people perish for lack of knowledge.

These members of the minority, with whom I confess I have a good deal of sympathy, are doubtful whether any of the other reasons urged in favour of the education of the people are of much value—whether, indeed, some of them are based upon either wise or noble grounds of action. They ques-tion if it be wise to tell people that you will do for them, out of fear of their power, what you have left undone, so long as your only motive was com-passion for their weakness and their sorrows. And, if ignorance of every-thing which it is needful a ruler should know is likely to do so much harm in the governing classes of the future, why is it, they ask reasonably enough, that such ignorance in the governing classes of the past has not been viewed with equal horror?

Compare the average artisan and the average country squire, and it may be doubted if you will find a pin to choose between the two in point of ignorance, class feeling, or prejudice. It is true that the ignorance is of a different sort—that the class feeling is in favour of a different class—and that the prejudice has a distinct savour of wrong-headedness in each case—but it is questionable if the one is either a bit better, or a bit worse, than the other. The old protectionist theory is the doctrine of trades unions as applied by the squires, and the modern trades unionism is the doctrine of the squires applied by the artisans. Why should we be worse off under one *régime* than under the other?

Again, this sceptical minority asks the clergy to think whether it is really want of education which keeps the masses away from their ministrations—whether the most completely educated men are not as open to reproach on this score as the workmen; and whether, perchance, this may not indicate that it is not education which lies at the bottom of the matter?

Once more, these people, whom there is no pleasing, venture to doubt whether the glory, which rests upon being able to undersell all the rest of the world, is a very safe kind of glory—whether we may not purchase it too dear; especially if we allow education, which ought to be directed to the making of men, to be diverted into a process of manufacturing human tools, wonderfully adroit in the exercise of some technical industry, but good for nothing else.

And, finally, these people inquire whether it is the masses alone who need a reformed and improved education. They ask whether the richest of our public schools might not well be made to supply knowledge, as well as gentlemanly habits, a strong class feeling, and eminent proficiency in cricket. They seem to think that the noble foundations of our old universities are hardly fulfilling their functions in their present posture of half-clerical seminaries, half racecourses, where men are trained to win a senior wranglership, or a double-first, as horses are trained to win a cup, with as little reference to the needs of after-life in the case of the man as in that of the racer. And, while as zealous for education as the rest, they affirm that, if the education of the richer classes were such as to fit them to be the leaders and the governors of the poorer; and, if the education of the poorer classes were such as to enable them to appreciate really wise guidance and good governance, the politicians need not fear mob-law, nor the clergy lament their want of flocks, nor the capitalists prognosticate the annihilation of the prosperity of the country.

Such is the diversity of opinion upon the why and the wherefore of education. And my hearers will be prepared to expect that the practical recommendations which are put forward are not less discordant. There is a loud cry for compulsory education. We English, in spite of constant experience to the contrary, preserve a touching faith in the efficacy of acts of Parliament; and I believe we should have compulsory education in the course of next session, if there were the least probability that half a dozen leading statesmen of different parties would agree what that education should be.

Some hold that education without theology is worse than none. Others maintain, quite as strongly, that education with theology is in the same predicament. But this is certain that those who hold the first opinion can by no means agree what theology should be taught; and that those who maintain the second are in a small minority.

At any rate "make people learn to read, write, and cipher," say a great many; and the advice is undoubtedly sensible as far as it goes. But, as has happened to me in former days, those who, in despair of getting anything better, advocate this measure, are met with the objection that it is very like making a child practise the use of a knife, fork, and spoon, without giving it a particle of meat. I really don't know what reply is to be made to such an objection.

But it would be unprofitable to spend more time in disentangling, or rather in showing up the knots in, the ravelled skeins of our neighbours. Much more to the purpose is it to ask if we possess any clue of our own which may guide us among these entanglements. And by way of a beginning, let us ask ourselves—What is education? Above all things, what is our ideal of a thoroughly liberal education?—of that education which, if we could begin life again, we would give ourselves—of that education which, if we could mould the fates to our own will, we would give our children? Well, I know not what may be your conceptions upon this matter, but I will tell you mine, and I hope I shall find that our views are not very discrepant.

Suppose it were perfectly certain that the life and fortune of every one of us would, one day or other, depend upon his winning or losing a game at chess. Don't you think that we should all consider it to be a primary duty to learn at least the names and the moves of the pieces; to have a notion of a gambit, and a keen eye for all the means of giving and getting out of check? Do you not think that we should look with a disapprobation amounting to scorn, upon the father who allowed his son, or the state which allowed its members, to grow up without knowing a pawn from a knight?

Yet it is a very plain and elementary truth, that the life, the fortune, and the happiness of every one of us, and, more or less, of those who are connected with us, do depend upon our knowing something of the rules of a game infinitely more difficult and complicated than chess. It is a game which has been played for untold ages, every man and woman of us being one of the two players in a game of his or her own. The chess-board is the world, the pieces are the phenomena of the universe, the rules of the game are what we call the laws of Nature. The player on the other side is hidden from us. We know that his play is always fair, just and patient. But also we know, to our cost, that he never overlooks a mistake, or makes the smallest allowance for ignorance. To the man who plays well, the highest stakes are paid, with that sort of overflowing generosity with which the strong shows delight in strength. And one who plays ill is checkmated—without haste, but without remorse.

My metaphor will remind some of you of the famous picture in which Retzsch has depicted Satan playing at chess with man for his soul. Substitute for the mocking fiend in that picture a calm, strong angel who is playing for love, as we say, and would rather lose than win—and I should accept it as an image of human life.

Well, what I mean by Education is learning the rules of this mighty game. In other words, education is the instruction of the intellect in the laws of Nature, under which name I include not merely things and their forces, but men and their ways; and the fashioning of the affections and of the will into an earnest and loving desire to move in harmony with those laws. For me, education means neither more nor less than this. Anything which professes to call itself education must be tried by this standard, and if it fails to stand the test, I will not call it education, whatever may be the force of authority, or of numbers, upon the other side.

It is important to remember that, in strictness, there is no such thing as an uneducated man. Take an extreme case. Suppose that an adult man, in the full vigour of his faculties, could be suddenly placed in the world, as Adma is said to have been, and then left to do as he best might. How long would he be left uneducated? Not five minutes. Nature would begin to teach him, through the eye, the ear, the touch, the properties of objects. Pain and pleasure would be at his elbow telling him to do this and avoid that; and by slow degrees the man would receive an education which, if narrow, would be thorough, real, and adequate to his circumstances, though there would be no extras and very few accomplishments.

And if to this solitary man entered a second Adam, or, better still, an Eve, a new and greater world, that of social and moral phenomena, would be revealed. Joys and woes, compared with which all others might seem but faint shadows, would spring from the new relations. Happiness and sorrow would take the place of the coarser monitors, pleasure and pain; but conduct would still be shaped by the observation of the natural consequences of actions; or, in others words, by the laws of the nature of man.

To every one of us the world was once as fresh and new as to Adam. And then, long before we were susceptible of any other mode of instruction, Nature took us in hand, and every minute of waking life brought its educational influence, shaping our actions into rough accordance with Nature's laws, so that we might not be ended untimely by too gross disobedience. Nor should I speak of this process of education as past for any one, be he as old as he may. For every man the world is as fresh as it was at the first day, and as full of untold novelties for him who has the eyes to see them. And Nature is still continuing her patient eduction of us in that great university, the universe, of which we are all members—Nature having no Test-Acts.

Those who take honours in Nature's university, who learn the laws which govern men and things and obey them, are the really great and successful men in this world. The great mass of mankind are the "Poll," who pick up just enough to get through without much discredit. Those who won't learn at all are plucked; and then you can't come up again. Nature's pluck means extermination.

Thus the question of compulsory education is settled so far as Nature is concerned. Her bill on that question was framed and passed long ago. But, like all compulsory legislation, that of Nature is harsh and wasteful in its operation. Ignorance is visited as sharply as wilful disobedience—incapacity meets with the same punishment as crime. Nature's discipline is not even a word and a blow, and the blow first; but the blow without the word. It is left to you to find out why your ears are boxed.

The object of what we commonly call education—that education in which man intervenes and which I shall distinguish as artificial education— is to make good these defects in Nature's methods; to prepare the child to receive Nature's education, neither incapably nor ignorantly, nor with wilful disobedience; and to understand the preliminary symptoms of her pleasure, without waiting for the box on the ear. In short, all artificial education ought to be an anticipation of natural education. And a liberal education is an artificial education which has not only prepared a man to escape the great evils of disobedience to natural laws, but has trained him to appreciate and to seize upon the rewards, which Nature scatters with as free a hand as her penalties.

That man, I think, has had a liberal education who has been so trained in youth that his body is the ready servant of his will, and does with ease and pleasure all the work that, as a mechanism, it is capable of; whose intellect is a clear, cold, logic engine, with all its parts of equal strength, and in smooth working order; ready, like a steam engine, to be turned to any kind of work, and spin the gossamers as well as forge the anchors of the mind; whose mind is stored with a knowledge of the great and fundamental truths of Nature and of the laws of her operations; one who, no stunted ascetic, is full of life and fire, but whose passions are trained to come to heel by a vigorous will, the servant of a tender conscience; who has learned to love all beauty, whether of Nature or of art, to hate all vileness, and to respect others as himself.

Such an one and no other, I conceive, has had a liberal education; for he is, as completely as a man can be, in harmony with Nature. He will make the best of her, and she of him. They will get on together rarely: she as his ever beneficent mother; he as her mouthpiece, her conscious self, her minister and interpreter.

Where is such an education as this to be had? Where is there any approximation to it? Has any one tried to found such an education? Looking over the length and breadth of these islands, I am afraid that all these questions must receive a negative answer. Consider our primary schools and what is taught in them. A child learns:—

1. To read, write, and cipher, more or less well; but in a very large pro-

portion of cases not so well as to take pleasure in reading, or to be able to write the commonest letter properly.

2. A quantity of dogmatic theology, of which the child, nine times out of ten, understands next to nothing.

3. Mixed up with this, so as to seem to stand or fall with it, a few of the broadest and simplest principles of morality. This, to my mind, is much as if a man of science should make the story of the fall of the apple in Newton's garden an integral part of the doctrine of gravitation and teach it as of equal authority with the law of the inverse squares.

4. A good deal of Jewish history and Syrian geography, and perhaps a little something about English history and the geography of the child's own country. But I doubt if there is a primary school in England in which hangs a map of the hundred in which the village lies, so that the children may be practically taught by it what a map means.

5. A certain amount of regularity, attentive obedience, respect for others: obtained by fear, if the master be incompetent or foolish; by love and reverence, it he be wise.

So fas as this school course embraces a training in the theory and practice of obedience to the moral laws of Nature, I gladly admit, not only that it contains a valuable educational element, but that, so far, it deals with the most valuable and important parts of all education. Yet, contrast what is done in this direction with what might be done; with the time given, to matters of comparatively no importance; with the absence of any attention to things of the highest moment; and one is tempted to think of Falstaff's bill and "the halfpenny worth of bread to all that quantity of sack."

Let us consider what a child thus "educated" knows, and what it does not know. Begin with the most important topic of all—morality, as the guide of conduct. The child knows well enough that some acts meet with approbation and some with disapprobation. But it has never heard that there lies in the nature of things a reason for every moral law, as cogent and as well defined as that which underlies every physical law; that stealing and lying are just as certain to be followed by evil consequences, as putting your hand in the fire, or jumping out of a garret window. Again, though the scholar may have been made acquainted, in dogmatic fashion, with the broad laws of morality, he has had no training in the application of those laws to the difficult problems which result from the complex conditions of modern civilisation. Would it not be very hard to expect any one to solve a problem in conic sections who had merely been taught the axioms and definitions of mathematical science?

A workman has to bear hard labour, and perhaps privation, while he sees others rolling in wealth, and feeding their dogs with what would keep his children from starvation. Would it not be well to have helped that man to calm the natural promptings of discontent by showing him, in his youth, the necessary connection of the moral law which prohibits stealing with the stability of society—by proving to him, once for all, that it is better for his own people, better for himself, better for future generations, that he should starve than steal? If you have no foundation of knowledge, or habit of thought, to work upon, what chance have you of persuading a hungry man that a capitalist is not a thief "with a circumbendibus?" And if he honestly believes that, of what avail is it to quote the commandment against stealing, when he proposes to make the capitalist disgorge?

Again, the child learns absolutely nothing of the history or the political organisation of his own country. His general impression is, that everything of much importance happened a very long while ago; and that the Queen and the gentlefolks govern the country much after the fashion of King David and the elders and nobles of Israel—his sole models. Will you give a man with this much information a vote? In easy times he sells it for a pot of beer. Why should he not? It is of about as much use to him as a chignon, and he knows as much what to do with it, for any other purpose. In bad times, on the contrary, he applies his simple theory of government, and believes that his rulers are the cause of his sufferings—a belief which sometimes bears remarkable practical fruits.

Least of all, does the child gather from this primary "education" of ours a conception of the laws of the physical world, or of the relations of cause and effect therein. And this is the more to be lamented, as the poor are especially exposed to physical evils, and are more interested in removing them than any other class of the community. If any one is concerned in knowing the ordinary laws of mechanics one would think it is the hand-labourer, whose daily toil lies among levers and pulleys; or among the other implements of artisan work. And if any one is interested in the laws of health, it is the poor workman, whose strength is wasted by ill-prepared food, whose health is sapped by bad ventilation and bad drainage, and half whose children are massacred by disorders which might be prevented. Not only does our present primary education carefully abstain from hinting to the workman that some of his greatest evils are traceable to mere physical agencies, which could be removed by energy, patience, and frugality; but it does worse—it renders him, so far as it can, deaf to those who could help him, and tries to substitute an Oriental submission to what is falsely declared to be the will of God, for his natural tendency to strive after a better condition.

What wonder, then, if very recently an appeal has been made to statistics for the profoundly foolish purpose of showing that education is of no good —that it diminishes neither misery nor crime among the masses of mankind? I reply, why should the thing which has been called education do either the one or the other? If I am a knave or a fool, teaching me to read and write won't make me less of either one or the other—unless somebody shows me how to put my reading and writing to wise and good purposes.

Suppose any one were to argue that medicine is of no use, because it could be proved statistically, that the percentage of deaths was just the same among people who had been taught how to open a medicine chest, and among those who did not so much as know the key by sight. The argument is absurd; but it is not more preposterous than that against which I am contending. The only medicine for suffering, crime, and all the other woes of mankind, is wisdom. Teach a man to read and write, and you have put into his hands the great keys of the wisdom box. But it is quite another matter whether he ever opens the box or not. And he is as likely to poison as to cure himself, if, without guidance, he swallows the first drug that comes to hand. In these times a man may as well be purblind, as unable to read—lame, as unable to write. But I protest that, if I thought the alternative were a necessary one, I would rather that the children of the poor should grow up ignorant of that knowledge to which these arts are means.

It may be said that all these animadversions may apply to primary schools, but that the higher schools at any rate, must be allowed to give a liberal education. In fact they professedly sacrifice everything else to this object.

Let us inquire into this matter. What do the higher schools, those to which the great middle class of the country sends its children, teach, over and above the instruction given in the primary schools? There is a little more reading and writing of English. But, for all that, every one knows that it is a rare thing to find a boy of the middle or upper classes who can read aloud decently, or who can put his thoughts on paper in clear and grammatical (to say nothing of good or elegant) language. The "ciphering" of the lower schools expands into elementary mathematics in the higher; into arithmetic, with a little algebra, a little Euclid. But I doubt if one boy in five hundred has ever heard the explanation of a rule of arithmetic, or knows his Euclid otherwise than by rote.

Of theology, the middle class schoolboy gets rather less than poorer children, less absolutely and less relatively, because there are so many other claims upon his attention. I venture to say that, in the great majority of cases, his ideas on this subject when he leaves school are of the most shadowy and vague description, and associated with painful impressions of the weary hours spent in learning collects and catechism by heart.

Modern geography, modern history, modern literature; the English language as a language; the whole circle of the sciences, physical, moral and social, are even more completely ignored in the higher than in the lower schools. Up till within a few years back, a boy might have passed through any one of the great public schools with the greatest distinction and credit, and might never so much as have heard of one of the subjects I have just mentioned. He might never have heard that the earth goes round the sun; that England underwent a great revolution in 1688, and France another in 1789; that there once lived certain notable men called Chaucer, Shakespeare, Milton, Voltaire, Goethe, Schiller. The first might be a German and the last an Englishman for anything he could tell you to the contrary. And as for Science, the only idea the word would suggest to his mind would be dexterity in boxing.

I have said that this was the state of things a few years back, for the sake of the few righteous who are to be found among the educational cities of the plain. But I would not have you too sanguine about the result, if you sound the minds of the existing generation of public schoolboys on such topics as those I have mentioned.

Now let us pause to consider this wonderful state of affairs; for the time will come when Englishmen will quote it as the stock example of the stolid stupidity of their ancestors in the nineteenth century. The most thoroughly commercial people, the greatest voluntary wanderers and colonists the world has ever seen, are precisely the middle classes of this country. If there be a people which has been busy making history on the great scale for the last three hundred years—and the most profoundly interesting history—history which, if it happened to be that of Greece or Rome, we should study with avidity—it is the English. If there be a people which, during the same period, has developed a remarkable literature, it is our own. If there be a nation whose prosperity depends absolutely and wholly upon their mastery over the forces of Nature, upon their intelligent apprehension of, and obedience to the laws of the creation and distribution of wealth, and of the stable equilibrium of the forces of society, it is precisely this nation. And yet this is what these wonderful people tell their sons:—"At the cost of from one to two thousand pounds of our hard-earned money, we devote twelve of the most precious years of your lives to school. There you shall toil, or be supposed to toil; but there you shall not learn one single thing of all those you will most want to know directly you leave school and enter upon the practical business of life. You will in all probability go into business, but you shall not know where, or how, any article of commerce is produced, or the difference between an export or an import, or the meaning of the word "capital." You will very likely settle in a colony, but you shall not know whether Tasmania is part of New South Wales, or *vice versâ*.

"Very probably you may become a manufacturer, but you shall not be provided with the means of understanding the working of one of your own steam-engines, or the nature of the raw products you employ; and, when you are asked to buy a patent, you shall not have the slightest means of judging whether the inventor is an impostor who is contravening the elementary principles of science, or a man who will make you as rich as Croesus.

"You will very likely get into the House of Commons. You will have to take your share in making laws which may prove a blessing or a curse to millions of men. But you shall not hear one word respecting the political organisation of your country; the meaning of the controversy between free-traders and protectionists shall never have been mentioned to you; you shall not so much as know that there are such things as economical laws.

"The mental power which will be of most importance in your daily life will be the power of seeing things as they are without regard to authority; and of drawing accurate general conclusions from particular facts. But at school and at college you shall know of no source of truth but authority; nor exercise your reasoning faculty upon anything but deduction from that which is laid down by authority.

"You will have to weary your soul with work, and many a time eat your bread in sorrow and in bitterness, and you shall not have learned to take refuge in the great source of pleasure without alloy, the serene resting-place for worn human nature,—the world of art."

Said I not rightly that we are a wonderful people? I am quite prepared to allow, that education entirely devoted to these omitted subjects might not be a completely liberal education. But is an education which ignores them all a liberal education? Nay, is it too much to say that the education which should embrace these subjects and no others would be a real education, though an incomplete one; while an education which omits them is really not an education at all, but a more or less useful course of intellectual gymnastics?

For what does the middle-class school put in the place of all these things which are left out? It substitutes what is usually comprised under the compendious title of the "classics"—that is to say, the languages, the literature, and the history of the ancient Greeks and Romans, and the geography of so much of the world as was known to these two great nations of antiquity. Now, do not expect me to depreciate the earnest and enlightened pursuit of classical learning. I have not the least desire to speak ill of such occupations, nor any sympathy with those who run them down. On the contrary, if my opportunities had lain in that direction, there is no investigation into which I could have thrown myself with greater delight than that of antiquity.

What science can present greater attractions than philology? How can a lover of literary excellence fail to rejoice in the ancient masterpieces? And with what consistency could I, whose business lies so much in the attempt to decipher the past, and to build up intelligible forms out of the scattered fragments of long-extinct beings, fail to take a sympathetic, though an unlearned, interest in the labours of a Niebuhr, a Gibbon, or a Grote? Classical history is a great section of the palaeontology of man; and I have the same double respect for it as for other kinds of palaeontology—that is to say, a respect for the facts which it establishes as for all facts, and a still greater respect for it as a preparation for the discovery of a law of progress.

But if the classics were taught as they might be taught—if boys and girls were instructed in Greek and Latin, not merely as languages, but as illustrations of philological science; if a vivid pucture of life on the shores of the Mediterranean two thousand years ago were imprinted on the minds of scholars; if ancient history were taught, not as a weary series of feuds and fights, but traced to its causes in such men placed under such conditions; if, lastly, the study of the classical books were followed in such a manner as to impress boys with their beauties, and with the grand simplicity of their statement of the everlasting problems of human life, instead of with their verbal and grammatical peculiarities; I still think it as little proper that they should form the basis of a liberal education for our contemporaries, as I should think it fitting to make that sort of palaeontology with which I am familiar the back-bone of modern education.

It is wonderful how close a parallel to classical training could be made out of that palaeontology to which I refer. In the first place I could get up an osteological primer so arid, so pedantic in its terminology, so altogether distasteful to the youthful mind, as to beat the recent famous production of the head-masters out of the field in all these excellences. Next, I could exercise my boys upon easy fossils, and bring out all their powers of memory and all their ingenuity in the application of my osteo-grammatical rules to the interpretation, or construing, of those fragments. To those who had reached the higher classes, I might supply odd bones to be built up into animals, giving great honour and reward to him who succeeded in fabricating monsters most entirely in accordance with the rules. That would answer to verse-making and essay-writing in the dead languages.

To be sure, if a great comparative anatomist were to look at these fabrications he might shake his head, or laugh. But what then? Would such a catastrophe destroy the parallel? What, think you, would Cicero, or Horace, say to the production of the best sixth form going? And would not Terence stop his ears and run out if he could be present at an English performance of his own plays? Would *Hamlet,* in the mouths of a set of French actors, who should insist on pronouncing English after the fashion of their own tongue, be more hideously ridiculous?

But it will be said that I am forgetting the beauty, and the human interest, which appertain to classical studies. To this I reply that it is only a very strong man who can appreciate the charms of a landscape as he is toiling up a steep hill, along a bad road. What with short-windedness, stones, ruts, and a pervading sense of the wisdom of rest and be thankful, most of us have little enough sense of the beautiful under these circumstances. The ordinary schoolboy is precisely in this case. He finds Parnassus uncommonly steep, and there is no chance of his having much time of inclination to look about him till he gets to the top. And nine times out of ten he does not get to the top.

But if this be a fair picture of the results of classical teaching at its best —and I gather from those who have authority to speak on such matters that it is so—what is to be said of classical teaching at its worst, or in other words, of the classics of our ordinary middle-class schools? I will tell you. It means getting up endless forms and rules by heart. It means turning Latin and Greek into English, for the mere sake of being able to do it, and without the smallest regard to the worth, or worthlessness, of the author read. It means the learning of innumerable, not always decent, fables in such a shape that the meaning they once had is tried up into utter trash; and the only impression left upon a boy's mind is, that the people who believed such things must have been the greatest idiots the world ever saw. And it means, finally, that after a dozen years spent at this kind of work, the sufferer shall be incompetent to interpret a passage in an author he has not already got up; that he shall loathe the sight of a Greek or Latin book; and that he shall never open, or think of, a classical writer again, until, wonderful to relate, he insists upon submitting his sons to the same process.

These be your gods, O Israel! For the sake of this net result (and respectability) the British father denies his children all the knowledge they might turn to account in life, not merely for the achievement of vulgar success, but for guidance in the great crises of human existence. This is the stone he offers to those whom he is bound by the strongest and tenderest ties to feed with bread.

If primary and secondary education are in this unsatisfactory state, what is to be said to the universities? This is an awful subject, and one I almost fear to touch with my unhallowed hands; but I can tell you what those say who have authority to speak.

The Rector of Lincoln College, in his lately published valuable "Suggestions for Academical Organisation with especial reference to Oxford," tells us:—

The colleges were, in their origin, endowments, not for the elements of a general liberal education, but for the prolonged study of special and professional faculties by men of riper age. The universities embraced both these objects. The colleges, while they incidentally aided in elementary education, were specially devoted to the highest learning. . . .

This was the theory of the middle-age university and the design of collegiate foundations in their origin. Time and circumstances have brought about a total change. The colleges no longer promote the researches of science, or direct professional study. Here and there college walls may shelter an occasional student, but not in larger proportions than may be found in private life. Elementary teaching of youths under twenty is now the only function performed by the university, and almost the only object of college endowments. Colleges were homes for the life-study of the highest and most abstruse parts of knowledge. They have become boarding schools in which the elements of the learned languages are taught to youths.

If Mr. Pattison's high position, and his obvious love and respect for his university, be insufficient to convince the outside world that language so severe is yet no more than just, the authority of the Commissioners who reported on the University of Oxford in 1850 is open to no challenge. Yet they write:—

It is generally acknowledged that both Oxford and the country at large suffer greatly from the absence of a body of learned men devoting their lives to the cultivation of science, and to the direction of academical education.

The fact that so few books of profound research emanate from the University of Oxford, materially impairs its character as a seat of learning, and consequently its hold on the respect of the nation.

Cambridge can claim no exemption from the reproaches addressed to Oxford. And thus there seems no escape from the admission that what we fondly call our great seats of learning are simply "boarding schools" for bigger boys; that learned men are not more numerous in them than out of them; that the advancement of knowledge is not the object of fellows of colleges; that, in the philosophic calm and meditative stillness of their greenswarded courts, philosophy does not thrive, and meditation bears few fruits.

It is my great fortune to reckon amongst my friends resident members of both universities, who are men of learning and research, zealous cultivators of science, keeping before their minds a noble ideal of a university, and doing their best to make that ideal a reality; and, to me, they would necessarily typify the universities, did not the authoritative statements I have quoted compel me to believe that they are exceptional, and not representative men. Indeed, upon calm consideration, several circumstances lead me to think that the Rector of Lincoln College and the Commissioners cannot be far wrong.

I believe there can be no doubt that the foreigner who should wish to become acquainted with the scientific, or the literary, activity of modern England, would simply lose his time and his pains if he visited our universities with that object.

And, as for works of profound research on any subject, and, above all, in that classical lore for which the universities profess to sacrifice almost everything else, why, a third-rate, poverty-stricken German university turns out more produce of that kind in one year, than our vast and wealthy foundations elaborate in ten.

Ask the man who is investigating any question, profoundly and thoroughly—be it historical, philosophical, philological, physical, literary, or theological; who is trying to make himself master of any abstract subject (except, perhaps, political economy and geology, both of which are intensely Anglican sciences), whether he is not compelled to read half a dozen times as many German as English books? And whether, of these English books, more than one in ten is the work of a fellow of a college, or a professor of an English university?

Is this from any lack of power in the English as compared with the German mind? The countrymen of Grote and of Mill, of Faraday, of Robert Brown, of Lyell, and of Darwin, to go no further back than the contemporaries of men of middle age, can afford to smile at such a suggestion. England can show now, as she has been able to show in every generation since civilisation spread over the West, individual men who hold their own against the world, and keep alive the old tradition of her intellectual eminence.

But, in the majority of cases, these men are what they are in virtue of their native intellectual force, and of a strength of character which will not recognise impediments. They are not trained in the courts of the Temple of Science, but storm the walls of that edifice in all sorts of irregular ways, and with much loss of time and power, in order to obtain their legitimate positions.

Our universities not only do not encourage such men; do not offer them positions, in which it should be their highest duty to do, thoroughly, that which they are most capable of doing; but, as far as possible, university training shuts out of the minds of those among them, who are subjected to it, the prospect that there is anything in the world for which they are specially fitted. Imagine the success of the attempt to still the intellectual hunger of any of the men I have mentioned, by putting before him, as the object of existence, the successful mimicry of the measure of a Greek song, or the roll of Ciceronian prose! Imagine how much success would be likely to attend the attempt to persuade such men that the education which leads to perfection in such elegances is alone to be called culture; while the facts of history, the process of thought, the conditions of moral and social exist-ence, and the laws of physical nature are left to be dealt with as they may by outside barbarians!

It is not thus that the German universities, from being beneath notice a century ago, have become what they are now—the most intensely culti-vated and the most productive intellectual corporations the world has ever seen.

The student who repairs to them sees in the list of classes and of profes-sors a fair picture of the world of knowledge. Whatever he needs to know there is some one ready to teach him, some one competent to discipline him in the way of learning; whatever his special bent, let him but be able and diligent, and in due time he shall find distinction and a career. Among his professors he sees men whose names are known and revered throughout the civilised world; and their living example infects him with a noble ambition, and a love for the spirit of work.

The Germans dominate the intellectual world by virtue of the same simple secret as that which made Napoleon the master of old Europe. They have declared *la carrière ouverte aux talents*, and every Bursch marches with a professor's gown in his knapsack. Let him become a great scholar, or a man of science, and ministers will compete for his services. In Ger-many, they do not leave the chance of his holding the office he would render illustrious to the tender mercies of a hot canvass, and the final wisdom of a mob of country parsons.

In short, in Germany, the universities are exactly what the Rector of Lincoln and the Commissioners tell us the English universities are not;

that is to say, corporations "of learned men devoting their lives to the cultivation of science, and the direction of academical education." They are not
"boarding schools for youths," nor clerical seminaries; but institutions for
the higher culture of men, in which the theological faculty is of no more
importance, or prominence, than the rest; and which are truly "universities,"
since they strive to represent and embody the totality of human knowledge,
and to find room for all forms of intellectual activity.

May zealous and clear-headed reformers like Mr. Pattison succeed in
their noble endeavours to shape our universities towards some such ideal as
this, without losing what is valuable and distinctive in their social tone!
But until they have succeeded, a liberal education will be no more obtainable in our Oxford and Cambridge Universities than in our public schools.

If I am justified in my conception of the ideal of a liberal education; and
if what I have said about the existing educational institutions of the country
is also true, it is clear that the two have no sort of relation to one another;
that the best of our schools and the most complete of our university train-
ings give but a narrow, one-sided, and essentially illiberal education—
while the worst give what is really next to no education at all. The South
London Working-Men's College could not copy any of these institutions if
it would; I am bold enough to express the conviction that it ought not if it
could.

For what is wanted is the reality and not the mere name of a liberal
education; and this College must steadily set before itself the ambition to
be able to give that education sooner or later. At present we are but beginning, sharpening our educational tools, as it were, and, except a modicum
of physical science, we are not able to offer much more than is to be found
in an ordinary school.

Moral and social science—one of the greatest and most fruitful of our
future classes, I hope—at present lacks only one thing in our programme,
and that is a teacher. A considerable want, no doubt; but it must be re-
collected that it is much better to want a teacher than to want the desire to
learn.

Further, we need what, for want of a better name, I must call Physical
Geography. What I mean is that which the Germans call "*Erdkunde.*" It
is a description of the earth, of its place and relation to other bodies; of its
general structure, and of its great features—winds, tides, mountains, plains:
of the chief forms of the vegetable and animal worlds, of the varieties of
man. It is the peg upon which the greatest quantity of useful and entertaining scientific information can be suspended.

Literature is not upon the College programme; but I hope some day to
see it there. For literature is the greatest of all sources of refined pleasure,
and one of the great uses of a liberal education is to enable us to enjoy that
pleasure. There is scope enough for the purposes of liberal education in the
study of the rich treasures of our own language alone. All that is needed is
direction, and the cultivation of a refined taste by attention to sound criti-

cism. But there is no reason why French and German should not be mastered sufficiently to read what is worth reading in those languages with pleasure and with profit.

And finally, by and by, we must have History; treated not as a succession of battles and dynasties; not as a series of biographies; not as evidence that Providence has always been on the side of either Whigs or Tories; but as the development of man in times past, and in other conditions than our own.

But, as it is one of the principles of our College to be self-supporting, the public must lead, and we must follow, in these matters. If my hearers take to heart what I have said about liberal education, they will desire these things, and I doubt not we shall be able to supply them. But we must wait till the demand is made.

The Emancipation of Reason: Friedrich Nietzsche

Friedrich Wilhelm Nietzsche, The Will to Power: an Attempted Transvaluation of All Values, ed. Oscar Levy, trans. Anthony M. Ludovici (London: George Allen & Unwin Ltd., 1910), Vol. II, Book III, Part III, pp. 183–238.

How many things a man can be! Friedrich Wilhelm Nietzsche (1844–1900) was philosopher, literary stylist (he ranked himself second only to Goethe), incisive critic of modern society and thought. He anticipates Freud and psychoanalysis; he anticipates the revolt against politics; he anticipates existentialism. Every aspirant to the status of intellectual finds comfort in Nietzsche. Here is a man who understood. Nietzsche recognized the growing power and importance of science. He saw the need for a new cultural metaphysic. Nietzsche conceived of himself as an emancipator, and Nietzscheans concur. He unfetters the mind.

Where does the mind go, once released? Nietzsche delighted in being considered dangerous and destructive by his critics. One scholar after another, in honorable pedigree running to the present and undoubtedly into the future, has demonstrated that Nietzsche did not advocate purification by war, did not justify the crude racism of subsequent years, did not believe in German nationalism, did not—— The list can run on almost indefinitely. The protests suggest a problem. It was, as more than one critic observes, Nietzsche's misfortune to be a better writer than philosopher. His phrases and aphorisms invite misuse.

Terribleness belongs to greatness: let us not deceive ourselves [1028].

In times of painful tension and vulnerability, choose war. War hardens and develops muscle [1040].

Nietzsche resists systematization of thought as his champions have discovered. The game that Nietzsche was playing with himself (Nietzsche—anti-Nietzsche) and his readers may be exciting; it is certainly dangerous. The problem of application and effect of Nietzsche's thought is quite different from the problem of what Nietzsche actually says. *The Will to Power* is posthumous (1901 and 1906). It was subjected to every abuse in editing and arrangement by Frau Förster-Nietzsche, his narrow-minded, anti-Semitic sister, and her colleagues, but it was a work that Nietzsche intended to write. It was also popular and helped to provide the rhetoric of tyranny and dictatorship. Nietzschean influence—which ran directly counter to Nietzsche's own beliefs—played out to become the school of the irrational, the denigration of democracy and the liberal state, the elevation of elites, and the cult of irresponsible will.

III

THE WILL TO POWER AS EXEMPLIFIED IN SOCIETY AND THE INDIVIDUAL

I. SOCIETY AND THE STATE

716

WE TAKE IT as a principle that only individuals feel any responsibility. Corporations are invented to do what the individual has not the courage to do. For this reason all communities are vastly more upright and instructive, as regards the nature of man, than the individual who is too cowardly to have the courage of his own desires.

All altruism is the prudence of the private man: societies are not mutually altruistic. The commandment, "Thou shalt love thy next-door neighbour," has never been extended to thy neighbour in general. Rather what Manu says is probably truer: "We must conceive of all the States on our own frontier, and their allies, as being hostile, and for the same reason we must consider all of their neighbours as being friendly to us."

The study of society is invaluable, because man in society is far more childlike than man individually. Society has never regarded virtue as anything else than as a means to strength, power, and order. Manu's words again are simple and dignified: "Virtue could hardly rely on her own strength alone. Really it is only fear of punishment that keeps men in their limits, and leaves every one in peaceful possession of his own."

717

The State, or *unmorality* organised, is from within—the police, the penal code, status, commerce, and the family; and from without, the will to war, to power, to conquest and revenge.

A multitude will do things an individual will not, because of the division of responsibility, of command and execution; because the virtues of obedience, duty, patriotism, and local sentiment are all introduced; because feelings of pride, severity, strength, hate, and revenge—in short, all typical traits are upheld, and these are characteristics utterly alien to the herd-man.

718

You haven't, any of you, the courage either to kill or to flog a man. But the huge machinery of the State quells the individual and makes him decline to be answerable for his own deed (obedience, loyalty, etc.).

Everything that a man does in the service of the State is against his own nature. Similarly, everything he learns in view of future service of the State. This result is obtained through division of labour (so that responsibility is subdivided too):—

The legislator—and he who fufils the law.

The teacher of discipline—and those who have grown hard and severe under discipline.

719

A division of labour among the emotions exists inside society, making individuals and classes produce an imperfect, but more useful, kind of soul. Observe how every type in society has become atrophied with regard to certain emotions with the view of fostering and accentuating other emotions.

Morality may be thus justified:—

Economically,—as aiming at the greatest possible use of all individual power, with the view of preventing the waste of exceptional natures.

Aesthetically,—as the formation of fixed types, and the pleasure in one's own.

Politically,—as the art of bearing with the severe divergencies of the degrees of power in society.

Psychologically,—as an imaginary preference for the bungled and the mediocre, in order to preserve the weak.

720

Man has one terrible and fundamental wish; he desires power, and this impulse, which is called freedom, must be the longest restrained. Hence ethics has instinctively aimed at such an education as shall restrain the desire for power; thus our morality slanders the would-be tyrant, and glorifies charity, patriotism, and the ambition of the herd.

721

Impotence to power,—how it disguises itself and plays the hypocrite, as obedience, subordination, the pride of duty and morality, submission, devotion, love (the idolisation and apotheosis of the commander is a kind of compensation, and indirect self-enhancement). It veils itself further under fatalism and resignation, objectivity, self-tyranny, stoicism, asceticism, self-abnegation, hallowing. Other disguises are: criticism, pessimism, indignation, susceptibility, "beautiful soul," virtue, self-deification, philosophic detachment, freedom from contact with the world (the realisation of impotence disguises itself as disdain).

There is a universal need to exercise some kind of power, or to create for one's self the appearance of some power, if only temporarily, in the form of intoxication.

There are men who desire power simply for the sake of the happiness it will bring; these belong chiefly to political parties. Other men have the same yearning, even when power means visible disadvantages, the sacrifice of their happiness, and well-being; they are the ambitious. Other men, again, are only like dogs in a manger, and will have power only to prevent its falling into the hands of others on whom they would then be dependent.

722

If there be justice and equality before the law, what would thereby be abolished?—Suspense, enmity, hatred. But it is a mistake to think that you thereby increase happiness; for the Corsicans rejoice in more happiness than the Continentals.

723

Reciprocity and the expectation of a reward is one of the most seductive forms of the devaluation of mankind. It involves that equality which depreciates any gulf as immoral.

724

Utility is entirely dependent upon the object to be attained,—the wherefore? And this wherefore, this purpose, is again dependent upon the degree of power. Utilitarianism is not, therefore, a fundamental doctrine; it is only a story of sequels, and cannot be made obligatory for all.

725

Of old, the State was regarded theoretically as a utilitarian institution; it has now become so in a practical sense. The time of kings has gone by, because people are no longer worthy of them. They do not wish to see the symbol of their ideal in a king, but only a means to their own ends. That's the whole truth.

726

I am trying to grasp the absolute sense of the communal standard of judgment and valuation, naturally without any intention of deducing morals.

The degree of psychological falsity and denseness required in order to sanctify the emotions essential to preservation and expansion of power, and to create a good conscience for them.

The degree of stupidity required in order that general rules and values may remain possible (including, formation of culture, and training).

The degree of inquisitiveness, suspicion, and intolerance required in order to deal with exceptions, to suppress them as criminals, and thus to give them bad consciences, and to make them sick with their own singularity.

727

Morality is essentially a shield, a means of defence; and, in so far, it is a sign of the imperfectly developed man (he is still in armour; he is still stoical).

The fully developed man is above all provided with *weapons*: he is a man who *attacks*.

The weapons of war are converted into weapons of peace (out of scales and carapaces grow feathers and hair).

728

The very notion, "living organism," implies that there must be growth,— that there must be a striving after an extension of power, and therefore a process of absorption of other forces. Under the drowsiness brought on by moral narcotics, people speak of the right of the individual to *defend* himself; on the same principle one might speak of his right to *attack*: for *both*— and the latter more than the former—are necessities where all living organisms are concerned: aggressive and defensive egoism are not questions of choice or even of "free will," but they are fatalities of life itself.

In this respect it is immaterial whether one have an individual, a living body, or "an advancing society" in view. The right to punish (or society's means of defence) has been arrived at only through a misuse of the word "right": a right is acquired only by contract,—but self-defence and self-preservation do not stand upon the basis of a contract. A people ought at least, with quite as much justification, to be able to regard its lust of power, either in arms, commerce, trade, or colonisation, as a right—the right of growth, perhaps. . . . When the instincts of a society ultimately make it give up war and renounce conquest, it is decadent: it is ripe for democracy and the rule of shopkeepers. In the majority of cases, it is true, assurances of peace are merely stupefying draughts.

729

The maintenance of the military State is the last means of adhering to the great tradition of the past; or, where it has been lost, to revive it. By means of it the superior or strong type of man is preserved, and all institutions and ideas which perpetuate enmity and order of rank in States, such as national feeling, protective tariffs, etc., may on that account seem justified.

730

In order that a thing may last longer than a person (that is to say, in order that a work may outlive the individual who has created it), all manner of limitations and prejudices must be imposed upon people. But how? By means of love, reverence, gratitude towards the person who created the work, or by means of the thought that our ancestors fought for it, or by virtue of the feeling that the safety of our descendants will be secured if we uphold the work—for instance, the *polis*. Morality is essentially the means of making something survive the individual, because it makes him of necessity a slave. Obviously the aspect from above is different from the aspect from below, and will lead to quite different interpretations. How is organised power *maintained?* —By the fact that countless generations sacrifice themselves to its cause.

731

Marriage, property, speech, tradition, race, family, people, and State, are each links in a chain—separate parts which have a more or less high or low origin. Economically they are justified by the surplus derived from the advantages of uninterrupted work and multiple production, as weighed against the disadvantages of greater expense in barter and the difficulty of making things last. (The working parts are multiplied, and yet remain largely idle. Hence the cost of producing them is greater, and the cost of maintaining them by no means inconsiderable.) The advantage consists in avoiding interruption and incident loss. Nothing is more expensive than a start. "The higher the standard of living, the greater will be the expense of maintenance, nourishment, and propagation, as also the risk and the probability of an utter fall on reaching the summit."

732

In bourgeois marriages, naturally in the best sense of the word marriage, there is no question whatsoever of love any more than there is of money. For on love no institution can be founded. The whole matter consists in society giving leave to two persons to satisfy their sexual desires under conditions obviously designed to safeguard social order. Of course there must be a certain attraction between the parties and a vast amount of good nature, patience, compatibility, and charity in any such contract. But the word love should not be misused as regards such a union. For two lovers, in the real and strong meaning of the word, the satisfaction of sexual desire is unessential; it is a mere symbol. For one side, as I have already said, it is a symbol of unqualified submission: for the other, a sign of condescension —a sign of appropriation of property. Marriage, as understood by the real old nobility, meant the breeding forth of the race (but are there any nobles nowadays? *Quaeritur*),—that is to say, the maintenance of a fixed definite type of ruler, for which object husband and wife were sacrificed. Naturally the first consideration here had nothing to do with love; on the contrary! It did not even presuppose that mutual sympathy which is the *sine qua non* of the bourgeois marriage. The prime consideration was the interest of the race, and in the second place came the interest of a particular class. But in the face of the coldness and rigour and calculating lucidity of such a noble concept of marriage as prevailed among every healthy aristocracy, like that of ancient Athens, and even of Europe during the eighteenth century, we warm-blooded animals, with our miserably oversensitive hearts, we "moderns," cannot restrain a slight shudder. That is why love as a passion, in the big meaning of this word, was invented for, and in, an aristocratic community—where convention and abstinence are most severe.

733

Concerning the future of marriage.—A super-tax on inherited property, a longer term of military service for bachelors of a certain minimum age within the community.

Privileges of all sorts for fathers who lavish boys upon the world, and perhaps plural votes as well.

A medical certificate as a condition of any marriage, endorsed by the parochial authorities, in which a series of questions addressed to the parties and the medical officers must be answered ("family histories").

As a counter-agent to prostitution, or as its ennoblement, I would recommend leasehold marriages (to last for a term of years or months), with adequate provision for the children.

Every marriage to be warranted and sanctioned by a certain number of good men and true, of the parish, as a parochial obligation.

734

Another commandment of philanthropy.—There are cases where to have a child would be a crime—for example, for chronic invalids and extreme neurasthenics. These people should be converted to chastity, and for this purpose the music of *Parsifal* might at all events be tried. For Parsifal himself, that born fool, had ample reasons for not resiring to propagate. Unfortunately, however, one of the regular symptoms of exhausted stock is the inability to exercise any self-restraint in the presence of stimuli, and the tendency to respond to the smallest sexual attraction. It would be quite a mistake, for instance, to think of Leopardi as a chaste man. In such cases the priest and moralist play a hopeless game: it would be far better to send for the apothecary. Lastly, society here has a positive duty to fulfil, and of all the demands that are made on it, there are few more urgent and necessary than this one. Society as the trustee of life, is responsible to life for every botched life that comes into existence, and as it has to atone for such lives, it ought consequently to make it impossible for them ever to see the light of day: it should in many cases actually prevent the act of procreation, and may, without any regard for rank, descent, or intellect, hold in readiness the most rigorous forms of compulsion and restrictsion, and, under certain circumstances have recoure to castration. The Mosaic law, "Thou shalt do no murder," is a piece of ingenuous pueriilty compared with the earnestness of this forbidding of life to decadents, "Thou shalt not beget"!!! . . . For life itself recognises no solidarity or equality of rights between the healthy and unhealthy parts of an organism. The latter must at all cost be *eliminated,* lest the whole fall to pieces. Compassion for decadents, equal rights for the physiologically botched—this would be the very pinnacle of immorality, it would be setting up Nature's mort formidable opponent as morality itself!

735

There are some delicate and morbid natures, the so-called idealists, who can never under any circumstances rise above a coarse, immature crime: yet it is the great justification of their anaemic little existence, it is the small requital for their lives of cowardice and falsehood to have been for one *instant* at least—strong. But they generally collapse after such an act.

736

In our civilised world we seldom hear of any but the bloodless, trembling criminal, overwhelmed by the curse and contempt of society, doubting even himself, and always belittling and belying his deeds—a misbegotten sort of criminal; that is why we are opposed to the idea that *all great men have been criminals* (only in the grand style, and neither petty nor pitiful), that crime must be inherent in greatness (this at any rate is the unanimous verdict of all those students of human nature who have sounded the deepest waters of great souls). To feel one's self adrift from all questions of ancestry, conscience, and duty—this is the danger with which every great man is confronted. Yet this is precisely what he desires: he desires the great goal, and consequently the means thereto.

737

In times when man is led by reward and punishment, the class of man which the legislator has in view is still of a low and primitive type: he is treated as one treats a child. In our latter-day culture, general degeneracy removes all sense from reward and punishment. This determination of action by the prospect of reward and punishment presupposes young, strong, and vigorous races. In effete races impulses are so irrepressible that a mere idea has no force whatever. Inability to offer any resistance to a stimulus, and the feeling that one must react to it: this excessive susceptibility of decadents makes all such systems of punshiment and reford altogether senseless.

.   .   .   .

The idea "amelioration" presupposes a normal and strong creature whose action must in some way be balanced or cancelled if he is not to be lost and turned into an enemy of the community.

738

The effect of prohibition.—Every power which forbids and which knows how to excite fear in the person forbidden creates a guilty conscience. (That is to say, a person has a certain desire but is conscious of the danger of gratifying it, and is consequently forced to be secretive, underhand, and cautious.) Thus any prohibition deteriorates the character of those who do not willingly submit themselves to it, but are constrained thereto.

739

"Punishment and reward."—These two things stand or fall together. Nowadays no one will accept a reward or acknowledge that any authority should have the power to punish. Warfare has been reformed. We have a desire: it meets with opposition: we then see that we shall most easily obtain it by coming to some agreement—by drawing up a contract. In modern society where every one has given his assent to a certain contract, the criminal is a man who breaks that contract. This at least is a clear concept. But in that case, anarchists and enemies of social order could not be tolerated.

740

Crimes belong to the category of revolt against the social system. A rebel is not punished, he is simply suppressed. He *may* be an utterly contemptible and pitiful creature; but there is nothing intrinsically despicable about rebellion—in fact, in our particular society revolt is far from being disgraeful. There are cases in which a rebel deserves honour precisely because he is conscious of certain elements in sociey which cry aloud for hostility; for such a man rouses us from our slumbers. When a criminal commits but one crime against a particular person, it does not alter the fact that all his instincts urge him to make a stand against the whole social sysem. His isolated act is merely a symptom.

The idea of punishment ought to be reduced to the concept of the suppression of revolt, a weapon against the vanquished (by means of long or short terms of imprisonment). But punishment should not be associated in any way with contempt. A criminal is at all events a man who has set his life, his honour, his freedom at stake; he is therefore a man of courage. Neither should punishment be regarded as penance or retribution, as though there were some recognised rate of exchange between crime and punishment. Punishment does not purify, simply because crime does not sully.

A criminal should not be prevented from making his peace with society, provided he does not belong to the race of criminals. In the latter case, however, he should be opposed even before he has committed an act of hostility. (As soon as he gets into the clutches of society the first operation to be performed upon him should be that of castration.) A criminal's bad manners and his low degree of intelligence should not be reckoned against him. Nothing is more common than that he should misunderstand himself (more particularly when his rebellious instinct—the rancour of the *unclassed*— has not reached consciousness simply because he has not read enough). It is natural that he should deny and dishonour his deed while under the influence of fear at its failure. All this is quite distinct from those cases in which, psychologically speaking, the criminal yields to an incomprehensible impulse, and attributes a motive to his deed by associating it with a merely incidental and insignificant action (for example, robbing a man, when his real desire was to take his blood).

The worth of a man should not be measured by any one isolated act. Napoleon warned us against this. Deeds which are only skin-deep are more particularly insignificant. If we have no crime—let us say no murder—on our conscience; why is it? It simply means that a few favourable circumstances have been wanting in our lives. And supposing we were induced to commit such a crime would our worth be materially affected? As a matter of fact, we should only be despised, if we were not credited with possessing the power to kill a man under certain circumstances. In nearly every crime certain qualities come into play without which no one would be a true man. Dostoievsky was not far wrong when he said of the inmates of the penal colonies in Siberia, that they constituted the strongest and most valuable portion of the Russian people. The fact that in our society the criminal happens to be a badly nourished and stunted animal is simply a condemnation of our system. In the days of the Renaissance the criminal was a flourishing specimen of humanity, and acquired his own virtue for himself. —Virtue in the sense of the Renaissance—that is to say, *virtù*; free from moralic acid.

It is only those whom we do not despise that we are able to elevate. Moral contempt is a far greater indignity and insult than any kind of crime.

741

Shame was first introduced into punishment when certain penalties were inflicted on persons held in contempt, such as slaves. It was a despised class that was most frequently punished, and thus it came to pass that punishment and contempt were associated.

742

In the ancient idea of punishment a religious concept was immanent, namely, the retributive power of chastisement. Penalties purified: in modern society, however, penalties degrade. Punishment is a form of paying off a debt: once it has been paid, one is freed from the deed for which one was so ready to suffer. Provided belief in the power of punishment exist, once the penalty is paid a feeling of relief and lightheartedness results, which is not so very far removed from a state of convalescence and health. One has made one's peace with society, and one appears to one's self more dignified—"pure." . . . To-day, however, punishment isolates even more than the crime; the fate behind the sin has become so formidable that it is almost hopeless. One rises from punishment still an enemy of society. Henceforward it reckons yet another enemy against it. The *jus talionis* may spring from the spirit of retribution (that is to say, from a sort of modification of the instinct of revenge); but in the Book of Manu, for instance, it is the need of having some equivalent in order to do penance, or to become free in a religious sense.

743

My pretty radical note of interrogation in the case of all more modern laws of punishment is this: should not the punishment fit the crime?—for in your heart of hearts thus would you have it. But then the susceptibility of the particular criminal to pain would have to be taken into account. In other words, there should be no such thing as a preconceived penalty for any crime—no fixed penal code. But as it would be no easy matter to ascertain the degree of sensitiveness of each individual criminal, punishment would have to be abolished in practice? What a sacrifice! Is it not? Consequently . . .

744

Ah! and the philosophy of jurisprudence! That is a science which, like all moral sciences, has not even been wrapped in swaddling-clothes yet. Even among jurists who consider themselves liberal, the oldest and most valuable significance of punishment is still misunderstood—it is not even known. So long as jurisprudence does not build upon a new foundation—on history and comparative anthropology—it will never cease to quarrel over the fundamentally false abstractions which are fondly imagined to be the "philosophy of law," and which have nothing whatever to do with modern man. The man of to-day, however, is such a complicated woof even in regard to his legal valuation that he allows of the most varied interpretation.

745

An old Chinese sage once said he had heard that when mighty empires were doomed they began to have numberless laws.

746

Schopenhauer would have all rapscallions castrated, and all geese shut up in convents. But from what point of view would this be desirable? The rascal has at least this advantage over other men—that he is not mediocre; and the fool is superior to us inasmuch as he does not suffer at the sight of mediocrity. It would be better to widen the gulf—that is to say, roguery and stupidity should be increased. In this way human nature would become broader . . . but, after all, this is Fate, and it will happen, whether we desire it or not. Idiocy and roguery are increasing: this is part of modern progress.

747

Society, to-day, is full of consideration, tact, and reticence, and of good-natured respect for other people's rights—even for the exactions of strangers. To an ever greater degree is there a certain charitable and instinctive depreciation of the worth of man as shown by all manner of trustful habits. Respect for men, and not only for the most virtuous, is perhaps the real parting of the ways between us and the Christian mythologists. We also have our good share of irony even when listening to moral sermons. He who preaches morality to us debases himself in our eyes and becomes almost comical. Liberal-mindedness regarding morality is one of the best signs of our age. In cases where it is most distinctly wanting, we regard it as a sign of a morbid condition (the case of Carlyle in England, of Ibsen in Norway, and Schopenhauer's pessimism throughout Europe). If there is anything which can reconcile us to our own age, it is precisely the amount of immorality which it allows itself without falling in its own estimation— very much the reverse! In what, then, does the superiority of culture over the want of culture consist—of the Renaissance, for instance, over the Middle Ages? In this alone: the greater quantity of acknowledged immorality. From this it necessarily follows that the very *zenith* of human development *must* be regarded by the moral fanatic as the *non plus ultra* of corruption (in this connection let us recall Savonarola's judgment of Florence, Plato's indictment of Athens under Pericles, Luther's condemnation of Rome, Rousseau's anathemas aganist the society of Voltaire, and German's hostility of Goethe).

748

A little more fresh air, for Heaven's sake! This ridiculous condition of Europe *must* not last any longer. Is there a single idea behind this bovine nationalism? What possible value can there be in encouraging this arrogant self-conceit when everything to-day points to greater and more common interests?—at a moment when the spiritual dependence and denationalisation, which are obvious to all, are paving the way for the reciprocal *rapprochements* and fertilisations which make up the real value and sense of present-day culture! . . . And it is precisely now that "the new German Empire" has beeen founded upon the most thread-bare and discredited of ideas—universal suffrage and equal right for all.

Think of all this struggling for advantage among conditions which are in every way degenerate: of this culture of big cities, of newspapers, of hurry and scurry, and of "aimlessness"! The economic unity of Europe must necessarily come—and with it, as a reaction, the pacivist movement.

A pacivist party, free from all sentimentality, which forbids its children to wage war; which forbids recourse to courts of justice; which forswears all fighting, all contradiction, and all persecution: for a while the party of the oppressed, and later the powerful party:—this party would be opposed to everything in the shape of revenge and resentment.

There will also be a war party, exercising the same thoroughness and severity towards self, which will proceed in precisely the opposite direction.

749

The princes of Europe should really consider whether as a matter of fact they can dispense with our services—with us, the immoralists. We are to-day the only power which can win a victory without allies: and we are there-fore far and away the strongest of the strong. We can even do without lying, and let me ask what other power can dispense with this weapon? A strong temptation fights for us; the strongest, perhaps, that exists—the tempta-tion of truth. . . . Truth? How do I come by this word? I must withdraw it: I must repudiate this proud word. But no. We do not even want it—we shall be quite able to achieve our victory of power without its help. The real charm which fights for us, the eye of Venus which our opponents them-selves deaden and blind—this charm is the magic of the extreme. The fas-cination which everything extreme exercises: we immoralists—we are in every way the extremists.

750

The corrupted ruling classes have brought ruling into evil odour. The State administration of justice is a piece of cowardice, because the great man who can serve as a standard is lacking. At last the feeling of insecurity becomes so great that men fall in the dust before any sort of will-power that commands.

751

"The will to power" is so loathed in democratic ages that the whole of the psychology of these ages seems directed towards its belittlement and slander. The types of men who sought the highest honours are said to have been Napoleon! Caesar! and Alexander!—as if these had not been precisely the greatest *scorners* of honour.

And Helvetius would fain show us that we strive after power in order to have those pleasures which are at the disposal of the mighty—that is to say, according to him, this striving after power is the will to pleasure—hedonism!

752

According as to whether a people feels: "the rights, the keenness of vision, and the gifts of leading, etc., are with the few" or "with the many"—it constitutes an oligarchic or a democratic community.

Monarchy represents the belief in a man who is completely superior—a leader, a saviour, a demigod.

Aristocracy represents the belief in a chose few—in a higher caste.

Democracy represents the disbelief in all great men and in all élite societies: everybody is everybody else's equal. "At bottom we are all herd and mob."

753

I am opposed to Socialism because it dreams ingenuously of "goodness, truth, beauty, and equal rights" (anarchy pursues the same ideal, but in a more brutal fashion).

I am opposed to parliamentary government and the power of the press, because they are the means whereby cattle become master.

754

The arming of the people means in the end the arming of the mob.

755

Socialists are particularly ridiculous in my eyes, because of their absurd optimism concerning the "good man" who is supposed to be waiting in their cupboards, and who will come into being when the present order of society has beeen overturned and has made way for natural instincts. But the opposing party is quite as ludicrous, because it will not see the act of violence which lies beneath every law, the severity and egoism inherent in every kind of authority. "I and my kind will rule and prevail. Whoever degenerates will be either expelled or annihilated."—This was the fundamental feeling of all ancient legislation. The idea of a higher order of man is hated much more profoundly than monarchs themselves. Hatred of aristocracy always uses hatred of monarchy as a mask.

756

How treacherous are all parties! They bring to light something concerning their leaders which the latter, perhaps, have hitherto kept hidden beneath a bushel with consummate art.

757

Modern Socialism would fain create a profane counterpart to Jesuitism: everybody a perfect instrument. But as to the object of it all, the purpose of it—this has not yet been ascertained.

758

The slavery of to-day: a piece of barbarism. Where are the master for whom these slaves work? One must not always expect the simultaneous appearance of the two complementary castes of society.

Utility and pleasure are slave theories of life. "The blessing of work" is an ennobling phrase for slaves. Incapacity for leisure.

759

There is no such thing as a right to live, a right to work, or a right to be happy: in this respect man is not different from the meanest worm.

760

We must undoubtedly think of these things as uncompromisingly as Nature does: they preserve the species.

761

We should look upon the needs of the masses with ironic compassion: they want something which we have got—Ah!

762

European democracy is only in a very slight degree the manifestation of unfettered powers. It represents, above all, the unfettering of laziness, fatigue, and *weakness*.

763

Concerning the future of the workman.—Workmen should learn to regard their duties as *soldiers* do. They receive emoluments, incomes, but they do not get wages!

There is on relationship between *work done* and money received; the individual should, *according to his kind*, be so placed as to *perform* the *highest* that is compatible with his powers.

764

Noblemen ought one day to live as the bourgeois do now—but above them, distinguishing themselves by the simplicity of their wants—the superior caste will then live in a poorer and simpler way and yet be in possession of power.

For lower orders of mankind the reverse valuations hold good: it is a matter of implanting "virtues" in them. Absolute commands, terrible compulsory methods, in order that they may rise above mere ease in life. The remainder may obey, but their vanity demands that they may feel themselves dependent, not upon great men, but upon principles.

765

"The Atonement of all Sin"

People speak of the "profound injustice" of the social arrangement, as if the fact that one man is born in favourable circumstances and that another is born in unfavourable ones—or that one should possess gifts the other has not, were on the face of it an injustice. Among the more honest of these opponents of society this is what is said: "We, with all the bad, morbid, criminal qualities which we acknowledge we possess, are only the inevitable result of the oppression for ages of the weak by the strong"; thus they insinuate their evil natures into the consciences of the ruling classes. They threaten and storm and surse. They become virtuous from sheer indignation—they don't want to have become bad men and *canaille* for nothing. The name for this attitude, which is an invention of the last century, is, if I am not mistaken, pessimism; and even that pessimism which is the outcome of indignation. It is in this attitude of mind that history is judged, that it is deprived of its inevitable fatality, and that responsibility and even guilt is discovered in it. For the great desideratum is to find guilty people in it. The botched and the bungled, the decadents of all kinds, are revolted at themselves, and require sacrifices in order that they may not slake their thirst for destruction upon themselves (which might, indeed, be the most reasonable procedure). But for this purpose they at least require a semblance of justification, *i.e.* a theory according to which the fact of their existence, and of their character, may be expiated by a scapegoat. This scapegoat may be God,—in Russia such resentful atheists are not wanting,—or the order of society, or education and upbringing, or the Jews, or the nobles, or, finally, the well-constituted of every kind. "It is a sin for a man to have been born in decent circumstances, for by so doing he disinherits the others, he pushes them aside, he imposes upon them the curse of vice and of work. . . . How can I be made answerable for my misery; surely some one must be responsible for it, or I could not bear to live." . . . In short, resentful pessimism discovers responsible parties in order to create a pleasurable sensation for itself—revenge. . . . "Sweeter than honey"—thus does even old Homer speak of revenge.

. . . .

The fact that such a theory no longer meets with understanding—or rather, let us say, contempt—is accounted for by that particle of Christianity which still circulates in the blood of every one of us; it makes us tolerant towards things simply because we scent a Christian savour about them. . . . The Socialists appeal to the Christian instincts; this is their really refined piece of cleverness. . . . Thanks to Christianity, we have now grown accustomed to the superstitious concept of a soul—of an immortal soul, of soul monads, which, as a matter of fact, hails from somewhere else, and which has only become inherent in certain cases—that is to say, become incarnate in them—by accident: but the nature of these cases is not altered, let alone determined by it. The circumstances of society, of relationship, and of history are only accidents for the soul, perhaps misadventures: in any case, the world is not their work. By means of the idea of soul the individual is made transcendental; thanks to it, a ridiculous amount of importance can be attributed to him.

As a matter of fact, it was Christianity which first induced the individual to take up this position of judge of all things. It made megalomania almost his duty: it has made everything temporary and limited subordinate to eternal rights! What is the State, what is society, what are historical laws, what is physiology to me? Thus speaks something from beyond Becoming, an immutable entity throughout history: thus speaks something immortal, something divine—it is the soul!

Another Christian, but no less insane, concept has percolated even deeper into the tissues of modern ideas: the concept of the equality of all souls before God. In this concept the prototype of all theories concerning equal rights is to be found. Man was first taught to stammer this proposition religiously: later, it was converted into a moral; no wonder he has ultimately begun to take it seriously, to take it *practically!*—that is to say, politically, socialistically, resento-pessimistically.

Wherever responsible circumstances or people have been looked for, it was the *instinct of revenge* that sought them. This instinct of revenge obtained such an ascendancy over man in the course of centuries that the whole of metaphysics, psychology, ideas of society, and, above all, morality, are tained with it. Man has nourished this idea of responsibility to such an extent that he has introduced the bacillus of vengeance into everything. By means of it he has made God Himself ill, and killed innocence in the universe, by tracing every condition of things to acts of will, to intentions, to responsible agents. The whole teaching of will, this most fatal fraud that has ever existed in psychology hitherto, was invented essentially for the purpose of punishment. It was the social utility of punishment that lent this concept its dignity, its power, and its truth. The originator of that psychology, that we shall call volitional psychology, must be sought in those classes which had the right of punishment in their hands; above all, therefore, among the priests who stood on the very pinnacle of ancient social systems: these people wanted to create for themselves the right to wreak revenge—they wanted to supply God with the privilege of vengeance. For this purpose; man was declared "free"; to this end every action had to be regarded as voluntary, and the origin of every deed had to be considered as lying in consciousness. But by such propositions as these ancient psychology is refuted.

To-day, when Europe seems to have taken the contrary direction; when we halcyonians would fain withdraw, dissipate, and banish the concept of guilt and punishment with all our might from the world; when our most serious endeavours are concentrated upon purifying psychology, morality, history, nature, social institutions and privileges, and even God Himself, from this filth; in whom must we recognise our most mortal enemeis? Precisely in those apostles of revenge and resentment, in those who are *par excellence* pessimists from indignation, who make it their mission to sanctify their filth with the name of "righteous indignation." . . . We others, whose one desire is to reclaim innocence on behalf of Becoming, would fain be the missionaries of a purer thought, namely, that no one is responsible for man's qualities; neither God, nor society, nor his parents, nor his ancestors, nor himself—in fact, that no one is to blame for him. . . . The being who might be made responsible for a man's existence, for the fact that he is constituted in a particular way, or for his birth in certain circumstances and in a certain environment, is absolutely lacking.—*And it is a great blessing that such a being is non-existent.* . . . We are *not* the result of an eternal design, of a will, of a desire: there is no attempt being made with us to attain to an "ideal of perfection," to an "ideal of happiness," to an "ideal of virtue,"—and we are just as little the result of a mistake on God's part in the presence of which He ought to feel uneasy (a thought which is known to be at the very root of the Old Testament). There is not a place nor a purpose nor a sense to which we can attribute our existence or our kind of existence. In the first place, no one is in a position to do this: it is quite impossible to judge, to measure, or to compare, or even to deny the whole universe! And why?—For five reasons, all accessible to the man of average intelligence: for instance, *because there is no existence outside the universe* . . . and let us say it again, this is a great blessing, for therein lies the whole innocence of our lives.

2. THE INDIVIDUAL

766

Fundamental errors: to regard the *herd* as an aim instead of the individual! The herd is only a means and nothing *more*! But nowadays people are trying to understand *the herd* as they would an individual, and to confer higher rights upon it than upon isolated personalities. Terrible mistake!! In addition to this, all that makes for gregariousness, *e.g.* sympathy, is regarded as the *more valuable* side of our natures.

767

The individual is something quite *new*, and capable of *creating new things*. He is something absolute, and all his actions are quite his own. The individual in the end has to seek the valuation for his actions in himself: because he has to give an individual meaning even to traditional words and notions. His interpretation of a formula is at least personal, even if he does not create the formula itself: at least as an interpreter he is creative.

768

The "ego" oppresses and kills. It acts like an organic cell. It is predatory and violent. It would fain regenerate itself—pregnancy. It would fain give birth to its God and see all mankind at its feet.

769

Every living organism gropes around as far as its power permits, and overcomes all that is weaker than itself: by this means it finds pleasure in its own existence. The *increasing "humanity"* of this tendency consists in the fact that we are beginning to feel ever more subtly how difficult it is really to *absorb* others: while we could show our power by injuring him, his will *estranges* him from us, and thus makes him less susceptible of being overcome.

770

The degree of resistance which has to be continually overcome in order to remain *at the top*, is the measure of *freedom*, whether for individuals or for societies: freedom being understood as positive power, as will to power. The highest form of individual freedom, of sovereignty, would, according to this, in all probability be found not five feet away from its opposite—that is to say, where the danger of slavery hangs over life, like a hundred swords of Damocles. Let any one go through the whole of history from this point of view: the ages when the individual reaches perfect maturity, *i.e.* the free ages, when the classical types, *sovereign man*, is attained to—these were certainly not humane times!

There should be no choice: either one must be uppermost or nethermost —like a worm, despised, annihilated, trodden upon. One must have tyrants against one in order to become a tyrant, *i.e.* in order to be free. It is no small advantage to have a hundred swords of Damocles suspended over one: it is only thus that one learns to dance, it is only thus that one attains to any freedom in one's movements.

771

Man more than any other animal was originally *altruistic*—hence his slow growth (child) and lofty development. Hence, too, his extraordinary and latest kind of egoism.—Beasts of prey are much more *individualistic*.

772

A criticism of *selfishness*. The involuntary ingenuousness of La Rochefoucauld, who believed that he was saying something bold, liberal, and paradoxical (in his days, of course, truth in psychological matters was something that astonished people) when he said: "*Les grandes âmes ne sont pas celles qui ont moins de passions et plus de vertus que les âmes communes, mais seulement celles qui ont de plus grands desseins.*" Certainly, John Stuart Mill (who calls Chamfort the *noble* and philosophical La Rochefoucauld of the eighteenth century) recognises in him merely an astute and keen-sighted observer of all that which is the result of habitual selfishness in the human breast, and he adds: "A noble spirit is unable to see the necessity of a constant observation of *baseness* and *contemptibility*, unless it were to show against what corrupting influences a lofty spirit and a noble character were able to triumph."

773

The Morphology of the Feelings of Self

First standpoint.—To what extent are *sympathy* or *communal feelings*, the lower or preparatory states, at a time when personal self-esteem and initiative in valuation, on the part of individuals, are not yet possible?

Second standpoint.—To what extent is the zenith of collective self-esteem, the pride in the distinction of the clan, the feeling of inequality and a certain abhorrence of mediation, of equal rights and of reconciliation, the school for individual self-esteem? It may be this in so far as it compels the individual to represent the pride of the community—he is obliged to speak and act with tremendous self-respect, because he stands for the community. And the same holds good when the individual regards himself as the instrument or speaking-tube of a godhead.

Third standpoint.—To what extent do these form of impersonality invest the individual with enormous importance? In so far as higher powers are using him as an intermediary: religious shyness towards one's self is the condition of prophets and poets.

Fourth standpoint.—To what extent does responsibility for a whole educate the individual in foresight, and give him a severe and terrible hand, a calculating and cold heart, majesty of bearing and of action—things which he would not allow himself if he stood only for his own rights?

In short, collective self-esteem is the great preparatory school for personal sovereignty. The noble caste is that which creates the heritage of this faculty.

774

The disguised forms of will to power:—

(1) *The desire for freedom*, for independence for equilibrim, for peace, for *co-ordination*. Also that of the anchorite, the "Free-Spirit." In its lowest form, the will to live at all costs—the instinct of self-preservation.

(2) Subordination, with the view of satisfying the will to power of a whole community; submissiveness, the making of one's self indispensable and useful to him who has the power; love, a secret path to the heart of the powerful, in order to become his master.

(3) The feeling of duty, conscience, the imaginary comfort of belonging to a higher order than those who actually hold the reins of power; the acknowledgment of an order of rank which allows of judging even the more powerful; self-depreciation; the discovery of new *codes of morality* (of which the Jews are a classical example).

775

Praise and gratitude as forms of will to power.—Praise and gratitude for harvests, for good weather, victories, marriages, and peace—all festivals need a subject on which feeling can be outpoured. The desire is to make all good things that happen to one appear as though they had been done to one: people will have a donor. The same holds good of the work of art: people are not satisfied with it alone, they must praise the artist.—What, then, is praise? It is a sort of compensation for benefits received, a sort of giving back, a manifestation of *our* power—for the man who praises assents to, blesses, values, *judges*: he arrogates to himself the right to give his consent to a thing, to be able to confer honours. An increased feeling of happiness or of liveliness is also an increased feeling of power, and it is as a result of this feeling that a man *praises* (it is as the outcome of this feeling that he invents a donor, a "subject"). Gratitude is thus revenge of a lofty kind: it is most severely exercised and demanded where equality and pride both require to be upheld—that is to say, where revenge is practised to its fullest extent.

776

Concerning the Machiavellism of Power

The *will to power* appears:—

(*a*) Among the oppressed and slaves of all kinds, in the form of will to "*freedom*": the mere fact of breaking loose from something seems to be an end in itself (in a religio-moral sense: "One is only answerable to one's own conscience"; "evangelical freedom," etc. etc.).

(*b*) In the case of a stronger species, ascending to power, in the form of the will to overpower. If this fails, then it shrinks to the "will to justice"— that is to say, to the will to the same measure of rights as the ruling caste possesses.

(*c*) In the case of the strongest, richest, most independent, and most courageous, in the form of "love of humanity," of "love of the people," of the "gospel," of "truth," of "God," of "pity," of "self-sacrifice," etc. etc.; in the form of overpowering, of deeds of capture, of imposing service on some one, of an instinctive reckoning of one's self as part of a great mass of power to which one attempts to give a direction: the hero, the prophet, the Caesar, the Saviour, the bell-wether. (The love of the sexes also belongs to this category; it will overpower something, possess it utterly, and it looks like self-abnegation. At bottom it is only the love of one's instrument, of one's "horse"—the conviction that things belong to one because one is in a position to use them.)

"*Freedom*," "*Justice*," "*Love*"!!!

777

Love.—Behold this love and pity of women—what could be more egoistic? . . . And when they do sacrifice themselves and their honour or reputation, to whom do they sacrifice themselves? To the man? Is it not rather to an unbridled desire? These desires are quite as selfish, even though they may be beneficial to others and provoke gratitude. . . . To what extent can such a hyperfoetation of one valuation sanctify everything else!!

778

"*Senses*," "*Passions*."—When the fear of the senses and of the passions and of the desires becomes so great as to warn us against them, it is already a symptom of *weakness*: extreme measures always characterise abnormal conditions. That which is lacking here, or more precisely that which is decaying, is the power to resist an impulse: when one feels instinctively that one must yield,—that is to say, that one must react,—then it is an excellent thing to avoid opportunities (temptations).

The stimulation of the senses is only a temptation in so far as those creatures are concerned whose systems are easily swayed and influenced:

on the other hand, in the case of remarkable constitutional obtuseness and hardness, strong stimuli are necessary in order to set the functions in motion. Dissipation can only be objected to in the case of one who has no right to it; and almost all passions have fallen into disrepute thanks to those who were not strong enough to convert them to their own advantage.

One should understand that passions are open to the same objections as illnesses: yet we should not be justified in doing without illnesses, and still less without passions. We require the abnormal; we give life a tremendous shock by means of these great illnesses.

In detail the following should be distinguished:—

(1) The *dominating passion*, which may even bring the supremest form of health with it: in this case the co-ordination of the internal system and its functions to perform one task is best attained,—but this is almost a definition of health.

(2) The antagonism of the passions—the double, treble, and multiple soul in one breast: this is very unhealthy; it is a sign of inner ruin and of disintegration, betraying and promoting an internal dualism and anarchy —unless, of course, one passion becomes master. *Return to health.*

(3) The juxtaposition of passions without their being either opposed or united with one another. Very often transitory, and then, as soon as order is established, this condition may be a healthy one. A most interesting class of men belong to this order, the chameleons; they are not necessarily at loggerheads with themselves, they are both happy and secure, but they cannot develop—their moods lie side by side, even though they may seem to lie far apart. They change, but they become nothing.

779

The quantitative estimate of aims and its influence upon the valuing standpoint: the *great* and the *small* criminal. The greatness or smallness of the aims will determine whether the doer feels respect for himself with it all, or whether he feels pusillanimous and miserable.

The degree of intellectuality manifested in the means employed may likewise influence our valuation. How differently the philosophical innovator, experimenter, and man of violence stands out against robbers, barbarians, adventurers!—There is a semblance of disinterestedness in the former.

Finally, noble manners, bearing, courage, self-confidence,—how they alter the value of that which is attained by means of them!

. . . .

Concerning the optics of valuation:—
The influence of the greatness or smallness of the aims.
The influence of the intellectuality of the means.
The influence of the behaviour in action.

The influence of success or failure.

The influence of opposing forces and their value.

The influence of that which is permitted and that which is forbidden.

780

The tricks by means of which actions, measures, and passions are legitimised, which from an individual standpoint are no longer good form or even in good taste:—

Art, which allows us to enter such strange worlds, makes them tasteful to us.

Historians prove its justification and reason; travels, exoticism, psychology, penal codes, the lunatic asylum, the criminal, sociology.

Impersonality (so that as media of a collective whole we allow ourselves these passions and actions—the Bar, juries, the bourgeois, the soldier, the minister, the prince, society, "critics") makes us feel that we are *sacrificing something*.

781

Preoccupations concerning one's self and one's eternal salvation are not expressive either of a rich or of a self-confident nature, for the latter lets all questions of eternal bliss go to the devil,—it is not interested in such matters of happiness; it is all power, deeds, desires; it imposes itself upon things; it even violates things. The Christian is a romantic hypochondriac who does not stand firmly on his legs.

Whenever hedonistic views come to the front, one can always presuppose the existence of pain and a certain ill-constitutedness.

782

"The growing autonomy of the individual"—Parisian philosophers like M. Fouillée talk of such things: they would do well to study the *race moutonnière* for a moment; for they belong to it. For Heaven's sake open your eyes, ye sociologists who deal with the future! The individual grew strong under quite opposite conditions: ye describe the extremest weakening and impoverishment of man; ye actually want this weakness and impoverishment, and ye apply the whole lying machinery of the old ideal in order to achieve your end. Ye are so constituted that ye actually regard your gregarious wants as an ideal! Here we are in the presence of an absolute lack of psychological honesty.

783

The two traits which characterise the modern European are apparently antagonistic—*individualism and the demand for equal rights*: this I am at last beginning to understand. The individual is an extremely vulnerable piece of vanity: this vanity, when it is conscious of its high degree of susceptibility to pain, demands that every one should be made equal; that the individual should only stand *inter pares*. But in this way a social race is depicted in which, as a matter of fact, gifts and powers are on the whole equally distributed. The pride which would have loneliness and but few appreciators is quite beyond comprehension: really "great" successes are only attained through the masses—indeed, we scarcely understand yet that a mob success is in reality only a small success; because *pulchrum est paucorum hominum.*

No morality will countenance order of rank among men, and the jurists know nothing of a communal conscience. The principle of individualism rejects *really great* men, and demands the most delicate vision for, and the speediest discovery of, a talent among people who are almost equal; and inasmuch as every one has some modicum of talent in such late and civilised cultures (and can, therefore, expect to receive his share of honour), there is a more general buttering-up of modest merits to-day than there has ever been. This gives the age the appearance of *unlimited justice*. Its want of justice is to be found not in its unbounded hatred of tyrants and demagogues, even in the arts; but in its detestation of noble natures who scorn the praise of the many. The demand for equal rights (that is to say, the privilege of sitting in judgment on everything and everybody) is anti-aristocratic.

This age knows just as little concerning the absorption of the individual, of his mergence into a great type of men who do not want to be personalities. It was this that formerly constituted the distinction and the zeal of many lofty natures (the greatest poets among them); or of the desire to be a *polis*, as in Greece; or of Jesuitism, or of the Prussian Staff Corps, and bureaucracy; or of apprenticeship and a continuation of the tradition of great masters: to all of which things, non-social conditions and the absence of *petty vanity* are necessary.

784

Individualism is a modest and still unconscious form of will to power; with it a single human unit seems to think it sufficient to free himself from the preponderating power of society (or of the State or Church). He does not set himself up in opposition as a *personality*, but merely as a unit; he represents the rights of all other individuals as against the whole. That is to say, he instinctively places himself on a level with every other unit: what he combats he does not combat as a person, but as a representative of units against a mass.

Socialism is merely an agitatory measure of individualism: it recognises the fact that in order to attain to something, men must organise themselves into a general movement—into a "power." But what the Socialist requires is not society as the object of the individual, *but society as a means of making many individuals possible*: this is the instinct of Socialists, though they frequently deceive themselves on this point (apart from this, however, in order to make their kind prevail, they are compelled to deceive others to an enormous extent). Altruistic moral preaching thus enters into the service of individual egoism,—one of the most common frauds of the nineteenth century.

Anarchy is also merely an agitatory measure of Socialism; with it the Socialist inspires fear, with fear he begins to fascinate and to terrorise: but what he does above all is to draw all courageous and reckless people to his side, even in the most intellectual spheres.

In spite of all this, individualism is the most modest stage of the will to power.

.   .   .   .

When one has reached a certain degree of independence, one always longs for more: separation in proportion to the degree of force; the individual is no longer content to regard himself as equal to everybody, he actually *seeks for his peer*—he makes himself stand out from others. Individualism is followed by a development in groups and organs; correlative tendencies join up together and become powerfully active: now there arise between these centres of power, friction, war, a reconnoitring of the forces on either side, reciprocity, understandings, and the regulation of mutual services. Finally, there appears an order of rank.

Recapitulation—

1. The individuals emancipate themselves.

2. They make war, and ultimately agree concerning equal rights (justice is made an end in itself).

3. Once this is reached, the actual differences in degrees of power begin to make themselves felt, and to a greater extent than before (the reason being that on the whole peace is established, and innumerable small centres of power begin to create differences which formerly were scarcely noticeable). Now the individuals begin to form groups, these strive after privileges and preponderance, and war starts afresh in a milder form.

People demand freedom only when they have no power. Once power is obtained, a preponderance thereof is the next thing to be coveted; if this is not achieved (owing to the fact that one is still too weak for it), then *"justice,"* i.e. *"equality* of power" become the objects of desire.

785

The rectification of the concept "egoism."—When one has discovered what an error the "individual" is, and that every single creature represents the whole process of evolution (not alone "inherited," but in "himself"), the individual then acquires *an inordinately great importance*. The voice of instinct is quite right here. When this instinct tends to decline, *i.e.* when the individual begins to seek his worth in his services to others, one may be sure that exhaustion and degeneration have set in. An altruistic attitude of mind, when it is fundamental and free from all hypocrisy, is the instinct of creating a second value for one's self in the service of other egoists. As a rule, however, it is only apparent—a circuitous path to the preservation of one's own feelings of vitality and worth.

786

The History of Moralisation and Demoralisation

Proposition one.—There are no such things as moral actions: they are purely imaginary. Not only is it impossible to demonstrate their existence (a fact which Kant and Christianity, for instance, both acknowledged)—but they are not even possible. Owing to psychological misunderstanding, a man invented an *opposite* to the instinctive impulses of life, and believed that a new species of instinct was thereby discovered: a *primum mobile* was postulated which does not exist at all. According to the valuation which gave rise to the antithesis "moral" and "immoral," one should say: *There is nothing else on earth but immoral intentions and actions.*

Proposition two.—The whole differentiation, "moral" and "immoral," arises from the assumption that both moral and immoral actions are the result of a spontaneous will—in short, that such a will exists; or in other words, that moral judgments can only hold good with regard to intuitions and actions *that are free.* But thise whole order of actions and intentions is purely imaginary: the only world to which the moral standard could be applied does not exist at all: *there is no such thing as a moral or an immoral action.*

. . . .

The *psychological error* out of which the antithesis "moral" and "immoral" arose is: "selfless," "unselfish," "self-denying"—all unreal and fantastic.

A false dogmatism also clustered around the concept "ego"; it was regarded as atomic, and falsely opposed to a non-ego; it was also liberated from Becoming, and declared to belong to the sphere of Being. The false materialisation of the ego: this (owing to the belief in individual immortality) was made an article of faith under the pressure of *religio-moral discipline.* According to this artificial liberation of the ego and its transference to the realm of the absolute, people thought that they had arrived at an antithesis in values which seemed quite irrefutable—the single ego and the vast non-ego. It seemed obvious that the value of the individual ego could only exist in conjunction with the vast non-ego, more particularly in the sense of being subject to it and existing only for its sake. Here, of course, the gregarious instinct determined the direction of thought: nothing is more opposed to this instinct than the sovereignty of the individual. Supposing, however, that the ego be absolute, then its value must lie in *self-negation.*

Thus: (1) the false emancipation of the "individual" as an atom;

(2) The gregarious self-conceit which abhors the desire to remain an atom, and regards it as hostile.

(3) As a result: the overcoming of the individual by changing his aim.

(4) At this point there appeared to be actions that were self-effacing: around these actions a whole sphere of antitheses was fancied.

(5) It was asked, in what sort of actions does man most strongly assert himself? Around these (sexuality, covetousness, lust for power, cruelty, etc. etc.) hate, contempt, and anathemas were heaped: it was believed that there could be such things as selfless impulses. Everything selfish was condemned, everything unselfish was in demand.

(6) And the result was: what had been done? A ban had been placed on the strongest, the most natural, yea, the only genuine impulses; henceforward, in order that an action might be praiseworthy, there must be no trace in it of any of those genuine impulses—*monstrous fraud in psychology.* Every kind of "self-satisfaction" had to be remodelled and made possible by means of misunderstanding and adjusting one's self *sub specie boni.* Conversely: that species which found its advantage in depriving mankind of its self-satisfaction, the representatives of the gregarious instincts, *e.g.* the priests and the philosophers, were sufficiently crafty and psychologically astute to show how selfishness ruled everywhere. The Christian conclusion from this was: "Everything is sin, even our virtues. Man is utterly undesirable. Selfless actions are impossible." Original sin. In short, once man had opposed his instincts to a purely imaginary world of the good, he concluded by despising himself as incapable of performing "good" actions.

N.B.—In this way Christianity represents a step forward in the sharpening of psychological insight: La Rochefoucauld and Pascal. It perceived the essential equality of human actions, and the equality of their values as a whole (all immoral).

. . . .

Now the first serious object was to rear men in whom self-seeking impulses were extinguished: *priests, saints.* And if people doubted that perfection was possible, they did not doubt what perfection was.

The psychology of the saint and of the priest and of the "good" man, must naturally have seemed purely phantasmagorical. The real motive of all action had been declared bad: therefore, in order to make action still possible, deeds had to be prescribed which, though not possible, had to be declared possible and sanctified. They now honoured and idealised things with as much falsity as they had previously slandered them.

Inveighing against the instincts of life came to be regarded as holy and estimable. The priestly ideal was: absolute chastity, absolute obedience, absolute poverty! The lay ideal: alms, pity, self-sacrifice, renunciation of the beautiful, of reason, and of sensuality, and a dark frown for all the strong qualities that existed.

. . . .

An advance is made: the slandered instincts attempt to re-establish their rights (*e.g.* Luther's Reformation, the coarsest form of moral falsehood under the cover of "Evangelical freedom"), they are rechristened with holy names.

The calumniated instincts try to demonstrate that they are necessary in order that the virtuous instincts may be possible. *Il faut vivre, afin de vivre pour autrui*: egoism as a means to an end.

But people go still further: they try to grant both the egoistic and altruistic impulses the right to exist—equal rights for both—from the utilitarian standpoint.

People go further: they see greater utility in placing the egoistic rights before the altruistic—greater utility in the sense of more happiness for the majority, or of the elevation of mankind, etc. etc. Thus the rights of egoism begin to preponderate, but under the cloak of an extremely altruistic standpoint—the collective utility of humanity.

An attempt is made to reconcile the altruistic mode of action with the natural order of things. Altruism is sought in the very roots of life. Altruism and egoism are both based upon the essence of life and nature.

The disappearance of the opposition between them is dreamt of as a future possibility. Continued adaptation, it is hoped, will merge the two into one.

At last it is seen that altruistic actions are merely a species of the egoistic —and that the degree to which one loves and spends one's self is a proof of the extent of one's individual power and personality. In short, that the more evil man *can* be made, the better he is, and that one cannot be the one without the other. . . . At this point the curtain rises which concealed the monstrous fraud of the psychology that has prevailed hitherto.

· · · · · · · · · · · · · · ·

Results.—There are only immoral intentions and actions; the so-called moral actions must be shown to be immoral. All emotions are traced to a single will, the will to power, and are called essentially equal. The concept of life: in the apparent antithesis good and evil, degrees of power in the instincts alone are expressed. A temporary order of rank is established according to which certain instincts are either controlled or enlisted in our service. Morality is justified: economicaly, etc.

· · · · · · · · · · · · · ·

Against proposition two.—Determinism: the attempt to rescue the moral world by transferring it to the unknown.

Determinism is only a manner of allowing ourselves to conjure our valuations away, once they have lost their place in a world interpreted mechanistically. Determinism must therefore be attacked and undermined at all costs: just as our right to distinguish between an absolute and phenomenal world should be disputed.

787

It is absolutely necessary to emancipate ourselves from motives: otherwise we should not be allowed to attempt to sacrifice ourselves or to neglect ourselves! Only the innocence of Becoming gives us the highest courage and the highest freedom.

788

A clean conscience must be restored to the evil man—has this been my involuntary endeavour all the time? for I take as the evil man him who is strong (Dostoievsky's belief concerning the convicts in prison should be referred to here).

789

Our new "freedom." What a feeling of relief there is in the thought that we emancipated spirits do not feel ourselves harnessed to any system of teleological aims. Likewise that the concepts reward and punishment have no roots in the essence of existence! Likewise that good and evil actions are not good or evil in themselves, but only from the point of view of the self-preservative tendencies of certain species of humanity! Likewise that our speculations concerning pleasure and pain are not of cosmic, far less then of metaphysical, importance! (That form of pessimism associated with the name of Hartmann, which pledges itself to put even the pain and pleasure of existence into the balance, with its arbitrary confinement in the prison and within the bounds of pre-Copernican thought, would be something not only retrogressive, but degenerate, unless it be merely a bad joke on the part of a "Berliner.")

790

If one is clear as to the "wherefore" of one's life, then the "how" of it can take care of itself. It is already even a sign of disbelief in the wherefore and in the purpose and sense of life—in fact, it is a sign of a lack of will—when the value of pleasure and pain step into the foreground, and hedonistic and pessimistic teaching becomes prevalent; and self-abnegation, resignation, virtue, "objectivity," *may*, at the very least, be signs that the most important factor is beginning to make its absence felt.

791

Hitherto there has been no German culture. It is no refutation of this assertion to say that there have been great anchorites in Germany (Goethe, for instance); for these had their own culture. But it was precisely around them, as though around mighty, defiant, and isolated rocks, that the remaining spirit of Germany, *as their antithesis,* lay—that is to say, as a soft, swampy, slippery soil, upon which every step and every footprint of the rest of Europe made an impression and created forms. German culture was a thing devoid of character and of almost unlimited yielding power.

792

Germany, though very rich in clever and well-informed scholars, has for some time been so excessively poor in great souls and in mighty minds, that it almost seems to have forgotten what a great soul or a mighty mind is; and to-day mediocre and even ill-constituted men place themselves in the market square without the suggestion of a conscience-prick or a sign of embarrassment, and declare themselves great men, reformers, etc. Take the case of Eugen Dühring, for instance, a really clever and well-informed scholar, but a man who betrays with almost every word he says that he has a miserably small soul, and that he is horribly tormented by narrow envious feelings; moreover, that it is no mighty overflowing, benevolent, and spend-thrift spirit that drives him on, but only the spirit of ambition! But to be ambitious in such an age as this is much more unworthy of a philosopher than ever it was: to-day, when it is the mob that rules, when it is the mob that dispenses the honours.

793

My "future": a severe polytechnic education. Conscription; so that as a rule every man of the higher classes should be an officer, whatever else he may be besides.

PART III

THE IRRESOLUTE PRESENT:
THE TWENTIETH CENTURY

A. *The Clash of Political Values*

Two Left Manifestos: British Socialism and German Communism

"Labour and the New Social Order," The Aims of Socialism *(London: 1918), pp. 111–28.*

"The Spartacist Manifesto" (December 26, 1918), New York Times, January 24, 1919, p. 3.

For some the First World War heralded the end of an old world and the promise of a new. The range of possibilities recapitulated the past and promised near or distant utopias. The promise of brave new worlds was held out for victors and vanquished alike. Form, content, and inspiration varied, but left-wing parties sought a new future, not a re-created past.

The British Labour party finally made its statement for socialism in its election platform, "Labour and the New Social Order." If the long-term view was revolutionary, the program was pacific and constitutional, appealing to the democratic electorate to accept its collectivist policies as a logical extension of nineteenth-century liberal social justice. The Labour party was conspicuously advanced on the radicalism of Joseph Chamberlain, but it remained within the same broad tradition. In six years, Labour would form its first government, albeit in coalition with the Liberals. This achievement made the Labour party a model for constitutional, revisionist social democratic parties in Europe.

In contrast, the Sparticist Manifesto was inspired by the Bolshevik Revolution of 1917 and summoned Germany to add its installment to the world revolution. These left-wing Socialists, led by Rosa Luxemburg and Karl Liebknecht, hoped to capitalize on the incapacity of the Social Democratic government of the new German Republic and the natural dislocation produced by defeat in war. Rosa Luxemburg preferred industrial action when the government lost the confidence of the workers, but Liebknecht precipitated an armed outbreak in Berlin in January, 1919. Force and a few trifling concessions restored order. Luxemburg and Liebknecht were murdered. Echoes of Sparticist week in Berlin (January 5–12, 1919) reverberated until March but were easily suppressed. Communist martyrology had its heroes, but this summons to international revolution, at least, ended in disaster.

LABOUR AND THE NEW SOCIAL ORDER

IT BEHOVES the Labour Party, in formulating its own programme for Reconstruction after the war, and in criticising the various preparations and plans that are being made by the present Government, to look at the problem as a whole. We have to make it clear what it is that we wish to construct. It is important to emphasise the fact that, whatever may be the case with regard to other political parties, our detailed practical proposals proceed from definitely held principles.

THE END OF A CIVILISATION

We need to beware of patchwork. The view of the Labour Party is that what has to be reconstructed after the war is not this or that Government Department, or this or that piece of social machinery; but, so far as Britain is concerned, society itself. The individual worker, or for that matter the individual statesman, immersed in daily routine—like the individual soldier in a battle—easily fails to understand the magnitude and far-reaching importance of what is taking place around him. How does it fit together as a whole? How does it look from a distance? Count Okuma, one of the oldest, most experienced and ablest of the statesmen of Japan, watching the present conflict from the other side of the globe, declares it to be nothing less than the death of European civilisation. Just as in the past the civilisations of Babylon, Egypt, Greece, Carthage, and the great Roman Empire have been successively destroyed, so, in the judgment of this detached observer, the civilisation of all Europe is even now receiving its death-blow. We of the Labour Party can so far agree in this estimate as to recognise, in the present world catastrophe, if not the death, in Europe, of civilisation itself, at any rate the culmination and collapse of a distinctive industrial civilisation, which the workers will not seek to reconstruct. At such times of crisis it is easier to slip into ruin than to progress into higher forms of organisation. That is the problem as it presents itself to the Labour Party to-day.

What this war is consuming is not merely the security, the homes, the livelihood and the lives of millions of innocent families, and an enormous proportion of all the accumulated wealth of the world, but also the very basis of the peculiar social order in which it has arisen. The individualist system of capitalist production, based on the private ownership and competitive administration of land and capital, with its reckless "profiteering" and wage-slavery; with its glorification of the unhampered struggle for the means of life and its hypocritical pretence of the "survival of the fittest"; with the monstrous inequality of circumstances which it produces and the degradation and brutalisation, both moral and spiritual, resulting therefrom, may, we hope, indeed have received a death-blow. With it must go the political system and ideas in which it naturally found expression. We of the Labour Party, whether in opposition or in due time called upon to form an Administration, will certainly lend no hand to its revival. On the contrary, we shall do our utmost to see that it is buried with the millions whom it has done to death. If we in Britain are to escape from the decay of civilisation itself, which the Japanese statesman foresees, we must ensure that what is presently to be built up is a new social order, based not on fighting, but on fraternity—not on the competitive struggle for the means of bare life, but on a deliberately planned co-operation in production and distribution for the benefit of all who participate by hand or by brain—not on the utmost possible inequality of riches, but on a systematic approach towards a healthy equality of material circumstances for every person born into the world—not on an enforced dominion over subject nations, subject races, subject Colonies, subject classes or a subject sex, but, in industry as well as in government, on that equal freedom, that general consciousness of consent, and that widest possible participation in power, both economic and political, which is characteristic of Democracy. We do not, of course pretend that it is possible, even after the drastic clearing away that is now going on, to build society anew in a year or two of feverish "Reconstruction." What the Labour Party intends to satisfy itself about is that each brick that it helps to lay shall go to erect the structure that it intends, and no other.

THE PILLARS OF THE HOUSE

We need not here recapitulate, one by one, the different items in the Labour Party's programme, which successive Party Conferences have adopted. These proposals, some of them in various publications worked out in practical detail, are often carelessly derided as impracticable, even by the politicians who steal them piecemeal from us! The members of the Labour Party, themselves actually working by hand or by brain, in close contact with the facts, have perhaps at all times a more accurate appreciation of what is practicable, in industry as in politics, than those who depend solely on academic instruction or are biased by great possessions. But to-day no man dares to say that anything is impracticable. The war, which has scared the old Political Parties right out of their dogmas, has taught every statesman and every Government official, to his enduring surprise, how very much more can be done along the lines that we have laid down than he had ever before thought possible. What we now promulgate as our policy, whether for opposition or for office, is not merely this or that specific reform, but a deliberately thought-out, systematic, and comprehensive plan for that immediate social rebuildnig which any Ministry, whether or not it desires to grapple with the problem, will be driven to undertake. The Four Pillars of the House that we propose to erect, resting upon the common foundation of the Democratic control of society in all its activities, may be termed, respectively:

(*a*) The Universal Enforcement of the National Minimum;

(*b*) The Democratic Control of Industry;

(*c*) The Revolution in National Finance; and

(*d*) The Surplus Wealth for the Common Good.

The various detailed proposals of the Labour Party, herein briefly summarised, rest on these four pillars, and can best be appreciated in connection with them.

THE UNIVERSAL ENFORCEMENT OF A NATIONAL MINIMUM

The first principle of the Labour Party—in significant contrast with those of the Capitalist System, whether expressed by the Liberal or by the Conservative Party—is the securing to every member of the community, in good times and bad alike (and not only to the strong and able, the well-born or the fortunate), of all the requisites of healthy life and worthy citizenship. This is in no sense a "class" proposal. Such an amount of social protection of the individual, however poor and lowly, from birth to death is, as the economist now knows, as indispensable to fruitful co-operation as it is to successful combination; and it affords the only complete safeguard against that insidious Degradation of the Standard of Life, which is the worst economic and social calamity to which any community can be subjected. We are members one of another. No man liveth to himself alone. If any, even the humblest is made to suffer, the whole community and every one of us, whether or not we recognise the fact, is thereby injured. Generation after generation this has been the corner-stone of the faith of Labour. It will be the guiding principle of any Labour Government.

THE LEGISLATIVE REGULATION OF EMPLOYMENT

Thus it is that the Labour Party to-day stands for the universal application of the Policy of the National Minimum, to which (as embodied in the successive elaborations of the Factory, Mines, Railways, Shops, Merchant Shipping, and Truck Acts, the Public Health, Housing, and Education Acts and the Minimum Wage Act—all of them aiming at the enforcement of at least the prescribed Minimum of Leisure, Health, Education, and Subsistence) the spokesmen of Labour have already gained the support of the enlightened statesmen and economists of the world. All these laws purporting to protect against extreme Degradation of the Standard of Life need considerable improvement and extension, whilst their administration leaves much to be desired. For instance, the Workmen's Compensation Act fails, shamefully, not merely to secure proper provision for all the victims of accident and industrial disease, but what is much more important, does not succeed in preventing their continual increase. The amendment and consolidation of the Factories and Workshop Acts, with their extension to all employed persons, is long overdue, and it will be the policy of Labour greatly to strengthen the staff of inspectors, especially by the addition of more men and women of actual experience of the workshop and the mine. The Coal Mines (Minimum Wage) Act must certainly be maintained in force, and suitably amended, so as both to ensure greater uniformity of conditions among the several districts, and to make the District Minimum in all cases an effective reality. The same policy will, in the interests of the agricultural labourers, dictate the perpetuation of the Legal Wage clauses of the new Corn Law just passed for a term of five years, and the prompt amendment of any defects that may be revealed in their working. And, in view of the fact that many millions of wage-earners, notably women and the less-skilled workmen in various occupations, are unable by combination to obtain wages adequate for decent maintenance in health, the Labour Party intends to see that the Trade Boards Act is suitably amended and made to apply to all industrial employments in which any considerable number of those employed obtain less than 30s. per week. This minimum of not less than 30s. per week (which will need revision according to the level of prices) ought to be the very lowest statutory base line for the least skilled adult workers, men or women, in any occupation, in all parts of the United Kingdom.

THE ORGANISATION OF DEMOBILISATION

But the coming industrial dislocation, which will inevitably follow the discharge from war service of half of all the working population, imposes new obligations upon the community. The demobilisation and discharge of the eight million wage-earners now being paid from public funds, either for service with the colours or in munition work and other war trades, will bring to the whole wage-earning class grave peril of Unemployment, Reduction of Wages, and a Lasting Degradation of the Standard of Life, which can be prevented only by deliberate National Organisation. The Labour Party has repeatedly called upon the present Government to formulate its plan, and to make in advance all arrangements necessary for coping with so unparalleled a dislocation. The policy to which the Labour Party commits itself is unhesitating and uncompromising. It is plain that regard should be had, in stopping Government orders, reducing the staff of the National Factories and demobilising the Army, to the actual state of employment in particular industries and in different districts, so as both to release first the kinds of labour most urgently required for the revival of peace production, and to prevent any congestion of the market. It is no less imperative that suitable provision against being turned suddenly adrift without resources should be made, not only for the soldiers, but also for the three million operatives in munition work and other war trades, who will be discharged long before most of the Army can be disbanded. On this important point, which is the most urgent of all, the present Government has, we believe, down to the present hour, formulated no plan, and come to no decision, and neither the Liberal nor the Conservative Party has apparently deemed the matter worthy of agitation. Any Government which should allow the discharged soldier or munition worker to fall into the clutches of charity or the Poor Law would have to be instantly driven from office by an outburst of popular indignation. What every one of them who is not wholly disabled will look for is a situation in accordance with his capacity.

SECURING EMPLOYMENT FOR ALL

The Labour Party insists—as no other political party has thought fit to do —that the obligation to find suitable employment in productive work for all these men and women rests upon the Government for the time being. The work of re-settling the disbanded soldiers and discharged munition workers into new situations is a national obligation; and the Labour Party emphatically protests against it being regarded as a matter for private charity. It strongly objects to this public duty being handed over either to committees of philanthropists or benevolent societies, or to any of the military or recruiting authorities. The policy of the Labour Party in this matter is to make the utmost use of the Trade Unions, and equally for the brain workers, of the various Professional Associations. In view of the fact that, in any trade, the best organisation for placing men in situations is a national Trade Union having local branches throughout the kingdom, every soldier should be allowed, if he chooses, to have a duplicate of his industrial discharge notice sent out, one month before the date fixed for his discharge, to the Secretary of the Trade Union to which he belongs or wishes to belong. Apart from this use of the Trade Union (and a corresponding use of the Professional Association) the Government must, of course, avail itself of some such public machinery as that of the Employment Exchanges; but before the existing Exchanges (which will need to be greatly extended) can receive the co-operation and support of the organised Labour Movement, without which their operations can never be fully successful, it is imperative that they should be drastically reformed, on the lines laid down in the Demobilisation Report of the "Labour after the War" Joint Committee; and, in particular, that each Exchange should be placed effectively under the supervision and control of a Joint Committee of Employers and Trade Unionists in equal numbers.

The responsiblity of the Government, for the time being, in the grave industrial crisis that demobilisation will produce, goes, however, far beyond the eight million men and women whom the various departments will suddenly discharge from their own service. The effect of this peremptory discharge on all the other workers has also to be taken into account. To the Labour Party it will seem the supreme concern of the Government of the day to see to it that there shall be, as a result of the gigantic "General Post" which it will itself have deliberately set going, nowhere any Degradation of the Standard of Life. The Government has pledged itself to restore the Trade Union conditions and "pre-war practices" of the workshop, which the Trade Unions patriotically gave up at the direct request of the Government itself; and this solemn pledge must be fulfilled, of course, in the spirit as well as in the letter. The Labour Party, moreover, holds it to be the duty of the Government of the day to take all necessary steps to prevent the Standard Rates of Wages, in any trade or occupation whatsoever, from suffering any reduction, relatively to the contemporary cost of living. Unfortunately, the present Government, like the Liberal and Conservative Parties, so far refuses to speak on this important matter with any clear voice. We claim that it should be a cardinal point of Government policy to make it plain to every capitalist employer that any attempt to reduce the customary rate of wages when peace comes, or to take advantage of the dislocation of demobilisation to worsen the conditions of employment in any grade whatsoever, will certainly lead to embittered industrial strife, which will be in the highest degree detrimental to the national interests; and that the Government of the day will not hesitate to take all necessary steps to avert such a calamity. In the great impending crisis the Government of the day should not only, as the greatest employer of both brainworkers and manual workers, set a good example in this respect but should also actively seek to influence private employers by proclaiming in advance that it will not itself attempt to lower the Standard Rates of conditions in public employment; by announcing that it will insist on the most rigorous observance of the Fair Wages Clause in all public contracts, and by explicitly recommending every Local Authority to adopt the same policy.

But nothing is more dangerous to the Standard of Life, or so destructive of those minimum conditions of healthy existence, which must in the interests of the community be assured to every worker, than any widespread or continued unemployment. It has always been a fundamental principle of the Labour Party (a point on which significantly enough it has not been followed by either of the other political parties) that in a modern industrial community, it is one of the foremost obligations of the Government to find, for every willing worker, whether by hand or by brain, productive work at Standard Rates.

It is accordingly the duty of the Government to adopt a policy of deliberately and systematically preventing the occurrence of unemployment, instead of (as heretofore) letting unemployment occur, and then seeking, vainly and expensively, to relieve the unemployed. It is now known that the Government can, if it chooses, arrange the Public Works and the orders of National Departments and Local Authorities in such a way as to maintain the aggregate demand for labour in the whole kingdom (including that of capitalist employers) approximately at a uniform level from year to year; and it is therefore a primary obligation of the Government to prevent any considerable or widespread fluctuations in the total numbers employed in times of good or bad trade. But this is not all. In order to prepare for the possibility of there being any unemployment, either in the course of demobilisation or in the first years of peace, it is essential that the Government should make all necessary preparations for putting instantly in hand, directly or through the Local Authorities, such urgently needed public works as (*a*) the rehousing of the population alike in rural districts, mining villages, and town slums, to the extent, possibly, of a million new cottages and an outlay of 300 millions sterling; (*b*) the immediate making good of the shortage of schools, training colleges, technical colleges, &c., and the engagement of the necessary additional teaching, clerical and administrative staffs; (*c*) new roads; (*d*) light railways; (*e*) the unification and reorganisation of the railway and canal system; (*f*) afforestation; (*g*) the reclamation of land; (*h*) the development and better equipment of our ports and harbours; (*i*) the opening up of access to land by co-operative small holdings and in other practicable ways. Moreover, in order to relieve any pressure of an overstocked labour market, the opportunity should be taken, if unemployment should threaten to become widespread, (*a*) im-

mediately to raise the school leaving age to sixteen; (b) greatly to increase
the number of scholarships and bursaries for Secondary and Higher Education; and (c) substantially to shorten the hours of labour of all young persons, even to a greater extent than the eight hours per week contemplated
in the new Education Bill, in order to enable them to attend technical and
other classes in the daytime. Finally, wherever practicable, the hours of
adult labour should be reduced to not more than forty-eight per week, without reduction of the Standard Rates of Wages. There can be no economic
or other justification for keeping any man or woman to work for long hours,
or at overtime, whilst others are unemployed.

SOCIAL INSURANCE AGAINST UNEMPLOYMENT

In so far as the Government fails to prevent Unemployment—wherever
it finds it impossible to discover for any willing worker, man or woman, a
suitable situation at the Standard Rate—the Labour Party holds that the
Government must, in the interest of the community as a whole, provide
him or her with adequate maintenance, either with such arrangements for
honourable employment or with such useful training as may be found practicable, according to age, health and previous occupation. In many ways the
best form of provision for those who must be unemployed, because the industrial organisation of the community so far breaks down as to be temporarily unable to set them to work, is the Out of Work Benefit afforded by
a well administered Trade Union. This is a special tax on the Trade Unionists themselves which they have voluntarily undertaken, but towards
which they have a right to claim a public subvention—a subvention which
was actually granted by Parliament (though only to the extent of a couple
of shillings or so per week) under Part II. of the Insurance Act. The arbitrary withdrawal by the Government in 1915 of this statutory right of the
Trade Unions was one of the least excusable of the war economies; and the
Labour Party must insist on the resumption of this subvention immediately
the war ceases, and on its increase to at least half the amount spent in Out of
Work Benefit. The extension of State Unemployment Insurance to other
occupations may afford a convenient method of providing for such of the
Unemployed, especially in the case of badly paid women workers, and the
less skilled men, whom it is difficult to organise in Trade Unions. But the
weekly rate of the State Unemployment Benefits needs, in these days of
high prices, to be considerably raised; whilst no industry ought to be com-
pulsorily brought within its scope against the declared will of the workers
concerned, and especially of their Trade Unions. In one way or another
remunerative employment or honourable maintenance must be found for
every willing worker, by hand or by brain, in bad times as well as in good.
It is clear that, in the twentieth century, there must be no question of driving
the Unemployed to anything so obsolete and discredited as either private
charity, with its haphazard and ill-considered doles, or the Poor Law, with
the futilities and barbarities of its "Stone Yard," or its "Able-bodied Test

Workhouse." Only on the basis of a universal application of the Policy of the National Minimum, affording complete security against destitution, in sickness and health, in good times and bad alike, to every member of the community of whatever age or sex, can any worthy social order be bulit up.

The Democratic Control of Industry

The universal application of the Policy of the National Minimum is, of course, only the first of the Pillars of the House that the Labour Party intends to see built. What marks off this Party most distinctively from any of the other political parties is its demand for the full and genuine adoption of the principle of Democracy. The first condition of Democracy is effective personal freedom. This has suffered so many encroachments during the war that it is necessary to state with clearness that the complete removal of all the wartime restrictions on freedom of speech, freedom of publication, freedom of the press, freedom of travel and freedom of choice of place of residence and kind of employment must take place the day after Peace is declared. The Labour Party declared emphatically against any continuance of the Military Service Acts a moment longer than the imperative requirements of the war excuse. But individual freedom is of little use without complete political rights. The Labour Party sees its repeated demands largely conceded in the present Representation of the People Act, but not yet wholly satisfied. The Party stands, as heretofore, for complete Adult Suffrage, with not more than a three months' residential qualification, for effective provision for absent electors to vote, for absolutely equal rights for both sexes, for the same freedom to exercise civic rights for the "common soldier" as for the officer, for Shorter Parliaments, for the complete Abolition of the House of Lords, and for a most strenuous opposition to any new Second Chamber, whether elected or not, having in it any element of Heredity or Privilege, or of the control of the House of Commons by any party or class. But unlike the Conservative and Liberal Parties, the Labour Party insists on Democracy in industry as well as in government. It demands the progressive elimination from the control of industry of the private capitalist, individual or joint-stock; and the setting free of all who work, whether by hand or by brain, for the service of the community, and of the community only. And the Labour Party refuses absolutely to believe that the British people will permanently tolerate any reconstruction or perpetuation of the disorganisation, waste and inefficiency involved in the abandonment of British industry to a jostling crowd of separate private employers, with their minds bent, not on the service of the community, but—by the very law of their being—only on the utmost possible profiteering. What the nation needs is undoubtedly a great bound onwards in its aggregate productivity. But this cannot be secured merely by pressing the manual workers to more strenuous toil, or even by encouraging the "Captains of Industry" to a less wasteful organisation of their several enterprises on a profit-making basis.

What the Labour Party looks to is a genuinely scientific reorganisation of the nation's industry, no longer deflected by individual profiteering, on the basis of the Common Ownership of the means of Production; the equitable sharing of the proceeds among all who participate in any capacity and only among these, and the adoption, in particular services and occupation, of those systems and methods of administration and control that may be found, in practice, best to promote, not profiteering, but the public interest.

IMMEDIATE NATIONALISATION

The Labour Party stands not merely for the principle of the Common Ownership of the nation's land, to be applied as suitable opportunities occur, but also, specifically, for the immediate Nationalisation of Railways, Mines, and the production of Electrical Power. We hold that the very foundation of any successful reorganisation of British Industry must necessarily be found in the provision of the utmost facilities for transport and communication, the production of power at the cheapest possible rate, and the most economical supply of both electrical energy and coal to every corner of the kingdom. Hence the Labour Party stands, unhesitatingly, for the National Ownership and administration of the Railways and Canals, and their union, along with Harbours and Roads and the Posts and Telegraphs—not to say also the great lines of steamers which could at once be owned, if not immediately directly managed in detail, by the Government—in a united national service of Communication and Transport; to be worked, unhampered by capitalist, private or purely local interests (and with a steadily increasing participation of the organised workers in the management, both central and local), exclusively for the common good. If any Government should be so misguided as to propose, when peace comes, to hand the railways back to the shareholders; or should show itself so spendthrift of the nation's property as to give these shareholders any enlarged franchise by presenting them with the economies of unification or the profits of increased railway rates; or so extravagant as to bestow public funds on the re-equipment of privately owned lines—all of which things are now being privately intrigued for by the railway interests—the Labour Party will offer any such project the most strenuous opposition. The railways and canals, like the roads, must henceforth belong to the public, and to the public alone.

In the production of Electricity, for cheap Power, Light and Heating, this country has so far failed, because of hampering private interests, to take advantage of science. Even in the largest cities we still "peddle" our Electricity on a contemptibly small scale. What is called for, immediately after the war, is the erection of a score of gigantic "super-power stations," which could generate, at incredibly cheap rates, enough electricity for the use of every industrialist establishment and every private household in Great Britain; the present municipal and joint-stock electrical plants being universally linked up and used for local distribution. This is inevitably the future of Electricity. It is plain that so great and so powerful an enterprise, affecting every industrial enterprise and, eventually every household, must not be allowed to pass into the hands of private capitalists. They are already pressing the Government for the concession, and neither the Liberal nor the Conservative Party has yet made up its mind to a refusal of such a new endowment of profiteering in what will presently be the lifeblood of modern productive industry. The Labour Party demands that the production of Electricity on the necessary gigantic scale shall be made, from the start (with suitable arrangements for municipal co-operation in local distribution), a national enterprise, to be worked exclusively with the object of supplying the whole kingdom with the cheapest possible Power, Light, and Heat.

But with the Railways and the generation of Electricity in the hands of the public, it would be criminal folly to leave to the present 1,500 colliery companies the power of "holding up" the coal supply. These are now all working under public control, on terms that virtually afford to their shareholders a statutory guarantee of their swollen incomes. The Labour Party demands the immediate Nationalisation of Mines, the extraction of coal and iron being worked as a public service (with a steadily increasing participation in the management, both central and local, of the various grades of persons employed); and the whole business of the retail distribution of household coal being undertaken, as a local public service, by the elected Municipal or County Councils. And there is no reason why coal should fluctuate in price any more than railway fares, or why the consumer should be made to pay more in winter than in summer, or in one town than another. What the Labour Party would aim at is, for household coal of standard quality, a fixed and uniform price for the whole kingdom, payable by rich and poor alike, as unalterable as the penny postage stamp.

But the sphere of immediate Nationalisation is not restricted to these great industries. We shall never succeed in putting the gigantic system of Health Insurance on a proper footing, or secure a clear field for the beneficent work of the Friendly Societies, or gain a free hand for the necessary development of the urgently called for Ministry of Health and the Local Public Health Service, until the nation expropriates the profit-making Industrial Insurance Companies, which now so tyrannously exploit the people with their wasteful house-to-house Industrial Life Assurance. Only by such an expropriation of Life Assurance Companies can we secure the universal provision, free from the burdensome toll of weekly pence, of the indispensable Funeral Benefit. Nor is it in any sense a "class" measure. Only by the assumption by a State Department of the whole business of Life Assurance can the millions of policy holders of all classes be completely protected against the possibly calamitous results of the depreciation of securities and suspension of bonuses which the war is causing. Only by this means can the great staff of insurance agents find their proper place as Civil Servants, with equitable conditions of employment, compensation for any disturbance and security of tenure, in a nationally organised public service for the discharge of the steadily increasing functions of the Government in Vital Statistics and Social Insurance.

In quite another sphere the Labour Party sees the key to Temperance Reform in taking the entire manufacture and retailing of alcoholic drink out of the hands of those who find profit in promoting the utmost possible consumption. This is essentially a case in which the people, as a whole, must assert its right to full and unfettered power for dealing with the licensing question in accordance with local opinion. For this purpose, localities should have conferred upon them facilities

(a) To prohibit the sale of liquor within their boundaries;

(b) To reduce the number of licences and regulate the conditions under which they may be held; and

(c) If a locality decides that licences are to be granted, to determine whether such licences shall be under private or any form of public control.

MUNICIPALISATION

Other main industries, especially those now becoming monopolised, should be nationalised as opportunity offers. Moreover, the Labour Party holds that the Municipalities should not confine their activities to the necessarily costly services of Education, Sanitation and Police; nor yet rest content with acquiring control of the local Water, Gas, Electricity, and Tramways; but that every facility should be afforded to them to acquire (easily, quickly and cheaply) all the land they require, and to extend their enterprises in Housing and Town Planning, Parks, and Public Libraries, the provision of music and the organisation of recreation; and also to undertake, besides the retailing of coal, other services of common utility, particularly the local supply of milk, wherever this is not already fully and satisfactorily organised by a Co-operative Society.

CONTROL OF CAPITALIST INDUSTRY

Meanwhile, however, we ought not to throw away the valuable experience now gained by the Government in its assumption of the importation of wheat, wool, metals, and other commodities, and in its control of the shipping, woollen, leather, clothing, boot and shoe, milling, baking, butchering, and other industries. The Labour Party holds that, whatever may have been the shortcomings of this Government importation and control, it has demonstrably prevented a lot of "profiteering." Nor can it end immediately on the Declaration of Peace. The people will be extremely foolish if they ever allow their indispensable industries to slip back into the unfettered control of private capitalists, who are, actually at the instance of the Government itself, now rapidly combining, trade by trade, into monopolist Trusts, which may presently become as ruthless in their extortion as the worst American examples. Standing as it does for the Democratic Control of Industry, the Labour Party would think twice before it sanctioned any abandonment of the present profitable centralisation of purchase of raw materials; of the present carefully organised "rationing," by joint committees of the trades concerned, of the several establishments with the materials they require; of the present elaborate system of "costing" and public audit of manufacturers' accounts, so as to stop the waste heretofore caused by the mechanical inefficiency of the more backward firms; of the present salutary publicity of manufacturing processes and expenses thereby ensured; and, on the information thus obtained (in order never again to revert to the old-time profiteering) of the present rigid fixing, for standardised products, of maximum prices at the factory, at the warehouse of the wholesale trader and in the retail shop. This question of the retail prices of household commodities is emphatically the most practical of all political issues to the woman elector. The male politicians have too long neglected the grievances of the small household, which is the prey of every profiteering combination; and neither the Liberal nor the Conservative party promises, in this respect, any amendment. This, too, is in no sense a "class" measure. It is, so the Labour Party holds, just as much the function of Government, and just as necessary a part of the Democratic Regulation of Industry, to safeguard the interests of the community as a whole, and those of all grades and sections of private consumers, in the matter of prices, as it is, by the Factory and Trade Boards Acts, to protect the rights of the wage-earning producers in the matter of wages, hours of labour, and sanitation.

A Revolution in National Finance

In taxation, also, the interests of the professional and housekeeping classes are at one with those of the manual workers. Too long has our National Finance been regulated, contrary to the teaching of Political Economy, according to the wishes of the possessing classes and the profits of the financiers. The colossal expenditure involved in the present war (of which, against the protest of the Labour Party, only a quarter has been raised by taxation, whilst three-quarters have been borrowed at onerous rates of interest, to be a burden on the nation's future) brings things to a crisis. When peace comes, capital will be needed for all sorts of social enterprises, and the resources of Government will necessarily have to be vastly greater than they were before the war. Meanwhile innumerable new private fortunes are being heaped up by those who take advantage of the nation's need; and the one-tenth of the population which owns nine-tenths of the riches of the United Kingdom, far from being made poorer, will find itself, in the aggregate, as a result of the war, drawing in rent and interest and dividends a larger nominal income than ever before. Such a position demands a revolution in national finance. How are we to discharge a public debt that may well reach the almost incredible figure of 7,000 million pounds sterling, and at the same time raise an annual revenue which, for local as well as central government, must probably reach 1,000 millions a year? It is over this burden of taxation that the various political parties will be found to be most sharply divided.

The Labour Party stands for such a system of taxation as will yield all the necessary revenue to the Government without encroaching on the Prescribed National Minimum Standard of Life of any family whatsoever; without hampering production or discouraging any useful personal effort, and with the nearest possible approximation to equality of sacrifice. We definitely repudiate all proposals for a Protective Tariff, in whatever specious guise they may be cloaked, as a device for burdening the consumer with unnecessarily enhanced prices, to the profit of the capitalist employer or landed proprietor, who avowedly expects his profits or rent to be increased thereby. We shall strenuously oppose any taxation, of whatever kind, which would increase the price of food or of any other necessary of life. We hold that indirect taxation on commodities, whether by Customs or Excise, should be strictly limited to luxuries; and concentrated principally on those of which it is socially desirable that the consumption should be actually discouraged. We are at one with the manufacturer, the farmer and the trader in objecting to taxes interfering with production or commerce, or hampering transport and communications. In all these matters— once more in contrast with the other political parties, and by no means in the interests of the wage-earners alone—the Labour Party demands that the very definite teachings of economic science should no longer be disregarded.

For the raising of the greater part of the revenue now required the Labour Party looks to the direct taxation of the incomes above the necessary cost of family maintenance; and for the requisite effort to pay off the National Debt, to the direct taxation of private fortunes both during life and at death. The Income Tax and Supertax ought at once to be thoroughly reformed in assessment and collection, in abatements and allowances, and in graduation and differentiation, so as to levy the required total sum in such a way as to make the real sacrifice of all the taxpayers as nearly as possible equal. This would involve assessment by families instead of by individual persons, so that the burden is alleviated in proportion to the number of persons to be maintained. It would involve the raising of the present unduly low minimum income assessable to the tax, and the lightening of the present unfair burden on the great mass of professional and small trading classes by a new scale of graduation, rising from a penny in the pound on the smallest assessable income up to sixteen or even nineteen shillings in the pound on the highest income of the millionaires. It would involve bringing into assessment the numerous windfalls of profit that now escape, and a further differentiation between essentially different kinds of income. The Excess Profits Tax might well be retained in an appropriate form; while so long as Mining Royalties exist the Mineral Rights Duty ought to be increased. The steadily rising unearned Increment of urban and mineral land ought, by an appropriate direct Taxation of Land Values, to be wholly brought into the Public Exchequer. At the same time, for the service and redemption of the National Debt, the Death Duties ought to be regraduated, much more strictly collected, and greatly increased. In this matter we need, in fact, completely to reverse our point of view, and to rearrange the whole taxation of inheritance from the standpoint of asking what is the maximum amount that any rich man should be permitted at death to divert, by his will, from the National Exchequer, which should normally be the heir to all private riches in excess of a quite moderate amount by way of family provision. But all this will not suffice. It will be imperative at the earliest possible moment to free the nation from any rate the greater part of its new load of interest-bearing debts for loans which ought to have been levied as taxation; and the Labour Party stands for a special Capital Levy to pay off; if not the whole, a very substantial part of the entire National Debt—a Capital Levy chargable like the Death Duties on all property, but (in order to secure approximate equality of sacrifice) with exemption of the smallest savings, and for the rest at rates very steeply graduated, so as to take only a small contribution from the little people and a very much larger percentage from the millionaires.

Over this issue of how the financial burden of the war is to be borne, and how the necessary revenue is to be raised, the greatest political battles will be fought. In this matter the Labour Party claims the support of four-fifths of the whole nation, for the interests of the clerk, the teacher, the doctor, the minister of religion, the average retail shopkeeper and trader, and all the mass of those living on small incomes are identical with those of the artisan. The landlords, the financial magnates, the possessors of great fortunes will not, as a class, willingly forego the relative immunity that they have hitherto enjoyed. The present unfair subjection of the Co-operative Society to an Excess Profits Tax on the "profits" which it has never made—specially dangerous as "the thin end of the wedge" of penal taxation of this laudable form of Democratic enterprise—will not be abandoned without a struggle. Every possible effort will be made to juggle with the taxes, so as to place upon the shoulders of the mass of labouring folk and upon the struggling households of the professional men and small traders (as was done after every previous war)—whether by Customs or Excise Duties, by industrial monopolies, by unnecessarily high rates of postage and railway fares, or by a thousand and one other ingenious devices—an unfair share of the national burden. Against these efforts the Labour Party will take the firmest stand.

The Surplus for the Common Good

In the disposal of the surplus above the Standard of Life society has hitherto gone as far wrong as in its neglect to secure the necessary basis of any genuine industrial efficiency or decent social order. We have allowed the riches of our mines, the rental value of the lands superior to the margin of cultivation, the extra profits of the fortunate capitalists, even the material outcome of scientific discoveries—which ought by now to have made this Britain of ours immune from class poverty or from any widespread destitution—to be absorbed by individual proprietors; and then devoted very largely to the senseless luxury of an idle rich class. Against this misappropriation of the wealth of the community, the Labour Party—speaking in the interests not of the wage-earners alone, but of every grade and section of producers by hand or by brain, not to mention also those of the generations that are to succeed us, and of the permanent welfare of the community—emphatically protests. One main Pillar of the House that the Labour Party intends to build is the future appropriation of the Surplus, not to the enlargement of any individual fortune, but to the Common Good. It is from this constantly arising Surplus (to be secured, on the one hand, by Nationalisation and Municipalisation and, on the other, by the steeply graduated Taxation of Private Income and Riches) that will have to be found the new capital which the community day by day needs for the perpetual improvement and increase of its various enterprises, for which we shall decline to be dependent on the usury-exacting financiers. It is from the same source that has to be defrayed the public provision for the Sick and Infirm of all kinds (including that for Maternity and Infancy) which is still so scandalously insufficient; for the Aged and those prematurely incapacitated by accident or disease, now in many ways so imperfectly cared for; for the Education alike of children, of adolescents and of adults, in which the Labour Party demands a genuine equality of opportunity, overcoming all differences of material circumstances; and for the organisation of public improvements of all kinds, including the brightening of the lives of those now condemned to almost ceaseless toil, and a great development of the means of recreation. From the same source must come the greatly increased public provision that the Labour Party will insist on being made for scientific investigation and original research, in every branch of knowledge, not to say also for the promotion of music, literature and fine art, which have been under Capitalism so greatly neglected, and upon which, so the Labour party holds, any real development of civilisation fundamentally depends. Society, like the individual, does not live by bread alone—does not exist only for perpetual wealth production. It is in the proposal for this appropriation of every surplus for the Common Good—in the vision of its resolute use for the building up of the community as a whole instead of for the magnification of individual fortunes—that the Labour Party, as the Party of the Producers by hand or by brain, most distinctively marks itself off from the older political parties, standing, as these do essentially for the maintenance, unimpaired of the perpetual private mortgage upon the annual product of the nation that is involved in the individual ownership of land and capital.

THE STREET OF TO-MORROW

The House which the Labour Party intends to build, the four Pillars of which have now been described, does not stand alone in the world. Where will it be in the Street of To-morrow? If we repudiate, on the one hand, the Imperialism that seeks to dominate other races, or to impose our own will on other parts of the British Empire, so we disclaim equally any conception of a selfish and insular "non-interventionism" unregarding of our special obligations to our fellow-citizens overseas; of the corporate duties of one nation to another; of the moral claims upon us of the non-adult races, and of our own indebtedness to the world of which we are part. We look for an ever-increasing intercourse, a constantly developing exchange of commodities, a steadily growing mutual understanding, and a continually expanding friendly co-operation among all the peoples of the world. With regard to that great Commonwealth of all races, all colours, all religions and all degrees of civilisation, that we call the British Empire, the Labour Party stands for its maintenance and its progressive development on the lines of Local Autonomy and "Home Rule All Round"; the fullest respect for the rights of each people, whatever its colour, to all the Democratic Self-Government of which it is capable, and to the proceeds of its own toil upon the resources of its own territorial home; and the closest possible co-operation among all the various members of what has become essentially not an Empire in the old sense, but a Britannic Alliance. We desire to maintain the most intimate relations with the Labour Parties overseas. Like them, we have no sympathy with the projects of "Imperial Federation," in so far as these imply the subjection to a common Imperial Legislature wielding coercive power (including dangerous facilities for coercive Imperial taxation and for enforced military service), either of the existing Self-Governing Dominions, whose autonomy would be thereby invaded; or of the United Kingdom, whose freedom of Democratic Self-development would be thereby hampered; or of India and the Colonial Dependencies, which would thereby run the risk of being further exploited for the benefit of a "White Empire." We do not intend, by any such "Imperial Senate," either to bring the plutocracy of Canada and South Africa to the aid of the British aristocracy or to enable the landlords and fiancers of the Mother Country to unite in controlling the growing Popular Democracies overseas. The absolute autonomy of each self-governing part of the Empire must be maintained intact. What we look for, besides a constant progress in Democratic Self-Government of every part of the Britannic Alliance, and especially in India, is a continuous participation of the Ministers of the Dominions of India, and eventually of other Dependencies (perhaps by means of their own Ministers specially resident in London for this purpose) in the most confidential deliberations of the Cabinet, so far as Foreign Policy and Imperial Affairs are concerned; and the annual assembly of an Imperial Council, representing all constituents of the Britannic Alliance and all parties in their Local Legislatures, which should discuss all matters of common intrest, but only in order to make recommendations for the simultaneous consideration of the various autonomous local legislatures of what should increasingly take the constitutional form of an Alliance of Free Nations. And we carry the idea further. As regards our relations to Foreign

Countries, we disavow and disclaim any desire or intention to dispossess or to impoverish any other State or Nation. We seek no increase of territory. We disclaim all idea of "economic war." We ourselves object to all Protective Customs Tariffs; but we hold that each nation must be left free to do what it thinks best for its own economic development, without thought of injuring others. We believe that nations are in no way damaged by each other's economic prosperity or commercial progress; but, on the contrary, that they are actually themselves mutually enriched thereby. We would therefore put an end to the old entanglements and mystifications of Secret Diplomacy and the formation of Leagues against Leagues. We stand for the immediate establishment, actually as a part of the Treaty of Peace with which the present war will end, of a Universal League or Society of Nations, a Supernational Authority, with an International High Court to try all justiciable issues between nations; an International Legislature to enact such common laws as can be mutually agreed upon, and an International Council of Mediation to endeavour to settle without ultimate conflict even those disputes which are not justiciable. We would have all the nations of the world most solemnly undertake and promise to make a common cause against any one of them that broke away from this fundamental agreement. The world has suffered too much from war for the Labour Party to have any other policy than that of lasting Peace.

MORE LIGHT—BUT ALSO MORE WARMTH!

The Labour Party is far from assuming that it possesses a key to open all locks; or that any policy which it can formulate will solve all the problems that beset us. But we deem it important to ourselves as well as to those who may, on the one hand, wish to join the Party, or, on the other, to take up arms against it, to make quite clear and definite our aim and purpose. The Labour Party wants that aim and purpose, as set forth in the preceding pages, with all its might. It calls for more warmth in politics, for much less apathetic acquiescence in the miseries that exist, for none of the cynicism that saps the life of leisure. On the other hand, the Labour Party has no belief in any of the problems of the world being solved by Good Will alone. Good Will without knowledge is Warmth without Light. Especially in all the complexities of politics, in the still undeveloped Science of Society, the Labour Party stands for increased study, for the scientific investigation of each suceeding problem, for the deliberate organisation of research, and for a much more rapid dissemination among the whole people of all the science that exists. And it is perhaps specially the Labour Party that has the duty of placing this Advancement of science in the forefront of its political programme. What the Labour Party stands for in all fields of life is, essentially, Democratic Co-operation; and Co-operation involves a common purpose which can be agreed to; a common plan which can be explained and discussed, and such a measure of success in the adaptation of means to ends as will ensure a common satisfaction. An autocratic Sultan may govern without science if his whim is law. A Plutocratic Party may choose to ignore science, if it is heedless whether its pretended solutions of social problems that may win political triumphs ultimately succeeed or fail. But no Labour Party can hope to maintain its position unless its proposals are, in fact, the outcome of the best Political Science of its time; or to fulfil its purpose unless that science is continually wresting new fields from human ignorance. Hence, although the purpose of the Labour Party must, by the law of its being, remain for all time unchanged, its Policy and its Programme will, we hope, undergo a perpetual development, as knowledge grows, and as new phases of the social problem present themselves, in a continually finer adjustment of our measures to our ends. If Law is the Mother of Freedom, Science, to the Labour Party, must be the Parent of Law.

SPARTICIST MANIFESTO

December 26, 1918

To the Workers of All Countries

Proletarians! Men and Women of labor! Comrades!

The revolution has made its entry into Germany. The masses of the soldiers who for four years were driven to the slaughterhouse for the sake of capitalistic profits; the masses of workers, who for four years were exploited, crushed, and starved, have revolted. That fearful tool of oppression —Prussian militarism, that scourge of humanity—lies broken on the ground. Its most noticeable representatives, and therewith the most noticeable of those guilty of this war, the Kaiser and the Crown Prince, have fled from the country. Workers' and Soldiers' Councils have been formed everywhere.

Proletarians of all countries, we do not say that in Germany all the power has really been lodged in the hands of the working people, that the complete triumph of the proletarian revolution has already been attained. There still sit in the Government all those Socialists who in August, 1914, abandoned our most precious possession, the International, who for four years betrayed the German working class and at the same time the International.

But, proletarians of all countries, now the German proletarian himself is speaking to you. We believe we have the right to appear before your forum in his name. From the first day of this war we endeavored to do our international duty by fighting that criminal Government with all our power and branding it as the one really guilty of the war.

Now at this moment we are justified before history, before the International and before the German proletariat. The masses agree with us enthusiastically, constantly widening circles of the proletariat share the knowledge that the hour has struck for a settlement with capitalist class rule.

But this great task cannot be accomplished by the German proletariat alone; it can only fight and triumph by appealing to the solidarity of the proletarians of the whole world.

Comrades of the belligerent countries, we are aware of your situation. We know very well that your Governments, now since they have won the victory, are dazzling the eyes of many strata of the people with the external brilliancy of the triumph. We know that they thus succeed through the success of the murdering in making its causes and aims forgotten.

But we also know something else. We know that also in your countries the proletariat made the most fearful sacrifices of flesh and blood, that it is weary of the dreadful butchery, that the proletarian is now returning to his home and is finding want and misery there, while fortunes amounting to billions are heaped up in the hands of a few capitalists. He has recognized, and will continue to recognize, that your Governments, too, have carried on the war for the sake of the big money bags. And he will further perceive that your Governments, when they spoke of "justice and civilization" and of the "protection of small nations," meant the profits of capital just as did ours when it talked about the 'defense of the home'; and that the peace of "justice" and of the "League of Nations" amounts to the same base brigandage as the peace of Brest-Litovsk. Here as well as there the same shameless lust for booty, the same desire for oppression, the same determination to exploit to the limit the brutal predominance of murderous steel.

The imperialism of all countries knows no "understanding," it knows only one right—capital's profits; it knows only one language—the sword; it knows only one method—violence. And if it is now talking in all countries, in yours as well as ours, about the "League of Nations," "disarmament," "rights of small nations," "self-determination of the peoples," it is merely using the customary lying phrases of the rulers for the purpose of lulling to sleep the watchfulness of the proletariat.

Proletarians of all countries! This must be the last war! We owe that to the 12,000,000 murdered victims, we owe that to our children, we owe that to humanity.

Europe has been ruined through the infamous international murder. Twelve million bodies cover the grewsome scenes of the imperialistic crime. The flower of youth and the best man power of the peoples have been mowed down. Uncounted productive forces have been annihilated. Humanity is almost ready to bleed to death from the unexampled bloodletting of history. Victors and vanquished stand at the edge of the abyss. Humanity is threatened with the most dreadful famine, a stoppage of the entire mechanism of production, plagues, and degeneration.

The great criminals of this fearful anarchy, of this chaos let loose—the ruling classes—are not able to control their own creation. The beast of capital that conjured up the hell of the world war is not capable of banishing it again, of restoring real order, of insuring bread and work, peace and civilization, justice and liberty to tortured humanity.

What is being prepared by the ruling classes as peace and justice is only a new work of brutal force from which the hydra of oppression, hatred and fresh, bloody wars raises its thousand heads.

Socialism alone is in a position to complete the great work of permanent peace, to heal the thousand wounds from which humanity is bleeding, to transform the plains of Europe, trampled down by the passage of the apocryphal horseman of war, into blooming gardens, to conjure up ten productive forces for every one destroyed, to awaken all the physical and moral energies of humanity, and to place hatred and dissension with fraternal solidarity, harmony, and respect for every human being.

If representatives of the proletarians of all countries stretch out their hands to each other under the banner of socialism for the purpose of making peace, then peace will be concluded in a few hours. Then there will be no disputed questions about the left bank of the Rhine, Mesopotamia, Egypt, or colonies. Then there will be only one people; the toiling human beings of all races and tongues. Then there will be only one right: the equality of all men. Then there will be only one aim: prosperity and progress for everybody.

Humanity is facing this alternative: Dissolution and downfall in capitalist anarchy, or regeneration through the social revolution. The hour for decision has struck. If you believe in socialism it is now time to show it by deeds. If you are Socialists, now is the time to act.

Proletarians of all countries, when we now summon you to a common struggle it is not done for the sake of the German capitalists who, under the label "German nation" are trying to escape the consequences of their own crimes; it is being done for our sake as well as for yours. Remember that your victorious capitalists stand ready to suppress in blood our revolution, which they fear as their own. You yourselves have not become any freer through the "victory," you have only become still more enslaved. If your ruling classes succeed in throttling the proletarian revolution in Germany, as well as in Russia, then they will turn against you with redoubled violence. Your capitalists hope that victory over us and over revolutionary Russia will give them the power to scourge you with a whip of scorpions and to erect the thousand-year empire of exploitation upon the grave of socialism.

Therefore the proletariat of Germany is looking toward you in this hour. Germany is pregnant with the social revolution, but socialism can only be realized by the proletariat of the world.

And therefore we call to you: "Arise for the struggle! Arise for action! The time for empty manifestos, platonic resolutions, and high-sounding words has gone by! The hour of action has struck for the International!" We ask you to elect Workers' and Soldiers' Councils everywhere that will seize political power and, together with us, will restore peace.

Not Lloyd George and Poincaré, not Sonnino, Wilson, and Erzberger or Scheidemann, must be allowed to make peace. Peace is to be concluded under the waving banner of the socialist world revolution.

Proletarians of all countries! We call upon you to complete the work of socialist liberation, to give a human aspect to the disfigured world and to make true those words with which we often greeted each other in the old days and which we sang as we parted: "And the Internationale shall be the human race!"

KLARA ZETKIN
ROSA LUXEMBURG
KARL LIEBKNECHT
FRANZ MEHRING

Revolutionary Thought and Practice: Bolshevism

Vladimir Ilich Ulyanov (Nikolai Lenin), The State and Revolution, Part V, chap. iii in part, in V. I. Lenin, Selected Works (Moscow: Foreign Languages Publishing House, 1947), chap. v, pp. 197–211.

Nikolai Lenin (1870–1924) is that rare combination of thinker and doer. His impact in each strengthened his influence in the other. Communist theoreticians today appeal to Lenin even more than to Marx and Engels for authority. Communism is a religion, and Communism—like the Roman Catholic Church—enjoys not only scriptural doctrine but continuing authoritative interpretation. Lenin is the greatest of Communist prophets. Notice throughout these selections the careful attention to the basic, unquestioned authority of Marx and Engels, the slashing attacks on doctrinal deviation, and the effort to define as precisely as possible the details necessary for the realization of the communist utopia.

The 1880's was no time for a liberal, sensitive young man to find himself in Russia. The brutal repression of Alexander III alienated most thinking Russians. Lenin's older brother, Alexander, was executed at the age of nineteen, having been implicated in an assassination plot. Harassed and watched by police, Lenin finally managed to secure a diploma in law from the University of St. Petersburg in 1891. Two years of legal practice, three more of Socialist agitation in St. Petersburg, then four in Siberian exile followed. Lenin moved to Switzerland in 1900 to work on the publication of Iskra (The Spark), an illegal publication for circulation in Russia. In July and August, 1903, he led the Bolshevik faction in the famous split with the Mensheviks at a Russian Socialist party congress held abroad. Lenin returned to St. Petersburg during the Duma Revolution of 1905, to work as an agitator and publicist, but fled again in December 1907. It was his last appearance in Russia for nine and a half years.

During his second exile abroad, Lenin devoted himself to the ideological purification of his party. Materialism and Empiro-Criticism (1909) was intended to check the philosophic move within the party towards idealism and religion. Other pamphlets were directed against revisionist tendencies in international socialist thought and practice. Lenin kept in close contact with all aspects of the Socialist and revolutionary movements within Russia and elsewhere in Europe. Thus in spite of his exile he was fully prepared to dispute the leadership of the Russian revolution when he returned to that country in April, 1917.

The State and Revolution, never completed, is one of the most important works in Communist ideology. Written during the months before the November Revolution in 1917, it was not actually published until early 1918. It was the guideline of revolution, accepted and endorsed by the Bolshevik party. The State and Revolution integrates Lenin's critique of capitalism and his plan for Communist organization. It proceeds from the Marx-Engels definition of the state as "a special organization of force; the organization of violence for the suppression of some class" to adumbrate both method and end through the dictatorship of the proletariat to the withering away of the state and the emergence of the classless society.

CHAPTER V

THE ECONOMIC BASIS OF THE WITHERING AWAY OF THE STATE

MARX EXPLAINS THIS QUESTION most thoroughly in his *Critique of the Gotha Program* (letter to Bracke, May 5, 1875, which was not printed until 1891 in *New Zeit*, Vol. IX, 1, and which has appeared in a special Russian edition). The polemical part of this remarkable work, which consists of a criticism of Lassalleanism, has, so to speak, overshadowed its positive part, namely, the analysis of the connection between the development of Communism and the withering away of the state.

1. MARX'S PRESENTATION OF THE QUESTION

From a superficial comparison of Marx's letter to Bracke of May 5, 1875, with Engels' letter to Bebel of March 28, 1875, which we examined above, it might appear that Marx was much more "pro-state" than Engels, and that the difference of opinion between the two writers on the question of the state was very considerable.

Engels suggested to Bebel that all the chatter about the state be dropped; that the word "state" be eliminated from the program altogether and the word "community" substituted for it. Engels even declared that the Commune was really no longer a state in the proper sense of the word. Yet Marx spoke of the "future state in Communist society," *i.e.*, as though he recognized the need for a state even under Communism.

But such a view would be fundamentally wrong. A closer examination shows that Marx's and Engels' views on the state and its withering away were completely identical, and that Marx's expression quoted above refers merely to this *withering away* of the state.

Clearly there can be no question of defining the exact moment of the *future* "withering away"—the more so since it must obviously be a rather lengthy process. The apparent difference between Marx and Engels is due to the different subjects they dealt with, the different aims they were pursuing. Engels set out to show Bebel plainly, sharply and in broad outline the absurdity of the prevailing prejudices concerning the state, which were shared to no small degree by Lassalle. Marx only touched upon *this* question in passing, being interested in another subject, *viz.*, the *development* of Communist society.

The whole theory of Marx is an application of the theory of development —in its most consistent, complete, thought-out and replete form—to modern capitalism. Naturally, Marx was faced with the question of applying this theory both to the *forthcoming* collapse of capitalism and to the *future* development of *future* Communism.

On the basis of what *data* can the question of the future development of future Communism be raised?

On the basis of the fact that *it has its origin* in capitalism, that it develops historically from capitalism, that it is the result of the action of a social force to which capitalism *has given birth*. There is no trace of an attempt on Marx's part to conjure up a utopia, to make idle guesses about what cannot be known. Marx treats the question of Communism in the same way as a naturalist would treat the question of the development, say, of a new biological species, if he knew that such and such was its origin and such and such the direction in which it was changing.

Marx, first of all, brushes aside the confusion the Gotha Program brings into the question of the relation between state and society. He writes:

"Present-day society" is capitalist society, which exists in all civilized countries, more or less free from mediaeval admixture, more or less modified by the special historical development of each country and more or less developed. On the other hand, the "present-day state" changes with a country's frontier. It is different in the Prusso-German Empire from what it is in Switzerland, it is different in England from what it is in the United States. The "present-day state" is therefore a fiction.

Nevertheless, the different states of the different civilized countries, in spite of their manifold diversity of form, all have this in common, that they are based on modern bourgeois society, only one more or less capitalistically developed. They have, therefore, also certain essential features in common. In this sense it is possible to speak of the "present-day state," in contrast to the future, in which its present root, bourgeois society, will have died away.

The question then arises: what transformation will the state undergo in Communist society? In other words, what social functions will remain in existence there that are analogous to the present functions of the state? This question can only be answered scientifically and one does not get a flea-hop nearer to the problem by a thousandfold combination of the word people with the word state. . . .

Having thus ridiculed all talk about a "people's state," Marx formulates the question and warns us, as it were, that to arrive at a scientific answer one must rely only on firmly established scientific data.

The first fact that has been established with complete exactitude by the whole theory of development, by science as a whole—a fact which the utopians forgot, and which is forgotten by the present-day opportunists who are afraid of the Socialist revolution—is that, historically, there must un-

doubtedly be a special stage or a special phase of *transition* from capitalism
to Communism.

2. The Transition from Capitalism to Communism

Marx continues:

Between capitalist and Communist society lies the period of the revolutionary transformation of the one into the other. There corresponds to this
also a political transition period in which the state can be nothing but the
revolutionary dictatorship of the proletariat.

Marx bases this conclusion on an analysis of the role played by the
proletariat in modern capitalist society, on the data concerning the development of this society, and on the irreconcilability of the antagonistic
interests of the proletariat and the bourgeoisie.

Earlier the question was put in this way: in order to achieve its emancipation, the proletariat must overthrow the bourgeoisie, conquer political
power and establish its revolutionary dictatorship.

Now the question is put somewhat differently: the transition from capitalist society—which is developing towards Communism—to a Communist society is impossible without a "political transition period," and the
state in this period can only be the revolutionary dictatorship of the proletariat.

What, then, is the relation of this dictatorship to democracy?

We have seen that *The Communis Manifesto* simply places the two
ideas side by side: "to raise the proletariat to the position of the ruling
class" and "to win the battle of democracy." On the basis of all that has
been said above, it is possible to determine more precisely how democracy
changes in the transition from capitalism to Communism.

In capitalist society, under the conditions most favourable to its development, we have more or less complete democracy in the democratic republic,
But this democracy is always restricted by the narrow framework of capitalist exploitation, and consequently always remains, in reality, a democracy
for the minority, only for the possessing classes, only for the rich. Freedom
in capitalist society always remains about the same as it was in the ancient
Greek republics: freedom for the slave-owners. Owing to the conditions
of capitalist exploitation the modern wage-slaves are so crushed by want
and poverty that "they cannot be bothered with democracy," "they cannot
be bothered with politics"; in the ordinary peaceful course of events the
majority of the population is debarred from participating in social and
political life.

The correctness of this statement is perhaps most clearly proved by Germany, precisely because in that country constitutional legality lasted and
remained stable for a remarkably long time—for nearly half a century

(1871–1914)—and Social-Democracy during this period was able to achieve far more in Germany than in other countries in the way of "utilizing legality," and was able to organize a larger proportion of the workers into a political party than anywhere else in the world.

What is this largest proportion of politically conscious and active wage-slaves that has so far been observed in capitalist society? One million members of the Social-Democratic Party—out of fifteen million wage workers! Three million organized in trade unions—out of fifteen million!

Democracy for an insignificant minority, democracy for the rich—that is the democracy of capitalist society. If we look more closely into the mechanism of the suffrage (residential qualification, exclusion of women, etc.), in the technique of the representative institutions, in the actual obstacles to the right of assembly (public building are not for "beggars"!), in the purely capitalist organization of the daily press, etc., etc.—we see restriction after restriction upon democracy. These restrictions, exceptions, exclusions, obstacles for the poor, seem slight, especially in the eyes of one who has never known want himself and has never been in close contact with the oppressed classes in their mass life (and nine-tenths if not ninety-nine hundredths, of the bourgeois publicists and politicians are of this category); but in their sum total these restrictions exclude and squeeze out the poor from politics, from taking an active part in democracy.

Marx grasped this *essence* of capitalist democracy splendidly, when, in analysing the experience of the Commune, he said that the oppressed are allowed once every few years to decide which particular representatives of the oppressing class should represent and repress them in parliament!

But from this capitalist democracy—inevitably narrow, tacitly repelling the poor, and therefore hypocritical and false to the core—forward development does not proceed simply, directly and smoothly to "greater and greater democracy," as the liberal professors and petty-bourgeois opportunists would have us believe. No, forward development, *i.e.*, towards Communism, proceeds through the dictatorship of the proletariat, and can not do otherwise, for the *resistance* of the capitalist exploiters cannot be *broken* by anyone else or in any other way.

But the dictatorship of the proletariat, *i.e.*, the organization of the vanguard of the oppressed as the ruling class for the purpose of crushing the oppressors, cannot result merely in an expansion of democracy. *Simultaneously* with an immense expansion of democracy, which *for the first time* becomes democracy for the poor, democracy for the people, and not democracy for the rich, the dictatorship of the proletariat imposes a series of restrictions on the freedom of the oppressors, the exploiters, the capitalists. We must crush them in order to free humanity from wage-slavery; their resistance must be broken by force; it is clear that where there is suppression, where there is coercion, there is no freedom and no democracy.

Engels expressed this splendidly in his letter to Bebel when he said, as the reader will remember, that

... so long as the proletariat still *uses* the state, it does not use it in the interests of freedom but in order to hold down its adversaries, and as soon as it becomes possible to speak of freedom the state as such ceases to exist.

Democracy for the vast majority of the people, and suppression by force, *i.e.*, exclusion from democracy, of the exploiters and oppressors of the people—this is the change democracy undergoes during the *transition* from capitalism to Communism.

Only in Communist society, when the resistance of the capitalists has been completely broken, when the capitalists have disappeared, when there are no classes (*i.e.*, when there is no difference between the members of society as regards their relation to the social means of production), *only* then does "the state . . . cease to exist," and it *"becomes possible to speak of freedom."* Only then will really complete democracy, democracy without any exceptions, be possible and be realized. And only then will democracy begin to *wither away,* owing to the simple fact that, freed from capitalist slavery, from the untold horrors, savagery, absurdities and infamies of capitalist exploitation, people will gradually *become accustomed* to observing the elementary rules of social intercourse that have been known for centuries and repeated for thousands of years in all copy-book maxims; they will become accustomed to observing them without force, without compulsion, without subordination, *without the special apparatus* for compulsion which is called the state.

The expression "the state *withers away*" is very well chosen, for it indicates both the gradual and the spontaneous nature of the process. Only habit can, and undoubtedly will, have such an effect; for we see around us millions of times how readily people become accustomed to observing the necessary rules of social intercourse if there is no exploitation, if there is nothing that causes indignation, nothing that calls forth protest and revolt or evokes the necessity for *suppression.*

Thus in capitalist society we have a democracy that is curtailed, wretched, false; a democracy only for the rich, for the minority. The dictatorship of the proletariat, the period of transition to Communism, will for the first time create democracy for the people, for the majority, in addition to the necessary suppression of the minority—the exploiters. Communism alone is capable of giving really complete democracy, and the more complete it is the more quickly will it become unnecessary and wither away of itself.

In other words: under capitalism we have a state in the proper sense of the word, that is, a special machine for the suppression of one class by another, and of the majority by the minority at that. Naturally, the successful discharge of such a task as the systematic suppression of the exploited majority by the exploiting minority calls for the greatest ferocity and savagery in the work of suppression, it calls for seas of blood through which mankind has to wade in slavery, serfdom and wage labour.

Furthermore, during the *transition* from capitalism to Communism suppression is *still* necessary; but it is now the suppression of the exploiting minority by the exploited majority. A special apparatus, a special machine for suppression, the "state," is *still* necessary, but this is now a transitory state; it is no longer a state in the proper sense; for the suppression of the minority of exploiters by the majority of the wage-slaves *of yesterday* is comparatively so easy, simple and natural a task that it will entail far less bloodshed than the suppression of the risings of slaves, serfs or wage labourers, and it will cost mankind far less. And it is compatible with the extension of democracy to such an overwhelming majority of the population that the need for a *special machine* of suppression will begin to disappear. The exploiters are naturally unable to suppress the people without a very complex machine for performing this task; but *the people* can suppress the exploiters even with a very simple "machine," almost without a "machine," without a special apparatus, by the simple *organization of the armed masses* (such as the Soviets of Workers' and Soldiers' Deputies, we may remark, running ahead a little).

Finally, only Communism makes the state absolutely unnecessary, for there is *nobody* to be suppressed—"nobody" in the sense of a *class*, in the sense of a systematic struggle against a definite section of the population. We are not utopians, and we do not in the least deny the possibility and inevitability of excesses on the part of *individual persons*, or the need to suppress *such* excesses. But, in the first place, no special machine, no special apparatus of repression is needed for this; this will be done by the armed people itself, as simply and as readily as any crowd of civilized people, even in modern society, parts two people who are fighting, or interferes to prevent a woman from being assaulted. And, secondly, we know that the fundamental social causes of excesses, which consist of violating the rules of social intercourse, is the exploitation of the masses, their want and their poverty. With the removal of this chief cause, excesses will inevitably begin to *"wither away."* We do not know how quickly and in what order, but we know that they will wither away. With their withering away the state *will also wither away*.

Without indulging in utopias, Marx defined more fully what can be defined *now* regarding this future, namely, the difference between the lower and higher phases (degrees, stages) of Communist society.

3. The First Phase of Communist Society

In the *Critique of the Gotha Program*, Marx goes into some detail to disprove Lassalle's idea that under Socialism the worker will receive the "undiminished" or "whole proceeds of his labour." Marx shows that from the whole of the social labour of society it is necessary to deduct a reserve fund, a fund for the expansion of production, for the replacement of "used up" machinery, and so on; then, also, from the means of consumption must be deducted a fund for the costs of administration, for schools, hospitals, homes for the aged, and so on.

Instead of Lassalle's hazy, obscure, general phrase ("the whole procceds of his labour to the worker") Marx makes a sober estimate of exactly how Socialist society will have to manage its affairs. Marx proceeds to make a *concrete* analysis of the conditions of life of a society in which there will be no capitalism, and says:

What we have to deal with here [in analysing the program of the workers' party] is a Communist society, not as it has *developed* on its own foundations, but, on the contrary, as it *emerges* from capitalist society; which is thus in every respect, economically, morally and intellectually, still stamped with the birthmarks of the old society from whose womb it emerges.

And it is this Communist society—a society whcih has just come into the world out of the womb of capitalism and which, in every respect, bears the birthmarks of the old society—that Marx terms the "first," or lower phase of Communist society.

The means of production are no longer the private property of individuals. The means of production belong to the whole of society. Every member of society, performing a certain part of the socially-necessary labour, receives a certificate from society to the effect that he has done such and such an amount of work. And with this certificate he draws from the social stock of means of consumption a corresponding quantity of products. After deduction of the amount of labour which goes to the public fund, every worker, therefore, receives from society as much as he has given it.

"Equality" apparently reigns supreme.

But when Lassalle, having such a social order in view (usually called Socialism, but termed by Marx the first phase of Communism), speaks of this as "equitable distribution," and says that this is "the equal right" of "all members of society" to "equal proceeds of labour," he is mistaken, and Marx exposes his error.

"Equal right," says Marx, we indeed have here; but it is *still* a "bourgeois right," which, like every right, *presupposes inequality.* Every right is an application of an *equal* standard to *different* people who in fact are not alike, are not equal to one another; that is why "equal right" is really a violation of equality and an injustice. As a matter of fact, every man, having performed as much social labour as another, receives an equal share of the social product (after the above-mentioned deductions).

But people are not alike: one is strong, another is weak; one is married, another is not; one has more children, another has less, and so on. And the conclusion Marx draws is:

. . . With an equal output, and hence an equal share in the social consumption fund, one will in fact receive more than another, one will be richer than another, and so on. To avoid all these defects, right, instead of being equal, would have to be unequal. . . .

Hence, the first phase of Communism cannot yet produce justice and equality; differences, and unjust differences, in wealth will still exist, but the *exploitation* of man by man will have become impossible, because it will be impossible to seize the *means of production*, the factories, machines, land, etc., as private property. In smashing Lassalle's petty-bourgeois con-fused phrases about "equality" and "justice" *in general*, Marx shows the *course of development* of Communist society, which at first is *compelled* to abolish *only* the "injustice" of the means of production having been seized by private individuals, and which *cannot* at once abolish the other injustice, which consists in the distribution of articles of consumption "according to the amount of labour performed" (and not according to needs).

The vulgar economists, including the bourgeois professors and also "our" Tugan-Baranovsky, constantly reproach the Socialists with forgetting the inequality of people and with "dreaming" of abolishing this inequality. Such a reproach, as we see, only proves the extreme ignorance of Messieurs the Bourgeois Ideologists.

Marx not only scrupulously takes into account the inevitable inequality of men but he also takes into account the fact that the mere conversion of the means of production into the common property of the wohle of society (usually called "Socialism") *does not remove* the defects of distribution and the inequality of "bourgeois right" which *continue to prevail* as long as products are divided "according to the amount of labour performed." Con-tinuing, Marx says:

But these defects are inevitable in the first phase of Communist society as it is when it has just emerged after prolonged birth pangs from capitalist society. Right can never be higher than the economic structure of society and the cultural development thereby determined.

And so, in the first phase of Communist society (usually called Social-ism) "bourgeois right" is *not* abolished in its entirety, but only in part, only in proportion to the economic transformation so far attained, *i.e.*, only in re-spect of the means of production. "Bourgeois right" recognizes them as the private property of individuals. Socialism converts them into *common* property. *To that extent*—and to that extent alone—"bourgeois right" disappears.

However, it continues to exist as far as its other part is concerned; it con-tinues to exist in the capacity of regulator (determining factor) in the dis-tribution of products and the allotment of labour among the members of society. The Socialist principle: "He who does not work, neither shall he eat," is *already* realized; the other Socialist principle: "An equal amount of products for an equal amount of labour," is also *already* realized. But this is not yet Communism, and it does not yet abolish "bourgeois right," which gives to unequal individuals, in return for an unequal (actually unequal) amount of labour, an equal amount of products.

This is a "defect," says Marx, but it is unavoidable in the first phase of Communism; for if we are not to indulge in utopianism, we must not think that having overthrown capitalism people will at once learn to work for society *without any standard of right*; and indeed the abolition of capitalism *does not immediately* create the economic premises for *such* a change.

And there is as yet no other standard than that of "bourgeois right." To this extent, therefore, there is still need for a state, which, while safeguarding the public ownership of the means of production would safeguard equality of labour and equality in the distribution of products.

The state withers away in so far as there are no longer any capitalists, any classes, and, consequently, no *class* can be *suppressed*.

But the state has not yet completely withered away, since there still remains the safeguarding of "bourgeois right," which sanctifies actual inequality. For the complete withering away of the state complete Communism is necessary.

4. THE HIGHER PHASE OF COMMUNIST SOCIETY

Marx continues:

In a higher phase of Communist society, after the enslaving subordination of individuals under division of labour, and therewith also the antithesis between mental and physical labour, has vanished; after labour, from a mere means of life, has itself become the prime necessity of life; after the productive forces have also increased with the all-round development of the individual, and all the springs of co-operative wealth flow more abundantly—only then can the narrow horizon of bourgeois right be fully left behind and society inscribe on its banners: From each according to his ability, to each according to his needs!

Only now can we appreciate to the full the correctness of Engels' remarks in which he mercilessly ridiculed the absurdity of combining the words "freedom" and "state." While the state exists there is no freedom. When there will be freedom, there will be no state.

The economic basis for the complete withering away of the state is such a high stage of development of Communism that the antithesis between mental and physical labour disappears, that is to say, when one of the principal sources of modern *social* inequality disappears—a source, moreover, which cannot be removed immediately by the mere conversion of the means of production into public property, by the mere expropriation of the capitalists.

This expropriation will *facilitate* an enormous development of productive forces. And seeing how capitalism is already *retarding* this development to an incredible degree, seeing how much progress could be achieved even on the basis of the present level of modern technique, we are entitled to say with the fullest confidence that the expropriation of the capitalists will inevitably result in an enormous development of the productive forces of human society. But how rapidly this development will proceed, how soon it will reach the point of breaking away from the division of labour, of removing the antithesis between mental and physical labour, or transforming labour into "the prime necessity of life"—we do not and *cannot* know.

That is why we are entitled to speak only of the inevitable withering away of the state, emphasizng the protracted nature of this process and its dependence upon the rapidity of development of the *higher phase* of Communism, and leaving the question of length of time, or the concrete forms of the withering away, quite open, because there is *no* material for an answer to these questions.

The state will be able to wither away completely when society applies the rule: "From each according to his abillity, to each according to his needs," *i.e.,* when people have become so accustomed to observing the fundamental rules of social intercourse and when their labour is so productive that they will voluntarily work *according to their ability.* "The narrow horizon of bourgeois right," which compels one to calculate with the stringency of a Shylock whether one has not worked half an hour more than another—this narrow horizon will then be left behind. There will then be no need for society to regulate the quantity of products to be distributed to each; each will take freely "according to his needs."

From the bourgeois point of view, it is easy to declare that such a social order is "a pure utopia" and to sneer at the Socialists for promisnig everyone the right to receive from society, without any control of the labour of the individual citizen, any quantity of truffles, automobiles, pianos, etc. Even now, most bourgeois "savants" confine themselves to sneering in this way, thereby displaying at once their ignorance and their mercenary defence of capitalism.

Ignorance—for it has never entered the head of any Socialist to "promise" that the higher phase of the development of Communism will arrive; but the great Socialists, in *foreseeing* its arrival, presuppose not the present productivity of labour *and not the present* ordinary run of people, who, like the seminary students in Pomyalovsky's stories,[1] are capable of damaging the stocks of social wealth "just for fun" and of demanding the impossible.

Until the "higher" phase of Communism arrives, the Socialists demand the *strictest* control by society *and by the state* of the measure of labour and the measure of consumption; but this control must *start* with the expropriation of the capitalists, with the establishment of workers' conrol over the capitalists, and must be carried out not by a state of bureaucrats, but by a state of *armed workers.*

[1] The reference here is to N. Pomyalovsky's *Sketches of Seminary Life* in which this Russian novelist exposed the absurd system of education and brutal customs which held sway in the Russian theological school in the fifties and sixties of the past century.—*Ed.*

The mercenary defence of capitalism by the bourgeois ideologists (and their hangers-on, like Messrs. Tsereteli, Chernov and Co.) lies in their *substituting* controversies and discussions about the distant future for the essential and imperative questions of *present-day* policy, *viz.*, the expropriation of the capitalists, the conversion of *all* citizens into workers and employees of *one* huge "syndicate"—the whole state—and the complete subordination of the whole of the work of this syndicate to the really democratic state, *the state of the Soviets of Workers' and Soldiers' Deputies.*

In reality, when a learned professor, and following him the philistine, and following him Messrs. Tsereteli and Chernov, talk of the unreasonable utopias, of the demagogic promises of the Bolsheviks, of the impossiblity of "introducing" Socialism, it is the higher stage or phase of Communism they have in mind, which no one has ever promised or even thought to "introduce," because generally speaking it cannot be "introduced."

And this brings us to the question of the scientific difference between Socialism and Communism, which Engels touched on in his above-quoted argument about the incorrectness of the name "Social-Democrat." The political difference between the first, or lower, and the higher phase of Communism will in time, probably, be tremendous; but it would be ridiculous to take cognisance of this difference now, under capitalism, and only isolated anarchists, perhaps, could invest it with primary importance (if there are still people among the anarchists who have learned nothing from the "Plekhanovite" conversion of the Kropotkins, the Graveses, the Cornelisens and other "leading lights" of anarchism into social-chauvinists or "anarcho-trenchists," as Gay, one of the few anarchists who has still preserved a sense of honour and a conscience, has expressed it).

But the scientific difference between Socialism and Communism is clear. What is usually called Socialism was termed by Marx the "first" or lower phase of Communist society. In so far as the means of production become *common* property, the word "Communism" is also applicable here, providing we do not forget that it is *not* complete Communism. The great significance of Marx's explanations is that here, too, he consistently applies materialist dialectics, the doctrine of development, and regards Communism as something which develops *out of* capitalism. Instead of scholastically invented, "concocted" definitions and fruitless disputes about words (what is Socialism? what is Communism?), Marx gives an analysis of what may be called the stages in the economic ripeness of Communism.

In its first phase, or first stage, Communism *cannot* as yet be fully ripe economically and entirely free from traditions and traces of capitalism. Hence the interesting phenomenon that Communism in its first phase retains "the narrow horizon of *bourgeois* right." Of course, bourgeois right in regard to the distribution of articles of *consumption* inevitably presupposes the existence of the *bourgeois state*, for right is nothing without an apparatus capable of *enforcing* the observance of the standards of right.

Consequently, not only bourgeois right, but even the bourgeois state for a certain time remains under Communism, without the bourgeoisie!

This may sound like a paradox or simply a dialetical puzzle, of which Marxism is often accused by people who do not take the slightest trouble to study its extraordinary profound content.

But as a matter of fact, remnants of the old surviving in the new confront us in life at every step, both in nature and in society. And Marx did not arbitrarily insert a scrap of "bourgeois" right into Communism, but indicated what is economically and politically inevitable in a society emerging *from the womb* of capitalism.

Democracy is of great importance to the working class in its struggle for emancipation from the capitalists. But democracy is by no means a boundary that must not be overstepped; it is only one of the stages on the road from feudalism to capitalism, and from capitalism to Communism.

Democracy means equality. The great significance of the proletariat's struggle for equality and the significance of equality as a slogan will be clear if we correctly interpret it as meaning the abolition of *classes*. But democracy means only *formal* equality. And as soon as equality is obtained for all members of society *in relation to* the ownership of the means of production, that is, equality of labour and equality of wages, humanity will inevitably be confronted with the question of going beyond formal equality to real equality, *i.e.*, to applying the rule, "from each according to his ability, to each according to his needs." By what stages, by what practical measures humanity will proceed to this higher aim—we do not and cannot know. But it is important to realize how infinitely mendacious is the ordinary bourgeois conception of Socialism as something lifeless, petrified, fixed once for all, whereas in reality *only* under Socialism will a rapid, genuine, really mass forward movement, embracing first the *majority* and then the whole of the population, commence in all spheres of social and personal life.

Democracy is a form of state, one of its varieties. Consequently, it, like every state, on the one hand represents the organized, systematic application of force against persons; but on the other hand it signifies the formal recognition of the equality of all citizens, the equal right of all to determine the structure and administration of the state. This, in turn, is connected with the fact that, at a certain stage in the development of democracy, it first rallies the proletariat as the revolutionary class against capitalism, and enables it to crush, smash to atoms, wipe off the face of the earth the bourgeois, even the republican bourgeois, state machine, the standing army, the police and bureaucracy, and to substitute for them a *more* democratic state machine, but a state machine nevertheless, in the shape of the armed masses of workers who are being transformed into a universal people's militia.

Here "quantity is transformed into quality": *such* a degree of democracy implies overstepping the boundaries of bourgeois society, the beginning of its Socialist reconstruction. If, indeed, *all* take part in the administration of the state, capitalism cannot retain its hold. And the development of capitalism, in turn, itself creates the *premises* that really enable "all" to take part in the administration of the state. Some of the premises are: universal literacy, which is already achieved in a number of the most advanced capitalist countries, then the "training and disciplining" of millions of workers by the huge, complex, socialized apparatus of the postoffice, railways, big factories, large-scale commerce, banking, etc., etc.

Given these *economic* premises it is quite possible, after the overthrow of the capitalists and bureaucrats, to proceed immediately, overnight, to supersede them in the *control* of production and distribution, in the work of *keeping account* of labour and products by the armed workers by the whole of the armed population. (The question of control and accounting must not be confused with the question of the scientifically trained staff of engineers, agronomists and so on. These gentlemen are working today and obey the capitalists; they will work even better to-morrow and obey the armed workers.)

Accounting and control—that is the *main* thing required for the "setting up" and correct functioning of the *first phase* of Communist society. *All* citizens are transformed into the salaried employees of the state, which consists of the armed workers. *All* citizens become employees and workers of a *single* national state "syndicate." All that is required is that they should work equally—do their proper share of work—and get paid equally. The accounting and control necessary for this have been *simplified* by capitalism to an extreme and reduced to the extraordinarily simple operations— which any literate person can perform—of checking and recording, knowledge of the four rules of arithmetic, and issuing receipts.[2]

When the *majority* of the people begin independently and everywhere to keep such accounts and maintain such control over the capitalists (now converted into employees) and over the intellectual gentry who preserve their capitalist habits, this control will really become universal, general, national; and there will be no way of getting away from it, there will be "nowhere to go."

The whole of society will have become a single office and a single factory, with equality of labour and equality of pay.

But this "factory" discipline, which the proletariat will extend to the whole of society after the defeat of the capitalists and the overthrow of the exploiters, is by no means our ideal, or our ultimate goal. It is but a necessary *step* for the purpose of thoroughly purging society of all the hideousness and foulness of capitalist exploitation, *and for further* progress.

From the moment all members of society, or even only the vast majority,

---

[2] When most of the functions of the state are reduced to this accounting and control by the workers themselves, it will cease to be a "political state" and the "public functions will lose their political character and be transformed into simple administrative functions." (*cf.* above, chap. 4, § 2, Engels' "Controversy with the Anarchists").

have learned to administer the state *themselves*, have taken this business into their own hands, have "set up" control over the insignificant minority of capitalists, over the gentry who wish to preserve their capitalist habits, and over the workers who have been profoundly corrupted by capitalism—from this moment the need for government begins to disappear altogether. The more complete democracy, the nearer the moment approaches when it becomes unnecessary. The more democratic the "state" which consists of the armed workers, and which is "no longer a state in the proper sense of the word," the more rapidly does *every form* of the state begin to wither away.

For when *all* have learned to administer and actually do administer social production independently, independently keep accounts and exercise control over the idlers, the gentlefolk, the swindlers and similar "guardians of capitalist traditions," the escape from this national accounting and control will inevitably become so incredibly difficult, such a rare exception, and will probably be accompanied by such swift and severe punishment (for the armed workers are practical men and not sentimental intellectuals, and they will scarcely allow anyone to trifle with them), that very soon the *necessity* of observing the simple, fundamental rules of human intercourse will become a *habit*.

And then the door will be wide open for the transition from the first phase of Communist society to its higher phase, and with it to the complete withering away of the state.

War Guilt and Economic Recovery

John Maynard Keynes, The Economic Consequences of the Peace
(New York: Harcourt, Brace and Howe, 1920), chap. vii, pp. 252-98.

John Maynard Keynes (1883-1946) has already secured his place as the
most influential economist of the twentieth century. Keynes was never lost
in a maze of statistics and graphs. He was a model gentleman-scholar, played
an active role in politics (albeit as one of the most eminent partisans of the
dying Liberal party), aided in the development of the Vic-Wells Ballet (now
the Royal Ballet), and proved a capable civil servant. Keynes first entered
government service in 1906, and his first book was a study of Indian currency and finance (1913). During the First World War he worked for the
British treasury, becoming by 1917 head of the Department on External
Finance. He went to the Paris Peace Conference as the principal Treasury
representative, although he had no place on the Reparations Commission.
He resigned in June, 1919, disgusted with the proceedings.

The Economic Consequences of the Peace, first published in December,
1919, was a master polemic. It was also one of the most important books
published between the wars. Étienne Mantoux wrote The Carthaginian
Peace, or the Economic Consequences of Mr. Keynes during the Second
World War in an effort to demonstrate that Keynes was wrong on the question of reparations and, by so discrediting the Paris conference and the
Treaty of Versailles, to show further that Keynes was instrumental in bringing about the Second World War. Whether the indictment can stand or not,
there is no question that The Economic Consequences of the Peace had
considerable impact upon economic negotiations in the subsequent years.
More important, Keynes had struck a devastating blow at the justice and
utility of what happened in Paris. Those among the victors, particularly in
Britain and the United States, who had nagging doubts about Versailles used
Keynes as a bible. The Germans, smarting under the humiliation of defeat
and the "war guilt" clause in the treaty, were delighted to accept Keynes's
arguments.

CHAPTER VII

REMEDIES

IT IS DIFFICULT to maintain true perspective in large affairs. I have criticized
the work of Paris, and have depicted in somber colors the condition and the
prospects of Europe. This is one aspect of the position and, I believe, a true
one. But in so complex a phenomenon the prognostics do not all point one
way; and we may make the error of expecting consequences to follow too
swiftly and too inevitably from what perhaps are not *all* the relevant
causes. The blackness of the prospect itself leads us to doubt its accuracy;
our imagination is dulled rather than stimulated by too woeful a narration,
and our minds rebound from what is felt "too bad to be true." But before

the reader allows himself to be too much swayed by these natural reflections, and before I lead him, as is the intention of this chapter, towards remedies and ameliorations and the discovery of happier tendencies, let him redress the balance of his thought by recalling two contrasts—England and Russia, of which the one may encourage his optimism too much, but the other should remind him that catastrophes can still happen, and that modern society is not immune from the very greatest evils.

In the chapters of this book I have not generally had in mind the situation or the problems of England. "Europe" in my narration must generally be interpreted to exclude the British Isles. England is in a state of transition, and her economic problems are serious. We may be on the eve of great changes in her social and industrial structure. Some of us may welcome such prospects and some of us deplore them. But they are of a different kind altogether from those impending on Europe. I do not perceive in England the slightest possibility of catastrophe or any serious likelihood of a general upheaval of society. The war has impoverished us, but not seriously;—I should judge that the real wealth of the country in 1919 is at least equal to what it was in 1900. Our balance of trade is adverse, but not so much so that the readjustment of it need disorder our economic life. The deficit in our Budget is large, but not beyond what firm and prudent statesmanship could bridge. The shortening of the hours of labor may have somewhat diminished our productivity. But it should not be too much to hope that this is a feature of transition, and no one who is acquainted with the British workingman can doubt that, if it suits him, and if he is in sympathy and reasonable contentment with the conditions of his life, he can produce at least as much in a shorter working day as he did in the longer hours which prevailed formerly. The most serious problems for England have been brought to a head by the war, but are in their origins more fundamental. The forces of the nineteenth century have run their course and are exhausted. The economic motives and ideals of that generation no longer satisfy us: we must find a new way and must suffer again the *malaise*, and finally the pangs, of a new industrial birth. This is one element. The other is that on which I have enlarged in Chapter II.;—the increase in the real cost of food and the diminishing response of nature to any further increase in the population of the world, a tendency which must be especially injurious to the greatest of all industrial countries and the most dependent on imported supplies of food.

But these secular problems are such as no age is free from. They are of an altogether different order from those which may afflict the peoples of Central Europe. Those readers who, chiefly mindful of the British conditions with which they are familiar, are apt to indulge their optimism, and still more those whose immediate environment is American, must cast their minds to Russia, Turkey, Hungary, or Austria, where the most dreadful material evils which men can suffer—famine, cold, disease, war, murder, and anarchy—are an actual present experience, if they are to apprehend the character of the misfortunes against the further extension of which it must surely be our duty to seek the remedy, if there is one.

What then is to be done? Then tentative suggestions of this chapter may appear to the reader inadequate. But the opportunity was missed at Paris during the six months which followed the Armistice, and nothing we can do now can repair the mischief wrought at that time. Great privation and great risks to society have become unavoidable. All that is now open to us is to re-direct, so far as lies in our power, the fundamental economic tendencies which underlie the events of the hour, so that they promote the re-establishment of prosperity and order, instead of leading us deeper into misfortune.

We must first escape from the atmosphere and the methods of Paris. Those who controlled the Conference may bow before the gusts of popular opinion, but they will never lead us out of our troubles. It is hardly to be supposed that the Council of Four can retrace their steps, even if they wished to do so. The replacement of the existing Governments of Europe is, therefore, an almost indispensable preliminary.

I propose then to discuss a program, for those who believe that the Peace of Versailles cannot stand, under the following heads:

1. The Revision of the Treaty.
2. The settlement of inter-Ally indebtedness.
3. An international loan and the reform of the currency.
4. The relations of Central Europe to Russia.

1. The Revision of the Treaty

Are any constitutional means open to us for altering the Treaty? President Wilson and General Smuts, who believe that to have secured the Covenant of the League of Nations outweighs much evil in the rest of the Treaty, have indicated that we must look to the League for the gradual evolution of a more tolerable life for Europe. "There are territorial settlements," General Smuts wrote in his statement on signing the Peace Treaty, "which will need revision. There are guarantees laid down which we all hope will soon be found out of harmony with the new peaceful temper and unarmed state of our former enemies. There are punishments foreshadowed over most of which a calmer mood may yet prefer to pass the sponge of oblivion. There are indemnities stipulated which cannot be enacted without grave injury to the industrial revival of Europe, and which it will be in the interests of all to render more tolerable and moderate. . . . I am confident that the League of Nations will yet prove the path of escape for Europe out of the ruin brought about by this war." Without the League, President Wilson informed the Senate when he presented the Treaty to them early in July, 1919, ". . . long-continued supervision of the task of reparation which Germany was to undertake to complete within the next generation might entirely break down; the reconsideration and revision of administrative arrangements and restrictions which the Treaty prescribed, but which it recognized might not provide lasting advantage or be entirely fair if too long enforced, would be impracticable."

Can we look forward with fair hopes to securing from the operation of the League those benefits which two of its principal begetters thus encourage us to expect from it? The relevant passage is to be found in Article XIX. of the Covenant, which runs as follows:

The Assembly may from time to time advise the reconsiderations by Members of the League of treaties which have become inapplicable and the consideration of international conditions whose continuance might endanger the peace of the world.

But alas! Article V. provides that "Except where otherwise expressly provided in this Covenant or by the terms of the present Treaty, decisions at any meeting of the Assembly or of the Council shall require the agreement of all the Members of the League represented at the meeting." Does not this provision reduce the League, so far as concerns an early reconsideration of any of the terms of the Peace Treaty, into a body merely for wasting time? If all the parties to the Treaty are unanimously of opinion that it requires alteration in a particular sense, it does not need a League and a Covenant to put the business through. Even when the Assembly of the League is unanimous it can only "advise" reconsideration by the members specially affected.

But the League will operate, say its suporters, by its influence on the public opinion of the world, and the view of the majority will carry decisive weight in practice, even though constitutionally it is of no effect. Let us pray that this be so. Yet the League in the hands of the trained European diplomatist may become an unequaled instrument for obstruction and delay. The revision of Treaties is entrusted primarily, not to the Council, which meets frequently, but to the Assembly, which will meet more rarely and must become, as any one with an experience of large Inter-Ally Conferences must know, an unwieldy polyglot debating society in which the greatest resolution and the best management may fail altogether to bring issues to a head against an opposition in favor of the *status quo*. There are indeed two disastrous blots on the Covenant,—Article V., which prescribes unanimity, and the much-criticized Article X., by which "The Members of the League undertake to respect and preserve as against external aggression the territorial integrity and existing political independence of all Members of the League." These two Articles together go some way to destroy the conception of the League as an instrument of progress, and to equip it from the outset with an almost fatal bias towards the *status quo*. It is these Articles which have reconciled to the League some of its original opponents, who now hope to make of it another Holy Alliance for the perpetuation of the economic ruin of their enemies and the Balance of Power in their own interests which they believe themselves to have established by the Peace.

But while it would be wrong and foolish to conceal from ourselves in the interests of "idealism" the real difficulties of the position in the special matter of revising treaties, that is no reason for any of us to decry the League, which the wisdom of the world may yet transform into a powerful instrument of peace, and which in Articles XI.–XVII. has already accomplished a great and beneficent achievement. I agree, therefore, that our first efforts for the Revision of the Treaty must be made through the League rather than in any other way, in the hope that the force of general opinion and, if necessary, the use of financial pressure and financial inducements, may be enough to prevent a recalcitrant minority from exercising their right of veto. We must trust the new Governments, whose existence I premise in the principal Allied countries, to show a profounder wisdom and a greater magnanimity than their predecessors.

We have seen in Chapters IV. and V. that there are numerous particles in which the Treaty is objectionable. I do not intend to enter here into details, or to attempt a revision of the Treaty clause by clause. I limit myself to three great changes which are necessary for the economic life of Europe, relating to Reparation, to Coal and Iron, and to Tariffs.

Reparation.—If the sum demanded for Reparation is less than what the Allies are entitled on a strict interpretation of their engagements, it is unnecessary to particularize the items it represents or to hear arguments about its compilation. I suggest, therefore, the following settlement:—

(1) The amount of the payment to be made by Germany in respect of Reparation and the costs of the Armies of Occupation might be fixed at $10,000,000,000.

(2) The surrender of merchant ships and submarine cables under the Treaty, of war material under the Armistice, of State property in ceded territory, of claims against such territory in respect of public debt, and of Germany's claims against her former Allies, should be reckoned as worth the lump sum of $2,500,000,000, without any attempt being made to evaluate them item by item.

(3) The balance of $7,500,000,000 should not carry interest pending its repayment, and should be paid by Germany in thirty annual instalments of $250,000,000, beginning in 1923.

(4) The Reparation Commission should be dissolved, or, if any duties remain for it to perform, it should become an appanage of the League of Nations and should include representatives of Germany and of the neutral States.

(5) Germany would be left to meet the annual instalments in such manner as she might see fit, any complaint against her for non-fulfilment of her obligations being lodged with the League of Nations. That is to say, there would be no further expropriation of German private property abroad, except so far as is required to meet private German obligations out of the proceeds of such property already liquidated or in the hands of Public Trustees and Enemy Property Custodians in the Allied countries and in the United States; and, in particular, Article 260 (which provides for the expropriation of German interests in public utility enterprises) would be abrogated.

(6) No attempt should be made to extract Reparation payments from Austria.

Coal and Iron.—(1) The Allies' options on coal under Annex V. should be abandoned, but Germany's obligation to make good France's loss of coal through the destruction of her mines should remain. That is to say, Germany should undertake "to deliver to France annually for a period not exceeding ten years an amount of coal equal to the difference between the annual production before the war of the coal mines of the Nord and Pas de Calais, destroyed as a result of the war, and the production of the mines of the same area during the years in question; such delivery not to exceed twenty million tons in any one year of the first five years, and eight million tions in any one year of the succeeding five years." This obligation should lapse, nevertheless, in the event of the coal districts of Upper Silesia being taken from Germany in the final settlement consequent on the plebiscite.

(2) The arrangement as to the Saar should hold good, except that, on the one hand, Germany should receive no credit for the mines, and, on the other, should receive back both the mines and the territory without payment and unconditionally after ten years. But this should be conditional on France's entering into an agreement for the same period to supply Germany from Lorraine with at least 50 per cent of the iron-ore which was carried from Lorraine into Germany proper before the war, in return for an undertaking from Germany to supply Lorraine with an amount of coal equal to the whole amount formerly sent to Lorraine from Germany proper, after allowing for the output of the Saar.

(3) The arrangement as to Upper Silesia should hold good. That is to say, a plebiscite should be held, and in coming to a final decision "regard will be paid (by the principal Allied and Associated Powers) to the wishes of the inhabitants as shown by the vote, and to the geographical and economic conditions of the locality." But the Allies should declare that in their judgment "economic conditions" require the inclusion of the coal districts in Germany unless the wishes of the inhabitants are decidedly to the contrary.

(4) The Coal Commission already established by the Allies should become an appanage of the League of Nations, and should be enlarged to include representatives of Germany and the other States of Central and Eastern Europe, of the Northern Neutrals, and of Switzerland. Its authority should be advisory only, but should extend over the distribution of the coal supplies of Germany, Poland, and the constituent parts of the former Austro-Hungarian Empire, and of the exportable surplus of the United Kingdom. All the States represented on the Commission should undertake to furnish it with the fullest information, and to be guided by its advice so far as their sovereignty and their vital interests permit.

Tariffs.—A Free Trade Union should be established under the auspices of the League of Nations of countries undertaking to impose no protectionist tariffs whatever against the produce of other members of the Union. Germany, Poland, the new States which formerly composed the Austro-Hungarian and Turkish Empires, and the Mandated States should be compelled to adhere to this Union for ten years, after which time adherence would be voluntary. The adherence of other States would be voluntary from the outset. But it is to be hoped that the United Kingdom, at any rate, would become an original member.

By fixing the Reparation payments well within Germany's capacity to pay, we make possible the renewal of hope and enterprise within her territory, we avoid the perpetual friction and opportunity of improper pressure arising out of Treaty clauses which are impossible of fulfilment, and we render unnecessary the intolerable powers of the Reparation Commission.

By a moderation of the clauses relating directly or indirectly to coal, and by the exchange of iron-ore, we permit the continuance of German's industrial life, and put limits on the loss of productivity which would be brought about otherwise by the interference of political frontiers with the natural localization of the iron and steel industry.

By the proposed Free Trade Union some part of the loss of organization and economic efficiency may be retrieved, which must otherwise result from the innumerable new political frontiers now created between greedy, jealous, immature, and economically incomplete nationalist States. Economic frontiers were tolerable so long as an immense territory was included in a few great Empires; but they will not be tolerable when the Empires of Germany, Austria-Hungary, Russia, and Turkey have been partitioned between some twenty independent authorities. A Free Trade Union, comprising the whole of Central, Eastern, and South-Eastern Europe, Siberia, Turkey, and (I should hope) the United Kingdom, Egypt, and India, might do as much for the peace and prosperity of the world as the League of Nations itself. Belgium, Holland, Scandinavia, and Switzerland might be expected to adhere to it shortly. And it would be greatly to be desired by their friends that France and Italy also should see their way to adhesion.

It would be objected, I suppose, by some critics that such an arrangement might go some way in effect towards realizing the former German dream of Mittel-Europa. If other countries were so foolish as to remain outside the Union and to leave to Germany all its advantages, there might be some truth in this. But an economic system, to which every one had the opportunity of belonging and which gave special privilege to none, is surely absolutely free from the objections of a privileged and avowedly imperialistic scheme of exclusion and discrimination. Our attitude to these criticisms must be determined by our whole moral and emotional reaction to the future of international relations and the Peace of the World. If we take the view that for at least a generation to come Germany cannot be trusted with even a modicum of prosperity, that while all our recent Allies are angels of light, all our recent enemies, Germans, Austrians, Hungarians, and the rest, are children of the devil, that year by year Germany must be kept impoverished and her children starved and crippled, and that she must be ringed round by enemies; then we shall reject all the proposals of this chapter, and particularly those which may assist Germany to regain a part of her former material prosperity and find a means of livelihood for the industrial population of her towns. But if this view of nations and of their relation to one another is adopted by the democracies of Western Europe, and is financed by the United States, heaven help us all. If we aim deliberately at the impoverishment of Central Europe, vengeance, I dare predict, will not limp. Nothing can then delay for very long that final civil war between the forces of Reaction and the despairing convulsions of Revolution, before which the horrors of the late German war will fade into nothing, and which will destroy, whoever is victor, the civilization and the progress of our generation. Even though the result disappoint us, must we not base our actions on better expectations, and believe that the prosperity and happiness of one country promotes that of others, that the solidarity of man is not a fiction, and that nations can still afford to treat other nations as fellow-creatures?

Such changes as I have proposed above might do something appreciable to enable the industrial populations of Europe to continue to earn a livelihood. But they would not be enough by themselves. In particular, France would be a loser on paper (on paper only, for she will never secure the actual fulfilment of her present claims), and an escape from her embarrassments must be shown her in some other direction. I proceed, therefore, to proposals, first, for the adjustment of the claims of America and the Allies amongst themselves; and second, for the provision of sufficient credit to enable Europe to re-create her stock of circulating capital.

2. The Settlement of Inter-Ally Indebtedness

In proposing a modification of the Reparation terms, I have considered them so far only in relation to Germany. But fairness requires that so great a reduction in the amount should be accompanied by a readjustment of its apportionment between the Allies themselves. The professions which our statesmen made on every platform during the war, as well as other considerations, surely require that the areas damaged by the enemy's invasion should receive a priority of compensation. While this was one of the ultimate objects for which we said we were fighting, we never included the recovery of separation allowances amongst our war aims. I suggest, therefore, that we should by our acts prove ourselves sincere and trustworthy, and that accordingly Great Britain should waive altogether her claims for cash payment in favor of Belgium, Serbia, and France. The whole of the payments made by Germany would then be subject to the prior charge of repairing the material injury done to those countries and provinces which suffered actual invasion by the enemy; and I believe that the sum of $7,500,-000,000 thus available would be adequate to cover entirely the actual costs of restoration. Further, it is only by a complete subordination of her own claims for cash compensation that Great Britain can ask with clean hands for a revision of the Treaty and clear her honor from the breach of faith for which she bears the main responsibility, as a result of the policy to which the General Election of 1918 pledged her representatives.

With the Reparation problem thus cleared up it would be possible to bring forward with a better grace and more hope of success two other financial proposals, each of which involves an appeal to the generosity of the United States.

The first is for the entire cancellation of Inter-Ally indebtedness (that is to say, indebtedness between the Governments of the Allied Associated countries) incurred for the purposes of the war. This proposal, which has been put forward already in certain quarters, is one which I believe to be absolutely essential to the future prosperity of the world. It would be an act of far-seeing statesmanship for the United Kingdom and the United States, the two Powers chiefly concerned, to adopt it. The sums of money which are involved are shown approximately in the following table:—

Loans to	By United States	By United Kingdom	By France	Total
	Million Dollars	Million Dollars	Million Dollars	Million Dollars
United Kingdom......	4,210	....	....	4,210
France	2,750	2,540	....	5,290
Italy	1,625	2,335	175	4,135
Russia	190	2,840 [1]	800	3,830
Belgium	400	490 [2]	450	1,340
Serbia and Jugo-Slavia.	100	100 [2]	100	300
Other Allies	175	395	250	820
Total	9,450 [3]	8,700	1,775	19,925

[1] This allows nothing for interest on the debt since the Bolshevik Revolution.

[2] No interest has been charged on the advances made to these countries.

[3] The actual total of loans by the United States up to date is very nearly $10,000,000,-000, but I have not got the latest details.

Thus the total volume of Inter-Ally indebtedness, assuming that loans from one Ally are not set off against loans to another, is nearly $20,000,-000,000. The United States is a lender only. The United Kingdom has lent about twice as much as she has borrowed. France has borrowed about three times as much as she has lent. The other Allies have been borrowers only.

If all the above Inter-Ally indebtedness were mutually forgiven, the net result on paper (*i.e.* assuming all the loans to be good) would be a surrender by the United States of about $10,000,000,000 and by the United Kingdom of about $4,500,000,000. France would gain about $3,500,000,000 and Italy about $4,000,000,000. But these figures overstate the loss to the United Kingdom and understate the gain to France; for a large part of the loans made by both these countries has been to Russia and cannot, by any stretch of imagination, be considered good. If the loans which the United Kingdom has made to her Allies are reckoned to be worth 50 per cent of their full value (an arbitrary but convenient assumption which the Chancellor of the Exchequer has adopted on more than one occasion as being as good as any other for the purposes of an approximate national balance sheet), the operation would involve her neither in loss nor in gain. But in whatever way the net result is calculated on paper, the relief in anxiety which such a liquidation of the position would carry with it would be very great. It is from the United States, therefore, that the proposal asks generosity.

Speaking with a very intimate knowledge of the relations throughout the war between the British, the American, and the other Allied Treasuries, I believe this to be an act of generosity for which Europe can fairly ask, provided Europe is making an honorable attempt in other directions, not to continue war, economic or otherwise, but to achieve the economic re-constitution of the whole Continent. The financial sacrifices of the United States have been, in proportion to her wealth, immensely less than those of the European States. This could hardly have been otherwise. It was a European quarrel, in which the United States Government could not have justified itself before its citizens in expending the whole national strength, as did the Europeans. After the United States came into the war her financial assistance was lavish and unstinted, and without this assistance the Allies could never have won the war, quite apart from the decisive influence of the arrival of the American troops. Europe, too, should never forget the extraordinary assistance afforded her during the first six months of 1919 through the agency of Mr. Hoover and the American Commission of Relief. Never was a nobler work of disinterested goodwill carried through with more tenacity and sincerity and skill, and with less thanks either asked or given. The ungrateful Governments of Europe owe much more to the statesmanship and insight of Mr. Hoover and his band of American workers than they have yet appreciated or will ever acknowledge. The American Relief Commission, and they only, saw the European position during those months in its true perspective and felt towards it as men should. It was their efforts, their energy, and the American resources placed by the President at their disposal, often acting in the teeth of European obstruction, which not only saved an immense amount of human suffering, but averted a widespread breakdown of the European system.

But in speaking thus as we do of American financial assistance, we tacitly assume, and America, I believe, assumed it too when she gave the money, that it was not in the nature of an investment. If Europe is going to repay the $10,000,000,000 worth of financial assistance which she has had from the United States with compound interest at 5 per cent, the matter takes on quite a different complexion. If America's advances are to be regarded in this light, her relative financial sacrifice has been very slight indeed.

Controversies as to relative sacrifice are very barren and very foolish also; for there is no reason in the world why relative sacrifice should neces-sarily be equal,—so many other very relevant considerations being quite different in the two cases. The two or three facts following are put for-ward, therefore, not to suggest that they provide any compelling argument

for Americans, but only to show that from his own selfish point of view
an Englishman is not seeking to avoid due sacrifice on his country's part in
making the present suggestion. (1) The sums which the British Treasury
borrowed from the American Treasury, after the latter came into the war,
were approximately offset by the sums which England lent to her other
Allies *during the same period* (*i.e.* excluding sums lent before the United
States came into the war); so that almost the whole of England's indebtedness to the United States was incurred, not on her own account, but to
enable her to assist the rest of her Allies, who were for various reasons not
in a position to draw their assistance from the United States direct. (2) The
United Kingdom has disposed of about $5,000,000,000 worth of her foreign
securities, and in addition has incurred foreign debt to the amount of
about $6,000,000,000. The United States, so far from selling, has bought
back upwards of $5,000,000,000, and has incurred practically no foreign
debt. (3) The population of the United Kingdom is about one-half that
of the United States, the income about one-third, and the accumulated
wealth between one-half and one-third. The financial capacity of the
United Kingdom may therefore be put at about two-fifths that of the
United States. This figure enables us to make the following comparison:—
Excluding loans to Allies in each case (as is right on the assumption that
these loans are to be repaid), the war expenditure of the United Kingdom
has been about three times that of the United States, or in proportion to
capacity between seven and eight times.

Having cleared this issue out of the way as briefly as possible, I turn to
the broader issues of the future relations between the parties to the late
war, by which the present proposal must primarily be judged.

Failing such a settlement as is now proposed, the war will have ended
with a network of heavy tribute payable from one Ally to another. The
total amount of this tirbute is even likely to exceed the amount obtainable
from the enemy; and the war will have ended with the intolerable result
of the Allies paying indemnities to one another instead of receiving them
from the enemy.

For this reason the question of Inter-Allied indebtedness is closely bound
up with the intense popular feeling amongst the European Allies on the
question of indemnities,—a feeling which is based, not on any reasonable
calculation of what Germany can, in fact, pay, but on a well-founded appreciation of the unbearable financial situation in which these countries will
find themselves unless she pays. Take Italy as an extreme example. If Italy
can reasonably be expected to pay $4,000,000,000, surely Germany can and
ought to pay an immeasurably higher figure. Or if it is decided (as it must
be) that Austria can pay next to nothing, is it not an intolerable conclusion
that Italy should be loaded with a crushing tribute, while Austria escapes?
Or, to put it slightly differently, how can Italy be expected to submit to
payment of this great sum and see Czecho-Slovakia pay little or nothing? At
the other end of the scale there is the United Kingdom. Here the financial

position is different, since to ask us to pay $4,000,000,000 is a very different proposition from asking Italy to pay it. But the sentiment is much the same. If we have to be satisfied without full compensation from Germany, how bitter will be the protests against paying it to the United States. We, it will be said, have to be content with a claim against the bankrupt estates of Germany, France, Italy, and Russia, whereas the United States has secured a first mortgage upon us. The case of France is at least as overwhelming. She can barely secure from Germany the full measure of the destruction of her countryside. Yet victorious France must pay her friends and Allies more than four times the indemnity which in the defeat of 1870 she paid Germany. The hand of Bismarck was light compared with that of an Ally or of an Associate. A settlement of Inter-Ally indebtedness is, therefore, an indispensable preliminary to the peoples of the Allied countries facing, with other than a maddened and exasperated heart, the inevitable truth about the prospects of an indemnity from the enemy.

It might be an exaggeration to say that it is impossible for the European Allies to pay the capital and interest due from them on these debts, but to make them do so would certainly be to impose a crushing burden. They may be expected, therefore, to make constant attempts to evade or escape payment, and these attempts will be a constant source of international friction and ill-will for many years to come. A debtor nation does not love its creditor, and it is fruitless to expect feelings of goodwill from France, Italy, and Russia towards this country or towards America, if their future development is stifled for many years to come by the annual tribute which they must pay us. There will be a great incentive to them to seek their friends in other directions, and any future rupture of peaceable relations will always carry with it the enormous advantage of escaping the payment of external debts. If, on the other hand, these great debts are forgiven, a stimulus will be given to the solidarity and true friendliness of the nations lately associated.

The existence of the great war debts is a menace to financial stability everywhere. There is no European country in which repudiation may not soon become an important political issue. In the case of internal debt, however, there are interested parties on both sides, and the question is one of the internal distribution of wealth. With external debts this is not so, and the creditor nations may soon find their interest inconveniently bound up with the maintenance of a particular type of government or economic organization in the debtor countries. Entangling alliances or entangling leagues are nothing to the entanglements of cash owing.

The final consideration influencing the reader's attitude to this proposal must, however, depend on his view as to the future place in the world's progress of the vast paper entanglements which are our legacy from war finance both at home and abroad. The war has ended with every one owing every one else immense sums of money. Germany owes a large sum to the Allies; the Allies owe a large sum to Great Britain; and Great Britain owes a large sum to the United States. The holders of war loan in every country are owed a large sum by the State; and the State in its turn is owed a large sum by these and other taxpayers. The whole position is in the highest degree artificial, misleading, and vexatious. We shall never be able to move again, unless we can free our limbs from these paper shackles. A general bonfire is so great a necessity that unless we can make of it an orderly and good-tempered affair in which no serious injustice is done to any one, it will, when it comes at last, grow into a conflagration that may destroy much else as well. As regards internal debt, I am one of those who believe that a capital levy for the extinction of debt is an absolute prerequisite of sound finance in every one of the European belligerent countries. But the continuance on a huge scale of indebtedness between Governments has special dangers of its own.

Before the middle of the nineteenth century no nation owed payments to a foreign nation on any considerable scale, except such tributes as were exacted under the compulsion of actual occupation in force and, at one time, by absentee princes under the sanctions of feudalism. It is true that the need for European capitalism to find an outlet in the New World has led during the past fifty years, though even now on a relatively modest scale, to such countries as Argentine owing an annual sum to such countries as England. But the system is fragile; and it has only survived because its burden on the paying countries has not so far been oppressive, because this burden is represented by real assets and is bound up with the property system generally, and because the sums already lent are not unduly large in relation to those which it is still hoped to borrow. Bankers are used to this system, and believe it to be a necessary part of the permanent order of society. They are disposed to believe, therefore, by analogy with it, that a comparable system between Governments, on a far vaster and definitely oppressive scale, represented by no real assets, and less closely associated with the property system, is natural and reasonable and in conformity with human nature.

I doubt this view of the world. Even capitalism at home, which engages many local sympathies, which plays a real part in the daily process of production, and upon the security of which the present organization of society largely depends, is not very safe. But however this may be, will the discontented people of Europe be willing for a generation to come so to order their lives that an appreciable part of their daily produce may be available to meet a foreign payment, the reason of which, whether as between Europe and America, or as between Germany and the rest of Europe, does not spring compellingly from their sense of justice or duty?

On the one hand, Europe must depend in the long run on her own daily labor and not on the largesse of America; but, on the other hand, she will not pinch herself in order that the fruit of her daily labor may go elsewhere. In short, I do not believe that any of these tributes will continue to be paid, at the best, for more than a very few years. They do not square with human nature or agree with the spirit of the age.

If there is any force in this mode of thought, expediency and generosity agree together, and the policy which will best promote immediate friendship between nations will not conflict with the permanent interests of the benefactor.

3. AN INTERNATIONAL LOAN

I pass to a second financial proposal. The requirement of Europe are *immediate*. The prospect of being relieved of oppressive interest payments to England and America over the whole life of the next two generations (and of receiving from Germany some assistance year by year to the costs of restoration) would free the future from excessive anxiety. But it would not meet the ills of the immediate present,—the excess of Europe's imports over her exports, the adverse exchange, and the disorder of the currency. It will be very difficult for European production to get started again without a temporary measure of external assistance. I am therefore a supporter of an international loan in some shape or form, such as has been advocated in many quarters in France, Germany, and England, and also in the United States. In whatever way the ultimate responsibility for repayment is distributed, the burden of finding the immediate resources must inevitably fall in major part upon the United States.

The chief objections to all the varieties of this species of project are, I suppose, the following. The United States is disinclined to entangel herself further (after recent experiences) in the affairs of Europe, and, anyhow, has for the time being no more capital to spare for export on a large scale. There is no guaranteee that Europe will put financial assistance to proper use, or that she will not squander it and be in just as bad case two or three years hence as she is in now;—M. Klotz will use the money to put off the day of taxation a little longer, Italy and Jugo-Slavia will fight one another on the proceeds, Poland will devote it to fulfilling towards all her neighbors the military rôle which France has designed for her, the governing classes of Roumania will divide up the booty amongst themselves. In short, America would have postponed her own capital developments and raised her own cost of living in order that Europe might continue for another year or two the practices, the poilcy, and the men of the past nine months. And as for assistance to Germany, is it reasonable or at all tolerable that the European Allies, having stripped Germany of her last vestige of working capital, in opposition to the arguments and appeals of the American financial representatives at Paris, should then turn to the United States for funds to rehabilitate the victim in sufficient measure to allow the spoliation to recommence in a year or two?

There is no answer to these objections as matters are now. If I had influence at the United States Treasury, I would not lend a penny to a single

one of the present Governments of Europe. They are not to be trusted with
resources which they would devote to the furtherance of policies in repugnance to which, in spite of the President's failure to assert either the might
or the ideals of the people of the United States, the Republican and the
Democratic parties are probably united. But if, as we must pray they will,
the souls of the European people turn away this winter from the false idols
which have survived the war that created them, and substitute in their
hearts for the hated and the nationalism, which now possess them,
thoughts and hopes of the happiness and solidarity of the European family,
—then should natural piety and filial love impel the American people to
put on one side all the smaller objections of private advantage and to complete the work, that they began in saving Europe from the tyranny of
organized force, by saving her from herself. And even if the conversion is
not fully accomplished, and some parties only in each of the European
countries have espoused a policy of reconciliation, America can still point
the way and hold up the hands of the party of peace by having a plan and
a condition on which she will give her aid to the work of renewing life.

The impulse which, we are told, is now strong in the mind of the United
States to be quit of the turmoil, the complication, the violence, the expense,
and, above all, the unintelligibility of the European problems, is easily
understood. No one can feel more intensely than the writer how natural it
is to retort to the folly and impracticability of the European statesmen,—
Rot, then, in your own malice, and we will go our way—

> Remote from Europe; from her blasted hopes;
> Her fields of carnage, and polluted air.

But if America recalls for a moment what Europe has meant to her and
still means to her, what Europe, the mother of art and of knowledge, in
spite of everything, still is and still will be, will she not reject these counsels
of indifference and isolation, and interest herself in what may prove decisive
issues for the progress and civilization of all mankind?

Assuming then, if only to keep our hopes up, that America will be prepared to contribute to the process of building up the good forces of Europe,
and will not, having completed the destruction of an enemy, leave us to
our misfortunes,—what form should her aid take?

I do not propose to enter on details. But the main outlines of all schemes
for an international loan are much the same. The countries in a position to
lend assistance, the neutrals, the United Kingdom, and, for the greater portion of the sum required, the United States, must provide foreign purchasing credits for all the belligerent countries of continental Europe, allied and
ex-enemy alike. The aggregate sum required might not be so large as is
sometimes supposed. Much might be done, perhaps, with a fund of $1,000,-
000,000 in the first instance. This sum, even if a precedent of a different
kind had been established by the cancellation of Inter-Ally War Debt,

should be lent and should be borrowed with the unequivocal intention of its being repaid in full. With this object in view, the security for the loan should be the best obtainable, and the arrangements for its ultimate repayment as complete as possible. In particular, it should rank, both for payment of interest and discharge of capital, in front of all Reparation claims, all Inter-Ally War Debt, all internal war loans, and all other Government indebtedness of any other kind. Those borrowing countries who will be entitled to Reparation payments should be required to pledge all such receipts to repayment of the new loan. And all the borrowing countries should be required to place their customs duties on a gold basis and to pledge such receipts to its service.

Expenditure out of the loan should be subject to general, but not detailed, supervision by the lending countries.

If, in addition to this loan for the purchase of food and materials, a guarantee fund were established up to an equal amount, namely $1,000,-000,000 (of which it would probably prove necessary to find only a part in cash), to which all members of the League of Nations would contribute according to their means, it might be practicable to base upon it a general reorganization of the currency.

In this manner Europe might be equipped with the minimum amount of liquid resources necessary to revive her hopes, to renew her economic organization, and to enable her great intrinsic wealth to function for the benefit of her workers. It is useless at the present time to elaborate such schemes in further detail. A great change is necessary in public opinion before the proposals of this chapter can enter the region of practical politics, and we must await the progress of events as patiently as we can.

4. THE RELATIONS OF CENTRAL EUROPE TO RUSSIA

I have said very little of Russia in this book. The broad character of the situation there needs no emphasis, and of the details we know almost nothing authentic. But in a discussion as to how the economic situation of Europe can be restored there are one or two aspects of the Russian question which are vitally important.

From the military point of view an ultimate union of forces between Russia and Germany is greatly feared in some quarters. This would be much more likely to take place in the event of reactionary movements being successful in each of the two countries, whereas an effective unity of purpose between Lenin and the present essentially middle-class Government of German in unthinkable. On the other hand, the same people who fear such a union are even more afraid of the success of Bolshevism; and yet they have to recognize that the only efficient forces for fighting it are, inside Russia, the reactionaries, and, outside Russia, the established forces of order and authority in Germany. Thus the advocates of intervention in Russia, whether direct or indirect, are at perpetual cross-purposes with themselves. They do not know what they want; or, rather, they want what they cannot help seeing to be incompatibles. This is one of the reasons why their policy is so inconstant and so exceedingly futile.

The same conflict of purpose is apparent in the attitude of the Council of the Allies at Paris towards the present Government of Germany. A victory of Spartacism in Germany might well be the prelude to Revolution everywhere: it would renew the forces of Bolshevism in Russia, and precipitate the dreaded union of Germany and Russia; it would certainly put an end to any expectations which have been built on the financial and economic clauses of the Treaty of Peace. Therefore Paris does not love Spartacus. But, on the other hand, a victory of reaction in Germany would be regarded by every one as a threat to the security of Europe, and as endangering the fruits of victory and the basis of the Peace. Besides, a new military power establishing itself in the East, with its spiritual home in Brandenburg, drawing to itself all the military talent and all the military adventurers, all those who regret emperors and hate democracy, in the whole of Eastern and Central and South-Eastern Europe, a power which would be geographically inaccessible to the military forces of the Allies, might well found, at least in the anticipations of the timid, a new Napoleonic domination, rising, as a phoenix, from the ashes of cosmopolitan militarism. So Paris dare not love Brandenburg. The argument points, then, to the sustentation of those moderate forces of order, which, somewhat to the world's surprise, still manage to maintain themselves on the rock of the German character. But the present Government of Germany stands for German unity more perhaps than for anything else; the signature of the Peace was, above all, the price which some Germans thought it worth while to pay for the unity which was all that was left them of 1870. Therefore Paris, with some hopes of disintegration across the Rhine not yet extinguished, can resist no opportunity of insult or indignity, no occasion of lowering the prestige or weakening the influence of a Government, with the continued stability of which all the conservative interests of Europe are nevertheless bound up.

The same dilemma affects the future of Poland in the rôle which France has cast for her. She is to be strong, Catholic, militarist, and faithful, the consort, or at least the favorite, of victorious France, prosperous and magnificent between the ashes of Russia and the ruin of Germany. Roumania, if only she could be persuaded to keep up appearances a little more, is a part of the same scatter-brained conception. Yet, unless her great neighbors are prosperous and orderly, Poland is an economic impossibility with no industry but Jew-baiting. And when Poland finds that the seductive policy of France is pure rhodomontade and that there is no money in it whatever, nor glory either, she will fall, as promptly as possible, into the arms of somebody else.

The calculations of "diplomacy" lead us, therefore, nowhere. Crazy dreams and childish intrigue in Russia and Poland and thereabouts are the favorite indulgence at present of those Englishmen and Frenchmen who seek excitement in its least innocent form, and believe, or at least behave as if foreign policy was of the same *genre* as a cheap melodrama.

Let us turn, therefore, to something more solid. The German Government has announced (October 30, 1919) its continued adhesion to a policy of non-intervention in the internal affairs of Russia, "not only on principle, but because it believes that this policy is also justified from a practical point of view." Let us assume that at last we also adopt the same standpoint, if not on principle, at least from a practical point of view. What are then the fundamental economic factors in the future relations of Central to Eastern Europe?

Before the war Western and Central Europe drew from Russia a substantial part of their imported cereals. Without Russia the importing countries would have had to go short. Since 1914 the loss of the Russian supplies has been made good, partly by drawing on reserves, partly from the bumper harvests of North America called forth by Mr. Hoover's guaranteed price, but largely by economies of consumption and by privation. After 1920 the need of Russian supplies will be even greater than it was before the war; for the guaranteed price in North America will have been discontinued, the normal increase of population there will, as compared with 1914, have swollen the home demand appreciably, and the soil of Europe will not yet have recovered its former productivity. If trade is not resumed with Russia, wheat in 1920-21 (unless the seasons are specially bountiful) must be scarce and very dear. The blockade of Russia, lately proclaimed by the Allies, is therefore a foolish and short-sighted proceeding; we are blockading not so much Russia as ourselves.

The process of reviving the Russian export trade is bound in any case to be a slow one. The present productivity of the Russian peasant is not believed to be sufficient to yield an exportable surplus on the pre-war scale. The reasons for this are obviously many, but amongst them are included the insufficiency of agricultural implements and accessories and the absence of incentive to production caused by the lack of commodities in the towns which the peasants can purchase in exchange for their produce. Finally, there is the decay of the transport system, which hinders or renders impossible the collection of local surpluses in the big centers of distribution.

I see no possible means of repairing this loss of productivity within any reasonable period of time except through the agency of German enterprise and organization. It is impossible geographically and for many other reasons for Englishmen, Frenchmen, or Americans to undertake it;—we have neither the incentive nor the means for doing the work on a sufficient scale. Germany, on the other hand, has the experience, the incentive, and to a large extent the materials for furnishing the Russian peasant with the goods of which he has been starved for the past five years, for reorganizing the business of transport and collection, and so for bringing into the world's pool, for the common advantage, the supplies from which we are now so disastrously cut off. It is in our interest to hasten the day when German agents and organizers will be in a position to set in train in every Russian village the impulses of ordinary economic motive. This is a process quite independent of the governing authority in Russia; but we may surely predict with some certainty that, whether or not the form of communism represented by the Soviet government proves permanently suited to the Russian temperament, the revival of trade, of the comforts of life and of ordinary economic motive are not likely to promote the extreme forms of those doctrines of violence and tyranny which are the children of war and of despair.

Let us then in our Russian policy not only applaud and imitate the policy of non-intervention which the Government of Germany has announced, but, desisting from a blockade which in injurious to our permanent interests, as well as illegal, let us encourage and assist Germany to take up again her place in Europe as a creator and organizer of wealth for her Eastern and Southern neighbors.

There are many persons in whom such proposals will raise strong prejudices. I ask them to follow out in thought the result of yielding to these prejudices. If we oppose in detail every means by which Germany or Russia can recover their material well-being, because we feel a national, racial, or political hatred for their populations or their Governments, we must be prepared to face the consequences of such feelings. Even if there is no moral solidarity between the nearly-related races of Europe, there is an economic solidarity which we cannot disregard. Even now, the world markets are one. If we do not allow Germany to exchange products with Russia and so feed herself, she must inevitably compete with us for the produce of the New World. The more successful we are in snapping economic relations between Germany and Russia, the more we shall depress the level of our own economic standards and increase the gravity of our own domestic problems. This is to put the issue on its lowest grounds. There are other arguments, which the most obtuse cannot ignore, against a policy of spreading and encouraging further the economic ruin of great countries.

I see few signs of sudden or dramatic developments anywhere. Riots and revolutions there may be, but not such, at present, as to have fundamental significance. Against political tyranny and injustice Revolution is a weapon, But what counsels of hope can Revolution offer to sufferers from economic privation, which does not arise out of the injustices of distribution but is general? The only safeguard against Revolution in Central Europe is indeed the fact that, even to the minds of men who are desperate, Revolution offers no prospect of improvement whatever. There may, therefore, be ahead of us a long, silent process of semi-starvation, and of a gradual, steady lowering of the standards of life and comfort. The bankruptcy and decay of Europe, if we allow it to proceed, will affect every one in the long-run, but perhaps not in a way that is striking or immediate.

This has one fortunate side. We may still have time to reconsider our courses and to view the world with new eyes. For the immediate future events are taking charge, and the near destiny of Europe is no longer in the hands of any man. The events of the coming year will not be shaped by the deliberate acts of statesmen, but by the hidden currents, flowing continually beneath the surface of political history, of which no one can predict the outcome. In one way only can we influence these hidden currents,—by setting in motion those forces of instruction and imagination which change *opinion*. The assertion of truth, the unveiling of illusion, the dissipation of hate, the enlargement and instruction of men's hearts and minds, must be the means.

In this autumn of 1919, in which I write, we are at the dead season of our fortunes. The reaction from the exertions, the fears, and the sufferings of the past five years is at its height. Our power of feeling or caring beyond the immediate questions of our own material well-being is temporarily eclipsed. The greatest events outside our own direct experiences and the most dreadful anticipations cannot move us.

> In each human heart terror survives
> The ruin it has gorged: the loftiest fear
> All that they would disdain to think were true:
> Hypocrisy and custom make their minds
> The fanes of many a worship, now outworn.
> They dare not devise good for man's estate,
> And yet they know not that they do not dare.
> The good want power but to weep barren tears.
> The powerful goodness want: worse need for them.
> The wise want love; and those who love want wisdom;
> And all best things are thus confused to ill.
> Many are strong and rich, and would be just,
> But live among their suffering fellow-men
> As if none felt: they know not what they do.

We have been moved already beyond endurance, and need rest. Never in the lifetime of men now living has the universal element in the soul of man burnt so dimly.

For these reasons the true voice of the new generation has not yet spoken, and silent opinion is not yet formed. To the formation of the general opinion of the future I dedicate this book.

From Ideas to Power:
Stalinism

Josef V. Stalin, "Strategy and Tactics," The Foundations of Leninism, in Works (Moscow: Foreign Languages Publishing House, 1953), Vol. VI, chap. vii, pp. 155–75.

Any living religion which rests upon scriptural sanction requires continual interpretation. Lenin claimed to "interpret" Marx and Engels. Iosif Djugashvili who became Josef Stalin (1879–1953) declared himself the true interpreter of Lenin. With Lenin and Leon Trotsky, Stalin played a role of considerable importance in the Russian Revolution. In 1924, with Lenin paralyzed, he was a claimant for the succession. While Stalin built his success on the capture of the Communist party machinery, it was still incumbent upon him to make his mark as an interpreter of Marxist-Leninism. Communist leadership imposed intellectual as well as practical political demands. *The Foundations of Leninism* (1924) is Stalin's principal claim to Communist doctrinal apostolic succession. The intellectual qualities of the book are so deceptively feeble that it suggests even in 1924 power in the Soviet Union rested upon practical, not intellectual claims. Stalin's success rested upon solid achievements: the successful implementation of planned economy and the careful elimination of old Bolsheviks and rival claimants for power, later fortified by his successful leadership in the Second World War. Human cost was never a significant factor, nor was truth.

In his life and work Stalin embodied the relativism of history. In an Orwellian sense, he who controls the present controls the past. History was rewritten, records and evidence forged, and the Communist world accepted the relative truth of power. Stalin did not have to be clever, a creative thinker, or honest. He had only to succeed—and he did. The dull, mechanical quality of Stalin's writings should never obscure his (or their) importance. Even in 1924 he was introducing significant departures from Lenin's doctrine. Stalin's methodology remained fixed by his experience in the Tiflis Theological Seminary (1894–99), which accounts for the categorical, dogmatic, brief questions and answers. In the chapter titled "The Party," subsequent to this selection, Stalin lays the ideological basis for absolute party dictatorship. In a seemingly unimaginative catechism, the departure from Lenin begins with the third response.

"What are the specific features of this new party [of Leninism]?"
    "The Party must be, first of all, the *vanguard* of the working class."
    "The Party is the political leader of the working class."
    "The Party is the General Staff of the proletariat."
    "The Party is an inseparable part of the working class."
    "The Party is the organized detachment of the working class."

Nowhere, of course, does Stalin say, "The Party is myself." But party control has meant national control in the Soviet Union since 1928. These plodding clichés, obviously no mark of intellectual sophistication, were as important to Stalin and Communist rule as his mastery of the party machinery.

Like "Socialism in one country," their impact on Russia and the world was crucial. Never belittle the importance of this rhetoric. Any Communist leader must attach his name, however fleetingly, to the ethical imperative of his political ideology.

VII

STRATEGY AND TACTICS

FROM THIS THEME I take six questions:

    a) strategy and tactics as the science of leadership in the class struggle of the proletariat;

    b) stages of the revolution, and strategy;

    c) the flow and ebb of the movement, and tactics;

    d) strategic leadership;

    e) tactical leadership;

    f) reformism and revolutionism.

    1. *Strategy and tactics as the science of leadership in the class struggle of the proletariat.* The period of the domination of the Second International was mainly a period of the formation and training of the proletarian political armies under conditions of more or less peaceful development. It was the period when parliamentarism was the principal form of class struggle. Questions of great class conflicts, of preparing the proletariat for revolutionary battles, of the means of achieving the dictatorship of the proletariat, did not seem to be on the order of the day at that time. The task was confirmed to utilizing all means of legal development for the purpose of forming and training the proletarian armies, to utilizing parliamentarism in conformity with the conditions under which the status of the proletariat was (and as it seemed then, had to remain) that of an Opposition. It need hardly be proved that in such a period and with such a conception of the tasks of the proletariat there could be neither an integral strategy nor any elaborated tactics. There were fragmentary and detached ideas about tactics and strategy, but no tactics or strategy as such.

    The mortal sin of the Second International was not that it pursued the tactics of utilizing the parliamentary forms of struggle, but that it over estimated the importance of these forms, that it considered them virtually the only forms; and that when the period of open revolutionary battles set in and the question of extraparliamentary forms of struggle came to the fore, the parties of the Second International turned their backs on these new tasks, refused to shoulder them.

    Only in the subsequent period, the period of direct action by the proletariat, the period of proletarian revolution, when the question of overthrowing the bourgeoisie became a question of immediate action; when the question of the reserves of the proletariat (strategy) became one of the most burning questions; when all forms of struggle and of organization, parliamentary and extraparliamentary (tactics), had fully manifested themselves and became well-defined—only in this period could an integral strategy and elaborated tactics for the struggle of the proletariat be drawn up. It was precisely in that period that Lenin brought out into the light of day the brilliant ideas of Marx and Engels on tactics and strategy that had been immured by the opportunists of the Second International. But Lenin did not confine himself to restoring certain tactical propositions of Marx and Engels. He developed them further and supplemented them with new ideas and propositions, combining them all into a system of rules and guiding principles for the leadership of the class struggle of the proletariat. Lenin's pamphlets, such as *What Is To Be Done? Two Tactics, Imperialism, State and Revolution, The Proletarian Revolution and the Renegade Kautsky, "Left-Wing" Communism,* etc., will undoubtedly always be treasured as priceless contributions to the general store of Marxism, to its revolutionary arsenal. The strategy and tactics of Leninism constitute the science of leadership in the revolutionary struggle of the proletariat.

2. *Stages of the revolution, and strategy.* Strategy is the determination of the direction of the main blow of the proletariat at a given stage of the revolution, the elaboration of a corresponding plan for the disposition of the revolutionary forces (main and secondary reserves), the fight to carry out this plan throughout the given stage of the revolution.

Our revolution had already passed through two stages, and after the October Revolution it entered a third one. Our strategy changed accordingly.

First Stage. 1903 to February 1917. Objective: to overthrow tsarism and completely wipe out the survivals of medievalism. The main force of the revolution: the proletariat. Immediate reserves: the peasantry. Direction of the main blow: the isolation of the liberal-monarchist bourgeoisie, which was striving to win over the peasantry and liquidate the revolution by *compromising* with tsarism. Plan for the disposition of forces: alliance of the working class with the peasantry. "The proletariat must carry to completion the democratic revolution, by allying to itself the mass of the peasantry in order to crush by force the resistance of the autocracy and to paralyze the instability of the bourgeoisie." (See Lenin, Vol. VIII, p. 96.)

Second Stage. March 1917 to October 1917. Objective: to overthrow imperialism in Russia and to withdraw from the imperialist war. The main force of the revolution: the proletariat. Immediate reserves: the poor peasantry. The proletariat of neighbouring countries as probable reserves. The protracted war and the crisis of imperialism as the favourable factor. Direction of the main blow: isolation of the petty-bourgeois democrats (Mensheviks and Socialist-Revolutionaries), who were striving to win over the toiling masses of the peasantry and to put an end to the revolution by *compromising* with imperialism. Plan for the disposition of forces: alliance of the proletariat with the poor peasantry. "The proletariat must accomplish the socialist revolution, by allying to itself the mass of the semi-proletarian elements of the population in order to crush by force the resistance of the bourgeoisie and to paralyze the instability of the peasantry and the petty bourgeoisie." (*Ibid.*)

Third Stage. Commenced after the October Revolution. Objective: to consolidate the dictatorship of the proletariat in one country, using it as a base for the defeat of imperialism in all countries. The revolution is spreading beyond the confines of one country; the epoch of world revolution has commenced. The main forces of the revolution: the dictatorship of the proletariat in one country, the revolutionary movement of the proletariat in all countries. Main reserves: the semiproletarian and small-peasant masses in the developed countries, the liberation movement in the colonies and dependent countries. Direction of the main blow: isolation of the petty-bourgeois democrats, isolation of the parties of the Second International, which constitute the main support of the policy of *compromise* with imperialism. Plan for the disposition of forces: alliance of the proletarian revolution with the liberation movement in the colonies and the dependent countries.

Strategy deals with the main forces of the revolution and their reserves. It changes with the passing of the revolution from one stage to another, but remains essentially unchanged throughout a given stage.

3. *The flow and ebb of the movement and tactics.* Tactics are the determination of the line of conduct of the proletariat in the comparatively short period of the flow or ebb of the movement, of the rise or decline of the revolution, the fight to carry out this line by means of replacing old forms of struggle and organization by new ones, old slogans by new ones, by combining these forms, etc. While the object of strategy is to win the war against tsarism, let us say, or against the bourgeoisie, to carry the struggle against tsarism or against the bourgeoisie to its end, tactics pursue less important objects, for the object of tactics is not the winning of the war as a whole, but the winning of some particular engagements or some particular battles, the carrying through successfully of some particular campaigns or actions corresponding to the concrete circumstances in the given period of rise or decline of the revolution. Tactics are a part of strategy, subordinate to it and serving it.

Tactics change according to flow and ebb. While the strategic plan remained unchanged during the first stage of the revolution (1903 to February 1917), tactics changed several times during that period. In the period from 1903 to 1905 the Party pursued offensive tactics, of the tide of the revolution was rising, the movement was on the upgrade, and tactics had to proceed from this fact. Accordingly, the forms of struggle were revolutionary, corresponding to the requirements of the rising tide of the revolution. Local political strikes, political demonstrations, the general political strike, boycott of the Duma, insurrection, revolutionary fighting slogans—such were the successive forms of the struggle during that period. These changes in the forms of struggle were accompanied by corresponding changes in the forms of organization. Factory committees, revolutionary peasant committees, strike committees, Soviets of workers' deputies, a workers' party operating more or less openly—such were the forms of organization during that period.

In the period from 1907 to 1912 the Party was compelled to resort to tactics of retreat; for we then experienced a decline in the revolutionary movement, the ebb of the revolution, and tactics necessarily had to take this fact into consideration. The forms of struggle, as well as the forms of organization, changed accordingly: instead of the boycott of the Duma there was participation in the Duma; instead of open, direct revolutionary action outside the Duma, there were parliamentary speeches and work in the Duma: instead of general political strikes, there were partial economic strikes, or simply a lull in activities. Of course, the Party had to go underground during that period, while the revolutionary mass organizations were superseded by cultural, educational, cooperative, insurance and other legal organizations.

The same must be said of the second and third stages of the revolution, during which tactics changed dozens of times, whereas the strategical plans remaind unchanged.

Tactics deal with the forms of struggle and the forms of organization of the proletariat, with their changes and combinations. During a given stage of the revolution tactics may change several times, depending on the flow or ebb, the rise or decline, of the revolution.

4. *Strategic leadership.* The reserves of the revolution can be:

direct: a) the peasantry and in general the intermediate strata of the population within the country; b) the proletariat of the neighbouring countries; c) the revolutionary movement in the colonies and dependent countries; d) the conquests and gains of the dictatorship of the proletariat —part of which the proletariat may give up temporarily, while retaining superiority of forces, in order to buy off a powerful enemy and gain a respite; and

indirect: a) the contradictions and conflicts among the non-proletarian classes within the country, which can be utilized by the proletariat to weaken the enemy and to strengthen its own reserves; b) contradictions, conflicts and wars (the imperialist war, for instance) among the bourgeois states hostile to the proletarian state, which can be utilized by the proletariat in its offensive or in manoeuvring in the event of a forced retreat.

There is no need to speak at length about the reserves of the first category, as their significance is understood by everyone. As for the reserves of the second categody, whose significance is not always clear, it must be said that sometimes they are of prime importance for the progress of the revolution. One can hardly deny the enormous importance, for example, of the conflict betweeen the petty-bourgeois democrats (Socialist-Revolutionaries) and the liberal-monarchist bourgeoisie (the Constitutional-Democrats) during the after the first revolution, which undoubtedly played its part in freeing the peasantry from the influence of the bourgeoisie. Still less reason is there for denying the colossal importance of the fact that the principal groups of imperialists were engaged in a deadly war during the period of the October Revolution, when the imperialists, engrossed in war among themselves, were unable to concentrate their forces against the young Soviet power, and the proletariat, for this very reason, was able to get down to the work of organizing its forces and consolidating its power, and to prepare the rout of Kolchak and Denikin. It must be presumed that now, when the contradictions among the imperialist groups are becoming more and more profound, and when a new war among them is becoming inevitable, reserves of this description will assume ever greater importance for the proletariat.

The task of strategic leadership is to make proper use of all these reserves for the achievement of the main object of the revolution at the given stage of its development.

What does making proper use of reserves mean?

It means fulfilling certain necessary conditions, of which the following must be regarded as the principal ones:

First. The concentration of the main forces of the revolution at the enemy's most vulnerable spot at the decisive moment, when the revolution has already become ripe, when the offensive is going full-team ahead, when insurrection is knocking at the door, and when bringing the reserves up to the vanguard is the decisive condition of success. The Party's strategy during the period from April to October 1917 well illustrates this manner of utilizing reserves. Undoubtedly, the enemy's most vulnerable spot at that time was the war. Undoubtedly, it was on this question, as the fundamental one, that the Party rallied the broadest masses of the population around the proletarian vanguard. The Party's strategy during that period was, while training the vanguard for street action by means of manifestations and demonstrations, to bring the reserves up to the vanguard through the medium of the Soviets in the rear and the soldiers' committees at the front. The outcome of the revolution has shown that the reserves were properly utilized.

Here is what Lenin, paraphrasing the well-known theses of Marx and Engels on insurrection, says about this condition of the strategic utilization of the forces of the revolution:

1) Never *play* with insurrection, but when beginning it firmly realize that you must *go to the end.*

2) Concentrate a *great superiority of forces* at the decisive point, at the decisive moment, otherwise the enemy, who has the advantage of better preparation and organization, will destroy the insurgents.

3) Once the insurrection has begin, you must act with the greatest *determination*, and by all means, without fail, take the *offensive.* "The defensive is the death of every armed rising."

4) You must try to take the enemy by surprise and seize the moment when his forces are scattered.

5) You must strive for *daily* successes, even if small (one might say

hourly, if it is the case of one town), and at all costs retain the *"moral ascendancy."* (See Vol. XXI, pp. 319–20.)

Second. The selection of the moment for the decisive blow, of the moment for starting the insurrection, so timed as to coincide with the moment when the crisis has reached its climax, when it is fully apparent that the vanguard is prepared to fight to the end, the reserves are prepared to support the vanguard, and maximum consternation reigns in the ranks of the enemy.

The decisive battle, says Lenin, may be deemed to have fully matured *when* "(1) all the class forces hostile to us have become sufficiently entangled, are sufficiently at loggerheads with each other, have sufficiently weakened themselves in a struggle which is beyond their strength"; *when* "(2) all the vacillating, wavering, unstable, intermediate elements—the petty bourgeoisie, the petty-bourgeois democrats as distinct from the bourgeoisie—have sufficiently exposed themselves in the eyes of the people, have sufficiently disgraced themselves through their practical bankruptcy"; *when* "(3) among the proletariat a mass sentiment in favour of supporting the most determined, supremely bold, revolutionary action against the bourgeoisie has arisen and begun vigorously to grow. Then revolution is indeed ripe; then, indeed, if we have correctly gauged all the conditions indicated . . . above, and if we have chosen the moment rightly, our victory is assured." (See Vol. XXV, p. 229.)

The manner in which the October insurrection was carried out may be taken as a model of such trategy.

Nonobservance of this condition leads to a dangerous error called "loss of tempo," when the Party lags behind the movement or runs far ahead of it, courting the danger of failure. An example of such "loss of tempo," of how the moment of insurrection should not be chosen, may be seen in the attempt made by a section of our comrades to begin the insurrection by arresting the Democratic Conference in September 1917, when hesitation was still rife in the Soviets, when the armies at the front were still at the crossroads, when the reserves had not yet been brought up to the vanguard.

Third. Undeviating pursuit of the course adopted, no matter what difficulties and complications are encountered on the road towards the goal; this is necessary in order that the vanguard may not lose sight of the main goal of the struggle and that the masses may not stray from the road while marching towards that goal and striving to rally around the vanguard. Failure to observe this condition leads to a grave error, well known to sailors as "losing the course." As an example of this "loss of course" we may mention the erroneous conduct of our Party when, immediately after the Democratic Conference, it adopted a resolution to participate in the Parliament. For the moment the Party, as it were, forgot that the Preparliament was an attempt of the bourgeoisie to switch the country from the path of the Soviets to the path of bourgeois parliamentarism, that the Party's participation in such a body might result in mixing up all the cards and confusing the workers and peasants, who were waging a revolutionary struggle under the slogan: "All Power to the Soviets." This mistake was rectified by the withdrawal of the Bolsheviks from the Parliament.

Fourth. Manoeuvring the reserves with a view to effecting a proper retreat when the enemy is strong, when retreat is inevitable, when to accept battle forced upon us by the enemy is obviously disadvantageous, when, with the given alignment of forces, retreat becomes the only way to ward off a blow against the vanguard and to keep the reserves intact.

"The revolutionary parties," says Lenin, "must complete their education. They have learned to attack. Now they have to realize that this knowledge must be supplemented with the knowledge how to retreat properly. They have to realize—and the revolutionary class is taught to realize it by its own bitter experience—that victory is impossible unless they have learned both how to attack and how to retreat properly." (See Vol. XXV, p. 177.)

The object of this strategy is to gain time, to demoralize the enemy, and to accumulate forces in order later to assume the offensive.

The signing of the Brest-Litovsk Peace may be taken as a model of this strategy, for it enable the Party to gain time, to take advantage of the conflicts in the camp of the imperialists, to demoralize the forces of the enemy, to retain the support of the peasantry, and to accumulate forces in preparation for the offensive against Kolchak and Denikin.

"In concluding a separate peace," said Lenin at that time, "we free ourselves as much *as is possible at the present moment* from both hostile imperialist groups, we take advantage of their mutual enmity and warfare, which hamper concerted action on their part against us, and for a certain period have our hands free to advance and to consolidate the socialist revolution." (See Vol. XXII, p. 198.)

"Now even the biggest fool," said Lenin, three years after the Brest-Litovsk Peace, "can see that the 'Brest Peace' was a concession that strengthened us and broke up the forces of international imperialism." (See Vol. XXVII, p. 7.)

Such are the phincipal conditions which ensure correct strategic leadership.

5. *Tactical leadership.* Tactical leadership is a part of strategic leadership, subordinated to the tasks and the requirements of the latter. The task of tactical leadership is to master all forms of struggle and organization of the proletariat and to ensure that they are used properly so as to achieve, with the given relation of forces, the maximum results necessary to prepare for strategic success.

What is meant by making proper use of the forms of struggle and organization of the proletariat?

It means fulfilling certain necessary conditions, of which the following must be regarded as the principal ones:

First. To put in the forefront precisely those forms of struggle and organization which are best suited to the conditions prevailing during the flow or ebb of the movement at a given moment, and which therefore can facilitate and ensure the bringing of the masses to the revolutionary positions, the bringing of the millions to the revolutionary front, and their disposition at the revolutionary front.

The point here is not that the vanguard shall realize the impossibility of preserving the old order of things and the inevitability of its overthrow. The point is that the masses, the millions, shall understand this inevitability and display their readiness to support the vanguard. But the masses can understand this only from their own experience. The task is to enable the vast masses to realize from their own exerience the inevitability of the overthrow of the old regime, to promote such methods of struggle and forms of organization as will make it easier for the masses to learn from experience to recognize the correctness of the revolutionary slogans.

The vanguard would have become detached from the working class, and the working class would have lost contact with the masses, if the Party had not decided at the time to participate in the Duma, if it had not decided to concentrate its forces on work in the Duma and to base the struggle on this work, in order to make it easier for the masses to realize from their own experience the futility of the Duma, the falsity of the promises of the Constitutional-Democrats, the impossibility of compromise with tsarism, and the inevitability of an aliance between the peasantry and the working class. Had the masses not gained their experience during the period of the Duma, the exposure of the Constitutional-Democrats and the hegemony of the proletariat would have been impossible.

The danger of the "Otzovist" tactics was that they threatened to detach the vanguard from the millions of its reserves.

The Party would have become detached from the working class, and the working class would have lost its influence among the broad masses of the peasants and soldiers, if the proletariat had followed the "left" Communists, who called for insurrection in April 1917, when the Mensheviks and the Socialist-Revolutionaries had not yet exposed themselves as advocates of war and imperialism, when the masses had not yet learned from their own experience to recognize the falsity of the speeches of the Mensheviks and the Socialist-Revolutionaries about peace, land and freedom. Had the masses not gained this experience during the Kerensky period, the Mensheviks and Socialist-Revolutionaries would not have been isolated and the dictatorship of the proletariat would have been impossible. Therefore, the tactics of "patiently explaining" the mistakes of the petty-bourgeois parties and of open struggle in the Soviets were the only correct tactics.

The danger of the tactics of the "left" Communists was that they threatened to transform the Party from the leader of the proletarian revolution into a handful of inane conspirators with no ground to stand on.

"Victory cannot be won with the vanguard alone," says Lenin. "To throw the vanguard alone into the decisive battle, before the whole class, before the broad masses have taken up a position either of direct support of the vanguard, or at least of benevolent neutrality towards it . . . would be not merely folly but a crime. And in order that actually the whole class, that actually the broad masses of the working people and those oppressed by capital may take up such a position, propoganda and agitation alone are not enough. For this the masses must have their own political experience. Such is the fundamental law of all great revolutions, now confirmed with astonishing force and vividness not only in Russia but also in Germany. Not only the uncultured, often illiterate masses of Russia, but the highly cultured, entirely literate masses of Germany had to realize through their own painful experience the absolute impotence and spinelessness, the absolute helplessness and servility to the bourgeoisie, the utter vileness of the government of the knights of the Second International, the absolute inevitability of a dictatorship of the extreme reactionaries (Kornilov in Russia, Kapp and Co. in Germany) as the only alternative to a dictatorship of the proletariat, in order to turn them resolutely toward communism." (See Vol. XXV, p. 228.)

Second. To locate at any given moment the particular link in the chain of processes which, if grasped, will enable us to hold the whole chain and to prepare the conditions for achieving strategic success.

The point here is to single out from all the problems confronting the Party the particular immediate problem, the answer to which constitutes the central point, and the solution of which will ensure the successful solution of the other immediate problems.

The importance of this thesis may be illustrated by two examples, one of which may be taken from the remote past (the period of the formation of the Party) and the other from the immediate present (the period of the New Economic Policy).

In the period of the formation of the Party, when the innumerable circles and organizations had not yet been linked together, when amateurishness and the parochial outlook of the circles were corroding the Party from top to bottom, when ideological confusion was the characteristic feature of the internal life of the Party, the main link and the main task in the chain of links and in the chain of tasks then confronting the Party proved to be the establishment of an all-Russian illegal newspaper (*Iskra*). Why? Because only by means of an all-Russian illegal newspaper was it possible under the conditions then prevailing to create a coherent Party nucleus capable of uniting the innumerable circles and organizations into a single organization, to prepare the conditions for ideological and tactical unity, and thus to lay the foundations for the formation of a real Party.

During the period of transition from war to economic construction, when industry was vegetating in prey to devastation and agriculture was suffering from a shortage of manufactured goods, when the establishment of a bond between state industry and peasant economy became the fundamental condition for successful socialist construction—in that period it turned out that the main link in the chain of processes, the main task among a number of tasks, was to develop trade. Why? Because under the conditions of the New Economic Policy (NEP) the bond between industry and peasant economy cannot be established except through trade; because under the conditions of NEP production without sale is fatal for industry; because industry can be expanded only by the expansion of sales as a result of developing trade; because only after we have consolidated our position in the sphere of trade, only after we have secured control of trade, only after we have secured this link can there be any hope of linking industry with the peasant market and successfully fulfiling the other immediate tasks in order to create the conditions for building the foundations of socialist economy.

"It is not enough to be a revolutionary and an adherent of socialism or a Communist in general," says Lenin. "One must be able at each particular moment to find the particular link in the chain which one must grasp with all one's might in order to hold the whole chain and to prepare firmly for the transition to the next link. . . ."

"At the present time . . . this link is the revival of internal *trade* under proper regulation (direction). Trade—that is the 'link' in the historical chain of events, in the transitional forms of our socialist construction in 1921–22, '*which we must grasp with all our might.*'" (See Vol. XXVII, p. 82.)

These are the principal conditions which ensure correct tactical leadership.

6. *Reformism and revolutionism.* What is the difference between revolutionary tactics and reformist tactics?

Some think that Leninism is opposed to reforms, opposed to compromises and to agreements in general. This is absolutely wrong. Bolsheviks know as well as anybody else that in a certain sense "every little helps," that under certain conditions reforms in general, and compromises and agreements in particular, are necessary and useful.

"To carry on a war for the overthrow of the international bourgeoisie," says Lenin, "a war which a hundred times more difficult, protracted and complicated than the most stubborn of ordinary wars between states, and to refuse beforehand to manoeuvre, to utilize the conflict of interests (even though temporary) among one's enemies, to refuse to temporize and compromise with possible (even though temporary, unstable, vacillating and conditional) allies—is not this ridiculous in the extreme? Is it not as though, when making a difficult asent of an unexplored and heretofore inaccessible mountain, we were to refuse beforehand ever to move in zigzags, ever to retrace our steps, ever to abandon the course once selected and to try others?" (See Vol. XXV, p. 210.)

Obviously, therefore, it is not a matter of reforms or of compromises and agreements, but of the use people make of reforms and compromises.

To a reformist, reforms are everything, while revolutionary work is something incidental, something just to talk about, mere eyewash. That is why, with reformist tactics under the bourgeois regime, reforms are inevitably transformed into an instrument for strengthening that regime, an instrument for disintegrating the revolution.

To a revolutionary, on the contrary, the main thing is revolutionary work and not reforms; to him reforms are by-products of the revolution. That is why, with revolutionary tactics under the bourgeois regime, reforms are naturally transformed into instruments for disintegrating this regime, into instruments for strengthening the revolution, into a base for the further development of the revolutionary movement.

The revolutionary will accept a reform in order to use it as an aid in combining legal work with illegal work, to intensify, under its cover, the illegal work for the revolutionary preparation of the masses for the overthrow of the bourgeoisie.

That is what making revolutionary use of reforms and agreements under the conditions of imperialism means.

The reformist, on the contrary, will accept reforms in order to renounce all illegal work, to thwart the preparation of the masses for the revolution and to rest in the shade of "bestowed" reforms.

That is what reformist tactics mean.

This is the position in regard to reforms and agreements under imperialism.

The situation changes somewhat, however, after the overthrow of imperialism, under the dictatorship of the proletariat. Under certain conditions, in a certain situation, the proletarian power may find itself constrained temporarily to leave the path of the revolutionary reconstruction of the existing order of things and to take the path of its gradual transformation, the "reformist path," as Lenin says in his well-known article "The Importance of Gold," the path of flanking movements, of reforms and concessions to the nonproletarian classes—in order to disintegrate these classes, to give the revolution a respite, to recuperate and prepare the conditions for a new offensive. It cannot be denied that in a sense this is a "reformist" path. But it must be borne in mind that there is a fundamental distinction here, which consists in the fact that in this case the reform emanates from the proletarian power, it strengthens the proletarian power, it procures for it a necessary respite; its purpose is to disintegrate, not the revolution, but the nonproletarian classes.

Under such conditions a reform is thus transformed into its opposite.

The proletarian power is able to adopt such a policy because, and only because, the sweep of the revolution in the preceding period was broad enough and therefore provided a sufficiently wide expanse within which to retreat, substituting for offensive tactics the tactics of temporary retreat, the tactics of flanking movements.

Thus, while formerly, under the bourgeois regime, reforms were a by-product of revolution, now, under the dictatorship of the proletariat, the source of reforms is the revolutionary gains of the proletariat, the reserves accumulated in the hands of the proletariat and consisting of these gains.

"Only Marxism," says Lenin, "has precisely and correctly defined the relation of reforms to revolutino. However, Marx was able to see this relation only from one aspect, namely, under the conditions preceding the first to any extent permanent and lasting victory of the proletariat, if only in a single country. Under those conditions, the basis of the proper relation was: reforms are a by-product of the revolutionary class struggle of the proletariat. . . . After the victory of the proletariat, if only in a single country, something new enters into the relation between reforms and revolution. In principle, it is the same as before, but a change in form takes place, which Marx himself could not foresee, but which can be appreciated only on the basis of the philosophy and politics of Marxism. . . . After the victory (while still remaining a 'by-product' on an international scale) they [i.e., reforms] are, in addition, for the country in which victory has been achieved, a necessary and legitimate respite in those cases when, after the utmost exertion of effort, it becomes obvious that sufficient strength is lacking for the revolutionary accomplishment of this or that transition. Victory creates such a 'reserve of strength' that it is possible to hold out even in a forced retreat, hold out both materially and morally." (See Vol. XXVII, pp. 84–85.)

Charisma and the Demagogue

Adolf Hitler, Mein Kampf, ed. John Chamberlain, Sidney B. Fay, et al. (unabridged ed.; Boston, Houghton Mifflin Co., 1939), Vol. II, chap. ii in part, pp. 630–51.

One of the unwritten principles of democratic politics, as more than one expert suggests, is that practitioners do not really mean what they say. Candidate A does not really believe that the victory of candidate B means ruin for the nation; he just says so. There are those who take their rhetoric seriously. Adolf Hitler (1889–1945) believed in himself and his ragbag of notions. He contributed nothing new save catastrophe on an unprecedented scale. Hitler was neither the first racist politician nor, regrettably, the last. Paranoid nationalism neither starts nor ends with him. But a sick man led a sick nation—and it was the strongest nation in Europe.

Fear and discontent elevated Hitler to power and maintained him there, and this negative popularity was not limited to Germany. "Better Hitler than Blum," was a candid comment in pre-Munich Paris. Guilt and rancor left from the First World War helped. Fundamentally, however, the rise of Hitler was testimony to European incapacity. Many men, not necessarily evil, connived in the rise of Nazism. Anti-Semitic fervor could be whipped up in good Lutheran families. The material achievement of the *Autobahnen* compensated in far too many minds for the gangsterism of the regime. If economic recovery was due to rearmament, it did provide employment.

Hitler was the nineteenth century run mad. The Third Reich was an aberrant realization of Treitschke's nationalism and doctrine of freedom through authority. Sorelian myth found its place. Corporate state, planned political economy might be realized. Even Nietzsche, wretchedly perverted and torn from context, would provide rhetorical flourishes for the New Order.

CHAPTER II

THE STATE

[The first part of this chapter has been omitted.]

SUMMING UP: the folkish State, therefore, has to give the general history lessons a shortened form that comprises all that is essential. Beyond this the possibility of a most thorough, specialized education has to be offered. It is enough that the individual receives a general knowledge, kept along broad outlines, as a basis, and enjoys a most thorough special and individual training only in the field which becomes later that of his life. Hereby the general education has to be compulsory in all fields, that of the specialty has to be left to the choice of the individual.

The shortening of the curriculum and of the number of hours, brought about in this way, will be of benefit to the training of the body, of the character, and of will power and determination.

How little bearing our present school education, especially that of the middle schools, has on the vocation of the future life, is best proved by the fact that today people from three entirely different kinds of schools can come into one and the same position. What is of decisive importance is actually only the general education and not the infiltrated special knowledge. But in instances where—as already said—actually a special knowledge is necessary, it can of course not be acquired within the curriculum of our present middle schools.

Some day the folkish State will have to do away with such half measures.

The second change in the scientific curriculum of the national State has to be the following:

It is a characteristic of our present materialized time that our scientific education turns more and more towards the subject of natural science only, namely, mathematics, physics, chemistry, etc. No matter how necessary this is for a time in which techniques and chemistry dominate in daily life and represent its symptoms, at least as far as outwardly recognizable, it is just as dangerous if the general education of a nation is always directed exclusively at this. On the contrary, this education has always to be an ideal one. It has to correspond more to the classic subjects and should only offer the foundations of a later training in a special field. Otherwise, one renounces forces which are still more important for the preservation of the nation than any technical or other ability. Especially in history instruction one should not let oneself be deterred from studying antiquity. Roman history, rightly conceived in very broad outlines, is and remains the best teacher not only for today but probably for all times. The Hellenic ideal of culture, too, should be preserved for us in its exemplary beauty. One must not allow the differences of the individual races to tear up the greater racial community. The struggle that rages today involves very great aims: a culture fights for its existence, which combines millenniums and embraces Hellenism and Germanity together.

A sharp difference should be made between general education and specialized knowledge. Since the latter, today more than ever, threatens to sink into the service of pure mammon, general education, at least in its more ideal orientation, has to be preserved as a counter-balance. Here, too, one has continuously to inculcate the principle *that industry and techniques, trade and professions are able to flourish only as long as an idealistically disposed national community offers the necessary presuppositions. But the latter do not lie in material egoism, but in a joyous readiness to renounce and to sacrifice.*

The present education of youth has by and large aimed at pumping into the young man that knowledge which he needs for his advancement in his future life. This is expressed in the following: 'The boy must sometime become a useful member of human society.' By this one understands his ability to earn some day his daily bread in a decent manner. The superficial civic education which goes along with this stands on a weak footing from the beginning. As the State in itself represents only a form, it is indeed very difficult to educate or even to obligate people with regard to the latter. A form can break too easily. But the concept 'State'—as we have seen— does not today possess a clear content. Thus there remains nothing but the traditional 'patriotic' education. In old Germany its emphasis, frequently little intelligent but mostly very stale, lay on an adoration of small and smallest potentates whose mass from the beginning made it necessary to renounce a comprehensive appreciation of the actually great men of our people. The result, therefore, was a very insufficient knowledge of German history on the part of our broad masses. Here, too, the great line was lacking.

It is obvious that in such a manner one could not arrive at a genuine national enthusiasm. Our education lacked the skill to lift out of the historical growth of our people a few names and to make them the common property of the entire German nation, so as to throw an equally unifying bond around the entire nation by equal knowledge and equal enthusiasm. One did not know how to make the really important men of our people appear, in the eyes of the present, as outstanding heroes, to concentrate the general attention on them and to create by this a uniform mood. In the various subjects one was not able to raise what was glorious for the nation above the level of objective presentation and to kindle the national pride by such shining examples. In those days this would have appeared as bad chauvinism which in this form one would have liked but little. Simply dynastic patriotism appeared more agreeable and more bearable than the fervent passion of highest national pride. The first was always ready to serve, the latter might some day become mistress. Monarchic patriotism resulted in veterans' clubs; national passion would have been more difficult to direct in its way. It is comparable to a thoroughbred horse which does not bear everyone on its back. No wonder that one preferred to keep back from such a danger. That some day a war would come which through drum fire and gas clouds would thoroughly test the inner steadfastness of patriotic feeling, nobody seemed to think possible. But when the War did come, the lack of highest national passion took its most terrible revenge. The gentlemen had but little inclination to die for their imperial and royal masters, but the 'nation' was unknown to most of them.

Since the revolution has made its entry into Germany and with it monarchic patriotism disappeared by itself, the purpose of history lessons is actually only that of a pure acquisition of knowledge. For *national enthusiasm* this State has no use, but what it wants it will never get. For just as little as there could be *dynastic patriotism* of ultimate *resistibility* in an era when the *principle of nationalities* is dominant, thus still less could there be *republican enthusiasm*. For about this there ought to be no doubt that with the slogan 'For the German Republic' the German people would not remain on the battlefield for four and a half years; least of all would those who have created this marvelous structure do so.

Actually, this Republic owes its unharmed existence to the readiness, assured everywhere, of voluntarily assuming all tributes and signing any renunciation of territory. This Republic is liked by the rest of the world; just as every weakling is considered more agreeable by those who need him than a rough man. *True, the very sympathy for just this State form implies its devastating criticism.* One likes the German Republic and lets it live because one could not find a better ally for the work of enslavement of our people. It is only to this that this glorious formation owes its present existence. Therefore it can renounce all really national education and be satisfied with the shouting of 'hoch' by the heroes of the Reichsbanner who, by the way, if they had to protect this banner with their blood, would run away like rabbits.

The folkish State will have to fight for its existence. It will not be able either to preserve or to defend its existence by Dawes signatures. But for its existence and its protection it will need just what now one believes that one can get along without. The more incomparable and valuable form and contents will be, the greater will also be the envy and the resistance of the opponents. Then the best protection will not be represented in its arms, but in its citizens; not fortress walls will protect it, but the living wall of men and women, filled with highest love for the country and with fanatical national enthusiasm.

As the third point, the following has to be considered in connection with scientific education:

Also in science the folkish State has to see a means for the promotion of national pride. Not only world history, but the entire culture history must be taught from this viewpoint. An inventor must appear great not only as an inventor, but greater still as a fellow citizen. The admiration for every great deed has to be recast into pride in the fortunate performer of this deed as a member of one's own nation. From the vast number of all the great names of German history the greatest have to be singled out and presented to youth so impressively as to become the pillars of an unshakable national sentiment.

The subjects to be taught must be built up systematically according to these viewpoints; education must be arranged systematically in such a way as to make the young man upon leaving school not half a pacifist, democrat or something of that kind, but a *genuine German.*

In order to render this national sentiment genuine from the beginning and to prevent it from being only pretense, as early as during youth an iron principle has to be hammered into the still pliable heads: *He who loves his people proves this solely by the sacrifices which he is ready to make for it. National sentiment that only seeks profit does not exist. Nor is there a nationalism that merely comprises classes. Shouting hurrah proves nothing and gives nobody the right to call himself national, if it is not backed by the great, loving care for the preservation of a general and sound nationality. A reason for pride in one's people exists only after one has no longer to be ashamed of any class. But a people one-half of which is miserable and careworn, or even depraved, gives such a bad picture that nobody should feel pride in it. Only if a nationality is sound in all its members, in body and soul, can the joy of belonging to it justly grow into that high feeling that we call national pride. But only he will feel this highest pride who knows the greatness of his nationality.*

The intimate coupling of nationalism and feeling of social justice must be planted in the young heart. Then there will some day arise a people of State citizens, bound to one another and forged together by a common love and a common pride, unshakable and invincible for all times.

Our time's fear of chauvinism is the sign of its impotence. Since it not only lacks but considers disagreeable all seething energy, Destiny has not chosen it for a great deed. For the greatest changes on this earth would not have been thinkable if their driving force, instead of fanatical, even hysterical passion, had been only the bourgeois virtues of peace and order.

It is certain, however, that this world approaches a great change. And there can be only the sole question whether it turns out for the benefit of Aryan mankind or for the profit of the eternal Jew.

The folkish State will have to see to it that by a suitable education of youth a mature generation is produced for the ultimate and greatest decisions on this globe.

That people, however, which as the first sets out on this way will be victorious.

The folkish State's entire work of education and training has some day to find its culmination in branding, through instinct and reason, the race sense and race feeling into the hearts and brains of the youth with whom it is entrusted. No boy or girl must leave school without having been led to the ultimate knowledge of the necessity and the nature of the purity of the blood. Thus the assumption is created for the racial foundations of our nationality and by it, in turn, the safeguarding of the presumptions for the future cultural development.

For all physical and spiritual training would still remain useless unless it benefited a human being who is fundamentally ready and determined to preserve himself and his kind.

In the reverse case there would happen what we Germans have to deplore greatly even now, without the entire size of this tragic misfortune having perhaps been understood so far: *that also in future we would remain only cultural fertilizer, not only in the meaning of the limited conception of our present bourgeois opinion, which sees in the individual lost national member only the lost citizen, but in the meaning of the most painful realization that then, despite all our knowledge and skill, our blood is nevertheless doomed to decline. By mating again and again with other*

*races, we may well lift those races out of their former cultural level to a
higher one, but we sink down from our own high level forever.*

*For the rest, this education, too, from the racial viewpoint, must find its
final completion in the military service. As on the whole the period of the
military service has to be considered the conclusion of the normal education
of the average German.*

*Great as the importance of the kind of physical and spiritual education in
the folkish State will be, just as important will it be for the folkish State to
select the right people.* Today this selection is treated very casually. Generally, it is the children of higher placed, momentarily well-to-do parents
who in turn are deemed worthy of a higher education. Hereby questions of
talent play a subordinate rôle. Strictly speaking a talent can always be
evaluated only relatively. A peasant boy can have many more talents than
a child of parents in a position that has been elevated through many generations, although in general knowledge he may be far behind the *bourgeois*
child. The greater knowledge of the latter has in itself nothing whatsoever to
do with greater or smaller talent, but it is rooted in the considerably greater
profusion of impressions which the child, in consequence of his many-
sided education and richer surroundings of life, receives uninterruptedly.
If the talented peasant boy had also grown up in such surroundings from
his early childhood, then his intellectual ability would be quite different.
Today there is perhaps only one domain in which family station is actually
less decisive than one's inborn ability: the domain of art. Here, where one
cannot just 'learn' and everything has to be originally inborn and is subject
to a more or less favorable development in the sense of wise promotion of
the existing abilities, the parents' money and property is almost irrelevant.
For this reason it is best proved in this field that genius is not bound to
higher spheres of life or even riches. The greatest artists not seldom come
from the poorest houses. And many a little village boy later becomes a
much celebrated master.

It does not speak for great depth of thinking in our time that one does not
make use of such knowledge for the entire intellectual life. One thinks that
what cannot be denied concerning art would not apply to the so-called
exact sciences. One can undoubtedly endow man with definite mechanical
abilities by education, just as by clever training it is possible to teach a
poodle the most incredible tricks. However, as with this animal training the
animal's understanding does not lead from itself to such exercises, the same
is the case with man. One can also teach man, without considering any other
talent, certain scientific tricks, but then it is exactly the same lifeless, inanimate procedure as with the animal. Based on a certain intellectual drill,
one can cram super-average knowledge into an average man, but this remains dead and ultimately unfruitful knowledge. The result then is that
kind of man who is perhaps a living dictionary, but who nevertheless fails
in the most deplorable manner in all special situations and decisive mo-

ments of life; he will have to be trained again for every, even the most modest demand, but out of himself he will not be able to give even the smallest contribution towards a development of mankind. Such a knowledge, acquired by mechanical training, will at the utmost suffice, in our time, for taking over State positions.

It is a matter of course that in the total sum of a nation's population there will be found talents for all kinds of domains of everyday life. It is a further matter of course that the value of knowledge will be the greater the more dead knowledge is animated by the adequate talent of the individual. *Creative achievements, in general, can arise only if ability and knowledge form a union.*

A further example may show how boundlessly today's mankind sins in this direction. From time to time it is demonstrated to the German petty *bourgeois* in illustrated periodicals that for the first time here or there a negro has become a lawyer, teacher, even clergyman, or even a leading opera tenor or something of that kind. While the stupid *bourgeoisie*, marveling, takes cognizance of this miraculous training, filled with respect for this fabulous result of our present educative skill, the Jew knows very slyly how to construe from this a new proof of the correctness of his theory of the *equality of men* which he means to instill into the nations. It does not dawn upon this depraved *bourgeois* world that here one has actually to do with a sin against all reason; that it is a criminal absurdity to train a born half-ape until one believes a lawyer has been made of him, while millions of members of the highest culture race have to remain in entirely unworthy positions; that it is a sin against the will of the eternal Creator to let hundreds and hundreds of thousands of His most talented beings degenerate in the proletarian swamp of today, while Hottentots and Zulu Kafirs are trained for intellectual vocations. For it is training, exactly as that of the poodle, and not a scientific 'education.' The same trouble and care, applied to intelligent races, would fit each individual a thousand times better for the same achievements.

Unbearable as this condition would be if it ever should concern anything but exceptions, it is equally unbearable today where it is not talent and abilities that decide for the higher education. Indeed, it is an unbearable idea that annually hundreds of thousands of completely untalented people are deemed worthy of a higher education, while other hundreds of thousands of great talent remain without any higher education. The loss the nation suffers from this cannot be estimated. If during the past decades the wealth of important inventions, especially in North America, increased extremely, then it was not in small measure due to the fact that there considerably more talent from the lowest layers find the possibility of a higher training than is the case in Europe.

For inventing, purely crammed knowledge is not sufficient, but only knowledge animated by talent. This is not evaluated by us today; the good mark alone is decisive.

Here, too, the folkish State will some day have to intervene by education. *Its task is not to preserve the decisive influence of an existing social class, but its task is to pick out of the sum of all fellow citizens the most able heads and to bring them to office and dignity.* It has not only the duty of giving the average child a definite education in public schools, but also the duty of placing the talent on the tracks on which it belongs. Above all it has to consider it its highest task to open the doors of the State's institutes of higher learning to every talent, no matter from what circles they may come. It has to fulfill this task, as only thus out of the stratum of representatives of dead knowledge can grow the talented leadership of the nation.

The State has to make provisions in this direction also for another reason: our intellectual classes, especially in Germany, are so secluded in themselves and so calcified that they lack the living connections towards the masses below. This takes its revenge in two directions: first, they lack by this the understanding of, and the feeling for, the great masses. They have been uprooted from this connection for so long a time that they can no longer have the necessary psychological understanding for the people. They have become estranged from the people. Secondly, however, these upper layers lack the necessary will power. For will power is always weaker in these secluded intellectual circles than in the masses of the primitive people. But God knows that we Germans never lacked scientific education; but all the more we lacked will power and determination. The more 'intellectual' for example our statesmen were, the weaker as a rule were their actual achievements. The political preparation as well as the technical armament for the World War were insufficient not for the reason that perhaps *too uneducated* heads ruled our people, but rather that those ruling were *over-educated* people, stuffed with knowledge and intellect, but bare of any sound instinct and devoid of all energy and courage. It was a disaster that our people had to fight its struggle for life under the Reichs chancellorship of a philosophizing weakling. If instead of a Bethmann Hollweg we had had a more robust man of the people as a leader, the heroic blood of the common grenadier would not have been shed in vain. Also, the exaggerated purely intellectual high-breeding of our leaders was the best ally for the revolutionary November rabble. By neglecting in the most wretched manner, the national good with which they were entrusted, these very intellectuals created the presumption for the success of the others.

Here the Catholic Church can be looked upon as a model example. In the celibacy of its priests roots the compulsion to draw the future generation of the clergy, instead of from its own ranks, again and again from the broad masses of the people. But this particular significance of celibacy is not recognized by most people. It is the origin of the incredibly vigorous power that inhabits this age-old institution. This gigantic host of clerical dignitaries, by uninterruptedly supplementing itself from the lowest layers of the nations, preserves not only its instinctive bond with the people's world of sentiment, but it also assures itself of a sum of energy and active force which in such a form will forever be present only in the broad masses of the people. From this results the astounding youthfulness of this giant organism, its spiritual pliability and its steel-like will power.

It will be the task of a folkish State to take care by its educational arrangements that, by fresh infusion of blood from below, a perpetual renovation of the existing intellectual layers takes place. The State has the obligation of selecting with utmost care and exactitude, out of the total of fellow citizens, that human material that is evidently favored by Nature and to employ it in the service of the community. For the object of the State and State positions is not to provide individual classes with a living, but to fulfill the tasks allotted to them. But this will only be possible if as its bearers, in principle, only able and strong-willed personalities are developed. This is valid not only for all official positions, but for the intellectual leadership of the nation in all domains in general. In this, too, lies a factor for the greatness of a people, that one succeeds in training the most able heads for the domains that are congenial to them, and in putting them into the service of the people's community. *If two nations that, generally speaking, are equally well endowed compete with each other, then that notion will win the victory that has its best talents represented in its intellectual leadership, and that nation will succumb whose leadership represents only one great common food crib for certain estates or classes, without consideration of the inborn abilities of the individual bearers.*

True, this seems impossible at first sight in our present world. One will immediately object that the small son of a higher State official for example cannot be expected to become, let us say, a craftsman, because some other boy whose parents were craftsmen, seems more able. This may be true for today's evaluation of manual work. For this reason the folkish State will have to arrive at an attitude that is different in principle in regard to the conception of work. *It will have to break, if necessary through centuries of education, with the absurdity of disrespecting physical activity. In principle, it will have to evaluate the individual, not according to his kind of work, but according to the form and the quality of his achievements.* This may appear monstrous to an era to which the most brainless columnist, solely for the reason that he works with the pen, is worth more than the most intelligent mechanic working with fine metals. This wrong evaluation, however, lies not in the nature of things, as said before, but has been artificially imposed by education and did not formerly exist. The present unnatural condition is based on the general symptoms of disease of our materialized time.

Fundamentally, the value of all work is a double one: *one that is purely material and one that is ideal.* The material value is based on the importance, that means the material importance, of a work for the life of the community. The more fellow citizens draw advantage from a certain completed achievement, that means, a direct and an indirect advantage, the greater must the material value be estimated. This evaluation finds plastic expression in turn in the material reward which the individual receives for his work. This purely material value is contrasted to the ideal value. This is not based on the importance of the work achieved, measured materially, but on its necessity in itself. As certainly as the material advantage of an invention may be greater than that of an everyday handyman's service, just as certainly is the community dependent on this smallest service as on that greatest. Materially it may make a difference in the evaluation of the advantage of the individual work for all, and it can express this in the corresponding reward; but ideally it has to establish the equality of all in the moment when every individual endeavors to do his best in his field, no matter what it may be. It is on this that the evaluation of a man must rest, and not on the reward.

Since in a sensible State care must be directed toward allotting to the individual an activity that corresponds to his abilities, or in other words, toward training the able heads for the work that is congenial to them, but as ability can fundamentally not be imposed by learning but has to be inborn, that means that it is a gift of Nature and not man's merit, the general civic appreciation cannot depend on the work that has been allotted, so to speak, to the individual. For this work comes on account of his birth and of the training conditioned by it which he received from the community. The evaluation of man must be founded on the kind and the manner in which he discharges the work that he has been given by the community. For the activity that the individual carries out is not the end of his existence, but only a means for it. Rather has he to continue his education as a man and to refine himself, but he can do so only within the frame of his cultural community which must always rest upon the foundation of a State. He must contribute his share to the preservation of this foundation. The form of this contribution is decided by Nature; it is up to him to return to the national community, by zeal and honesty, what it once itself had given to him. He who does so earns highest esteem and highest respect. *Material reward may be granted to one whose achievement bears corresponding profit for the community; ideal reward, however, must lie in the evaluation which every man can claim who devotes to the service of his nationality the forces which Nature gave him and which the national community developed.* But then it is no longer a disgrace to be a decent craftsman, but it is a disgrace, as an incapable official, to steal the day from the Lord and the daily bread from the nation. Then one will also consider it a matter of course that a man is not allotted tasks to which he is not suited from the beginning.

Furthermore, such an activity offers the only yardstick for the law with regard to the general, equal, legal and civil activity.

The present time is liquidating itself: it introduces general suffrage, it talks of equal rights but it does not find a justification for them. In the material reward it sees the expression of a man's value and by this it smashes the foundation of the most noble equality which can at all exist. For equality is not based and can never be based upon the achievements of the individuals in themselves, but it is possible in the form in which everyone fulfills his special obligations. Only by this is Nature's chance in the evaluation of man's value eliminated and the individual becomes the forger of his own significance.

In the present time, when entire groups of human beings know only how to evaluate one another merely according to salary classes, one has—as already said—no understanding for this. But this must not be a reason for us to renounce the presentation of our ideas. On the contrary: *He who wants to cure this time which is intrinsically sick and rotten has first of all to have the courage to expose the causes of this disease. But this should be the care of the National Socialist movement: ignoring all petty bourgeoisism, to collect out of, and to arrange in, our nationality those forces which are capable of being the protagonists of a new view of life.*

Of course one will now raise the objection that in general it is difficult to separate the ideal evaluation from the material one, that even the diminishing evaluation of physical labor is brought about just by its inferior reward. That this inferior reward in turn is again the cause of the limitations of the individual's participation in the cultural treasures of his nation. That it is precisely the ideal culture of man, which does not necessarily have to have anything to do with his activity in itself, that is impaired thereby. That the dread of physical labor is all the more founded in the fact that in consequence of the lower reward, the cultural level of the manual laborer is necessarily lowered and that by this the justification of a general, lower evaluation is given.

In this lies a good deal of truth. But for this very reason one will have to guard in future against a too great differentiation in salary levels. One should not say that with this the achievements will disappear. This would be the most sorrowful symptom of the decay of a time if the impulse for a higher intellectual achievement were to be found only in the higher salary. If this viewpoint had been the only decisive one in the world so far, mankind would never have received its greatest scientific and cultural goods. For the greatest inventions, the greatest discoveries, the most revolutionary scientific works, the most glorious monuments of human culture have not been given to the world out of greed for money. On the contrary their birth not infrequently meant the very reunuciation of the worldly happiness of riches.

It may be that today gold has become the exclusive ruler of life, but man will some day again bow to higher gods. Many things may today owe their existence only to the longing for money and property, but among them are only few the non-existence of which would make mankind poorer.

This, too, is one of the tasks of our movement that as early as today it announces a time which will give to the individual what he needs for living, but at that same time upholding the principle that man does not live exclusively for material enjoyments. This must some day find its expression in a wisely limited sliding scale of earnings, which in any case will make possible for even the most humble honest worker a decent, orderly existence as fellow citizen and man.

One must on no account say that this is an ideal condition which, if carried out in practice, the world would not bear and would actually never attain.

We, too, are not so simple as to believe that one could ever succeed in bringing about a faultless era. But this does not relieve us of the obligation of fighting recognized mistakes, of overcoming weaknesses and of striving toward the ideal. Crude reality will of itself bring about only too many limitations. For that very reason man has to try all the more to serve the ultimate aim, and failures must deter him from his intention just as little as he can renounce justice merely because the latter, too, is liable to make mistakes, and just as little as one rejects medicine because there will nevertheless always be sickness.

One should beware of evaluating the force of an ideal too little. Those who today become faint-hearted in this regard, I would like to remind, in case they once were soldiers, of a time the heroism of which was the most overwhelming profession of the force of ideal motives. For, what made people die at that time was not care for their daily bread, but the love of their country, the confidence in its greatness, the general feeling for the honor of the nation. And only after the German people turned its back on these ideals in order to follow the material promises of the Revolution, and after it exchanged the gun for the knapsack it came, instead of into an earthly heaven, into the purgatory of general disdain and not less, of general distress.

Therefore it is all the more necessary to oppose the calculating masters of the erstwhile *material Republic* with the faith in an *ideal Reich*.

Faith and Totalitarianism

Pius XI, Mit brennender Sorge: *Encyclical Letter (March 14, 1937)* . . . *on the Condition of the Church in Germany,* in Henri Lichtenberger, *The Third Reich: Germany and National Socialism,* trans. Koppel S. Pinson and Nicholas Murray Butler *(New York: Greystone Press, 1937),* pp. 345–49, 351–53, 356–62.

Pius XI, Divini Redemptoris: *Encyclical Letter (March 19, 1937)* . . . *on Atheistic Communism,* in Oswald von Nell-Breuning, *Reorganization of Social Economy: the Social Encyclicals Developed and Explained (New York, Milwaukee, and Chicago: Bruce Publishing Co., 1936–37),* pp. 446–68.

The *Syllabus of Errors* entrenched the papacy on the extreme right of the European political spectrum in 1864. Significant modification in that position took place in only social and economic policy. From *Rerum Novarum* (1891) to *Quadragesimo Anno* (1931), the Roman Catholic hierarchy has demonstrated a capacity to recognize and offer cures for some of the fundamental ills of man as a social animal. The political position shifted very slowly before the Second World War. Pius XI (1857–1939) assumed the papal throne in 1922 as determined as his predecessors to make no truce with socialism, particularly with Bolshevik Russia. Fascism was another matter. The Lateran Treaties (1929) finally liquidated the struggle between the papacy and the Italian state, a struggle subsisting since the *Risorgimento.* In 1931, Pope Pius agreed to end Catholic Action and all political activity in the state. The papacy was less happy with Nazi Germany than Fascist Italy. While Pius XI concluded a Concordat in 1933 with the new Nazi government, the relationship was strained from the beginning. There was never, however, a total break or the same uncompromising resistance that the papacy displayed towards the Soviet Union.

To illustrate the point and problem, parts of two encyclicals—the first directed against Nazi anticlericalism and paganism, the second restating Catholic incompatibility with communism—are given here. The differences merit examination, for just as the Communist parties of western Europe advocated a popular front against fascism, so the papacy was willing to reach far and compromise much for an Anti-Communist alliance.

ENCYCLICAL OF POPE PIUS XI

TO THE VENERABLE ARCHBISHOPS AND BISHOPS OF GERMANY AND OTHER
ORDINARIES IN PEACE AND COMMUNION WITH THE APOSTOLIC SEE

On the Condition of the Church in Germany

POPE PIUS XI

VENERABLE BRETHREN, GREETING AND APOSTOLIC BENEDICTION

1. With deep anxiety and increasing dismay, We have for some time past beheld the sufferings of the Church, and the steadily growing oppres-

sion of those men and women who, loyally professing their faith in thought and deed, have remained true to her amidst the people of that land to which St. Boniface once brought the light and glad tidings of Christ and the Kingdom of God.

2. This anxiety of Ours has not been lessened by the accurate reports dutifully brought to Us by the representatives of the most reverend episcopate, who came to visit at Our sick-bed. They related much that is consoling and edifying about the struggle for religion that is being waged by the faithful, and yet, despite their love for their people and their fatherland, with every possible attempt to reach a dispassionate judgment, they could not pass over much that is bitter and sad. After receiving their accounts, We could say in great thankfulness to God: "I have no greater grace than this, to hear that my children walk in truth." But the frankness befitting Our responsible apostolic office, and the desire to place before your eyes and those of the entire Christian world the actual facts in all their gravity, require Us to add: A greater anxiety, a more bitter suffering in Our pastoral care, We have not, than to hear "many leave the way of truth."

3. In the summer of 1933, Venerable Brethren, We accepted the offer made by the Government of the Reich to institute negotiations for a Concordant in connection with a proposal of the previous year, and to the satisfaction of you all brought them to a conclusion with a solemn agreement. In this We were guided by the solicitude incumbent on Us to safeguard the freedom of the Church in the exercise of her apostolic ministry in Germany and the salvation of the souls entrusted to her, and at the same time by the sincere wish of rendering an essential service to the progress and prosperity of the German people.

4. In spite of many serious misgivings at the time, We forced Ourselves to decide that We should not withhold Our consent. We wished to spare Our faithful sons and daughters in Germany, so far as was humanly possible, the anxiety and suffering which, in the given circumstances, We would certainly have otherwise had to expect. Through Our act We wished to prove to all, that seeking only Christ and the things of Christ, We do not refuse the hand of peace of Mother Church to anyone who does not himself reject it.

5. If the tree of peace which We planted with pure intention in German soil has not borne the fruit We desired in the interests of your people, no one in the wide world who has eyes to see and ears to hear can say today that the fault lies with the Church and her Head. The lessons of the past years make it clear where the responsibility lies. They disclose machinations that from the beginning had no other aim than a war of extermination. In the furrows where We labored to plant the seeds of sincere peace, others were sowing—like the enemy in Holy Scripture—the tares of distrust, of discord, hatred, calumny, of secret and open enmity against Christ and His Church, an enmity in principle, fed from a thousand springs and working with every means at its disposal. With them and only with them, as well as

with their open and silent supporters, lies the responsibility that now, instead of the rainbow of peace, the storm-clouds of destructive religious conflicts are visible on the German horizon.

6. We have not tired, Venerable Brethren, of portraying to the responsible guides of the destinies of your country the consequences that necessarily follow if such trends are left unhindered and much more if they are viewed with favor. We have done everything to defend the sanctity of a word solemnly pledged, to protect the inviolability of obligations, freely undertaken, against theories and practices which, if officially approved, must destroy all confidence and render valueless any word that might also be pledged in the future. When once the time shall have come to place before the eyes of the world these Our endeavors, all right minded persons will know where they have to look for those who kept the peace, and where for those who broke it. Everyone in whose mind there is left the least perception of the truth, in whose heart there is a trace of feeling for justice, will then have to admit that in these grievous and eventful years after the signing of the Concordat, in every word and in every action of Ours, We have stood faithful to the terms of the agreement. But with amazement and deep aversion he will be obliged to admit that to change the meaning of the agreement, to evade the agreeement, to empty the agreement of all its significance, and finally more or less openly to violate the agreement, has been made the unwritten law of conduct by the other party.

7. The moderation We have shown in spite of everything was neither dictated by considerations of human expediency nor motivated by unseemly weakness, but simply by the desire that We might not perchance tear up valuable wheat with the tares; by the intention not to pronounce judgment openly until minds were made ready for the inevitability of this judgment; by the determination not to deny definitively the good faith of others before the hard language of facts had torn away the coverings under which a systematic camouflage has been able and is able to disguise the attack on the Church. Even today, when the opening campaign waged against the denominational school guaranteed by the Concordat, when the nullification of the freedom of the vote for Catholics who should have the right to decide in the matter of education, shows the dreadful seriousness of the situation in a most important field of the Church's life and the unparalleled torment of conscience of believing Christians, Our pastoral care for the salvation of souls counsels Us not to leave unheeded even the slight prospects of return to a loyal adherence to a responsible agreement. In compliance with the prayers of the Most Reverend Episcopate, We shall not weary in the future also of pleading the cause of outraged right with the rulers of your people. Unconcerned with the success or failure of the day and obeying only Our conscience and in accordance with Our pastoral mission, We shall oppose an attitude of mind that seeks to stifle chartered right with open or covered violence.

8. The purpose of the present letter, however, Venerable Brethren, is a

different one. As you kindly visited Us as We lay on Our bed of sickness, so today We turn to you and through you to the Catholic faithful of Germany, who, like all suffering and oppressed children, are particularly close to the heart of the Common Father. In this hour, when their faith is being tried like pure gold in the fire of tribulation and concealed and open persecution, when they are surrounded by a thousand forms of organized bondage in matters of religion, when the lack of true information and absence of the customary means of defense weigh heavy on them, they have a double right to words of truth and spiritual comfort from him, to whose first predecessor the significant words of the Saviour were spoken: "But I have prayed for thee, that thy faith fail not; and thou being once converted, confirm thy brethren."

True Belief in God

9. Take care, Venerable Brethren, that first of all belief in God, the primary and irreplaceable foundation of all religion, be preserved true and unadulterated in German lands. He is not a believer in God who uses the word of God rhetorically but he who associates with the sacred word the true and worthy idea of God.

10. He who, in pantheistic vagueness, equates God with the universe, and identifies God with the world and the world with God does not belong to believers in God.

11. He who replaces a personal God with a weird impersonal Fate supposedly according to ancient pre-Christian German concepts denies the wisdom and providence of God, that "reacheth from end to end mightily and ordereth all things sweetly" and directs everything for the best. Such a one cannot claim to be numbered among those who believe in God.

12. He who takes the race, or the people, or the State, or the form of Government, the bearers of the power of the State or other fundamental elements of human society—which in the temporal order of things have an essential and honorable place—out of the system of their earthly valuation, and makes them the ultimate norm of all, even of religious, values, and defies them with an idolatrous worship, perverts and falsifies the order of things created and commanded by God. Such a one is far from true belief in God and a conception of life corresponding to true belief.

13. Beware, Venerable Brethren, of the growing abuse in speech and writing, of using the thrice holy name of God as a meaningless label for a more or less capricious form of human search and longing. Work among your faithful that they may be vigilant to reject this aberration as it deserves. Our God is the personal, superhuman, almighty, infinitely perfect God, one in the Trinity of persons, threefold in the unity of the Divine essence, the Creator of the universe, the Lord and King in whom the history of the world finds fulfillment, Who suffers and can suffer no other god beside Him.

14. This God has given His commandments in His capacity as Sovereign. They apply regardless of time and space, country or race. As God's sun

shines on all that bear human countenance, so does His law know no privileges or exceptions. The rulers and the ruled, crowned and uncrowned, high and low, rich and poor, all alike are subject to His law. From the sum total of His rights as Creator flows connaturally the sum total of His claims to obedience on the part of the individual and every kind of society. This claim to obedience comprehends every walk of life, in which moral questions demand a settlement in harmony with God's law and consequently the adjustment of transistory human legislation to the structure of the immutable law of God. Only superficial minds can lapse into the heresy of speaking of a national God, of a national religion; only such can make the mad attempt of trying to confine within the boundaries of a single people, within the narrow blood stream of a single race, God the Creator of the world, the King and Lawgiver of all peoples before whose greatness all peoples are small as a drop of a bucket.

15. The Bishops of the Church of Christ set up "for the things that appertain to God" must be watchful that such pernicious errors, which are usually followed by more pernicious practices, find no foothold among the faithful. It is the holy duty of your office, as far as in you lies, to do everything to bring it about that the commandments of God shall be regarded and obeyed as the obligatory basis of morally ordered private and public life, that the sovereign rights of God, the name and the word of God, be not blasphemed; that the blasphemies—in word, writing and picture, at times countless as the sands by the sea—be made to cease; that over against the defying Promethean spirit of deniers, scorners and haters of God the propitiatory prayer of the faithful never falters but that, like incense, it may rise hour after hour to the Most High and stay His hand raised to punish.

16. We thank you, Venerable Brethren, your priests and all the faithful, who have done and continue to do their duty in defending the sovereign rights of God against the aggressive neo-paganism—that unfortunately in many instances is favored in influential quarters. Our thanks are doubly sincere and coupled with admiration and approval of those who in the exercise of their duty were found worthy of making earthy sacrifices for God's sake and of enduring earthly suffering.

.   .   .   .

22. The divine mission of the Church that works among men and must work through men may be lamentably obscured by human failings that again and again sprout up as tares amid the wheat of God's kingdom. He who has heard the Saviour's word about scandals and those who give scandal, knows how the Church and each indivdual has to judge on what was sin and is sin. But because of these deplorable discrepancies between believing and living, between word and deed, between the outward conduct and the interior disposition of individuals—even though there might be many such—to forget the immense sum of sincere pursuit of virtue, of the spirit of sacrifice, of brotherly love, of heroic striving after holiness; or worse, to conceal all this knowingly, is to display regrettable blindness and

injustice. When it becomes perfectly clear that the hard standard applied to the hated Church is forgotten the very moment there is question of societies of a different nature, felt to be akin in sentiment or interest, then the one who so acts and pretends that he has been offended in his sense of cleanliness, shows that he is related to those who in the cutting words of the Saviour see the mote in their brother's eye, but do not see the beam in their own. Questionable as is the intention of those who make a career, and in many instances a low profession, of busying themselves with human failings in the Church, and though it be true that the authority of him who holds ecclesiastical office is founded on God and is independent of his human or moral standing; nevertheless, no period of time, no individual, no community is free from the duty of sincere examination of conscience, of unrelenting, of thorough renewal in mind and deed. In Our encyclical on the priesthood, in Our letters on Catholic Action, We pointed out with adjuring insistence the sacred duty of all members of the Church, and particularly members of the priesthood and religious state, that they should bring their belief and conduct into the agreement required by the law of God and demanded by the Church with emphasis. And today We earnestly repeat: It is not enough to be counted a member of the Church of Christ. One must be also a living member of this Church—in spirit and in truth. And only they are such, who are in the grace of the Lord and ever walk in His presence—in innocence or in sincere and efficacious penance. If the Apostle of the Gentiles, the "Vessel of Election," kept his body under the rod of chastisement and mortification in order that he might not, after preaching to others, become himself a castaway, can there be any other way but that of the closest union of apostolate and personal sanctification for the others to whose hands is committed the keeping and increase of the kingdom of God? Only in this way can it be proved to the present generation, and especially to the adversaries of the Church, that the salt of the earth has not lost its savor, that the leaven of Christendom has not become stale, but is capable and ready to bring to the people of today who are caught in doubt and error, in indifference and perplexity, in weariness in believing and in separation from God, the spiritual renewal and rejuvenation of which they stand, whether they admit it or not, in greater need than ever before. A Christianity that enters into itself in all its members, that strips off all mere outward show and worldliness, that takes the commandments of God seriously, and proves itself in love of God and active love of one's neighbor, can and must be the pattern and leader to a world sick to its very heart and seeking for support and guidance if unspeakable misfortune and a cataclysm far beyond all imagination is not to burst over it.

23. In the final analysis every true and lasting reform has proceeded from the sanctuary; from men who were inflamed and driven by love of God and their neighbor. From their magnanimity and readiness to hearken to every call of God and to realize that call first of all in themselves, they grew in humility and in the conviction of their calling to be luminaries and re-

newers of their times. When zeal for reform did not spring from the pure source of personal singleness of heart, but was the expression and outbreak of passionate frenzy, it caused confusion instead of bringing light, tore down instead of building up; and not seldom was the point of departure for errors more disastrous than were the evils that it was the intention or the pretended intention to correct. True, the spirit of God breatheth where He will. He can raise up stones to prepare the way for His design. He chooses the instruments of His will according to His Own plans, and not according to those of men. But He Who founded His Church and called it into being in the storm of Pentecost, does not blast the foundation of the establishment He Himself intended for salvation. Those who are moved by the spirit of God have of themselves the proper inward and outward attitude towards the Church, which is the precious fruit on the tree of the Cross, the Pentecostal gift of God's spirit to a world in need of guidance.

24. In your districts, Venerable Brethren, voices are raised in ever louder chorus urging men on to leave the Church. Among the spokesmen there are many who, by reason of their official position, seek to create the impression that leaving the Church, and the disloyalty to Christ the King which it entails, is a particularly convincing and meritorious form of profession of loyalty to the present State. With cloaked and with manifest methods of coercion, by intimidation, by holding out the prospect of economic, professional, civic and other advantages, the loyalty of Catholics and especially of certain classes of Catholic officials to their faith is put under a pressure that is as unlawful as it is unworthy of human beings. All Our fatherly sympathy and deepest condolence We offer to those who pay so high a price for their fidelity to Christ and the Church. But here We reach the point of supreme importance, where it is a question of safety or destruction, and where, consequently, for the believer the way of heroic fortitude is the only way of salvation. When the tempter or oppressor comes to him with the Judas-like suggestion to leave the Church, then, even at the cost of heavy, earthly sacrifices he can only reply in the words of the Saviour: "Begone, Satan: for it is written: The Lord thy God thou shalt adore and Him only shalt thou serve." But to the Church he will say: Thou my Mother from the days of my childhood, my comfort in life, my intercessor in death, may my tongue cleave to my palate, if I, yielding to earthly enticements or threats, should turn traitor to the promises of my baptism. But to those who think that they can continue outward leaving of the Church with inward loyalty to the Church, let the Saviour's words be earnest warning: "He that shall deny Me before men, I will also deny him before My Father Who is in heaven."

.   .   .   .

Recognition of the Natural Law

35. It is part of the trend of the day to sever more and more not only morality but also the foundation of law and jurisprudence, from true belief

in God and from His revealed commandments. Here We have in mind particularly the so-called natural law that is written by the finger of the Creator Himself in the tables of the hearts of men and which can be read on these tables by sound reason not darkened by sin and passion. Every positive law, from whatever lawgiver it may come, can be examined as to its moral implications, and consequently as to its moral authority to bind in conscience, in the light of the commandments of the natural law. The laws of man that are in direct contradiction with the natural law bear an initial defect that no violent means, no outward display of power can remedy. By this standard must we judge the principle: "What helps the people is right." A right meaning may be given to this sentence if understood as expressing that what is morally illicit can never serve the true interests of the people. But even ancient paganism recognized that the sentence, to be perfectly accurate, should be inverted and read: "Never is anything useful, if it is not at the same time morally good. And not because it is useful, is it morally good, but because it is morally good, it is also useful." Cut loose from this rule of morality, that principle would mean, in international life, a perpetual state of war between the different nations. In political life within the State, since it confuses considerations of utility with those of right, it mistakes the basic fact that man as a person possesses God-given rights, which must be preserved from all attacks aimed at denying, suppressing or disregarding them. To pay no heed to this truth is to overlook the fact that the true public good is finally determined and recognized by the nature of man, with his harmonious coordination of personal rights and social obligations, as well as by the purpose of the community which in turn is conditioned by the same human nature. The community is willed by the Creator as the means to the full development of the individual and social attainments, which the individual in give and take has to employ to his own good and that of others. Also those higher and more comprehensive values, that cannot be realized by the individual but only by the community, in the final analysis are intended by the Creator for the sake of the individual, for his natural and supernatural development and perfection. A deviation from this order loosens the supports on which the community is placed, and thereby imperils the tranquillity, security and even the existence of the community itself.

36. The believer has an inalienable right to profess his faith and put it into practice in the manner sutied to him. Laws that suppress or make this profession and practice difficult contradict the natural law.

37. Conscientious parents, aware of their duty in the matter of education, have a primary and original right to determine the education of the children given to them by God in the spirit of the true faith and in agreement with its principles and ordinances. Laws or other regulations concerning schools that disregard the rights of parents guaranteed to them by the natural law, or by threat and violence nullify those rights, contradict the natural law and are utterly and essentially immoral,

38. The Church, the guardian and exponent of the divine natural law, cannot do otherwise than declare that the registrations which have just taken place in circumstances of notorious coercion are the result of violence and void of all legality.

To Youth

39. As the vice regent of Him who said to the young man of the gospel: "If thou wilt enter into life, keep the commandments," do We especially address fatherly words to youth. By a thousand tongues today a gospel is preached in your ears that is not revealed by your Heavenly Father. A thousand pens write in the service of a sham Christianity that is not the Christianity of Christ. Day by day the press and the radio overwhelm you with productions hostile to your faith and Church and, with no consideration or reverence, attack what must be to you sacred and holy.

40. We know that many, very many, of you for the sake of loyalty to your religion and Church, for the sake of belonging to Church associations guaranteed by the Concordat, have borne and still endure bitter days of misunderstanding, of suspicion, of contempt, of denial of your patriotism, of manifold injury in your professional and social life. We are aware that many an unknown soldier of Christ stands in your ranks, who with heavy heart but head erect bears his lot and finds comfort solely in the thought of suffering reproach for the Name of Jesus.

41. Today, when new perils and conflicts threaten, We say to this youth: "If anyone preach to you a gospel, besides that which you have received" at the knees of a pious mother, from the lips of a Catholic father, from the education of a teacher true to his God and his church, "let him be anathema." If the State founds a State-Youth to which all are obliged to belong, then it is—without prejudice to the rights of Church associations—an obvious, an inalienable right of the young men themselves, and of their parents responsible for them before God, to demand that this obligatory organization should be cleansed of all manifestations of a spirit hostile to Christianity and the Church, which, up to the recent past and even at the present moment, place Catholic parents in hopeless conflicts of conscience, since they cannot give to the State what is demanded in the name of the State without robbing God of what belongs to God.

42. No one has any intention of obstructing the youth of Germany on the road that is meant to bring them to the realization of true popular union, to the fostering of the love of freedom, to steadfast loyalty to the fatherland. What We object to, and what We must object to, is the intentional and systematically fomented opposition which is set up between these educational purposes and those of religion. Therefore we call out to youth: Sing your songs of freedom, but do not forget the freedom of the sons of God while singing them. Do not allow this noble freedom, for which there is no substitute, to pine away in the slave chains of sin and sensuality. He who sings the song of loyalty to his earthly country must not, in disloyalty to

God, to his church, to his eternal country, become a deserter and a traitor. You are told a great deal about heroic greatness, in designed and false contrast to the humility and patience of the Gospel. Why is silence kept about the heroism of moral struggle? Why is it not told you that the preservation of baptismal innocence represents an heroic action which should be assured of the appreciation is deserves in the religious and moral sphere? A great deal is told you of human weaknesses in the history of the Church. Why is nothing said of the great deeds that accompany her on her way through the centuries, of the Saints she has produced, of the blessings which came from the living union between this Church and your people and enriched the culture of the west? You are told a great deal of the exercises of sport. Undertaken with discretion, the cult of physical fitness is a benefit for youth. But now so much time is devoted to it, in many cases, that no account is taken of the harmonious development of mind and body, of what is due to family life, of the commandment to keep holy the Lord's day. With a disregard bordering on indifference, the sacredness and peace that are in the best tradition of the German Sunday are taken from it. With confidence We expect from practicing Catholic youth that, in the difficult circumstances of obligatory State organization, they will insist unflinchingly on their right to keep Sunday in a Christian manner, that in the cult of physical fitness they will not forget the interests of their immortal souls; that they will not allow themselves to be overcome by evil, but will strive to overcome evil by good; that their highest and holiest ambition will be so to run the race towards immortal life as to achieve the crown of victory.

To Priests and Religious

43. We address a special word of recognition, encouragement and exhortation to the priests of Germany, on whom, in subordination to their Bishops, there rests the task of showing the flock of Christ in a trying time and under difficult circumstances, the right paths, by precept and example, by daily sacrifice and apostolic patience. Be not weary, beloved sons and sharers in the holy mysteries, in following the eternal High Priest, Jesus Christ, Who bestows love and care like the good Samaritan. Keep yourselves day by day in conduct undefiled before God, in unremitting discipline and perfection, in merciful care for all entrusted to you, especially for those endangered, the weak and the wavering. Be the leaders of the faithful, the support of the stumbling, the teachers of the doubtful, the consolers of those who mourn, the unselfish helpers and counsellors of all. The trials and sorrows through which your people have passed since the war have left their mark on its soul. They have left behind conflicts and bitterness that can be healed only slowly, that can be overcome only in the spirt of unselfish and active charity. This charity, which is the indispensable armor of the apostle, especially in the world of the present day stirred up and distorted with hate, We pray and beg the Lord to bestow on you in superabundant measure. This apostolic love will make you, if not forget,

at least forgive the many undeserved offenses that more plentifully than ever before are strewn in the path of your priestly ministration. This comprehending and merciful charity towards the erring, and even towards the contemptuous, does not mean and cannot mean, that you renounce in any way the proclaiming of, the insisting on, and the courageous defense of the truth and its free and unhindered application to the realities about you. The first and obvious duty the priest owes to the world about him is service to the truth, the whole truth, the unmasking and refutation of error in whatever form or disguise it conceals itself.

44. To Catholic religious of both sexes We likewise express Our fatherly thanks, together with our utmost sympathy in the fate that, in consequence of regulations against the religious Orders, has taken them out of the work of their chosen career, which they had loved and made rich in blessing. If individuals have fallen short and proved themselves unworthy, their misdeeds, punished by the Church herself, do not lessen the merits of the overwhelming majority, who, in unselfishness and voluntary poverty, were striving to serve their God and people in the spirit of sacrifice. The zeal, fidelity, striving after virtue, active charity and readiness to help on the part of the Orders engaged in the ministry, hospitals and schools are, and remain, a praiseworthy contribution to private and public prosperity, to which undoubtedly a later and quieter time will accord more justice than the troubled present. We feel confident that Superiors of religious communities will take occasion from their trials and difficulties to call down from the Almighty fresh blessing and fruitfulness on their heavy work through redoubled zeal, deepened life of prayer, holy earnestness in their vocation and religious discipline.

To the Faithful of the Laity

45. Before our eyes stands the countless throng of faithful sons and daughters, for whom the suffering of the Church in Germany and their own suffering has in no way diminished their devotion to the cause of God, their tender love for the Father of Christendom, their obedience to their Bishops and priests, their cheerful readiness, come what may, to remain true in the future to what they have believed and have received from their forefathers as a sacred inheritance. From a heart that is deeply moved We send them all our paterial greeting.

46. And this, first and foremost, to the members of the Church associations, who courageously and oftentimes at the cost of painful sacrifice have kept true to Christ and did not give up the rights which a formal agreement, made in good faith and trust, had guaranteed to the Church and themselves.

47. We address a particularly heartfelt greeting to Catholic parents. Their God-given rights and duties in education are this present moment at the very center of a struggle which could not conceivably be fraught with graver consequences for the future. The Church of Christ cannot wait until

her altars have been overthrown, until sacrilegious hands have set the houses of God on fire, before she begins to mourn and lament. When the attempt is made to desecrate the tabernacle of a child's soul sanctified in baptism by an education that is hostile to Christ; when from this living temple of God the eternal lamp of belief in Christ is cast out and in its place is brought the false light of a substitute faith that has nothing in common with the faith of the Cross, then the time of spiritual profanation of the temple is at hand, then it is the duty of every professing Christian to separate clearly his responsibility from that of the other side, to keep his conscience clear of any culpable cooperation in such dreadful work and corruption. The more the opponents are at pains to deny and gloss over their dark intentions, all the more is vigilant distrust called for, and distrustful vigilance that has been aroused by bitter experience. The formal maintaining of religious instruction, especially when controlled and shackled by those who are not competent, in the framework of a school that in other departments systematically and invidiously works against the same religion, can never be a justification for a beliving Christian to give his free approval to such a school that aims at destroying religion. We know, beloved Catholic parents, that there can be no question of such willingness on your part. We know that a free and secret ballot would in your case be equivalent to an overwhelming vote for the religious school. And therefore We shall not weary in the future of representing to responsible parties the injustice of the coercive measures so far adopted, and the obligation of allowing free expression of a free will. Meanwhile do not forget this: from the bond of responsibility established by God that binds you to your children, no earthly power can loose you. No one of those who today are oppressing you in the exercise of your rights in education and pretend to free you from your duty in this matter, will be able to answer for you to the Eternal Judge when He asks you the question: "Where are those I have given you?" May everyone of you be able to answer: "Of them thou hast given me, I have not lost anyone."

48. Venerable Brethren, We are certain that the words which We address to you, and through you to the Catholics of the German Reich, in this decisive hour, will awaken in the hearts and actions of Our loyal children the echo that answers to the loving solicitude of the Common Father. If there is anything that We beseech of the Lord with particular fervor, it is this, that Our words may also reach the ears and hearts of those who have already begun to allow themselves to be inveigled by the enticements and threats of those who take their stand against Christ and His holy Gospel and cause them to reflect.

49. Every word of this letter has been weighed in the scales of truth and of charity. We did not desire to share any accountability, by reason of untimely silence, for want of enlightenment, nor, by needless severity, for the hardening of heart of any one of those who are placed under Our pastorial responsibility and are no less included in Our pastoral charity because at the moment they are walking estranged in the ways of error.

Though many of those who adapt themselves to the ways of their new environment, who have for their deserted Father's house and for the Father Himself only words of disloyalty, ingratitude or even insult; though they forget what they have cast behind them, the day will dawn when the horror of being in spiritual dereliction far from God will strike the hearts of these prodigal sons, when homesickness will drive them back to the "God who rejoiced their youth" and to the Church whose maternal hand pointed out for them the way to the Heavenly Father. To hasten this hour is the object of Our unceasing prayers.

ENCYCLICAL LETTER . . .

On Atheistic Communism

POPE PIUS XI

VENERABLE BRETHREN, HEALTH AND APOSTOLIC BENEDICTION

THE PROMISE OF a Redeemer brightens the first page of the history of mankind, and the confident hope aroused by this promise softened the keen regret for a paradise which had been lost. It was this hope that accompanied the human race on its weary journey, until in the fullness of time the expected Saviour came to begin a new universal civilization, the Christian civilization, far superior even to that which up to this time had been laboriously achieved by certain more privileged nations.

2. Nevertheless, the struggle between good and evil remained in the world as a sad legacy of the original fall. Nor has the ancient tempter ever ceased to deceive mankind with false promises. It is on this account that one convulsion following upon another has marked the passage of the centuries, down to the revolution of our own days. This modern revolution, it may be said, has actually broken out or threatens everywhere, and it exceeds in amplitude and violence anything yet experienced in the preceding persecutions launched against the Church. Entire peoples find themselves in danger of falling back into a barbarism worse than that which oppressed the greater part of the world at the coming of the Redeemer.

3. This all too imminent danger, Venerable Brethren, as you have already surmised, is bolshevistic and atheistic Communism, which aims at upsetting the social order and at undermining the very foundations of Christian civilization.

I

ATTITUDE OF THE CHURCH TOWARDS COMMUNISM

Previous Condemnations

4. In the face of such a threat, the Catholic Church could not and does not remain silent. This Apostolic See, above all, has not refrained from raising its voice, for it knows that its proper and social mission is to defend

truth, justice, and all those eternal values which Communism ignores or attacks. Ever since the days when groups of "intellectuals" were formed in an arrogant attempt to free civilization from the bonds of morality and religion. Our Predecessors overtly and explicitly drew the attention of the world to the consequences of the de-Christianization of human society. With reference to Communism, Our Venerable Predecessor, Pius IX, of holy memory, as early as 1846 pronounced a solemn condemnation, which he confirmed in the words of the Syllabus directed against "that infamous doctrine of so-called Communism which is absolutely contrary to the natural law itself, and if once adopted would utterly destroy the rights, property, and possessions of all men, and even society itself." Later on, another of Our Predecessors, the immortal Leo XIII, in his Encyclical *Quod Apostolici Muneris,* defined Communism as "the fatal plague which insinuates itself into the very marrow of human society only to bring about its ruin." With clear intuition he pointed out that the atheistic movements existing among the masses of the Machine Age had their origin in that school of philosophy which for centuries had sought to divorce science from the life of the Faith and of the Church.

Acts of Present Pontificate

5. During Our Pontificate We too have frequently and with urgent insistence denounced the current trend to atheism which is alarmingly on the increase. In 1924 when Our relief-mission returned from the Soviet Union We condemned Communism in a special Allocution which We addressed to the whole world. In our Encyclicals *Miserentissimus Redemptor, Quadragesimo Anno, Caritate Christi, Acerba Animi, Dilectissima Nobis,* We raised a solemn protest against the persecutions unleashed in Russia, in Mexico, and now in Spain. Our two Allocutions of last year, the first on the occasion of the opening of the International Catholic Press Exposition, and the second during Our audience to the Spanish refugees, along with Our message of last Christmas, have evoked a world-wide echo which is not yet spent. In fact, the most persistent enemies of the Church, who from Moscow are directing the struggle against Christian civilization, themselves bear witness, by their unceasing attacks in word and act, that even to this hour the Papacy has continued faithfully to protect the sanctuary of the Christian religion, and that it has called public attention to the perils of Communism more frequently and more effectively than any other public authority on earth.

Need of Another Solemn Pronouncement

6. To Our great satisfaction, Venerable Brethren, you have, by means of individual and even joint pastorial Letters, accurately transmitted and explained to the Faithful these admonitions. Yet despite Our frequent and paternal warning the peril only grows greater from day to day because of the pressure exerted by clever agitators. Therefore, We believe it to be Our duty to raise Our voice once more, in a still more solemn missive, in

accord with the tradition of this Apostolic See, the Teacher of Truth, and in accord with the desire of the whole Catholic world, which makes the appearance of such a document but natural. We trust that the echo of Our voice will reach every mind free from prejudice and every heart sincerely desirous of the good of mankind. We wish this the more because Our words are now receiving sorry confirmation from the spectacle of the bitter fruits of subversive ideas, which We foresaw and foretold, and which are in fact multiplying fearfully in the countries already stricken, or threatening every other country of the world.

7. Hence, We wish to expose once more in a brief synthesis the principles of atheistic Communism as they are manifested chiefly in bolshevism. We wish also to indicate its method of action and to contrast with its false principles the clear doctrine of the Church, in order to inculcate anew and with greater insistence the means by which the Christian civilization, the true *civitas kumana*, can be saved from the satanic scourge, and not merely saved, but better developed for the well-being of human society.

II

COMMUNISM IN THEORY AND PRACTICE

Doctrine

FALSE IDEAL

8. The Communism of today, more emphatically than similar movements in the past, conceals in itself a false messianic idea. A pseudo-ideal of justice, of equality and fraternity in labor inpregnates all its doctrine and activity with a deceptive mysticism, which communicates a zealous and contagious enthusiasm to the multitudes entrapped by delusive promises. This is especially true in an age like ours, when unusual misery has resulted from the unequal distribution of the goods of this world. This pseudo-ideal is even boastfully advanced as if it were responsible for a certain economic progress. As a matter of fact, when such progress is at all real, its true causes are quite different, as for instance the intensification of industrialism in countries which were formerly almost without it, the exploitation of immense natural resouces, and the use of the most brutal methods to insure the achievement of gigantic projects with a minimum of expense.

MARXIST EVOLUTIONARY MATERIALISM

9. The doctrine of modern Communism, which is often concealed under the most seductive trappings, is in substance based on the principles of dialectical and historical materialism previously advocated by Marx, of which the theoricians of bolshevism claim to possess the only genuine interpretation. According to this doctrine there is in the world only one reality, matter, the blind forces of which evolve into plant, animal, and man. Even human society is nothing but a phenomenon and form of matter, evolving in the same way. By a law of inexorable necessity and through a perpetual conflict

of forces, matter moves towards the final synthesis of a classless society. In such a doctrine, as is evident, there is no room of the idea of God; there is no difference between matter and spirit, between soul and body; there is neither survival of the soul after death nor any hope in a future life. Insisting on the dialectical aspect of their materialism, the Communists claim that the conflict which carries the world towards its final synthesis can be accelerated by man. Hence, they endeavor to sharpen the antagonisms which arise between the various classes of society. Thus, the class-struggle with its consequent violent hate and destruction takes on the aspects of a crusade for the progress of humanity. On the other hand, all other forces whatever, as long as they resist such systematic violence, must be annihilated as hostile to the human race.

MAN AND THE FAMILY UNDER COMMUNISM

10. Communism, moreover, strips man of his liberty, robs human personality of all its dignity, and removes all the moral restrains that check the eruptions of blind impulse. There is no recognition of any right of the individual in his relations to the collectivity; no natural right is accorded to human personality, which is a mere cog-wheel in the Communist system. In man's relations with other individuals, besides, Communists hold the principle of absolute equality, rejecting all hierarchy and divinely constituted authority, including the authority of parents. What men call authority and subordination is derived from the community as its first and only font. Nor is the individual granted any property rights over material goods or the means of production, for inasmuch as these are the source of further wealth, their possession would give one man power over another. Precisely on this score, all forms of private property must be eradicated, for they are at the origin of all economic enslavement.

11. Refusing to human life any sacred or spiritual character, such a doctrine logically makes of marriage and the family a purely artificial and civil institution, the outcome of a specific economic system. There exists no matrimonial bond of a juridico-moral nature that is not subject to the whim of the individual or' of the collectivity. Naturally, therefore, the notion of an indissoluble marriage tie is scouted. Communism is particularly characterized by the rejection of any link that binds woman to the family and the home, and her emancipation is proclaimed as a basic principle. She is withdrawn from the family and the care of her children, to be thrust instead into public life and collective production under the same conditions as man. The care of home and children then devotes upon the collectivity. Finally, the right of education is denied to parents, for it is conceived as the exclusive prerogative of the community, in whose name and by whose mandate alone parents may exercise this right.

COMMUNIST SOCIETY

12. What woud be the condition of a human society based on such materialistic tenents? It would be a collectivity with no other hierarchy than

that of the economic system. It would have only one mission: the production of material things by means of collective labor, so that the goods of this world might be enjoyed in a paradise where each would "give according to his powers" and would "receive according to his needs." Communism recognizes in the collectivity the right, or rather, unlimited discretion, to draft individuals for the labor of the collectivity with no regard for their personal welfare; so that even violence could be legitimately execised to dragoon the recalcitrant against their wills. In the Communistic commonwealth morality and law would be nothing but a derivation of the existing economic order, purely earthly in origin and unstable in character. In a word, the Communists claim to inaugurate a new era and a new civilization which is the result of blind evolutionary forces culminating in a humanity without God.

13. When all men have finally acquired the collectivist mentality in this Utopia of a really classless society, the political State, which is now conceived by Communists merely as the instrument by which the proletariat is oppressed by the capitalists, will have lost all reason for its existence and will "wither away." However, until that happy consummation is realized, the State and the powers of the State furnish Communism with the most efficacious and most extensive means for the achievement of its goal.

14. Such, Venerable Bretheren, is the new gospel which bolshevistic and atheistic Communism offers the world as the glad tidings of deliverance and salvation! It is a system full of errors and sophisms. It is in opposition both to reason and to Divine Revelation. It subverts the social order, because it means the destruction of its foundations; because it ignores the true origin and purpose of the State; because it denies the rights, dignity, and liberty of human personality.

Spread of Communism Explained

ALLURING PROMISES

15. How is it possible that such a system, long since rejected scientifically and now proved erroneous by experience, how is it, We ask, that such a system could spread so rapidly in all parts of the world? The explanation lies in the fact that too few have been able to grasp the nature of Communism. The majority instead succumb to its deception, skillfully concealed by the most extravagant promises. By pretending to desire only the betterment of the condition of the working classes, by urging the removal of the very real abuses chargeable to the liberalistic economic order, and by demanding a more equitable distribution of this world's goods (objectives entirely and undoubtedly legitimate), the Communist takes advantage of the present world-wide economic crisis to draw into the sphere of his influence even those sections of the populace which on principle reject all forms of materialism and terrorism. And as every error contains its element of truth, the partial truths to which We have referred are astutely presented according to the needs of time and place, to conceal, when convenient, the

repulsive crudity and inhumanity of Communistic principles and tactics. Thus the Communist ideal wins over many of the better-minded members of the community. These in turn become the apostles of the movement among the younger intelligentsia who are still too immature to recognize the intrinsic errors of the system. The preachers of Communism are also proficient in exploiting racial antagonisms and political divisions and oppositions. They take advantage of the lack of orientation characteristic of modern agnostic science in order to burrow into the universities, where they bolster up the principles of their doctrine with pseudo-scientific arguments.

LIBERALISM PREPARES THE WAY

16. If we would explain the blind acceptance of Communism by so many thousands of workmen, we must remember that the way had been already prepared for it by the religious and moral destitution in which wage-earners had been left by liberal economics. Even on Sundays and holy days, labor-shifts were given no time to attend to their essential religious duties. No one thought of building churches within convenient distance of factories, nor of facilitating the work of the priest. On the contrary, laicism was actively and persistently promoted, with the result that we are now reaping the fruits of the errors so often denounced by Our Predecessors and by Ourselves. It can surprise no one that the Communistic fallacy should be spreading in a world already to a large extent de-Christianized.

SHREWD AND WIDESPREAD PROPAGANDA

17. There is another explanation for the rapid diffusion of the Communistic ideas now seeping into every nation, great and small, advanced and backward, so that no corner of the earth is free from them. This explanation is to be found in a propaganda so truly diabolical that the world has perhaps never witnessed its like before. It is directed from one common center. It is shrewdly adapted to the varying conditions of diverse peoples. It has at its disposal great financial resources, gigantic organizations, international congresses, and countless trained workers. It makes use of pamphlets and reviews, of cinema, theatre, and radio, of schools and even universities. Little by little it penetrates into all classes of the people and even reaches the better-minded groups of the community, with the result that few are aware of the poison which increasingly prevades their minds and hearts.

SILENCE OF THE PRESS

18. A third powerful factor in the diffusion of Communism is the conspiracy of silence on the part of a large section of the non-Catholic press of the world. We say conspiracy, because it is impossible otherwise to explain how a press usually so eager to exploit even the little daily incidents of life has been able to remain silent for so long about the horrors per-

petrated in Russia, in Mexico and even in a great part of Spain; and that it should have relatively so little to say concerning a world organization as vast as Russian Communism. This silence is due in part to short-sighted political policy, and is favored by various occult forces which for a long time have been working for the overthrow of the Christian Social Order.

Sad Consequences

RUSSIA AND MEXICO

19. Meanwhile the sorry effects of this propaganda are before our eyes. Where Communism has been able to asert its power—and here We are thinking with special affection of the people of Russia and Mexico—it has striven by every possible means, as its champions openly boast, to destroy Christian civilization and the Christian religion by banishing every remembrance of them from the hearts of men, especially of the young. Bishops and priests were exiled, condemned to forced labor, shot and done to death in inhuman fashion; laymen suspected of defending their religion were vexed, persecuted, dragged off to trial and thrown into prison.

HORRORS OF COMMUNISM IN SPAIN

20. Even where the scourge of Communism has not yet had time enough to exercise to the full its logical effect, as witness Our beloved Spain, it has, alas, found compensation in the fiercer violence of its attack. Not only this or that church or isolated monastery was sacked, but as far as possble every church and every monastery was destroyed. Every vestige of the Christian religion was eradicated, even though intimately linked with the rarest monuments of art and science. The fury of Communism has not confined itself to the indiscriminate slaughter of Bishops, of thousands of priests, and religious of both sexes; it searches out above all those who have been devoting their lives to the welfare of the working classes and the poor. But the majority of its victims have been laymen of all conditions and classes. Even up to the present moment, masses of them are slain almost daily for no other offense than the fact that they are good Christians or at least opposed to atheistic Communism. And this fearful destruction has been carried out with a hatred and a savage barbarity one would not have believed possible in our age. No man of good sense, nor any statesman conscious of his responsibility can fail to shudder at the thought that what is happening today in Spain may perhaps be repeated tomorow in other civilized countries.

LOGICAL RESULT OF SYSTEM

21. Nor can it be said that these atrocities are a transitory phenomenon, the usual accompaniment of all great revolutions, the isolated excesses common to every war. No, they are the natural fruit of a system which lacks all inner restraint. Some restraint is necessary for man considered either as

an individual or in society. Even the barbaric peoples had this inner check in the natural law written by God in the heart of every man. And where this natural law was held in higher esteem, ancient nations rose to a grandeur that still fascinates—more than it should!—certain superficial students of human history. But tear the very idea of God from the hearts of men, and they are necessarily urged by their passions to the most atrocious barbarity.

STRUGGLE AGAINST ALL THAT IS DIVINE

22. This, unfortunately, is what we now behold. For the first time in history we are witnessing a struggle, cold-blooded in purpose and mapped out to the least detail, between man and "all that is called God." Communism is by its nature anti-religious. It considers religion as "the opiate of the people" because the principles of religion which speak of a life beyond the grave dissuade the proletariat from the dream of a soviet paradise which is of this world.

TERRORISM

23. But the law of nature and its Author cannot be flouted with impunity. Communism has not been able, and will not be able, to achieve its objectives even in the merely economic sphere. It is true that in Russia it has been a contributing factor in rousing men and materials from the intertia of centuries, and in obtaining by all manner of means, often without scruple, some measure of material success. Nevertheless We know from reliable and even recent testimony that not even there, in spite of slavery imposed on millions of men, has Communism reached its promised goal. After all, even the sphere of economics needs some morality, some moral sense of responsibility, which can find no place in a system so thoroughly materialistic as Communism. Terrorism is the only possible substitute, and it is terrorism that reigns today in Russia, where former comrades in revolution are exterminating each other. Terrorism, having failed despite all to stem the tide of moral corruption, cannot even prevent the dissolution of society itself.

FATHERLY CONCERN FOR OPPRESSED RUSSIANS

24. In making these observations it is no part of Our intention to condemn *en masse* the peoples of the Soviet Union. For them We cherish the warmest paternal affection. We are well aware that not a few of them groan beneath the yoke imposed on them by men who in very large part are strangers to the real interests of the country. We recognize that many others were deceived by fallacious hopes. We blame only the system, with its authors and abettors who considered Russia the best-prepared field for experimenting with a plan elaborated decades ago, and who from there continue to spread it from one end of the world to the other.

Muted Socialism:
The Humane Vision of Léon Blum

In many ways Léon Blum (1872–1950) as a man and *For All Mankind* as a work are more important for demonstrating the aspirations of a generation that failed than for documenting a new departure in modern thought.

> Now entertain conjecture of a time
> When creeping murmur and the poring dark
> Fills the wide vessel of this universe.

And then you have Léon Blum, Socialist premier of France (1936–37), seized by Vichy authorities and shortly to be dispatched to the brutality of a Nazi concentration camp. Blum, like Péguy before him, deeply believed in the soul of France and its mystique. Blum was also the heir of Jean Jaurès— the great French revisionary Socialist leader, murdered on the eve of the First World War by his political opponents (a fate Blum narrowly avoided). Blum was an implacable foe of the flaws of his nation but certain of its capacity to overcome them.

The manuscript of *For All Mankind* was smuggled from prison early in 1942. France had fallen. Vichy dictatorship seemed a sordid climax to the degradation of a proud state. An earlier French politician, Adolf Thiers, cynically observed the collapse of the tinsel empire of Napoleon III and remarked, "There are no errors left to commit." Léon Blum might have commented in the same vein, for he understood the moral rot in the French upper classes which sapped the character of the nation. Falling back on mystique, on his infinite faith in the soul of France, Blum saw his nation and the western world rising like the phoenix.

Remembering that Blum was writing a defense of democracy in days of totalitarian ascendancy—remembering, in short, that he had a specific end in view, to counter the effect of Vichy propaganda—much of the naïveté, the groundless optimism, seems less awkward. *For All Mankind*, in spite of patent weaknesses, was a dying generation's hope for the future.

CHAPTER EIGHT

I FULLY REALIZE that to look forward in this way to an international society ruling the world of tomorrow is to arouse not only the facile skepticism of those who, at bottom, are only overcredulous (and who can therefore be left out of accout), but also the perfectly honorable and legitimate feeling that we call patriotism. Patriotic feeling, always more acute and sensitive after a defeat, becomes, by the same fact of defeat, more touchy and more jealous. I can hear the objections that will be put forward: "What! France has not yet arisen from her ruins, her wounds are not yet healed, and you talk about Europe and the world! You invoke all over again the humanitarian softheartedness from which we have suffered so much in the past, and that at a time when our sense of patriotic duty should be our one clear-cut, imperative, and exclusive preoccupation. No! France first, France above all! France's only chance of salvation lies in the egoistic devotion of all her children."

It is true that in our country's misfortune we become more deeply and clearly conscious of the love we all bear her, even though at other times it may go unrecognized within us. It is true that the history of recent years ought to have taught us how to preserve all the natural dignity and vigor of patriotic feeling. And yet I believe that when I try to show that the Europe and the world of tomorrow must be organized within a larger framework than that of the nation if they are not once again to revert to chaos and war, I have said nothing that need offend, injure, or lessen patriotic feeling. I am not suggesting that patriotism must go, that it must give way, as if it were an old-fashioned instinct belonging to a past age and no longer corresponding to the aspirations of the modern mind. Nor do I think that it must be absorbed—which, in effect, means dissipated—in a more general and, if you like, more noble sentiment, such as faith in human solidarity, love of humanity. Love of country is eternal. It is on the same plane as love of family, love of one's native town or village, of all the fundamental realities that in our heart of hearts we hold nearest and dearest. But I am quite sure that there is nothing incompatible between patriotism and humanism—or, if you like, between national and international loyalties. Love of a nation and love of the human race, as one great man once said, can co-exist in the same patriotism and religious belief.

For evidence of this we need look no further than the citizens and soldiers of the Revolution of '89. It was not only their ideal, but their positive and well-considered intention, to set up one comprehensive human society, founded on universal principles. Yet never at any period in our history was patriotism more ardent and unyielding. Never was the soil of France defended with more heroic tenacity. The explanation is simple. It is that the irreducible basic element of any international structure must be free peoples, independent nations. The primary objective of every international community is to guarantee the liberty and independence of the separate nations of which it is made up. Nations will join together and organize themselves in communities, while yet remaining themselves, formed by their particular history and traditions, with their own tastes, preferences, national characteristics, and peculiarities. National characteristics are the necessary constituents of human harmony; they will be respected and, indeed, encouraged within the international organization, just as individual characteristics are preserved within the organization of society. In neither case does the existence of a community require, or even imply, any kind of official or compulsory uniformity. When I look forward to the future Comity of Nations, I cannot help recalling an expression of

Hugo: "I see them," he said, "gathered around the common source of Justice and Peace like sisters round the fireside," sisters of the same blood, but distinguished from one another by their clothes, gestures, accent, and facial expressions. Jaurès once said that while a little internationalism took one further away from patriotism, much internationalism brought one closer to it again. The real meaning of these words, as I understand them, is that the individuality of nations can flower most freely and luxuriantly in the serene atmosphere of peace and comfort which international solidarity carries with it, that men become conscious of its full value only when they can feel its impact in the deepest fibers of their being. I add, and with some pride, that this harmonizing of humanism and patriotism comes more naturally and easily to a Frenchman than to the citizens of any other nation, for it is a French characteristic, as I have already remarked, to understand—as France has always understood and still understands today—the noble urge to think and act for universal causes.

The risk of friction and internal conflict will, no doubt, still exist and will never be completely eliminated. It is not always an easy matter to order even one's personal life and place in proper hierarchy the diverse passions that make up a human character. But an effort of integrity and intelligence can usually find some way of harmonizing them, and that effort will almost always take the form of freeing either patriotism or humanism from the natural impurities that had corrupted it. For there is an instinct, as old as the history of men, akin to the spirit of the tribe or of the clan, which leads us to abandon and almost to condemn every attempt at rationality and objectivity where the relations of our own and other countries are concerned. "I do not need to look further; my country cannot be wrong, because it is my country." Or again: "My country is the natural and predestined leader of others. . . ." This instinct is mistakenly called patriotism, but it can be described accurately only by the pejorative terms of chauvinism and nationalism. It breeds arrogance and hatred, it holds sway in other countries just as it does in our own, and the conflicts between peoples to which it gives rise admit neither of arbitration nor—more important—of reconciliation. Alongside this instinct there is another sentiment, of much more recent origin, for it has developed only under the impetus of certain forms of revolutionary propaganda, that is the exact opposite of chauvinism. In any international dispute its exponents disavow in advance, on *a priori* principles, the attitude and interests of their country. "My country must be wrong, because it is my country." Those who hold such sentiments become alienated from the national community just as surely as the blind nationalists become imprisoned within it. But it would be wrong to describe it as internationalism; for in reality it is no more than inverted nationalism. Any attempt to distinguish real nationalism from chauvinism and real internationalism from inverted nationalism will reveal that the two authentic sentiments are not only compatible, but almost always co-existent. Real patriotism and internationalism both imply a readiness to judge international relations and all the problems arising from them by the criteria of reason and moral principle, which are common to all men, and to do so, not with absolute impartiality—for that would be unnatural—but with an effort to achieve as much impartiality as is humanly possible. And, looking at the problem in this way, no honest man can fail to come to the conclusion that, at the present stage of human evolution, the liberty and the prosperity of one nation are virtually inseparable from those of others, and that love of country cannot, either rationally or emotionally, be separated from certain other beliefs which are vaild for the whole human race.

The foundations of the new world should therefore be laid in this order: within the nation, political democracy will prove its worth and strengthen its position by becoming also a social democracy; together, the national democracies will maintain an international order that completes their structure and keeps a balance between them. When this was has freed humanity from the last convulsions of barbarism and despotism—and that will surely be the meaning and the result of the allied victory—men will have to turn their efforts toward the construction of some world order of this kind. It is in this sense that I interpret the Atlantic Charter, signed by Mr. Winston Churchill and President Roosevelt in the names of the two great Anglo-Saxon powers, and agreed to unreservedly by all the other allied states. The triumph of liberty and justice in war will lead naturally to the organization of liberty and justice in peace. I can see, indeed, no other road for the world to take in its search, either for the satisfaction of its imediate needs or for the attainment of its future security.

I have given careful consideration to the possibility that in expressing this belief in the logic of history, I have perhaps erred on the side of overconfidence or have succumbed to the temptation, to which men who have been in public life are peculiarly prone, to cast the present and the future into the mold of the past. It is true that all that I have done, in outlining this picture of the world of the future, is to return to conceptions more than twenty-five years old, and that all my plans and hopes for the postwar years are merely a repetition of the hopes entertained by my contemporaries at the time of the signing of the Treaty of Versailles—hopes which we showed ourselves, later, unable to realize. Why should the picture be original? While problems remain essentially the same, their solutions cannot be expected to undergo any fundamental modifications either, A generation cannot change at will the nature of the problems with which history is to confront it. On the other hand, it is no less true that progress such as I have outlined assumes peaceful labor, friendly understandings between nations, and a solidarity which approximates union, and I am fully aware that, to many minds, the realities of the future appear in a totally different light. "How," I shall be asked, "can you expect the ordered beauty of classical architecture to spring from a soil that will be torn by popular upheavals, once peace has liberated the forces whose expansion has been so long held in check? No doubt humanity will discover some day an order of its own, but only after an inevitable period of dislocation and chaos and through means very different from the peaceful and considered will of nations! There has been too much misery and suffering, there will remain too much legitimate anger, and none of those can be appeased by the serene contemplation of an ideal! Then again, we shall certainly have to take account of the force of attraction exercised by the Soviet Union and of the natural prestige of a power which, if not the sole conqueror, was certainly the first to check the military might of Germany. We shall have to reckon with the work of propaganda and organization carried out in the face of every kind of danger by the Communist parties of all the occupied countries. Europe cannot escape a revolutionary crises after the war, and it is from this crisis alone and by methods which, like the crisis itself, are essentially revolutionary, that justice and peace can be born." This is the kind of historical development that my arguments would seem to have left entirely out of account. I understand the views of those who think that this is what is most likely to happen, but I cannot share them.

Nor do I hold that war—and particularly a long war—creates a revolutionary situation, that it bring to victor and vanquished alike the opportunity to make a revolution. Twenty-three years ago, in 1918, I found it difficult to accept this mechanical association of the conclusion of a war and the outbreak of a revolution, and today I have still no hesitation in rejecting it. Not that experience or age have deadened my revolutionary ardor. How, indeed, could a profession of revolutionary principles cause alarm to anyone, in an age when everyone, everywhere, including even the most barefaced reactionaries, is labeled "revolutionary"? I reject it because I perceive more and more clearly that the essence of all revolutions lies in their aims and achievements and not in the means by which they obtain their results. Any fundamental change in political structure—and so *a fortiori* in the systems governing production and property—even obtained by eminently legal and peaceful means, is a revolutionary process; violent insurrection, the seizure of power by force of arms, even terror, would be merely unsuccessful attempts at revolution if they did not bring about a clearly marked political or social transformation. Now, war can, in certain circumstances, create conditions favorable to insurrection and to the seizure of power, but it cannot create conditions favorable to revolutionary transfomation. This conclusion reinforces my previous arguments, which gave us grounds for the fear that allied victory would be followed by a Communist propaganda campaign in France in favor of insurrectional violence. The most forcible and urgent collective feelings throughout Europe at that time will doubtless be much simpler than we tend to assume. Men are the same everywhere, and what they want, first and foremost, is the satisfaction of the elementary human needs, material, emotional, and even intellectual, which war does not eliminate, though it makes them seem less important, and for which the coming of peace seems to promise immediate relief.

Men have been separated from their families and forced to leave their homes, and they want to see them again. They have been hungry, and they want to eat their fill. They have been bound and gagged by every kind of violence and they want to live their own lives again and to speak their minds freely. For months and years they suffered from "the world's insomnia"; now they want peace and rest. These are the fundamental feelings that will emerge from the froth of demand, anger, and reprisal. There is only one collective need that a long war can inflame to the point of transforming it into a revolutionary passion, and that is quite simply the need of peace. It was this need that Communism exploited so efficiently, both inside and outside Russia, during the last stages of the last war and during the early postwar period, and that the leaders of the National Revolution did their best to exalt and to exploit before and after the armistice. It exists and will continue to exist for some time after victory has been won. Overtaxed and worn out by war, men will want to be sure— as they did in 1918—that their sacrifice is at least of some benefit to their children. Then it will be the duty of those who have some influence over them to take this potential enthusiasm, to keep it alive, and so prevent it from exhausting itself in impotent convulsion during the period, in all probability short, before it is submerged by habit and routine.

It will not be difficult to convince the peoples of the world that true peace can be built up only on the threefold foundation of political democracy, social democracy, and international order. It is, indeeed, almost mathematically certain that the work of world construction will move toward that goal, for its starting point will be the destruction of the totalitarian dictatorships and it will be controlled by the two greatest democracies in the world. Nor do I think that nations will take long, in the face of the overwhelming evidence, to realize that history is offering them a chance of a fresh start. Material obstacles have collapsed and will crumble at the first onslaught. The political power of the bourgeoisie no longer exists, and its economic power will, in all probability, vanish as soon as it is attacked. In France, and indeed throughout the European continent, the whole bourgeois structure is buried beneath its own ruins. In the great Anglo-Saxon countries the bourgeoisie has already consented to an infusion of new blood that is equivalent to abdication. The winds of history are favorable, and everywhere the workers are conscious of being carried by the tide. But this is where the real difficulty arises. Will they be worthy of their destiny? Will they be able to play the parts for which history has cast them? Will they understand, or can they be made to understand, that favorable material conditions, even if they are overwhelmingly favorable, cannot alone carry them into power, much less keep them there? Can they understand that if, to seize power, they will need both the force and the authority that come from being in harmony with the nature and the trend of economic evolution, they will have no less need of dignity, of the ascendancy, in a word, that comes from moral superiority and efficiency? For a transfer of power to be consolidated and established before history, it must be acceptable to the conscience of mankind no less than to human emotion and to human reason. It must call forth from every sincere man the spontaneous tribute, "It had to be," but not that alone. He must also say, "It is right, it is good, and it is beautiful." Like all other peoples, the French people will fulfill their mission—in other words, they will build the world of their ideals— only if they show themselves able to cultivate and cherish in themselves those virtues that must be present to justify any form of human supremacy, the virtues of courage, generosity of heart, righteousness of mind and conscience, abnegation of self in favor of the good of all.

This is what we should be preaching. This is the task we ought now to be undertaking, and we may have only a short time in which to accomplish it. In human affairs new roads must be taken boldly and quickly. Otherwise there is always the danger that the attraction of the old ruts will be so strong that men will be pulled back almost automatically into them. There is, therefore, not a moment to lose. Above all, it must be borne in mind that the effort will be incomplete and fruitless if it is limited to the sum of individual *examens de conscience*. The ethics of the group—of political, social, and moral groups—are no less real than individual ethics, and it is precisely the organs of collective life that need thorough moral renewal. It is evident, for example, that national democracy would undergo a sea change if the interplay of forces within the nation were not in the future to be judged according to criteria of good faith, integrity, and honor. Democracy everywhere presupposes freedom of action and, consequenly, political conflict. But it does not follow that there are no rules in this civil conflict, that no holds are barred or that its ends justify any means, and this is as true of parties, social groups, and the press as it is of individuals. No advantage won, no plea of necessity, can justify lies, slander, dishonesty, the abuse of force, failure to fulfill obligations or to keep one's word. The argument becomes even stronger if we turn to the international order, for its foundations *must* be the belief in the validity and the sacredness of contracts; if that foundation is lacking, it is built on sand and must collapse. No doubt contracts will still be violated in the international sphere, just as crimes are still committed in civil society. What is essential is that the injured nation shall at least be able to count with certainty on the support of others against the offender. In other words, morality must remain the law and the offending nation the exception.

Moreover, at every stage of this collective life subordination of private interests to those of the community must be recognized as an inescapable obligation and treated as such. Social life would be impossible if the individual did not subordinate his particular and temporary interests to the more general and permanent interests of the group. The difficulty is to secure from political and social groups what is required of the individual— namely, voluntary subordination to the general and permanent interests of humanity. Obstinate partisanship, narrow-minded clannishness, and jingo nationalism are essentially the same as the selfishness of the individual. This renunciation of rivalry and of claims arising from the divergence of immediate interests, this spontaneous surrender to a higher will, this consciousness of permanent contact with and dependence on a higher order of reality extending by stages to embrace the broadest of all concepts, is what Socrates and Plato meant by wisdom and what a Christian thinker like Pascal called humility. But humility of this kind should be a source of strength, and then men should be proud to feel it. In the past men felt that it implied faith and obedience. We must see that it leads to faith and action.

Can it be a Socialist who is putting forward this view? Indeed it can, and one, moreover, who flatters himself that he is being perfectly consistent. The aim of Socialism is to set up a universal society founded on equal justice for all men and on equal peace for all nations. Many means must work together to this end, but no Socialist worthy of the name would claim that the end could be achieved unless human personality is perfected, enriched, and deepened in the process, or unless the spirit of discipline and sacrifice is continually developed and more widely spread. Socialism has never denied either "moral" or "spiritual" values and has never repudiated either the sentiment of virtue or that of honor. All that it has done, like Christianity before it, is to interpret these concepts differently.

Socialism has often been reproached for attracting only the unfortunate multitudes by holding out to them the prospect of what Renan in the last century called "the satisfaction of their purely material needs" and of what we call "jouissances." The suppression of poverty, of the scourges of cold, hunger, and disease, are not "purely material ends." What is there about belief in social justice that could make it more materialist than belief in charity? When a worker demands better wages, he is not thinking of piling his table a little higher with food, but only of a larger and healthier home, of better-clad and better-educated children. Life, family, home, the healthy growth of children, and security in old age are not "material" preoccupations. All the same, if Socialism had restricted itself to demands like these, noble and selfish at the same time, it would not have attracted the mass support it now has. Socialism teaches its followers that their own individual and selfish needs are inextricably related to those of their fellow-men, that their rights and their liberty are inseparable from the rights and the liberty of others. It teaches men that they can satisfy their own needs only together with those of others, by a common effort on the part of all to create a whole as full, coherent, and harmonious as that which obtains in the physical realms of the universe. Socialist philosophy is therefore inseparable from the most comprehensive of human ideals, the belief in the universality of ordered life and human bonds. Jaurès, for instance, always regarded the concept of humanity as the essential principal of all human progress. It afforded a new basis for virtually immutable moral precepts, as well as for ever changing customs and rights and a new raw material for artists and philosophers. The idea of humanity, like that of God in the Middle Ages, could inform all the different aspects of individual life and all forms of social existence. This "complete Socialism" is in no sense of the word a religion, for it has neither dogma nor rites nor priests, but it does appeal to and satisfy the religious urge in men. It teaches its own concepts of what is good and right, encourages the practice of conscientious scruple, and asks its followers to base their conduct on ideals that transcend the sphere of the individual and are their own reward, and it can do so because the assent it receives comes near to the kind of religious faith to which the sacrifice of individual interest is normal and legitimate.

How is it that Socialism has been so misunderstood? How have fair-minded people come so to depreciate ideas that millions of people throughout the world cultivated in their own hearts as the highest of human aspirations? I have already tried to show the extent to which we Socialists must ourselves be held responsible for this misconception which does us so much harm, but I think I can explain in a few words the real reason for the mistake. The development of great human ideas, and even of religions, is influenced as much by the resistance they encouter as by the nature of their own initial impetus. Socialism had first to survive, then to make a niche for itself and to make its way; in order to establish its right to live, it had first to criticize its opponents, and, to protect its early achievements, it had to struggle. Capitalist society, misled by the instinct of self-preservation, treated Socialism as an implacable enemy with which no compromise was possible and which must be overthrown and destroyed without mercy. Attack was held to be the best form of self-defense, and so the pulpit gave way to the battlefield, and battles inevitably call forth all man's most primitive instincts, including fear—on both sides—greed, and intolerance.

This polemical phase now belongs to the past. Socialism can move from the militant to the victorious period. The social system which it attacked and by which it was in turn attacked is now falling into ruin, and even where it still survives does so without belief in itself and in contradiction with its own laws. The men and parties who have most bitterly opposed Socialist assumptions and axioms have now taken them over for their own purposes. Today, whether consciously or not, society is being reconstituted everywhere on principles laid down by the Socialists. Even the Catholic Church, although it has never withdrawn its condemnation of the principles of Socialism, has, in the course of the last fifty years, adopted points of view, particularly on the problems of labor and property, that take it along a road parallel with ours and perhaps even converging with ours, in a way that at least rules out all real incompatibility. In such a situation polemics are almost pointless and conflict baseless. The task of the Socialist movement is now only one of preaching and conversion. Like the Church in those periods of history when its temporal interests dangerously obscured the real pur-

pose for which it existed, it must now rediscover the purity of its initial inspiration.

Does that mean that religious propaganda is one of the tasks of Socialism? In a sense it does. Spinoza said, "If we have a concept of God, every
action that falls within our control must be based on our religion." If for
what Spinoza calls "the concept of God," we substitute the concept of Humanity, of all mankind, of the universe seen as a whole, the statement remains true. There is no doubt that in this form it corresponds to the peculiar
genius of France, whose people have, throughout their history, from the
Crusades to the French Revolution, held that human solidarity and a desire for universalism constituted the highest form of patriotism. This is what
men and nations must teach—I am almost tempted to say preach—if they
are to be worthy of their historic mission. The aim of their mutual efforts
must be to improve man and society, to stimulate and encourage man's
potentialities for good, so that he can make his personal contribution toward
the creation of the best possible society. Now is the time to undertake these
great tasks, when the ground has been prepared by the political crisis which
shook Europe before the war, by the war itself, and by defeat. Hemmed
round as we are by day-to-day responsibilities and anxieties, we are never
optimistic enough in our outlook, for optimism in world affairs demands
appreciation and understanding of the time factor. Who can be sure that
a century or two hence, when philosophers can regard the events of our
time with complete detachment, they will not conclude that even Nazism
and Fascism had some share in the providential march of progress?

Only a short time ago I reread a work of Renan, published only a few
months before the war of 1870, in which he foretold and seemed to hope for
an outbreak of those barbarian forces that he regarded as a kind of latent
residue, a dynamic vitality, that humanity holds perpetually in reserve. If,
he says, these barbarian forces are released, more than that, if they spread
widely over highly civilized countries at a time when their vitality is temporarily exhausted, then the effect may very well be one of stimulation and
renewal. The flood passes, the barbarian elements are driven back to their
Stygian retreats, but the fertility, the renewal, are none the less real and
lasting. I have already explained why I cannot admit that totalitarian barbarism possesses this stimulating the fertilizing virtue. Renan was thinking
of possible historical developments of a totally different kind. He was thinking of the tides of youth and freshness that for thousands of years at periodic
intervals have submerged the known forms of civilization, of the alluvium
spread by the German tribes at the time of the Roman Empire and, in
modern times, by the spread of the Slav and even of the Oriental races. But
he was not thinking, and could never have thought, of looking upon the
destruction of civilization as an ideal, nor of suggesting that one section of
civilized humanity might come deliberately to adopt as its own ideal a
return to primitive savagery. This kind of development is no river bringing
down its fertile mud, but a desert wind that scatters in sterile dust the

strata of soil slowly built up through the ages. Some poisons can cure, but others are always fatal. I therefore refuse categorically to apply Renan's argument to totalitarian dictatorships. But let us assume for a moment, even though the assumptoin is rationally inadmissible, that this barbarian fertilizer has renewed the productive capacity of an exhausted sail. Let us admit that by some historical accident incomprehensible to contemporary minds the plunder of the soil of Europe by Nazism and Fascism has made it possible for the Socialist way of life to come at last to its full flowering in the lives of all men. What a restitution, what a magnificent revenge that would be! It would point to the existence within the universe of a harmony of design that made the *raison d'être* of the totalitarian dictatorships the ultimate emergence in France of that democratic Socialism which is the living and creative element of international democracy!

In the work of Renan to which I have just referred, after emphasizing the "uniqueness" and "decisiveness" of the French Revolution—which he calls "the glory of France, and most French of all epics"—and after claiming that for centuries "the Revolution will divide men and be one of the pretexts of their loves and hates," Renan goes on to add these strangely prophetic words: "Wherever we find, in the history of a nation, some unique event, its cost is almost always a long period of suffering and sometimes the very eclipse of the nation itself. It was so in the case of Judea, of Greece, of Italy. These nations created something unique, in which the human race itself has found life and profit, but they did so only at a cost of centuries of humiliation and of eclipse as nations. The nations that created religion, art, science, the Empire, the Papacy—all of which are universal rather than national creations—were more than nations, but they were also, and by virtue of the same fact, less than nations, in the sense that they were the victims of their own achievement." The word expiation has become familiar to us; we are always being told that our country today is expiating the Revolution of 1789 and the train of errors that has followed it for more than a century! But these claims are no more than vulgar polemics; Renan, who is a historian and a philosopher, uses the term in a way that makes it both nobler and more just.

What France is expiating, in his view, is not a false or evil work, but one which was too fine, too vast, and, above all, too wide in scope for one nation to accomplish alone, and he sees its consequences as a sacrifice rather than an expiation. A nation which was the first to conceive of and to introduce universal truths sacrifices itself to all mankind in so doing. But Renan held that the consequences of this holocaust would not be as lasting in the case of France as they were in those of Judea, Greece, and Italy, precisely because France's revolutionary achievement was less significant and less "universal." He thought that the expiation for the French Revolution would last throughout the nineteenth century, after which, having paid for her noble recklessness, France would rise again, younger and stronger, just as Germany recovered after the period of political decline

which was her way of expiating the Reformation. Renan's calculations
were inaccurate; the expiation lasted half a century longer. Today France
has recovered her former status among nations; now it is her turn to receive the deferred reward for the sacrifice from which the whole of humanity had benefited.

All these reflections must surely combine to justify our confidence, to
give us comfort and encouragement, and to convince us that justice will be
done. If we should ever be tempted to discouragement in the face of the
miseries and evils of our times, then we have only to look beyond the present brief moment of time toward the past and the future; we must learn to
see, beyond the little world of our immediate surroundings, the universe
that is a harmonious whole. This does not mean that immediate tasks are
to be neglected in favor of empty speculation. We are not dreamers; we cannot afford to dream. But this moment will pass, the dictatorships that now
hold Europe in their grip will pass, present sufferings and ills will pass, and
the eternal truths will remain. There is a human destiny which is linked to
the laws of the universe, into which we must write our own brief fate. We
are working *in* the present but not *for* the present. How many times in
public meetings have I quoted these words of Nietzsche: "Let the future
and what it holds in the far distance be your guide today and every day. My
advice to you is to love, not just your neighbor today, but those who will
come long after you." Why should the human race, or the French people,
prove unworthy in the future of all that they have achieved in the past?
Wisdom, science, and art are human creations. Why, then, should the
human race be incapable of creating justice, fraternity, and peace? Humanity produced Plato, Homer, Shakespeare, Hugo, Michelangelo, Beetho-
ven, Pascal, and Newton—all human heroes whose genius lay essentially
in their contact with essential truths, with the central reality of the universe. Why should humanity not produce guides who can lead us forward
toward those forms of social life most in harmony with universal laws?
The social system, like the stellar system, must have its laws of attraction
and gravitation. Man is not a dual personality, with one side of his nature
that sings and learns while the other acts; one that feels beauty and understands truth and another to feel brotherhood and understand justice. Nobody who sees mankind and the universe in this way can fail to be conscious
of an invincible hope. Let man only keep his gaze fixed on his goal, let him
keep his faith in his destiny, let him not shrink from using the strength that
is his, and in times of anxiety and discouragement, let all his thought be for
all mankind.

B. *Cultural, Social, and Economic Distress*

Mind and Culture:
The Psychoanalyst Looks at War

Sigmund Freud, "Thoughts for the Times on War and Death," Collected Papers, authorized translation under the supervision of Joan Riviere (New York: Basic Books, 1959), Vol. IV, Papers on Metapsychology, Papers on Applied Psycho-Analysis, pp. 288–317.

Sigmund Freud, 1865–1939), the father of psychoanalysis, was one of the greatest thinkers of modern times. The strengths and limitations of his psychiatric views were and remain a subject of considerable debate. Freud's thought and teaching ranged far beyond medicine or psychoanalysis. He saw the dangers of overspecialization, the threat that science would forge too far ahead of culture, and he sought the union of the life sciences and natural sciences. There was a place for the psychoanalytic approach in cultural anthropology and sociology. In his great work, *Civilization and Its Discontents* (1930), Freud attempted to come to grips with the problem of civilization and instinctual life.

"Thoughts for the Times on War and Death" was written in 1915 during the First World War. The problems Freud examined are still topical; they are studies of the place of man in culture—what, how, and why he acts as he does. The dislocation of war offered a testing ground for theory. War, by its very nature, peels away most of the layers of civilization from man, for civilization is only achieved by the renunciation of instinctual drives. War— that fault in the fabric of culture—not only permits, it demands the reappearance of savage man. He is neither good nor evil; he merely satisfies primal needs.

Many of Freud's ablest followers would argue the need for more complex reasoning and explanation than Freud allows in "Thoughts for the Times." Many other psychologists and psychiatrists disliked Freud's biological determinism. Environmental factors to which Freud had devoted considerable attention between 1880 and 1900 deserved more weight. But the message of "Thoughts for the Times" was clear; the problems raised still unresolved.

THOUGHTS FOR THE TIMES ON WAR AND DEATH

I

The Disillusionment of the War

Swept as we are into the vortex of this war-time, our information one-sided, ourselves too near to focus the mighty transformations which have already taken place or are beginning to take place, and without a glimmering of the inchoate future, we are incapable of apprehending the significance of the thronging impressions, and know not what value to attach to the judgements we form. We are constrained to believe that never has any event been destructive of so much that is valuable in the common wealth of humanity, nor so misleading to many of the clearest intelligences, nor so debasing to the highest that we know. Science herself has lost her passionless impartiality; in their deep embitterment her servants seek for weapons from her with which to contribute towards the defeat of the enemy. The anthropologist is driven to declare the opponent inferior and degenerate; the psychiatrist to publish his diagnosis of the enemy's disease of mind or spirit. But probably our sense of these immediate evils is disproportionately strong, and we are not entitled to compare them with the evils of other times of which we have not undergone the experience.

The individual who is not himself a combatant—and so a wheel in the gigantic machinery of war—feels conscious of disorientation, and of an inhibition in his powers and activities. I believe that he will welcome any indication, however slight, which may enable him to find out what is wrong with himself at least. I propose to distinguish two among the most potent factors in the mental distress felt by non-combatants, against which it is such a heavy task to struggle, and to treat of them here: the disillusionment which this war has evoked; and the altered attitude towards death which this—like every other war—imposes on us.

When I speak of disillusionment, everyone at once knows what I mean. One need not be a sentimentalist; one may perceive the biological and psychological necessity of suffering in the economics of human life, and yet condemn war both in its means and in its aims, and devoutly look forward to the cessation of all wars. True, we have told ourselves that wars can never cease so long as nations live under such widely differing conditions, so long as the value of individual life is in each nation so variously computed, and so long as the animosities which divide them represent such powerful instinctual forces in the mind. And we were prepared to find that wars between the primitive and the civilized peoples, between those races whom a colour-line divides, nay, wars with and among the undeveloped nationalities of Europe or those whose culture has perished— that for a considerable period such wars would occupy mankind. But we permitted ourselves to have other hopes. We had expected the great ruling powers among the white nations upon whom the leadership of the human species has fallen, who were known to have cultivated world-wide interests, to whose creative powers were due our technical advances in the direction of dominating nature, as well as the artistic and scientific acquisitions of the mind—peoples such as these we had expected to succeed in discovering another way of settling misunderstandings and conflicts of interest. Within each of these nations there prevailed high standards of accepted custom for the individual, to which his manner of life was bound to conform if he desired a share in communal privileges. These ordinances, frequently too stringent, exacted a great deal from him, much self-restraint, much renunciation of instinctual gratification. He was especially forbidden to make use of the immense advantages to be gained by the practice of lying and deception in the competition with his fellow-men. The civilized state regarded these accepted standards as the basis of its existence; stern were its proceedings when an impious hand was laid upon them; frequent the pronouncement that to subject them even to examination by a critical intelligence was entirely impracticable. It could be assumed, therefore, that the state itself would respect them, nor would contemplate undertaking any infringement of what it acknowledged as the basis of its own existence. To be sure, it was evident that within these civilized states were mingled remnants of certain other races who were universally unpopular and had therefore been only reluctantly, and even so not to the fullest extent, admitted to participation in the common task of civilization, for which they had shown themselves suitable enough. But the great nations themselves, it might have been supposed, had acquired so much comprehension of their common interests, and enough tolerance for the differences that existed between them, that 'foreigner' and 'enemy' could no longer, as still in antiquity, be regarded as synonymous.

Relying on this union among the civilized races, countless people have exchanged their native home for a foreign dwelling-place, and made their existence dependent on the conditions of intercourse between friendly nations. But he who was not by stress of circumstances confined to one spot, could also confer upon himself, through all the advantages and attractions of these civilized countries, a new, a wider fatherland, wherein he moved unhindered and unsuspected. In this way he enjoyed the blue sea, and the grey; the beauty of the snow-clad mountains and of the green pasture-lands; the magic of the northern forests and the splendour of the southern vegetation; the emotion inspired by landscapes that recall great historical events, and the silence of nature in her inviolate places. This new fatherland was for him a museum also, filled with all the treasures which the artists among civilized communities had in the successive centuries created and left behind. As he wandered from one gallery to another in this museum, he could appreciate impartially the varied types of perfection that miscegenation, the course of historical events, and the special characteristics of their mother-earth had produced among his more remote compatriots. Here he would find a cool inflexible energy developed to the highest point; there, the gracious art of beautifying existence; elsewhere, the sense of order and fixed law—in short, any and all of the qualities which have made mankind the lords of the earth.

Nor must we forget that each of these citizens of culture had created for himself a personal 'Parnassus' and 'School of Athens'. From among the great thinkers and artists of all nations he had chosen those to whom he conceived himself most deeply indebted for what he had achieved in enjoyment and comprehension of life, and in his veneration had associated them with the immortals of old as well as with the more familiar masters of his own tongue. None of these great figures had seemed to him alien because he had spoken another language—not the incomparable investigator of the passions of mankind, nor the intoxicated worshipper of beauty, nor the vehement and threatening prophet, nor the subtle mocking satirist; and never did he on this account rebuke himself as a renegade towards his own nation and his beloved mother-tongue.

The enjoyment of this fellowship in civilization was from time to time disturbed by warning voices, which declared that as a result of long-prevailing differences wars were unavoidable, even among the members of a fellowship such as this. We refused to believe it; but if such a war indeed must be, what was our imaginary picture of it? We saw it as an opportunity for demonstrating the progress of mankind in communal feeling since the era when the Greek Amphictyones had proclaimed that no city of the league might be demolished, nor its olive-groves hewn down, nor its water cut off. As a chivalrous crusade, which would limit itself to establishing the superiority of one side in the contest, with the least possible infliction of dire sufferings that could contribute nothing to the decision, and with complete immunity for the wounded who must of necessity withdraw from the contest, as well as for the physicians and nurses who devoted themselves to the task of healing. And of course with the utmost precautions for the non-combatant classes of the population— for women who are debarred from war-work, and for the children who, grown older, should be enemies no longer but friends and co-operators. And again, with preservation of all the international undertakings and institutions in which the mutual civilization of peace-time had been embodied.

Even a war like this would have been productive of horrors and sufferings enough; but it would not have interrupted the development of ethical relations between the greater units of mankind, between the peoples and the states.

Then the war in which we had refused to believe broke out, and brought —disillusionment. Not only is it more sanguinary and more destructive than any war of other days, because of the enormously increased perfection of weapons of attack and defence; but it is at least as cruel, as embittered, as implacable as any that has preceded it. It sets at naught all those restrictions known as International Law, which in peace-time the states had bound themselves to observe; it ignores the prerogatives of the wounded and the medical service, the distinction between civil and military sections of the population, the claims of private property. It tramples in blind fury on all that comes in its way, as though there were to be no future and no goodwill among men after it has passed. It rends all bonds of fellowship between the contending peoples, and threatens to leave such a legacy of embitterment as will make any renewal of such bonds impossible for a long time to come.

Moreover, it has brought to light the almost unbelievable phenomenon of a mutual comprehension between the civilized nations so slight that the one can turn with hate and loathing upon the other. Nay, more—that one of the great civilized nations is so universally unpopular that the attempt can actually be made to exclude it from the civilized community as 'barbaric', although it long has proved its fitness by the most magnificent co-operation in the work of civilization. We live in the hope that the impartial decision of history will furnish the proof that precisely this nation, this in whose tongue we now write, this for whose victory our dear ones are fighting, was the one which least transgressed the laws of civilization—but at such a time who shall dare present himself as the judge of his own cause?

Nations are in a measure represented by the states which they have formed; these states, by the governments which administer them. The individual in any given nation has in this war a terrible opportunity to convince himself of what would occasionally strike him in peace-time—that the state has forbidden to the individual the practice of wrong-doing, not because it desired to abolish it, but because it desires to monopolize it, like salt and tobacco. The warring state permits itself every such misdeed, every such act of violence, as would disgrace the individual man. It practises not only the accepted stratagems, but also deliberate lying and deception against the enemy; and this, too, in a measure which appears to surpass the usage of former wars. The state exacts the utmost degree of obedience and sacrifice from its citizens, but at the same time treats them as children by maintaining an excess of secrecy, and a censorship of news and expressions of opinion that renders the spirits of those thus intellectually oppressed defenceless against every unfavourable turn of events and every sinister rumour. It absolves itself from the guarantees and contracts it had formed with other states, and makes unabashed confession of its rapacity and lust for power, which the private individual is then called upon to sanction in the name of patriotism.

Nor may it be objected that the state cannot refrain from wrong-doing, since that would place it at a disadvantage. It is no less disadvantageous, as a general rule, for the individual man to conform to the customs of morality and refrain from brutal and arbitrary conduct; and the state but seldom proves able to indemnify him for the sacrifices it exacts. It cannot be a matter for astonishment, therefore, that this relaxation of all the moral ties between the greater units of mankind should have had a seducing influence on the morality of individuals; for our conscience is not the inflexible judge that ethical teachers are wont to declare it, but in its origin is 'dread of the community' and nothing else. When the community has no rebuke to make, there is an end of all suppression of the baser passions, and men perpetrate deeds of cruelty, fraud, treachery and barbarity so incompatible with their civilization that one would have held them to be impossible.

Well may that civilized cosmopolitan, therefore, of whom I spoke, stand helpless in a world grown strange to him—his all-embracing patrimony disintegrated, the common estates in it laid waste, the fellow-citizens embroiled and debased!

In criticism of his disillusionment, nevertheless, certain things must be said. Strictly speaking, it is not justified, for its consists in the destruction of—an illusion! We welcome illusions because they spare us emotional distress, and enable us instead to indulge in gratification. We must not then complain if now and again they come into conflict with some portion of reality, and are shattered against it.

Two things in this war have evoked our sense of disillusionment: the destitution shown in moral relations externally by the states which in their interior relations pose as the guardians of accepted moral usage, and the brutality in behaviour shown by individuals, whom, as partakers in the highest form of human civilization, one would not have credited with such a thing.

Let us begin with the second point and endeavour to formulate, as succinctly as may be, the point of view which it is proposed to criticize. How do we imagine the process by which an individual attains to a higher plane of morality? The first answer is sure to be: He is good and noble from his very birth, his very earliest beginnings. We need not consider this any further. A second answer will suggest that we are concerned with a developmental process, and will probably assume that this development consists in eradicating from him the evil human tendencies and, under the influence of education and a civilized environment, replacing them by good ones. From that standpoint it is certainly astonishing that evil should show itself to have such power in those who have been thus nurtured.

But this answer implies the thesis from which we propose to dissent. In reality, there is no such thing as 'eradicating' evil tendencies. Psychological—more strictly speaking, psycho-analytic—investigation shows instead that the inmost essence of human nature consists of elemental instincts, which are common to all men and aim at the satisfaction of certain primal needs. These instincts in themselves are neither good nor evil. We but classify them and their manifestations in that fashion, according as they meet the needs and demands of the human community. It is admitted that all those instincts which society condemns as evil—let us take as representatives the selfish and the cruel—are of this primitive type.

These primitive instincts undergo a lengthy process of development before they are allowed to become active in the adult being. They are inhibited, directed towards other aims and departments, become commingled, alter their objects, and are to some extent turned back upon their possessor. Reaction-formations against certain instincts take the deceptive form of a change in content, as though egoism had changed into altruism, or cruelty into pity. These reaction-formations are facilitated by the circumstance that many instincts are manifested almost from the first in pairs of opposites, a very remarkable phenomenon—and one strange to the lay public—which is termed the 'ambivalence of feeling'. The most easily observable and comprehensible instance of this is the fact that intense love and intense hatred are so often to be found together in the same person. Psycho-analysis adds that the conflicting feelings not infrequently have the same person for their object.

It is not until all these 'vicissitudes to which instincts are subject' have been surmounted that what we call the character of a human being is formed, and this, as we know, can only very inadequately be classified as 'good' or 'bad'. A human being is seldom altogether good or bad; he is usually 'good' in one relation and 'bad' in another, or 'good' in certain external circumstances and in others decidedly 'bad'. It is interesting to learn that the existence of strong 'bad' impulses in infancy is often the actual condition for an unmistakable inclination towards 'good' in the adult person. Those who as children have been the most pronounced egoists may well become the most helpful and self-sacrificing members of the community; most of our sentimentalists, friends of humanity, champions of animals, have been evolved from little sadists and animal-tormentors.

The transformation of 'bad' instincts is brought about by two co-operating factors, an internal and an external. The internal factor consists in an influence on the bad—say, the egoistic—instincts exercised by erotism, that is, by the human need for love, taken in its widest sense. By the admixture of *erotic* components the egoistic instincts are transmuted into *social* ones. We learn to value being loved as an advantage for which we are willing to sacrifice other advantages. The external factor is the force exercised by up-bringing, which advocates the claims of our cultural environment, and this is furthered later by the direct pressure of that civilization by which we are surrounded. Civilization is the fruit of renunciation of instinctual satisfaction, and from each new-comer in turn it exacts the same renunciation. Throughout the life of the individual there is a constant replacement of the external compulsion by the internal. The influences of civilization cause an ever-increasing transmutation of egoistic trends into altruistic and social ones, and this by an admixture of erotic elements. In the last resort it may be said that every internal compulsion which has been of service in the development of human beings was originally, that is, in the evolution of the human race, nothing but an external one. Those who are born to-day bring with them as an inherited constitution some degree of a tendency (disposition) towards transmutation of egoistic into social instincts, and this disposition is easily stimulated to achieve that effect. A further measure of this transformation must be accomplished during the life of the individual himself. And so the human being is subject not only to the pressure of his immediate environment, but also to the influence of the cultural development attained by his forefathers.

If we give the name of *cultural adaptability* to a man's personal capacity for transformation of the egoistic impulses under the influence of the erotic, we may further affirm that this adaptability is made up of two parts, one innate and the other acquired through experience, and that the relation of the two to each other and to that portion of the instinctual life which remains untransformed is a very variable one.

Generally speaking, we are apt to attach too much importance to the innate part, and in addition to this we run the risk of overestimating the general adaptability to civilization in comparison with those instincts which have remained in their primitive state—by which I mean that in this way we are led to regard human nature as 'better' than it actually is. For there is, besides, another factor which obscures our judgement and falsifies the issue in too favourable a sense.

The impulses of another person are naturally hidden from our observation. We deduce them from his actions and behaviour, which we trace to motives born of his instinctual life. Such a conclusion is bound to be, in many cases, erroneous. This or that action which is 'good' from the civilized point of view may in one instance be born of a 'noble' motive, in another not so. Ethical theorists class as 'good' actions only those which are the outcome of good impulses; to the others they refuse their recognition. But society, which is practical in its aims, is little troubled on the whole by this distinction; it is content if a man regulates his behaviour and actions by the precepts of civilization, and is little concerned with his motives.

We have seen that the external compulsion exercised on a human being by his up-bringing and environment produces a further transformation towards good in his instinctual life—a turning from egoism towards altruism. But this is not the regular or necessary effect of the external compulsion. Education and environment offer benefits not only in the way of love, but also employ another kind of premium system, namely, reward and punishment. In this way their effect may turn out to be that he who is subjected to their influence will choose to 'behave well' in the civilized sense of the phrase, although no ennoblement of instinct, no transformation of egoistic into altruistic inclinations, has taken place within. The result will, roughly speaking, be the same; only a particular concatenation of circumstances will reveal that one man always acts rightly because his instinctual inclination compels him so to do, and the other is 'good' only in so far and for so long as such civilized behaviour is advantageous for his own egoistic purposes. But superficial acquaintance with an individual will not enable us to distinguish between the two cases, and we are certainly misled by our optimism into grossly exaggerating the number of human beings who have been transformed in a civilized sense.

Civilized society, which exacts good conduct and does not trouble itself about the impulses underlying it, has thus won over to obedience a great many people who are not thereby following the dictates of their own natures. Encouraged by this success, society has suffered itself to be led into straining the moral standard to the highest possible point, and thus it has forced its members into a yet greater estrangement from their instinctual dispositions. They are consequently subjected to an unceasing suppression of instinct, the resulting strain of which betrays itself in the most remarkable phenomena of reaction and compensation formations. In the domain of sexuality, where such suppression is most difficult to enforce, the result is seen in the reaction-phenomena of neurotic disorders. Elsewhere the pressure of civilization brings in its train no pathological results, but is shown in malformations of character, and in the perpetual readiness of the inhibited instincts to break through to gratification at any suitable opportunity. Anyone thus compelled to act continually in the sense of precepts which are not the expression of instinctual inclinations, is living, psychologically speaking, beyond his means, and might objectively be designated a hypocrite, whether this difference be clearly known to him or not. It is undeniable that our contemporary civilization is extraordinarily favourable to the production of this form of hypocrisy. One might venture to say that it is based upon such hypocrisy, and that it would have to submit to far-reaching modifications if people were to undertake to live in accordance with the psychological truth. Thus there are very many more hypocrites than truly civilized persons—indeed, it is a debatable point whether a certain degree of civilized hypocrisy be not indispensable for the maintenance of civilization, because the cultural adaptability so far attained by those living to-day would perhaps not prove adequate to the task. On the other hand, the maintenance of civilization even on so questionable a basis offers the prospect of each new generation achieving a farther-reaching transmutation of instinct, and becoming the pioneer of a higher form of civilization.

From the foregoing observations we may already derive this consolation —that our mortification and our grievous disillusionment regarding the uncivilized behaviour of our world-compatriots in this war are shown to be unjustified. They were based on an illusion to which we had abandoned ourselves. In reality our fellow-citizens have not sunk so low as we feared, because they had never risen so high as we believed. That the greater units of humanity, the peoples and states, have mutually abrogated their moral restraints naturally prompted these individuals to permit themselves relief for a while from the heavy pressure of civilization and to grant a passing satisfaction to the instincts it holds in check. This probably caused no breach in the relative morality within their respective national frontiers.

We may, however, obtain insight deeper than this into the change brought about by the war in our former compatriots, and at the same time receive a warning against doing them an injustice. For the evolution of the mind shows a peculiarity which is present in no other process of development. When a village grows into a town, a child into a man, the village and the child become submerged in the town and the man. Memory alone can trace the earlier features in the new image; in reality the old materials or forms have been superseded and replaced by new ones. It is otherwise with the development of the mind. Here one can describe the state of affairs, which is a quite peculiar one, only by saying that in this case every earlier stage of development persists alongside the later stage which has developed from it; the successive stages condition a co-existence, although it is in reference to the same materials that the whole series of transformations has been fashioned. The earlier mental state may not have manifested itself for years, but none the less it is so far present that it may at any time again become the mode of expression of the forces in the mind, and that exclusively, as though all later developments had been annulled, undone. This extraordinary plasticity of the evolution that takes place in the mind is not unlimited in its scope; it might be described as a special capacity for retroversion—for regression—since it may well happen that a later and higher stage of evolution, once abandoned, cannot be reached again. But the primitive stages can always be re-established; the primitive mind is, in the fullest meaning of the word, imperishable.

What are called mental diseases inevitably impress the layman with the idea of destruction of the life of mind and soul. In reality, the destruction relates only to later accretions and developments. The essence of mental disease lies in a return to earlier conditions of affective life and functioning. An excellent example of the plasticity of mental life is afforded by the state of sleep, which every night we desire. Since we have learnt to interpret even absurd and chaotic dreams, we know that whenever we sleep we cast off our hard-won morality like a garment, only to put it on again next morning. This divestiture is naturally unattended by any danger because we are paralysed, condemned to inactivity, by the state of sleep. Only through a dream can we learn of the regression of our emotional life to one of the earliest stages of development. For instance, it is noteworthy that all our dreams are governed by purely egoistic motives. One of my English friends put forward this proposition at a scientific meeting in America, whereupon a lady who was present remarked that that might be the case in Austria, but she could maintain for herself and her friends that *they* were altruistic even in their dreams. My friend, although himself of English race, was obliged to contradict the lady emphatically on the ground of his personal experience in dream-analysis, and to declare that in their dreams high-minded American ladies were quite as egoistical as the Austrians.

Thus the transformations of instinct on which our cultural adaptability is based, may also be permanently or temporarily undone by the experiences of life. Undoubtedly the influences of war are among the forces that can bring about such regression; therefore we need not deny adaptability for culture to all who are at the present time displaying uncivilized behaviour, and we may anticipate that the refinement of their instincts will be restored in times of peace.

There is, however, another symptom in our world-compatriots which has perhaps astonished and shocked us no less than the descent from their ethical nobility which has so greatly distressed us. I mean the narrow-mindedness shown by the best intellects, their obduracy, their inaccessibility to the most forcible arguments, their uncritical credulity for the most disputable assertions. This indeed presents a lamentable picture, and I wish to say emphatically that in this I am by no means a blind partisan who finds all the intellectual shortcomings on one side. But this phenomenon is much easier to account for and much less disquieting than that which we have just considered. Students of human nature and philosophers have long taught us that we are mistaken in regarding our intelligence as an independent force and in overlooking its dependence upon the emotional life. Our intelligence, they teach us, can function reliably only when it is removed from the influences of strong emotional impulses; otherwise it behaves merely as an instrument of the will and delivers the inference which the will requires. Thus, in their view, logical arguments are impotent against affective interests, and that is why reasons, which in Falstaff's phrase are 'as plenty as blackberries', produce so few victories in the conflict with interests. Psycho-analytic experience has, if possible, further confirmed this statement. It daily shows that the shrewdest persons will all of a sudden behave like imbeciles as soon as the needful insight is confronted by an emotional resistance, but will completely regain their wonted acuity once that resistance has been overcome. The logical infatuations into which this war has deluded our fellow-citizens, many of them the best of their kind, are therefore a secondary phenomenon, a consequence of emotional excitement, and are destined, we may hope, to disappear with it.

Having in this way come to understand once more our fellow-citizens who are now so greatly alienated from us, we shall the more easily endure the disillusionment which the nations, those greater units of the human race, have caused us, for we shall perceive that the demands we make upon them ought to be far more modest. Perhaps they are reproducing the course of individual evolution, and still to-day represent very primitive phases in the organization and formation of higher unities. It is in agreement with this that the educative factor of an external compulsion towards morality, which we found to be so effective for the individual, is barely discernible in them. True, we had hoped that the extensive community of interests established by commerce and production would constitute the germ of such a compulsion, but it would seem that nations still obey their immediate passions far more readily than their interests. Their interests serve them, at most, as rationalizations for their passions; they parade their interests as their justification for satisfying their passions. Actually why the national units should disdain, detest, abhor one another, and that even when they are at peace, is indeed a mystery. I cannot tell why it is. It is just as though when it becomes a question of a number of people, not to say millions, all individual moral acquirements were obliterated, and only the most primitive, the oldest, the crudest mental attitudes were left. Possibly only future stages in development will be able in any way to alter this regrettable state of affairs. But a little more truthfulness and upright dealing on all sides, both in the personal relations of men to one another and between them and those who govern them, should also do something towards smoothing the way for this transformation.

II
Our Attitude towards Death

The second factor to which I attribute our present sense of estrangement in this once lovely and congenial world is the disturbance that has taken place in our attitude towards death, an attitude to which hitherto we have clung so fast.

This attitude was far from straightforward. We were of course prepared to maintain that death was the necessary outcome of life, that everyone owes a debt to Nature and must expect to pay the reckoning—in short, that death was natural, undeniable and unavoidable. In reality, however, we were accustomed to behave as if it were otherwise. We displayed an unmistakable tendency to 'shelve' death, to eliminate it from life. We tried to hush it up; indeed we even have the saying, "To think of something as we think of death'.[1] That is our own death, of course. Our own death is indeed unimaginable, and whenever we make the attempt to imagine it we can perceive that we really survive as spectators. Hence the psycho-analytic school could venture on the assertion that at bottom no one believes in his own death, or to put the same thing in another way, in the unconscious every one of us is convinced of his own immortality.

As to the death of another, the civilized man will carefully avoid speaking of such a possibility in the hearing of the person concerned. Children alone disregard this restriction; unabashed they threaten one another with the eventuality of death, and even go so far as to talk of it before one whom they love, as for instance: 'Dear Mamma, it will be a pity when you are dead but then I shall do this or that.' The civilized adult can hardly even entertain the thought of another's death without seeming to himself hard or evil-hearted; unless, of course, as a physician, lawyer or something of the sort, he has to deal with death professionally. Least of all will he permit himself to think of the death of another if with that event some gain to himself in freedom, means or position is connected. This sensitiveness of ours is of course impotent to arrest the hand of death; when it has fallen, we are always deeply affected, as if we were prostrated by the overthrow of our expectations. Our habit is to lay stress on the fortuitous causation of the death—accident, disease, infection, advanced age; in this way we betray our endeavour to modify the significance of death from a necessity to an accident. A multitude of simultaneous deaths appears to us exceedingly terrible. Towards the dead person himself we take up a special attitude, something like admiration for one who has accomplished a very

[1] [The German saying is used as an equivalent for 'incredible' or 'unlikely'.—Trans.]

difficult task. We suspend criticism of him, overlook his possible misdoings, issue the command: *De mortuis nil nisi bene,* and regard it as justifiable to set forth in the funeral-oration and upon the tombstone only that which is most favourable to his memory. Consideration for the dead, who no longer need it, is dearer to us than the truth, and certainly, for most of us, is dearer also than consideration for the living.

The culmination of this conventional attitude towards death among civilized persons is seen in our complete collapse when death has fallen on some person whom we love—a parent or a partner in marriage, a brother or sister, a child, a dear friend. Our hopes, our pride, our happiness, lie in the grave with him, we will not be consoled, we will not fill the loved one's place. We behave then as if we belonged to the tribe of the Asra, who must die too when those die whom they love.

But this attitude of ours towards death has a powerful effect upon our lives. Life is impoverished, it loses in interest, when the highest stake in the game of living, life itself, may not be risked. It becomes as flat, as superficial, as one of those American flirtations in which it is from the first understood that nothing is to happen, contrasted with a Continental love-affair in which both partners must constantly bear in mind the serious consequences. Our ties of affection, the unbearable intensity of our grief, make us disinclined to court danger for ourselves and for those who belong to us. We dare not contemplate a great many undertakings which are dangerous but quite indispensable, such as attempts at mechanical flight, expeditions to far countries, experiments with explosive substances. We are paralysed by the thought of who is to replace the son with his mother, the husband with his wife, the father with his children, if there should come disaster. The tendency to exclude death from our calculations brings in its train a number of other renunciations and exclusions. And yet the motto of the Hanseatic League declared: '*Navigare necesse est, vivere non necesse*'! (It is necessary to sail the seas, it is not necessary to live.)

It is an inevitable result of all this that we should seek in the world of fiction, of general literature and of the theatre compensation for the impoverishment of life. There we still find people who know how to die, indeed, who are even capable of killing someone else. There alone too we can enjoy the condition which makes it possible for us to reconcile ourselves with death—namely, that behind all the vicissitudes of life we preserve our existence intact. For it is indeed too sad that in life it should be as it is in chess, when one false move may lose us the game, but with the difference that we can have no second game, no return-match. In the realm of fiction we discover that plurality of lives for which we crave. We die in the person of a given hero, yet we survive him, and are ready to die again with the next hero just as safely.

It is evident that the war is bound to sweep away this conventional treatment of death. Death will no longer be denied; we are forced to believe in him. People really are dying, and now not one by one, but many

at a time, often ten thousand in a single day. Nor is it any longer an accident. To be sure, it still seems a matter of chance whether a particular
bullet hits this man or that; but the survivor may easily be hit by another
bullet; and the accumulation puts an end to the impression of accident.
Life has, in truth, become interesting again; it has regained its full significance.

Here a distinction should be made between two groups—those who
personally risk their lives in battle, and those who have remained at home
and have only to wait for the loss of their dear ones by wounds, disease,
or infection. It would indeed be very interesting to study the changes in
the psychology of the combatants, but I know too little about it. We must
stop short at the second group, to which we ourselves belong. I have said
already that in my opinion the bewilderment and the paralysis of energies,
now so generally felt by us, are essentially determined in part by the
circumstance that we cannot maintain our former attitude towards death,
and have not yet discovered a new one. Perhaps it will assist us to do this
if we direct our psychological inquiry towards two other relations with
death—the one which we may ascribe to primitive, prehistoric peoples, and
that other which in every one of us still exists, but which conceals itself,
invisible to consciousness, in the deepest-lying strata of our mental life.

The attitude of prehistoric man towards death is known to us, of course,
only by inferences and reconstruction, but I believe that these processes
have furnished us with tolerably trustworthy information.

Primitive man assumed a very remarkable attitude towards death. It
was far from consistent, was indeed extremely contradictory. On the one
hand, he took death seriously, recognized it as the termination of life and
used it to that end; on the other hand, he also denied death, reduced it to
nothingness. This contradiction arose from the circumstance that he took
up radically different attitudes towards the death of another man, of a
stranger, of an enemy, and towards his own. The death of the other man
he had no objection to; it meant the annihilation of a creature hated, and
primitive man had no scruples against bringing it about. He was, in truth,
a very violent being, more cruel and more malign than other animals. He
liked to kill, and killed as a matter of course. That instinct which is said
to restrain the other animals from killing and devouring their own species
we need not attribute to him.

Hence the primitive history of mankind is filled with murder. Even
to-day, the history of the world which our children learn in school is essentially a series of race-murders. The obscure sense of guilt which has been
common to man since prehistoric times, and which in many religions has
been condensed into the doctrine of original sin, is probably the outcome
of a blood-guiltiness incurred by primitive man. In my book *Totem und
Tabu* (1913) I have, following clues given by W. Robertson Smith,
Atkinson and Charles Darwin, attempted to surmise the nature of this
primal guilt, and I think that even the contemporary Christian doctrine

enables us to deduce it. If the Son of God was obliged to sacrifice his life to redeem mankind from original sin, then by the law of the talion, the requital of like for like, that sin must have been a killing, a murder. Nothing else could call for the sacrifice of a life in expiation. And if the original sin was an offence against God the Father, the primal crime of mankind must have been a parricide, the killing of the primal father of the primitive human horde, whose image in memory was later transfigured into a deity.

His own death was for primitive man certainly just as unimaginable and unreal as it is for any one of us to-day. But there was for him a case in which the two opposite attitudes towards death came into conflict and joined issue; and this case was momentous and productive of far-reaching results. It occurred when primitive man saw someone who belonged to him die—his wife, his child, his friend, whom assuredly he loved as we love ours, for love cannot be much younger than the lust to kill. Then, in his pain, he had to learn that one can indeed die oneself, an admission against which his whole being revolted; for each of these loved ones was, in very truth, a part of his own beloved ego. But even so, on the other hand, such deaths had a rightfulness for him, since in each of the loved persons something of the hostile stranger had resided. The law of ambivalence of feeling, which to this day governs our emotional relations with those whom we love most, had assuredly a very much wider validity in primitive periods. Thus these beloved dead had also been enemies and strangers who had aroused in him a measure of hostile feeling.

Philosophers have declared that the intellectual enigma presented to primitive man by the picture of death was what forced him to reflection, and thus that it became the starting-point of all speculation. I believe that here the philosophers think too philosophically, and give too little consideration to the primarily effective motives. I would therefore limit and correct this assertion: By the body of his slain enemy primitive man would have triumphed, without racking his brains about the enigma of life and death. Not the intellectual enigma, and not every death, but the conflict of feeling at the death of loved, yet withal alien and hated persons was what disengaged the spirit of inquiry in man. Of this conflict of feeling psychology was the direct offspring. Man could no longer keep death at a distance, for he had tasted of it in his grief for the dead; but still he did not consent entirely to acknowledge it, for he could not conceive of himself as dead. So he devised a compromise; he conceded the fact of death, even his own death, but denied it the significance of annihilation,which he had had no motive for contesting where the death of his enemy had been concerned. During his contemplation of his loved one's corpse he invented ghosts, and it was his sense of guilt at the satisfaction mingled with his sorrow that turned these new-born spirits into evil, dreaded demons. The changes wrought by death suggested to him the disjunction of the individuality into a body and a soul—first of all into several souls; in this way his train of thought ran parallel with the process of disintegration which sets in with death. The enduring remembrance of the dead became the basis for assuming other modes of existence, gave him the conception of life continued after apparent death.

These subsequent modes of existence were at first no more than appendages to that life which death had brought to a close—shadowy, empty of content, and until later times but slightly valued; they showed as yet a pathetic inadequacy. We may recall the answer made to Odysseus by the soul of Achilles:

Erst in the life on the earth, no less than a god we revered thee,
We the Achaeans; and now in the realm of the dead as a monarch
Here dost thou rule; then why should death thus grieve thee, Achilles?
Thus did I speak: forthwith then answering thus he addressed me,
Speak not smoothly of death, I beseech, O famous Odysseus,
Better by far to remain on the earth as the thrall of another;
E'en of a portionless man that hath means right scanty of living,
Rather than reign sole king in the realm of the bodiless phantoms.[1]

Or in the powerful, bitterly burlesque rendering by Heine, where he makes Achilles say that the most insignificant little Philistine at Stuckert-on-the-Neckar, in being alive, is far happier than he, the son of Peleus, the dead hero, the prince of shadows in the nether world.

It was not until much later that the different religions devised the view of this after-life as the more desirable, the truly valid one, and degraded the life which is ended by death to a mere preparation. It was then but consistent to extend life backward into the past, to conceive of former existences, transmigrations of the soul and reincarnation, all with the purpose of depriving death of its meaning as the termination of life. So early did the denial of death, which above we designated a convention of civilization, actually originate.

Beside the corpse of the beloved were generated not only the idea of the soul, the belief in immortality, and a great part of man's deep-rooted sense of guilt, but also the earliest inkling of ethical law. The first and most portentous prohibition of the awakening conscience was: Thou shalt not kill. It was born of the reaction against that hate-gratification which lurked behind the grief for the loved dead, and was gradually extended to unloved strangers and finally even to enemies.

This final extension is no longer experienced by civilized man. When the frenzied conflict of this war shall have been decided, every one of the victorious warriors will joyfully return to his home, his wife and his children, undelayed and undisturbed by any thought of the enemy he has slain either at close quarters or by distant weapons of destruction. It is worthy of note that such primitive races as still inhabit the earth, who are undoubtedly closer than we to primitive man, act differently in this respect,

---

[1] *Odyssey*, xi. 484-491; translated by H. B. Cotterill.

or did so act until they came under the influence of our civilization. The savage—Australian, Bushman, Tierra del Fuegan—is by no means a remorseless murderer; when he returns victorious from the war-path he may not set foot in his village nor touch his wife until he has atoned for the murders committed in war by penances which are often prolonged and toilsome. This may be presumed, of course, to be the outcome of superstition; the savage still goes in fear of the avenging spirits of the slain. But the spirits of the fallen enemy are nothing but the expression of his own conscience, uneasy on account of his blood-guiltiness; behind this superstition lurks a vein of ethical sensitiveness which has been lost by us civilized men.

Pious souls, who cherish the thought of our remoteness from whatever is evil and base, will be quick to draw from the early appearance and the urgency of the prohibition of murder gratifying conclusions in regard to the force of these ethical stirrings, which must consequently have been implanted in us. Unfortunately this argument proves even more for the opposite contention. So powerful a prohibition can only be directed against an equally powerful impulse. What no human soul desires there is no need to prohibit; it is automatically excluded. The very emphasis of the commandment *Thou shalt not kill* makes it certain that we spring from an endless ancestry of murderers, with whom the lust for killing was in the blood, as possibly it is to this day with ourselves. The ethical strivings of mankind, of which we need not in the least depreciate the strength and the significance, are an acquisition accompanying evolution; they have then become the hereditary possession of those human beings alive to-day, though unfortunately only in a very variable measure.

Let us now leave primitive man, and turn to the unconscious in our own mental life. Here we depend entirely upon the psycho-analytic method of investigation, the only one which plumbs such depths. We ask what is the attitude of our unconscious towards the problem of death. The answer must be: Almost exactly the same as primitive man's. In this respect, as in many others, the man of prehistoric ages survives unchanged in our unconscious. Thus, our unconscious does not believe in its own death; it behaves as if immortal. What we call our 'unconscious' (the deepest strata of our minds, made up of instinctual impulses) knows nothing whatever of negatives or of denials—contradictories coincide in it—and so it knows nothing whatever of our own death, for to that we can give only a negative purport. It follows that no instinct we possess is ready for a belief in death. This is even perhaps the secret of heroism. The rational explanation for heroism is that it consists in the decision that the personal life cannot be so precious as certain abstract general ideals. But more frequent, in my view, is that instinctive and impulsive heroism which knows no such motivation, and flouts danger in the spirit of Anzengruber's Hans the Road-Mender: 'Nothing can happen to *me*.' Or else that motivation serves but to clear away the hesitation which might delay an heroic reaction in accord with the unconscious. The dread of death which dominates us oftener than we know, is on the other hand something secondary, being usually the outcome of the sense of guilt.

On the other hand, for strangers and for enemies, we do acknowledge death, and consign them to it quite as readily and unthinkingly as did primitive man. Here there does, indeed, appear a distinction which in practice shows for a decisive one. Our unconscious does not carry out the killing; it merely thinks it and wishes it. But it would be wrong entirely to depreciate this psychical reality as compared with actual reality. It is significant and pregnant enough. In our unconscious we daily and hourly deport all who stand in our way, all who have offended or injured us. The expression: 'Devil take him!' which so frequently comes to our lips in joking anger, and which really means 'Death take him!' is in our unconscious an earnest deliberate death-wish. Indeed, our unconscious will murder even for trifles; like the ancient Athenian law of Draco, it knows no other punishment for crime than death; and this has a certain consistency, for every injury to our almighty and autocratic ego is at bottom a crime of *lèse-majesté*.

And so, if we are to be judged by the wishes in our unconscious, we are, like primitive man, simply a gang of murderers. It is well that all these wishes do not possess the potency which was attributed to them by primitive men; in the cross-fire of mutual maledictions mankind would long since have perished, the best and wisest of men and the loveliest and fairest of women with the rest.

Psycho-analysis finds little credence among laymen for assertions such as these. They reject them as calumnies which are confuted by conscious experience, and adroitly overlook the faint indications through which the unconscious is apt to betray itself even to consciousness. It is therefore relevant to point out that many thinkers who could not have been influenced by psycho-analysis have quite definitely accused our unspoken thoughts of a readiness, heedless of the murder-prohibition, to get rid of anyone who stands in our way. From many examples of this I will choose one very famous one:

In *Le Père Goriot*, Balzac alludes to a passage in the works of J. J. Rousseau where that author asks the reader what he would do if—without leaving Paris and of course without being discovered—he could kill, with great profit to himself, an old mandarin in Peking by a mere act of the will. Rousseau implies that he would not give much for the life of this dignitary. *'Tuer son mandarin'* has passed into a proverb for this secret readiness even on the part of ourselves to-day.

There is as well as whole array of cynical jests and anecdotes which testify in the same sense, such as, for instance, the remark attributed to a husband: 'If one of us dies, I shall go and live in Paris.' Such cynical jokes would not be possible unless they contained an unacknowledged verity which could not be countenanced if seriously and baldly expressed. In joke, as we know, even the truth may be told.

As for primitive man, so also for us in our unconscious, there arises a case in which the two contrasted attitudes towards death, that which acknowledges it as the annihilation of life and the other which denies it as ineffectual to that end, conflict and join issue—and this case is the same as in primitive ages—the death, or the endangered life, of one whom we love, a parent or partner in marriage, a brother or sister, a child or dear friend. These loved ones are on the one hand an inner possession, an ingredient of our personal ego, but on the other hand are partly strangers, even enemies. With the exception of only a very few situations, there adheres to the tenderest and closest of our affections a vestige of hostility which can excite an unconscious death-wish. But this conflict of ambivalence does not now, as it did then, find issue in theories of the soul and of ethics, but in neuroses, which afford us deep insight into normal mental life as well. How often have those physicians who practise psycho-analysis had to deal with the symptom of an exaggeratedly tender care for the well-being of relatives, or with entirely unfounded self-reproaches after the death of a loved person. The study of these cases has left them in no doubt about the extent and the significance of unconscious death-wishes.

The layman feels an extraordinary horror at the possibility of such feelings, and takes this repulsion as a legitimate ground for disbelief in the assertions of psycho-analysis. I think, mistakenly. No depreciation of our love is intended, and none is actually contained in it. It is indeed foreign to our intelligence as also to our feelings thus to couple love and hate, but Nature, by making use of these twin opposites, contrives to keep love ever vigilant and fresh, so as to guard it against the hate which lurks behind it. It might be said that we owe the fairest flowers of our love-life to the reaction against the hostile impulse which we divine in our breasts.

To sum up: Our unconscious is just as inaccessible to the idea of our own death, as murderously minded towards the stranger, as divided or ambivalent towards the loved, as was man in earliest antiquity. But how far we have moved from this primitive state in our conventionally civilized attitude towards death!

It is easy to see the effect of the impact of war on this duality. It strips us of the later accretions of civilization, and lays bare the primal man in each of us. It constrains us once more to be heroes who cannot believe in their own death; it stamps the alien as the enemy, whose death is to be brought about or desired; it counsels us to rise above the death of those we love. But war is not to be abolished; so long as the conditions of existence among the nations are so varied, and the repulsions between peoples so intense, there will be, must be, wars. The question then arises: Is it not we who must give in, who must adapt ourselves to them? Is it not for us to confess that in our civilized attitude towards death we are once more living psychologically beyond our means, and must reform and give truth its due? Would it not be better to give death the place in actuality and in our thoughts which properly belongs to it, and to yield a little more prominence to that unconscious attitude towards death which we have hitherto so carefully suppressed? This hardly seems indeed a greater achievement, but rather a backward step in more than one direction, a regression; but it has the merit of taking somewhat more into account the true state of affairs, and of making life again more endurable for us. To endure life remains, when all is said, the first duty of all living beings. Illusion can have no value if it makes this more difficult for us.

We remember the old saying: *Si vis pacem, para bellum.* If you desire peace, prepare for war.

It would be timely thus to paraphrase it: *Si vis vitam, para mortem.* If you would endure life, be prepared for death.

Progress Refuted:
Spengler's World View

Oswald Spengler, "The State. (C) Philosophy of Politics," Perspectives of World-History, trans. Charles Francis Atkinson (New York: Alfred A. Knopf, 1928), Vol. II, The Decline of the West, chap. xii, pp. 439–65.

One effect of the First World War was to reinforce intellectual criticism of nineteenth-century culture and values. Forces of the left and right were fortified by the disgust of intellectuals for nineteenth-century civilization. The carnage and waste of the war reduced ideals to wishful thinking. For many, to be sure, the 1920's were a stumbling search for the certainties of the "good old days." The cataclysm of war made the present unthinkable. Others sought alternatives, indicting the values (particularly the materialism) of the past and suggested or reinforced the move in new directions.

Oswald Spengler (1880–1936) was neither the first nor last to seek for answers in a cosmic philosophy of history. His *Decline of the West* was a product of the First World War. The first version was completed in 1918, the final edition in 1922–23. Commentators have debated the intellectual genealogy of *The Decline*, but it seems evident that Spengler was generally oblivious to Freud's psychology, Pareto's sociology, the work of Sorel and Bergson, the historical system of Croce (even Vico), or the brothers Henry and Brooks Adams save insofar as they were part of the general cultural pattern of the age. Spengler was clearly Nietzsche's disciple, extending his philosophy rather crudely and narrowly to world history. And, in spite of his arguments to the contrary, Spengler was in the tradition of Darwin's popularizers with his "morphological history."

Spengler rejected nineteenth-century materialism and eighteenth-century rationalism, drawing a distinction between culture and civilization. Culture was healthy, dynamic, an evolving organism inspired by a metaphysic. Civilization, on the other hand, being "external and artificial," lacked an inner dynamic. The "life force" was spiritual and philosophical. In Spengler's neoromanticism, "Faustian man," always aspiring and searching, reached his apex in the sixteenth and seventeenth centuries. Sterile rationalism, the triumph of money, popular materialism were hallmarks of decline. While Spengler was a prophet of doom—the new age was to be one of perpetual strife—salvation might be found with revitalized leadership and renewed aristocratic values.

All grand events of history are carried by beings of the cosmic order, by peoples, parties, armies, and classes, while the history of the intellect runs its course in loose associations and circles, schools, levels of education, 'tendencies' and 'isms.' And here again it is a question of destiny whether such aggregates at the decisive moments of highest effectiveness find a leader or are driven blindly on, whether the chance headmen are men of the first order or men of no real significance tossed up, like Robespierre or Pompey, by the surge of events. It is the hall-mark of the statesman that he has a sure and penetrating eye for these mass-souls that form and dissolve on the tide of the times, their strength and their duration, their direction and purpose. And even so, it is a question of incident whether he is one who *can* master them or one who is swept away by them. [Vol. II, p. 19.]

Spengler attempted to apply his broad historical philosophy, one section of which is included here, to the German state. In *Prussianism and Socialism* (1920), he rejected socialism as the crude pursuit of material gain and adulated the eighteenth-century Hohenzollerns as the true socialists and efficient rulers. Conservatives and socialists should therefore unite to overthrow the bourgeois, materialistic Weimar Republic and revive the potential greatness of Faustian man.

CHAPTER XII

THE STATE

(c)

Philosophy of Politics

I

To politics as an idea we have given more thought than has been good for us, since, correspondingly, we have understood all the less about the observation of Politics as a reality. The great statesmen are assustomed to act immediately and on the basis of a sure flair for facts. This is so self-evident, to them, that it simply never enters their heads to reflect upon the basic general principles of their action—supposing indeed that such exist. In all ages they have known what they had to do, and any theory of this knowledge has been foreign to both their capacities and their tastes. But the professional thinkers who have turned their attention to the *faits accomplis* of men have been so remote, inwardly, from these actions that they have just spun for themselves a web of abstractions—for preference, abstraction-myths like justice, virtue, freedom—and then applied them as criteria to past and, especially, future historical happening. Thus in the end they have forgotten that concepts are only concepts, and brought themselves to the conclusion that there is a political science whereby we can form the course of the world according to an ideal recipe. As nothing of the kind has ever or anywhere happened, political doing has come to be considered as so trivial in comparison with abstract thinking that they debate in their books whether there is a "genius of action" at all.

Here, on the contrary, the attempt will be made to give, instead of an ideological system, a *physiognomy* of politics as it has actually been practised in the course of general history, and not as it might or ought to have been practised. The problem was, and is, to penetrate to the final meaning of great events, to "see" them, to fell and to transcribe the symbolically important in them. The projects of world-improvers and the actuality of History have nothing to do with one another.[1]

The being-streams of humanity are called History when we regard them as movement, and family, estate, people, nation, when we regard them as the object moved. Politics is the way in which this fluent Being maintains itself, *grows*, triumphs over other life-streams. *All living is politics*, in every trait of instinct, in the inmost marrow. That which we nowadays like to call life-energy (vitality), the "it" in us that at all costs strives forward and upward, the blind cosmic drive to validity and power that at the same time remains plantwise and racewise, bound up with the earth, the "home"-land; the directedness, the need to actualize—it is this that appears in every higher mankind, as its political life, seeking naturally and inevitably the great decisions that determine whether it shall be, or shall suffer, a Destiny. For it grows or *it dies out*; there is no third possibility.

For this reason the nobility, as expression of a strong race-quality, is the truly political Order, and training and not shaping is the truly political sort of education. Every great politician, a centre of forces in the stream of happening, has something of the noble in his feeling of self-vocation and inward obligation. On the other hand, all that is microcosmic and "intellect" is unpolitical, and so there is a something of priestliness in all program-politics and ideology. The best diplomats are the children; in their play, or when they want something, a cosmic "it" that is bound up in the individual being breaks out immediately and with the sure tread of the sleep-walker. They do not learn, but unlearn, this art of early years as they grow older— hence the rarity in the world of adults of the Statesman.

It is only in and between these being-streams that fill the field of the high Culture that high policy exists. They are only possible, therefore, in the plural. A people *is*, really, only in relation to peoples. But the natural, "race," relation between them is for that very reason a relation of war—this is a fact that no truths avail to alter. War is the primary politics of *everything* that lives, and so much so that in the deeps battle and life are one, and being and will-to-battle expire together. Old Germanic words for this, like "*orusta*" and "*orlog*," mean seriousness and destiny in contrast to jest and play —and the contrast is one of intensity, not of qualitative difference. And even though all high politics tries to be a substitution of more intellectual weapons for the sword and though it is the ambition of the statesman at the culminations of all the Cultures to feel able to dispense with war, yet the primary relationship between diplomacy and the war-art endures. The character of battle is common to both, and the tactics and stratagems, and the necessity of material forces in the background to give weight to the

---

[1] "Empires perish, but a good verse stands," said W. von Humboldt on the field of Waterloo. But, all the same, the personality of Napoleon performed the history of the next century. Good verses!—he should have questioned a peasant by the way-side. They "stand"—for literary teaching. Plato is eternal—for philologists. But Napoleon inwardly rules *us*, all of *us*, our states and our armies, our public opinion, the whole of our political outlook, and the more effectually the less we are conscious of it.

operations. The aim, too, remains the same—namely, the growth of one's own life-unit (class or nation) at the cost of the other's. And every attempt to eliminate the "race" element only leads to its transfer to other ground; instead of the conflict of states we have that of parties, or that of areas, or (if there also the will to growth is extinct) that of the adventurers' retinues, to whose doings the rest of the population unresistingly adjusts itself.

In every war between life-powers the question at issue is which is to govern the whole. It is always a life, never a system, law, or program that gives the beat in the stream of happening.[2] To be the centre of action and effective focus of a multitude, to make the inward form of one's own personality into that of whole peoples and periods, to be history's commanding officer, with the aim of bringing one's own people or family or purposes to the top of events—that is the scarce-conscious but irresistible impulse in every individual being that has a historical vocation in it. There is only *personal* history, and consequently only *personal* politics. The struggle of, not principles but men, not ideals but race-qualities, for executive power is the alpha and omega. Even revolutions are no exception, for the "sovereignty of the people" only expresses the fact that the ruling power has assumed the title of people's leader instead of that of king. The method of governing is scarcely altered thereby, and the position of the governed not at all. And even world-peace, in every case where it has existed, has been nothing but the slavery of an entire humanity under the regimen imposed by a few strong natures determined to rule.

The conception of executive power implies that the life-unit—even in the case of the animals—is subdivided into subjects and objects of government. This is so self-evident that no mass-unit has ever for a moment, even in the severest crises (such as 1789), lost the sense of this inner structure of itself. Only the incumbent vanishes, not the office, and if a people does actually, in the tide of events, lose all leadership and float on haphazard, it only means that control has passed to outside hands, that it has become *in its entirety* the mere object.

Politically gifted *peoples* do not exist. Those which are supposed to be so are simply peoples that are firmly in the hands of a ruling minority and in consequence feel themselves to be in good form. The English as a people are just as unthinking, narrow, and unpractical in political matters as any other nation, but they possess—for all their liking for public debate—a *tradition of confidence*. The difference is simply that the Englishman is the object of a regimen of very old and successful habits, in which he acquiesces because experience has shown him their advantage. From an acquiescence that has the outward appearance of agreement, it is only one step to the conviction that this government depends upon his will, although paradoxically it is the government that, for technical reasons of its own, unceasingly hammers the notion into his head. The ruling class in England has de-

---

[2] This is what is expressed in the English proverb: "Men, not measures," which is the very key to the secrets of all political achievement.

veloped its aims and methods quite independently of the "people," and it works with and within an unwritten constitution of which the refinements —which have arisen from practice and are wholly innocent of theory—are to the uninitiated as opaque as they are unintelligible. But the courage of a troop depends on its confidence in the leadership, and confidence means involuntary abstention from criticism. It is the officer who makes cowards into heroes, or heroes into cowards, and this holds good equally for armies, peoples, classes, and parties. *Political talent in a people* is nothing but confidence in its leading. But that confidence has to be acquired; it will ripen only in its own good time, and success will stabilize it and make it into a tradition. What appears as a lack of the feeling of certainty in the ruled is really lack of leadership-talent in the ruling classes, which generates that sort of uninstinctive and meddlesome criticism which by its very existence shows that a people has got "out of condition."

II

How is politics *done?* The born statesman is above all a valuer—a valuer of men, situations, and things. He has the "eye" which unhesitatingly and inflexibly embraces the round of possibilities. The judge of horses takes in an animal with one glance and knows what prospects it will have in a race. To do the correct thing without "knowing" it, to have the hands that imperceptibly tighten or ease the bit—his talent is the very opposite to that of the man of theory. The secret pulse of all being is one and the same in him and in the things of history. They sense one another, they exist for one another. The fact-man is immune from the risk of practising sentimental or program politics. He does not believe in the big words. Pilate's question is constantly on his lips—truths? The born statesman stands beyond true and false. He does not confuse the logic of events with the logic of systems. "Truths" or "errors"—which here amount to the same—only concern him as intellectual currents, and in resect of *workings.* He surveys their potency, durability, and direction, and duly books them in his calculations for the destiny of the power that he directs. He has convictions, certainly, that are dear to him, but he has them as a private person; no real politician ever felt himself tied to them when in action. "The doer is always conscienceless; no one has a conscience except the spectator," said Goethe, and it is equally true of Sulla and Robespierre as it is of Bismarck and Pitt. The great Popes and the English party-leaders, so long as they had still to strive for the mastery of things, acted on the same principles as the conquerors and upstarts of all ages. Take the dealings of Innocent III, who very nearly succeeded in creating a world-dominion of the Church, and deduce therefrom the catechism of success; it will be found to be in the extremest contradiction with all religious moral. Yet without it there could have been no bearable existence for any Church, not to mention English Colonies, American fortunes, victorious revolutions, or, for that matter, states or parties of peoples in general. It is *life,* not the individual, that is conscienceless.

The essential, therefore, is to understand the time *for* which one is born.
He who does not sense and understand its most secret forces, who does not
feel in himself something cognate that drives him forward on a path neither
hedged nor defined by concepts, who believes in the surface, public opinion,
large phrases and ideals of the day—he is not of the stature for its events.
He is in their power, not they in his. Look not back to the past for measuring-
rods! Still less sideways for some system or other! There are times, like our
own present and the Gracchan age, in which there are two most deadly
kinds of idealism, the reactionary and the democratic. The one believes in
the reversibility of history, the other in a teleology of history. But it makes
no difference to the inevitable failure with which both burden a nation over
whose destiny they have power, whether it is to a memory or to a concept
that they sacrifice it. The genuine statesman is incarnate history, its directedness expressed as individual will and its organic logic as character.

But the true statesman must also be, in a large sense of the word, an educator—not the representative of a moral or a doctrine, but an exemplar in
doing. It is a patent fact that a religion has never yet altered the style of an
existence. It penetrated the waking-consciousness, the *intellectual* man, it
threw new light on another world, it created an immense happiness by way
of humanity, resignation, and patience unto death, but over the forces of
life it possessed no power. In the sphere of the living only the great personality—the "it," the race, the cosmic force bound up in that personality—has
been creative (not shaping, but breeding and training) and has effectively
modified the type of entire classes and peoples. It is not "the" truth or "the"
good or "the" upright, but "the" Roman or "the" Puritan or "the" Prussian
that is a fact. The sum of honour and duty, discipline, resolution, is a thing
not learned from books, but *awakened* in the stream of being by a living
exemplar; and that is why Frederick William I was one of those educators,
great for all time, whose personal race-forming conduct does not vanish in
the course of the generations. The genuine statesman is distinguished from
the "mere politician"—the player who plays for the pleasure of the game,
the *arriviste* on the heights of history, the seeker after wealth and rank—as
also from the schoolmaster of an ideal, by the fact that he dares to demand
sacrifices—*and* obtains them, because his feeling that he is necessary to
the time and the nation is shared by thousands, transforms them to the core,
and renders them capable of deeds to which otherwise they could never
have risen.[3]

Highest of all, however, is not action, but the *ability to command*. It is
this that takes the individual up out of himself and makes him the centre
of a world of action. There is one kind of commanding that makes obedi-

---

[3] The same, too, holds good of the Churches, which are different in kind from the
Religion—namely, elements of the world of facts and, therefore, political and not religious in the type of their leadership. It was not the Christian evangel, but the Christian martyr, who conquered the world, and that which gave him his strength was not
the doctrine, but the example, of the Man on the Cross.

ence a proud, free, and noble habit. That kind Napoleon, for example, did *not* possess. A residue of subaltern outlook in him prevented him from training men to be men and not bureau-personnel, and led him to govern through edicts instead of through personalities; as he did not understand this subtlest tact of command and, therefore, was obliged to do everything really decisive himself, he slowly collapsed from inability to reconcile the demands of his position with the limit of human capabilities. But one who, like Caesar or Frederick the Great, possesses this last and highest gift of complete humanity feels—on a battle-evening when operations are sweeping to the willed conclusion, and the victory is turning out to be conclusive of the campaign; or when the last signature is written that rounds off a historical epoch—a wondrous sense of power that the man of truths can never know. There are moments—and they indicate the maxima of cosmic flowings—when the individual feels himself to be identical with Destiny, the centre of the world, and his own personality seems to him almost as a covering in which the history of the future is about to clothe itself.

The first problem is to make oneself somebody; the second—less obvious, but harder and greater in its ultimate effects—*to create a tradition,* to bring on others so that one's work may be continued with one's own pulse and spirit, to release a current of like activity that does not need the original leader to maintain it in form. And here the statesman rises to something that in the Classical world would doubtless have been called divinity. He becomes the creator of a new life, the *spirit*-ancestor of a young race. He himself, as a unit, vanishes from the stream after a few years. But a minority called into being by him takes up his course and maintains it indefinitely. This cosmic something, this soul of a ruling stratum, an individual *can* generate and leave as a heritage, and throughout history it is this that has produced the durable effects. The great statesman is rare. Whether he comes, or wins through, too soon or too late, incident determines. Great individuals often destroy more than they have built up—by the gap that their death makes in the flow of happening. But *the creation of tradition means the elimination of the incident.* A tradition breeds a high average, with which the future can reckon—no Caesar, but a Senate, no Napoleon, but an incomparable officer-corps. A strong tradition attracts talents from all quarters, and out of small gifts produces great results. The schools of painting of Italy and Holland are proof of this, no less than the Prussian army and the diplomacy of the Roman Curia. It was the great flaw in Bismarck, as compared with Frederick William I, that he could achieve, but could not form a tradition; that he did not parallel Moltke's officer-corps by a corresponding race of politicans who would identify themselves in feeling with his State and its new tasks, would constantly take up good men from below and so provide for the continuance of the Bismarckian action-pulse for ever. If this creation of a tradition does not come off, then instead of a homogeneous ruling stratum we have a congeries of heads that are helpless when confronted by the unforeseen. If it does, we have a *Sovereign People* in the one sense of the phrase that is worthy of a people and possible in the world of fact—a highly trained, self-replenishing minority with sure and slowly ripened traditions, which attracts every talent into the charmed circle and uses it to the full, and *ipso facto* keeps itself in harmony with the remainder of the nation that it rules. Such a minority slowly developes into a true "breed," even when it had begun merely as a party, and the sureness of its decisions comes to be that of blood, not of reason. But this means that what happens in it happens "of itself" and does not need the Genius. *Great politics, so to put it, takes the place of the great politician.*

What, then, *is* politics? It is the art of the possible—an old saying, and almost an all-inclusive saying. The gardener can obtain a plant from the seed, or he can improve its stock. He can bring to bloom, or let languish, the dispositions hidden in it, its growths and colour, its flower and fruit. On his eye for possibilities—and, therefore, necessities—depends its fulfilment, its strength, its whole Destiny. But the basic form and direction of its being, the stages and tempo and direction thereof, are *not* in his power. It must accomplish them or it decays, and the same is true of the immense plant that we call a "Culture" and the being-streams of human families that are bound up in its form-world. The great statesman is the gardener of a people.

Every doer is born in a time and for a time, and thereby the ambit of *his* attainable achievement is fixed. For his grandfather, for his grandson, the data, and therefore the task and the object, are not the same. The circle is further narrowed by the limits of his personality, the properties of his people, the situation, and the men with whom he has to work. Is it the hallmark of the high politician that he is rarely caught out in a misappreciation of this limit, and equally rarely overlooks anything realizable within it. With this—one cannot too often repeat, especially to Germans—goes a sure discrimination between what "ought" to be and what *will* be. The basic forms of the state and of political life, the direction and the degree of their evolution, are given values unalterably dependent on the given time. They are the track of political success and not its goal. On the other hand the worshippers of political ideals create out of nothing. Their intellectual freedom is astounding, but their castles of the mind, built of airy concepts like wisdom and righteousness, liberty and equality, are in the end all the same; they are built from the top storey downwards. The master of fact, for his part, is content to direct imperceptibly that which he sees and accepts as plain reality. This does not seem very much, yet it is the very starting-point of freedom, in a grand sense of the word. The knack lies in the little things, the last careful touch of the helm, the fine sensing of the most delicate oscillations of collective and individual souls. The art of the statesman consists not only in a clear idea of the main lines drawn undeviably before him, *but also* in the sure handling of the single occurrences and the single persons, encountered along those lines, which can turn an impending disaster into a decisive success. The secret of all victory lies in the organization of the non-obvious. An adept in the game can, like Talleyrand, go to Vienna as ambassador of the vanquished party and make himself master of the victor.

At the Lucca meeting, Caesar, whose position was wellnigh desperate, not only made Pompey's power serviceable to his own ends, but undermined it at the same time, and without his opponent's becoming aware of the fact. But the domain of the possible has dangerous edges, and if the finished tact of the great Baroque diplomatists almost always managed to keep clear, it is the very privilege of the ideologues to be always stumbling over it. There have been turns in history in which the statescraftman has let himself drift with the current awhile, in order not to lose the leadership. Every situation has its elastic limit, and in the estimation of that limit not the smallest error is permissible. A revolution that reaches explosion-point is always a proof of lack of the political pulse in the governors *and* in their opponents.

Further, the necessary must be done *opportunely*—namely, while it is a present wherewith the governing power can buy confidence in itself, whereas if it has to be conceded as a sacrifice, it discloses a weakness and excites contempt. Political forms are living forms whose changes inexorably follow a definite direction, and to attempt to prevent this course or to divert it towards some ideal is to confess oneself "out of condition." The Roman nobility possessed this congruence of pulse, the Spartan did not. In the period of mounting democracy we find again and again (as in France before 1789 and Germany before 1918) the arrival of a fatal moment when it is too late for the necessary reform to be given as a free gift; *then* that which should be refused with the sternest energy is given as a *sacrifice*, and so becomes the sign of dissolution. But those who fail to detect the first necessity in good time will all the more certainly fail to misunderstand the second situation. Even a journey to Canossa can be made too soon or too late—the timing may settle the future of whole peoples, whether they shall be Destiny for others, or themselves the objects of another's Destiny. But the declining democracy also repeats the same error of trying to hold what was the ideal of yesterday. This is the danger of our twentieth century. On the path towards Caesarism there is ever a Cato to be found.

The influence that a statesman—even one in an exceptionally strong position—possesses over the *methods* of politics is very small, and it is one of the characteristics of the high-grade statesman that he does not deceive himself on this matter. His task is to work in and with the historical form that he finds in existence; it is only the theorist who enthusiatically searches for more ideal forms. But to be politically "in form" means necessarily, amongst other things, an unconditional *command of the most modern means*. There is no choice about it. The means and methods are premisses pertaining to the time and belong to the inner form of the time—and one who grasps at the inapposite, who permits his taste or his feelings to overpower the pulse in him, loses at once his grip of realities. The danger of an aristocracy is that of being conservative in its means, the danger of a democracy is the confusion of formula and form. The means of the present are, and will be for many years, parliamentary—elections and the press. He may think what he pleases about them, he may respect them or despise them, but he *must command them.* Bach and Mozart *commanded* the musical means of their times. This is the hall-mark of mastery in any and every field, and statecraft is no exception. Now, the publicly visible outer form thereof is not the essential but merely the disguise, and consequently it may be altered, rationalized, and brought down to constitutional texts—without its actualities being necessarily affected in the slightest—and hence the ambitions of all revolutionaries expend themselves in playing the game of rights, principles, and franchises on the surface of history. But the states-man knows that the extension of a franchise is quite unimportant in com-parison with the technique—Athenian or Roman, Jacobin or American or present-day German—of *operating* the votes. How the English constitution reads is a matter of small import compared with the fact that it is managed by a small stratum of high families, so that an Edward VII is simply a minister of his Ministry. And as for the modern Press, the sentimentalist may beam with contentment when it is constitutionally "free"—but the realist merely asks at whose disposal it is.

Politics, lastly, is the form in which is accomplished the history of a nation within a plurality of nations. The great art is to maintain ones' own nation inwardly "in form" for events outside; this is the natural relation of home and foreign politics, holding not only for Peoples and States and Es-tates, but for living units of every kind, down to the simplest animal swarms and down into the individual bodies. And, as between the two, *the first exists exclusively for the second and not vice versa.* The true democrat is accustomed to treat home politics as an end in itself; the rank and file of diplomats think solely of foreign affairs; but just because of this the indi-vidual successes of either "cut no ice." No doubt, the political master ex-hibits his powers most obviously in the tactics of home reform; in his eco-nomic and social activities; in his cleverness in maintaining the public form of the whole, the "rights and liberties," both in tune wth the tastes of the period and *at the same time* effective; and in the education of the feelings without which it is impossible for a people to be "in condition"—namely, trust, respect for the leading, consciousness of power, contentment, and (when necessary) enthusiasm. But the value of all this depends upon its relation to this basic fact of higher history—that a people is not alone in the world, and that its future will be decided by its force-relationships towards other peoples and powers and not by its mere internal ordering. And, since the ordinary man is not so long-sighted, it is the ruling minority that must possess this quality on behalf of the rest, and not unless there is such a minority does the stateman find the instrument wherewith he can carry his purposes into effect.[4]

---

[4] It should scarcely need to be emphasized that this is the basic principle, not of an aristocratic régime, but of government itself. Cleon, Robespierre, Lenin, every gifted mass-leader, has treated his office thus. Anyone who genuinely felt himself as the dele-gate of the multitude, instead of as the regent of such as do not know what they want, would not remain master of his house for one day. The only question is whether the great popular leaders apply their powers for their own benefit or for that of others; and on that much might be said,

III

In the early politics of all Cultures the governing powers are pre-established and unquestioned. The whole being is strictly in patriarchal and symbolic form. The connexions with the mother soil are so strong, the feudal tie, and even its successor the aristocratic state, so self-evident to the life held in their spell, that politics in a Homeric or Gothic age is limited to plain action within the cadre of the given forms. In so far as these forms change, they do so more or less spontaneously, and the idea that it is a *task* of politics to bring about the changes never definitely emerges into anyone's mind, even if a kingdom be overthrown or a nobility reduced to subjection. There is only class-politics, Imperial- or Papal- or vassal-politics. Blood and race speak in actions undertaken instinctively or half-consciously —even the priest behaves, *qua* politician, as the man of race. The "problems" of the State are not yet awakened. The sovereignty, the primary orders, the entire early form-world, are God-given, and it is on them as premisses, not about them as objects of dispute, that the organic minorities fight their battles. These minorities we call *Factions*.

It is of the essence of the Faction that it is wholly inaccessible to the idea that the order of things can be changed to a plan. Its object is to win for itself status, power, or possessions within this order—like all growing things in a growing world. There are groups in which relationships of houses, honour and loyalty, bonds of union of almost mythic inwardness, play a part, and from which abstract ideas are totally excluded. Such were the factions of the Homeric and Gothic periods, Telemachus and the suitors in Ithaca, the Blues and Greens under Justinian, the Guelphs and Ghibellines, the House of Lancaster and York, the Protestants, the Huguenots, and even later the motive forces of Fronde and First Tyrannis. Machiavelli's book rests entirely on this spirit.

The change sets in as soon as, with the great city, the Non-Estate, the bourgeoisie, takes over the leading rôle. Now it is the reverse, the political *form* becomes the object of conflict, the problem. Heretofore it was ripened, now it must needs be shaped. Politics becomes awake, not merely comprehended, but reduced to comprehensible ideas. The powers of intellect and money set themselves up against blood and tradition. In place of the organic we have the organized; *in place of the Estate, the Party*. A party is not a growth of race, but an aggregate of heads, and therefore as superior to the old estates in intellect as it is poorer in instinct. It is the mortal enemy of naturally matured class-ordering, the mere existence of which is in contradiction with its essence. Consequently, the notion of party is always bound up with the unreservedly negative, disruptive, and socially levelling notion of *equality*. Noble ideals are no longer recognized, but only vocational interests.[5] It is the same with the freedom-idea, which is likewise a

---

[5] Hence it is that on the soil of burgher equality the possession of money immediately takes the place of genealogical rank.

negative. *Parties are a purely urban phenomenon.* With the emancipation of the city from the country, everywhere (whether we happen to know it evidentially or not) Estate politics gives way to party politics—in Egypt at the end of the Middle Kingdom, in China with the Contending States, in Baghdad and Byzantium with the Abbassid period. In the capitals of the West the parties form in the parliamentary style, in the city-states of the Classical they are forum-parties, and we recognize parties of the Magian style in the Mavali and the monks of Theodore of Studion.

But always it is the Non-Estate, the unit of protest against the essence of Estate, whose leading minority—"educated" and "well-to-do"—comes forward as a party with a program, consisting of aims that are not felt but defined, and of the rejection of everything that cannot be rationally grasped. *At bottom, therefore, there is only one party,* that of the bourgeoisie, the liberal, and it is perfectly conscious of its position as such. It looks on itself as coextensive with "the people." Its opponents (above all, the genuine Estates—namely, "squire and parson") are enemies and traitors to "the people," and its opinions are the "voice of the people"—which is inoculated by all the expedients of party-political nursing, oratory in the Forum, press in the West, until these opinions do fairly represent it.

The prime Estates are nobility and priesthood. The prime Party is that of money and mind, the liberal, the megalopolitan. Herein lies the profound justification, in *all* Cultures, of the ideas of Aristocracy and Democracy. Aristocracy despises the mind of the cities, Democracy despises the boor and hates the countryside.[6] It is the difference between Estate politics and party politics, class-consciousness and party inclination, race and intellect, growth and construction. Aristocracy in the completed Culture, and Democracy in the incipient cosmopolitan Civilization, stand opposed till both are submerged in Caesarism. As surely as the nobility is *the* Estate (and the Tiers État never manages to get itself into real form in this fashion), so surely the nobility fails to feel as a party, though it may organize itself as one.

It has in fact no choice but to do so. All modern constitutions repudiate the Estates and are built on the Party as self-evidently the basic form of politics. The nineteenth century—correspondingly, therefore, the third century B.C.—is the heyday of party politics. Its democratic character compels the formation counter-parties, and whereas formerly, as late even as the eighteenth century, the "Tiers" constituted itself in imitation of the nobility as an Estate, now there arises the *defensive* figure of the Conservative party, copied from the Liberal,[7] dominated completely by the latter's

[6] It is an important factor in the democracy of England and America that in the first the yeomanry had died out and in the second has never existed. The "farmer" is spiritually a suburban and in practice carries on his farming as an industry. Instead of villages, there are only fragments of megalopolis.

[7] And wherever, as in Egypt, India, and the West, there exists a *political* opposition between the two primary Estates, there is also a clerical party—the party, 50 to speak, of the Church as distinct from religion and of the priest as distinct from the believer.

forms, bourgeois-ized without being bourgeois, and obliged to fight with rules and methods that liberalism has laid down. It has the choice of handling these means better than its adversary[8] or of perishing; but it is of the intimate structure of an Estate that it does not understand the situation and challenges the form instead of the foe, and is thus involved in that use of extreme methods which we see dominating the inner politics of whole states in the early phases of every Civilization, and delivering them help- less into the hands of the enemy. The compulsion that there is upon every party to be bourgeois, at any rate in appearance, turns to sheer caricature when below the bourgeoisie of education and possessions the Residue also organizes itself as a party. Marxism, for example, is in theory a negation of burgeoisie, but as a party it is in attitude and leadership essentially middle- class. There is a continuous conflict between its will—which necessarily steps outside the bounds of party politics and therefore of constitutionalism (both being exclusively liberal phenomena), and can in honesty only be called civil war—and the appearances which it feels obliged, in justice to itself, to keep up. But for Marxism, again, these appearances are in- dispensable, at this particular period, if durable success is to be attained. A noble party in a parliament is inwardly just as spurious as a proletarian. Only the bourgeoisie is in its natural place there.

In Rome, from the introduction of the Tribunes, in 471, to the recogni- tion of their legislative omnipotence, in the revolution of 287, patricians and plebians had fought their fight essentially as Estates, classes. But thereafter these opposite terms possessed hardly more than genealogical significance, and there developed instead parties, to which the terms liberal and con- servative respectively may quite reasonably be applied—namely, the Populus,[9] supreme in the forum, and the nobility, with its fulcrum in the Senate. The latter had transformed itself (about 287) from a family council of the old clans into a state council of the administrative aristocracy. The associations of the Populus are with the property-graded Comitia Centuriata and the big-money group of the Equites, those of the nobility with the yeomanry that was influential in the Comitia Tributa. Think on the one hand of the Gracchi and Marius, and on the other of C. Flaminius, and a little penetration will disclose the complete change in the position of the Consuls and the Tribunes. They are no longer the chosen trustees of the first and third Estates, with lines of conduct determined by that fact, but they represent party, and on occasion change it. There were "liberal" con- suls like the Elder Cato and "conservative" Tribunes like the Octavius who opposed Ti. Gracchus. Both parties put up candidates at elections, and used

---

[8] And with its content of race-strength it has an excellent chance of successfully doing so.

[9] *Plebs* corresponds to the "Tiers" (burghers and yeomen) of the eighteenth century, *populus* to the megalopolitan masses of the nineteenth. The difference manifested itself in their respective attitudes towards the freed slaves, mostly of non-Italian origin. These the Plebs, as an order, sought to thrust away into as few tribes as possible, but in the Populus as a party they very soon came to play the decisive rôle.

every sort of demagogic operation to get them in—and when money had failed to win an election, it got to work afterwards with (increasing) success upon the person elected.

In England Tories and Whigs constituted themselves, from the beginning of the nineteenth century, as parties, both becoming in form bourgeois and both taking up the liberal program literally, whereby public opinion as usual was completely convinced and set at rest. This was a master-stroke, delivered at the correct moment, and prevented the formation of a party hostile to the Estate-principle such as arose in France in 1789. The members of the lower House, hitherto emissaries of the ruling stratum, became popular representatives, but still continued to depend financially upon it. The leading remained in the same hands, and the opposition of the parties, which from 1830 assumed the titles of Liberal and Conservative almost as a matter of course, was always one of pluses and minuses, never of blank alternatives. In these same years the literary freedom-movement of "young Germany" changed into a party-movement, and in America under Andrew Jackson the National-Whig and Democratic parties organized themselves as opposites, and open recognition was given to the principle that elections were a business, and state offices from top to bottom the "spoils of the victors."[10]

But the form of the governing minority *develops steadily from that of the Estate, through that of the Party, towards that of the Individual's following.* The outward sign of the end of Democracy and its transition into Caesarism is not, for example, the disappearance of the party of the Tiers État, the Liberal, but the disappearance of party itself as a form. The sentiments, the popular aim, the abstract ideals that characterize all genuine party politics, dissolve and are supplanted by *private* politics, the unchecked will-to-power of the race-strong few. An Estate has instincts, a party has a program, but a following has a master. That was the course of events from Patricians and Plebeians, through Optimates and Populares, to Pompeians and Caesarians. The period of real party government covers scarcely two centuries, and in our own case is, since the World War, well on the decline. That the entire mass of the electorate, actuated by a common impulse, should send up men who are capable of managing their affairs— which is the naïve assumption in all constitutions—is a possibility only in the first rush, and presupposes that not even the rudiments of organization by definite groups exists. So it was in France in 1789 and in 1848. An assembly has only to *be*, and tactical units will form at once within it, whose

---

[10] Simultaneously, too, the Roman Catholic Church quietly changed the basis of its politics from a class to a party, and did so with a strategic sureness that cannot be too much admired. In the eighteenth century it had been, as regards the style of its diplomacy, the allocation of its offices and the spirit of its higher circles, aristocratic through and through. Think of the type of the abbé, and of the prince-prelates who became ministers and ambassadors, like the young Cardinal Rohan. Now, in the true liberal fashion, opinions took the place of origins, working-power that of taste, and the great weapons of democracy—press, elections, money—were handled with a skill that liberalism proper rarely equalled and never surpassed.

cohesion depends upon the will to *maintain* the dominant position once won, and which, so far from regarding themselves as the mouthpieces of their constituents, set about making all the expedients of agitation amenable to their influence and usable for their purposes. A tendency that has organized itself in the people, has already *ipso facto* become the *tool* of the organization, and continues steadily along the same path until the organization also becomes in turn the tool of the leader. The will-to-power is stronger than any theory. In the beginning the leading and the apparatus come into existence for the sake of the program. Then they are held on to defensively by their incumbents for the sake of power and booty—as is already universally the case to-day, for thousands in every country live on the party and the offices and functions that it distributes. Lastly the program vanishes from memory, and the organization works for its own sake alone.

With the elder Scipoior Quinctius Flamininus comradeship on campaign is still the implication when we speak of their "friends." But the younger Scipio went further and his "Cohors Amicorum" was no doubt the first example of an organized following whose activity extended to the law-courts and the elections. In the same way the old purely *patriarchal and aristocratic relation of loyalty* between patron and client evolved into a community of interest based on very material foundations, and even before Caesar there were written compacts between candidates and electors with specific provisions as to payment and performances. On the other side, just as in present-day America, clubs and election committees were formed, which so controlled or frightened the mass of the electors of their wards as to be able to do election business with the great leaders, the pre-Caesars, as one power with another. Far from this being the shipwreck of democracy, it is its very meaning and necessary issue, and the lamentations of unworldly idealists over this destruction of their hopes only show their blind ignorance of the inexorable duality of truths and facts and of the intimate linkage of intellect and money.

Politico-social theory is only one of the bases of party politics, but it is a necessary one. The proud series that runs from Rousseau to Marx has its anti-type in the line of the Classical Sophists up to Plato and Zeno. In the case of China the characteristics of the corresponding doctrines have still to be extracted from Confucian and Taoist literature; it suffices to name the Socialist Moh-ti. In the Byzantine and Arabian literature of the Abbassid period—in which radicalism, like everything else, is orthodox-religious in constitution—they hold a large place, and they were driving forces in all the crises of the ninth century. That they existed in Egypt and in India also is proved by the spirit of events in the Hyksos time and in Buddha's. Literary form is not essential to them—they are just as effectively disseminated by word of mouth, by sermon and propaganda in sects and associations, which indeed is the standard method at the close of the Puritan movements (Islam an Anglo-American Christianity amongst them).

Whether these doctrines are "true" or "false" is—we must reiterate and emphasize—a question without meaning for political history. The refutation of, say, Marxism belongs to the realm of academic dissertation and public debates, in which everyone is always right and his opponents always wrong. But whether they are *effective*—from when, and for how long, the belief that actuality can be ameliorated by a system of concepts is a real force that politics must reckon with—that does matter. We of to-day find ourselves in a period of boundless confidence in the omnipotence of reason. Great general ideas of freedom, justice, humanity, progress are sacrosanct. The great theories are gospels. Their power to convince does not rest upon logical premisses, for the mass of a party possesses neither the critical energy nor the detachment seriously to test them, but upon the sacramental hypostasis in their keywords. At the same time, the spell is limited to the population of the great cities and the period of Rationalism as the "educated man's religion." On a peasantry it has no hold, and even on the city masses its effect lasts only for a certain time. But *for* that time it has all the irresistibleness of a new revelation. They are converted to it, hang fervently upon the words and the preachers thereof, go to martyrdom on barricades and battle-field and gallows; their gaze is set upon a political and social other-world, and dry sober criticism seems base, impious, worthy of death.

But for this very reason documents like the *Contrat Social* and the *Communist Manifesto* are engines of highest power in the hands of forceful men who have come to the top in party life and know how to form and to use the convictions of the dominated masses.

The power that these abstract ideals possess, however, scarcely extends in time beyond the two centuries that belong to party politics, and their end comes not from refutation, but from boredom—which has killed Rousseau long since and will shortly kill Marx. Men finally give up, not this or that theory, but the belief in theory of any kind and with it the sentimental optimism of an eighteenth century that imagined that unsatisfactory actualities could be improved by the application of concepts. When Plato, Aristotle, and their contemporaries defined and blended the various kinds of Classical constitution so as to obtain a wise and beautiful resultant, all the world listened, and Plato himself tried to transform Syracuse in accordance with an idealogical recipe—and sent the city downhill to its ruin. It appears to me equally certain that it was philosophical experimentation of this kind that put the Chinese southern states out of condition and delivered them up to the imperialism of Tsin. The Jacobin fanatics of liberty and equality delivered France, from the Directory onward, into the hands of Army and Bourse for ever, and every Socialistic outbreak only blazes new paths for Capitalism. But when Cicero wrote his *De re publica* for Pompey, and Sallust his two comminations for Caesar, nobody any longer paid attention. In Tiberius Gracchus we may discover perhaps an influence derived from the Stoic enthusiast Blossius, who later committed suicide after having similarly brought Aristonicus of Pergamum to ruin;[11] but in the first century B.C. theories had become a threadbare school-exercise, and thenceforward power and power alone mattered.

For us, too—let there be no mistake about it—the age of theory is draw-ing to its end. The great systems of Liberalism and Socialism all arose between about 1750 and 1850. That of Marx is already half a century old, and it has had no successor. Inwardly it means, with its materialist view of history, that Nationalism has reached its extreme logical conclusion; it is therefore an end-term. But, as belief in Rousseau's Rights of Man lost its force from (say) 1848, so belief in Marx lost its force from the World War. When one contrasts the devotion unto death that Rousseau's ideas found in the French Revolution with the attitude of the Socialists of 1918, who had to keep up before and in their adherents a conviction that they themselves no longer possessed—for the sake, not of the idea, but of the power that de-pended on it—one discerns also the stretches of the road ahead, where what still remains of program is doomed to fall by the way as being henceforth a mere handicap in the struggle for power. Belief in program was the mark and the *glory* of our grandfathers—in our grandsons it will be a proof of provincialism. In its place is developing even now the seed of a new re-signed piety, sprung from tortured conscience and spiritual hunger, whose task will be to found a new Hither-side that looks for secrets instead of steel-bright concepts and in the end will find them in the deeps of the "Second Religiousness."

IV

This is the one side, the verbal side, of the great fact Democracy. It re-mains now to consider the other, the decisive side, that of race. Democracy would have remained in minds and on paper had there not been amongst its champions true master-natures for whom—unconscious though they may be, and often have been, of the fact—the people is nothing but an object and the ideal nothing but a means. All, even the most irresponsible, methods of demagogy—which inwardly is exactly the same as the diplo-macy of the *ancien régime,* but designed for application to masses instead of to princes and ambassadors, to wild opinions and sentiments and will-out-bursts instead of to choice spirits, an orchestra of brass instead of old chamber-music—have been worked out by honest but practical democrats, and it was from them that the parties of tradition learnt them.

It is characteristic, however, of the course of democracy, that the authors of popular constitutions have never had any idea of the actual workings of their schemes—neither the authors of the "Servian" Constitution in Rome nor the National Assembly in Paris. Since these forms of theirs are not, like

---

[11] For this "Sun-state" formed of slaves and day-labourers see Pauly-Wissowa, *Realencyel.,* 2, 961. Similarly, the revolutionary King Cleomenes III of Sparta was like-wise under the influence of a Stoic, Sphaerus. One can understand why "philosophers and rhetors"—i.e., professional politicians, fantastics and subverters—were expelled again and again by the Roman Senate.

feudalism, the result of growth, but of thought (and based, moreover, not on deep knowledge of men and things, but on abstract ideas of right and justice), a gulf opens between the intellectual side of the laws and—the practical habits that silently form under the pressure of them, and either adapt them to, or fend them off from, the rhythm of actual life. Only experience has ever taught the lesson, and only at the end of the whole development has it been assimilated, that the rights of the people and the influence of the people are two different things. The more nearly universal a franchise is, the *less* becomes the power of the electorate.

In the beginning of a democracy the field belongs to intellect alone. History has nothing nobler and purer to show than the night session of the 4th August 1789 and the Tennis-Court Oath, or the assembly in the Frankfurt Paulskirche on the 18th May 1848—when men, with power in their very hands, debated general truths so long that the forces of actuality were able to rally and thrust the dreamers aside. But, meantime, that other democratic quantity lost no time in making its appearance and reminding men of the fact that one can make use of constitutional rights only when one has money.[12] That a franchise should work even approximately as the idealist supposes it to work presumes the absence of any organized leadership operating on the electors (in *its* interest) to the extent that its available money permits. As soon as such leadership does appear, the vote ceases to possess anything more than the significance of a censure applied by the multitude to the individual organizations, over whose structure it possesses in the end not the slightest positive influence. So also with the ideal thesis of Western constitutions, the fundamental right of the mass to choose its own representatives—it remains pure theory, for in actuality every developed organization recruits itself. Finally the feeling emerges that the universal franchise contains no effective rights at all, not even that of choosing between parties. For the powerful figures that have grown up on their soil control, through money, all the intellectual machinery of speech and script, and are able, on the one hand, to guide the individual's opinions as they please *above* the parties, and, on the other, through their patronage, influence, and legislation, to create a firm body of whole-hearted supporters (the "Caucus") which excludes the rest and induces in it a vote-apathy which at the last it cannot shake off even for the great crises.

In appearance, there are vast differences between the Western, parliamentary, democracy and the democracies of the Egyptian, Chinese, and Arabian Civilizations, to which the idea of a universal popular franchise is wholly alien. But in reality, for us in this age of ours, the mass is "in form" as an *electorate* in exactly the same sense as it used to be "in form" as a

---

[12] The early democracy, which in our case reaches up to Lincoln, Bismarck, and Gladstone, has to learn this by *experience*. The later democracy, in our case mature parliamentarism, starts out from it; here truths and facts finally separate out in the form of party ideals and party funds. It is the money that gives the real parliamentarian his sense of being freed from the dependence which is implicit in the naïve idea that the elector has of his delegate.

collectivity of obedience—namely, as an *object for a subject*—as it was "in form" in Baghdad as the sects, and in Byzantium in its monks, and elsewhere again as a dominant army or a secret society or a "state within a state." Freedom is, as always, purely *negative*. It consists in the repudiation of tradition, dynasty, Caliphate; but the executive power passes, at once and undiminished, from these institutions to new forces—party leaders, dictators, presidents, prophets, and their adherents—towards which the multitude continues to be unconditionally the passive object.[13] "Popular self-determination" is a courteous figure of speech—in reality, under a universal-inorganic franchise, election has soon ceased to possess its original meaning. The more radical the political elimination of the matured old order of Estates and callings, the more formless and feckless the electoral mass, the more completely is it delivered into the hands of the new powers, the party leaders, who dictate their will to the people through all the machinery of intellectual compulsion; fence with each other for primacy by methods which in the end the multitude can neither perceive nor comprehend; and treat public opinion merely as a weapon to be forged and used for blows at each other. But this very process, viewed from another angle, is seen as an irresistible tendency driving every democracy further and further on the road to suicide.[14]

The fundamental rights of a Classical people (demos, populus) extended to the holding of the highest state and judicial offices.[15] For the exercise of these the people was "in form" in its Forum, where the Euclidean point-mass was corporeally assembled, and there it was the object of an influencing process in the Classical style; namely, by bodily, near, and sensuous means—by a rhetoric that worked upon every ear *and eye;* by devices many of which to us would be repellent and almost intolerable, such as rehearsed sob-effects and the rending of garments;[16] by shameless flattery of the audi-

---

[13] That the mass of the same *feels* itself as freed is simply another outcome of the profound incompatibility between megalopolitan spirit and mature tradition. Its *acts*, so far from being independent, are in inward relation with its subjection to money-rule.

[14] The German Consitution of 1919—standing by virtue of its date on the verge of the *decline* of democracy—most naïvely admits a dictature of the party machines, which have attracted all rights into themselves and are seriously responsible to no one. The notorious system of proportional election and the Reichslist [see *Ency. Brit.*, 1922 Supplement, II, 249.—*Tr.*] secures their self-recruitment. In place of the "people's" rights, which were axiomatic in the Frankfurt Constitution of 1848, there is now only the right of parties, which, harmless as it sounds, really nurses within itself a Caesarism of the organizations. It must be allowed, however, that in this respect it is the most advanced of all the constitutions. Its issue is visible already. A few quite small alterations and it confers unrestricted power upon individuals.

[15] And *legislation*, too, was bound up with an office. Even when, as a formality, acceptance or rejection by an assembly was requisite, the law in question could be brought in only by an official; for example, a Tribune. The constitutional demands of the masses, therefore (which in any case were mostly instigated by the real power-holders), expressed themselves in the issue of the elections to office, as the Gracchan period shows.

[16] Even Caesar, at fifty years of age, was obliged to play this comedy at the Rubicon for his soldiers because they were used to it and expected it when anything was asked of them. It corresponds to the "chest-tones of deep conviction" of our political assemblies.

ence, fantastic lies about opponents; by the employment of brilliant phrases and resounding cadenzas (of which there came to be a perfect repertory for this place and purpose) by games and presents; by threats and blows; but, above all, by money. We have its beginnings in the Athens of 400,[17] and its appalling culmination in the Rome of Caesar and Cicero. As everywhere, the elections, from being nominations of class-representatives, have become the battle-ground of party candidates, an arena ready for the intervention of money, and, from Zama onwards, of ever bigger and bigger money. "The greater became the wealth which was capable of concentration in the hands of individuals, the more the fight for political power developed into a question of money." It is unnecessary to say more. And yet, in a deeper sense, it would be wrong to speak of corruption. It is not a matter of degeneracy, it is the democratic ethos itself that is foredoomed of necessity to take such forms when it reaches maturity. In the reforms of the Censor Appius Claudius (310), who was beyond doubt a true Hellenist and constitutional ideologue of the type of Madame Roland's circle, there was certainly no question but that of the franchise as such, and not at all of the arts of gerrymandering—but the effect was simply to prepare the way for those arts. Not in the scheme as such, but from the first applications of it, race-quality emerged, and very rapidly it forced its way to complete dominance. And, after all, in a dictatorship of money it is hardly fair to describe the employment of money as a sign of decadence.

The career of office in Rome from the time when its course took form as a series of elections, required so large a capital that every politician was the debtor of his entire entourage. Especially was this so in the case of the ædileship, in which the incumbent had to outbid his predecessors in the magnificence of his public games, in order later to have the votes of the spectators. (Sulla failed in his first attempt on the praetorship precisely because he had not previously been aedile.) Then again, to flatter the crowd of loafers it was necessary to show oneself in the Forum daily with a brilliant following. A law forbade the maintenance of paid retainers, but the acquisition of persons in high society by lending them money, recommending them for official and commercial employments, and covering their litigation expenses, in return for their company in the Forum and their attendance at the daily levee, was more expensive still. Pompey was *patronus* to half the world. From the peasant of Picenum to the kings of the Orient, he represented and protected them all, and this was his political capital which he could stake against the non-interest-bearing loans of Crassus and the "gilding" of every ambitious fellow by the conqueror of Gaul. Dinners were offered to the electors of whole wards, or free seats for the gladiatorial shows, or even (as in the case of Milo) actual cash, delivered at home—out of respect, Cicero says, for traditional morals. Election-capital rose to American dimensions, sometimes hundreds of millions of sesterces; vast as was the stock of cash available in Rome, the elections of 54 locked up so

[17] But the Cleon type must obviously have existed also in contemporary Sparta, and in Rome at the time of the Consular Tribunes.

much of it that the rate of interest rose from four to eight per cent. Caesar paid out so much as aedile that Crassus had to underwrite him for twenty millions before his creditors would allow him to depart to his province, and in his candidature for the office of Pontifex Maximus he so overstrained his credit that failure would have ruined him, and his opponent Catulus could seriously offer to buy him off. But the conquest and exploitation of Gaul—this also an undertaking motived by finance—made him the richest man in the world. In truth, Pharsalus was won there in advance.[18] For it was for *power* that Caesar amassed these milliards, like Cecil Rhodes, and not because he delighted in wealth like Verres or even like Crassus, who was first and foremost a financier and only secondarily a politician. Caesar grasped the fact that on the soil of a democracy constitutional rights signify nothing without money and everything with it. When Pompey was still dreaming that he could evoke legions by stamping on the ground, Caesar had long since condensed the dream to reality with his money. It must be clearly understood, however, that he did not introduce these methods but found them in existence, that he made himself master of them but never identified himself with them. For practically a century parties grouped on principles had been dissolving into personal followings grouped upon men who pursued private political aims and were expert in handling the political weapons of their time.

Amongst these means, besides money, was influence upon the courts. Since Classical assemblies voted, but did not debate, the trial before the rostra was *a form of party battle* and the school of schools for political persuasiveness. The young politician began his career by indicting and if possible annihilating some great personage, as the nineteen-year-old Crassus annihilated the renowned Papirius Carbo, the friend of Gracchi, who had later gone over to the Optimates. This was why Cato was tried no less than forty-four times, though acquitted in every case. The legal side of the question was entirely subordinate in these affairs.[19] The decisive factors

[18] For from that time sesterces flowed through his hands by the million. The votive treasures of the Gallic temples which he put up for sale in Italy sent down the value of gold with a rush. From King Ptolemy he and Pompey exorted 144,000,000 (and Gabinius another 240,000,000) as the price of recognition. The Consul Aemilius Paullus (50) was bought for 36,000,000, Curio for 60,000,000. We can guess from such figures how enviable was the position of his closer associates. At the triumph of 46 every soldier in an army of well over 100,000 men received 24,000 sesterces, officers and other leaders much more. Yet at his death the state treasury was still full enough to secure Antony's position.

[19] Extortion and corruption were the usual charges. As in those days these things were identical with politics, and the judges and plaintiffs had acted precisely in the same way as the defendants, the art consisted in using the forms of a well-acted ethical passion to cover a party speech, of which the real import was only comprehensible to the initiated. This corresponds entirely with the modern parliamentary usage. The "people" would be very much astonished to see party opponents, after delivering wild speeches in the chamber (for the reporters) chatting together in the lobbies, or to be told how a party passionately champions a proposal after it has made certain by agreement with the other side that it will not be passed. In Rome, too, the judgment was not the important thing in these "trials"; it was enough if a defendant voluntarily left the city and so retired from the occupancy of, or candidature for, office.

were the party affinities of the judges, the number of patrons, and the size of the crowd of backers—the number of the witnesses was really only paraded in order to bring the financial and political power of the plaintiff into the limelight. The intention in all Cicero's oratory against Verres was to convince the judges, under the veil of fine ethical passion, that the condemnation of the accused was *in the interests of their order*. Given the general outlook of the Classical, the courts self-evidently existed to serve private and party interests. Democratic complainants in Athens were accustomed at the end of their speeches to remind the jurymen from the people that they would forfeit their fees by acquitting the wealthy defendant. The tremendous power of the Roman Senate consisted mainly in their occupancy of every seat of the judicial (jurors') bench, which placed the destinies of every citizen at their mercy; hence the far-reachingness of the Gracchan law of 122 which handed over the judicature to the Equites and delivered over the nobility—that is, the official class—to the financial world. In 83 Sulla, simultaneously with his proscription of the financial magnates, restored the judicature to the Senate, *as political weapon*, of course, and the final duel of the potentates finds one more expression in the ceaseless changing of the judges selected.

Now, whereas the Classical, and supremely the Forum of Rome, drew the mass of the people together as a visible body in order to compel it to make that use of its rights which was desired of it, the "contemporary" English-American politics have created *through the press* a force-field of world-wide intellectual and financial tensions in which every individual unconsciously takes up the place allotted to him, so that he must think, will, and act as a ruling personality somewhere or other in the distance thinks fit. This is dynamics against statics, Faustian against Apollinian world-feeling, the passion of the third dimension against the pure sensible present. Man does not speak to man; the press and its associate, the electrical news-service, keep the waking-consciousness of whole peoples and continents under a deafening drum-fire of theses, catchwords, standpoints, scenes, feelings, day by day and year by year, so that every Ego becomes a mere function of a monstrous intellectual Something. Money does not pass, politically, from one hand to the other. It does not turn itself into cards and wine. It is turned into *force*, and its quantity determines the intensity of its working influence.

Gunpowder and printing belong together—both discovered at the culmination of the Gothic, both arising out of Germanic technical thought—as *the two* grand means of Faustian distance-tactics. The Reformation in the beginning of the Late period witnessed the first flysheets and the first field-guns, the French Revolution in the beginning of the Civilization witnessed the first tempest of pamphlets of the autumn of 1788 and the first mass-fire of artillery at Valmy. But with this the printed word, produced in vast quantity and distributed over enormous areas, became an uncanny weapon in the hands of him who knew how to use it. In France it was still in 1788 a matter of expressing private convictions, but England was already past that, and deliberately seeking to produce impressions on the reader. The war of articles, flysheets, spurious memoirs, that was waged from London on French soil against Napoleon is the first great example. The scattered sheets of the Age of Enlightenment transformed themselves into "the Press"—a term of most significant anonymity. Now the *press campaign* appears as the prolongation—or the preparation—of war by other means, and in the course of the nineteenth century the strategy of outpost fights, feints, surprises, assaults, is developed to such a degree that a war may be lost ere the first shot is fired—because the Press has won it meantime.

To-day we live so cowed under the bombardment of this intellectual artillery that hardly anyone can attain to the inward detachment that is required for a clear view of the monstrous drama. The will-to-power operat-ing under a pure democratic disguise has finished off its masterpiece so well that the object's sense of freedom is actually flattered by the most thorough-going enslavement that has ever existed. The liberal bourgeois mind is *proud* of the abolition of censorship, the last restraint, while the dictator of the press—Northcliffe!—keeps the slave-gang of his readers under the whip of his leading articles, telegrams, and pictures. *Democracy has by its newspaper completely expelled the book from the mental life of the people.* The book-world, with its profusion of standpoints that compelled thought to select and criticize, is now a real possession only for a few. The people reads the *one* paper, "its" paper, which forces itself through the front doors by millions daily, spellbinds the intellect from morning to night, drives the book into oblivion by its more engaging layout, and if one or another specimen of a book does emerge into visibility, forestalls and eliminates its possible effects by "reviewing" it.

What is truth? For the multitude, that which it continually reads and hears. A forlorn little drop may settle somewhere and collect grounds on which to determine "the truth"—but what it obtains is just *its* truth. The other, the public truth of the moment, which alone matters for effects and successes in the fact-world, is to-day a product of the Press. What the Press wills, is true. Its commanders evoke, transform, interchange truths. Three weeks of press work, and the truth is acknowledged by everybody.[20] Its bases are irrefutable for just so long as money is available to maintain them intact. The Classical rhetoric, too, was designed for effect and not content—as Shakespeare brilliantly demonstrates in Antony's funeral oration—but it did limit itself to the bodily audience and the moment. What the dynamism of our Press wants is *permanent* effectiveness. It must keep men's minds continuously under its influence. Its arguments are overthrown as soon as the advantage of financial power passes over to the counter-argu-

[20] The most striking example of this for future generations will be the "War-guilt" question, which is the question—*who* possesses the power, through control of press and cable in all parts of the world, to establish in world-opinion that truth which he needs for his political ends and to maintain it for so long as he needs? An altogether different question (which only in Germany is confused with the first) is the purely scientific one—to *whose* interest was it that an event about which there was already a whole literature should occur in the summer of 1914 in particular?

ments and brings these still oftener to men's eyes and ears. At that moment the needle of public opinion swings round to the stronger pole. Everybody convinces himself at once of the new truth, and regards himself awakened out of error.

With the political press is bound up the need of universal school-education, which in the Classical world was completely lacking. In this demand there is an element—quite unconscious—of desiring to shepherd the masses, as the object of party politics, into the newspaper's power-area. The idealist of the early democracy regarded popular education, without *arrière pensée*, as enlightenment pure and simple, and even to-day one finds here and there weak heads that become enthusiastic on the Freedom of the Press—but it is precisely this that smooths the path for the coming Caesars of the world-press. Those who have learnt to read succumb to their power, and the visionary self-determination of Late democracy issues in a thorough-going determination of the people by the powers whom the printed word obeys.

In the contests of to-day tactics consists in depriving the opponent of this weapon. In the unsophisticated infancy of its power the newspaper suffered from official censorship which the champions of tradition wielded in self-defence, and the bourgeoisie cried out that the freedom of the spirit was in danger. Now the multitude placidly goes its way; it has definitely won for itself this freedom. But in the background, unseen, the new forces are fighting one another by buying the press. Without the reader's observing it, the paper, *and himself with it,* changes masters.[21] Here also money triumphs and forces the free spirits into its service. No tamer has his animals more under his power. Unleash the people as reader-mass and it will storm through the streets and hurl itself upon the target indicated, terrifying and breaking windows; a hint to the press-staff and it will become quiet and go home. The Press to-day is an army with carefully organized arms and branches, with journalists as officers, and readers as soldiers. But here, as in every army, the soldier obeys blindly, and war-aims and operation-plans change without his knowledge. The reader neither knows, nor is allowed to know, the purposes for which he is used, nor even the rôle that he is to play. A more appalling caricature of freedom of thought cannot be imagined. Formerly a man did not dare to think freely. Now he dares, but cannot; his will to think is only a willingness to think to order, and this is what he feels as *his* liberty.

And the other side of this belated freedom—it is permitted to everyone to say what he pleases, *but* the Press is free to take notice of what he says or not. It can condemn any "truth" to death simply by not undertaking its communication to the world—a terrible censorship of silence, which is all the

---

[21] In preparation for the World War the press of whole countries was brought financially under the command of London and Paris, and the peoples belonging to them reduced to an unqualified intellectual slavery. The more democratic the inner form of a nation is, the more readily and completely it succumbs to this danger. This is the style of the twentieth century. To-day a democrat of the old school would demand, not freedom for the press, but freedom from the press; but mean-time the leaders have changed themselves into parvenus who have to secure their position *vis-à-vis* the masses.

more potent in that the masses of newspaper readers are absolutely unaware that it exists. Here, as ever in the birth-pangs of Caesarism, emerges a trait of the buried springtime. The arc of happening is about to close on itself. Just as in the concrete and steel buildings the expression-will of early Gothic once more bursts forth, but cold, controlled, and Civilized, so the iron will of the Gothic Church to power over souls reappears as—the "freedom of democracy." The age of the "book" is flanked on either hand by that of the sermon and that of the newspaper. Books are a personal expression, sermon and newspaper obey an impersonal *purpose*. The years of Scholasticism afford the only example in world-history of an intellectual discipline that was applied universally and permitted no writing, no speech, no thought to come forth that contradicted the *willed* unity. This is spiritual dynamics. Classical, Indian, or Chinese mankind would have been horrified at this spectacle. But the same things recur, and as a *necessary* result of the European-American liberalism—"the despotism of freedom against tyranny," as Robespierre put it. In lieu of stake and faggots there is the great silence. The dictature of party leaders supports itself upon that of the Press. The competitors strive by means of money to detach readers—nay, peoples—*en masse* from the hostile allegiance and to bring them under their own mind-training. And all that they learn in this mind-training, is what it is considered that they should know—a higher will puts together the picture of their world for them. There is no need now, as there was for Baroque princes, to impose military-service liability on the subject—one whips their souls with articles, telegrams, and pictures (Northcliffe!) until they *clamour* for weapons and force their leaders into a conflict to which they *willed* to be forced.

This is the end of Democracy. If in the world of truths it is *proof* that decides all, in that of facts it is *success*. Success means that one being triumphs over the others. Life has won through, and the dreams of the world-improvers have turned out to be but the tools of *master*-natures. In the Late Democracy, *race* bursts forth and either makes ideals its slaves or throws them scornfully into the pit. It was so, too, in Egyptian Thebes, in Rome, in China—but in no other Civilization has the will-to-power manifested itself in so inexorable a form as in this of ours. The thought, and consequently the action, of the mass are kept under iron pressure—for which reason, and for which reason only, men are permitted to be readers and voters—that is, in a dual slavery—while the parties become the obedient retinues of a few, and the shadow of coming Caesarism already touches them. As the English kingship became in the nineteenth century, so parliaments will become in the twentieth, a solemn and empty pageantry. As then sceptre and crown, so now peoples' rights are paraded for the multitude, and all the more punctiliously the less they really signify—it was for this reason that the *cautious* Augustus never let pass an opportunity of emphasizing old and venerated customs of Roman freedom. But the power is migrating even today, and correspondingly elections are degenerating for us into the farce that they were in Rome. Money organizes the process in the interests of those who possess it,[22] and election affairs become a preconcerted game that is staged as popular self-determination. If election was originally *revolution in legitimate forms,* it has exhausted those forms, and what takes place is that mankind "elects" its Destiny again by the primitive methods of bloody violence when the politics of money become intolerable.

Through money, democracy becomes its own destroyer, after money has destroyed intellect. But, just *because* the illusion that actuality can allow itself to be improved by the ideas of any Zeno or Marx has fled away; because men have learned that in the realm of reality one power-will *can be overthrown only by another* (for that is the great human experience of Contending States periods); there wakes at last a deep yearning for all and worthy tradition that still lingers alive. Men are tired to disgust of money-economy. They hope for salvation from somewhere or other, for some real thing of honour and chivalry, of inward nobility, of unselfishness and duty. And now dawns the time when the form-filled powers of the blood, which the rationalism of the Megalopolis has suppressed, reawakens in the depths. Everything in the order of dynastic tradition and old nobility that has saved itself up for the future, everything that there is of high money-disdaining ethic, everything that is intrinsically sound enough to be, in Frederick the Great's words, the *servant*—the hard-working, self-sacrificing, caring *servant*—of the State, all that I have described elsewhere in one word as Socialism in contrast to Capitalism—all this becomes suddenly the focus of immense life-forces. Caesarism *grows* on the soil of Democracy, but its roots thread deeply into the underground of blood tradition. The Classical Caesar derived his power from the Tribunate, and his dignity and therewith his permanency from his being the Princeps. Here too the soul of old Gothic wakens anew. The spirit of the knightly orders overpowers plunderous Vikingism. The mighty ones of the future may possess the earth as their private property—for the great political form of the Culture is irremediably in ruin—but it matters not, for, formless and limitless as their power may be, it has a task. And this task is the unwearying care for this world as it is, which is the very opposite of the interestedness of the money-power age, and demands high honour and conscientiousness. But for this very reason there now sets in the final battle between Democracy and Caesarism, between the leading forces of dictatorial money-economics and the *purely political* will-to-order of the *Caesars.* And in order to understand this *final battle between Economics and Politics,* in which the latter *reconquers* its realm, we must now turn our glance upon the physiognomy of economic history.

[22] Herein lies the secret of why all racial (i.e., poor) parties necessarily become the tools of the money-powers, the Equites, the Bourse. Theoretically their enemy is capital, but practically they attack, not the Bourse, but Tradition on behalf of the Bourse. This is as true of to-day as it was for the Gracchan age, and in all countries. Fifty per cent of mass-leaders are procurable by money, office, or opportunities to "come in on the ground-floor," and with them they bring their whole party.

Liberalism Revisited:
John Maynard Keynes

John Maynard Keynes, "The End of Laissez-Faire," Essays in Persuasion (New York: Harcourt, Brace & Co., 1932), pp. 312–22.

John Maynard Keynes (1883–1946) was born into an academic family; demonstrated his youthful capacities in mathematics, classics, and philosophy; was culturally broadened in that circle of English intellectuals called the Bloomsbury group; and made a mark for himself as a civil servant in the India Office and as an academic economist. As editor of the *Economic Journal* he exerted great influence on the younger generation of economists who developed their ideas in the years surrounding the First World War. Keynes was also an active political figure. He headed the Liberal *Nation and Athenaeum* until it merged with the *New Statesman*, and he was the principal author of the Liberal "Yellow Book," *Britain's Industrial Future* (1928). Thinking about this problem brought Keynes back to the question of savings and investment and their role in the rise and fall of prices—work that would bear fruit in *A Treatise on Money* (1930) and *The General Theory of Employment, Interest, and Money* (1936).

While the depression of 1929 underscored Keynes's arguments, he had been thinking and writing in these terms for some years. "The End of Laissez-Faire" was written in 1926. The faltering European and world economy had not yet collapsed, but the clear-headed were well aware of the danger signals that were flying. Keynes never argued that economic answers were ends in themselves. In a speech, "Liberalism and Labour," to the Manchester Reform Club in February, 1926, he attempted to place the issue in proper perspective.

The political problem of mankind is to combine three things: Economic Efficiency, Social Justice, and Individual Liberty. The first needs criticism, precaution, and technical knowledge; the second, an unselfish and enthusiastic spirit which loves the ordinary man; the third, tolerance, breadth, appreciation of the excellencies of variety and independence, which prefers above everything, to give unhindered opportunity to the exceptional and to the aspiring. The second ingredient is the best possession of the great party of the Proletariat. The first and third require the qualities of the party which, by its traditions and ancient sympathies, has been the home of Economic individualism and Social Liberty. [pp. 344–45.]

Thus Keynes stated his case, to become the heir of John Stuart Mill and the British liberal tradition.

THE END OF LAISSEZ-FAIRE (1926)

LET US CLEAR from the ground the metaphysical or general principles upon which, from time to time, *laissez-faire* has been founded. It is *not* true that individuals possess a prescriptive "natural liberty" in their economic activities. There is *no* "compact" conferring perpetual rights on those who Have

or on those who Acquire. The world is *not* so governed from above the
private and social interest always coincide. It is *not* so managed here below
that in practice they coincide. It is *not* a correct deduction from the Principles of Economics that enlightened self-interest always operates in the public interest. Nor is it true that self-interest generally *is* enlightened; more
often individuals acting separately to promote their own ends are too
ignorant or too weak to attain even these. Experience does *not* show that
individuals, when they make up a social unit, are always less clear-sighted
than when they act separately.

We cannot, therefore, settle on abstract grounds, but must handle on its
merits in detail, what Burke termed "one of the finest problems in legislation, namely, to determine what the State ought to take upon itself to direct
by the public wisdom, and what it ought to leave, with as little interference
as possible, to individual exertion." We have to discriminate between what
Bentham, in his forgotten but useful nomenclature, used to term *Agenda*
and *Non-Agenda*, and to do this without Bentham's prior presumption that
interference is, at the same time, "generally needless" and "generally pernicious." Perhaps the chief task of Economists at this hour is to distinguish
afresh the *Agenda* of Government from the *Non-Agenda*; and the companion task of Politics is to devise forms of Government within a Democracy which shall be capable of accomplishing the *Agenda*. I will illustrate what I have in mind by two examples.

(1) I believe that in many cases the ideal size for the unit of control and
organisation lies somewhere between the individual and the modern State.
I suggest, therefore, that progress lies in the growth and the recognition of
semi-autonomous bodies within the State—bodies whose criterion of action
within their own field is solely the public good as they understand it, and
from whose deliberations motives of private advantage are excluded, though
some place it may still be necessary to leave, until the ambit of men's
altruism grows wider, to the separate advantage of particular groups,
classes, or faculties—bodies which in the ordinary course of affairs are
mainly autonomous within their prescribed limitations, but are subject in
the last resort to the sovereignty of the democracy expressed through
Parliament.

I propose a return, it may be said, towards mediaeval conceptions of
separate autonomies. But, in England at any rate, corporations are a mode
of government which has never ceased to be important and is sympathetic
to our institutions. It is easy to give examples, from what already exists, of
separate autonomies which have attained or are approaching the mode I
designate—the Universities, the Bank of England, the Port of London
Authority, even perhaps the Railway Companies.

But more interesting than these is the trend of Joint Stock Institutions,
when they have reached a certain age and size, to approximate to the status
of public corporations rather than that of individualistic private enterprise.
One of the most interesting and unnoticed developments of recent decades

has been the tendency of big enterprise to socialise itself. A point arrives in the growth of a big institution—particularly a big railway or big public utility enterprise, but also a big bank or a big insurance company—at which the owners of the capital, *i.e.* the shareholders, are almost entirely dissociated from the management, with the result that the direct personal interest of the latter in the making of great profit becomes quite secondary. When this stage is reached, the general stability and reputation of the institution are more considered by the management than the maximum of profit for the shareholders. The shareholders must be satisfied by conventionally adequate dividends; but once this is secured, the direct interest of the management often consists in avoiding criticism from the public and from the customers of the concern. This is particularly the case if their great size or semi-monopolistic position renders them conspicuous in the public eye and vulnerable to public attack. The extreme instance, perhaps, of this tendency in the case of an institution, theoretically the unrestricted property of private persons, is the Bank of England. It is almost true to say that there is no class of persons in the Kingdom of whom the Governor of the Bank of England thinks less when he decides on his policy than of his shareholders. Their rights, in excess of their conventional dividend, have already sunk to the neighbourhood of zero. But the same thing is partly true of many other big institutions. They are, as time goes on, socialising themselves.

Not that this is unmixed gain. The same causes promote conservatism and a waning of enterprise. In fact, we already have in these cases many of the faults as well as the advantages of State Socialism. Nevertheless we see here, I think, a natural line of evolution. The battle of Socialism against unlimited private profit is being won in detail hour by hour. In these particular fields—it remains acute elsewhere—this is no longer the pressing problem. There is, for instance, no so-called important political question so really unimportant, so irrelevant to the reorganisation of the economic life of Great Britain, as the Nationalisation of the Railways.

It is true that many big undertakings, particularly Public Utility enterprises and other business requiring a large fixed capital, still need to be semi-socialised. But we must keep our minds flexible regarding the forms of this semi-socialism. We must take full advantage of the natural tendencies of the day, and we must probably prefer semi-autonomous corporations to organs of the Central Government for which Ministers of State are directly responsible.

I criticise doctrinaire State Socialism, not because it seeks to engage men's altruistic impulses in the service of Society, or because it departs from *laissez-faire*, or because it takes away from man's natural liberty to make a million, or because it has courage for bold experiments. All these things I applaud. I criticise it because it misses the significance of what is actually happening; because it is, in fact, little better than a dusty survival of a plan to meet the problems of fifty years ago, based on a misunderstanding of

what some one said a hundred years ago. Nineteenth-century State Socialism sprang from Bentham, free competition, etc., and is in some respects a
clearer, in some respects a more muddled, version of just the same philosophy as underlies nineteenth-century individualism. Both equally laid all
their stress on freedom, the one negatively to avoid limitations on existing
freedom, the other positively to destroy natural or acquired monopolies.
They are different reactions to the same intellectual atmosphere.

(2) I come next to a criterion of *Agenda* which is particularly relevant to
what it is urgent and desirable to do in the near future. We must aim at
separating those services which are technically social from those which are
technically individual. The most important *Agenda* of the State relate not to
those activities which private individuals are already fulfilling, but to those
functions which fall outside the sphere of the individual, to those decisions
which are made by *no one* if the State does not make them. The important
thing for Government is not to do things which individuals are doing already, and to do them a little better or a little worse; but to do those things
which at present are not done at all.

It is not within the scope of my purpose on this occasion to develop
practical policies. I limit myself, therefore, to naming some instances of
what I mean from amongst those problems about which I happen to have
thought most.

Many of the greatest economic evils of our time are the fruits of risk,
uncertainty, and ignorance. It is because particular individuals, fortunate
in situation or in abilities, are able to take advantage of uncertainty and
ignorance, and also because for the same reason big business is often a
lottery, that great inequalities of wealth come about; and these same factors
are also the cause of the Unemployment of Labour, or the disappointment
of reasonable business expectations, and of the impairment of efficiency
and production. Yet the cure lies outside the operations of individuals; it
may even be to the interest of individuals to aggravate the disease. I believe
that the cure for these things is partly to be sought in the deliberate control
of the currency and of credit by a central institution, and partly in the collection and dissemination on a great scale of data relating to the business
situation, including the full publicity, by law if necessary, of all business
facts which it is useful to know. These measures would involve Society in
exercising directive intelligence through some appropriate organ of action
over many of the inner intricacies of private business, yet it would leave
private initiative and enterprise unhindered. Even if these measures prove
insufficient, nevertheless they will furnish us with better knowledge than
we have now for taking the next step.

My second example relates to Savings and Investment. I believe that
some co-ordinated act of intelligent judgment is required as to the scale
on which it is desirable that the community as a whole should save, the scale
on which these savings should go abroad in the form of foreign investments,
and whether the present organisation of the investment market distributes

savings along the most nationally productive channels. I do not think that
these matters should be left entirely to the chances of private judgment and
private profits, as they are at present.

My third example concerns Population. The time has already come when
each country needs a considerable national policy about what size of Population, whether larger or smaller than at present or the same, is most
expedient. And having settled this policy, we must take steps to carry it into
operation. The time may arrive a little later when the community as a whole
must pay attention to the innate quality as well as to the mere numbers of
its future members.

These reflections have been directed towards possible improvements in
the technique of modern Capitalism by the agency of collective action.
There is nothing in them which is seriously incompatible with what seems
to me to be the essential characteristic of Capitalism, namely the dependence upon an intense appeal to the money-making and money-loving
instincts of individuals as the main motive force of the economic machine.
Nor must I, so near to my end, stray towards other fields. Nevertheless, I
may do well to remind you, in conclusion, that the fiercest contests and the
most deeply felt divisions of opinion are likely to be waged in the coming
years not round technical questions, where the arguments on either side
are mainly economic, but round those which, for want of better words, may
be called psychological or, perhaps, moral.

In Europe, or at least in some parts of Europe—but not, I think, in the
United States of America—there is a latent reaction, somewhat widespread,
against basing Society to the extent that we do upon fostering, encouraging,
and protecting the money-motives of individuals. A preference for ar-
ranging our affairs in such a way as to appeal to the money-motive as little
as possible, rather than as much as possible, need not be entirely *a priori,*
but may be based on the comparison of experiences. Different persons,
according to their choice of profession, find the money-motive playing a
large or a small part in their daily lives, and historians can tell us about
other phases of social organisation in which this motive has played a much
smaller part than it does now. Most religions and most philosophies dep-
recate, to say the least of it, a way of life mainly influenced by considerations of personal money profit. On the other hand, most men to-day reject
ascetic notions and do not doubt the real advantages of wealth. Moreover
it seems obvious to them that one cannot do without the money-motive,
and that, apart from certain admitted abuses, it does its job well. In the
result the average man averts his attention from the problem, and has no
clear idea what he really thinks and feels about the whole confounded
matter.

Confusion of thought and feeling leads to confusion of speech. Many
people, who are really objecting to Capitalism as a way of life, argue as
though they were objecting to it on the ground of its inefficiency in attain-

ing its own objects. Contrariwise, devotees of Capitalism are often unduly conservative, and reject reforms in its technique, which might really strengthen and preserve it, for fear that they may prove to be first steps away from Capitalism itself. Nevertheless a time may be coming when we shall get clearer than at pesent as to when we are talking about Capitalism as an efficient or inefficient technique, and when we are talking about it as desirable or objectionable in itself. For my part, I think that Capitalism, wisely managed, can probably be made more efficient for attaining economic ends than any alternative system yet in sight, but that in itself it is in many ways extremely objectionable. Our problem is to work out a social organisation which shall be as efficient as possible without offending our notions of a satisfactory way of life.

The next step forward must come, not from political agitation or premature experiments, but from thought. We need by an effort of the mind to elucidate our own feelings. At present our sympathy and our judgement are liable to be on different sides, which is a painful and paralysing state of mind. In the field of action reformers will not be successful until they can steadily pursue a clear and definite object with their intellects and their feelings in tune. There is no party in the world at present which appears to me to be pursuing right aims by right methods. Material Poverty provides the incentive to change precisely in situations where there is very little margin for experiments. Material Prosperity removes the incentive just when it might be safe to take a chance. Europe lacks the means, America the will, to make a move. We need a new set of convictions which spring naturally from a candid examination of our own inner feelings in relation to the outside facts.

The Church and the Depression: Quadragesimo Anno

Pius XI, Quadragesimo Anno: Encyclical Letter (May 15, 1931) of His Holiness . . . on Reconstructing the Social Order and Perfecting It Conformably to the Precepts of the Gospel, in Commemoration of the Fortieth Anniversary of the Encyclical Rerum Novarum, *in Oswald von Nell-Breuning, Reorganization of Social Economy: The Social Encyclicals Developed and Explained (Milwaukee: Bruce Publishing Co., 1936–37), pp. 401–42.*

Economists and statesmen moved like men in a nightmare trying to understand and escape the chaos of depression. Some proposed drastic expedients, other merely hoped for an upswing in the economic cycle. Pope Pius XI, using *Rerum Novarum* as a starting point, expanded the economic and social statement while rejecting secular collectivist answers. The position of the Catholic Church remained basically unchanged in political terms. Communism and Socialism were impossible, Godless creeds. Catholic and Socialist were hynonyms. Secular liberalism had opened a Pandora's box, and the world was paying the penalty. All of the spiritual and secular ills of the day could be found in the general category, "modernism." The basic issue revolved around human perfectibility. In the eyes of the Church, human perfectibility was impossible, for man was ever limited by original sin. Such a state of grace was possible only in the afterlife. Liberal, Socialist, and Communist doctrine reasoned in terms of the perfectibility of man upon earth.

Pius XI, like Leo XIII before him, sought to extract what remained as morally safe social and economic doctrine from liberalism and socialism, and then to demonstrate that this was neither liberal nor socialist. The residue was error. The contention arises from divergent conceptions of society. *Quadragesimo Anno* was a cogent, practical response to the depression for those who wished to preserve their Catholic faith and survive in a hectic world. The emphasis on corporate theory was in the spirit of the age, whether the coming New Deal in the United States or the Fascist states of Europe.

ENCYCLICAL LETTER OF HIS HOLINESS PIUS XI

BY DIVINE PROVIDENCE, POPE

TO OUR VENERABLE BRETHREN: THE PATRIARCHS, PRIMATES, ARCHBISHOPS, BISHOPS AND OTHER ORDINARIES, IN PEACE AND COMMUNION WITH APOSTOLIC SEE, AND TO ALL THE FAITHFUL OF THE CATHOLIC WORLD

on Reconstructing the Social Order and Perfecting It Conformably to the Precepts of the Gospel, in Commemoration of the Fortieth Anniversary of the Encyclical Rerum Novarum.

FORTY YEARS have elapsed since the incomparable Encyclical of Leo
XIII of happy memory, *Rerum Novarum*, first saw the light. The whole
Catholic world gratefully recalls the event, and prepares to celebrate it with
befitting solemnity.

2. The way for this remarkable document of pastoral solicitude, it is
true, had been in a measure prepared by other pronouncements of Our
Predecessor. His letters on the foundation of human society, The Family
and the Holy Sacrament of Matrimony, On the Origin of Civil Power; and
its proper co-ordination with the Church; on the Chief Duties of Christian
Citizens, Against the Tenets of Socialism; and the False Notions of Human
Liberty, these and others of the kind had unmistakably revealed the mind
of Leo XIII. *Rerum Novarum*, however, stood out in this, that it laid down
for all mankind unerring rules for the right solution of the difficult problem
of human solidarity, called the social question, at the very time when such
guidance was most opportune and necessary.

[Paragraphs 16–40 summarize the achievements of *Rerum Norvarum*,
characterizing it as "the Magna Carta on which all Christian activities
in social matters are ultimately based."]

THE AUTHORITY OF THE CHURCH IN SOCIAL AND ECONOMIC SPHERES

41. But before proceeding to discuss these problems We lay down the
principle long since clearly established by Leo XIII that it is Our right and
Our duty to deal authoritatively with social and economic problems. It is
not, of course, the office of the Church to lead men to transient and perishable happiness only, but to that which is eternal. Indeed "the Church believes that it would be wrong for her to interfere without just cause in such
earthly concerns", but she never can relinquish her God-given task of interposing her authority, not indeed in technical matters, for which she has
neither the equipment nor the mission, but in all those that have a bearing
on moral conduct. For the deposit of truth entrusted to Us by God, and Our
weighty office of propagating, interpreting, and urging, in season and out of
season, the entire moral law, demand that both social and economic questions be brought within Our supreme jurisdiction, insofar as they refer to
moral issues.

42. For, though economic science and moral discipline are guided each
by its own principles in its own sphere, it is false that the two orders are so
distinct and alien that the former in no way depends on the latter. The so-
called laws of economics, derived from the nature of earthly goods and from
the qualities of the human body and soul, determine what aims are unattainable or attainable in economic matters and what means are thereby

necessary, while reason itself clearly deduces from the nature of things and from the individual and social character of man, what is the end and object of the whole economic order assigned by God the Creator.

43. For it is the moral law alone which commands us to seek in all our conduct our supreme and final end, and to strive directly in our specific actions for those ends which nature, or rather, the Author of Nature, has established for them, duly subordinating the particular to the general. If this law be faithfully obeyed, the result will be that particular economic aims, whether of society as a body or of individuals, will be intimately linked with the universal teleological order, and as a consequence we shall be led by progressive stages to the final end of all, God Himself, our highest and lasting good.

THE RIGHT OF PROPERTY

44. Descending now in details, We commence with ownership, or the right of property. You are aware, Venerable Brethren and Beloved Children, how strenuously Our Predecessor of happy memory defended the right of property against the teachings of the Socialists of His time, showing that the abolition of private ownership would prove to be not beneficial, but grievously harmful to the working classes. Yet, since there are some who falsely and unjustly accuse the Supreme Pontiff and the Church as upholding, both then and now, the wealthier classes against the proletariat, and since controversy has arisen among Catholics as to the true sense of Pope Leo's teaching, We have thought it well to defend from calumny the Leonine doctrine in this matter, which is also the Catholic doctrine, and to safeguard it against false interpretations.

ITS INDIVIDUAL AND SOCIAL CHARACTER

45. First, let it be made clear beyond all doubt that neither Leo XIII, nor those theologians who have taught under the guidance and direction of the Church, have ever denied or called in question the two-fold aspect of ownership, which is individual or social accordingly as it regards individuals or concerns the common good. This unanimous contention has always been that the right to own private property has been given to many by nature or rather by the Creator Himself, not only in order that individuals may be able to provide for their own needs and those of their families, but also that by means of it, the goods which the Creator has destined for the human race may truly serve this purpose. Now these ends cannot be secured unless some definite and stable order is maintained.

46. There is, therefore, a double danger to be avoided. On the one hand, if the social and public aspect of ownership be denied or minimized, the logical consequence is "Individualism," as it is called; on the other hand, the rejection or diminution of its private and individual character necessarily leads to some form of "Collectivism." To disregard these dangers

would be to rush headlong into the quicksands of Modernism in the moral, juridical, and social order which We condemned in the Encyclical Letter issued at the beginning of Our Pontificate.

Let this be noted particularly by those seekers after novelties who launch against the Church the odious calumny that she has allowed a pagan concept of ownership to creep into the teachings of her theologians and that another concept must be substituted, which in their astounding ignorance they call Christian.

THE OBLIGATIONS OF OWNERSHIP

47. That we may keep within bounds the controversies which have arisen concerning ownership and the duties attaching to it, We reassert in the first place the fundamental principle laid down by Leo XIII, that the right of property must be distinguished from its use. It belongs to what is called communtative justice faithfully to respect the possessions of others, not encroaching on the rights of another and thus exceeding one's rights of ownership. The putting of one's own possessions to proper use, however, does not fall under this form of justice, but under certain other virtues, and therefore it is "a duty not enforced by courts of justice." Hence it is idle to contend that the right of ownership and its proper use are bounded by the same limits; and it is even less true that the very misuse or even the non-use of ownership destroys or forfeits the right itself.

48. Most helpful, therefore, and worthy of all praise are the efforts of those who, in a spirit of harmony and with due regard for the traditions of the Church, seek to determine the precise nature of these duties and to define the boundaries imposed by the requirements of social life upon the right of ownership itself or upon its use. On the contrary, it is a grievous error so to weaken the individual character of ownership as actually to destroy it.

THE POWER OF THE STATE

49. It follows from the two-fold character of ownership, which We have termed individual and social, that men must take into account in this matter not only their own advantage but also the common good. To define in detail these duties, when the need occurs and when the natural law does not do so, is the function of the government. Provided that the natural and divine law be observed, the public authority, in view of the common good, may specify more accurately what is licit and what is illicit for property owners in the use of their possessions. Moreover, Leo XIII had wisely taught that "the defining of private possession has been left by God to man's own industry and to the laws of individual peoples."

History proves that the right of ownership, like other elements of social life, is not absolutely rigid, and this doctrine We ourselves have given utterance to on a previous occasion in the following terms: "How varied are the forms which the right of property has assumed! First, the primitive form used amongst rude and savage peoples, which still exists in certain localities even in our own day; then, that of the patriarchal age; later came various tyrannical types (We use the word in its classical meaning); finally, the feudal and monarchic system down to the varieties of more recent times."

"It is plain, however, that the state may not discharge this duty in an arbitrary manner. Man's natural right of possessing and transmitting property by inheritance must remain intact and cannot be taken away by the state from man." "For man precedes the state and the domestic household is antecedent, as well in idea as in fact, to the gathering of men into a community."

Hence the prudent Pontiff had already declared it unlawful for the state to exhaust the means of individuals by crushing taxes and tributes. "The right to possess private property is derived from nature, not from man; and the state has by no means the right to abolish it, but only to control its use and bring it into harmony with the inerests of the public good."

However, when civil authority adjusts ownership to meet the needs of the public good it acts not as an enemy, but as the friend of private owners; for thus it effectively prevents the possessions of private property, intended by Nature's Author in His Wisdom for the sustaining of human life, from creating intolerable burdens and so rushing to its own destruction. It does not therefore abolish, but protects private ownership, and, far from weakening the right of private property, it gives new strength.

OBLIGATIONS REGARDING SUPERFLUOUS INCOME

50. At the same time a man's superfluous income is not left entirely to his own discretion. We speak of that portion of his income which he does not need in order to live as becomes his station. On the contrary, the grave obligations to charity, beneficence and liberality which rest upon the wealthy are constantly insisted upon in telling words by Holy Scripture and the Fathers of the Church.

51. However, the investment of superfluous income in securing favorable opportunities for employment, provided the labor emloyed produces results which are really useful, is to be considered, according to the teaching of the Angelic Doctor, an act of real liberality particularly appropriate to the needs of our time.

TITLES IN ACQUIRING OWNERSHIP

52. The original acquisition of property takes place by first occupation and by industry, or, as it is called, specification. This is the universal teaching of tradition and the doctrine of Our Predecessor, despite unreasonable assertions to the contrary, and no wrong is done to any man by the occupation of gods unclaimed and which belong to nobody. The only form of labor, however, which gives the workingman a title to its fruits is that which a man exercises as his own master, and by which some new form or new value is produced.

2. *Capital and Labor*

53. Altogether different is the labor one man hires out to another, and which is expended on the property of another. To it apply appositely the words of Leo XIII: "It is only by the labor of workingmen that states grow rich." Is it not indeed apparent that the huge possessions which constitute human wealth are begotten by and flow from the hands of the workingman, toiling either unaided or with the assistance of tools and machinery which wonderfully intensify his efficiency?

Universal experience teaches us that no nation has ever yet risen from want and poverty to a better and loftier station without the unremitting toil of all its citizens, both employers and employed. But it is no less self-evident that these ceaseless labors would have remained ineffective, indeed could never have been attempted, had not God, the Creator of all things, in His goodness bestowed in the first instance the wealth and resources of nature, its treasures and its powers. For what else is work but the application of one's forces of soul and body to these gifts of nature for the development of one's powers by their means?

Now, the natural law, or rather, God's Will manifested by it, demands that right order be observed in the application of natural resources to human needs; and this order consists in everything having its proper owner.

NEITHER CAN ACCOMPLISH ANYTHING WITHOUT THE OTHER

Hence it follows that unless a man apply his labor to his own property, an alliance must be formed between his toil and his neighbor's property, for each is helpless without the other. This was what Leo XIII had in mind when He wrote: "Capital cannot do without labor, nor labor without capital." It is therefore entirely false to ascribe the results of their combined efforts to either party alone; and it is flagrantly unjust that either should deny the efficacy of the other and seize all the profits.

UNJUST CLAIMS OF CAPITAL

54. Capital, however, was long able to appropriate to itself excessive advantages; it claimed all the products and profits and left to the laborer the barest minimum necessary to repair his strength and to ensure the continuation of his class. For by an inexorable economic law, it was held, all accumulation of riches must fall to the share of the wealthy, while the workingman must remain perpetually in indigence or reduced to the minimum needed for existence. It is true that the actual state of things was not always and everywhere as deplorable as the liberalistic tenets of the so-called Manchester School might lead us to conclude; but it cannot be denied that a steady drift of economic and social tendencies was in this direction. These false opinions and specious axioms were vehemently attacked, as was to be expected, and by others also than merely those whom such principles deprived of their innate right to better the condition.

UNJUST CLAIMS OF LABOR

55. The cause of the harassed workingman was espoused by the "intellectuals," as they are called, who set up in opposition to this fictitious law another equally false moral principle: that all products and profits, excepting those required to repair and replace invested capital, being by every right to the workingman. This error, more subtle than that of the socialists who hold that all means of production should be transferred to the state (or, as they term it, socialized), is for that reason more dangerous and apt to deceive the unwary. It is an alluring poison, consumed with avidity by many not deceived by open Socialism.

PRINCIPLE OF JUST DISTRIBUTION

56. To prevent erroneous doctrines of this kind from blocking the path of justice and peace, the advocates of these opinions should have hearkened to the wise words of Our Professor: "The earth even though apportioned amongst private owners, ceases not thereby to minister to the needs of all." This teaching We ourselves have reaffirmed above when We wrote that the division of goods which is effected by private ownership is ordained by nature itself and has for its purpose that created things may minister to man's needs in orderly and stable fashion. These principles must be constantly borne in mind if we would not wander from the path of truth.

57. Now, not every kind of distribution of wealth and property amongst men is such that it can at all, and still less can adequately, attain the end intended by God. Wealth, therefore, which is constantly being augmented by social and economic progress, must be so distributed amongst the various individuals and classes of society that the common good of all, of which Leo XIII spoke, be thereby promoted. In other words, the good of the whole community must be safeguarded. By these principles of social justice one class is forbidden to exclude the other from a share in the profits. This sacred law is violated by an irresponsible wealthy class who, in the excess of their good fortune, deem it a just state of things that they should receive everything and the laborer nothing; it is violated also by a propertyless wage-earning class who demand for themselves all the fruits of production, as being the work of their hands. Such men, vehemently incensed against the violation of justice by capitalists, go too far in vindicating the one right of which they are conscious; they attack and seek to abolish all forms of ownership and all profits not obtained by labor, whatever be their nature of significance in human socity, for the sole reason that they are not acquired by toil. In this connection it must be noted that the appeal made by some to the words of the Apostle: "If any man will not work, neither let him eat," is as inept as it is unfounded. The Apostle is here passing judgment on those who refuse to work though they could and ought to do so; he admonishes us to use diligently our time and our powers of body and mind, and not to become burdensome to others as long as we are able to provide for our-

selves. In no sense does he teach that labor is the sole title which gives a right to a living or to profits.

58. Each class, then, must receive its due share, and the distribution of created goods must be brought into conformity with the demands of the common good and social justice, for every sincere observer is conscious that the vast differences between the few who hold excessive wealth and the many who live in destitution constitute a grave evil in modern society.

3. The Uplifting of the Proletariat

59. This is the aim which Our Predecessor urged as the necessary object of our efforts: the uplifting of the proletariat. It calls for more emphatic assertion and more insistent repetition on the present occasion because these salutary injunctions of the Pontiff have not infrequently been forgotten, deliberately ignored, or deemed impracticable, though they were both feasible and imperative. They have lost none of their force or wisdom for our own age, even though the horrible "pauperism" of the days of Leo XIII is less prevalent today. The condition of the workingman has indeed been improved and rendered more equitable in many respects, particularly in the larger and more civilized states, where the laboring class can no longer be said to be universally in misery and want. But after modern machinery and modern industry had progressed with astonishing speed and taken possession of many newly colonized countries no less than of the ancient civilizations of the Far East, the number of the dispossessed laboring masses, whose groans mount to Heaven from these lands increased beyond all measure.

Moreover, there is the immense army of hired rural laborers, whose condition is depressed in the extreme, and who have no hope of ever obtaining a share in the land. These too, unless efficacious remedies be applied will remain perpetually sunk in their proletarian condition.

60. It is true that there is a formal difference between pauperism and proletarianism. Nevertheless, the immense number of propertyless wage-earners on the one hand, and the superabundant riches of the fortunate few on the other, is an unanswerable argument that the earthly goods so abundantly produced in this age of industrialism are far from rightly distributed and equitably shared among the various classes of men.

PROLETARIAN CONDITIONS TO BE OVERCOME BY WAGE-EARNER OWNERSHIP

61. Every effort, therefore, must be made at least in future a just share only of the fruits of production be permitted to accumulate in the hands of the wealthy, and that an ample sufficiency be supplied to the workingmen. The purpose is not that these become slack at their work, for man is born to labor as the bird to fly, but that by thrift they may increase their possessions and by the prudent management of the same may be enabled to bear the family burden with greater ease and security, being freed from that

hand-to-mouth uncertainty which is the lot of the proletarian. Thus they will not only be in a position to support life's changing fortunes, but will also have the reassuring confidence that when their lives are ended, some little provision will remain for those whom they leave behind them.

62. These ideas were not merely suggested, but stated in frank and open terms by Our Predecessor. We emphasize them with renewed insistence in this present Encyclical; for unless serious attempts be made, with all energy and without delay to put them into practice, let nobody persuade himself that the peace and tranquillity of human society can be effectively defended against the forces of revolution!

4. A Just Wage

63. This program cannot, however, be realized unles the propertyless wage-earner be placed in such circumstances that by skill and thrift he can acquire a certain moderate ownership, as was already declared by Us, following the footsteps of Our Predecessor. But how can he ever save money, except from his wages and by living sparingly, who has nothing but his labor by which to obtain food and the necessaries of life? Let us turn, therefore, to the question of wages, which Leo XIII held to be "of great importance," stating and explaining where necessary its principles and precepts.

WAGE CONTRACT NOT ESSENTIALLY UNJUST

64. And first of all, those who hold that the wage contract is essentially unjust, and that in its place must be introduced the contract of partnership, are certainly in error. They do a grave injury to Our Predecessor, whose Encyclical not only admits this contract, but devotes much space to its determination according to the principles of justice.

65. In the present state of human society, however, We deem it advisable that the wage contract should, when possible, be modified somewhat by a contract of partnership, as is already being tried in various ways to the no small gain both of the wage-earners and of the employers. In this way wage-earners are made sharers in some sort in the ownership, or the management, or the profits.

66. In estimating a just wage, not one consideration alone but many must be taken into account, according to the wise words of Leo XIII: "Before deciding whether wages are fair, many things have to be considered."

67. In this way He refuted the irresponsible view of certain writers who declare that this momentous question can easily be solved by the application of a single principle, and that not even a true one.

68. Entirely false is the principle, widely propagated today, that the worth of labor and therefore the equitable return to be made for it, should equal the worth of its net result. Thus the right to the full product of his toil is claimed for the wage-earner. How erroneous this is appears from what We have written above concerning capital and labor,

INDIVIDUAL AND SOCIAL CHARACTER OF LABOR

69. The obvious truth is that in labor, especially hired labor, as in owner-ship, there is a social as well as a personal or individual aspect to be con-sidered. For unless human society forms a truly social and organic body; unless labor be protected in the social and juridical order; unless the various forms of human endeavor, dependent one upon the other, are united in mutual harmony and mutual support; unless, above all, brains, capital and labor combine together for common effort, man's toil cannot produce due fruit. Hence, if the social and individual character of labor be overlooked, it can be neither equitably appraised nor properly recompensed according to strict justice.

THREE FACTORS TO BE CONSIDERED

70. From this double aspect, growing out of the very notion of human labor, follow important conclusions for the regulation and fixing of wages.

A) SUPPORT OF THE WORKINGMAN AND HIS FAMILY

71. In the first place, the wage paid to the workingman must be sufficient for the support of himself and of his family. It is right indeed that the rest of the family contribute according to their power towards the common main-tenance, as in the rural home or in the families of many artisans and small shop keepers. But it is wrong to abuse the tender years of children or the weakness of woman. Mothers will above all devote their work to the home and the things connected with it. Intolerable, and to be opposed with all our strength, is the abuse whereby mothers of families, because of the in-sufficiency of the father's salary, are forced to engage in gainful occupations outside the domestic walls, to the neglect of their own proper cares and duties, particularly the education of their children.

Every effort must therefore be made that fathers of families receive a wage sufficient to meet adequately ordinary domestic needs. If in the pres-ent state of society this is not always feasible, social justice demands that re-forms be introduced without delay which will guarantee every adult work-ingman just such a wage. In this connection We might utter a word of praise for various systems devised and attempted in practice, by which an increased wage is paid in view of increased family burdens, and a special provision is made for special needs.

B) THE STATE OF BUSINESS

72. The condition of any particular business and of its owner must also come into question in settling the scale of wages; for it is unjust to demand wages so high that an employer cannot pay them without ruin, and without consequent distress amongst the working people themselves. If the business make smaller profit on account of bad management, want of enterprise or out-of-date methods, this is not a just reason for reducing the workingmen's

wages. If, however, the business does not make enough money to pay the workman a just wage, either because it is overwhelmed with unjust burdens, or because it is overwhelmed with unjustly low price, those who thus injure it are guilty of grievous wrong; for it is they who deprive the workingmen of the just wage, and force them to accept lower terms.

73. Let employers, therefore, and employed join in their plans and efforts to overcome all difficulties and obstacles, and let them be aided in this wholesome endeavor by the wise measures of the public authority. In the last extreme, counsel must be taken whether the business can continue, or whether some other provision should be made for the workers. The guiding spirit in this crucial decision should be one of mutual understanding and Christian harmony between employers and workers.

c) THE EXIGENCIES OF THE COMMON GOOD

74. Finally, the wage scale must be regulated with a view to the economic welfare of the whole people. We have already shown how conducive it is to the common good that wage-earners of all kinds be enabled by economizing that portion of their wage which remains after necessary expenses have been met, to attain to the possession of a certain modest fortune. Another point, however, of no less importance must not be overlooked, in these our days especially, namely, that opportunities for work be provided for those who are willing and able to work. This depends in large measure upon the scale of wages, which multiplies opportunities for work as long as it remains within proper limits, and reduces them if allowed to pass these limits. All are aware that a scale of wages too low, no less than a scale excessively high, causes unemloyment. Now unemployment, particularly if widespread and of long duration, as We have been forced to experience it during Our Pontificate, is a dreadful scourge; it causes misery and temptation to the laborer, ruins the prosperity of nations, and endangers public order, peace and tranquillity the world over. To lower or raise wages unduly, with a view to private profit, and with no consideration for the common good, is contrary to social justice which demands that by union of effort and good will such a scale of wages be set up, if possible, as to offer to the greatest number opportunities of employment and of securing for themselves suitable means of livelihood.

75. A reasonable relationship between different wages here enters into consideration. Intimately connected with this is a reasonable relationship between the prices obtained for the products of the various economic groups: agrarian, industrial, etc. Where this harmonious proportion is kept, man's various economic activities combine and unite into one single organism and become members of a common body, lending each other mutual help and service. For then only will the economic and social organism be soundly established and attain its end, when it secures for all and each those goods which the wealth and resources of nature, technical achievement, and the social organization of economic affairs can give. These goods should

be sufficient to supply all needs and an honest livelihood, and to uplift men to that higher level of prosperity and culture which, provided it be used with prudence, is not only no hindrance but is of singular help to virtue.

5. *The Reconstruction of the Social Order*

76. What We have written thus far regarding a right distribution of property and a just scale of wages is concerned directly with the individual, and deals only indirectly with the social order. To this latter, however, Our Predecessor, Leo XIII, devoted special thought and care in his efforts to reconstruct and perfect it according to the principles of sound philosophy and the sublime precepts of the Gospel.

77. A happy beginning has here been made. But in order that what has been well begun may be rendered stable, that what has not yet been accomplished may now be achieved, and that still richer and brighter blessings may descend upon mankind, two things are particularly necessary: the reform of the social order and the correction of morals.

78. When We speak of the reform of the social order it is principally the state We have have in mind. Not indeed that all salvation is to be hoped for from its intervention; but because on account of the evil of Individualism, as We called it, things have come to such a pass that the highly developed social life which once flourished in a variety of prosperous institutions organically linked with each other, has been damaged and all but ruined, leaving thus virtually only individuals and the state. Social life lost entirely its organic form. The state, which now was encumbered with all the burdens once borne by associations rendered extinct by it, was in consequence submerged and overwhelmed by an infinity of affairs and duties.

79. It is indeed true, as history clearly proves, that owing to the change in social condition, much that was formerly done by small bodies can nowadays be accomplished only by large corporations. None the less, just as it is wrong to withdraw from the individual and commit to the community at large what private enterprise and industry can accomplish, so too it is an injustice, a grave evil, and a disturbance of right order for a larger and higher organization to arrogate to itself functions which can be performed efficiently by smaller and lower bodies. This is a fundamental principle of social philosophy, unshaken and unchangeable, and it retains its full truth today. Of its very nature, the true aim of all social activity should be to help individual members of the social body, but never to destroy or absorb them.

80. The state should leave to these smaller groups the settlement of business of minor importance. It will thus carry out with greater freedom, power, and success the tasks belonging to it, because it alone can effectively accomplish these, directing, watching, stimulating and restraining, as circumstances suggest or necessity demands. Let those in power, therefore, be convinced that the more faithfully this principle be followed, and a graded hierarchial order exist between the various subsidiary organizations, the more excellent will be both the authority and the efficiency of the social

organization as a whole and the happier and more prosperous the condition of the state.

HARMONY BETWEEN RANKS IN SOCIETY

81. Now this is the primary duty of the state and of all good citizens: to abolish conflict between classes with divergent interests, and thus foster and promote harmony between the various ranks of society.

82. The aim of social legislation must therefore be the re-establishment of vocational groups. Society today still remains in a strained and therefore unstable and uncertain state, being founded on classes with contradictory interests and hence opposed to each other, and consequently prone to enmity and strife.

83. Labor, indeed, as has been well said by Our Predecessor in his Encyclical, is not a mere chattel, since the human dignity of the workingman must be recognized in it, and consequently it cannot be bought and sold like any piece of merchandise. None the less the demand and supply of labor divides men on the labor market into two classes, as into two camps, and the bargaining between these parties transforms this labor market into an arena where the two armies are engaged in combat. To this grave disorder, which is leading society to ruin, a remedy must evidently be applied as speedily as possible. But there cannot be question of any perfect cure, except this opposition be done away with, and well-ordered members of the social body come into being anew, vocational groups namely, binding men together not according to the position they occupy in the labor market, but according to the diverse functions which they exercise in society. For as nature induces those who dwell in close proximity to unite into municipalities, so those who practice the same trade or profession, economic or otherwise, combine into vocational groups. These groups, in a true sense autonomous, are considered by many to be, if not essential to civil society, at least its natural and spontaneous development.

84. Order, as the Angelic Doctor well defines, is unity arising from the apt arrangement of a plurality of objects; hence, true and genuine social order demands various members of society, joined together by a common bond. Such a bond of union is provided on the one hand by the common effort of employers and employees of one and the same group joining forces to produce goods or give service; on the other hand, by the common good which all groups should unite to promote, each in its own sphere, with friendly harmony. Now this union will become powerful and efficacious in proportion to the fidelity with which the individuals and the groups strive to discharge their professional duties and to excel in them.

85. From this it is easy to conclude that in these associations the common interests of the whole group must predominate; and among these interests the most important is the directing of the activities of the group to the common good. Regarding cases in which interests of employers and employees call for special care and protection against opposing interests,

separate deliberation will take place in their respective assemblies and separate votes will be taken as the matter may require.

86. It is hardly necessary to note that what Leo XIII taught concerning the form of political government can, in due measure, be applied also to vocational groups. Here, too, men may choose whatever form they please, provided that both justice and the common good be taken into account.

87. Just as the citizens of the same municipality are wont to form associations with diverse aims, which various individuals are free to join or not, similarly, those who are engaged in the same trade or profession will form free associations among themselves, for purposes connected with their occupations. Our Predecessor has explained clearly and lucidly the nature of these free associations. We are content, therefore, to emphasize this one point: Not only is man free to institute these unions which are of a private character, but he has a right "further to adopt such organization and such rules as may best conduce to the attainment of their respective objects." The same liberty must be claimed for the founding of associations which extend beyond the limits of a single trade. Let those free associations which already flourish and produce salutary fruits make it the goal of their endeavors, in accordance with Christian social doctrine, to prepare the way and to do their part towards the realization of that ideal type of vocational groups which We have mentioned above.

THE RESTORATION OF THE TRUE GUIDING PRINCIPLE OF ECONOMICS

88. Still another aim intimately connected with the preceding must be kept in view. Just as the unity of human society cannot be built upon class warfare, so the proper ordering of economic affairs cannot be left to free competition alone. From this source have proceeded in the past all the errors of the "Individualistic" school. This school, ignorant or forgetful of the social and moral aspects of economic matters, teaches that the state should refrain in theory and practice from interfering therein, because these possess in free competition and open markets a principle of self-direction better able to control them than any created intellect. Free competition, however, though within certain limits just and productive of good results, cannot be the ruling principle of the economic world; this has been abundantly proved by the consequences that have followed from the free rein given to these dangerous individualistic ideals. It is therefore very necessary that economic affairs be once more subjected to and governed by a true and effective guiding principle. Still less can this function be exercised by the economic supremacy which within recent times has taken the place of free competition; for this is a headstrong and vehement power, which, if it is to prove beneficial to mankind, needs to be curbed strongly and ruled with prudence. It cannot, however, be curbed and governed by itself. More loftily and noble principles must therefore be sought in order to control this supremacy sternly and uncompromisingly; to wit, social justice and social charity.

To that end all the institutions of public and social life must be imbued with the spirit of justice, and this justice must above all be truly operative, must build up a juridical and social order able to pervade all economic activity. Social charity should be, as it were, the soul of this order and the duty of the state will be to protect and defend it effectively. This task it will perform the more readily if it free itself from those burdens which, as We have readily declared, are not properly its own.

89. Further, it would be well if the various nations in common counsel and endeavor strove to promote a healthy economic co-operation by prudent pacts and institutions, since in economic matters they are largely dependent one upon the other, and need one another's help.

90. If then the members of the social body be thus reformed, and if the true directive principle of social and economic activity be thus re-established, it will be possible to say, in a sense, of this body what the Apostle said of the Mystical Body of Christ: "The whole body, being compacted and fitly joined together, by what every joint supplieth, according to the operation in the measure of every part maketh increase of the body, unto the edifying of itself in charity."

91. Within recent times, as all are aware, a special syndical and corporative organization has been inaugurated which, in view of the subject of the present Encyclical, demands of Us some mention and opportune comment.

92. The state here grants legal recognition to the syndicate or union, and thereby confers on it some of the features of a monopoly, for in virtue of this recognition, it alone can represent respectively workingmen and employers, and it alone can conclude labor contracts and labor agreements. Affiliation to the syndicate is optional for everyone; but in this sense only can the syndical organization be said to be free, since the contribution to the union and other special taxes are obligatory for all who belong to a given branch, whether workingmen or employers, and the labor-contracts drawn up by the legal syndicate are likewise obligatory. It is true that it has been authoritatively declared that the legal syndicate does not exclude the existence of unrecognized trade associations.

93. The corporations are composed of representatives of the unions of workingmen and employers of the same trade or profession, and as true and genuine organs and institutions of the state, they direct and co-ordinate the activities of the unions in all matters of common interest.

94. Srikes and lockout are forbidden. If the contending parties cannot come to an agreement, public authority intervenes.

95. Little reflection is required to perceive the advantage of the institution thus summarily described: peaceful collaboration of the classes, repression of socialist organizations and efforts, the moderating influence of a special ministry.

But in order to overlook nothing in a matter of such importance, and in the light of the general principles stated above, as well as of that which We are now about to formulate, We feel bound to add that to Our knowledge there are some who fear that the state is substituting itself in the place of private initiative, instead of limiting to necessary and sufficient help and assistance. It is feared that the new syndical and corporative institution possesses an excessively bureaucratic and political character, and that, notwithstanding the general advantages referred to above, it risks serving particular political aims rather than contributing to the initiation of a better social order.

96. We believe that to attain this last-named lofty purpose for the true and permanent advantage of the commonwealth, there is need before and above all else of the blessing of God, and, in the second place, of the cooperation of all men of good will. We believe, moreover, as a necessary consequence, that the end intended will be the more certainly attained, the greater the contribution furnished by men of technical, commercial, and social competence, and, more still, by Catholic principles and their application. We look for this contribution, not to Catholic Action (which has no intention of displaying any strictly syndical or political activities), but to Our sons, whom Catholic Action imbues with these principals and trains for the Apostolate under the guidance and direction of the Church, of the Church, We say, which in the above-mentioned sphere, as in all others where moral questions are discussed and regulated, cannot forget or neglect its mandate as custodian and teacher, given it by God.

97. However, all that We have taught about reconstructing and perfecting the social order will be of no avail without a reform of manners; of this, history affords the clearest evidence. At one period there existed a social order which, though by no means perfect in every respect, corresponded nevertheless in a certain measure to right reason according to the needs and conditions of the times. That this order has long since perished, is not due to the fact that it was incapable of development and adaptation to changing needs and circumstances, but rather to the wrongdoing of men. Men were hardened in excessive self-love and refused to extend that order, as was their duty, to the increasing numbers of the people; or else, deceived by the attractions of false liberty and other errors, they grew impatient of every restraint and endeavored to throw off all authority.

98. It remains for Us then to turn Our attention to the actual condition of the economic order and to its bitterest adversary and accures—We mean Socialism. On these We shall pronounce a frank and just sentence, shall examine more closely the root of the present grave evils, and shall indicate the first and most necessary remedy, which lies in a reform of morals.

CHANGES SINCE LEO XIII

99. Since the time of Leo XIII important changes have taken place both in economic conditions and in regard to Socialism.

100. In the first place, it is obvious to all that the entire economic scene has greatly changed. You are aware, Venerable Brethren and Beloved Children, that Our Predecessor, of happy memory, had chiefly in mind that eco-

nomic regime in which were provided by different people the capital and labor jointly needed for production. He described it in a happy phrase: "Capital cannot do without labor, nor labor without capital."

1. *Changes in Economic Conditions*

101. Leo XIII's whole endeavor was to adjust this economic regime to the standards of true order; whence it follows that the system itself is not to be condemned. And surely it is not vicious of its very nature; but it violates right order whenever capital so employs the working or wage-earning classes as to divert business and economic activity entirely to its own arbitrary will and advantage without any regard to the human dignity of the workers, the social character of economic life, social justice and the common good.

102. It is true that even today these economic conditions do not everywhere exist exclusively, for there is another economic system which still embraces a very large and influential group of men. There are, for instance, the agricultural classes, who form the larger portion of the human family and who find in their occupation the means of obtaining honestly and justly what is needful for their maintenance. This system, too, has its difficulties and problems, of which Our Predecessor spoke repeatedly in his Encyclical, and to which We Ourselves have more than once referred in the present Letter.

103. But it is the capitalist economic regime that, with the world-wide diffusion of industry, has penerated everywhere, particularly since the publication of Leo XIII's Encyclical. It has invaded and pervaded the economic and social sphere even of those who live outside its ambit, influencing them, and, as it were, intimately affecting them by its advantages, inconveniences, and vices.

104. When We turn Our attention, therefore, to the changes which this capitalistic economic order has undergone since the days of Leo XIII, We have regard to the interests, not of those only who live in countries where "capital" and industry prevail, but of the whole human race.

DOMINATION HAS FOLLOWED FROM FREE COMPETITION

105. In the first place, then, it is patent that in our days not alone is wealth accumulated, but immense power and despotic economic domination is concentrated in the hands of a few, and that those few are frequently not the owners, but only the trustees and directors of invested funds, who administer them at their good pleasure.

106. This power becomes particularly irresistible when exercised by those who, because they hold and control money, are able also to govern credit and determine its allotment, for that reason supplying, so to speak, the lifeblood to the entire economic body, and grasping, as it were, in their hands the very soul of production, so that no one dare breathe against their will.

107. This accumulation of power, the characteristic note of the modern economic order, is a natural result of limitless free competition which permits the survival of those only who are the strongest, which often means those who fight most relentlessly, who pay least heed to the dictates of conscience.

108. This concentration of power has led to a threefold struggle for domination. First, there is the struggle for dictatorship in the economic sphere itself; then, the fierce battle to acquire control of the state, so that its resources and authority may be abused in the economic struggles; finally, the clash between states themselves.

This latter arises from two causes: because the nations apply their power and political influence, regardless of circumstances, to promote the economic advantages of their citizens; and because, vice versa, economic forces and economic domination are used to decide political controversies between peoples.

DISASTROUS CONSEQUENCES

109. You assuredly know, Venerable Brethren and Beloved Children, and you lament the ultimate consequences of this Individualistic spirit in economic affairs. Free competition is dead; economic dictatorship has taken its place.

Unbridled ambition for domination has succeeded the desire for gain; the whole economic life has become hard, cruel, and relentless in a ghastly measure. Furthermore, the intermingling and scandalous confusing of the duties and offices of civil authority and of economics have produced crying evils and have gone so far as to degrade the majesty of the state. The state which should be the supreme arbiter, ruling in kingly fashion far above all party contention, intent only upon justice and the common good, has become instead a slave, bound over to the service of human passion and greed. As regards the relations of peoples among themselves, a double stream has issued forth from this one fountainhead: on the one hand, economic Nationalism or economic Imperialism; on the other, a not less noxious and detestable Internationalism or international Imperialism in financil affairs, which holds that where a man's fortune is, there is his country.

110. The remedies for these great evils We have exposed in the second part of the present Encyclical, where We explicitly dwelt upon their doctrinal aspect. It will, therefore, be sufficient to recall them briefly here. Since the present economic regime is based mainly upon capital and labor, it follows that the principles of right reason and Christian social philosophy regarding capital, labor, and their mutual co-operation must be accepted in theory and reduced to practice. In the first place, due consideration must be had for the double character, individual and social, of capital and labor, in order that the dangers of Individualism and of Collectivism be avoided. The mutual relations between capital and labor must be determined according to the laws of the strictest justice, called commutative justice, sup-

ported however by Christian charity. Free competition and still more economic domination must be kept within just and definite limits, and must be brought under the effective control of the public authority, in matters appertaining to this latter's competence. The public institutions of the nations must be such as to make the whole of human society conform to the common good, i.e., to the standard of social justice. If this is done, the economic system, the most important branch of social life, will necessarily be restored to sanity and right order.

2. *Changes in Socialism*

111. Since the days of Leo XIII, Socialism too, the great enemy with which his battles were waged, has undergone profound changes, no less than economics. At that time Socialism could fairly be termed a single system, which defended certain definite and mutually coherent doctrines. Nowadays it has in the main become divided into two opposing, and often bitterly hostile camps, neither of which, however, has abandoned the principle peculiar to Socialism, namely, opposition to the Christian Faith.

A) THE MORE VIOLENT SECTION—COMMUNISM

112. One section of Socialism has undergone approximately the same change through which, as We have described, the capitalistic economic regime has passed; it has degenerated into Communism. Communism teaches and pursues a twofold aim: merciless class warfare and complete abolition of private ownership; and this it does, not in secret and by hidden methods, but openly, frankly, and by every means, even the most violent. To obtain these ends, communists shrink from nothing and fear nothing; and when they have attained power it is unbelievable, indeed it seems portentous, how cruel and inhuman they show themselves to be. Evidence for this is the ghastly destruction and ruin with which they have laid waste immense tracts of Eastern Europe and Asia, while their antagonism and open hostility to Holy Church and to God Himself are, alas! but too well known and proved by their deeds. We do not think it necessary to warn upright and faithful children of the Church against the impious and nefarious character of Communism. But We cannot contemplate without sorrow the heedlessness of those who seem to make light of these imminent dangers and with stolid indifference allow the propagation far and wide of those doctrines which seek by violence and bloodshed the destruction of all society. Even more severely must be condemned the foolhardiness of those who neglect to remove or modify such conditions as exasperate the minds of the people, and so prepare the way for the overthrow and ruin of the social order.

B) THE MORE MODERATE SECTION

113. The other secon, which has retained the name of Socialism, is much less radical in its views. Not only does it condemn recourse to physical

force; it even mitigates and moderates to some extent class warfare and the abolition of private property, it does not reject them entirely. It would seem as if Socialism were afraid of its own principles and of the conclusion drawn therefrom by the communists, and in consequence were drifting towards the truth which Christian tradition has always held in respect; for it cannot be denied that its programs often strikingly approach the just demands of Christian social reformers.

It recedes somewhat from class war and the extinction of ownership.

114. Class war, provided it abstains from enmities and mutual hatred, is changing gradually to an honest discussion of differences based upon the desire of social justice. If this is by no means the blessed social peace which we all long for it, it can be and must be an approach towards the mutual co-operation of vocational groups. The war declared against private ownership has also abated more and more in such a way that nowadays it is not really the possession of the means of production which is attacked but that type of social rulership, which, in violation of all justice, has been seized and usurped by the owners of wealth. This rulership in fact belong, not to the individual owners, but to the state.

If these changes continue, it may well come about that gradually the tenets of mitigated Socialism will no longer be different from the program of those who seek to reform human society according to Christian principles.

For it is rightly contended that certain forms of property must be reserved to the state, since they carry with them an opportunity of domination too great to be left to private individuals without injury to the community at large.

115. Just demands and desires of this kind contain nothing opposed to Christian truth, nor are they in any sense peculiar to Socialism. Those therefore who look for nothing else, have no reason for becoming socialists.

THE POSSIBILITY OF A MIDDLE COURSE

116. It must not be imagined, however, that all the socialist sects or factions which are not communist, have in fact or in theory uniformly returned to this reasonable position. For the most part, they do not reject class warfare and the abolition of property, but merely are more moderate in regard to them. Now, when false principles are thus mitigated and in some sense waived, the question arises, or is unwarrantably proposed in certain quarters, whether the principles of Christian truth also could not be somewhat moderated and attenuated, so as to meet Socialism, as it were, halfway upon common ground. Some are enticed by the empty hope of gaining in this way the socialists to our cause. But such hopes are vain. Those who wish to be apostles amongst the socialists should preach the Christian truth whole and entire, openly and sincerely, without any connivance with error. If they wish in truth to be heralds of the Gospel, let their endeavor be to convince socialists that their demands, in so far as they are just, are defended much more cogently by the principles of Christian

faith, and are promoted much more efficaciously by the power of Christian charity.

117. But what if, in questions of class war and private ownership, Socialism were to become so mitigated and amended, that nothing reprehensible could any longer be found in it? Would it by that very fact have laid aside its character of hostility to the Christian religion? This is a question which holds many minds in suspense; and many are the Catholics who, realizing clearly that Christian principles can never be either sacrificed or minimized, seem to be raising their eyes towards the Holy See, and earnestly beseeching Us to decide whether or not this form of Socialism has retracted so far its false doctrines that it can now be accepted without the loss of any Christian principle, and be baptized into the Church. In Our fatherly solicitude We desire to satisfy these petitions, and We pronounce as follows: Whether Socialism be considered as a doctrine, or as a historical fact, or as a movement, if it really remain Socialism, it cannot be brought into harmony with the dogmas of the Catholic Church, even after it has yielded to truth and justice in the points We have mentioned; the reason being that it conceives human society in a way utterly alien to Christian truth.

SOCIALISM CONCEIVES SOCIETY AND SOCIAL CHARACTER OF MEN FOREIGN TO CHRISTIAN TRUTH

118. For according to Christian doctrine, man, endowed with a social nature, is placed here on earth in order that he may spend his life in the society, and under an authority ordained by God; that he may develop and evolve to the full all his faculties to the praise and glory of his Creator; and that, by fulfilling faithfully the duties of his station, he may attain to temporal and eternal happiness. Socialism, on the contrary, entirely ignorant of or unconcerned about this sublime end both of individuals and of society, affirms that living in community was instituted merely for the sake of the advantages which it brings to mankind.

119. Goods are produced more efficiently by a suitable distributor of labor than by the scattered efforts of individuals. Hence the socialists argue that economic production, of which they see only the material side, must necessarily be carried on collectively, and that because of this necessity men must surrender and submit themselves wholly to society with a view to the production of wealth. Indeed, the possession of the greatest possible amount of temporal goods is esteemed so highly, that man's higher goods, not excepting liberty, must, they claim, be subordinated and even sacrificed to the exigencies of efficient production. They affirm that the loss of human dignity, which results from these socialized methods of production, will be easily compensated for by the abundance of goods produced in common and accruing to the individual who can turn them at his will to the comforts and culture of life. Society, therefore, as the socialist conceives it, is, on the one hand, impossible and unthinkable without the use of compul-

sion of the most excessive kind; on the other, it fosters a false liberty, since in such a scheme no place is found for true social authority, which is not based on temporal and material advantages, but descends from God alone, the Creator and Last End of all things.

CATHOLIC AND SOCIALIST ARE CONTRADICTORY TERMS

120. If, like all errors, Socialism contains a certain element of truth (and this all Sovereign Pontiffs have never denied), it is nevertheless founded upon a doctrine of human society peculiarly its own, which is opposed to true Christianity. "Religious Socialism," "Christian Socialism" are expressions implying a contradiction in terms. No one can be at the same time a sincere Catholic and a true socialist.

CULTURAL SOCIALISM

121. All the We have thus far laid down and established by Our sovereign authority bears application also to a certain new socialist phenomenon, hitherto little known, but nowadays common to many sections of Socialism. Its main aim is the formation of minds and manners. Under the appearance of friendship, it attracts little children in particular and attaches them to itself, though its activity extends to all the people, to make of them convinced socialists, upon whom to build society modeled on socialistic principles.

122. In Our Encyclical Letter *Divini Illius Magistri*, We have expounded at length the true principles on which Christian education rests and the end which it pursues; the contradiction between these and the actions and aims of cultural Socialism is so clear and evident as to require no comment. Nevertheless, the formidable dangers which this form of Socialism brings in its train seem to be ignored or underestimated by those who are little concerned to resist it with strength and zeal, as the gravity of the situation demands.

It is a duty of Our pastoral office to warn these men of the grave danger which threatens. Let all bear in mind that the parent of this cultural Socialism was Liberalism, and that its offspring will be Bolshevism.

CATHOLIC DESERTERS TO SOCIALISM

123. This being so, you can understand, Venerable Brethren and Beloved Children, with what grief We perceive, in certain countries particularly, not a few of Our children, who, while still preserving, as We are convinced, their true faith and good will, have deserted the camp of the Church and passed over to the ranks of Socialism. Some openly boast of its name and profess socialistic doctrines; others, either through indifference or even almost inspite of themselves, join associations which, in theory or in fact, are socialist.

124. In Our paternal solicitude, therefore, We have meditated and sought to understand what can have been the reason of their going so far astray; and We seem to hear what many of them allege in excuse: The Church and

those professing attachment to the Church favor the rich and neglect workingmen and have no care for them: they were obliged therefore in their own interest to join the socialist ranks.

125. What a lamentable fact, Venerable Brethren and Beloved Children, that there have been, and that there are even now some who, while professing the Catholic Faith, are well-nigh unmindful of that sublime law of justice and charity which binds us not only to give each man his due, but to succor Our brethren as Christ Our Lord Himself; worse still, that there are those who out of greed for gain do not shame to oppress the workingman. Indeed there are some who even abuse religion itself cloaking their own unjust impositions under its name, that they may protect themselves against the clearly just demands of their employees.

We shall never desist from gravely censuring such conduct. Such men are the cause that the Church, without deserving it, may have the appearance and be accused of taking sides with the wealthy, and of being little moved by the needs and sufferings of the disinherited. That these appearances and these accusations are undeserved and unjust, the whole history of the Church clearly shows. The very Encyclical, the anniversary of which we are celebrating affords the clearest evidences that these calumnies and contumelies have been most unfairly passed upon the Church and upon her teaching.

THE INVITATION TO RETURN

126. But We are far indeed from being exasperated by these injustices or dejected by Our pastoral sorrow. We have no wish to drive away or repel Our children who have been so unhappily deceived, and who are wandering so far from the paths of truth and salvation. On the contrary, We invite them with all possible solicitude to return to the maternal bosom of the Church. God grant that they listen to Our voice. God grant that whence they set out, thither they may return, to their Father's house; that where their true place is, there they may remain, amongst the ranks of those who, zealously following the directions promulgated by Leo XIII and solemnly repeated by Ourselves, unremittingly endeavor to reform society according to the mind of the Church on a firm basis of social justice and social charity. Let it be their firm persuasion that nowhere, even on earth, can they find an ampler happiness than in company with Him, who being rich became poor for our sakes. That through His poverty We might become rich; Who was poor and in labors from His youth; Who invites to Himself all who labor and are burdened that He may refresh them bounteously in the love of His Heart; who, in fine, without any respect for persons, will require more of him to whom more has been given, and will render to every man according to his works.

3. *Moral Renovation*

127. However, if We examine matters diligently and thoroughly We shall perceive clearly that this longed-for social reconstruction must be preceded

by a profound renewal of the Christian spirit, from which multitudes engaged in industry in every country have unhappily departed. Otherwise, all our endeavors will be futile, and our social edifice will be built, not upon a rock, but upon shifting sand.

128. We have passed in review, Venerable Brethren and Beloved Children, the state of the modern economic world, and have found it suffering from the greatest evils. We have investigated anew Socialism and Communism, and have found them, even in their mitigated forms, far removed from the precepts of the Gospel.

129. "And if society is to be healed now"—we use the words of Our Predecessor—"in now way can it be healed save by a return to Christian life and Christian institutions," for Christianity alone can apply an efficacious remedy for the excessive solicitude for transitory things, which is the origin of all vices. When men are fascinated and completely absorbed in the things of the world, it alone can draw away their attention and raise it to Heaven. And who will deny that this remedy is not urgently needed by society?

THE CHIEF DISORDER OF THE MODERN WORLD: THE RUIN OF SOULS

130. For most men are affected almost exclusively by temporal upheavals, disasters, and ruins. Yet if we view things with Christian eyes, as we should, what are they all in comparison with the ruin of souls?

Nevertheless, it may be said with all truth that nowadays the conditions of social and economic life are such that vast multitudes of men can only with great difficulty pay attention to that one thing necessary, namely, their eternal salvation.

131. Constituted Pastor and Protector of these innumerable sheep by the Prince of Pastors Who redeemed them by His blood, We can scarcely restrain Our tears when We reflect upon the dangers which threaten them. Our pastoral office, moreover, reminds Us to search constantly, with paternal solicitude, for means of coming to their assistance, appealing to the unwearying zeal of others who are bound to this cause by justice and charity. For what will it profit men that a more prudent distribution and use of riches make it possible for them to gain even the whole world, if thereby they suffer the loss of their own souls? What will it profit to teach them sound principles in economics, if they permit themselves to be so swept away by selfishness, by unbridled and sordid greed, that "hearing the Commandments of the Lord, they do all things contrary"?

THE CAUSE OF LOSS OF SOULS

132. The fundamental cause of this defection from the Christian law in social and economic matters, and of the apostasy of many workingmen from the Catholic Faith which has resulted from it, is the disorderly affection of the soul, a sad consequence of original sin, the source of these and of all other evils. By original sin the marvelous harmony of man's faculties

has been so deranged that now he is easily led astray by low desires, and strongly tempted to prefer the transient goods of this world to the lasting goods of heaven.

Hence comes that unquenchable thirst for riches and temoral possessions, which at all times has impelled men to break the law of God and trample on the rights of their neighbor; but the condition of the economic world today lays more snares than ever for human frailty. For the uncertainty of economic conditions and of the whole economic regime demands the keenest and most unceasing straining of energy on the part of those engaged therein; and as a result, some have become so hardened against the stings of conscience as to hold all means good which enable them to increase their profits, and to safeguard against sudden changes of fortune the wealth amassed by unremitting toil. Easy returns, which an open market offers to anyone, lead many to interest themselves in trade and exchange, their one aim being to make clear profits with the least labor. By their unchecked speculation prices are raised and lowered out of mere greed for gain, making voil all the most prudent calculations of manufacturers.

The regulations legally enacted for corporations, with their divided responsibility and limited liability, have given occasion to abominable abuses. The greatly weakened accountability makes little impression, as is evident, upon the conscience. The worst injustices and frauds take place beneath the obscurity of the common name of a corporative, firm. Boards of directors proceed in their unconscionable methods even to the violation of their trust in regard to those whose savings they administer. In the last place must still be mentioned the unscrupulous but well-calculated speculation of men who, without seeking to answer real needs, appeal to the lowest human passions. These are aroused in order to turn their satisfaction into gain.

133. A stern insistence on the moral law, enforced wtih vigor by civil authority, could have dispelled or perhaps averted these enormous evils. This, however, was too often lamentably wanting. For at the time when the new social order was beginning, the doctrines of rationalism had already taken firm hold of large numbers, and an economic science alien to the true moral law had soon arisen, whence it followed that free rein was given to human avarice.

134. As a result, a much greater number than ever before, solely concerned with adding to their wealth by any means whatsoever, sought their own selfish interests above all things; they had no scruple in committing the gravest injustices against others.

Those who first entered upon this broad way which leads to destruction, easily found many imitators of their iniquity because of their manifest success, their extravagant display of wealth, their derision of the scruples of more delicate consciences and the crushing of more cautious competitors.

135. With the leaders of business abandoning the true path, it is not surprising that in every country multitudes of workingmen too sank in the same morass; all the more so, because very many employers treated their

workmen as mere tools, without any concern for the welfare of their souls, indeed, without the slightest thought of higher interests. The mind shudders if we consider the frightful perils to which the morals of workers (of boys and young men particularly), and the virtue of girls and women are exposed in modern factories; if we recall how the present economic regime and above all the disgraceful housing conditions prove obstacles to the family tie and family life; if we remember the insuperable difficulties placed in the way of a proper observance of the holydays.

How universally has the true Christian spirit become impaired, which formerly produced such lofty sentiments even in uncultured and illiterate men! In its stead, man's one solicitude it to obtain his daily bread in any way he can. And so bodily labor, which was decreed by Providence for the good of man's body and soul even after original sin, has everywhere been changed into an instrument of strange perversion: for dead matter leaves the factory ennobled and transformed, where men are corrupted and degraded.

THE REMEDIES
A) ECONOMIC LIFE MUST BE INSPIRED BY CHRISTIAN PRINCIPLES

136. For this pitiable ruin of souls, which, if it continue, will frustrate all efforts to reform society, there can be no other remedy than a frank and sincere return to the teaching of the Gospel. Men must observe anew the precepts of Him who alone has the words of eternal life, words which, even though heaven and earth be changed, shall not pass away.

All those versed in social matters demand a rationalization of economic life which will introduce sound and true order. But this order, which We Ourselves desire and make every effort to promote, will necessarily be quite faulty and imperfect, unless all man's activities harmoniously unite to imitate and, as far as is humanly possible attain the marvelous unity of the divine plan. This is the perfect order which the Church preaches with intense earnestness, and which right reason demands; which places God as the first and supreme end of all created activity, and regards all created goods as mere instruments under God, to be used only in so far as they help towards the attainment of our supreme end.

Nor is it to be imagined that remunerative occupations are thereby belittled or deemed less consonant with human dignity. On the contrary, we are taught to recognize and reverence in them the manifest will of God the Creator, who placed man upon earth to work it and use it in various ways in order to supply his needs. Those who are engaged in production are not forbidden to increase their fortunes in a lawful and just manner; indeed it is just that he who renders service to society and develops its wealth should himself have his proportionate share of the increased public riches, provided always that he respect the laws of God and the rights of his neighbor, and uses his property in accord with faith and right reason. If these principles be observed by all, everywhere and at all times, not merely the production and acquisition of goods, but also the use of wealth, now so often uncontrolled, will within a short time be brought back again to the standards of equity and just distribution.

Mere sordid selfishness, which is the disgrace and the great crime of the present age, will be opposed in very deed by the kindly and forcible law of Christian moderation, whereby man is commanded to seek first the Kingdom of God and His Justice, confiding in God's liberality and definite promise that temporal goods also, in so far as he has need of them, will be added unto him.

B) THE LAW OF CHARITY MUST OPERATE

137. Now, in effect this reform, charity "which is the bond of perfection," must play a leading part. How completely deceived are those inconsiderate reformers who, zealous only for commutative justice, proudly disdain the help of charity! Clearly charity cannot take the place of justice unfairly withheld. But, even though a state of things be pictured in which every man receives at last all that is his due, a wide field will nevertheless remain open for charity. For, justice alone, even though most faithfully observed, can remove indeed the cause of social strife, but can never bring about a union of hearts and minds. Yet this union, binding men together, is the main principle of stability in all institutions, no matter how perfect they may seem, which aim at establishing social peace and promoting mutual aid. In its absence, as repeated experience proves, the wisest regulations come to nothing. Then only will it be possible to unite all in harmonious striving for the common good, when all sections of socity have the intimate conviction that they are members of a single family and children of the same Heavenly Father, and further, that they are "one body in Christ and every one members one of another," so that "if one member suffer anything, all members suffer with it." Then the rich and others in power will change their former negligence of their poorer brethren into solicitous and effective regard; will listen with kindly feeling to their just complaints, and will readily forgive them the faults and mistakes they possibly make. Workingmen too will lay aside all feelings of hatred or envy, which the instigators of social strife arouse so skillfully. Not only will they cease to feel weary of the position assigned them by divine Providence in human society; they will become proud of it, well aware that every man by doing his duty is working usefully and honorably for the common good, and is following in the footsteps of Him, Who, being in the form of God, chose to become a carpenter among men, and to be known as the Son of a carpenter.

A DIFFICULT TASK

138. Because of this new diffusion throughout the world of the Gospel spirit, which is a spirit of Christian moderation and of universal charity, We confidently look forward to that complete and much-desired renewal of human society, and to "the Peace of Christ in the Kingdom of Christ," to

which We firmly resolved at the very beginning of Our Pontificate to devote all Our care and all Our pastorial solicitude. You, Venerable Brethren, who by ordinance of the Holy Spirit rule with Us the Church of God, are laboring strenuously and with admirable zeal in all parts of the world, not exclusive of the sacred missions among the pagans, towards this same end of capital importance and necessity today. Receive your well-deserved meed of praise; and with you all those, of the clergy and laity, whom We rejoice to see daily taking part in this great work and affording valuable help: Our beloved sons devoted to Catholic Action, who with extraordinary zeal aid Us in the solution of social problems, in so far as the Church in virtue of her divine institution has the right and the duty to concern herself with them. With repeated insistence We exhort all these in the Lord to spare no labor and be overcome by no difficulty, but daily more to take courage and be valiant.

The task We propose to them is truly difficult, for well do We know that many are the obstacles to be overcome on either side, whether amongst the higher classes of society or the lower. Still, let them not lose heart, nor in any way allow themselves to be diverted by any art from their purpose. To face stern combats is the part of a Christian, and to endure labor is the lot of those, who, as good soldiers of Christ, follow closely in His footsteps.

139. Relying therefore solely on the assistance of Him Who "will have all men be saved," let us devote all our energies to helping those unhappy souls who are turned away from God; let us withdraw them from the temporal cares in which they are too much involved, and teach them to aspire with confidence to things that are eternal. At times, indeed, this will be easier to accomplish than appears at first sight; for if in the depths of even the most abandoned hearts, there lurk, like sparks beneath the ashes, spiritual forces of unexpected strength—a clear testimony of a "naturally Christian soul"— how much more then must these abide in the hearts of the many who largely through ignorance and unfavorable surroundings have wandered into error!

140. For the rest, the associations of the workingmen themselves provide glad signs of coming social reconstruction. To the great joy of Our heart We discern amongst them dense masses of young workers who listen readily to the call of divine grace and strive with splendid zeal to win their fellows to Christ. No less praise is due to those leaders of workingmens' organizations who, sacrificing their own interests, and anxious only for the good of their companions, strive with prudence to bring their just demands into harmony with the prosperity of their entire vocational group, nor by any obstacle or misgiving do they permit themselves to be deterred from this noble task. Further, many young men, destined soon by reason of their talents or their wealth to hold distinguished places in the foremost ranks of society, are studying social problems with growing earnestness. These youths encourage the fairest hopes that they will devote themselves wholly to social reforms.

141. Present circumstances therefore, Venerable Brethren and Beloved Children, indicate clearly the course to be followed. Nowadays, as more than once in the history of the Church, we are confronted with a world which in large measure has almost fallen back into paganism. In order to bring back to Christ these whole classes of men who have denied Him, we must gather and train from amongst their very ranks auxiliary soldiers of the Church, men who know their mentality and their aspirations, and who with kindly fraternal charity will be able to win their hearts. Undoubtedly the first and immediate apostles of the workingman must themselves be workingmen, while the apostles of the industrial and commercial world should themselves be employers and merchants. It is your chief duty, Venerable Brethren, and that of your clergy, to seek diligently, to select prudently, and train fittingly these lay apostles, amongst workingmen and amongst emloyers.

142. No easy task is here imposed upon the clergy, wherefore all candidates for the sacred priesthood must be adequately prepared to meet it by intense study of social matters. It is particularly necessary, however, that they whom you specially select and devote to this work should show themselves endowed with a keen sense of justice, ready to oppose with real manly constancy unjust claims and unjust actions; that they avoid every extreme with consummate prudence and discretion; above all, that they be thoroughly imbued with the charity of Christ, which alone has power to incline men's hearts and wills firmly and gently to the laws of equity and justice. This course, already productive of success in the past, we must follow now with alacrity.

143. Further, We earnestly exhort in the Lord the beloved sons who are chosen for this task, to devote themselves wholeheartedly to the formation of the men entrusted to them. In the execution of this most priestly and apostolic work, let them make opportune use of the powerful resources of Christian training, by instructing youth, by founding Christian associations, by forming study circles on Christian lines.

Above all, let them hold in high esteem and employ with diligence for the benefit of their disciples the spiritual exercises, a most precious means of personal and of social reform, as We said in Our encyclical *Mens Nostra.* These exercises We declare in express terms to be most useful for the laity in general and especially for workingmen, and We warmly recommended them; for in that school of the spirit not only are excellent Christians formed, but real apostles of every state of life are trained and enkindled with the fire of the Heart of Christ. From that school they will go forth, as the Apostles from the Cenacle in Jerusalem, strong in faith, unconquerable in steadfastness under trials, aflame with zeal, eager only for the spread in every way of the Kingdom of Christ.

144. And in truth, the world has nowadays sore need of valiant soldiers

of Christ, who strain every thew and sinew to preserve the human family from the dire havoc which would befall it were the teaching of the Gospel to be flouted, and a social order permitted to prevail, which spurns no less the laws of nature than those of God. For herself the Church of Christ, built upon the solid rock, has nothing to fear, for she knows that the Gates of Hell shall not prevail against her; and the experience of centuries has taught her that storms, even the most violent, pass, leaving her stronger and triumphantly victorious. But her maternal bosom cannot but be stirred at the though of the countless ills which tempests of the kind would occasion to so many thousands; at the thought, above all, of the immense spiritual evils which would ensue, entailing the eternal ruin of so many souls redeemed by the Blood of Christ.

145. No stone, then, must be left unturned to avert these grave misfortunes from human society.

Towards this one aim must tend all our effort and endeavor, supported by assiduous and fervent prayers to God. For, with the assistance of Divine Grace, the destiny of the human family lies in our hands.

146. Let us not permit, Venerable Brethren and Beloved Children, the children of this world to seem wiser in their generation than We, who by God's goodness are children of Light. We see these men cunningly select and train resolute disciples, who spread their false doctrines daily more widely amongst men of every station and of every clime.

And when it becomes a question of attacking more vehemently the Church of Christ, we see them lay aside their internal quarrels, link up harmoniously into a single battle-line, and strive with united forces towards this common aim.

INTIMATE UNION AND HARMONY BETWEEN ALL GOOD MEN

147. No one indeed is unaware of the many and splendid works in the social and economic field, as well as in education and religion, laboriously set in motion with indefatigable zeal by Catholics. But this admirable and self-sacrificing activity not unfrequently loses some of its effectiveness by being directed into too many different channels. Let, then, all men of good will stand united. Let all those who, under the pastors of the Church, wish to fight this good and peaceful fight of Christ, as far as talents, powers and station allow, strive to play their part in the Christian renewal of human society, which Leo XIII inaugurated in his immortal Encyclical *Rerum Novarum*. Let them seek, not themselves and the things that are their own, but the things that are Jesus Christ's. Let them not urge their own ideas with undue persistence, but be ready to abandon them, however admirable, should the greater common good seem to require it: that in all and above all Christ may reign and rule, to Whom be honor and glory and power forever and ever.

That this happy result may be attained, Venerable Brethren and Beloved Children, We impart to you all members of the great Catholic family entrusted to Our care, but with special affection of Our heart to artisans and other workingmen engaged in manual labor, by Divine Providence committed to Us in a particular manner, and to Christian employers and masters, with paternal affection, the Apostolic Benediction.

148. Given at Rome, at Saint Peter's, the fifteenth day of May in the year 1931, the tenth of Our pontificate.

Pius Pp. xi

The Depression:
A Statement of Conditions

George Orwell, The Road to Wigan Pier (New York: Harcourt, Brace & Co., 1937), chaps. v–vi, pp. 75–104.

The depression of 1929 was the culmination of many basic economic flaws triggered by the collapse of the American speculative boom. It remained unresolved until the rearmament of the 1930's, preceding the Second World War. The residual effects, psychological and social, are still felt today. What does it mean to be out of work? What does it mean to have no real prospect for steady employment? What does it mean to have lost status and pride? The psychological impact of depression cannot be measured, nor can one assess the impact of this economic collapse upon social values. If savings and thrift were the way to material salvation, what use were worthless securities or defaulted savings accounts? How could self-help apply to a world of chronic and growing unemployment and uncertainty? To what spiritual and social values does a man turn when the economic framework of life disappears? Hysteria is one response, for reactions are emotional, not rational. Xenophobia, anti-Semitism, even antifeminism are partial by-products from the factory of economic disorder. When confronted with a choice between liberty and security, the result is predictable. Nazism and European fascism owe much of their rise and persistence to the dislocation of economic and social life. Communist and Socialist alternatives assume a greater appeal within the liberal state. Above all, a depression contributes to the dehumanization of man.

This is not to say that depressions are universally bad. If you happen to have work or if you happen to retain capital, you are better off than you were before. Your real standard of living improves dramatically and thus the growing hysteria and ultra-conservatism within the ranks of the better-to-do. Status, too, is precious. George Orwell (1903–50) found, to no one's great surprise, that the middle classes tended to cling the more strongly to their position in society as its economic basis eroded. This Etonian and former civil servant in the colonial service found his world inadequate, but even he, penetrating critic that he was, found alternatives displeasing. *The Road to Wigan Pier* is two books in one. It is a moving catalogue of the condition of life in the old industrial heart of England, particularly mining districts in the West Riding of Yorkshire and southern Lancashire. It is also a confession of faith and doubt—an acceptance of socialism and rejection of Socialists. Orwell's brilliance lay in his critical capacities—of imperialism in "Shooting an Elephant," of middle-class snob education in "Such, Such Were the Joys," of cultural barbarism in "Politics and the English Language," of the Spanish civil war in *Homage to Catalonia*. His novel, *1984*, is among the great antiutopian works. All deserve careful reading.

These chapters from *The Road to Wigan Pier* are simple analysis. They are a statement of facts and of the difficulty of finding answers. They are lucid and grim.

CHAPTER V

WHEN YOU SEE the unemployment figures quoted at two millions, it is fatally easy to take this as meaning that two million people are out of work and the rest of the population is comparatively comfortable. I admit that till recently I was in the habit of doing so myself. I used to calculate that if you put the registered unemployed at round about two millions and threw in the destitute and those who for one reason and another were not registered, you might take the number of underfed people in England (for *everyone* on the dole or thereabouts is underfed) as being, at the very most, five millions.

This is an enormous under-estimate, because, in the first place, the only people shown on unemployment figures are those actually drawing the dole—that is, in general, heads of families. An unemployed man's dependants do not figure on the list unless they too are drawing a separate allowance. A Labour Exchange officer told me that to get at the real number of people *living on* (not drawing) the dole, you have got to multiply the official figures by something over three. This alone brings the number of unemployed to round about six millions. But in addition there are great numbers of people who are in work but who, from a financial point of view, might equally well be unemployed, because they are not drawing anything that can be described as a living wage. Allow for these and their dependants, throw in as before the old-age pensioners, the destitute and other nondescripts, and you get an *underfed* population of well over ten millions. Sir John Orr puts it at twenty millions.

Take the figures for Wigan, which is typical enough of the industrial and mining districts. The number of insured workers is round about 36,000 (26,000 men and 10,000 women). Of these, the number unemployed at the beginning of 1936 was about 10,000. But this was in winter when the mines are working full time; in summer it would probably be 12,000. Multiply by three, as above, and you get 30,000 or 36,000. The total population of Wigan is a little under 87,000; so that at any moment more than one person in in three out of the whole population—not merely the registered workers—is either drawing or living on the dole. Those ten or twelve thousand unemployed contain a steady core of from four to five thousand miners who have been continuously unemployed for the past seven years. And Wigan is not especially badly off as industrial towns go. Even in Sheffield, which has been doing well for the last year or so because of wars and rumours of war, the proportion of unemployment is about the same—one in three of registered workers unemployed,

When a man is first unemployed, until his insurance stamps are exhausted, he draws "full benefit," of which the rates are as follows:

	per week
Single man	17s.
Wife	9s.
Each child below 14	3s.

Thus in a typical family of parents and three children of whom one was over 14, the total income would be 32s. per week, plus anything that might be earned by the eldest child. When a man's stamps are exhausted, before being turned over to the P.A.C. (Public Assistance Committee), he receives twenty-six weeks' "transitional benefit" from the U.A.B. (Unemployment Assistance Board), the rates being as follows:

	per week
Single man	15s.
Man and wife	24s.
Children, 14–18	6s.
Children, 11–14	4s. 6d.
Children, 8–11	4s.
Children, 5–8	3s. 6d.
Children, 3–5	3s.

Thus on the U.A.B. the income of the typical family of five persons would be 37s. 6d. a week if no child was in work. When a man is on the U.A.B. a quarter of his dole is regarded as rent, with a minimum of 7s. 6d. a week. If the rent he is paying is more than a quarter of his dole he receives an extra allowance, but if it is less than 7s. 6d., a corresponding amount is deducted. Payments on the P.A.C. theoretically come out of the local rates, but are backed by a central fund. The rates of benefit are:

	per week
Single man	12s. 6d.
Man and wife	23s.
Eldest child	4s.
Any other child	3s.

Being at the discretion of the local bodies these rates vary slightly, and a single man may or may not get an extra 2s. 6d. weekly, bringing his benefit up to 15s. As on the U.A.B., a quarter of a married man's dole is regarded as rent. Thus in the typical family considered above the total income would be 33s. a week, a quarter of this being regarded as rent. In addition, in most districts a coal allowance of 1s. 6d. a week (1s. 6d. is equivalent to about a hundredweight of coal) is granted for six weeks before and six weeks after Christmas.

It will be seen that the income of a family on the dole normally averages round about thirty shillings a week. One can write at least a quarter of this off as rent, which is to say that the average person, child or adult, has got to be fed, clothed, warmed, and otherwise cared-for for six or seven shillings a week. Enormous groups of people, probably at least a third of the whole population of the industrial areas, are living at this level. The Means Test is very strictly enforced, and you are liable to be refused relief at the slightest hint that you are getting money from another source. Dock-labourers, for instance, who are generally hired by the half day, have to sign on at a Labour Exchange twice daily; if they fail to do so it is assumed that they have been working and their dole is reduced correspondingly. I have seen cases of evasion of the Means Test, but I should say that in the industrial towns, where there is still a certain amount of communal life and everyone has neighbours who know him, it is much harder than it would be in London. The usual method is for a young man who is actually living with his parents to get an accommodation address, so that supposedly he has a separate establishment and draws a separate allowance. But there is much spying and tale-bearing. One man I knew, for instance, was seen feeding his neighbour's chickens while the neighbour was away. It was reported to the authorities that he "had a job feeding chickens" and he had great difficulty in refuting this. The favourite joke in Wigan was about a man who was refused relief on the ground that he "had a job carting firewood." He had been seen, it was said, carting firewood at night. He had to explain that he was not carting firewood but doing a moonlight flit. The "firewood" was his furniture.

The most cruel and evil effect of the Means Test is the way in which it breaks up families. Old people, sometimes bedridden, are driven out of their homes by it. An old age pensioner, for instance, if a widower, would normally live with one or other of his children; his weekly ten shillings goes towards the household expenses, and probably he is not badly cared for. Under the Means Test, however, he counts as a "lodger" and if he stays at home his children's dole will be docked. So, perhaps at seventy or seventy-five years of age, he has to turn out into lodgings, handing his pension over to the lodging-house keeper and existing on the verge of starvation. I have seen several cases of this myself. It is happening all over England at this moment, thanks to the Means Test.

Nevertheless, in spite of the frightful extent of unemployment, it is a fact that poverty—extreme poverty—is less in evidence in the industrial North than it is in London. Everything is poorer and shabbier, there are fewer motor-cars and fewer well-dressed people; but also there are fewer people who are obviously destitute. Even in a town the size of Liverpool or Manchester you are struck by the fewness of the beggars. London is a sort of whirlpool which draws derelict people towards it, and it is so vast that life there is solitary and anonymous. Until you break the law nobody will take any notice of you, and you can go to pieces as you could not possibly do in a place where you had neighbours who knew you. But in the industrial towns the old communal way of life has not yet broken up, tradition is still strong and almost everyone has a family—potentially, therefore, a home. In a town of 50,000 or 100,000 inhabitants there is no casual and as it were unaccounted-for population; nobody sleeping in the streets, for instance.

Moreover, there is just this to be said for the unemployment regulations, that they do not discourage people from marrying. A man and wife on twenty-three shillings a week are not far from the starvation line, but they can make a home of sorts; they are vastly better off than a single man on fifteen shillings. The life of a single unemployed man is dreadful. He lives sometimes in a common lodging-house, more often in a "furnished" room for which he usually pays six shillings a week, finding himself as best he can on the other nine (say six shillings a week for food and three for clothes, tobacco and amusements). Of course he cannot feed or look after himself properly, and a man who pays six shillings a week for his room is not encouraged to be indoors more than is necessary. So he spends his days loafing in the public library or any other place where he can keep warm. That—keeping warm—is almost the sole preoccupation of a single unemployed man in winter. In Wigan a favourite refuge was the pictures, which are fantastically cheap there. You can always get a seat for fourpence, and at the matinee at some houses you can even get a seat for twopence. Even people on the verge of starvation will readily pay twopence to get out of the ghastly cold of a winter afternoon. In Sheffield I was taken to a public hall to listen to a lecture by a clergyman, and it was by a long way the silliest and worst-delivered lecture I have ever heard or ever expect to hear. I found it physically impossible to sit it out; indeed my feet carried me out, seemingly of their own accord, before it was half way through. Yet the hall was thronged with unemployed men; they would have sat through far worse drivel for the sake of a warm place to shelter in.

At times I have seen unmarried men on the dole living in the extreme of misery. In one town I remember a whole colony of them who were squatting, more or less illicitly, in a derelict house which was practically falling down. They had collected a few scraps of furniture, presumably off refuse-tips, and I remember that their sole table was an old marble-topped wash-handstand. But this kind of thing is exceptional. A working-class bachelor is a rarity, and so long as a man is married unemployment makes comparatively little alteration in his way of life. His home is impoverished but it is still a home, and it is noticeable everywhere that the anomalous position created by unemployment—the man being out of work while the woman's work continues as before—has not altered the relative status of the sexes. In a working-class home it is the man who is the master and not, as in a middle-class home, the woman or the baby. Practically never, for instance, in a working-class home, will you see the man doing a stroke of the housework. Unemployment has not changed this convention, which on the face of it seems a little unfair. The man is idle from morning to night but the woman is as busy as ever—more so, indeed, because she has to manage with less money. Yet so far as my experience goes the women do not protest. I believe that they, as well as the men, feel that a man would lose his manhood if, merely because he was out of work, he developed into a "Mary Ann."

But there is no doubt about the deadening, debilitating effect of unemployment upon everybody, married or single, and upon men more than upon women. The best intellects will not stand up against it. Once or twice it has happened to me to meet unemployed men of genuine literary ability; there are others whom I haven't met but whose work I occasionally see in the magazines. Now and again, at long intervals, these men will produce an article or a short story which is quite obviously better than most of the stuff that gets whooped up by the blurb-reviewers. Why, then, do they make so little use of their talents? They have all the leisure in the world; why don't they sit down and write books? Because to write books you need not only comfort and solitude—and solitude is never easy to attain in a working-class home—you also need peace of mind. You can't settle to anything, you can't command the spirit of *hope* in which anything has got to be created, with that dull evil cloud of unemployment hanging over you. Still, an unemployed man who feels at home with books can at any rate occupy himself by reading. But what about the man who cannot read without discomfort? Take a miner, for instance, who has worked in the pit since childhood and has been trained to be a miner and nothing else. How the devil is he to fill up the empty days? It is absurd to say that he ought to be looking for work. There is no work to look for, and everybody knows it. You can't go on looking for work every day for seven years. There are allotments, which occupy the time and help to feed a family, but in a big town there are only allotments for a small proportion of the people. Then there are the occupational centres which were started a few years ago to help the unemployed. On the whole this movement has been a failure, but some of the centres are still flourishing. I have visited one or two of them. There are shelters where the men can keep warm and there are periodical classes in carpentering, boot-making, leather-work, handloom-weaving, basket-work, sea-grass work, etc., etc.; the idea being that the men can make furniture and so forth, not for sale but for their own homes, getting tools free and materials cheaply. Most of the Socialists I have talked to denounce this movement as they denounce the project—it is always being talked about but it never comes to anything—to give the unemployed small-holdings. They say that the occupational centres are simply a device to keep the unemployed quiet and give them the illusion that something is being done for them. Undoubtedly that *is* the underlying motive. Keep a man busy mending boots and he is less likely to read the *Daily Worker*. Also there is a nasty Y.M.C.A. atmosphere about these places which you can feel as soon as you go in. The unemployed men who frequent them are mostly of the cap-touching type—the type who tells you oilily that he is "Temperance" and votes Conservative. Yet even here you feel yourself torn both ways. For probably it is better that a man should waste his time even with such rubbish as sea-grass work than that for years upon end he should do absolutely *nothing*.

By far the best work for the unemployed is being done by the N.U.W.M.

—National Unemployed Workers' Movement. This is a revolutionary organisation intended to hold the unemployed together, stop them backlegging during strikes and give them legal advice against the Means Test. It is a movement that has been built out of nothing by the pennies and efforts of the unemployed themselves. I have seen a good deal of the N.U.W.M., and I greatly admire the men, ragged and underfed like the others, who keep the organisation going. Still more I admire the tact and patience with which they do it; for it is not easy to coax even a penny-a-week subscription out of the pockets of people on the P.A.C. As I said earlier, the English working class do not show much capacity for leadership, but they have a wonderful talent for organisation. The whole trade union movement testifies to this; so do the excellent working-men's clubs—really a sort of glorified co-operative pub, and splendidly organised—which are so common in Yorkshire. In many towns the N.U.W.M. have shelters and arrange speeches by Communist speakers. But even at these shelters the men who go there do nothing but sit round the stove and occasionally play a game of dominoes. If this movement could be combined with something along the lines of the occupational centres, it would be nearer what is needed. It is a deadly thing to see a skilled man running to seed, year after year, in utter, hopeless idleness. It ought not to be impossible to give him the chance of using his hands and making furniture and so forth for his own home, without turning him into a Y.M.C.A. cocoa-drunkard. We may as well face the fact that several million men in England will—unless another war breaks out—never have a real job this side the grave. One thing that probably could be done and certainly ought to be done as a matter of course, is to give every unemployed man a patch of ground and free tools if he chose to apply for them. It is disgraceful that men who are expected to keep alive on the P.A.C. should not even have the chance to grow vegetables for their families.

To study unemployment and its effects you have got to go to the industrial areas. In the South unemployment exists, but it is scattered and queerly unobtrusive. There are plenty of rural districts where a man out of work is almost unheard-of, and you don't anywhere see the spectacle of whole blocks of cities living on the dole and the P.A.C. It is only when you lodge in streets where nobody has a job, where getting a job seems about as probable as owning an aeroplane and much *less* probable than winning fifty pounds in the Football Pool, that you begin to grasp the changes that are being worked in our civilisation. For a change *is* taking place, there is no doubt about that. The attitude of the submerged working class is profoundly different from what it was seven or eight years ago.

I first became aware of the unemployment problem in 1928. At that time I had just come back from Burma, where unemployment was only a word, and I had gone to Burma when I was still a boy and the post-war boom was not quite over. When I first saw unemployed men at close quarters, the thing that horrified and amazed me was to find that many of them were *ashamed* of being unemployed. I was very ignorant, but not so ignorant as to imagine that when the loss of foreign markets pushes two million men out of work, those two million are any more to blame than the people who draw blanks in the Calcutta Sweep. But at that time nobody cared to admit that unemployment was inevitable, because this meant admitting that it would probably continue. The middle classes were still talking about "lazy idle loafers on the dole" and saying that "these men could all find work if they wanted to," and naturally these opinions percolated to the working class themselves. I remember the shock of astonishment it gave me, when I first mingled with tramps and beggars, to find that a fair proportion, perhaps a quarter, of these beings whom I had been taught to regard as cynical parasites, were decent young miners and cotton-workers gazing at their destiny with the same sort of dumb amazement as an animal in a trap. They simply could not understand what was happening to them. They had been brought up to work and behold! it seemed as if they were never going to have the chance of working again. In their circumstances it was inevitable, at first, that they should be haunted by a feeling of personal degradation. That was the attitude towards the unemployment in those days: it was a disaster which happened to *you* as an individual and for which *you* were to blame.

When a quarter of a million miners are unemployed, it is part of the order of things that Alf Smith, a miner living in the back streets of Newcastle, should be out of work. Alf Smith is merely one of the quarter million, a satistical unit. But no human being finds it easy to regard himself as a statistical unit. So long as Bert Jones across the street is still at work, Alf Smith is bound to feel himself dishonoured and a failure. Hence that frightful feeling of impotence and despair which is almost the worst evil of unemployment—far worse than any hardship, worse than the demoralisation of enforced idleness, and only less bad than the physical degeneracy of Alf Smith's children, born on the P.A.C. Everyone who saw Greenwood's play *Love on the Dole* must remember that dreadful moment when the poor, good, stupid working man beats on the table and cries out, "O God, send me some work!" This was not dramatic exaggeration, it was a touch from life. That cry must have been uttered, in almost those words, in tens of thousands, perhaps hundreds of thousands of English homes, during the past fifteen years.

But, I think not again—or at least, not so often. That is the real point: people are ceasing to kick against the pricks. After all, even the middle classes—yes, even the bridge clubs in the country towns—are beginning to realise that there is such a thing as unemployment. The "My dear, I don't *believe* in all this nonsense about unemployment. Why, only last week we wanted a man to weed the garden, and we simply couldn't get one. They don't *want* to work, that's all it is!" which you heard at every decent tea-table five years ago, is growing perceptibly less frequent. As for the working class themselves, they have gained immensely in economic knowledge.

I believe that the *Daily Worker* has accomplished a great deal here: its influence is out of all proportion to its circulation. But in any case they have had their lesson well rubbed into them, not only because unemployment is so widespread but because it has lasted so long. When people live on the dole for years at a time they grow used to it, and drawing the dole, though it remains unpleasant, ceases to be shameful. Thus the old, independent, workhouse-fearing tradition is undermined, just as the ancient fear of debt is undermined by the hire-purchase system. In the back streets of Wigan and Barnsley I saw every kind of privation, but I probably saw much less *conscious* misery than I should have seen ten years ago. The people have at any rate grasped that unemployment is a thing they cannot help. It is not only Alf Smith who is out of work now; Bert Jones is out of work as well, and both of them have been "out" for years. It makes a great deal of difference when things are the same for everybody.

So you have whole populations settling down, as it were, to a lifetime on the P.A.C. And what I think is admirable, perhaps even hopeful, is that they have managed to do it without going spiritually to pieces. A working man does not disintegrate under the strain of poverty as a middle-class person does. Take, for instance, the fact that the working class think nothing of getting married on the dole. It annoys the old ladies in Brighton, but it is a proof of their essential good sense; they realise that losing your job does not mean that you cease to be a human being. So that in one way things in the distressed area are not so bad as they might be. Life is still fairly normal, more normal than one really has the right to expect. Families are impoverished, but the family-system has not broken up. The people are in effect living a reduced version of their former lives. Instead of raging against their destiny they have made things tolerable by lowering their standards.

But they don't necessarily lower their standards by cutting out luxuries and concentrating on necessities; more often it is the other way about—the more natural way, if you come to think of it. Hence the fact that in a decade of unparalleled depression, the consumption of all cheap luxuries has increased. The two things that have probably made the greatest difference of all are the movies and the mass-production of cheap smart clothes since the war. The youth who leaves school at fourteen and gets a blind-alley job is out of work at twenty, probably for life; but for two pounds ten on the hire-purchase system he can buy himself a suit which, for a little while and at a little distance, looks as though it had been tailored in Savile Row. The girl can look like a fashion plate at an even lower price. You may have three halfpence in your pocket and not a prospect in the world, and only the corner of a leaky bedroom to go home to; but in your clothes you can stand on the street corner, indulging in a private daydream of yourself as Clark Gable or Greta Garbo, which compensates you for a great deal. And even at home there is generally a cup of tea going—a "nice cup of tea"—and

Father, who has been out of work since 1929, is temporarily happy because he has a sure tip for the Cesarewitch.

Trade since the war has had to adjust itself to meet the demands of underpaid, underfed people, with the result that a luxury is nowadays almost always cheaper than a necessity. One pair of plain solid shoes costs as much as two ultra-smart pairs. For the price of one square meal you can get two pounds of cheap sweets. You can't get much meat for threepence, but you can get a lot of fish-and-chips. Milk costs threepence a pint and even "mild" beer costs fourpence, but aspirins are seven a penny and you can wring forty cups of tea out of a quarter-pound packet. And above all there is gambling, the cheapest of all luxuries. Even people on the verge of starvation can buy a few days' hope ("Something to live for," as they call it) by having a penny on a sweeepstake. Organised gambling has now risen almost to the status of a major industry. Consider, for instance, a phenomenon like the Football Pools, with a turnover of about six million pounds a year, almost all of it from the pockets of working-class people. I happened to be in Yorkshire when Hitler re-occupied the Rhineland. Hitler, Locarno, Fascism and the threat of war aroused hardly a flicker of interest locally, but the decision of the Football Association to stop publishing their fixtures in advance (this was an attempt to quell the Football Pools) flung all Yorkshire into a storm of fury. And then there is the queer spectacle of modern electrical science showering miracles upon people with empty bellies. You may shiver all night for lack of bedclothes, but in the morning you can go to the public library and read the news that has been telegraphed for your benefit from San Francisco and Singapore. Twenty million people are underfed but literally everyone in England has access to a radio. What we have lost in food we have gained in electricity. Whole sections of the working class who have been plundered of all they really need are being compensated, in part, by cheap luxuries which mitigate the surface of life.

Do you consider all this desirable? No, I don't. But it may be that the psychological adjustment which the working class are visibly making is the best they could make in the circumstances. They have neither turned revolutionary nor lost their self-respect; merely they have kept their tempers and settled down to make the best of things on a fish-and-chip standard. The alternative would be God knows what continued agonies of despair; or it might be attempted insurrections which, in a strongly governed country like England, could only lead to futile massacres and a régime of savage repression.

Of course the post-war development of cheap luxuries has been a very fortunate thing for our rulers. It is quite likely that fish and chips, art-silk stockings, tinned salmon, cut-price chocolate (five two-ounce bars for sixpence), the movies, the radio, strong tea and the Football Pools have between them averted revolution. Therefore we are sometimes told the whole thing is an astute manoeuvre by the governing class—a sort of "bread and circuses" business—to hold the unemployed down. What I have seen of our governing class does not convince me that they have that much intelligence. The thing has happened, but by an unconscious process—the quite natural interaction between the manufacturer's need for a market and the need of half-starved people for cheap palliatives.

CHAPTER VI

WHEN I WAS a small boy at school a lecturer used to come once a term and deliver excellent lectures on famous battles of the past, such as Blenheim, Austerlitz, etc. He was fond of quoting Napoleon's maxim "An army marches on its stomach," and at the end of his lecture he would suddenly turn to us and demand, "What's the most important thing in the world?" We were expected to shout "Food!" and if we did not do so he was disappointed.

Obviously he was right in a way. A human being is primarily a bag for putting food into; the other functions and faculties may be more godlike, but in point of time they come afterwards. A man dies and is buried, and all his words and actions are forgotten, but the food he has eaten lives after him in the sound or rotten bones of his children. I think it could be plausibly argued that changes of diet are more important than changes of dynasty or even of religion. The Great War, for instance, could never have happened if tinned food had not been invented. And the history of the past four hundred years in England would have been immensely different if it had not been for the introduction of root-crops and various other vegetables at the end of the Middle Ages, and a little later the introduction of non-alcoholic drinks (tea, coffee, cocoa) and also of distilled liquors to which the beer-drinking English were not accustomed. Yet it is curious how seldom the all-importance of food is recognised. You see statues everywhere to politicians, poets, bishops, but none to cooks or bacon-curers or market-gardeners. The Emperor Charles V is said to have erected a statue to the inventor of bloaters, but that is the only case I can think of at the moment.

So perhaps the really important thing about the unemployed, the really basic thing if you look to the future, is the diet they are living on. As I said earlier, the average unemployed family lives on an income of round about thirty shillings a week, of which at least a quarter goes in rent. It is worth considering in some detail how the remaining money is spent. I have here a budget which was made out for me by an unemployed miner and his wife. I asked them to make a list which represented as exactly as possible their expenditure in a typical week. This man's allowance was thirty-two shillings a week, and besides his wife he had two children, one aged two years and five months and the other ten months. Here is the list:

											s.	d.
Rent	.	.	.	.	.	.	.	.	.	.	9	0½
Clothing Club	.	.	.	.	.	.	.	.	.	3	0
Coal	.	.	.	.	.	.	.	.	.	.	2	0
Gas	.	.	.	.	.	.	.	.	.	.	1	3
Milk	.	.	.	.	.	.	.	.	.	.	0	10½
Union fees	.	.	.	.	.	.	.	.	.	0	3
Insurance (on the children)	.	.	.	.	.	.	.	0	2
Meat	.	.	.	.	.	.	.	.	.	.	2	6
Flour (2 stone)	.	.	.	.	.	.	.	.	3	4
Yeast	.	.	.	.	.	.	.	.	.	.	0	4
Potatoes	.	.	.	.	.	.	.	.	.	1	0
Dripping	.	.	.	.	.	.	.	.	.	0	10
Margarine	.	.	.	.	.	.	.	.	.	0	10
Bacon	.	.	.	.	.	.	.	.	.	.	1	2
Sugar	.	.	.	.	.	.	.	.	.	.	1	9
Tea	.	.	.	.	.	.	.	.	.	.	1	0
Jam	.	.	.	.	.	.	.	.	.	.	0	7½
Peas and cabbage	.	.	.	.	.	.	.	.	0	6
Carrots and onions	.	.	.	.	.	.	.	0	4
Quaker oats	.	.	.	.	.	.	.	.	0	4½
Soap, powders, blue, etc.	.	.	.	.	.	.	0	10

Total £1 12 0

In addition to this, three packets of dried milk were supplied weekly for the baby by the Infants' Welfare Clinic.

One or two comments are needed here. To begin with, the list leaves out a great deal—blacking, pepper, salt, vinegar, matches, kindling-wood, razor blades, replacements of utensils and wear and tear of furniture and bedding, to name the first few that come to mind. Any money spent on these would mean reduction on some other item. A more serious charge is tobacco. This man happened to be a small smoker, but even so his tobacco would hardly cost less than a shilling a week, meaning a further reduction on food. The "clothing clubs" into which unemployed people pay so much a week are run by big drapers in all the industrial towns. Without them it would be impossible for unemployed people to buy new clothes at all. I don't know whether or not they buy bedding through these clubs. This particular family, as I happen to know, possessed next to no bedding.

In the above list, if you allow a shilling for tobacco and deduct this and the other non-food items, you are left with sixteen and fivepence half-penny. Call it sixteen shillings and leave the baby out of account—for the baby was getting its weekly packets of milk from the Welfare Clinic. This sixteen shillings has got to provide the entire nourishment, *including fuel,* of three persons, two of them adult. The first question is whether it is even theoretically possible for three persons to be properly nourished on sixteen shillings a week. When the dispute over the Means Test was in progress there was a disgusting public wrangle about the minimum weekly sum on which a human being could keep alive. So far as I remember, one school of dietitians worked it out at five and ninepence, while another school, more

generous, put it at five and ninepence halfpenny. After this there were letters to the papers from a number of people who claimed to be feeding themselves on four shillings a week. Here is a weekly budget (it was printed in
the *New Statesman* and also in the *News of the World*) which I picked
out from among a number of others:

									s.	d.
3 wholemeal loaves	.	.	.	.	.	.	.	.	1	0
½ lb. margarine	.	.	.	.	.	.	.	.	0	2½
½ lb. dripping	.	.	.	.	.	.	.	.	0	3
1 lb. cheese	.	.	.	.	.	.	.	.	0	7
1 lb. onions	.	.	.	.	.	.	.	.	0	1½
1 lb. carrots	.	.	.	.	.	.	.	.	0	1½
1 lb. broken biscuits	.	.	.	.	.	.	.	.	0	4
2 lb. dates	.	.	.	.	.	.	.	.	0	6
1 tin evaporated milk	.	.	.	.	.	.	.	.	0	5
10 oranges	.	.	.	.	.	.	.	.	0	5
Total	.	.	.	.	.	.	.	.	3	11½

Please notice that this budget contains *nothing for fuel.* In fact, the writer
explicitly stated that he could not afford to buy fuel and ate all his food raw.
Whether the letter was genuine or a hoax does not matter at the moment.
What I think will be admitted is that this list represents about as wise an
expenditure as could be contrived; if you *had* to live on three and eleven-
pence halfpenny a week, you could hardly extract more food-value from it
than that. So perhaps it is possible to feed yourself adequately on the
P.A.C. allowance if you concentrate on essential foodstuffs; but not otherwise.

Now compare this list with the unemployed miner's budget that I gave
earlier. The miner's family spend only tenpence a week on green vegetables and tenpence halfpenny on milk (remember that one of them is a
child less than three years old), and nothing on fruit; but they spend one
and nine on sugar (about eight pounds of sugar, that is) and a shilling on
tea. The half-crown spent on meat *might* represent a small joint and the
materials for a stew; probably as often as not it would represent four or
five tins of bully beef. The basis of their diet, therefore, is white bread
and margarine, corned beef, sugared tea and potatoes—an appalling diet.
Would it not be better if they spent more money on wholesome things like
oranges and wholemeal bread or if they even, like the writer of the letter to
the *New Statesman*, saved on fuel and ate their carrots raw? Yes, it would,
but the point is that no ordinary human being is ever going to do such a
thing. The ordinary human being would sooner starve than live on brown
bread and raw carrots. And the peculiar evil is, that the less money you
have, the less inclined you feel to spend it on wholesome food. A millionaire
may enjoy breakfasting off orange juice and Ryvita biscuits; an unemployed
man doesn't. Here the tendency of which I spoke at the end of the last
chapter comes into play. When you are unemployed, which is to say when

you are underfed, harassed, bored and miserable, you don't *want* to eat dull wholesome food. You want something a little bit "tasty." There is always some cheaply pleasant thing to tempt you. Let's have three pennorth of chips! Run out and buy us a twopenny ice-cream! Put the kettle on and we'll all have a nice cup of tea! *That* is how your mind works when you are at the P.A.C. level. White bread-and-marg and sugared tea don't nourish you to any extent, but they are *nicer* (at least most people think so) than brown bread-and-dripping and cold water. Unemployment is an endless misery that has got to be constantly palliated, and especially with tea, the Englishman's opium. A cup of tea or even an aspirin is much better as a temporary stimulant than a crust of brown bread.

The results of all this are visible in a physical degeneracy which you can study directly, by using your eyes, or inferentially, by having a look at the vital statistics. The physical average in the industrial towns is terribly low, lower even than in London. In Sheffield you have the feeling of walking among a population of troglodytes. The miners are splendid men, but they are usually small, and the mere fact that their muscles are toughened by constant work does not mean that their children start life with a better physique. In any case the miners are physically the pick of the population. The most obvious sign of under-nourishment is the badness of everybody's teeth. In Lancashire you would have to look for a long time before you saw a working-class person with good natural teeth. Indeed, you see very few people with natural teeth at all, apart from the children; and even the children's teeth have a frail bluish appearance which means, I suppose, calcium deficiency. Several dentists have told me that in industrial districts a person over thirty with any of his or her own teeth is coming to be an abnormality. In Wigan various people gave me their opinion that it is best to "get shut of" your teeth as early in life as possible. "Teeth is just a misery," one woman said to me. In one house where I stayed there were, apart from myself, five people, the oldest being forty-three and the youngest a boy of fifteen. Of these the boy was the only one who possessed a single tooth of his own, and his teeth were obviously not going to last long. As for the vital statistics, the fact that in any large industrial town the death rate and infant mortality rate of the poorest quarters are always about double those of the well-to-do residential quarters—a good deal more than double in some cases—hardly needs commenting on.

Of course one ought not to imagine that the prevailing bad physique is due solely to unemployment, for it is probable that the physical average has been declining all over England for a long time past, and not merely among the unemployed in the industrial areas. This cannot be proved statistically, but it is a conclusion that is forced upon you if you use your eyes, even in rural places and even in a prosperous town like London. On the day when King George V's body passed through London on its way to Westminster, I happened to be caught for an hour or two in the crowd in Trafalgar Square. It was impossible, looking about one then, not to be

struck by the physical degeneracy of modern England. The people surrounding me were *not* working-class people for the most part; they were the
shopkeeper-commercial-traveller type; with a sprinkling of the well-to-do.
But what a set they looked! Puny limbs, sickly faces, under the weeping
London sky! Hardly a well-built man or a decent-looking woman, and not
a fresh complexion anywhere. As the King's coffin went by, the men took
off their hats, and a friend who was in the crowd at the other side of the
Strand said to me afterwards, "The only touch of colour anywhere was the
bald heads." Even the Guards, it seemed to me—there was a squad of
guardsmen marching besides the coffin—were not what they used to be.
Where are the monstrous men with chests like barrels and moustaches like
the wings of eagles who strode across my childhood's gaze twenty or thirty
years ago? Buried, I suppose, in the Flanders mud. In their place there are
these pale-faced boys who have been picked for their height and consequently look like hop-poles in overcoats—the truth being that in modern
England a man over six feet high is usually skin and bone and not much
else. If the English physique has declined, this is no doubt partly due to
the fact that the Great War carefully selected the million best men in
England and slaughtered them, largely before they had had time to breed.
But the process must have begun earlier than that, and it must be due ultimately to unhealthy ways of living, i.e. to industrialism. I don't mean the
habit of living in towns—probably the town is healthier than the country,
in many ways—but the modern industrial technique which provides you
with cheap substitutes for everything. We may find in the long run that
tinned food is a deadlier weapon than the machine gun.

It is unfortunate that the English working class—the English nation
generally, for that matter—are exceptionally ignorant about and wasteful
of food. I have pointed out elsewhere how civilised is a French navvy's idea
of a meal compared with an Englishman's, and I cannot believe that you
would ever see such wastage in a French house as you habitually see in
English ones. Of course, in the very poorest homes, where everybody is
unemployed, you don't see much actual waste, but those who can afford to
waste food often do so. I could give startling instances of this. Even the
Northern habit of baking one's own bread is slightly wasteful in itself, because an overworked woman cannot bake more than once or, at most, twice
a week and it is impossible to tell beforehand how much bread will be
wasted, so that a certain amount generally has to be thrown away. The
usual thing is to bake six large loaves and twelve small ones at a time. All
this is part of the old, generous English attitude to life, and it is an amiable
quality, but a disastrous one at the present moment.

English working people everywhere, so far as I know, refuse brown
bread; it is usually impossible to buy wholemeal bread in a working-class
district. They sometimes give the reason that brown bread is "dirty." I
suspect the real reason is that in the past brown bread has been confused
with black bread, which is traditionally associated with Popery and wooden

shoes. (They have plenty of Popery and wooden shoes in Lancashire. A pity they haven't the black bread as well!) But the English palate, especially the working-class palate, now rejects good food almost automatically. The number of people who *prefer* tinned peas and tinned fish to real peas and real fish must be increasing every year, and plenty of people who could afford real milk in their tea would much sooner have tinned milk—even that dreadful tinned milk which is made of sugar and cornflour and has UNFIT FOR BABIES on the tin in huge letters. In some districts efforts are now being made to teach the unemployed more about food-values and more about the intelligent spending of money. When you hear of a thing like this you feel yourself torn both ways. I have heard a Communist speaker on the platform grow very angry about it. In London, he said, parties of Society dames now have the cheek to walk into East End houses and give shopping-lessons to the wives of the unemployed. He gave this as an instance of the mentality of the English governing class. First you condemn a family to live on thirty shillings a week, and then you have the damned impertinence to tell them how they are to spend their money. He was quite right—I agree heartily. Yet all the same it *is* a pity that, merely for the lack of a proper tradition, people should pour muck like tinned milk down their throats and not even know that it is inferior to the product of the cow.

I doubt, however, whether the unemployed would ultimately benefit if they learned to spend their money more economically. For it is only the fact that they are *not* economical that keeps their allowances so high. An Englishman on the P.A.C. gets fifteen shillings a week because fifteen shillings is the smallest sum on which he can conceivably keep alive. If he were, say, an Indian or Japanese coolie, who can live on rice and onions, he wouldn't get fifteen shillings a week—he would be lucky if he got fifteen shillings a month. Our unemployment allowances, miserable though they are, are framed to suit a population with very high standards and not much notion of economy. If the unemployed learned to be better managers they would be visibly better off, and I fancy it would not be long before the dole was docked correspondingly.

There is one great mitigation of unemployment in the North, and that is the cheapness of fuel. Anywhere in the coal areas the retail price of coal is about one and sixpence a hundredweight; in the South of England it is about half a crown. Moreover, miners in work can usually buy coal direct from the pit at eight or nine shillings a ton, and those who have a cellar in their homes sometimes store a ton at a time and sell it (illicitly, I suppose) to those who are out of work. But apart from this there is immense and systematic thieving of coal by the unemployed. I call it thieving because technically it is that, though it does no harm to anybody. In the "dirt" that is sent up from the pits there is a certain amount of broken coal, and unemployed people spend a lot of time picking it out of the slag-heaps. All day long over those strange grey mountains you see people wandering to and fro with sacks and baskets among the sulphurous smoke (many slag-heaps are on fire under the surface), prising out the tiny nuggets of coal which are buried here and there. You meet men coming away, wheeling strange and wonderful homemade bicycles—bicycles made of rusty parts picked off refuse-tips, without saddles, without chains and almost always without tyres—across which are slung bags containing perhaps half a hundredweight of coal, fruit of half a day's searching. In times of strikes, when everybody is short of fuel, the miners turn out with pick and shovel and burrow into the slag-heaps, whence the hummocky appearance which most slag-heaps have. During long strikes, in places where there are out-crops of coal, they have sunk surface mines and carried them scores of yards into the earth.

In Wigan the competition among unemployed people for the waste coal has become so fierce that it has led to an extraordinary custom called "scrambling for the coal," which is well worth seeing. Indeed I rather won-der that it has never been filmed. An unemployed miner took me to see it one afternoon. We got to the place, a mountain range of ancient slag-heaps with a railway running through the valley below. A couple of hundred ragged men, each with a sack and coal-hammer strapped under his coat-tails, were waiting on the "broo." When the dirt comes up from the pit it is loaded on to trucks and an engine runs these to the top of another slag-heap a quarter of a mile away and there leaves them. The process of "scrambling for the coal" consists in getting on to the train while it is moving; any truck which you have succeeded in boarding while it is in motion counts as "your" truck. Presently the train hove in sight. With a wild yell a hundred men dashed down the slope to catch her as she rounded the bend. Even at the bend the train was making twenty miles an hour. The men hurled them-selves upon it, caught hold of the rings at the rear of the trucks and hoisted themselves up by way of the bumpers, five or ten of them on each truck. The driver took no notice. He drove up to the top of the slag-heap, un-coupled the trucks and run the engine back to the pit presently returning with a fresh string of trucks. There was the same wild rush of ragged figures as before. In the end only about fifty men had failed to get on to either train.

We walked up to the top of the slag-heap. The men were shovelling the dirt out of the trucks, while down below their wives and children were kneeling, swiftly scrabbling with their hands in the damp dirt and picking out lumps of coal the size of an egg or smaller. You would see a woman pounce on a tiny fragment of stuff, wipe it on her apron, scrutinise it to make sure it was coal and pop it jealously into her sack. Of course, when you are boarding a truck you don't know beforehand what is in it; it may be actual "dirt" from the roads or it may merely be shale from the roofing. If it is a shale truck there will be no coal in it, but there occurs among the shale another inflammable rock called cannel, which looks very like ordi-nary shale but is slightly darker and is known by splitting in parallel lines, like slate. It makes tolerable fuel, not good enough to be commercially valuable but good enough to be eagerly sought after by the unemployed.

The miners on the shale trucks were picking out the cannel and splitting it up with their hammers. Down at the bottom of the "broo" the people who had failed to get on to either train were gleaning the tiny chips of coal that came rolling down from above—fragments no bigger than a hazel nut, these, but the people were glad enough to get them.

We stayed there till the train was empty. In a couple of hours the people had picked the dirt over to the last grain. They slung their sacks over shoulder or bicycle, and started on the two-mile trudge back to Wigan. Most of the families had gathered about half a hundredweight of coal or cannel, so that between them they must have stolen five or ten tons of fuel. This business of robbing the dirt trains takes place every day in Wigan, at any rate in winter, and at more collieries than one. It is of course extremely dangerous. No one was hurt the afternoon I was there, but a man had had both his legs cut off a few weeks earlier, and another man lost several fingers a week later. Technically it is stealing but, as everybody knows, if the coal were not stolen it would simply be wasted. Now and again, for form's sake, the colliery companies prosecute somebody for coal-picking, and in that morning's issue of the local paper there was a paragraph saying that two men had been fined ten shillings. But no notice is taken of the prosecutions—in fact, one of the men named in the paper was there that afternoon—and the coal-pickers subscribe among themselves to pay the fines. The thing is taken for granted. Everyone knows that the unemployed have got to get fuel somehow. So every afternoon several hundred men risk their necks and several hundred women scrabble in the mud for hours—and all for half a hundredweight of inferior fuel, value ninepence.

That scene stays in my mind as one of my pictures of Lancashire: the dumpy, shawled women, with their sacking aprons and their heavy black clogs, kneeling in the cindery mud and the bitter wind, searching eagerly for tiny chips of coal. They are glad enough to do it. In winter they are desperate for fuel; it is more important almost than food. Meanwhile all round, as far as the eye can see, are the slag-heaps and hoisting gear of collieries, and not one of those collieries can sell all the coal it is capable of producing. This ought to appeal to Major Douglas.

The Scientist and Humanist: Albert Einstein

Albert Einstein, "Principles of Research," "Inaugural Address to the Prussian Academy of Sciences," "On Scientific Truth," and "What Is the Theory of Relativity?" The World as I See It, trans. Alan Harris (New York: Convici, Friede Inc., 1934), pp. 19–30, 73–81.

Every schoolchild encounters $E = mc^2$, recognizes the name Albert Einstein (1879–1955), and knows that the world is different because of them. On no man did greatness sit better. Humble and simple in tastes and values, he was dedicated to truth, freedom, peace, and the Judaism of his forbears. There was nothing narrow about Einstein. His whimsical wit crept into his most serious pursuits. When denounced as a Socialist and pacifist by the Daughters of the American Revolution during an early visit to the United States, he reminded those formidable ladies that perhaps they were right. Rome, too, had once been saved by the clacking of geese.

Einstein was born at Ulm and studied art before turning to the Polytechnic Academy at Zurich. At the age of twenty-six he published his first statement of the theory of relativity—perhaps the most striking advance in pure science in this century—in the Annals of Physics. Shortly before the outbreak of the First World War he was appointed director of the Kaiser Wilhelm Institute for Physics in Berlin. His General Theory of Relativity appeared in 1916; Unitary Field Theory in 1929. He had accomplished a scientific revolution. Academic and world acclaim poured down on him. He won the Nobel Prize for physics in 1921.

Einstein was aware of a serious problem: the growing complexity of science required specialization and limited the capacity of the scientist to communicate with the general public. For a man dedicated not only to science but to the cause of humanity this would not do. To the end of his life he continued to write and to speak on science and the many problems of human welfare that concerned him. These brief essays and addresses were intended not merely for specialists but also for the educated public. They are sensitive and perceptive, and they reflect the quality of his intellectual greatness.

PRINCIPLES OF RESEARCH

(Address on the occasion of Max Planck's sixtieth birthday delivered at the Physical Society in Berlin)

IN THE TEMPLE of Science are many mansions, and various indeed are they that dwell therein and the motives that have led them thither. Many take to science out of a joyful sense of superior intellectual power; science is their own special report to which they look for vivid experience and the satisfaction of ambition; many others are to be found in the temple who have offered the products of their brains on this altar for purely utilitarian purposes. Were an angel of the Lord to come and drive all the people belonging to these two categories out of the temple, it would be noticeably emptier, but there would still be some men, of both present and past times, left inside. Our Planck is one of them, and that is why we love him.

I am quite aware that we have just now light-heartedly expelled in imagination many excellent men who are largely, perhaps chiefly, responsible for the building of the temple of Science; and in many cases our angel would find it a pretty ticklish job to decide. But of one thing I feel sure: if the types we have just expelled were the only types there were, the temple would never have existed, any more than one can have a wood consisting of nothing but creepers. For these people any sphere of human activity will do, if it comes to a point; whether they become officers, tradesmen or scientists depends on circumstances. Now let us have another look at those who have found favour with the angel. Most of them are somewhat odd, uncommunicative, solitary fellows, really less like each other, in spite of these common characteristics, than the hosts of the rejected. What has brought them to the temple? That is a difficult question and no single answer will cover it. To begin with I believe with Schopenhauer that one of the strongest motives that lead men to art and science is escape from everyday life with its painful crudity and hopeless dreariness, from the fetters of one's own ever shifting desires. A finely tempered nature longs to escape from personal life into the world of objective perception and thought; this desire may be compared with the townsman's irresistible longing to escape from his noisy, cramped surroundings into the silence of high mountains, where the eye ranges freely through the still, pure air and fondly traces out the restful contours apparently built for eternity. With this negative motive there goes a personal one. Man tries to make for himself in the fashion that suits him best a simplified and intelligible picture of the world; he then tries to some extent to substitute this cosmos of his for the world of experience, and thus to overcome it. This is what the painter, the poet, the speculative philosopher and the natural scientist do, each in his own fashion. He makes this cosmos and its construction the pivot of his emotional life, in order to find in this way the peace and security which he cannot find in the narrow whirlpool of personal experience.

What place does the theoretical physicist's picture of the world occupy among all these possible pictures? It demands the highest possible standard of rigorous precision in the description of relations, such as only the use of mathematical language can give. In regard to his subject matter, on the other hand, the physicist has to limit himself very severely: he must content himself with describing the most simple events which can be brought within the domain of our experience; all events of a more complex order are beyond the power of the human intellect to reconstruct with the subtle accuracy and logical perfection which the theoretical physicist demands. Supreme purity, clarity and certainty at the cost of completeness. But what can be the attraction of getting to know such a tiny section of nature thoroughly, while one leaves everything subtler and more complex shyly and timidly alone? Does the product of such a modest effort deserve to be called by the proud name of a theory of the Universe?

In my belief the name is justified; for the general laws on which the structure of theoretical physics is based claim to be valid for any natural phenomenon whatsoever. With them, it ought to be possible to arrive at the description, that is to say, the theory, of every natural process, including life, by means of pure deduction, if that process of deduction were not far beyond the capacity of the human intellect. The physicist's renunciation of completeness for his cosmos is therefore not a matter of fundamental principle.

The supreme task of the physicist is to arrive at those universal elementary laws from which the cosmos can be built up by pure deduction. There is no logical path to these laws; only intuition, resting on sympathetic understanding of experience, can reach them. In this methodological uncertainty, one might suppose that there were any number of possible systems of theoretical physics all with an equal amount to be said for them; and this opinion is no doubt correct, theoretically. But evolution has shown that at any given moment, out of all conceivable constructions, a single one has always proved itself absolutely superior to all the rest. Nobody who has really gone deeply into the matter will deny that in practice the world of phenomena uniquely determines the theoretical system, in spite of the fact that there is no logical bridge between phenomena and their theoretical principles; this is what Leibnitz described so happily as a 'pre-established harmony.' Physicists often accuse epistemologists of not paying sufficient attention to this fact. Here, it seems to me, lie the roots of the controversy carried on some years ago between Mach and Planck.

The longing to behold this pre-established harmony is the source of the inexhaustible patience and endurance with which Planck has devoted himself, as we see, to the most general problems of our science, refusing to let himself be diverted to more grateful and more easily attained ends. I have often heard colleagues try to attribute this attitude of his to extraordinary will-power and discipline—wrongly, in my opinion. The state of mind which enables a man to do work of this kind is akin to that of the religious worshipper or the lover; the daily effort comes from no deliberate intention or programme, but straight from the heart. There he sits, our beloved Planck, and smiles inside himself at my childish playing-about with the lantern of Diogenes. Our affection for him needs no threadbare explanation. May the love of science continue to illumine his path in the future and lead him to the solution of the most important problem in present-day physics, which he has himself posed and done so much to solve. May he succeed in uniting the quantum theory and electrodynamics in a single logical system,

INAUGURAL ADDRESS TO THE PRUSSIAN
ACADEMY OF SCIENCES (1914)

GENTLEMEN,

First of all, I have to thank you most heartily for conferring the greatest benefit on me that anybody can confer on a man like myself. By electing me to your Academy you have freed me from the distractions and cares of a professional life and so made it possible for me to devote myself entirely to scientific studies. I beg that you will continue to believe in my gratitude and my industry even when my efforts seem to you to yield but a poor result.

Perhaps I may be allowed à propos of this to make a few general remarks on the relation of my sphere of activity, which is theoretical physics, towards experimental physics. A mathematician friend of mine said to me the other day half in jest: 'The mathematician can do a lot of things, but never what you happen to want him to do just at the moment'. Much the same often applies to the theoretical physicist when the experimental physicist calls him in. What is the reason for this peculiar lack of adaptability?

The theorist's method involves his using as his foundation general postulates or 'principles' from which he can deduce conclusions. His work thus falls into two parts. He must first discover his principles and then draw the conclusions which follow from them. For the second of these tasks he receives an admirable equipment at school. Once, therefore, he has performed the first task in some department, or for some complex of related phenomena, he is certain of success, provided his industry and intelligence are adequate. The first of these tasks, namely, that of establishing the principles which are to serve as the starting point of his deduction, is of an entirely different nature. Here there is no method capable of being learnt and systematically applied so that it leads to the goal. The scientist has to worm these general principles out of nature by perceiving certain general features which permit of precise formulation, amidst large complexes of empirical facts.

Once this formulation is successfully accomplished, inference follows on inference, often revealing relations which extend far beyond the province of the reality from which the principles were drawn. But as long as the principles capable of serving as starting points for the deduction remain undiscovered, the individual fact is of no use to the theorist; indeed he cannot even do anything with isolated empirical generalisations of more or less wide application. No, he has to persist in his helpless attitude towards the separate results of empirical research, until principles which he can make the basis of deductive reasoning have revealed themselves to him.

This is the kind of position in which theory finds itself at present in regard to the laws of heat, radiation, and molecular movement at low temperatures. About fifteen years ago nobody had yet doubted that a correct account of the electrical, optical and thermal properties of bodies was possible on the basis of Galileo-Newtonian mechanics applied to the movement of molecules and of Clerk Maxwell's theory of the electro-magnetic field. Then Planck showed that in order to establish a law of heat radiation consonant with experience, it was necessary to employ a method of calculation the incompatibility of which with the principles of classical physics became clearer and clearer. For with this method of calculation Planck introduced the quantum hypothesis into physics, which has since received brilliant confirmation. With this quantum hypothesis he dethroned classical physics as applied to the case where sufficiently small masses are moved at sufficiently low speeds and high rates of acceleration, so that today the laws of motion propounded by Galileo and Newton can only be allowed validity as limiting laws. In spite of assiduous efforts, however, the theorists have not yet succeeded in replacing the principles of mechanics by others which fit in with Planck's law of heat radiation or the quantum hypothesis. No matter how definitely it has been proved that heat is to be explained by molecular movement, we have nevertheless to admit today that our position in regard to the fundamental laws of this motion resembles that of astronomers before Newton in regard to the motions of the planets.

I have just now referred to a group of facts for the theoretical treatment of which the principles are lacking. But it may equally well happen that clearly formulated principles lead to conclusions which fall entirely, or almost entirely, outside the sphere of reality at present accessible to our experience. In that case it may need many years of empirical research to ascertain whether the theoretical principles correspond with reality. We have an instance of this in the theory of relativity.

An analysis of the fundamental concepts of space and time has shown us that the principle of the constant velocity of light in empty space, which emerges from the optics of bodies in motion, by no means forces us to accept the theory of a stationary luminiferous ether. On the contrary, there is nothing to prevent our framing a general theory which takes account of the fact that in experiments carried out on the earth we are wholly unconscious of the translatory motion of the earth. This involves using the principle of relativity, which says that the laws of nature do not alter their form when one proceeds from the original (legitimate) system of co-ordinates to a new one which is in uniform translatory motion with respect to it. This theory has received impressive confirmation from experience and has led to a simplification of the theoretical description of groups of facts already connected together.

On the other hand, from the theoretical point of view this theory is not wholly satisfactory, because the principle of relativity just formulated prefers *uniform* motion. If it is true that no absolute significance can be attached to *uniform* motion from the physical point of view, the question arises whether this statement must not also be extended to non-uniform motions. It became clear that one arrives at a quite definite enlargement of the relativity theory if one postulates a principle of relativity in this extended sense. One is led thereby to a general theory of gravitation which includes dynamics. For the present, however, we have not the necessary array of facts to test the legitimacy of our introduction of the postulated principle.

We have ascertained that inductive physics asks questions of deductive, and vice versa, to answer which demands the exertion of all our energies. May we soon succeed in making permanent progress by our united efforts!

ON SCIENTIFIC TRUTH

(1) It is difficult even to attach a precise meaning to the term 'scientific truth'. So different is the meaning of the word 'truth' according to whether we are dealing with a fact of experience, a mathematical proposition or a scientific theory. 'Religious truth' conveys nothing clear to me at all.

(2) Scientific research can reduce superstition by encouraging people to think and survey things in terms of cause and effect. Certain it is that a conviction, akin to religious feeling, of the rationality or intelligibility of the world lies behind all scientific work of a higher order.

(3) This firm belief, a belief bound up with deep feeling, in a superior mind that reveals itself in the world of experience, represents my conception of God. In common parlance this may be described as 'pantheistic' (Spinoza).

(4) Denominational traditions I can only consider historically and psychologically; they have no other significance for me.

WHAT IS THE THEORY OF RELATIVITY?

I GLADLY ACCEDE to the request of your colleague to write something for *The Times* on relativity. After the lamentable break-down of the old active intercourse between men of learning, I welcome this opportunity of expressing my feelings of joy and gratitude towards the astronomers and physicists of England. It is thoroughly in keeping with the great and proud traditions of scientific work in your country that eminent scientists should have spent much time and trouble, and your scientific institutions have spared no expense, to test the implications of a theory which was perfected and published during the War in the land of your enemies. Even though the investigation of the influence of the gravitational field of the sun on light rays is a purely objective matter, I cannot forbear to express my personal thanks to my English colleagues for their work; for without it I could hardly have lived to see the most important implication of my theory tested.

We can distinguish various kinds of theories in physics. Most of them are constructive. They attempt to build up a picture of the more complex phenomena out of the materials of a relatively simple formal scheme from which they start out. Thus the kinetic theory of gases seeks to reduce mechanical, thermal and diffusional processes to movements of molecules —i.e., to build them up out of the hypothesis of molecular motion. When we say that we have succeeded in understanding a group of natural processes, we invariably mean that a constructive theory has been found which covers the processes in question.

Along with this most important class of theories there exists a second, which I will call 'principle-theories'. These employ the analytic, not the synthetic, method. The elements which form their basis and starting-point are not hypothetically constructed but empirically discovered ones, general characteristics of natural processes, principles that give rise to mathematically formulated criteria which the separate processes or the theoretical representations of them have to satisfy. Thus the science of thermodynamics seeks by analytical means to deduce necessary connections, which separate events have to satisfy, from the universally experienced fact that perpetual motion is impossible.

The advantages of the constructive theory are completeness, adaptability and clearness, those of the principle theory are logical perfection and security of the foundations.

The theory of relativity belongs to the latter class. In order to grasp its nature, one needs first of all to become acquainted with the principles on which it is based. Before I go into these, however, I must observe that the theory of relativity resembles a building consisting of two separate storeys, the special theory and the general theory. The special theory, on which the general theory rests, applies to all physical phenomena with the exception of gravitation; the general theory provides the law of gravitation and its relations to the other forces of nature.

It has, of course, been known since the days of the ancient Greeks that in order to describe the movement of a body, a second body is needed to which the movement of the first is referred. The movement of a vehicle is considered in reference to the earth's surface, that of a planet to the totality of the visible fixed stars. In physics the body to which events are spatially referred is called the co-ordinate system. The laws of the mechanics of Galileo and Newton, for instance, can only be formulated with the aid of a co-ordinate system.

The state of motion of the co-ordinate system may not, however, be arbitrarily chosen, if the laws of mechanics are to be valid (it must be free from rotation and acceleration). A co-ordinate system which is admitted in mechanics is called an 'inertial system'. The state of motion of an inertial system is according to mechanics not one that is determined uniquely by nature. On the contrary, the following definition holds good:—a co-ordinate system that is moved uniformly and in a straight line relatively to an inertial system is likewise an inertial system. By the 'special principle of relativity' is meant the generalisation of this definition to include any natural event whatever: thus, every universal law of nature which is valid in relation to a co-ordinate system C, must also be valid, as it stands, in relation to a co-ordinate system C', which is in uniform translatory motion relatively to C.

The second principle, on which the special theory of relatively rests, is the 'principle of the constant velocity of light in vacuo.' This principle asserts that light in vacuo always has a definite velocity of propagation (independent of the state of motion of the observer or of the source of the light). The confidence which physicists place in this principle springs from the successes achieved by the electro-dynamics of Clerk Maxwell and Lorentz.

Both the above-mentioned principles are powerfully supported by experience, but appear not to be logically reconcileable. The special theory of relativity finally succeeded in reconciling them logically by a modification of kinematics—i.e., of the doctrine of the laws relating to space and time (from the point of view of physics). It became clear that to speak of the simultaneity of two events had no meaning except in relation to a given co-ordinate system, and that the shape of measuring devices and the speed at which clocks move depend on their state of motion with respect to the co-ordinate system.

But the old physics, including the laws of motion of Galileo and Newton, did not fit in with the suggested relativist kinematics. From the latter, general mathematical conditions issued, to which natural laws had to conform, if the above-mentioned two principles were really to apply. To these, physics had to be adapted. In particular, scientists arrived at a new law of motion for (rapidly moving) mass points, which was admirably confirmed in the case of electrically charged particles. The most important upshot of the special theory of relativity concerned the inert mass of corporeal systems. It turned out that the inertia of a system necessarily depends on its energy-content, and this led straight to the notion that inert mass is simply latent energy. The principle of the conservation of mass lost its independence and became fused with that of the conservation of energy.

The special theory of relativity, which was simply a systematic development of the electro-dynamics of Clerk Maxwell and Lorentz, pointed beyond itself, however. Should the independence of physical laws of the state of motion of the co-ordinate system be restricted to the uniform translatory motion of co-ordinate systems in respect to each other? What has nature to do with our co-ordinate systems and their state of motion? If it is necessary for the purpose of describing nature, to make use of a co-ordinate system arbitrarily introduced by us, then the choice of its state of motion ought to be subject to no restriction; the laws ought to be entirely independent of this choice (general principle of relativity).

The establishment of this general principle of relativity is made easier by a fact of experience that has long been known, namely that the weight and the inertia of a body are controlled by the same constant. (Equality of inertial and gravitational mass.) Imagine a co-ordinate system which is rotating uniformly with respect to an inertial system in the Newtonian manner. The centrifugal forces which manifest themselves in relation to this system must, according to Newton's teaching, be regarded as effects of inertia. But these centrifugal forces are, exactly like the forces of gravity, proportional to the masses of the bodies. Ought it not to be possible in this case to regard the co-ordinate system as stationary and the centrifugal forces as gravitational forces? This seems the obvious view, but classical mechanics forbid it.

This hasty consideration suggests that a general theory of relativity must supply the laws of gravitation, and the consistent following up of the idea has justified our hopes.

But the path was thornier than one might suppose, because it demanded the abandonment of Euclidean geometry. This is to say, the laws according to which fixed bodies may be arranged in space, do not completely accord with the spatial laws attributed to bodies by Euclidean geometry. This is what we mean when we talk of the 'curvature of space'. The fundamental concepts of the 'straight line', the 'plane', etc., thereby lose their precise significance in physics.

In the general theory of relativity the doctrine of space and time, or kinematics, no longer figures as a fundamental independent of the rest of physics. The geometrical behaviour of bodies and the motion of clocks rather depend on gravitational fields, which in their turn are produced by matter.

The new theory of gravitation diverges considerably, as regards principles, from Newton's theory. But its practical results agree so nearly with those of Newton's theory that it is difficult to find criteria for distinguishing them which are accessible to experience. Such have been discovered so far:—

(1) In the revolution of the ellipses of the planetary orbits round the sun (confirmed in the case of Mercury).

(2) In the curving of light rays by the action of gravitational fields (confirmed by the English photographs of eclipses).

(3) In a displacement of the spectral lines towards the red end of the spectrum in the case of light transmitted to us from stars of considerable magnitude (unconfirmed so far).[1]

The chief attraction of the theory lies in its logical completeness. If a single one of the conclusions drawn from it proves wrong, it must be given up; to modify it without destroying the whole structure seems to be impossible.

Let no one suppose, however, that the mighty work of Newton can really be superseded by this or any other theory. His great and lucid ideas will retain their unique significance for all time as the foundation of our whole modern conceptual structure in the sphere of natural philosophy.

[1] This criterion has also been confirmed in the meantime.